FUNDAMENTALS OF
HUMAN RESOURCE MANAGEMENT

FUNDAMENTALS OF
HUMAN RESOURCE MANAGEMENT

Second Edition

RAYMOND A. NOE
The Ohio State University

JOHN R. HOLLENBECK
Michigan State University

BARRY GERHART
University of Wisconsin–Madison

PATRICK M. WRIGHT
Cornell University

McGraw-Hill
Irwin

Boston   Burr Ridge, IL   Dubuque, IA   Madison, WI   New York   San Francisco   St. Louis
Bangkok   Bogotá   Caracas   Kuala Lumpur   Lisbon   London   Madrid   Mexico City
Milan   Montreal   New Delhi   Santiago   Seoul   Singapore   Sydney   Taipei   Toronto

Higher Education

FUNDAMENTALS OF HUMAN RESOURCE MANAGEMENT

Published by McGraw-Hill/Irwin, a business unit of The McGraw-Hill Companies, Inc., 1221 Avenue of the Americas, New York, NY, 10020. Copyright © 2007 by The McGraw-Hill Companies, Inc. All rights reserved. No part of this publication may be reproduced or distributed in any form or by any means, or stored in a database or retrieval system, without the prior written consent of The McGraw-Hill Companies, Inc., including, but not limited to, in any network or other electronic storage or transmission, or broadcast for distance learning.

Some ancillaries, including electronic and print components, may not be available to customers outside the United States.

The book is printed on acid-free paper.

6 7 8 9 0 WCK/WCK 0 9 8

ISBN: 978-0-07-293425-0
MHID: 0-07-293425-5

Editorial director: *John E. Biernat*
Executive editor: *John Weimeister*
Developmental editor: *Sarah Reed*
Associate marketing manager: *Margaret A. Beamer*
Producer, Media technology: *Damian Moshak*
Project manager: *Marlena Pechan*
Senior production supervisor: *Sesha Bolisetty*
Senior designer: *Adam Rooke*
Photo research coordinator: *Lori Kramer*
Photo researcher: *Robin Sand*
Lead media project manager: *Brian Nacik*
Typeface: *10.5/12 Goudy*
Compositor: *ElectraGraphics, Inc.*
Printer: *Quebecor World Versailles Inc.*
Cover Illustration: *Jim Frazier/Images.com*

Library of Congress Cataloging-in-Publication Data

Fundamentals of human resource management / Raymond A. Noe . . . [et al.].—2nd ed.
    p. cm.
   Includes bibliographical references and index.
   ISBN: 978-0-07-293425-0
   MHID: 0-07-293425-5 (alk. paper)
   1. Personnel management. I. Title: Human resource management. II. Noe, Raymond A.
HF5549.F86 2007
658.3—dc22

2005052292

www.mhhe.com

ABOUT THE AUTHORS

Raymond A. Noe is the Robert and Anne Hoyt Professor of Management at The Ohio State University. He was previously a professor in the Department of Management at Michigan State University and the Industrial Relations Center of the Carlson School of Management, University of Minnesota. He received his BS in psychology from The Ohio State University and his MA and PhD in psychology from Michigan State University. Professor Noe conducts research and teaches undergraduate as well as MBA and PhD students in human resource management, managerial skills, quantitative methods, human resource information systems, training, employee development, and organizational behavior. He has published articles in the *Academy of Management Journal, Academy of Management Review, Journal of Applied Psychology, Journal of Vocational Behavior,* and *Personnel Psychology.* Professor Noe is currently on the editorial boards of several journals including *Personnel Psychology, Journal of Applied Psychology,* and *Journal of Organizational Behavior.* Professor Noe has received awards for his teaching and research excellence, including the Herbert G. Heneman Distinguished Teaching Award in 1991 and the Ernest J. McCormick Award for Distinguished Early Career Contribution from the Society for Industrial and Organizational Psychology in 1993. He is also a fellow of the Society for Industrial and Organizational Psychology.

John R. Hollenbeck is currently the Eli Broad Professor of Management at the Eli Broad Graduate School of Business Administration at Michigan State University. He received his PhD in Management from New York University in 1984 and joined the Michigan State faculty that year. Dr. Hollenbeck has published over 60 articles and book chapters, with more than 35 of these appearing in the most highly cited refereed outlets (*Journal of Applied Psychology, Academy of Management Journal, Personnel Psychology,* and *Organizational Behavior and Human Decision Processes*). Dr. Hollenbeck was the acting editor at *Organizational Behavior and Human Decision Processes* in 1995, the associate editor at *Decision Sciences* from 1999 to 2004, and the editor of *Personnel Psychology* between 1996 and 2002. Prior to serving as editor, he served on the editorial board of these journals, as well as the boards of the *Academy of Management Journal, Academy of Management Review, Journal of Applied Psychology,* and *Journal of Management.* Dr. Hollenbeck was the first recipient of the Ernest J. McCormick Award for Early Contributions to the field of Industrial and Organizational Psychology in 1992 and is a Fellow of the American Psychological Association.

Barry Gerhart is Professor of Management and Human Resources, the Bruce R. Ellig Distinguished Chair in Pay and Organizational Effectiveness, and Director of the Strategic Human Resources Program, School of Business, University of Wisconsin–Madison. His previous faculty appointments include serving as Area Coordinator of the Organization Studies area at Vanderbilt University's Owen Graduate School of Management and as Chair of the Department of Human Resource Studies, Cornell University. His major fields of interest are human resource management and strategy, compensation, and business performance. Professor Gerhart received his BS in Psychology from Bowling Green State University and his PhD in Industrial Relations from the University of Wisconsin–Madison. Current and past editorial board appointments include the *Academy of Management Journal*, *Administrative Science Quarterly*, *Industrial and Labor Relations Review*, the *International Journal of Human Resource Management*, the *Journal of Applied Psychology*, and *Personnel Psychology*. In 1991, Professor Gerhart received the Scholarly Achievement Award from the Human Resources Division, Academy of Management. He is also a Fellow of the American Psychological Association and of the Society for Industrial and Organizational Psychology. Professor Gerhart is co-author of the book, *Compensation: Theory, Evidence, and Strategic Implications*, as well as co-editor of *Compensation in Organizations*.

Patrick M. Wright is Professor of Human Resource Studies and Director of the Center for Advanced Human Resource Studies in the School of Industrial and Labor Relations, Cornell University. He holds a BA in psychology from Wheaton College, and an MBA and a PhD in Organizational Behavior/Human Resource Management from Michigan State University. Professor Wright teaches, conducts research, and consults in the area of Strategic Human Resource Management (SHRM), particularly focusing on how firms use people as a source of competitive advantage. He has published over 50 research articles in journals such as *Academy of Management Journal*, *Academy of Management Review*, *Strategic Management Journal*, *Organizational Behavior and Human Decision Processes*, *Journal of Applied Psychology*, *Personnel Psychology*, and *Journal of Management* as well as over 20 chapters in books and edited volumes such as *Research in P/HRM* and *Handbook of I/O Psychology*. He currently serves on the editorial boards of *Personnel Psychology*, *Human Resource Management Journal*, *Human Resource Management Review*, *Journal of Management*, *Human Resource Planning*, *Management and Organization Review*, *Journal of Management Studies*, and *Journal of Managerial Issues*.

He has co-authored two textbooks, has co-edited a number of special issues of journals dealing with the future of Strategic HRM as well as Corporate Social Responsibility. He has taught in Executive Development programs and has conducted programs and/or consulted for a number of large public and private sector organizations. Dr. Wright served as the Chair of the HR Division of the Academy of Management, and on the Board of Directors for SHRM Foundation, World at Work, and Human Resource Planning Society.

PREFACE

The "good, the bad, and the ugly" appropriately describes how human resource management practices have recently appeared in the media. If you have watched television or read any newspapers or magazines in the last several months you have undoubtedly come across reports dealing with ethics and legal challenges to business practices (such as the discrimination lawsuits against Wal-Mart), and offshoring and outsourcing of jobs (such as IBM plans to send 5,000 jobs to India). On the bright side, companies such as Wegmans Food Markets (the supermarket chain), J. M. Smucker (the jam and jelly company), Container Store (the storage and organization store), and A. G. Edwards (financial services firm) give employees a chance to make a difference at work and as a result have received positive media attention for being included on Fortune magazine's list of "The 100 Best Companies to Work For." These media reports highlight how choices that companies have made about human resource management practices influence employees, managers, shareholders, the community, and ultimately, the success of the company.

◈ FOCUS AND APPROACH OF *FUNDAMENTALS OF HUMAN RESOURCE MANAGEMENT*

Following graduation most students will find themselves working in businesses or not-for-profit organizations. Regardless of their position or career aspirations, their role in either directly managing other employees or understanding human resource management practices is critical for insuring both company and personal success. As a result, *Fundamentals of Human Resource Management* focuses on human resource issues and how HR is used at work. *Fundamentals of Human Resource Management* is applicable to both HR majors and students from other majors or colleges who are taking a human resource course as an elective or a requirement. An important feature of *Fundamentals of Human Resource Management* is that the book is rich with examples and engages the student with applications. Students not only learn about best human resource practices but they are actively engaged in learning about human resource issues through cases and decision-making. This is critical for helping students learn how to find, develop, and nurture talent, one of the most important tasks in organizations but one which according to a recent *Fast Company* article titled "Why we hate HR," is woefully performed in most companies. For example, as described in detail in the guided tour of the book, each chapter includes "Thinking Ethically" which confronts students with ethical issues regarding managing human resources and asks them to make and justify their decisions, and several different cases (*BusinessWeek* Cases and additional end-of-chapter cases) which look at events of real companies and encourage students to critically evaluate each situation and apply the chapter concepts. "Did You Know" boxes are included in each chapter. The information provided in these boxes shows students how the issues raised in the chapter play out in companies. Some examples include the top ten causes of workplace injuries, the importance of first impressions in the interview, and the effects of the glass ceiling on the number of women CEOs. Adopters of *Fundamentals* have access to Manager's Hot Seat exercises which include video segments showing scenarios that are critical for HR success including ethics, diversity, working in teams, and the virtual workplace. Students assume the role of manager as they watch the video and answer questions that appear during the segment—forcing them to make on-the-spot decisions. *Fundamentals of Human Resource Management* also provides students with "how to" perform HR activities such as interviewing that they are likely to have to perform in their jobs. Finally, *Fundamentals of Human Resource Management* shows how the Internet can be useful for managing human resources.

While other books may have similar coverage of HR topics, the author team believes that three features distinguish this book from the rest: timely coverage of important HR issues, easy to read, and features that grab students' attention and get them actively involved in learning. For those of you who adopted the first edition of *Fundamentals* we thank you and hope you will continue to use the second edition! For those of you considering *Fundamentals* for adoption we hope you agree that the book's features make *Fundamentals* your text of choice for human resource management!

◈ ORGANIZATION

Fundamentals of Human Resource Management includes an introductory chapter (Chapter 1) and five parts.

Chapter 1 discusses why human resource management is an essential element for an organization's success. The chapter introduces human resource management practices and human resource professionals and managers' roles and responsibilities in managing human resources. Also, ethics in human resource management is emphasized.

Part 1 discusses the environmental forces that companies face in trying to effectively utilize their human resources. These forces include economic, technological, social trends, employment laws, and work design. Employers typically have more control over work design than development of equal employment law or economic, technological, or social trends but all affect how employers attract, retain, and motivate human resources. Some of the major trends discussed in Chapter 2 include greater availability of new and inexpensive technology for human resource management, the growth of the use of human resources on a global scale, changes in the labor force and the types of skills needed in today's jobs, and a focus on aligning human resource management with the company's strategy. Chapter 3, "Providing Equal Employment Opportunity and a Safe Workplace," presents an overview of the major laws affecting employers in these areas and ways that organizations can develop human resource practices that are in compliance with the laws. Chapter 4, "Analyzing Work and Designing Jobs," shows how jobs and work systems determine the knowledge, skills, and abilities that employees need to provide services or produce products and influence employees' motivation, satisfaction, and safety at work. The process of analyzing and designing jobs is discussed.

Part 2 deals with identifying the types of employees needed, recruiting and choosing them, and training them to perform their jobs. Chapter 5, "Planning for and Recruiting Human Resources," discusses how to develop a human resource plan. The strengths and weaknesses of different employment options for dealing with shortage or excesses of human resources including outsourcing, use of contract workers and downsizing are emphasized. Strategies for recruiting talented employees including use of electronic recruiting sources such as job boards and blogs are emphasized. Chapter 6, "Selecting Employees and Placing Them in Jobs," emphasizes that selection is a process starting with screening applications and résumés and concluding with a job offer. The chapter takes a look at the most widely used methods for minimizing errors in choosing employees including applications and résumés, employment tests, and interviews. Selection method standards such as reliability and validity are discussed in understandable terms. Chapter 7, "Training Employees," covers the features of effective training systems. Effective training includes not only creating a good learning environment, but managers who encourage employees to use training content in their jobs and employees who are motivated to learn. The advantages and disadvantages of different training methods, including e-learning, are discussed.

Part 3 discusses how to assess employee performance and capitalize on their talents through retention and development. In "Managing Employees' Performances," (Chapter 8) we examine the strengths and weaknesses of different performance management systems including controversial forced distribution or ranking systems. "Developing Employees for Future Success" (Chapter 9) shows the student how assessment, job experiences, formal courses, and mentoring relationships can be used to develop employees for future success. Chapter 10, "Separating and Retaining Employees," discusses how to maximize employee satisfaction and productivity and retain valuable employees as well as how to fairly and humanely separate employees if the need arises because of poor performance or economic conditions.

Part 4 covers rewarding and compensating human resources, including how to design pay structures, recognize good performers, and provide benefits. In Chapter 11, "Establishing a Pay Structure," we discuss how managers weigh the importance and costs of pay to develop a compensation structure and levels of pay for each job given the worth of the jobs, legal requirements, and employee's judgments about the fairness of pay levels. The advantages and disadvantages of different types of incentive pay including merit pay, gainsharing, and stock ownership are discussed in Chapter 12, "Recognizing Employee Contributions with Pay." Chapter 13, "Providing Employee Benefits," highlights the contents of employee benefit packages, the ways that organizations administer benefits, and what companies can do to help employees understand the value of benefits and control benefits costs.

Part 5 covers other HR goals including collective bargaining and labor relations, managing human resource globally, and creating and maintaining high-performance organizations. "Collective Bargaining and Labor Relations" (Chapter 14) explores human resource activities where employees belong to unions or are seeking to join unions. Traditional issues in labor-management relations such as union structure and membership, the labor organizing process, and contract negotiations are discussed, as well as new ways unions and management are working together in less adversarial and more cooperative relationships. In "Managing Human Resources Globally" (Chapter 15) HR planning, selection, training, and compensating in international settings are discussed. We show how global differences among countries affect decisions about human resources. The role of human resources in creating an organization that achieves a high level of performance for employees, customers, community, shareholders, and managers is the focus of Chapter 16 "Creating and Maintaining High Performance Work Organizations." The chapter describes high-performance work systems, the conditions that contribute to high performance, and introduces students to the ways to measure the effectiveness of human resource management.

fundamentals of human
resource
management

NOE
HOLLENBECK
GERHART
WRIGHT

2

fundamentals of human
resource
management

focused.
engaging.
applied.

The second edition of
*Fundamentals of Human
Resource Management*
continues to offer students
a brief introduction to
HRM that is rich with
examples and engaging in
its application.

**Please take a moment to
page through some of the
highlights of this new
edition.**

FEATURES

The well-known author team of Noe, Hollenbeck, Gerhart, and Wright have revised their successful first edition for students and classes that want to learn more about how human resource management is used in the everyday work environment.

WHAT DO I NEED TO KNOW?

Student learning objectives open each chapter. They bring attention to the key topics in the chapter and are then referenced in the page margins of the chapter discussion so students can easily see where each topic is explored. Learning objectives are referenced in the page margins where the relevant discussion begins.

CHAPTER 7

TRAINING EMPLOYEES

After reading this chapter, you should be able to:

What Do I Need to Know?

1. Discuss how to link training programs to organizational needs.

2. Explain how to assess the need for training.

3. Explain how to assess employees' readiness for training.

4. Describe how to plan an effective training program.

5. Compare widely used training methods.

6. Summarize how to implement a successful training program.

7. Evaluate the success of a training program.

8. Describe training methods for employee orientation and diversity management.

◈ INTRODUCTION

The problem facing Espresso Connection was that sales were flat. The chain of drive-through coffee stands, based in Everett, Washington, used a variety of advertising media, but the customers attracted by the ads simply weren't coming back. Espresso Connection's owner, Christian Kar, identified the source of this problem as poor customer service. He decided he needed to teach employees how to impress customers.

Espresso Connection hired several part-time trainers and set up a practice facility. Newly hired employees no longer rely on their coworkers to teach them what to do. Instead, they spend a week in the practice facility, learning to use the equipment, followed by another week of on-the-job training at a store. The first week prepares employees to work fast, a goal that quickly affects Espresso Connection's bottom line. Says Kar, "Our locations are really, really small. Unless our staff really focuses on getting customers through there more efficiently, we quickly would hit a brick wall in terms of revenues." Moving fast also cuts the waiting time for Espresso Connection's customers. The other major goal of the training is to teach employees specific skills related to customer service—for example, keeping the window open while serving customers. A few years after Espresso Connection started the training, the company saw its sales nearly double.[1]

Training consists of an organization's planned efforts to help employees acquire job-related knowledge, skills, abilities, and behaviors, with the goal of

thinking ETHICALLY

Carrying Ethics Standards Abroad

The "Best Practices" box in this chapter described how Deloitte Touche Tohmatsu is applying ethical standards to its employees, who work in almost 150 different countries. The firm has one advantage, at least: Its professional employees share the values of their profession, even if they come from a variety of cultural backgrounds. For other companies, the political, cultural, and economic realities of a host country may be extremely different from those of the parent country, causing ethical dilemmas.

Consider companies that market clothing in the United States that is manufactured in low-wage countries where living standards are far from those in the United States. Critics have objected to the practice of selling goods made in "sweatshops," factories where working conditions are unhealthy and unsafe. Typically, the U.S. marketer doesn't hire its own manufacturing employees but instead contracts with manufacturing firms in low-wage countries, so the U.S. company has limited direct control over working conditions. Nike has addressed the criticism by joining the Fair Labour Association, an international group that monitors factory conditions, and it issues reports of working conditions. For example, in 2005, the company published a report indicating, for example, that abuses of employees occurred in one-fourth of its factories in South Asia and that over one-fourth of those factories restricted access to toilets and drinking water during the workday. The Gap has issued similar reports about working conditions in the factories of its suppliers. The retailer conducts initial evaluations of potential suppliers and has reported that about 90 percent fail that evaluation. The Gap also trains suppliers in its requirements for working conditions, and it helps them set up compliance programs.

Paul Fireman, the chairman and chief executive officer of Reebok International,

NEW!

THINKING ETHICALLY

The "Thinking Ethically" feature at the end of each chapter confronts students with ethical issues regarding managing human resources and asks them to make and justify their decisions. Examples include: "Gays and Lesbians in the Picture at Eastman Kodak", and "Whose Business is it When you Blog?"

BEST PRACTICES

The "Best Practices" boxes give specific company examples of what is working well in HRM. Illustrating real-world examples of policies that have been put in place and have been successful helps students understand how to apply what they're learning in the text. Examples include: "Building a Common Culture at PriceWaterhouseCoopers," "Pregnancy no Barrier at Plante & Moran," and "Jobs Without Titles Promote Innovation at W.L. Gore."

HR HOW TO

The "HR How To" boxes discuss steps to creating HRM programs and include examples of how companies have tackled challenges. This feature helps students to understand the common functions of human resource professionals. Examples include: "Putting Interns on the Payroll," "Writing a Job Description," and "Interviewing Effectively."

e-HRM

The "e-HRM" boxes appear throughout the book and emphasize the increasing use of technology in human resource management today and how it is changing the way things are getting done. Examples include: "At Sun Microsystems, Offices are 'Virtual'," "Reebok Application to Shed Light on Working Conditions," and "New Technology Redefines Personnel Selection."

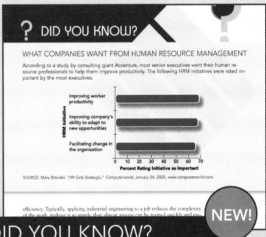
DID YOU KNOW?

"Did You Know?" boxes within the chapters provide a snapshot of interesting statistics related to chapter topics. The information provided here shows students how the issues raised in the chapter play out in companies. Examples include: "Top Ten Causes of Workplace Injuries," "Importance of First Impressions in the Interview," and "The Effects of the Glass Ceiling on the Number of Women CEOs."

CHAPTER SUMMARIES recap the "What Do I Need to Know?" objectives from the beginning of each chapter with brief summary discussions.

BUSINESSWEEK CASES look at events at real companies as reported by the nation's number one business weekly and encourage students to critically evaluate each situation and apply the chapter concepts.

KEY TERMS and definitions appear in the text margins, so purposes of terms are highlighted where they are discussed and students can get to know the language of HRM.

---

thinking ETHICALLY

Can You Teach People to Be Ethical?

This chapter looked at training as a way to ensure that employees have a variety of skills and abilities, such as knowing how to perform the tasks involved in a particular trade and being able to work constructively with a diverse group of people. Some organizations also provide training to help their employees make ethical decisions.

Molson Coors Brewing Company offers its employees several resources related to ethics, including interactive e-learning, ethics leadership training, and a visual "map" to guide ethical decision making. These training resources support detailed ethics policies and supplement a company help line to call for guidance in specific situations. According to Warren Malmquist, who developed the ethics training for Adolph Coors Company before its 2005 acquisition of Molson, "The goal of the program is to step beyond rules and guidelines and teach employees how to think, clarify, and analyze situations." The e-learning program presents scenarios and provides feedback to help employees see the ethical principles related to their decisions. The program includes a series of modules presented as an "expedition" from a base camp to the top of the mountain. As the employee ascends through the modules, the topics become more complex and the choices less obvious. All new hires must complete this course within 90 days, and existing employees must take refresher courses.

SOURCE: Based on Samuel Greengard, "Golden Values," Workforce Management, March 2005, pp. 52–53.

Questions

1. To make ethical decisions, what skills and abilities do you need? What else do you need besides skills and abilities?
2. Do you think the ethics training described here will help make Molson Coors employees more ethical? Explain.
3. Suppose you became responsible for providing ethics training at Molson Coors. What additional ideas from the chapter or your own experience would you want to apply to the program described here?

SUMMARY

1. Discuss how to link training programs to organizational needs.
   Organizations need to establish training programs that are effective. In other words, they teach what they are designed to teach, and they teach skills and behaviors that will help the organization achieve its goals. Organizations create such program through instructional design. This process begins with a needs assessment. The organization then ensures readiness for training, including employee characteristics and organizational support. Next, the organization plans a training program, implements the program, and evaluates the results.

2. Explain how to assess the need for training.
   Needs assessment consists of an organization analysis, person analysis, and task analysis. The organization analysis determines the appropriateness of training by

---

9. How can organizations improve the quality of their interviewing so that interviews provide valid information?
10. Some organizations set up a selection process that is long and complex. In some people's opinion, this kind of selection process not only is more valid but also has symbolic value. What can the use of a long, complex selection process symbolize to job seekers? How do you think this would affect the organization's ability to attract the best employees?

WHAT'S YOUR HR IQ?

The text Web site offers two more ways to check what you've learned so far. Use the Self-Assessment exercise to practice behavioral interview questions. Go online with the Web Exercise to analyze a selection tool used by some convenience stores.

BusinessWeek CASE

BusinessWeek How Google Searches for Talent

March 26, 2005, heralds the opening of the spring season in India, a day celebrated with riotous color and revelry. But in one corner of Bangalore, India's info tech hub, the sunny Saturday is heavy with tension. At an Internet café, a group of engineers and math majors, all in their twenties, hunch over terminals, ready to write some killer code—and, with luck, launch careers with one of the world's premier tech companies, Google Inc.

It's the Google India Code Jam, a contest to find the most brilliant coder in South and Southeast Asia. The fastest will win $6,900—and more important, the offer of a coveted job at one of Google's research and development centers. At the stroke of 10:30 A.M., the contestants begin, emerging exhausted three hours later. "It's been incredibly difficult and awesome," says Nitin Gupta, a computer science undergrad at the Indian Institute of Technology at Bombay.

Google has staged Code Jams in the United States, but this is its first such bakeoff in Asia, and the response is huge. Some 14,000 aspirants registered from all over South and Southeast Asia for the first round in February. The top 50 were selected for the finals in Bangalore: 39 from India, 8 from Singapore, and 3 from Indonesia. "It's a dog-eat-dog world," says Robert Hughes, president of TopCoder Inc., the Glastonbury, Connecticut, testing company that runs the Code Jam. "Wherever the best talent is, Google wants them."

And the winner is . . . one of those clever IIT grads from India, right? Surprisingly, no. Ardian Poernomo, a third-year undergrad computer engineering student at Singapore's Nanyang Technological University, lands in first place. The number two finisher, Pascal Alfadian, a

second-year student at the Universitas Katolik Parahyangan in West Java, is Indonesian, too. Poernomo didn't commit to taking a job with Google, however. He may go for a doctorate degree in computer science in the United States.

Still, Google now has a new pool of Asian talent to choose from. According to Krishna Bharat, head of Google's India research and development center, all the finalists will be offered jobs. And Google needs them. The search company has been frustrated by its inability to find top-notch engineers for its year-old Indian center, according to industry insiders. Its Bangalore staff now totals 25, but it was hoping to have signed up at least 100 engineers by December 2004.

Google's frustrations in India stem from two factors. One is the red-hot job market in Indian tech. Engineering students are assured of a job a year before they graduate. But Google makes things hard for itself by having some of the most exacting hiring standards going. The contest is an example. Participants are tested on aptitude in problem solving, on designing and writing code, and on testing peer-written work. Finalists are asked to create and test software for unique Web searches and to get from point A to B in a city with a minimum number of turns. The final challenge is programming a war-based board game, a task so complex that only winner Poernomo completed it.

For Google, the Code Jam will serve as a shortcut through its hiring regime. Candidates normally go through a seven-stage process that can last months—and, at the end of it, they're more likely to be rejected than hired. Much of that screening can be set aside for Code Jam winners.

Typically, an industrial union represents many in the union is the result of working for a particular employer. ng employers is less common than it is among craft e employers remain members of the same union r employers covered by that union. Another dif- may restrict the nu es, industrial union possible. d with the **Ameri** s **(AFL-CIO)**. The vance the shared i hamber of Commu ember employers.

American Federation of Labor and Congress of

Outsourcing

Many organizations are increasingly outsourcing business activities. Ou refers to the practice of having another company (a vendor, third-party pr consultant) provide services. For instance, a manufacturing company might its accounting and transportation functions to businesses that specialize in

outsourcing
The practice of having another company (a vendor, third-party provider, or consultant) provide services

---

ress wrote and passed Title VII, and President Lyndon n 1964. The law is enforced by the **Equal Employment** (EEOC), an agency of the Department of Justice. oyers from discriminating against individuals because of ex, or national origin. An employer may not use these r not hiring someone, for firing someone, or for discrim- terms of their pay, conditions of employment, or privi- dition, an employer may not use these characteristics in mployees or job applicants in any way that would deprive nt opportunities or otherwise adversely affect his or her act applies to organizations that employ 15 or more per- eeks a year and that are involved in interstate commerce, rnments, employment agencies, and labor organizations. employers may not retaliate against employees for either al employment practice or "participating in a proceeding" employment practice. Opposition refers to expressing to

Equal Employment Opportunity Commission (EEOC)
Agency of the Department of Justice charged with enforcing Title VII of the Civil Rights Act of 1964 and other antidiscrimination laws.

REVIEW AND DISCUSSION
QUESTIONS
at the end of each chapter help
students nail down the concepts
presented in the chapter and understand
potential applications of the chapter
material.

FINAL CASES in each chapter
take another look at companies
and how their practices illustrate
or apply concepts from the
chapter. They provide external
examples to bring into a
lecture, along with questions
for assignments or classroom
discussion. Oriented Online.

WHAT'S YOUR HR IQ? sections at
the end of each chapter reference the
assessment activities and web exercises
included on the text Web site (www.
mhhe.com/noefund2e)—these are
activities to reinforce the specific
chapter content.

supplements for students and instructors

INSTRUCTOR'S MANUAL
The Instructor's Manual includes chapter summaries, learning objectives, an extended chapter outline, key terms, description of text boxes, discussion questions, summary of end-of-chapter cases, video notes and additional activities, and references to Annual Editions articles.

TEST BANK
The test bank includes multiple choice, true/false, and essay questions for each chapter. Rationales and page references are also provided for the answers.

INSTRUCTOR PRESENTATION CD-ROM
This multimedia CD-ROM allows instructors to create dynamic classroom presentations by incorporating PowerPoint, videos and the Instructor's Manual and Test Bank.

BROWNSTONE'S DIPLOMA FOR WINDOWS
This test generator allows instructors to add and edit questions, create new versions of the test, and more.

VIDEOS
12 new videos on HRM issues accompany this edition. The accompanying video cases are included on the text Web site. Teaching notes are included in the Instructor's Manual.

POWERPOINT
This presentation program features slides that include lecture material, key terms, additional content to expand concepts in the text, hotlinks, video clips, and discussion questions that can be used in CPS (see below). The PowerPoint is found on the Instructor CD-ROM and on the Instructor and student Center of the Online Learning Center. The PPT also now includes detailed teaching notes.

CPS (WIRELESS CLASSROOM PERFORMANCE SYSTEM)
by eInstruction
If you've ever asked yourself, "How can I measure class participation, or "How do I encourage class participation?" then CPS might be the product for you. CPS enables you to record responses from students to questions posed in a PowerPoint slide, even record attendance, and offers a variety of reporting features, including easy export to WebCT or Blackboard grade books. For your students, it's as easy as using buttons on a remote control. Questions can be designed by you, or questions are already included in the Fundamentals of Human Resource Management PowerPoint. Ask your local sales representative how to get CPS for your classroom.

ONLINE LEARNING CENTER
(www.mhhe.com/noefund2e)
This text-specific Web site follows the text chapter by chapter. Students can go online to take self-grading quizzes, access professional resources, watch video clips and answer discussion questions, read relevant, current HR news and work through interactive exercises. There is a new guide linking the PHR/SPHR certification exam with the text. Instructors can also access the downloadable supplements such as the instructor's manual and Hot Seat DVD notes. OLCs can be delivered multiple ways—professors and students can access them directly through the textbook Web site, through PageOut, or within a course management system (i.e., WebCT, Blackboard, TopClass, or eCollege).

POWERWEB
Harness the assets of the Web to keep your course current with PowerWeb! This online resource provides high-quality , peer-reviewed content including up-to-date articles from leading periodicals and journals, current news, weekly updates with assessment, interactive exercises, Web research guide, study tips, and much more! Visit the text Web site to access the material.

MANAGER'S HOT SEAT DVD
The Manager's Hot Seat is an interactive DVD that allows students to watch as 15 real managers apply their years of experience to confront these issues. Students assume the role of the manager as they watch the video and answer multiple choice questions that pop up during the segment — forcing them to make decisions on the spot. Students learn from the manager's mistakes and successes, and then do a report critiquing the manager's approach by defending their reasoning. Reports can be e-mailed or printed out for credit. If you choose to package the Hot Seat DVD with this text, there are individual and group exercises related to most of the segments on the online learning center, as well as accompanying teaching notes in the Instructor's Manual.

ACKNOWLEDGMENTS

The second edition of *Fundamentals of Human Resource Management* would not have been possible without the staff of McGraw-Hill/Irwin and Elm Street Publishing Services. John Weimeister, our editor, helped us in developing the vision for the book and gave us the resources we needed to develop a top-of-the-line HRM teaching package. Sarah Reed's organizational skills kept the author team on deadline and made the book more visually appealing than the authors could have ever done on their own. Karen Hill of Elm Street worked diligently to make sure that the book was interesting, practical, and readable, and remained true to findings of human resource management research. We also thank Meg Beamer for her marketing efforts for this new book.

Our supplements' authors deserve thanks for helping us create a first-rate teaching package. Amit Shah of Frostburg State University wrote the *Instructor's Manual* and created the Test Bank. He also authored content for the text Web site. Paige Wolf of George Mason University authored the new PowerPoint presentation and the PHR/SPHR resource guide on the Web site.

We would like to extend our sincere appreciation to all of the professors who gave of their time to offer their suggestions and insightful comments that helped us to develop and shape this new edition:

Michelle Alarcon
Hawaii Pacific University

Lydia Anderson
Fresno City College

Brenda Anthony
Tallahassee Community College

Barry Armandi
SUNY–Old Westbury

Kristin Backhaus
State University of New York at New Paltz

Charlene Barker
Spokane Falls Community College

Melissa Woodard Barringer
University of Massachusetts at Amherst

Jerry Bennett
Western Kentucky University

Tom Bilyeu
Southwestern Illinois College

Genie Black
Arkansas Tech University

Larry Borgen
Normandale Community College

Kay Braguglia
Hampton University

John Brau
Alvin Community College

Susan Burroughs
Roosevelt University

Tony Cafarelli
Ursuline College

Jerry Carbo
Fairmont State College

Kevin Carlson
Virginia Tech

Xiao-Ping Chen
University of Washington

Sharon Clark
Lebanon Valley College

Gary Corona
Florida Community College

Suzanne Crampton
Grand Valley State University

Denise Daniels
Seattle Pacific University

K. Shannon Davis
North Carolina State University

Cedric Dawkins
Ashland University

Tom Diamante
Adelphi University

Anita Dickson
Northampton Community College

Robert Ericksen
Craven Community College

Dave Erwin
Athens State University

Philip Ettman
Westfield State College

Angela Farrar
University of Nevada at Las Vegas

Ronald Faust
University of Evansville

David Foote
Middle Tennessee State University

Lucy Ford
Rutgers University

Wanda Foster
Calumet College of St. Joseph

Marty Franklin
Wilkes Community College

Rusty Freed
Tarleton State University

Walter Freytag
University of Washington

Donald Gardner
University of Colorado–Colorado Springs

Michael Gavlik
Vanderbilt University

Treena Gillespie
California State University–Fullerton

Kris Gossett
Ivy Tech State College

Samuel Hazen
Tarleton State University

James Hess
Ivy Tech State College

Kim Hester
Arkansas State University

Chad Higgins
University of Washington

Nancy Higgins
Montgomery College

Charles Hill
UC Berkeley

Mary Hogue
Kent State University

MaryAnne Hyland
Adelphi University

Linda Isenhour
University of Central Florida

Henry Jackson
Delaware County Community College

Pamela Johnson
California State University–Chico

Coy Jones
The University of Memphis

Gwendolyn Jones
University of Akron

Kathleen Jones
University of North Dakota

Jordan Kaplan
Long Island University

Jim Kennedy
Angelina College

Shawn Komorn
University of Texas Health Sciences Center

Lee W. Lee
Central Connecticut State University

Leo Lennon
Webster University

Dan Lybrook
Purdue University

Patricia Martinez
University of Texas at San Antonio

Jalane Meloun
Kent State University

Angela Miles
Old Dominion University

James Morgan
California State University–Chico

Cliff Olson
Southern Adventist University

Laura Paglis
University of Evansville

Teresa Palmer
Illinois State University

Jack Partlow
Northern Virginia Community College

Dana Partridge
University of Southern Indiana

Brooke Quizz
Peirce College

Barbara Rau
University of Wisconsin–Oshkosh

Mike Roberson
Eastern Kentucky University

Foreman Rogers, Jr.
Northwood University

Joseph Salamone
State University of New York at Buffalo

Lucian Spataro
Ohio University

Steven Thomas
Southwest Missouri State University

Alan Tilquist
West Virginia State College

Tom Tudor
University of Arkansas

Fraya Wagner-Marsh
Eastern Michigan University

Richard Wagner
University of Wisconsin–Whitewater

Gary Waters
Hawaii Pacific University

Bill Waxman
Edison Community College

John Zietlow
Lee University

John Zummo
York College

We would also like to thank the professors who gave of their time to review the first edition text through various stages of development.

Cheryl Adkins
Longwood University

Wendy Becker
University of Albany

Jon Bryan
Bridgewater State College

Craig Cowles
Bridgewater State College

Vicki Mullenex
Davis &Elkins College

Mary Ellen Rosetti
Hudson Valley Community College

James Tan
University of Wisconsin–Stout

Steve Thomas
Southwest Missouri State University

Melissa Waite
SUNY Brockport

Barbara Warschawski
Schenectady County Community College

Steven Wolff
Marist College

Raymond A. Noe
John R. Hollenbeck
Barry Gerhart
Patrick M. Wright

BRIEF CONTENTS

CONTENTS

ⓟⓐⓡⓣ ②

**Acquiring and Preparing Human
Resources 135**

ᴘᴀʀᴛ 3

Assessing Performance
and Developing Employees 247

MANAGING HUMAN RESOURCES

After reading this chapter, you should be able to:

What Do I Need to Know?

1. Define human resource management and explain how HRM contributes to an organization's performance.

2. Identify the responsibilities of human resource departments.

3. Summarize the types of skills needed for human resource management.

4. Explain the role of supervisors in human resource management.

5. Discuss ethical issues in human resource management.

6. Describe typical careers in human resource management.

❧ INTRODUCTION

Imagine trying to run a business where you have to replace every employee two or three times a year. If that sounds chaotic, you can sympathize with the challenge facing Rob Cecere when he took the job of regional manager for a group of eight Domino's Pizza stores in New Jersey. In Cecere's region, store managers were quitting after a few months on the job. The lack of consistent leadership at the store level contributed to employee turnover rates of up to 300 percent a year (one position being filled three times in a year). In other words, new managers constantly had to find, hire, and train new workers—and rely on inexperienced people to keep customers happy. Not surprisingly, the stores in Cecere's new territory were failing to meet sales goals.

Cecere made it his top goal to build a stable team of store managers who in turn could retain employees at their stores. He held a meeting with the managers and talked about improving sales, explaining, "It's got to start with people": hiring good people and keeping them on board. He continues to coach his managers, helping them build sales and motivate their workers through training and patience. In doing so, he has the backing of Domino's headquarters. When the company's current chief executive, David Brandon, took charge in 1999, he was shocked by the high employee turnover (then 158 percent nationwide), and he made

LO1
Define human resource management and explain how HRM contributes to an organization's performance.

human resource management (HRM)
The policies, practices, and systems that influence employees' behavior, attitudes, and performance.

that problem his priority. Brandon doubts the pay rates are what keeps employees with any fast-food company; instead, he emphasizes careful hiring, extensive coaching, and opportunities to earn promotions. In the years since Brandon became CEO, employee turnover at Domino's has fallen. And in New Jersey, Cecere is beginning to see results from his store managers as well.[1]

The challenges faced by Domino's are important dimensions of **human resource management (HRM),** the policies, practices, and systems that influence employees' behavior, attitudes, and performance. Many companies refer to HRM as involving "people practices." Figure 1.1 emphasizes that there are several important HRM practices: analyzing work and designing jobs, attracting potential employees (recruiting), choosing employees (selection), teaching employees how to perform their jobs and preparing them for the future (training and development), evaluating their performance (performance management), rewarding employees (compensation), creating a positive work environment (employee relations), and supporting the organization's strategy (HR planning and change management). An organization performs best when all of these practices are managed well. At companies with effective HRM, employees and customers tend to be more satisfied, and the companies tend to be more innovative, have greater productivity, and develop a more favorable reputation in the community.[2]

In this chapter, we introduce the scope of human resource management. We begin by discussing why human resource management is an essential element of an organization's succcess. We then turn to the elements of managing human resources: the roles and skills needed for effective human resource management. Next, the chapter describes how all managers, not just human resource professionals, participate in the activities related to human resource management. The following section of the chapter addresses some of the ethical issues that arise with regard to human resource management. We then provide an overview of careers in human resource management. The chapter concludes by highlighting the HRM practices covered in the remainder of this book.

Figure 1.1
Human Resource Management Practices

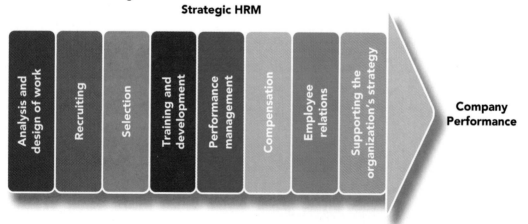

≫ HUMAN RESOURCES AND COMPANY PERFORMANCE

Managers and economists traditionally have seen human resource management as a necessary expense, rather than as a source of value to their organizations. Economic value is usually associated with *capital*—cash, equipment, technology, and facilities. However, research has demonstrated that HRM practices can be valuable.[3] Decisions such as whom to hire, what to pay, what training to offer, and how to evaluate employee performance directly affect employees' motivation and ability to provide goods and services that customers value. Companies that attempt to increase their competitiveness by investing in new technology and promoting quality throughout the organization also invest in state-of-the-art staffing, training, and compensation practices.[4]

The concept of "human resource management" implies that employees are *resources* of the employer. As a type of resource, **human capital** means the organization's employees, described in terms of their training, experience, judgment, intelligence, relationships, and insight—the employee characteristics that can add economic value to the organization. In other words, whether it manufactures automobiles or forecasts the weather, for an organization to succeed at what it does, it needs employees with certain qualities, such as particular kinds of training and experience. This view means employees in today's organizations are not interchangeable, easily replaced parts of a system but the source of the company's success or failure. By influencing *who* works for the organization and *how* those people work, human resource management therefore contributes to such basic measures of an organization's success as quality, profitability, and customer satisfaction. Figure 1.2 shows this relationship.

Athleta Corporation, a catalog and Internet retailer of sports apparel, based in Petaluma, California, demonstrates the importance of human capital to the company's bottom line. Athleta's workforce is so committed to the company that turnover is less than 1 percent (1 out of 100 employees leave the company in an average year), productivity (output per worker) is increasing, and the company's growth is skyrocketing—it grew by five times in 2000 alone. One way the company has built a committed workforce

human capital
An organization's employees, described in terms of their training, experience, judgment, intelligence, relationships, and insight.

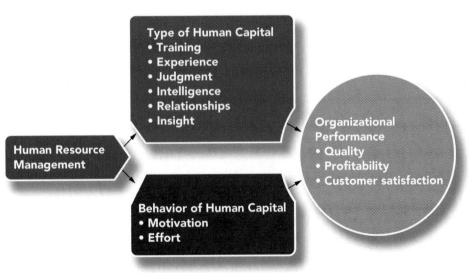

figure 1.2

Impact of Human Resource Management

LONG-TERM VIEW PAYS DIVIDENDS FOR VANGUARD GROUP

Vanguard Group, the money management and mutual-fund company based in Valley Forge, Pennsylvania, takes a long-term view not only in its investment advice but also in terms of employee relationships. Although Vanguard's HRM focus has shifted over the 28 years of the company's life, its ultimate goal has always been to retain and develop its valued employees.

At different times, Vanguard has been concerned with work/life programs, career management, and leadership programs. Today, the focus is on how employees are feeling about the company. Vanguard has faced difficult times because of recent scandals in the mutual-fund industry, which have raised worries among investors. Vanguard has avoided layoffs, because they would conflict with the company's position that retaining and motivating employees is at the root of the company's success.

Rather than a strict no-layoff policy, Vanguard's policy is to "do what is right for the crew," meaning its employees. According to this view, showing commitment to its crew in tough times goes a long way toward attracting, motivating, and retaining employees. For example, to adjust to new investment trends, the company redeployed staff to positions where they could be most useful, rather than firing and hiring to meet the new needs.

In addition, company policy is to grow from within. In other words, when Vanguard hires someone, it is not hiring for one position but for a career with the company. As a result, Vanguard does not cut funds for training when the economy slows, as it recently did. About 60 percent of Vanguard's 250 human resource staff are involved in training activities. This emphasis fits well with employees' concerns. Although the employees report

satisfaction with Vanguard's "do the right thing" philosophy, they want to know what they can do to prepare themselves for the next opportunity within Vanguard. Along with the training, Vanguard has had its managers meet more frequently with crew members to discuss these and other issues.

Vanguard does not pretend to believe that employees are unconcerned about money. The company's managing director of human resources says, "People always want to be paid at a competitive rate." But he adds that money is not the main reason people join an organization and stay there: "They stay because of the culture and a career opportunity [and] because of the people they work with." Vanguard's human resource management practices are well positioned to address those concerns.

SOURCE: R. Stolz, "Keeping the Crew," *Human Resource Executive*, December 2003, pp. 20–26.

is by cultivating a positive work environment. Most of Athleta's 60 employees set their own work schedules and are permitted to take personal time during the day. Employees take the initiative to learn one another's jobs, so they can fill in for one another during the day. Those who take time off for personal reasons willingly work odd hours. The company encourages employees to take breaks for physical activity, and employees can even bring along their dogs, which join employees outside for a run or to play catch. Employees use the open space preserve behind Athleta's facility to run, or they work out with the gym equipment set up in the company's storage area.[5] The "Best Practices" box tells about another company that appreciates the importance of human capital.

Human resource management is critical to the success of organizations because human capital has certain qualities that make it valuable. In terms of business strategy, an organization can succeed if it has a *sustainable competitive advantage* (is better than

At Southwest Airlines, the company's focus is on keeping employees loyal, motivated, trained, and compensated. In turn, there is a low turnover rate and a high rate of customer satisfaction.

competitors at something, and can hold that advantage over a sustained period of time). Therefore, we can conclude that organizations need the kind of resources that will give them such an advantage. Human resources have these necessary qualities:

- Human resources are *valuable*. High-quality employees provide a needed service as they perform many critical functions.
- Human resources are *rare* in the sense that a person with high levels of the needed skills and knowledge is not common. An organization may spend months looking for a talented and experienced manager or technician.
- Human resources *cannot be imitated*. To imitate human resources at a high-performing competitor, you would have to figure out which employees are providing the advantage and how. Then you would have to recruit people who can do precisely the same thing and set up the systems that enable those people to imitate your competitor.
- Human resources have *no good substitutes*. When people are well trained and highly motivated, they learn, develop their abilities, and care about customers. It is difficult to imagine another resource that can match committed and talented employees.

These qualities imply that human resources have enormous potential. An organization realizes this potential through the ways it practices human resource management.

Effective management of human resources can form the foundation of a **high-performance work system**—an organization in which technology, organizational structure, people, and processes all work together to give an organization an advantage in the competitive environment. As technology changes the ways organizations manufacture, transport, communicate, and keep track of information, human resource management must ensure that the organization has the right kinds of people to meet the new challenges. Maintaining a high-performance work system may include development of training programs, recruitment of people with new skill sets, and establishment of rewards for such behaviors as teamwork, flexibility, and learning. In the next chapter, we will see some of the changes that human resource managers are planning for, and Chapter 16 examines high-performance work systems in greater detail.

high-performance work system
An organization in which technology, organizational structure, people, and processes all work together to give an organization an advantage in the competitive environment.

◈ RESPONSIBILITIES OF HUMAN RESOURCE DEPARTMENTS

In all but the smallest organizations, a human resource department is responsible for the functions of human resource management. On average, an organization has one HR staff person for every 100 employees served by the department. Table 1.1 details

LO2
Identify the responsibilities of human resource departments.

FUNCTION	RESPONSIBILITIES
Analysis and design of work	Work analysis; job design; job descriptions
Recruitment and selection	Recruiting; job postings; interviewing; testing; coordinating use of temporary labor
Training and development	Orientation; skills training; career development programs
Performance management	Performance measures; preparation and administration of performance appraisals; discipline
Compensation and benefits	Wage and salary administration; incentive pay; insurance; vacation leave administration; retirement plans; profit sharing; stock plans
Employee relations	Attitude surveys; labor relations; employee handbooks; company publications; labor law compliance; relocation and outplacement services
Personnel policies	Policy creation; policy communication; record keeping; HR information systems
Compliance with laws	Policies to ensure lawful behavior; reporting; posting information; safety inspections; accessibility accommodations
Support for strategy	Human resource planning and forecasting; change management

SOURCE: Based on SHRM-BNA Survey No. 66, "Policy and Practice Forum: Human Resource Activities, Budgets, and Staffs, 2000-2001," *Bulletin to Management,* Bureau of National Affairs Policy and Practice Series (Washington, DC: Bureau of National Affairs, June 28, 2001).

the responsibilities of human resource departments. These responsibilities include the practices introduced in Figure 1.1 plus two areas of responsibility that support those practices: (1) establishing and administering personnel policies and (2) ensuring compliance with labor laws.

Although the human resource department has responsibility for these areas, many of the tasks may be performed by supervisors or others inside or outside the organization. No two human resource departments have precisely the same roles because of differences in organization sizes and characteristics of the workforce, the industry, and management's values. In some companies, the HR department handles all the activities listed in Table 1.1. In others, it may share the roles and duties with managers of other departments such as finance, operations, or information technology. In some companies, the HR department actively advises top management. In others, the department responds to top-level management decisions and implements staffing, training, and compensation activities in light of company strategy and policies.

Let's take an overview of the HR functions and some of the options available for carrying them out. Human resource management involves both the selection of which options to use and the activities of using those options. Later chapters of the book will explore each function in greater detail.

Analyzing and Designing Jobs

To produce their given product or service (or set of products or services) companies require that a number of tasks be performed. The tasks are grouped together in various combinations to form jobs. Ideally, the tasks should be grouped in ways that help the organization to operate efficiently and to obtain people with the right qualifications to do the jobs well. This function involves the activities of job analysis and job design. **Job analysis** is the process of getting detailed information about jobs. **Job design** is the process of defining the way work will be performed and the tasks that a given job requires.

In general, jobs can vary from having a narrow range of simple tasks to having a broad array of complex tasks requiring multiple skills. At one extreme is a worker on an assembly line at a poultry-processing facility; at the other extreme is a doctor in an emergency room. In the past, many companies have emphasized the use of narrowly defined jobs to increase efficiency. With many simple jobs, a company can easily find workers who can quickly be trained to perform the jobs at relatively low pay. However, greater concern for innovation and quality have shifted the trend to more use of broadly defined jobs. Also, as we will see in Chapters 2 and 4, some organizations assign work even more broadly, to teams instead of individuals.

Recruiting and Hiring Employees

Based on job analysis and design, an organization can determine the kinds of employees it needs. With this knowledge, it carries out the function of recruiting and hiring employees. **Recruitment** is the process through which the organization seeks applicants for potential employment. **Selection** refers to the process by which the organization attempts to identify applicants with the necessary knowledge, skills, abilities, and other characteristics that will help the organization achieve its goals. An organization makes selection decisions in order to add employees to its workforce, as well as to transfer existing employees to new positions.

Approaches to recruiting and selection involve a variety of alternatives. Some organizations may actively recruit from many external sources, such as Internet job postings, newspaper want-ads, and college recruiting events. Other organizations may rely heavily on promotions from within, applicants referred by current employees, and the availability of in-house people with the necessary skills. During the height of the Dot.com days, Freddie Mac, the Mclean, Virginia based secondary mortgage company, faced employee shortages in its information technology area. The company responded by retraining existing, non-technical talent into IT professionals. Freddie Mac offered interested employees who displayed a technical aptitude with an intense,

job analysis
The process of getting detailed information about jobs.

job design
The process of defining the way work will be performed and the tasks that a given job requires.

recruitment
The process through which the organization seeks applicants for potential employment.

selection
The process by which the organization attempts to identify applicants with the necessary knowledge, skills, abilities, and other characteristics that will help the organization achieve its goals.

SOURCE: Courtesy of Freddie Mac.

As a mortgage company, Freddie Mac has not only helped numerous families afford new homes, they have also invested in the young adults of America when they hired 20 recent graduates whom they trained in IT during an employee shortage at the company.

1. Communication skills (written and verbal)
2. Honesty/integrity
3. Interpersonal skills
4. Strong work ethic
5. Teamwork skills
6. Analytical skills
7. Motivation/initiative
8. Flexibility/adaptability
9. Computer skills
10. Detail orientation

SOURCE: Reprinted from Job Outlook 2005, with permission of the National Association of Colleges and Employers, copyright holder.

three-month training program that prepared them for a variety of positions within the information technology department. In general, these employees had liberal arts degrees, knowledge of the company and its products, and demonstrated communications, organizational, and project skills. None were in technical positions. During their training, they all received benefits and a salary equivalent to their current pay. When the program ended, all 20 participants took new positions within Freddie Mac as IT professionals.[6]

At some organizations the selection process may focus on specific skills, such as experience with a particular programming language or type of equipment. At other organizations, selection may focus on general abilities, such as the ability to work as part of a team or find creative solutions. The focus an organization favors will affect many choices, from the way the organization measures ability, to the questions it asks in interviews, to the places it recruits. Table 1.2 lists the top 10 qualities that employers say they are looking for in job candidates, based on a survey by the National Association of Colleges and Employers.

Training and Developing Employees

Although organizations base hiring decisions on candidates' existing qualifications, most organizations provide ways for their employees to broaden or deepen their knowledge, skills, and abilities. To do this, organizations provide for employee training and development. **Training** is a planned effort to enable employees to learn job-related knowledge, skills, and behavior. For example, many organizations offer safety training to teach employees safe work habits. **Development** involves acquiring knowledge, skills, and behavior that improve employees' ability to meet the challenges of a variety of new or existing jobs, including the client and customer demands of those jobs. Development programs often focus on preparing employees for management responsibility. Likewise, if a company plans to set up teams to manufacture products, it might offer a development program to help employees learn the ins and outs of effective teamwork. Figure 1.3 illustrates examples of training and development designed to increase the value of an organization's human capital.

Decisions related to training and development include whether the organization will emphasize enabling employees to perform their current jobs, preparing them for future jobs, or both. An organization may offer programs to a few employees in whom the organization wants to invest, or it may have a philosophy of investing in the training of all its workers. Some organizations, especially large ones, may have extensive

training
A planned effort to enable employees to learn job-related knowledge, skills, and behavior.

development
The acquisition of knowledge, skills, and behaviors that improve an employee's ability to meet changes in job requirements and in customer demands.

Figure 1.3

How Training and Development Can Increase the Value of Human Capital

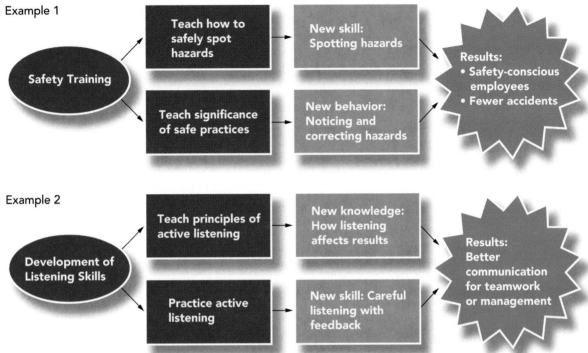

formal training programs, including classroom sessions and training programs on CD-ROM. Other organizations may prefer a simpler, more flexible approach of encouraging employees to participate in outside training and development programs as needs are identified.

Managing Performance

Managing human resources includes keeping track of how well employees are performing relative to objectives such as job descriptions and goals for a particular position. The process of ensuring that employees' activities and outputs match the organization's goals is called **performance management.** The activities of performance management include specifying the tasks and outcomes of a job that contribute to the organization's success. Then various measures are used to compare the employee's performance over some time period with the desired performance. Often, rewards—the topic of the next section—are developed to encourage good performance.

The human resource department may be responsible for developing or obtaining questionnaires and other devices for measuring performance. The performance measures may emphasize observable behaviors (for example, answering the phone by the second ring), outcomes (number of customer complaints and compliments), or both. When the person evaluating performance is not familiar with the details of the job, outcomes tend to be easier to evaluate than specific behaviors.[7] The evaluation may focus on the short term or long term and on individual employees or groups. Typically, the person who completes the evaluation is the employee's supervisor. Often employees also evaluate their own performance, and in some organizations, peers and subordinates participate, too.

performance management
The process of ensuring that employees' activities and outputs match the organization's goals.

Planning and Administering Pay and Benefits

The pay and benefits that employees earn play an important role in motivating them. This is especially true when rewards such as bonuses are linked to the individual's or group's achievements. Decisions about pay and benefits can also support other aspects of an organization's strategy. For example, a company that wants to provide an exceptional level of service or be exceptionally innovative might pay significantly more than competitors in order to attract and keep the best employees. At other companies, a low-cost strategy requires knowledge of industry norms, so that the company does not spend more than it must.

Planning pay and benefits involves many decisions, often complex and based on knowledge of a multitude of legal requirements. An important decision is how much to offer in salary or wages, as opposed to bonuses, commissions, and other performance-related pay. Other decisions involve which benefits to offer, from retirement plans to various kinds of insurance to time off with pay. All such decisions have implications for the organization's bottom line, as well as for employee motivation.

Pay and benefits have the greatest impact when they are based on what employees really want and need. Sherman Assembly Systems, located in San Antonio, Texas, hires many unskilled workers, including a large number who moved off the welfare rolls to take jobs at Sherman. These employees need benefits that help them enter the world of earning a regular paycheck. Sherman arranges to have its bank send representatives to the worksite to help employees apply for checking accounts with low minimum balances. In addition, the company gives workers without a high school diploma an opportunity to take Internet-based courses so they can earn their GED.[8] The work situation at Cronin and Company, a small advertising agency in Glastonbury, Connecticut, is far different. With Cronin's offices located midway between Boston and New York, the challenge is to keep talent from leaving for the many attractions of those major cities. Cronin makes it a priority that the workplace be comfortable and attractive, with an environment that makes people want to linger. The company has a posh employee lounge with leather chairs, piped-in jazz, and a cappucino machine. The lounge is meant not only to keep employees happy but to stimulate creative interaction.[9]

Administering pay and benefits is another big responsibility. Organizations need systems for keeping track of each employee's earnings and benefits. Employees need information about their health plan, retirement plan, and other benefits. Keeping track of this involves extensive record keeping and reporting to management, employees, the government, and others.

Maintaining Positive Employee Relations

Organizations often depend on human resource professionals to help them maintain positive relations with employees. This function includes preparing and distributing employee handbooks that detail company policies, and in large organizations company publications such as a monthly newsletter or a Web site on the organization's intranet. Preparing these communications may be a regular task for the human resource department.

The human resource department can also expect to handle certain kinds of communications from individual employees. Employees turn to the HR department for answers to questions about benefits and company policy. If employees feel they have been discriminated against, see safety hazards, or have other problems and are dissatisfied with their supervisor's response, they may turn to the HR department for help. Members of the department should be prepared to address such problems.

In organizations where employees belong to a union, employee relations entail additional responsibilities. The organization periodically conducts collective bargaining to negotiate an employment contract with union members. The HR department maintains communication with union representatives to ensure that problems are resolved as they arise.

Establishing and Administering Personnel Policies

All the human resource activities described so far require fair and consistent decisions, and most require substantial record keeping. Organizations depend on their HR department to help establish policies related to hiring, discipline, promotions, and benefits. For example, with a policy in place that an intoxicated worker will be immediately terminated, the company can handle such a situation more fairly and objectively than if it addressed such incidents on a case-by-case basis. The company depends on its HR professionals to help develop and then communicate the policy to every employee, so that everyone knows its importance. If anyone violates the rule, a supervisor can quickly intervene—confident that the employee knew the consequences and that any other employee would be treated the same way. Not only do such policies promote fair decision making, but they also promote other objectives, such as workplace safety and customer service.

All aspects of human resource management require careful and discreet record keeping, from processing job applications, to performance appraisals, benefits enrollment, and government-mandated reports. Handling records about employees requires accuracy as well as sensitivity to employee privacy. Whether the organization keeps records in file cabinets or on a sophisticated computer information system, it must have methods for ensuring accuracy and for balancing privacy concerns with easy access for those who need information and are authorized to see it.

Ensuring Compliance with Labor Laws

As we will discuss in later chapters, especially Chapter 3, the government has many laws and regulations concerning the treatment of employees. These laws govern such matters as equal employment opportunity, employee safety and health, employee pay

One reason W. L. Gore & Associates is repeatedly named one of the 100 Best Companies to Work for in America is their unusual corporate culture where all employees are known as associates and bosses are not to be found. How do you think this boosts morale in the workplace?

and benefits, employee privacy, and job security. Government requirements include filing reports and displaying posters, as well as avoiding unlawful behavior. Most managers depend on human resource professionals to help them keep track of these requirements.

Ensuring compliance with laws requires that human resource personnel keep watch over a rapidly changing legal landscape. For example, the increased use of and access to electronic databases by employees and employers suggest that in the near future legislation will be needed to protect employee privacy rights. Currently, no federal laws outline how to use employee databases in such a way as to protect employees' privacy while also meeting employers' and society's concern for security.

The requirement that employers give people with disabilities access to the workplace is a topic of continuing debate and court action. The Americans with Disabilities Act (ADA), discussed in Chapter 3, covers access of disabled persons to the physical work environment and attempts to eliminate discrimination against these persons in hiring and other HRM practices. However, no law helps eliminate disabled persons' disadvantages in access to technology such as the Internet, cell phones, and other electronic devices. Disabled people's computer usage and Internet access are only about half the level of persons without disabilities. Future laws may require that persons with disabilities receive access to such technology.[10] Accessibility might include adding screen readers to Web sites, providing voice recognition technology to computer users, or changing computer design to make computers easier for employees with limited mobility to use.

Another area of continued debate likely will be laws designed to prohibit discrimination by employers and health insurers against employees based on their genetic makeup. Advances in medicine and genetics allow scientists to predict from DNA samples a person's likelihood of contracting certain diseases. To reduce health care costs, companies may want to use this information to screen out job candidates or reassign current employees who have a genetic predisposition to a disease that is triggered by exposure to certain working conditions. Congress has debated laws that restrict genetic testing to monitoring the adverse effects of exposure to hazardous workplace substances (such as chemicals) and that prohibit employers from requiring employees or job candidates to provide predictive genetic information.

Also in the realm of fair employment practices, we are likely to see more attention to sex and race discrimination focusing on lack of access to training and development opportunities needed for an employee to be considered for top management. Although women and minorities are advancing into top management positions, "glass ceilings" still exist for female and minority employees. A recent survey showed that women held only 10 percent of the top corporate officer positions in companies listed by *Fortune* magazine as the 50 largest corporations.[11]

Lawsuits that will continue to influence HRM practices concern job security. As companies are forced to close facilities and lay off employees because of economic or competitive conditions, cases dealing with the illegal discharge of employees have increased. The issue of "employment at will"—that is, the principle that an employer may terminate employment at any time without notice—will be debated. As the age of the overall workforce increases, as described in the next chapter, the number of cases dealing with age discrimination in layoffs, promotions, and benefits will likely rise. Employers will need to review work rules, recruitment practices, and performance evaluation systems, revising them if necessary to ensure that they do not falsely communicate employment agreements the company does not intend to honor (such as lifetime employment) or discriminate on the basis of age.

Supporting the Organization's Strategy

At one time, human resource management was primarily an administrative function. The HR department focused on filling out forms and processing paperwork. As more organizations have come to appreciate the significance of highly skilled human resources, however, many HR departments have taken on a more active role in supporting the organization's strategy.

An important element of this responsibility is **human resource planning,** identifying the numbers and types of employees the organization will require in order to meet its objectives. Using these estimates, the human resource department helps the organization forecast its needs for hiring, training, and reassigning employees. Planning also may show that the organization will need fewer employees to meet anticipated needs. In that situation, human resource planning includes how to handle or avoid layoffs.

Often, an organization's strategy requires some type of change—for example, adding, moving, or closing facilities; applying new technology; or entering markets in other regions or countries. Common reactions to change include fear, anger, and confusion. The organization may turn to its human resource department for help in managing the change process. Skilled human resource professionals can apply knowledge of human behavior, along with performance management tools, to help the organization manage change constructively.

human resource planning
Identifying the numbers and types of employees the organization will require to meet its objectives.

SKILLS OF HRM PROFESSIONALS

With such varied responsibilities, the human resource department needs to bring together a large pool of skills. These skills fall into the four basic categories shown in Figure 1.4: human relations skills, decision-making skills, leadership skills, and technical skills.

LO3
Summarize the types of skills needed for human resource management.

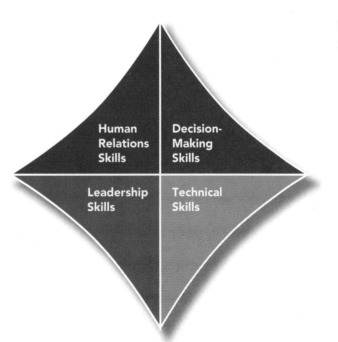

Figure 1.4
Skills of HRM Professionals

Human Relations Skills

The ability to understand and work well with other people is important to virtually any career, but human relations skills have taken on new significance for human resource management today. As organizations' managers increasingly appreciate the significance of human resources, many are calling for HRM to become the "source of people expertise" in the organization.[12] HR managers therefore need knowledge of how people can and do play a role in giving the organization an advantage against the competition, as well as of the policies, programs, and practices that can help the organization's people do so. Some of the human relations skills that are particularly important for today's HR professionals are communicating, negotiating, and team development.

Decision-Making Skills

Human resource managers must make a wide variety of decisions that affect whether employees are qualified and motivated and whether the organization is operating efficiently and complying with the law. Especially at organizations that give HRM departments a role in supporting strategy, HR decision makers also must be able to apply decision-making skills to strategic issues. This requires knowledge of the organization's line of business and the ability to present options in terms of costs and benefits to the organization, stated in terms of dollars.[13] Decisions must also take into account social and ethical implications of the alternatives. The "HR How To" box describes some of the decisions involved when a company wants to include interns in its workforce.

Leadership Skills

Through their knowledge, communication skills, and other abilities, HR managers need to play a leadership role with regard to the organization's human resources. In today's environment, leadership often requires helping the organization manage change. Fulfilling this leadership role includes diagnosing problems, implementing organizational changes, and evaluating results, especially in terms of employees' skills and attitudes. Changes typically produce conflict, resistance, and confusion among the people who must implement the new plans or programs. HR professionals must oversee the change in a way that ensures success. HRM provides tools for overcoming resistance to change, teaching employees to operate under new conditions, and even encouraging innovation. A survey of large corporations found that in 87 percent of the companies, organization development and change were managed by the HR department.[14]

Technical Skills

In any field, including management, "technical skills" are the specialized skills of that field. In human resource management, professionals need knowledge of state-of-the-art practices in such areas as staffing, development, rewards, organizational design, and communication. New selection techniques, performance appraisal methods, training programs, and incentive plans are constantly being developed. These developments often include the use of new software and computer systems. New laws are passed every year, and technical skills require knowledge of how to comply.

HR HOW TO

PUTTING INTERNS ON THE PAYROLL

Your budget is tight and your workload is overwhelming. It's the norm today at companies across America. Some managers decide they can solve this problem, find bright people, and contribute to developing the labor force all at the same time by hiring college students as interns. The idea can work, but only with careful decision making.

The first challenge is to identify which candidates are truly goal oriented and motivated to learn and contribute at work. Larina Kase, a small-business coach as well as a psychologist at the University of Pennsylvania School of Medicine, recommends that managers develop relationships with professors and career counselors at nearby schools. Offering guest lectures and participating at career fairs can strengthen ties with the people who know the students best. Another option is to work with colleges that have internship training programs.

Cary Catalano used this type of program to find interns for his marketing firm, Catalano Fenske & Associates. Interns have helped Catalano design his Web site and set up filing and billing systems. Before he hired any of the interns, Catalano defined the skills he was looking for and worked with a local college to clarify how it screened and trained internship candidates. He interviewed the candidates as he would for a permanent job, looking for a personality match as well as a particular set of skills.

Another challenge is to define the work for which the intern will be responsible. From the student's point of view, the internship is a chance to gain valuable work experience; standing at a photocopier all day would not attract the brightest, most ambitious candidates. Small businesses also face the disadvantage that many students will want a chance to put a famous corporation's name on their résumé; without that lure, employers need to craft a set of responsibilities that add up to a significant experience. In Santa Barbara, California, Chic Boutique, which designs fashion dolls, involves its interns in marketing decisions. A former intern later returned to the company as its director of product development.

Other decisions involve training and pay. An intern, by definition, is relatively inexperienced, so careful training and supervision are necessary to prevent expensive mistakes. Development Counsellors International, a New York marketing firm, assigns junior staff members to manage its interns, viewing this responsibility as a chance for the staff members to develop their management skills at the same time the interns are learning job skills. Finally, even though interns are students, they must be paid fairly. Failure to pay at least the minimum wage causes the employer to run afoul of labor laws. At Chic Boutique, managing partner Sarah Nguyen considers interns to be possible future employees, so good employee relations is as important with interns as with permanent employees.

SOURCE: Alison Stein Wellner, "Getting the Most out of Interns," *Inc.*, September 2004, www.inc.com.

Professionals must be able to evaluate the worth of the techniques that are available for carrying out HRM activities. Some of the new methods and tools will provide value to the organization, whereas others may be no more than the HRM equivalent of snake oil. HRM professionals must be able to critically evaluate new techniques in light of HRM principles and business value to determine which are beneficial.

❧ HR RESPONSIBILITIES OF SUPERVISORS

Although many organizations have human resource departments, HR activities are by no means limited to the specialists who staff those departments. In large organizations, HR departments advise and support the activities of the other departments. In small organizations, there may be an HR specialist, but many HR activities are carried out by line supervisors. Either way, non-HR managers need to be familiar with the basics of HRM and their role with regard to managing human resources.

At a start-up company, the first supervisors are the company's founders. Not all founders recognize their HR responsibilities, but those who do have a powerful advantage. When Rene Larrave and two partners founded the consulting firm they called Tactica, Larrave felt certain that the only way the firm could grow profitably was with a clear vision of the numbers and kinds of employees who could enable that growth. Larrave and his partners drew up career paths for all the employees they planned to hire, including the requirements for the jobs to which they would be promoted during the company's first few years. To help their future employees find their way along those career paths, they published the details in their company's Employee Atlas. The partners also set up a plan for reviewing performance by collecting feedback from peers as well as supervisors. Using this plan, implemented by its HR department, Tactica in several years grew to a $40 million firm, staffed by almost 200 highly committed, hardworking employees—most of them holding the positions that Larrave and his partners had planned for them.[15]

As we will see in later chapters, supervisors typically have responsibilities related to all the HR functions. Figure 1.5 shows some HR responsibilities that supervisors are likely to be involved in. Organizations depend on supervisors to help them determine what kinds of work need to be done (job analysis and design) and in what quantities (HR planning). Supervisors typically interview job candidates and participate in the decisions about which candidates to hire. Many organizations expect supervisors to train employees in some or all aspects of the employees' jobs. Supervisors conduct performance appraisals and may recommend pay increases. And, of course, supervisors play a key role in employee relations, because they are most often the voice of management for their employees, representing the company on a day-to-day basis. In all these activities, supervisors can participate in HRM by taking into consideration the ways that decisions and policies will affect their employees. Understanding the principles of communication, motivation, and other elements of human behavior can help supervisors inspire the best from the organization's human resources.

figure 1.5

Supervisors' Involvement in HRM: Common Areas of Involvement

❦ ETHICS IN HUMAN RESOURCE MANAGEMENT

Whenever people's actions affect one another, ethical issues arise, and business decisions are no exception. **Ethics** refers to fundamental principles of right and wrong; ethical behavior is behavior that is consistent with those principles. Business decisions, including HRM decisions, should be ethical, but the evidence suggests that is not always what happens. Recent surveys indicate that the general public and managers do not have positive perceptions of the ethical conduct of U.S. businesses. For example, in a survey conducted by *The Wall Street Journal,* 4 out of 10 executives reported they had been asked to behave unethically.[16] The nearby "Did You Know . . . ?" box shows survey results suggesting that most Americans have a low opinion of business executives' honesty and ethical standards.

As a result of unfavorable perceptions of U.S. business practices and an increased concern for better serving customers, U.S. companies are becoming more aware of the need for all company representatives to act responsibly.[17] They have an interest in the way their employees behave because customer, government agency, and vendor perceptions of the company affect the relationships necessary to sell goods and services.

Many ethical issues in the workplace involve human resource management. Nationwide Insurance has a three-person ethics office that offers a confidential "help line" for employees. About two-thirds of the calls to the help line involve issues related to human resource management—for example, conflicts with coworkers or supervisors or complaints of sexual harassment. When employees raise these concerns, the human resource team investigates them and takes action when necessary. Other departments handle other issues, such as those involving security or legal matters. The goal of these efforts is to keep employees focused on living up to the company's values, rather than just staying out of legal trouble.[18]

LO5
Discuss ethical issues in human resource management.

ethics
The fundamental principles of right and wrong.

Employee Rights

In the context of ethical human resource management, HR managers must view employees as having basic rights. Such a view reflects ethical principles embodied in the U.S. Constitution and Bill of Rights. A widely adopted understanding of human rights, based on the work of the philosopher Immanuel Kant, as well as the tradition of the Enlightenment, assumes that in a moral universe, every person has certain basic rights:

- *Right of free consent*—People have the right to be treated only as they knowingly and willingly consent to be treated. An example that applies to employees would be that employees should know the nature of the job they are being hired to do; the employer should not deceive them.
- *Right of privacy*—People have the right to do as they wish in their private lives, and they have the right to control what they reveal about private activities. One way an employer respects this right is by keeping employees' medical records confidential.
- *Right of freedom of conscience*—People have the right to refuse to do what violates their moral beliefs, as long as these beliefs reflect commonly accepted norms. A supervisor who demands that an employee do something that is unsafe or environmentally damaging may be violating this right if it conflicts with the employee's values. (Such behavior could be illegal as well as unethical.)
- *Right of freedom of speech*—People have the right to criticize an organization's ethics, if they do so in good conscience and their criticism does not violate the rights of individuals in the organization. Many organizations address this right by

BUSINESS LEADERS' IMAGE NEEDS A MAKEOVER

In a Gallup survey of American adults, opinions of business executives' ethical standards lagged far behind opinions about nurses, pharmacists, and teachers.

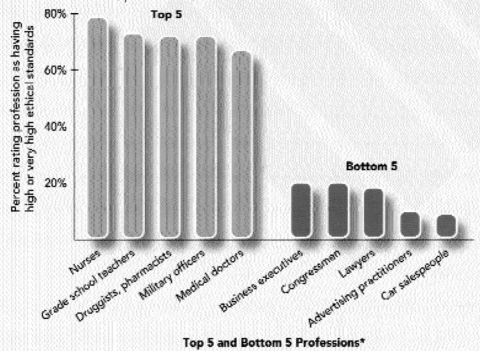

*Out of 21 named in the survey.

SOURCE: Miranda Hitti, "Nurses Top List for Honesty," CBS News, December 8, 2004, www.cbsnews.com; "Most Honest? Least Honest? The Envelope, Please . . . ," Yahoo News, December 8, 2004, http://story.news.yahoo.com; and The Polling Report, Inc., "Values," PollingReport.com, www.pollingreport.com, downloaded March 21, 2005.

offering hot lines or policies and procedures designed to handle complaints from employees.

- *Right to due process*—If people believe their rights are being violated, they have the right to a fair and impartial hearing. As we will see in Chapter 3, Congress has addressed this right in some circumstances by establishing agencies to hear complaints when employees believe their employer has not provided a fair hearing. For example, the Equal Employment Opportunity Commission may prosecute complaints of discrimination if it believes the employer did not fairly handle the problem.

One way to think about ethics in business is that the morally correct action is the one that minimizes encroachments on and avoids violations of these rights.

As the examples above suggest, organizations often face situations in which the rights of employees are affected. In particular, the right of privacy has received much attention in recent years. Computerized record keeping and computer networks have greatly increased the ways people can gain (authorized or unauthorized) access to records about individuals. Human resource records can be particularly sensitive. HRM responsibilities therefore include the ever-growing challenge of maintaining confidentiality.

Standards for Ethical Behavior

Ethical, successful companies act according to four principles.[19] First, in their relationships with customers, vendors, and clients, ethical and successful companies emphasize mutual benefits. Second, employees assume responsibility for the actions of the company. Third, such companies have a sense of purpose or vision that employees value and use in their day-to-day work. Finally, they emphasize fairness; that is, another person's interests count as much as their own.

United Parcel Service (UPS) has made a commitment to ensuring that every employee takes responsibility for ethical behavior. At the top of the organization, UPS's chief executive officer emphasizes that employees who get results by violating laws or ethical principles harm the company by undermining its customer relationships and ability to grow. The company has developed a set of ethics-related processes and procedures, embodied in a Code of Business Conduct. All employees must read and agree to follow that code, which describes the kinds of behavior required in a variety of business situations. UPS has also hired a company to provide a hotline employees can call if they have concerns that ethical standards have been violated. All information received by the hotline is forwarded to UPS's compliance department, whose employees investigate and ensure that appropriate action is taken. Managers of business units are evaluated based on ethical as well as financial standards. Each year, managers evaluate their unit's employee and business relationships in terms of ethical issues.[20]

For human resource practices to be considered ethical, they must satisfy the three basic standards summarized in Figure 1.6.[21] First, HRM practices must result in the greatest good for the largest number of people. Second, employment practices must respect basic human rights of privacy, due process, consent, and free speech. Third, managers must treat employees and customers equitably and fairly. These standards are most vexing when none of the alternatives in a situation meets all three of them.

Figure 1.6

Standards for Identifying Ethical Practices

For instance, most employers hesitate to get involved in the personal affairs of employees, and this attitude is in keeping with employees' right to privacy. But when personal matters include domestic violence, employees' safety may be in jeopardy, both at home and in the workplace. For Barbara Marlowe of the Boston law firm Mintz Levin Cohn Ferris Glovsky and Popeo, the choice is clear: Helping employees protect themselves does good for employees and also helps employees do better on the job, she says. Mintz Levin set up a group called Employers Against Domestic Violence. Companies that join the group take measures such as posting the phone number of a victim help line, allowing employees to keep flexible hours (to shake off stalkers), and removing victims' names from dial-by-name directories (so harassers can't easily call and disturb them at work).[22]

To explore how ethical principles apply to a variety of decisions, throughout the book we will highlight ethical dilemmas in human resource management practices.

LO6
Describe typical careers in human resource management.

❧ CAREERS IN HUMAN RESOURCE MANAGEMENT

There are many different types of jobs in the HRM profession. Figure 1.7 shows selected HRM positions and their salaries. The salaries vary depending on education and experience, as well as the type of industry in which the person works. As you can see from Figure 1.7, some positions involve work in specialized areas of HRM such as recruiting, training, or labor and industrial relations. Usually, HR generalists make between $60,000 and $80,000, depending on their experience and education level. Generalists usually perform the full range of HRM activities, including recruiting, training, compensation, and employee relations.

Figure 1.7

Median Salaries for HRM Positions

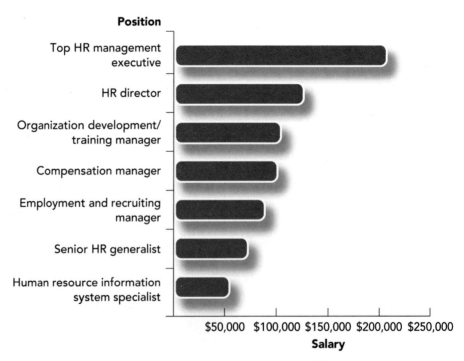

SOURCE: Based on Society for Human Resource Management–Mercer Survey 2003 as reported in J. Vocino, "On the Rise," *HR Magazine*, November 2003, pp. 75–84; and F. Hansen, "2003 Data Bank Annual," *Workforce Management* 82, no. 13 (2003), p. 88.

The vast majority of HRM professionals have a college degree, and many also have completed postgraduate work. The typical field of study is business (especially human resources or industrial relations), but some HRM professionals have degrees in the social sciences (economics or psychology), the humanities, and law programs. Those who have completed graduate work have master's degrees in HR management, business management, or a similar field. A well-rounded educational background will serve a person well in an HRM position.

HR professionals can increase their career opportunities by taking advantage of training and development programs. General Motors offers its human resource employees a curriculum designed to improve their ability to contribute to the company's business success. The training program details the goals of HRM at General Motors, explains how these relate to business changes at the company, and teaches business topics such as finance and the management of change.[23]

Some HRM professionals have a professional certification in HRM, but many more are members of professional associations. The primary professional organization for HRM is the Society for Human Resource Management (SHRM). SHRM is the world's largest human resource management association, with more than 190,000 professional and student members throughout the world. SHRM provides education and information services, conferences and seminars, government and media representation, and online services and publications (such as *HR Magazine*). You can visit SHRM's Web site to see their services at www.shrm.org.

ORGANIZATION OF THIS BOOK

This chapter has provided an overview of human resource management, to give you a sense of its scope. In this book, the topics are organized according to the broad areas of human resource management shown in Table 1.3. The numbers in the table refer to the part and chapter numbers.

Part 1 discusses several aspects of the human resource environment. To be effective, human resource management must begin with an awareness of the trends shaping this field, including changes in the workforce, technology, and society. Such trends are the topic of Chapter 2. On a more detailed level, human resource management must also ensure that the organization's actions comply with legal requirements, the topic of Chapter 3. And within the organization itself, human resource management looks at the types of work required and designs jobs that meet a variety of objectives, balancing safety, efficiency, mental demands, and motivation. Chapter 4 covers the topics of analyzing work and designing jobs.

Part 2 explores the responsibilities involved in acquiring and preparing human resources. Chapter 5 explains how to plan for human resource needs and recruit candidates to meet those needs. Chapter 6 discusses the selection of employees and their

SHRM provides education, information services (such as this conference), seminars, government and media representation, and online services and publications.

TABLE 1.3

Topics Covered in This Book

I.	The Human Resource Environment
2.	Trends in Human Resource Management
3.	Providing Equal Employment Opportunity and a Safe Workplace
4.	Analyzing Work and Designing Jobs
II.	Acquiring and Preparing Human Resources
5.	Planning for and Recruiting Human Resources
6.	Selecting Employees and Placing Them in Jobs
7.	Training Employees
III.	Assessing Performance and Developing Employees
8.	Managing Employees' Performance
9.	Developing Employees for Future Success
10.	Separating and Retaining Employees
IV.	Compensating Human Resources
11.	Establishing a Pay Structure
12.	Recognizing Employee Contributions with Pay
13.	Providing Employee Benefits
V.	Meeting Other HR Goals
14.	Collective Bargaining and Labor Relations
15.	Managing Human Resources Globally
16.	Creating and Maintaining High-Performance Organizations

placement into jobs or teams. Chapter 7 addresses various ways organizations train their employees to perform their jobs.

In Part 3, the discussion turns to the assessment and development of human resources. Chapter 8 describes the various activities involved in managing performance, including regular performance appraisals. Chapter 9 describes practices related to employee development—preparing employees for future jobs and helping to establish career paths that take into account employees' work interests, goals, values, and other career issues. Despite these activities, organizations at times determine they no longer need certain positions or no longer wish to retain certain employees. To address these situations, Chapter 10 discusses appropriate ways to handle employee separation. It also discusses the flip side: how organizations can keep valuable employees from wanting to leave.

An important element of employee satisfaction is the employee's belief that he or she is being fairly compensated for the work performed. Part 4 addresses several topics related to compensation. Chapter 11 explores decisions related to the organization's overall pay structure. Chapter 12 discusses ways organizations can use pay to recognize individual and group contributions to the organization's performance. Chapter 13 considers benefits—forms of compensation other than pay (for example, insurance and paid vacation time).

The last part of the book addresses a number of special topics that human resource managers face today. Chapter 14 discusses responsibilities of human resource management in organizations where employees have or are seeking union representation. Chapter 15 explores issues that arise when the organization has human resources working in more than one nation. And Chapter 16, the last chapter, returns to the topic of high-performance organizations, taking a closer look at how human resource management can contribute to creating and maintaining such an organization.

Each chapter includes examples highlighting how the human resource management practice covered in that chapter helps a company maintain high performance. "Best

Practices" boxes tell success stories related to the chapter's topic. "HR How To" boxes provide a more detailed look at how to carry out a practice in each HR area. "Did You Know . . . ?" boxes provide a snapshot of interesting statistics related to a chapter topic. Many chapters also include an "e-HRM" box identifying the ways that human resource professionals are applying information technology and the Internet to help their organizations excel in the fast-changing modern world. Finally, "Thinking Ethically" at the end of each chapter demonstrates ethical issues in managing human resources.

thinking ETHICALLY

HRM Theft Prevention

A persistent problem at many companies, especially stores, is theft. Shoplifters help themselves to merchandise and dishonest employees take items from store inventories. Losses from stolen merchandise directly hurt a store's ability to serve customers and keep prices low. Theft often costs a retail chain millions of dollars and affects customers (through higher prices), the company's managers and shareholders (through lower profits), and honest employees, who may pay the price indirectly if the company's reputation and performance suffer.

Big Lots, a chain of stores that buys closeout lots of clothes, electronics, food, and household items and sells them at deep discounts, addressed the problem of theft by tapping the skills of human resource management. In contrast to most retailers, which put their finance department in charge of theft prevention, Big Lots charged HRM with that responsibility. Its idea was that building a committed, honest team of employees is a goal that HRM should already be pursuing as its area of expertise. Loyal employees not only refrain from stealing but also help prevent mistakes and accidents that cause inventory losses. Explains Big Lots' executive vice president of human resources, Brad A. Waite, "If someone in the company is violating company policy or acting in a dishonest way, then human resources and loss prevention have the identical goal of ridding the company of the problem." He must be right; under his leadership, inventory losses at Big Lots have fallen by several million dollars a year.

SOURCE: F. Hansen, "The CFO Connection," *Workforce Management*, July 2003, pp. 50–54.

Questions

1. Which HRM responsibilities can contribute to reducing employee theft? Suggest a technique Big Lots might use to reduce employee theft.
2. Can theft prevention at a store invade employees' or customers' privacy? Explain. Describe how you would handle a potential conflict between privacy rights and enforcement of honest behavior.

SUMMARY

1. Define human resource management and explain how HRM contributes to an organization's performance. Human resource management consists of an organization's "people practices"—the policies, practices, and systems that influence employees' behavior, attitudes, and performance. HRM influences who works for the organization and how those people work. These human resources, if well managed, have the potential to be a

source of sustainable competitive advantage, contributing to basic objectives such as quality, profits, and customer satisfaction.

2. Identify the responsibilities of human resource departments.

By carrying out HR activities or supporting line management, HR departments have responsibility for a variety of functions related to acquiring and managing employees. The HRM process begins with analyzing and designing jobs, then recruiting and selecting employees to fill those jobs. Training and development equip employees to carry out their present jobs and follow a career path in the organization. Performance management ensures that employees' activities and outputs match the organization's goals. Human resource departments also plan and administer the organization's pay and benefits. They carry out activities in support of employee relations, such as communications programs and collective bargaining. Conducting all these activities involves the establishment and administration of personnel policies. Management also depends on human resource professionals for help in ensuring compliance with labor laws, as well as for support for the organization's strategy—for example, human resource planning and change management.

3. Summarize the types of skills needed for human resource management.

Human resource management requires substantial human relations skills, including skill in communicating, negotiating, and team development. Human resource professionals also need decision-making skills based on knowledge of the HR field as well as the organization's line of business. Leadership skills are necessary, especially for managing conflict and change. Technical skills of human resource professionals include knowledge of current techniques, applicable laws, and computer systems.

4. Explain the role of supervisors in human resource management.

Although many organizations have human resource departments, non-HR managers must be familiar with the basics of HRM and their own role with regard to managing human resources. Supervisors typically have responsibilities related to all the HR functions. Supervisors help analyze work, interview job candidates, participate in selection decisions, provide training, conduct performance appraisals, and recommend pay increases. On a day-to-day basis, supervisors represent the company to their employees, so they also play an important role in employee relations.

5. Discuss ethical issues in human resource management.

Like all managers and employees, HR professionals should make decisions consistent with sound ethical principles. Their decisions should result in the greatest good for the largest number of people; respect basic rights of privacy, due process, consent, and free speech; and treat employees and customers equitably and fairly. Some areas in which ethical issues arise include concerns about employee privacy, protection of employee safety, and fairness in employment practices (for example, avoiding discrimination).

6. Describe typical careers in human resource management.

Careers in human resource management may involve specialized work in fields such as recruiting, training, or labor relations. HR professionals may also be generalists, performing the full range of HR activities described in this chapter. People in these positions usually have a college degree in business or the social sciences. Human resource management means enhancing communication with employees and concern for their well-being, but also involves a great deal of paperwork, and a variety of non–people skills as well as knowledge of business and laws.

REVIEW AND DISCUSSION QUESTIONS

1. How can human resource management contribute to a company's success?

2. Imagine that a small manufacturing company decides to invest in a materials resource planning (MRP) system. This is a computerized information system that improves efficiency by automating such work as planning needs for resources, ordering materials, and scheduling work on the shop floor. The company hopes that with the new MRP system, it can grow by quickly and efficiently processing small orders for a variety of products. Which of the human resource functions are likely to be affected by this change? How can human resource

management help the organization carry out this change successfully?

3. What skills are important for success in human resource management? Which of these skills are already strengths of yours? Which would you like to develop?

4. Traditionally, human resource management practices were developed and administered by the company's human resource department. Line managers are now playing a major role in developing and implementing HRM practices. Why do you think non-HR managers are becoming more involved?

5. If you were to start a business, which aspects of human resource management would you want to entrust to specialists? Why?
6. Why do all managers and supervisors need knowledge and skills related to human resource management?
7. Federal law requires that employers not discriminate on the basis of a person's race, sex, national origin, or age over 40. Is this also an ethical requirement? A competitive requirement? Explain.
8. When a restaurant employee slipped on spilled soup and fell, requiring the evening off to recover, the owner realized that workplace safety was an issue to which she had not devoted much time. A friend warned the owner that if she started creating a lot of safety rules and procedures, she would lose her focus on customers and might jeopardize the future of the restaurant. The safety problem is beginning to feel like an ethical dilemma. Suggest some ways the restaurant owner might address this dilemma. What aspects of human resource management are involved?
9. Does a career in human resource management, based on this chapter's description, appeal to you? Why or why not?

WHAT'S YOUR HR IQ?

The text Web site offers two more ways to check what you've learned so far. Use the Self-Assessment exercise to see whether you have what it takes for a career in HR. Go online with the Web Exercise to learn about the Society for Human Resource Management and its publication *HR Magazine*.

BusinessWeek CASE

BusinessWeek Why Business Should Make AIDS Its Business

British mining company Anglo American PLC has extensive operations in Africa, and it knows the devastation caused by AIDS. It estimates that 30,000 of its 125,000 employees in South Africa are infected with HIV. That's not unexpected, given that at least 22 percent of South Africa's entire workforce is HIV positive. Anglo American isn't counting on the South African government to solve its problems, however. In the early 1990s, the company started its own AIDS treatment and prevention program for workers and their families. And in 2002, Anglo American began administering highly effective anti-retroviral drugs to its infected employees—medicines that are still rare in Africa. It expects to treat 3,000 people this year, up from 223 in 2003. In a report delivered to the International AIDS Conference held in Bangkok, Thailand, in 2004, the company said the treatment costs were "offset by the sharp decline in mortality—from 30 percent to 3.4 percent in the first year—and in absenteeism due to illness."

Both Anglo American and its employees benefit from its concern, and the company is not alone. A handful of other multinationals have realized that the governments of many developing nations lack the resources or the will to mount effective AIDS programs. Nike, ChevronTexaco, BMW, Heineken, and Coca-Cola, among others, have concluded that they must actively work to control AIDS among their own employees in Asia and Africa, or profits and economic progress could be severely hampered.

Unfortunately, far more corporations are doing nothing. According to a report by the World Economic Forum, two-thirds of 1,620 companies operating in Africa expect AIDS to affect their profits over the next five years, but only 12 percent have an AIDS policy. A UN survey found that just 21 of 100 large multinationals have AIDS programs.

Such apathy is self-defeating. If multinationals don't embrace aggressive anti-AIDS tactics, both their employees and their customers in emerging markets could fall victim to the epidemic. The dimensions of the disaster are laid out in a new study by the UN-affiliated International Labor Organization (ILO), which estimates that, out of 38 million people infected with HIV globally, at least 26 million are workers. In sub-Saharan Africa, 7.7 percent of the workforce is infected with HIV, with rates in Swaziland and Botswana as high as 38 percent. In China and India, HIV infection rates are beginning to rise at the same pace seen in Africa 20 years ago. By the end of this decade, 6 million workers in India and an additional 1.8 million in China will have been killed by AIDS.

Few governments are adequately addressing the crisis. The UN predicts that global spending on AIDS by governments and nongovernmental organizations (NGOs) will total only half of the $12 billion needed by 2005. Will companies respond to entreaties from AIDS organizations to pick up the slack?

It is not an easy sell. "The last things most companies want to discuss in the workplace are sex and death," says Diana Barrett, until recently a senior lecturer at Harvard Business School, who has done extensive surveys on AIDS in the workforce. When a company does start down that road, there is no easy exit strategy. Says Barrett, "Once you offer testing, you have to provide anti-retrovirals, and that means you have to rethink your whole medical capability. You also have to guard against workplace stigma."

Successful models do exist, however. Two years ago, General Motors Corporation set up a pilot AIDS program in Thailand, where it has 2,500 employees, with an emphasis on prevention. All employees receive training and contraceptive supplies to protect against the disease and information on avoiding discrimination against infected coworkers. GM provides voluntary and free on-site testing and counseling and pays for treatment at local hospitals for employees with AIDS. The company next plans to expand the program to operations in India, Indonesia, and China.

The cost of such an effort is far lower than might be expected. GM budgeted $50,000 over two years for Thailand and India, about $8 per year per employee. Still, plenty of companies hesitate to make even that small commitment. "We often get the comment that 'It's not our problem. We're not [a welfare organization], we're a business,'" says Simon Graham, regional program coordinator of the Thailand Business Coalition on AIDS.

But it is their problem. Lafarge Group, a French building materials multinational, says AIDS is the leading cause of death for its 7,500 employees in Africa and a major industrial risk in terms of absenteeism, loss of skills, and reduced productivity. Other multinationals must be suffering the same losses—or soon will. Nonprofit organizations and local clinics are eager to help companies develop AIDS programs. The alternative—doing nothing—is too terrible to consider.

SOURCE: Catherine Arnst, "Why Business Should Make AIDS Its Business," *BusinessWeek*, August 9, 2004, downloaded from Infotrac at http://web1.infotrac.galegroup.com.

QUESTIONS

1. Which ethics principles from the chapter have Anglo American and General Motors applied? Suggest additional ethics principles that might apply to this situation.
2. Which human resource management specialties and skills could help a company make decisions about offering AIDS-related benefits?
3. This case emphasizes AIDS-related benefits in Africa and Asia, where a large percentage of the population is infected and may not have access to health care. How would decisions about AIDS-related benefits be similar or different in the United States? Which (if any) HRM issues in the United States are as sensitive as the AIDS issue is in Africa and Asia?

CASE: HRM Excellence Helps Xerox Rebound

In 2000, Xerox was $17 billion in debt, its stock price was tumbling, and it was losing money. Along with these financial woes, the Securities and Exchange Commission was investigating the way the company had been accounting for copier leases. Since then, the company has made a remarkable comeback. It has returned to profitability, and the stock price has increased.

How did the company turn around? Along with cost cutting, top management refocused the company on its commitment to quality. In terms of products, this has meant a shift away from small copiers that compete mainly on price in favor of office copiers and high-end printers. It also requires a focus on people. According to Xerox's chief executive officer, Anne M. Mulcahy, the company's strategy of offering "world-class products and services" requires "world-class people." One unusual expression of this commitment has been to create a "brand" for employment, *eXpress yourself*. Just as a product brand is meant to convey an image of the product, the employment brand is intended to signal what working for Xerox is like. In Mulcahy's words, the eXpress yourself brand "distinguishes Xerox as a place where the passion, diversity, ideas and contributions of every member of the Xerox family define our capability for bold innovation and a leading edge work environment."

To put these ideas into practice, Xerox's headquarters relies on its HR Service Center. The center started by handling routine transactions such as job changes and address changes, and then it added Web-based services. Now the center also provides research and analysis services for employees in Xerox's many operating units.

Even during the difficult phase of cost cutting, the human resource professionals at Xerox stayed focused on positive employee relations. The HR professionals helped ensure that employees were treated with dignity. For example, if laid-off employees were near retirement age, they could add up to a year of unpaid, inactive status to their records so that they could qualify for retirement benefits. The company also continued its yearly employee attitude surveys during the layoff period, which helped the company evaluate whether it was effectively communicating the company's direction. HR also set up various communication programs to emphasize a message of "we really care."

Now, having weathered these difficult times, Xerox depends on its HR staff to help talented employees add valuable skills. To prepare future leaders, Xerox offers development through work experiences, job assignments (including international positions), and learning opportunities. Internal training and development at Xerox includes computer-based learning, which makes it affordable to offer training to more employees. Xerox set up a two-month management development program that includes computer-based learning, coaching, and a week of classroom training.

HR is also charged with ensuring the employees understand the "new" Xerox and how to achieve success. HR has focused on three key programs: an employee value proposition, building a high-performance culture, and developing a pipeline of three candidates for every position within the company. The employee value proposition states the expectations an employee should have of the company and what Xerox can expect in return. According to Xerox's vice president of human resources, acquiring and keeping the best talent is a matter of inclusion in the broad sense of "[allowing] an employee to bring his or her uniqueness to the table and . . . to make a difference." Without this, adds the vice president, "we'll be in trouble."

SOURCE: T. Starner, "Processing a Turnaround," *Human Resource Executive*, May 16, 2004, pp. 1, 16–24, www.xerox.com.

QUESTIONS

1. Which areas of human resource management are necessary for Xerox to attract and retain valuable employees? Does this effort go beyond simply recruiting and hiring people with the necessary skills?

2. How would you expect a period of cutbacks and layoffs to affect a company's human resource professionals? Would their goals and activities need to shift to meet this challenge? If so, how?

3. Suggest one or two ways in which HR professionals at Xerox might work with line managers to build loyalty to the company and a commitment to providing "world-class products and services."

NOTES

1. Erin White, "To Keep Employees, Domino's Decides It's Not All about Pay," *The Wall Street Journal*, February 17, 2005, http://online.wsj.com.

2. A. S. Tsui and L. R. Gomez-Mejia, "Evaluating Human Resource Effectiveness," in *Human Resource Management: Evolving Rules and Responsibilities*, ed. L. Dyer (Washington, DC: BNA Books, 1988), pp. 1187–227; M. A. Hitt, B. W. Keats, and S. M. DeMarie, "Navigating in the New Competitive Landscape: Building Strategic Flexibility and Competitive Advantage in the 21st Century," *Academy of Management Executive* 12, no. 4 (1998), pp. 22–42; J. T. Delaney and M. A. Huselid, "The Impact of Human Resource Management Practices on Perceptions of Organizational Performance," *Academy of Management Journal* 39 (1996), pp. 949–69.

3. W. F. Cascio, *Costing Human Resources: The Financial Impact of Behavior in Organizations*, 3rd ed. (Boston: PWS-Kent, 1991).

4. S. A. Snell and J. W. Dean, "Integrated Manufacturing and Human Resource Management: A Human Capital Perspective," *Academy of Management Journal* 35 (1992), pp. 467–504; M. A. Youndt, S. Snell, J. W. Dean Jr., and D. P. Lepak, "Human Resource Management, Manufacturing Strategy, and Firm Performance," *Academy of Management Journal* 39 (1996), pp. 836–66.

5. Athleta Corporation Web site, www.athleta.com, September 22, 2001; K. Dobbs, "Knowing How to Keep Your Best and Brightest," *Workforce*, April 2001, pp. 56–60.

6. C. Patton, "Future Shock," *Human Resource Executive*, March 16, 2003, pp. 16–22.

7. S. Snell, "Control Theory in Strategic Human Resource Management: The Mediating Effect of Administrative Information," *Academy of Management Journal* 35 (1992), pp. 292–327.

8. Leigh Buchanan, "City Lights," *Inc.*, May 2001, pp. 66–71.

9. Jill Hecht Maxwell, "New to the HR Brew," *Inc.*, April 2001, p. 100.

10. J. Britt, "Disability Advocates Aim at Technology Barriers," *HR News* 20, no. 9 (2001), pp. 1, 9.

11. *Women in U.S. Corporate Leadership: 2003* (New York: Catalyst, 2003).

12. G. McMahan and R. Woodman, "The Current Practice of Organization Development within the Firm: A Survey of Large Industrial Corporations," *Group and Organization Studies* 17 (1992), pp. 117–34.

13. G. Jones and P. Wright, "An Economic Approach to Conceptualizing the Utility of Human Resource Management Practices," *Research in Personnel/Human Resources* 10 (1992), pp. 271–99.

14. R. Schuler and J. Walker, "Human Resources Strategy: Focusing on Issues and Actions," *Organizational Dynamics*, Summer 1990, pp. 5–19.

15. Kate O'Sullivan, "Why You're Hiring All Wrong," *Inc.*, February 2002, p. 86.

16. R. Ricklees, "Ethics in America," *The Wall Street Journal*, October 31–November 3, 1983, p. 33.

17. C. Lee, "Ethics Training: Facing the Tough Questions," *Training*, March 31, 1986, pp. 33, 38–41.

18. D. Buss, "Working It Out," *HR Magazine*, June 2004, www.shrm.org.

19. M. Pastin, *The Hard Problems of Management: Gaining the Ethics Edge* (San Francisco: Jossey-Bass, 1986);

and T. Thomas, J. Schermerhorn Jr., and J. Dienhart, "Strategic Leadership of Ethical Behavior in Business," *Academy of Management Executive* 18 (2004), pp. 56–66.

20. R. Stolz, "What HR Will Stand For," *Human Resource Executive*, January 2003, pp. 20–28.

21. G. F. Cavanaugh, D. Moberg, and M. Velasquez, "The Ethics of Organizational Politics," *Academy of Management Review* 6 (1981), pp. 363–74.

22. Mike Hofman, "The Shadow of Domestic Violence," *Inc.*, March 2001, p. 85.

23. S. Caudron, "HR Is Dead, Long Live HR," *Workforce*, January 2003, pp. 26–29; and S. Bates, "Business Partners," *HR Magazine*, March 2003, pp. 50–57.

If you are using the Manager's Hot Seat DVD with this book, consider finishing case 2: Ethics: Let's Make a Fourth Quarter Deal, for this chapter.

THE HUMAN RESOURCE ENVIRONMENT

CHAPTER 2

TRENDS IN HUMAN RESOURCE MANAGEMENT

What Do I Need to Know?

1. Describe trends in the labor force composition and how they affect human resource management.

2. Summarize areas in which human resource management can support the goal of creating a high-performance work system.

3. Define employee empowerment and explain its role in the modern organization.

4. Identify ways HR professionals can support organizational strategies for quality, growth, and efficiency.

5. Summarize ways in which human resource management can support organizations expanding internationally.

6. Discuss how technological developments are affecting human resource management.

7. Explain how the nature of the employment relationship is changing.

8. Discuss how the need for flexibility affects human resource management.

▧ INTRODUCTION

The early years of the 21st century shook the complacency of U.S. workers and forced them to take a fresh look at the ways they are working. The previous decade of turbulent growth gave way to caution as hiring slowed and many companies created jobs overseas. Terrorist attacks on U.S. soil followed by wars in two countries forced a new sense of life's uncertainties. And a revolution in information technology redefined such fundamental notions as what it means to be "in touch" or "at work." More and more voices in the workplace, in the community, and in the media tell of people who are mulling over why they work the way they do, what the future holds, and how they want to change to meet new demands and opportunities.

More than ever, organizations today must be able to respond creatively to uncertainty and change. For some companies, the challenge involves juggling the workload when some employees who are military reservists or National Guard members are called into active duty. When these service members return home, their employers must return them to their jobs at the pay level they would have received had they not been away, and they must try to make accommodations for them if they have become disabled. That means many employers either hire people to fill the vacant positions temporarily or ask their other employees to handle the service members' work as well as they can. When Navy reservist Warren White returned to his sales job after six months of duty in Iraq, he needed six months to rebuild his sales to their level before his military service. Facing similar difficulties, some companies have stumbled in fulfilling legal requirements. When National Guard Pfc. Ron Vander Wal returned to his job in tech support after 15 months of active duty, his employer told him his job was unavailable; he filed a lawsuit to get the job back. And in Thomasville, Alabama, a police officer returning from military service in Iraq initially learned that he could not be reemployed because he had sustained a foot injury. Other employers are taking a much different point of view, seeing reservists and National Guard members as individuals whose experiences give them an added level of maturity and leadership ability. For example, Harley-Davidson pays employees on active duty the difference between their military pay and what they had been earning on the job, including benefits. The company also sends care packages to their employees, who make up 14 percent of the company's workforce.[1]

While some employees are coming and going because of military service, a sizable chunk of the U.S. workforce is retiring. Persons over the age of 65 represent a growing share of the U.S. population, and as they retire, they are taking years of experience with them. Employers are challenged not only to fill the jobs but also to make important knowledge available to the new people. Defense contractor Northrop Grumman is one company that has met this challenge; the average age of its aerospace engineers is 54. Before these experienced workers retire, the company has been hiring new engineers at a rapid pace. The company established a "community of practice"—a group whose members are invited to meet in person and online to share ideas—for new employees. The group has arranged for project managers to lead seminars and for young engineers to shadow experienced ones, accompanying them throughout the workday to see how they handle various situations. One of those benefiting is Tamra Johnson, a young engineer working on a project to provide NASA with orbiters for Jupiter's moons. Johnson says she is learning from her more experienced colleagues and also teaching Northrop about how to orient new employees, "so the knowledge transfer really goes both ways."[2]

As more and more of the workforce reaches retirement age, some companies have set up mentoring programs between older and younger workers so that knowledge is not lost but passed on. How does the company benefit from these mentoring programs?

Another face of change is the temporary executive—a top-level employee hired to carry out a special assignment or to fill a post until the company makes a long-term hiring decision. Stephen McElfresh, who headed the Saratoga Institute until it was acquired by a larger firm, now accepts temporary management assignments of up to 18 months in companies' HR divisions. In his positions, McElfresh has the authority to hire and fire, but he avoids major staff shakeups, seeing that responsibility as more appropriate for a company insider. Instead, he leads new projects, such as product launches or the opening of a facility. Although McElfresh enjoyed his years of experience as a corporate insider, he says, "There is more opportunity to make a real difference in an interim role, because I am touching people and organizations at the moment of change."[3]

These creative responses to change and uncertainty illustrate the kinds of people and situations that shape the nature of human resource management today. This chapter describes major trends that are affecting human resource management. It begins with an examination of the modern labor force, including trends that are determining who will participate in the workforce of the future. Next, we explore ways HRM can support a number of trends in organizational strategy, from efforts to maintain high-performance work systems to changes in the organization's size and structure. Often, growth includes the use of human resources on a global scale, as more and more organizations hire immigrants or open operations overseas. The chapter then turns to major changes in technology, especially the role of the Internet. As we will explain, the Internet is changing organizations themselves, as well as providing new ways to carry out human resource management. Finally, we explore the changing nature of the employment relationship, in which careers and jobs are becoming more flexible.

CHANGE IN THE LABOR FORCE

LO1
Describe trends in the labor force composition and how they affect human resource management.

internal labor force
An organization's workers (its employees and the people who have contracts to work at the organization).

external labor market
Individuals who are actively seeking employment.

The term *labor force* is a general way to refer to all the people willing and able to work. For an organization, the **internal labor force** consists of the organization's workers—its employees and the people who have contracts to work at the organization. This internal labor force has been drawn from the organization's **external labor market,** that is, individuals who are actively seeking employment. The number and kinds of people in the external labor market determine the kinds of human resources available to an organization (and their cost). Human resource professionals need to be aware of trends in the composition of the external labor market, because these trends affect the organization's options for creating a well-skilled, motivated internal labor force.

An Aging Workforce

In the United States, the Bureau of Labor Statistics (BLS), an agency of the Department of Labor, tracks changes in the composition of the U.S. labor force and forecasts employment trends. The BLS has projected that from 2002 to 2012, the total U.S. labor force will grow from 128 million to 162 million workers.[4] This 12 percent increase represents slightly lower growth than during the previous decade.

Some of the expected change involves the distribution of workers by age. During the 2002–2012 period, the fastest-growing age groups are expected to be workers 55 and older. Young workers will enter the labor force, but at a much slower rate. The 35- to 44-year-old age group is actually expected to shrink, as baby boomers move into the older age groups and fewer workers enter this group. This combination of trends will cause the overall workforce to age. Figure 2.1 shows the change in age distribution, as forecast by the Bureau of Labor Statistics, between 2002 and 2012. By 2010, more than half of U.S. workers will be older than 40, and a significant share will be nearing retirement.[5] Human resource professionals will therefore spend much of their time on concerns related to retirement planning, retraining older workers, and motivating workers whose careers have plateaued. Organizations will struggle with ways to control the rising costs of health care and other benefits. At the same time, organizations will have to find ways to attract, retain, and prepare the youth labor force.

In doing so, organizations will be reminded that values tend to change from one generation to the next, as well as when people reach different life stages.[6] For example, members of Generation Y (born between 1976 and 1995) begin their career with the assumption that they will frequently change jobs. They are likely to place a high value on money as well as on helping others. Most employees, however, value several aspects of work, regardless of their age. Employees view work as a means to self-fulfillment—that is, a means to more fully use their skills and abilities, meet their interests, and live a desirable lifestyle.[7] One report indicates that if employees receive opportunities to fully use and develop their skills, have greater job responsibilities, believe the promotion system is fair, and have a trustworthy manager who represents employees' best interests, they are more committed to their companies.[8]

Employers will likely find that many talented older workers want to continue contributing through their work, though not necessarily in a traditional nine-to-five job. For organizations to attract and keep talented older workers, many will have to rethink the ways they design jobs. In Princeton, Minnesota, Lucille Decker retired after 60 years as a first-grade teacher, but she missed the action and returned as a substitute teacher. In Saint Louis, endoscopy nurse Josephine Godfrey returned to St. Mary's Health Center to work part-time after her early retirement. She appreciates being able to schedule work around visits with her two dozen grandchildren and says, "I'll continue working as long as I'm productive." And Lloyd Baker, a civil engineer and surveyor in his nineties, continues to operate his business, partly for the income but also to continue providing work for his company's employees.[9]

Older employees may be more likely to stay in jobs with limited physical demands, fewer work hours, and less stress. Especially for jobs requiring a college degree, today's jobs are less likely to be physically difficult, which may help employers fill positions by keeping older workers.[10]

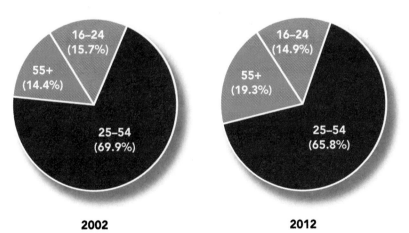

2002   **2012**

Figure 2.1

Age Distribution of U.S. Labor Force, 2002 and 2012

SOURCE: Bureau of Labor Statistics, "Labor Force," *Occupational Outlook Quarterly,* Winter 2003–2004, pp. 42–48, downloaded at www.bls.gov.

A Diverse Workforce

Another kind of change affecting the U.S. labor force is that it is growing more diverse in racial, ethnic, and gender terms. As Figure 2.2 shows, the 2012 workforce is expected to be 66 percent white (and non-Hispanic), 15 percent Hispanic (any race), 12 percent black (non-Hispanic), and 7 percent Asian and other minorities. The fastest-growing of these categories are "Asian and other" and Hispanics because these groups are experiencing immigration and birth rates above the national average. Along with greater racial and ethnic diversity, there is also greater gender diversity. More women are in the paid labor force than in the past. Thus far in the current decade, women have made up 47 percent of the U.S. labor force, up slightly from the 1990s.[11]

The greater diversity of the U.S. labor force challenges employers to create HRM practices that ensure they fully utilize the talents, skills, and values of all employees. The growth in the labor market of female and minority populations will exceed the growth of white non-Hispanic persons. As a result, organizations cannot afford to ignore or discount the potential contributions of women and minorities. Employers will have to ensure that employees and HRM systems are free of bias and value the perspectives and experience that women and minorities can contribute to organizational goals such as product quality and customer service. As we will discuss further in the next chapter, managing cultural diversity involves many different activities. These include creating an organizational culture that values diversity, ensuring that HRM systems are bias-free, encouraging career development for women and minorities, promoting knowledge and acceptance of cultural differences, ensuring involvement in education both within and outside the organization, and dealing with employees' resistance to diversity.[12] Figure 2.3 summarizes ways in which HRM can support the management of diversity for organizational success.

Many U.S. companies have already committed themselves to ensuring that they recognize the diversity of their internal labor force and use it to gain a competitive advantage. According to a recent survey of HR professionals, the most common approaches include recruiting efforts with the goal of increasing diversity and training programs related to diversity.[13] The majority of respondents believed that these efforts were beneficial; 91 percent said they helped the company maintain a competitive advantage.

For Home Depot, diversity in the ranks of employees is an obvious way to provide top-notch customer service. Hiring people with diverse backgrounds helps build a

Figure 2.2

Projected Racial/Ethnic Makeup of the U.S. Workforce, 2012

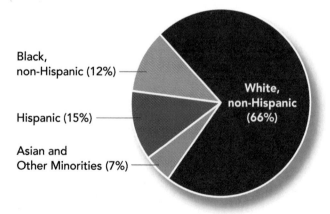

Black, non-Hispanic (12%)

Hispanic (15%)

Asian and Other Minorities (7%)

White, non-Hispanic (66%)

SOURCE: Bureau of Labor Statistics, "Tomorrow's Jobs," *Occupational Outlook Handbook*, last modified June 2, 2004, downloaded at www.bls.gov/oco/.

Figure 2.3

HRM Practices That Support Diversity Management

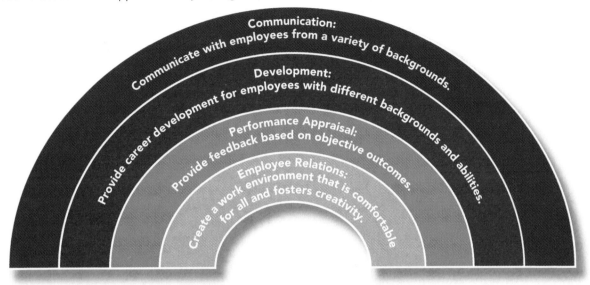

Communication:
Communicate with employees from a variety of backgrounds.

Development:
Provide career development for employees with different backgrounds and abilities.

Performance Appraisal:
Provide feedback based on objective outcomes.

Employee Relations:
Create a work environment that is comfortable for all and fosters creativity.

SOURCE: Based on M. Loden and J. B. Rosener, *Workforce America!* (Homewood, IL: Business One Irwin, 1991).

sales force that understands customers' needs and communicates effectively. And extra effort to recruit from many groups widens the pool of talent, so the company can hire the best people. Home Depot arranged a partnership with four Hispanic organizations to increase the company's visibility as an employer. The company hopes the effort will allow it to hire more bilingual employees. Home Depot has also arranged hiring partnerships to recruit senior citizens (through a partnership with the AARP) and military veterans (through a partnership with the U.S. Departments of Defense, Labor, and Veterans Affairs). According to Dennis Donovan, Home Depot's executive vice president of human resources, "Sales have increased substantially over the four years that we've really been at a lot of these things." He adds, "Talented associates are the customer service differentiator."[14]

The practices required for successfully managing diversity do more than meet employee needs; they reduce turnover costs and ensure that customers receive the best service possible. For instance, Molina Healthcare operates clinics whose clients are mostly African American, Hispanic, and Southeast Asian. The company tries to hire staffers who live in the clinics' neighborhoods and speak their patients' languages. This commitment to diversity helps improve communications and the quality of health care provided by the company.[15]

Throughout this book, we will show how diversity affects HRM practices. For example, from a staffing perspective, it is important to ensure that tests used to select employees are not unfairly biased against minority groups. From the perspective of work design, employees need flexible schedules that allow them to meet nonwork needs. In terms of training, it is clear that employees must be made aware of the damage that stereotypes can do. With regard to compensation, organizations are providing benefits such as elder care and day care as a way to accommodate the needs of a diverse workforce. As we will see later in the chapter, successfully managing diversity is also critical for companies that compete in international markets.

Skill Deficiencies of the Workforce

The increasing use of computers to do routine tasks has shifted the kinds of skills needed for employees in the U.S. economy. Such qualities as physical strength and mastery of a particular piece of machinery are no longer important for many jobs. More employers are looking for mathematical, verbal, and interpersonal skills, such as the ability to solve math or other problems or reach decisions as part of a team. Often, when organizations are looking for technical skills, they are looking for skills related to computers and using the Internet. Today's employees must be able to handle a variety of responsibilities, interact with customers, and think creatively.

To find such employees, most organizations are looking for educational achievements. A college degree is a basic requirement for many jobs today. Competition for qualified college graduates in many fields is intense. At the other extreme, workers with less education often have to settle for low-paying jobs. Some companies are unable to find qualified employees and instead rely on training to correct skill deficiencies.[16] Other companies team up with universities, community colleges, and high schools to design and teach courses ranging from basic reading to design blueprint reading.

Not all the skills employers want require a college education. Employers surveyed by the National Association of Manufacturers report a deficiency in qualified production workers—not just engineers and computer experts. In the words of Bill Bachman, president of Bachman Machine Company in St. Louis, "Kids think these are dirty, dead-end jobs. . . . When we find someone good, we try to hang onto them. When we lose them, they're extremely hard to replace."[17] Part of the challenge is that today's U.S. production jobs rely on intelligence and skills as much as on strength. Workers often must operate sophisticated computer-controlled machinery and monitor quality levels. In some areas, companies and communities have set up apprenticeship and training programs to fix the worker shortage. The gap between skills needed and skills available has decreased U.S. companies' ability to compete because as a consequence of the deficiency they sometimes lack the capacity to upgrade technology, reorganize work, and empower employees.

LO2
Summarize areas in which human resource management can support the goal of creating a high-performance work system.

high-performance work systems
Organizations that have the best possible fit between their social system (people and how they interact) and technical system (equipment and processes).

❧ HIGH-PERFORMANCE WORK SYSTEMS

Human resource management is playing an important role in helping organizations gain and keep an advantage over competitors by becoming **high-performance work systems.** These are organizations that have the best possible fit between their social system (people and how they interact) and technical system (equipment and processes).[18] As the nature of the workforce and the technology available to organizations have changed, so have the requirements for creating a high-performance work system. Customers are demanding high quality and customized products, employees are seeking flexible work arrangements, and employers are looking for ways to tap people's creativity and interpersonal skills. Such demands require that organizations make full use of their people's knowledge and skill, and skilled human resource management can help organizations do this.

Among the trends that are occurring in today's high-performance work systems are reliance on knowledge workers; the empowerment of employees to make decisions; and the use of teamwork. The following sections describe those three trends, and Chapter 16 will explore the ways HRM can support the creation and maintenance of a high-performance work system. HR professionals who keep up with change are well positioned to help create high-performance work systems. The nearby "HR How To"

HR HOW TO

KEEPING UP WITH CHANGE

Many of the changes in today's business environment have a direct impact on human resource management. Changes in the population, in technology, in employees' expectations, and other aspects of the business environment place heavy demands on modern HR professionals—and anyone else involved in management. The career advantage goes to those who keep an eye on what's happening in the business environment. Here are some ways to keep up with change:

Know Your Specialty Join and participate in trade and professional groups. In human resource management, the largest group is the Society for Human Resource Management. Attendance at meetings and visits to the SHRM home page will help you stay abreast of the latest ideas in the field.

Know Your Business To support your organization's strategy, you have to know the company's line of work. Read industry and general business publications, with an eye on news about what's happening in your company's industry. You can customize Web portals and news Web sites to deliver headlines related to your industry.

Follow Trends Government agencies publish news releases and data related to their area of responsibility. Pay regular visits to relevant agency Web sites, such as those for the Bureau of Labor Statistics (www.bls.gov), the Equal Employment Opportunity Commission (www.eeoc.gov), and the Occupational Safety and Health Administration (www.osha.gov) to find the latest information.

Listen at Work When employees and management are talking about their work and the organization's performance, listen for the HR implications. Does the organization have the right amounts and kinds of knowledge, skills, and motivation to carry out its goals? Can some of the new ideas in your field help your organization?

Keep Your Résumé Up-to-Date If new job or career opportunities become available with your current employer (or another organization), you will be ready to take advantage of them.

Take Time Out to Relax Change creates long work hours and stress. Work can become all-consuming. If you are stressed out, you are not a valuable employee or a happy person to be around. Make sure you take time for leisure activities you enjoy. Dance, read, exercise—have fun!

box suggests ways HR professionals can make a commitment to adapt to change in order to keep up with a fast-changing work environment.

Knowledge Workers

The growth in e-commerce, plus the shift from a manufacturing to a service and information economy, has changed the nature of employees that are most in demand. The Bureau of Labor Statistics forecasts that between 2002 and 2012, most new jobs will be in-service occupations, especially education and health services.

The number of service jobs has important implications for human resource management. Research shows that if employees have a favorable view of HRM practices—say, their career opportunities, training, pay, and feedback on performance—they are more likely to provide good service to customers. Therefore, quality HRM for service employees can translate into customer satisfaction. The second-largest category of new

TOP 10 OCCUPATIONS FOR JOB GROWTH

The following graph shows the occupations that are expected to add the most new jobs between 2002 and 2012. These jobs require widely different levels of training and responsibility, and pay levels vary considerably.

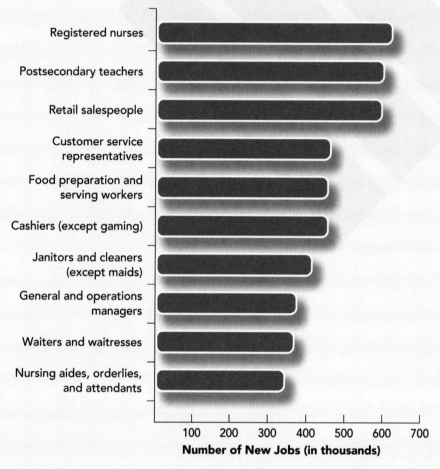

Number of New Jobs (in thousands)

SOURCE: Bureau of Labor Statistics, "Occupational Employment," *Occupational Outlook Quarterly*, Winter 2003–2004, pp. 6–27; and Bureau of Labor Statistics, "Tomorrow's Jobs," *Occupational Outlook Handbook*, last modified June 2, 2004, both downloaded at www.bls.gov.

jobs is professional and business services, with the fastest growth expected to come from employment services. Among goods-producing industries, the fastest job growth is expected in construction. Also, even though some industries, such as mining, manufacturing, and agriculture, are expected to have fewer jobs by 2012, companies in those industries still need to fill jobs when workers retire. And as noted in the previ-

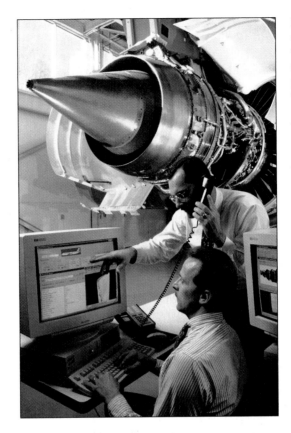

Knowledge workers are employees whose value to their employers stems primarily from what they know. Engineers such as the ones pictured here have in-depth knowledge of their field and are hard to replace because of their special knowledge.

ous section, finding qualified people to fill these jobs is not always easy, especially when new workers avoid these industries.

Besides differences among industries, job growth varies according to the type of job. The "Did You Know . . . ?" box lists the 10 occupations expected to gain the most jobs between 2002 and 2012. Of the jobs expected to have the greatest percentage increases, most are related to health care and computers. The fastest-growing occupations are medical assistants, network systems and data communications analysts, and physician assistants.[19] Most of these occupations require a college degree. In contrast, the occupations expected to have the largest numerical increases more often require only on-the-job training. (Exceptions are registered nurses, postsecondary teachers, and general and operations managers.) This means that many companies' HRM departments will need to provide excellent training as well as hiring.

What most of these high-growth jobs have in common is specialized knowledge. To meet their human capital needs, companies are increasingly trying to attract, develop, and retain knowledge workers. **Knowledge workers** are employees whose main contribution to the organization is specialized knowledge, such as knowledge of customers, a process, or a profession. Knowledge workers are especially needed for jobs in health services, business services, social services, engineering, and management.

Knowledge workers are in a position of power, because they own the knowledge that the company needs in order to produce its products and services, and they must share their knowledge and collaborate with others in order for their employer to succeed. An employer cannot simply order these employees to perform tasks. Managers depend on the employees' willingness to share information. Furthermore, skilled

knowledge workers
Employees whose main contribution to the organization is specialized knowledge, such as knowledge of customers, a process, or a profession.

knowledge workers have many job opportunities, even in a slow economy. If they choose, they can leave a company and take their knowledge to another employer. Replacing them may be difficult and time-consuming.

As more organizations become knowledge-based, they must promote and capture learning at the level of employees, teams, and the overall organization. Buckman Laboratories, for example, is known for its knowledge management practices.[20] Buckman Laboratories develops and markets specialty chemicals. Buckman's CEO, Robert Buckman, has developed an organizational culture, technology, and work processes that encourage the sharing of knowledge. Employees have laptop computers so they can share information anywhere and anytime via the Internet. The company set up rewards for innovation and for creating and exchanging knowledge. The rewards are based on performance measures related to the percentage of sales of new products. Buckman also changed the focus of the company's information systems department, renaming it the "knowledge transfer department" to better match the service it is supposed to provide.

The reliance on knowledge workers also affects organizations' decisions about the kinds of people they are recruiting and selecting.[21] They are shifting away from focusing on specific skills, such as how to operate a particular kind of machinery, and toward a greater emphasis on general cognitive skills (thinking and problem solving) and interpersonal skills. Employers are more interested in evidence that job candidates will excel at working in teams or interacting with customers. These skills also support an employee's ability to gather and share knowledge, helping the organization to innovate and meet customer needs. To the extent that technical skills are important, employers often are most interested in the ability to use information technology, including the Internet and statistical software.

Employee Empowerment

LO3
Define employee empowerment and explain its role in the modern organization.

To completely benefit from employees' knowledge, organizations need a management style that focuses on developing and empowering employees. **Employee empowerment** means giving employees responsibility and authority to make decisions regarding all aspects of product development or customer service.[22] Employees are then held accountable for products and services. In return, they share the resulting losses and rewards.

employee empowerment
Giving employees responsibility and authority to make decisions regarding all aspects of product development or customer service.

HRM practices such as performance management, training, work design, and compensation are important for ensuring the success of employee empowerment. Jobs must be designed to give employees the necessary latitude for making a variety of decisions. Employees must be properly trained to exert their wider authority and use information resources such as the Internet, as well as tools for communicating information. Employees also need feedback to help them evaluate their success. Pay and other rewards should reflect employees' authority and be related to successful handling of their responsibility. In addition, for empowerment to succeed, managers must be trained to link employees to resources within and outside the organization, such as customers, coworkers in other departments, and Web sites with needed information. Managers must also encourage employees to interact with staff throughout the organization, must ensure that employees receive the information they need, and must reward cooperation.

As with the need for knowledge workers, use of employee empowerment shifts the recruiting focus away from technical skills and toward general cognitive and interpersonal skills. Employees who have responsibility for a final product or service must be able to listen to customers, adapt to changing needs, and creatively solve a variety of problems.

Teamwork

Modern technology places the information that employees need for improving quality and providing customer service right at the point of sale or production. As a result, the employees engaging in selling and producing must also be able to make decisions about how to do their work. Organizations need to set up work in a way that gives employees the authority and ability to make those decisions. One of the most popular ways to increase employee responsibility and control is to assign work to teams. **Teamwork** is the assignment of work to groups of employees with various skills who interact to assemble a product or provide a service. Work teams often assume many activities traditionally reserved for managers, such as selecting new team members, scheduling work, and coordinating work with customers and other units of the organization. Work teams also contribute to total quality by performing inspection and quality-control activities while the product or service is being completed.

In some organizations, technology is enabling teamwork even when workers are at different locations or work at different times. These organizations use *virtual teams*—teams that rely on communications technology such as videoconferences, e-mail, and cell phones to keep in touch and coordinate activities.

Teamwork can motivate employees by making work more interesting and significant. At organizations that rely on teamwork, labor costs may be lower as well. Spurred by such advantages, a number of companies are reorganizing assembly operations—abandoning the assembly line in favor of operations that combine mass production with jobs in which employees perform multiple tasks, use many skills, control the pace of work, and assemble the entire final product. One example of this type of teamwork is the Marion, North Carolina, factory of Rockwell Automation's Power Systems Division, where almost every employee works on a team. The facility is organized into 20 manufacturing cells; 16 make routine products accounting for 80 percent of the division's revenue, and the other 4 make special-order products in lots as small as one unit. These machining and assembly employees are cross-trained to perform at least three jobs, so they can step in wherever they are needed. Management also is carried out by teams, each of which brings together a supervisor, an engineer, and a planner. These management teams are responsible for buying materials, hiring employees, providing customer service, and scheduling overtime. Employees and management are all involved in monitoring product data and introducing improvements to products and processes. This setup has enabled Power Systems to produce excellent quality with fast turnaround times, exceptionally low costs, high customer satisfaction, and no accidents.[23]

teamwork
The assignment of work to groups of employees with various skills who interact to assemble a product or provide a service.

◈ FOCUS ON STRATEGY

As we saw in Chapter 1, traditional management thinking treated human resource management primarily as an administrative function, but managers today are beginning to see a more central role for HRM. They are beginning to look at HRM as a means to support a company's *strategy*—its plan for meeting broad goals such as profitability, quality, and market share.[24] This strategic role for HRM has evolved gradually. At many organizations, managers still treat HR professionals primarily as experts in designing and delivering HR systems. But at a growing number of organizations, HR professionals are strategic partners with other managers.

This means they use their knowledge of the business and of human resources to help the organization develop strategies and to align HRM policies and practices with those strategies. To do this, human resource managers must focus on the future as well

LO4
Identify ways HR professionals can support organizational strategies for quality, growth, and efficiency.

Figure 2.4

Business Strategy:
Issues Affecting
HRM

as the present, and on company goals as well as human resource activities. They may, for example, become experts at analyzing the business impact of HR decisions or at developing and keeping the best talent to support business strategy. An example of an HRM professional who understands this new role is Kiyoski Shinozaki, a manager with Nikkei, a Japanese business publishing company. Shinozaki's education includes a master's degree in human resource management, and he is adding to his business credentials by taking further courses in finance and accounting. He predicts that deeper business knowledge will help him plan and suggest initiatives, rather than merely reacting to strategies devised by other managers.[25]

The specific ways in which human resource professionals support the organization's strategy vary according to their level of involvement and the nature of the strategy. Strategic issues include emphasis on quality and decisions about growth and efficiency. Human resource management can support these strategies, including efforts such as quality improvement programs, mergers and acquisitions, and restructuring. Decisions to use reengineering and outsourcing can make an organization more efficient and also give rise to many human resource challenges. International expansion presents a wide variety of HRM challenges and opportunities. Figure 2.4 summarizes these strategic issues facing human resource management.

High Quality Standards

total quality management (TQM)
A companywide effort to continuously improve the ways people, machines, and systems accomplish work.

To compete in today's economy, companies need to provide high-quality products and services. If companies do not adhere to quality standards, they will have difficulty selling their product or service to vendors, suppliers, or customers. Therefore, many organizations have adopted some form of **total quality management (TQM)**—a companywide effort to continuously improve the ways people, machines, and systems accomplish work.[26] TQM has several core values:[27]

- Methods and processes are designed to meet the needs of internal and external customers (that is, whomever the process is intended to serve).
- Every employee in the organization receives training in quality.
- Quality is designed into a product or service so that errors are prevented from occurring, rather than being detected and corrected in an error-prone product or service.
- The organization promotes cooperation with vendors, suppliers, and customers to improve quality and hold down costs.
- Managers measure progress with feedback based on data.

Based on these values, the TQM approach provides guidelines for all the organization's activities, including human resource management. To promote quality, organizations need an environment that supports innovation, creativity, and risk taking to meet customer demands. Problem solving should bring together managers, employees, and customers. Employees should communicate with managers about customer needs.

Human resource management supports the strong commitment to quality at TRW Automotive Holdings Corporation's factory in Fowlerville, Michigan. The facility produces automotive slip-control units, a category that encompasses automobile components such as antilock brakes and vehicle stability systems. Auto companies are always looking for product and price improvements, but in spite of constant changes, the Fowlerville plant continues to operate efficiently and with an amazing defect rate of just three customer rejections out of every million items. In addition, all deliveries have been made on time. The company credits its efficient plant layout and its workforce for the exceptional practices. With low turnover, the facility benefits from employees' experience, and training ensures that its people are knowledgeable. Plant manager Bob Holman comments, "People here know what to do without being told," and manufacturing employee Andrew Bogdan explains, "This is probably the most multitasked plant floor you'll ever see. Seventy percent of our people can do 90 percent of the jobs here." In addition, the organization fosters employee involvement and teamwork. For example, production workers serve on Policy and Procedure Panels, which have a voice in administrative decisions.[28]

Mergers and Acquisitions

Increasingly, organizations are joining forces through mergers (two companies becoming one) and acquisitions (one company buying another). Some mergers and acquisitions result in consolidation within an industry, meaning that two firms in one industry join to hold a greater share of the industry. For example, British Petroleum's acquisition of Amoco Oil represented a consolidation, or reduction of the number of companies in the oil industry. Other mergers and acquisitions cross industry lines. In a merger to form Citigroup, Citicorp combined its banking business with Traveller's Group's insurance business. Furthermore, these deals more frequently take the form of global megamergers, or mergers of big companies based in different countries (as in the case of BP-Amoco).

These deals do not always meet expectations, however. According to a report by the Conference Board, one of the major reasons for their failure may be "people issues." Recognizing this, some companies now heavily weigh the other organization's culture before they embark on a merger or acquisition. For example, before acquiring ValueRx, executives at Express Scripts interviewed senior executives and middle managers at ValueRx in order to get a sense of its values and practices.[29] Even so, in a recent survey, fewer than one-third of the HRM executives said they had a major influence in how mergers are planned. Not surprisingly, 80 percent of them said people issues have a significant impact after the deals go through.[30]

HRM should have a significant role in carrying out a merger or acquisition. Differences between the businesses involved in the deal make conflict inevitable. Training efforts should therefore include development of skills in conflict resolution. Also, HR professionals have to sort out differences in the two companies' practices with regard to compensation, performance appraisal, and other HR systems. Settling on a consistent structure to meet the combined organization's goals may help to bring employees together. Cisco Systems heads off conflict following its acquisitions by preparing employees at the firm to be acquired. Cisco tries to make sure that employees of the acquired firm understand that major change will follow the acquisition, so that they will not be surprised afterward. Cisco also addresses career paths. It provides significant roles for the acquired company's top talent in order to keep them on board with challenging opportunities. With such HR-related efforts, Cisco outperforms most firms in retaining talented employees after an acquisition.[31]

Downsizing

It would have been hard to ignore the massive "war for talent" that went on during the late 1990s, particularly with the dot-com craze, as Internet-based companies seemingly became rich overnight. During this time, organizations sought to become "employers of choice," to establish "employment brands," and to develop "employee value propositions." All these slogans were meant as ways to ensure that the organizations would be able to attract and retain talented employees. However, what was less noticeable was that in spite of the hiring craze, massive layoffs also were occurring. In fact, as shown in Figure 2.5, 1998, the height of the war for talent, also saw the largest number of layoffs in the decade.[32]

This pattern seems to represent a "churning" of employees. In other words, organizations apparently were laying off employees with outdated skills or cutting whole

Figure 2.5

Number of Employees Laid Off during the 1990s

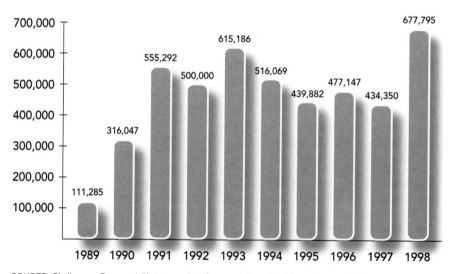

SOURCE: Challenger, Gray, and Christmas, Outplacement Firm, Workforce Reports 1998.

businesses that were in declining markets while simultaneously building businesses and employee bases in newer, higher-growth markets. For example, IBM cut 69,256 people yet increased its workforce by 16,000 in 1996. Although downsizing always poses problems for human resource management, the impact can be especially confusing in an organization that "churns" employees. How can such an organization develop a reputation as an employer of choice and motivate employees to care about the organization? The way organizations answer such questions will play a significant part in determining the quality of employees on the payroll.

Whether or not the organization is churning employees, downsizing presents a number of challenges and opportunities for HRM. In terms of challenges, the HRM function must "surgically" reduce the workforce by cutting only the workers who are less valuable in their performance. Achieving this is difficult because the best workers are most able (and often willing) to find alternative employment and may leave voluntarily before the organization lays off anyone. In 1992 General Motors and the United Auto Workers agreed to an early-retirement program for individuals between the ages of 51 and 65 who had been employed for 10 or more years. For those who agreed to retire, even if they obtained employment elsewhere, the program provided full pension benefits and as much as $13,000 toward the purchase of a GM car.[33] Such early-retirement programs are humane, but they essentially reduce the workforce with a "grenade" approach—not distinguishing good from poor performers but rather eliminating an entire group of employees. In fact, research indicates that when companies downsize by offering early-retirement programs, they usually end up rehiring to replace essential talent within a year. Often the company does not achieve its cost-cutting goals because it spends 50 to 150 percent of the departing employee's salary in hiring and retraining new workers.[34]

Another HRM challenge is to boost the morale of employees who remain after the reduction; this is discussed in greater detail in Chapter 5. Survivors may feel guilt over keeping their jobs when their friends were laid off. Or they may envy their friends who retired with attractive severance and pension benefits. Their reduced satisfaction and lower commitment to the organization may interfere with their performance of their work. To address these problems, HR professionals should maintain open communication with remaining employees to build their trust and commitment, rather than withholding information.[35] All employees should be informed why the downsizing is necessary, what costs are to be cut, how long the downsizing will last, and what strategies the organization intends to pursue. Finally, HRM can provide downsized employees with outplacement services to help them find new jobs. Such services are ways an organization can show that it cares about its employees, even though it cannot afford to keep all of them on the payroll.

Reengineering

Rapidly changing customer needs and technology have caused many organizations to rethink the way they get work done. For example, when an organization adopts new technology, its existing processes may no longer result in acceptable quality levels, meet customer expectations for speed, or keep costs to profitable levels. Therefore, many organizations have undertaken **reengineering**—a complete review of the organization's critical work processes to make them more efficient and able to deliver higher quality.

Ideally, reengineering involves reviewing all the processes performed by all the organization's major functions, including production, sales, accounting, and human

reengineering
A complete review of the organization's critical work processes to make them more efficient and able to deliver higher quality.

resources. Therefore, reengineering affects human resource management in two ways. First, the way the HR department itself accomplishes its goals may change dramatically. Second, the fundamental change throughout the organization requires the HR department to help design and implement change so that all employees will be committed to the success of the reengineered organization. Employees may need training for their reengineered jobs. The organization may need to redesign the structure of its pay and benefits to make them more appropriate for its new way of operating. It also may need to recruit employees with a new set of skills. Often, reengineering results in employees being laid off or reassigned to new jobs, as the organization's needs change. HR professionals should help with this transition, as described above in the case of downsizing.

Outsourcing

outsourcing
The practice of having another company (a vendor, third-party provider, or consultant) provide services.

Many organizations are increasingly outsourcing business activities. **Outsourcing** refers to the practice of having another company (a vendor, third-party provider, or consultant) provide services. For instance, a manufacturing company might outsource its accounting and transportation functions to businesses that specialize in these activities. Outsourcing gives the company access to in-depth expertise and is often more economical as well.

Not only do HR departments help with a transition to outsourcing, but many HR functions are being outsourced. A recent study suggests that 8 out of 10 companies outsource at least one human resource activity.[36] HR functions that are commonly outsourced include payroll administration, training, and recruitment and selection of employees. For example, Bank of America signed a 10-year contract with Exult Inc. to manage much of the bank's HR function.[37] Among the functions that Bank of America is outsourcing are payroll, accounts payable, and benefits administration. Other services Exult is handling include delivery of HR services and a call center to provide employees with information about human resources and benefits. Bank of America retained the HR functions of recruiting and compensation, as well as legal counsel. This arrangement frees HR managers at Bank of America to work on strategy and vision, focusing them on HRM responsibilities that add value to the business.

Expanding into Global Markets

LO5
Summarize ways in which human resource management can support organizations expanding internationally.

Companies are finding that to survive they must compete in international markets as well as fend off foreign competitors' attempts to gain ground in the United States. To meet these challenges, U.S. businesses must develop global markets, keep up with competition from overseas, hire from an international labor pool, and prepare employees for global assignments.

Study of companies that are successful and widely admired suggests that these companies not only operate on a multinational scale, but also have workforces and corporate cultures that reflect their global markets.[38] These companies, which include General Electric, Coca-Cola, Microsoft, Walt Disney, and Intel, focus on customer satisfaction and innovation. In addition, they operate on the belief that people are the company's most important asset. Placing this value on employees requires the companies to emphasize human resource practices, including rewards for superior performance, measures of employee satisfaction, careful selection of employees, promotion from within, and investment in employee development.

The Global Workforce

For today's and tomorrow's employers, talent comes from a global workforce. Organizations with international operations hire at least some of their employees in the foreign countries where they operate. In fact, regardless of where their customers are located, more and more organizations are looking overseas to hire talented people willing to work for less pay than the U.S. labor market requires. Intel, for example, has projected that most of its future employees will be hired outside U.S. borders. The efforts to hire workers in other countries are common enough that they have spurred the creation of a popular name for the practice: **offshoring.** Just a few years ago, most offshoring involved big manufacturers building factories in countries with lower labor costs. But today it is so easy to send information and software around the world that even start-ups are hiring overseas. In one study, almost 4 out of 10 new companies employed foreign analysts, marketers, engineers, and other employees. In contrast to computer and printer manufacturer Hewlett-Packard, which hired its first foreign workers 20 years after its founding in 1939, search engine Google employed people outside the United States just three years after its 1998 start.[39]

Technology is lowering barriers to overseas operations. OfficeTiger, which provides business services to banks, insurance companies, and other clients, has 200 employees in the United States and 2,000 in southern India. Whether its clients need typesetting or marketing research, the Indian employees can readily submit their work over the Internet. Because Indian workers are generally paid only about one-fifth of U.S. earnings for comparable jobs, OfficeTiger offers attractive prices. The company is growing, and it expects that two-thirds of its future hires will be in India, Sri Lanka, and countries other than the United States.[40]

Hiring in developing nations such as India, Mexico, and Brazil gives employers access to people with potential who are eager to work yet who will accept lower wages than elsewhere in the world. Challenges, however, may include employees' lack of familiarity with technology and corporate practices, as well as political and economic instability in the areas. Important issues that HR experts can help companies weigh include whether workers in the offshore locations can provide the same or better skills, how offshoring will affect motivation and recruitment of employees needed in the United States, and whether managers are well prepared to manage and lead offshore employees.

Despite the risks, many organizations that have hired globally are realizing high returns. General Electric has been a pioneer in offshoring and is reaping its rewards.[41] The foundation was laid in 1989, when most U.S. companies viewed India as too underdeveloped to be an attractive investment. GE's first attempt was to establish a partnership to develop an ultrasound machine. Sales to the Indian market were disappointing, but from the business relationship, GE executives discovered the engineering and programming talent India had to offer. They soon began arranging to have work done in India at far lower costs than if the same work had been done in the United States—not only through contracts but also by setting up GE operations in India. Besides engineers and programmers, GE has hired customer service representatives, accountants, and market researchers.

For an organization to operate in other countries, its HR practices must take into consideration differences in culture and business practices. Consider how Starbucks Coffee handled its expansion into Beijing, China.[42] Demand for qualified managers in Beijing exceeds the local supply. Employers therefore have to take steps to attract and retain managers. Starbucks researched the motivation and needs of potential

offshoring
Moving operations from the country where a company is headquartered to a country where pay rates are lower but the necessary skills are available.

BUILDING A COMMON CULTURE AT PRICEWATERHOUSECOOPERS

PricewaterhouseCoopers (PWC) is a global organization that provides tax and accounting services through offices in 769 cities spread across 144 countries. Of the company's more than 120,000 employees, about one-fourth are located in North America. To create a common culture, develop leaders, and encourage innovation, the company offers a global training program it calls Genesis Park, held in Washington, D.C.

The five-month Genesis Park program is designed to remove any cultural biases its participants may have about teamwork and creative thinking. It builds them into an effective multinational team that can help solve problems for the organization and its clients. The unique program exposes the participants, drawn from many of the countries where PWC operates, to goals that are universal throughout the company, including effective communications and mentoring.

The program helps participants develop skills in many areas, including coaching, strategic thinking, and global networking. They learn to offer feedback, listen effectively, and understand personality differences. Participants are actively engaged, working on projects and interacting with company leaders as they explore topics such as how the company should be structured in the future and what its objectives should be.

What's really special about Genesis Park is the learning that comes when individuals of different cultural backgrounds interact. In the projects and exercises, participants are expected to influence one another through their leadership abilities, rather than their job titles. For some participants, the lack of a "boss" and a hierarchy is challenging. For example, participants from Singapore, Malaysia, and other Asian countries sometimes feel awkward selling their ideas because their cultures en-

courage people to defer to those with higher status. Also, the business issues of most importance may differ from one country to another. As participants struggle with these differences, they learn to be effective across countries and cultures.

PWC has enjoyed several benefits from Genesis Park. Not only do participants learn the subject matter, but they also develop professional networks of colleagues who can help them in the future. Genesis Park graduates often contact graduates from other countries when they need help on projects in those countries. They also develop greater confidence and willingness to challenge the status quo. Through Genesis Park, PWC is shaping leaders for its role in a global economy.

SOURCE: Based on C. Patton, "The Genesis of Talent," *Human Resource Executive*, February 2004, pp. 34–38; and PricewaterhouseCoopers, "About Us," PWC Web site, www.pwcglobal. com, accessed March 29, 2005.

---

managers. The company learned that in traditional Chinese-owned companies, rules and regulations allowed little creativity and self-direction. Also, in many joint U.S.-China ventures, local managers were not trusted. Starbucks distinguished itself as an employer by emphasizing its casual culture and opportunities for career development. The company also spends considerable time training employees. It sends new managers to Tacoma, Washington, where they learn the corporate culture as well as the secrets of brewing flavorful coffee. Another company that trains foreign workers in the United States is PricewaterhouseCoopers, described in the "Best Practices" box.

Even hiring at home may involve selection of employees from other countries. The 1990s and the beginning of the 21st century, like the beginning of the last century,

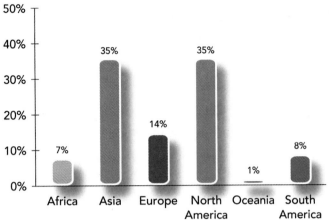

Figure 2.6
Where Immigrants
to the United States
Came from in 2003

SOURCE: Department of Homeland Security, Office of Immigration Statistics, *Yearbook of Immigration Statistics: 2003*, Table 3, downloaded at http://uscis.gov (March 23, 2005).

have been years of significant immigration. Immigrants will likely account for an additional million persons in the U.S. workforce each year through 2012.[43] Figure 2.6 shows the distribution of immigration by continent of origin. The impact of immigration will be especially large in some regions of the United States. In the states on the Pacific Coast, 7 out of 10 entrants to the labor force are immigrants.[44] About 70 percent of immigrant workers will be Hispanics and Asians. Employers in tight labor markets—such as those seeking experts in computer science, engineering, and information systems—are especially likely to recruit international students.[45] The war against terrorism has not changed the use of immigrants by U.S. employers, but heightened concern for national security has resulted in longer waits for visas to be approved by the government and for hiring decisions to be approved.

International Assignments

Besides hiring an international workforce, organizations must be prepared to send employees to other countries. This requires HR expertise in selecting employees for international assignments and preparing them for those assignments. Employees who take assignments in other countries are called **expatriates.**

U.S. companies must better prepare employees to work in other countries. The failure rate for U.S. expatriates is greater than that for European and Japanese expatriates.[46] To improve in this area, U.S. companies must carefully select employees to work abroad based on their ability to understand and respect the cultural and business norms of the host country. Qualified candidates also need language skills and technical ability. In Chapter 15, we discuss practices for training employees to understand other cultures.

expatriates
Employees who take assignments in other countries.

TECHNOLOGICAL CHANGE IN HRM

Advances in computer-related technology have had a major impact on the use of information for managing human resources. Large quantities of employee data (including training records, skills, compensation rates, and benefits usage and cost) can easily be stored on personal computers and manipulated with user-friendly spreadsheets

LO6
Discuss how technological developments are affecting human resource management.

TABLE 2.1

New Technologies
Influencing HRM

TECHNOLOGY	WHAT IT DOES	EXAMPLE
Internet portal	Combines data from several sources into a single site; lets user customize data without programming skills.	A company's manager can track labor costs by work group.
Shared service centers	Consolidate different HR functions into a single location; eliminate redundancy and reduce administrative costs; process all HR transactions at one time.	AlliedSignal combined more than 75 functions, including finance and HR, into a shared service center.
Application service provider (ASP)	Lets companies rent space on a remote computer system and use the system's software to manage its HR activities, including security and upgrades.	KPMG Consulting uses an ASP to host the company's computerized learning program.
Business intelligence	Provides insight into business trends and patterns and helps businesses improve decisions.	Managers use the system to analyze labor costs and productivity among different employee groups.

human resource information system (HRIS)
A computer system used to acquire, store, manipulate, analyze, retrieve, and distribute information related to an organization's human resources.

or statistical software. Often these features are combined in a **human resource information system (HRIS),** a computer system used to acquire, store, manipulate, analyze, retrieve, and distribute information related to an organization's human resources.[47] An HRIS can support strategic decision making, help the organization avoid lawsuits, provide data for evaluating programs or policies, and support day-to-day HR decisions. Table 2.1 describes some of the new technologies that may be included in an organization's HRIS.

The support of an HRIS can help HR professionals navigate the challenges of today's complex business environment. For example, rapidly changing technology can cause employees' skills to become obsolete. Organizations must therefore carefully monitor their employees' skills and the organization's needed skills. Often the employees and needs are distributed among several locations, perhaps among several countries. Florida Power & Light Company, based in Juno Beach, Florida, uses HRIS applications to provide information to employees and to support decision making by managers. More than 10,000 employees in 20 states can use the information system to learn about their benefits. Managers use the system to track employees' vacation and sick days and to make changes in staffing and pay. If managers want a personnel report, they no longer have to call the human resource department to request one; the HRIS will prepare it automatically.[48]

electronic business (e-business)
Any process that a business conducts electronically, especially business involving use of the Internet.

The Internet Economy

The way business is conducted has changed rapidly during the past decade and will continue to do so. Much of the change is related to the widespread adoption of the Internet by businesses and individuals. More than two-thirds of the U.S. population uses the Internet, and their numbers have more than doubled over the first half of this decade.[49] Greater use of the Internet has prompted the spread of **electronic business (e-business)**—any process that a business conducts electronically, especially business

The internet and e-HRM are helpful for employees who work outside the office because they can receive and share information online easily. The benefits of products such as PDAs' and Blackberrys' are enormous but is it possible to be too accessible?

involving use of the Internet. E-business includes several forms of buying and selling goods and business services:

- Business-to-consumer transactions, such as purchasing books and tickets and conducting services, including banking, online.
- Business-to-business transactions, including sales among manufacturers, retailers, wholesalers, and construction firms.
- Consumer-to-consumer transactions—in particular, individuals buying and selling through auctions.

E-business relies on the Internet to enable buyers to obtain product information online, directly order products and services, receive after-sale technical support, and view the status of orders and deliveries. Internet sites may also allow the customer and seller to communicate with each other through e-mail, chat, and voice connections. Companies may set up customer service centers offering e-mail and live telephone connections to provide help, advice, or product information not found on their Web sites.

E-business creates many HRM challenges.[50] The fast pace of change in information technology requires companies to continually update their skill requirements and then recruit and train people to meet those requirements. The competition for such employees may be stiff and, as described earlier, often involves recruiting on an international scale.

Motivation can also be a challenge. A decade ago, many e-business organizations were small start-up companies founded by young, forward-looking people who saw the potential of a then-new technology. These companies sometimes made up for inexperienced management with a culture based on creativity, enthusiasm, and intense commitment. Policies and procedures sometimes took a backseat to team spirit and workplace fun. But as competition from established companies heated up and as investors withdrew funding, the start-up companies were acquired, went out of business, or had to radically cut back hiring and spending. In this changed environment, employees no longer believed the vision that they could invest long hours at modest pay for the hope of a huge payoff when their company became the next Amazon or Google. In this less frenzied, more practical environment, programmers and game designers are beginning to demand overtime pay for their 60-hour workweeks and refusing stock options as substitutes for pay raises. In an extreme case, current and former employees of videogame company Electronic Arts filed a lawsuit complaining that it had not paid them overtime wages to which they were entitled.[51] In this environment, HRM needs to help companies comply with labor laws, motivate employees, and craft human resource policies that seem fair to workers and meet employers' competitive demands.

Electronic Human Resource Management (e-HRM)

The development of e-business has included ways to move HRM activities onto the Internet. Electronic HRM applications let employees enroll in and participate in training programs online. Employees can go online to select from items in a benefits package and enroll in the benefits they choose. They can look up answers to HR-related questions and read company news. This processing and transmission of digitized HR information is called **electronic human resource management (e-HRM).**

> **electronic human resource management (e-HRM)**
> The processing and transmission of digitized HR information, especially using computer networking and the Internet.

E-HRM has the potential to change all traditional HRM functions. Table 2.2 shows some major implications of e-HRM. For example, employees in different geographic areas can work together. Use of the Internet lets companies search for talent without geographic limitations. Recruiting can include online job postings, applications, and candidate screening from the company's Web site or the Web sites of companies that specialize in online recruiting, such as Monster.com or HotJobs. Employees from different geographic locations can all receive the same training over the company's computer network.

Privacy is an important issue in e-HRM. A great deal of HR information is confidential and not suitable for posting on a Web site for everyone to see. One solution is to set up e-HRM on an *intranet*, which is a network that uses Internet tools but limits access to authorized users in the organization. However, to better draw on the Internet's potential, organizations are increasingly replacing intranets with Web portals (Web sites designed to serve as a gateway to the Internet, highlighting links to relevant information).[52] Whether a company uses an intranet or a Web portal, it must ensure that it has sufficient security measures in place to protect employees' privacy.

Another issue that involves privacy concerns, the Internet, and personnel policy is employees' use of e-mail. Many employees believe that the e-mail messages they send are private and not accessible once they delete them. In fact, employers legitimately point out that they have a right to see and control communications employees create on company time and send from the company's address. Over half of U.S. companies recently surveyed said they monitor incoming and outgoing e-mail.[53] Some companies also monitor e-mail messages sent within the company. Scanning

TABLE 2.2

Implications of e-HRM for HRM Practices

HRM PRACTICES	IMPLICATIONS OF E-HRM
Analysis and design of work	Employees in geographically dispersed locations can work together in virtual teams using video, e-mail, and the Internet.
Recruiting	Post job openings online; candidates can apply for jobs online.
Training	Online learning can bring training to employees anywhere, anytime.
Selection	Online simulations, including tests, videos, and e-mail, can measure job candidates' ability to deal with real-life business challenges.
Compensation and benefits	Employees can review salary and bonus information and seek information about and enroll in benefit plans.

software can flag messages that use potentially embarrassing words or that mention sensitive topics such as competitors, client or patient files, or code names for products under development. Webcor Builders, a California construction company, uses scanning software that can search for keywords, word patterns, and names of competitors. Few states have laws requiring companies to notify employees of such practices, but ethical principles and good employee relations call upon HR personnel to ensure that the company is clear about its policy and the reasons for it.

Sharing of Human Resource Information

Information technology is changing the way HR departments handle record keeping and information sharing. Today, HR employees use modern technology to automate much of their work in managing employee records and giving employees access to information and enrollment forms for training, benefits, and other programs. As a result, HR employees play a smaller role in maintaining records, and employees now get information through **self-service.** This means employees have online access to information about HR issues such as training, benefits, compensation, and contracts; go online to enroll themselves in programs and services; and provide feedback through online surveys. Today, employees routinely look up workplace policies and information about their benefits online, and they may receive electronic notification when deposits are made directly to their bank accounts.

self-service
System in which employees have online access to information about HR issues and go online to enroll themselves in programs and provide feedback through surveys.

Mapics, a software developer based in Atlanta, provides self-service software geared to managers as well as nonmanagement employees. Self-service at Mapics includes enrollment in benefits plans, and managers use the system for such tasks as performance appraisals and payroll planning. Mapics lacked reliable information on vacation time used by its employees, many of whom work from home or at client sites. The company used HR self-service to solve this information problem. Not only was the existing information tracked on paper inaccurate, but many employees were too engrossed in their work to take their vacations, and the days rolled over year after year, until the company was recording a liability of a million dollars' worth of accrued, unused vacation time. Mapics set up a vacation management system in which managers can look up the amount of vacation time their employees have used and the amount of remaining vacation. Employees keep track of their vacation time too. This helps with scheduling and also enables managers to encourage employees to use their remaining time. Mapics changed its vacation policy to require that employees take their vacation or lose the time at the end of the year. At Mapics, self-service has improved management and employee satisfaction with HR services at the same time it has cut costs.[54]

Like Mapics, a growing number of companies are combining employee self-service with management self-service, such as the ability to go online to authorize pay increases, approve expenses, and transfer employees to new positions. More sophisticated systems extend management applications to decision making in areas such as compensation and performance management. For example, managers can schedule job interviews or performance appraisals, guided by the system to provide the necessary information and follow every step called for by the company's procedures.[55]

Linking Employees and Teams Electronically

Business today operates on a global scale. Many organizations therefore need employees throughout the world, and employees need to collaborate with coworkers in different places. HR professionals must identify potential recruits, provide training, and assess skills in many parts of the world. Organizations can save travel costs and time by applying e-HRM to a variety of HR practices. For example, members of a team could make hiring decisions during an online videoconference or chat session, and training technologies range from downloadable text files to streaming video.

Electronic links pose a challenge that is especially significant for human resource management: They lack the personal touch of face-to-face communication. When e-HRM includes sensitive matters, such as discrimination complaints, the lack of a personal touch can prevent an organization from seeing important problems or meeting important needs. In Detroit, two former employees filed a sexual harassment lawsuit against a software company that had arranged for an outside company to provide its HR services online. In their complaint, the former employees said the software company's human resource provider had failed to respond appropriately when they reported the harassment. As a result, the former employer might be held responsible for the e-HRM provider's inaction.[56] The lesson for organizations interested in e-HRM is to plan how they will hear and respond to employees' concerns when most communications take place online.

LO7
Explain how the nature of the employment relationship is changing.

⬙ CHANGE IN THE EMPLOYMENT RELATIONSHIP

Economic downturns will continue to occur, resulting in layoffs in all industries. In addition, renewed interest in mergers and acquisitions suggests that layoffs may follow. Following a merger or acquisition, companies typically look for ways to become more efficient by eliminating positions where two sets of employees are handling the same responsibilities. Whatever the circumstances, the use of layoffs for improving efficiency has played a major role in changing the basic relationship between employers and employees.

A New Psychological Contract

psychological contract
A description of what an employee expects to contribute in an employment relationship and what the employer will provide the employee in exchange for those contributions.

We can think of that relationship in terms of a **psychological contract,** a description of what an employee expects to contribute in an employment relationship and what the employer will provide the employee in exchange for those contributions.[57] Unlike a written sales contract, the psychological contract is not formally put into words. Instead, it describes unspoken expectations that are widely held by employers and employees. In the traditional version of this psychological contract, organizations expected their employees to contribute time, effort, skills, abilities, and loyalty. In return, the organizations would provide job security and opportunities for promotion.

However, this arrangement is being replaced with a new type of psychological contract.[58] To stay competitive, modern organizations must frequently change the quality, innovation, creativeness, and timeliness of employee contributions and the skills needed to make those contributions. This need has led to organizational restructuring, mergers and acquisitions, layoffs, and longer hours for many employees. Companies demand excellent customer service and high productivity levels. They expect employees to take more responsibility for their own careers, from seeking training to balancing work and family. These expectations result in less job security for employees, who can count on working for several companies over the course of a career. The average length of time a person holds a job has declined during this decade from nine years to just seven.[59]

In exchange for top performance and working longer hours without job security, employees want companies to provide flexible work schedules, comfortable working conditions, more control over how they accomplish work, training and development opportunities, and financial incentives based on how the organization performs.

(Figure 2.7 provides a humorous look at an employee who seems to have benefited from this modern psychological contract by obtaining a family-friendly work arrangement.) Employees realize that companies cannot provide employment security, so they want *employability*. This means they want their company to provide training and job experiences to help ensure that they can find other employment opportunities.

MTW, an information technology company, is exceptional in that it puts its psychological contracts into writing. Whenever a new employee joins the company, that person writes an "expectations agreement" stating his or her most important goals. Every six months or so, the employee and the team leader of the employee's project team review the expectations agreement and modify it if the employee's expectations have changed. For example, Dan Carier's expectations agreement said he would stay knowledgeable about a type of software and that the company would let him continue work on his project, even if he had to move out of state (his wife had a job that might require relocation). Says Carier of the agreement, "I felt I was in control of my destiny." MTW's treatment of employees has translated into business success. Employee turnover is just 6.7 percent a year, in contrast to an industry average of 30 percent, and in a tough job market, most of the company's new hires come from referrals by existing employees. Revenues have grown at a rate of 50 percent a year, and an impressive 14 percent of that revenue is profits.[60]

Flexibility

The new psychological contract largely results from the HRM challenge of building a committed, productive workforce in turbulent economic conditions that offer opportunity for financial success but can also quickly turn sour, making every employee expendable. From the organization's perspective, the key to survival in a fast-changing environment is flexibility. Organizations want to be able to change as fast as customer needs and economic conditions change. Flexibility in human resource management includes flexible staffing levels and flexible work schedules. The "e-HRM" box describes how Sun Microsystems uses technology to create a flexible work environment.

LO8

Discuss how the need for flexibility affects human resource mangement.

SPEED BUMP   **Dave Coverly**

Figure 2.7

A Family-Friendly Work Arrangement

By permission of Dave Coverly and Creators Syndicate, Inc.

E-HRM

AT SUN MICROSYSTEMS, OFFICES ARE "VIRTUAL"

The employees of Sun Microsystems live out the company's slogan "Everyone and everything connected to the Net." Because their work and information are available online, they can work almost anywhere and anytime. Based on the idea that flexibility can help employees accomplish their goals, Sun has set up a program called iWork, which uses both flexible hours and flexible workspaces.

Under the iWork program, an employee sits at a customized computer and uses a smart card (called a Sun Ray) to obtain access to the company's computer network via the Internet. The Sun Ray gives employees access to applications and files needed for their work. They can work independently or with one another online through videoconferencing and collaboration software.

Employees eligible for iWork can work in any of several locations. They may use Sun's flexible offices, located in 12 drop-in centers, as well as 115 other locations around the world. They also may receive approval to use the system from home up to five days per week. The locations of the drop-in centers enable employees to reduce the time they spend commuting into a central location. Working closer to home also helps employees set up flexible arrangements where they can go to and from work to pick up and drop off family members, perhaps finishing the day's work at home.

Employees who want to participate in the iWork program take an assessment that evaluates their suitability for this work arrangement. Nearly all of them are eligible, and more

than three-quarters connect to the company from remote locations, rather than sitting in conventional offices. Most are pleased with the flexibility—both the convenience of choosing a location and the greater control to balance work and personal time. In addition, Sun is saving money by reducing its office space. The company estimates that iWork has eliminated the need for about 7,700 cubicles and workstations and has saved millions of dollars it would have spent for real estate, power consumption, and other expenses related to a conventional office arrangement.

SOURCE: Samuel Greengard, "Sun's Shining Example," *Workforce Management*, March 2005, pp. 48–49.

Flexible Staffing Levels

A flexible workforce is one the organization can quickly reshape and resize to meet its changing needs. To be able to do this without massive hiring and firing campaigns, organizations are using more alternative work arrangements. **Alternative work arrangements** are methods of staffing other than the traditional hiring of full-time employees. There are a variety of methods, with the following being most common:

- *Independent contractors* are self-employed individuals with multiple clients.
- *On-call workers* are persons who work for an organization only when they are needed.
- *Temporary workers* are employed by a temporary agency; client organizations pay the agency for the services of these workers.
- *Contract company workers* are employed directly by a company for a specific time specified in a written contract.

alternative work arrangements
Methods of staffing other than the traditional hiring of full-time employees (for example, use of independent contractors, on-call workers, temporary workers, and contract company workers).

Multitasking has become a way of life for many employees who need to make the most of every minute. This is a new, but prevalent, trend that is affecting human resource management and the employees it supports.

The Bureau of Labor Statistics estimates that there are 12.2 million "nontraditional workers," including 8.2 million independent contractors, 2 million on-call workers, 1.2 million temporary workers, and approximately 800,000 contract company workers. According to one estimate, workers with alternative work arrangements make up more than one-fourth of the total workforce.[61] FedEx Ground, a subsidiary of Federal Express Corporation, depends on a team of 14,300 independent contractors who work as either pickup and delivery contractors or long-haul contractors. During peak delivery season, the company adds up to 2,800 temporary drivers and up to 2,000 part-time package handlers.[62]

More workers in alternative employment relationships are choosing these arrangements, but preferences vary. Most independent contractors and contract workers have this type of arrangement by choice. In contrast, temporary agency workers and on-call workers are likely to prefer traditional full-time employment. There is some debate about whether nontraditional employment relationships are good or bad. Some labor analysts argue that alternative work arrangements are substandard jobs featuring low pay, fear of unemployment, poor health insurance and retirement benefits, and dissatisfying work. Others claim that these jobs provide flexibility for companies and employees alike. With alternative work arrangements, organizations can more easily modify the number of their employees. Continually adjusting staffing levels is especially cost-effective for an organization that has fluctuating demand for its products and services. And when an organization downsizes by laying off temporary and part-time employees, the damage to morale among permanent full-time workers is likely to be less severe.

From employees' perspective, alternative work arrangements provide some flexibility for balancing work and nonwork activities. A study by the Families and Work Institute found that more than one out of six workers would prefer to work part-time.[63] Some employers permit part-time work in principle, but the people on part-time schedules discover that work pressures keep them on the job longer than their scheduled hours—sometimes full-time. Legal and accounting firms have been establishing policies designed to retain part-time professionals without limiting their future careers. Some, including PricewaterhouseCoopers and Ernst & Young, have hired coordinators to oversee these arrangements.

Flexible Work Schedules

The globalization of the world economy and the development of e-commerce have made the notion of a 40-hour work week obsolete. As a result, companies need to be staffed 24 hours a day, seven days a week. Employees in manufacturing environments and service call centers are being asked to work 12-hour days or to work afternoon or midnight shifts. Similarly, professional employees face long hours and work demands that spill over into their personal lives. E-mail, pagers, and cell phones bombard employees with information and work demands. In the car, on vacation, on planes, and even in the bathroom, employees can be interrupted by work demands. The Bureau of Labor Statistics recently found that on workdays, one out of five employed persons do some or all of their work at home.[64] More demanding work results in greater employee stress, less satisfied employees, loss of productivity, and higher turnover—all of which are costly for companies.

Many organizations are taking steps to provide more flexible work schedules, to protect employees' free time, and to more productively use employees' work time. Workers consider flexible schedules a valuable way to ease the pressures and conflicts of trying to balance work and nonwork activities. Employers are using flexible schedules to recruit and retain employees and to increase satisfaction and productivity. For example, Deloitte & Touche offers flexible work arrangements if employees can continue meeting clients' needs and the arrangement makes business sense. Employees who want such an arrangement must demonstrate they can meet job requirements. At Household International, flexibility is designed into the company's benefits package. Employees select from a menu of benefits that include flexible hours, training opportunities, and discounts for services, as well as the usual insurance and paid time off.[65]

To protect employees' nonwork time, some companies, such as the consulting firm Ernst & Young, allow employees to wait until they return to work to answer weekend or vacation voice mail and e-mail messages.[66] At SCJohnson in Racine, Wisconsin, employees often had to take work home on the weekends because they were so tied up in meetings from Monday through Friday that they had to finish duties on their own time.[67] SCJohnson now bans all meetings for two Fridays each month. The policy helps employees rest on at least two weekends and work at home on those Fridays because they won't be afraid of missing a meeting.

Flexible work schedules and flexible job assignments also provide organizations with a way to adjust to slow periods without laying off valued workers. Lincoln Electric Company responded to slow demand by moving salaried employees to clerical jobs at hourly wages that vary according to the assignment. Lincoln's production workers also are trained to handle different jobs, according to the size and types of orders the company receives from its customers. In the recession of the early 1980s, which hit the company hard, engineers and factory workers from Lincoln went on the road to try peddling Lincoln's welding and cutting parts to potential customers. Of course, employees prefer the higher-paying jobs, not the demands of lean times. Still, they are glad for Lincoln's commitment to keep them on the payroll—and on the receiving end of benefits like pensions and insurance.[68]

thinking ETHICALLY

Whose Business Is It When You Blog?

Just as companies have become used to the idea of warning employees that their e-mail messages are not private, along come blogs (Web logs), with their own set of privacy issues. Although some companies have begun to use blogs as a marketing tool, most blogs are written by individuals who enjoy posting their thoughts online. The privacy issue involves the line between what people do as employees and what they do on their own time.

Consider the case of Mark Jen. After he obtained a job with Google, he began posting his observations about the company in a blog he named Ninetyninezeros. (Coincidentally or not, this title has one less zero than the number of zeros in a googol, the number that inspired Google's name.) About a week after the entries began, they disappeared temporarily, and they reappeared after some editing. Jen noted that Google was "pretty cool about" his blog, but a few days later, word leaked that he was no longer working for Google.

Other bloggers weighed in. Jeremy Zawodny, who works for Yahoo! and said he spoke to Jen, wrote, "He doesn't believe he was doing anything wrong (neither do I based on what he told me)." Robert Scoble, a Microsoft employee, cautioned, "It's not easy writing in public. All it takes is one paragraph to lose credibility, have people laugh at you, get you sued, create a PR firestorm, or get your boss mad at you."

Jen is not the first blogger to lose his job. Ellen Simonetti was fired after her Queen of the Sky blog posted pictures of herself posed humorously and a little provocatively in her flight attendant uniform. Bank employee Peter Whitney was fired after coworkers came across his Gravity Spike blog, which included complaints about work. Heather Armstrong's blog at www.dooce.com included exaggerated stories about work. They were intended to amuse her family and friends, but her boss, alerted by an anonymous tip, was not amused.

SOURCE: Evan Hansen, "Google Blogger Has Left the Building," *CNet News.com,* February 8, 2005, www.news.com; Neville Hobson, "Google Blogger Firing Highlights Why Guidelines Are Essential," *WebProNews.com,* February 10, 2005, www.webpronews.com; and Todd Wallack, "Beware if Your Blog Is Related to Work," *San Francisco Chronicle,* January 24, 2005, downloaded at www.sfgate.com.

Questions

1. Who might be affected by a blog written about a company? What kinds of work-related information are public? What information does a company have a right to keep private?
2. Imagine that you work in human resources and you learn that an employee of your company has mentioned work-related topics in a blog. What would you do?

SUMMARY

1. Describe trends in the labor force composition and how they affect human resource management.
An organization's internal labor force comes from its external labor market—individuals who are actively seeking employment. In the United States, this labor market is aging and becoming more racially and ethnically diverse. The share of women in the U.S. workforce has grown to nearly half of the total. To compete for talent, organizations must be flexible enough to meet the needs of older workers, possibly redesigning jobs. Organizations must recruit from a diverse population, establish bias-free HR systems, and help employees understand and appreciate cultural differences.

Organizations also need employees with skills in decision making, customer service, and teamwork, as well as technical skills. The competition for such talent is intense. Organizations facing a skills shortage often hire employees who lack certain skills, then train them for their jobs.

2. Summarize areas in which human resource management can support the goal of creating a high-performance work system.
HRM can help organizations find and keep the best possible fit between their social system and technical system. Organizations need employees with broad skills

and strong motivation. Recruiting and selection decisions are especially important for organizations that rely on knowledge workers. Job design and appropriate systems for assessment and rewards have a central role in supporting employee empowerment and teamwork.

3. Define employee empowerment and explain its role in the modern organization.
Employee empowerment means giving employees responsibility and authority to make decisions regarding all aspects of product development or customer service. The organization holds employees accountable for products and services, and in exchange, the employees share in the rewards (or losses) that result. Selection decisions should provide the organization people who have the necessary decision-making and interpersonal skills. HRM must design jobs to give employees latitude for decision making and train employees to handle their broad responsibilities. Feedback and rewards must be appropriate for the work of empowered employees. HRM can also play a role in giving employees access to the information they need.

4. Identify ways HR professionals can support organizational strategies for quality, growth, and efficiency.
HR professionals should be familiar with the organization's strategy and may even play a role in developing the strategy. Specific HR practices vary according to the type of strategy. Job design is essential for empowering employees to practice total quality management. In organizations planning major changes such as a merger or acquisition, downsizing, or reengineering, HRM must provide leadership for managing the change in a way that includes skillful employee relations and meaningful rewards. HR professionals can bring "people issues" to the attention of the managers leading these changes. They can provide training in conflict resolution skills, as well as knowledge of the other organization involved in a merger or acquisition. HR professionals also must resolve differences between the companies' HR systems, such as benefits packages and performance appraisals. For a downsizing, the HR department can help to develop voluntary programs to reduce the workforce or can help identify the least valuable employees to lay off. Employee relations can help maintain the morale of employees who remain after a downsizing. Organizations with international operations hire employees in foreign countries where they operate, so they need knowledge of differences in culture and business practices. Even small businesses serving domestic markets discover that qualified candidates include immigrants, as they account for a significant and growing share of the U.S. labor market, so HRM requires knowledge of different cultures. Organizations also must be able to select and prepare employees for overseas assignments. In reengineering,

the HR department can lead in communicating with employees and providing training. It will also have to prepare new approaches for recruiting and appraising employees that are better suited to the reengineered jobs. Outsourcing presents similar issues related to job design and employee selection.

5. Summarize ways in which human resource management can support organizations expanding internationally.
Organizations with international operations hire employees in foreign countries where they operate, so they need knowledge of differences in culture and business practices. Even small businesses discover that qualified candidates include immigrants, as they account for a significant and growing share of the U.S. labor market. HRM needs to understand and train employees to deal with differences in cultures. HRM also must be able to help organizations select and prepare employees for overseas assignments. To support efficiency and growth, HR staff can prepare companies for offshoring, in which operations are moved to lower-wage countries. HR experts can help organizations determine whether workers in offshore locations can provide the same or better skills, how offshoring will affect motivation and recruitment of employees needed in the United States, and whether managers are prepared to manage offshore employees.

6. Discuss how technological developments are affecting human resource management.
Information systems have become a tool for more HR professionals, and often these systems are provided through the Internet. In addition, e-business plays a role in a growing number of organizations. The widespread use of the Internet includes HRM applications. Organizations search for talent globally using online job postings and screening candidates online. Organizations' Web sites feature information directed toward potential employees. Employees may receive training online. At many companies, online information sharing enables employee self-service for many HR needs, from application forms to training modules to information about the details of company policies and benefits. Online communications also may link employees and teams, enabling organizations to structure work that involves collaboration among employees at different times and places. In such situations, HR professionals must ensure that communications remain effective enough to detect and correct problems when they arise.

7. Explain how the nature of the employment relationship is changing.
The employment relationship takes the form of a "psychological contract" that describes what employees and employers expect from the employment relation-

ship. It includes unspoken expectations that are widely held. In the traditional version, organizations expected their employees to contribute time, effort, skills, abilities, and loyalty in exchange for job security and opportunities for promotion. Today, modern organizations' needs are constantly changing, so organizations are requiring top performance and longer work hours but cannot provide job security. Instead, employees are looking for flexible work schedules, comfortable working conditions, greater autonomy, opportunities for training and development, and performance-related financial incentives. For HRM, the changes require planning for flexible staffing levels.

8. Discuss how the need for flexibility affects human resource management.

Organizations seek flexibility in staffing levels through alternatives to the traditional employment relationship. They may use outsourcing as well as temporary and contract workers. The use of such workers can affect job design, as well as the motivation of the organization's permanent employees. Organizations also may seek flexible work schedules, including shortened workweeks. They may offer flexible schedules as a way for employees to adjust work hours to meet personal and family needs. Organizations also may move employees to different jobs to meet changes in demand.

REVIEW AND DISCUSSION QUESTIONS

1. How does each of the following labor force trends affect HRM?
   a. Aging of the labor force.
   b. Diversity of the labor force.
   c. Skill deficiencies of the labor force.
2. At many organizations, goals include improving people's performance by relying on knowledge workers, empowering employees, and assigning work to teams. How can HRM support these efforts?
3. Merging, downsizing, and reengineering all can radically change the structure of an organization. Choose one of these changes, and describe HRM's role in making the change succeed. If possible, apply your discussion to an actual merger, downsizing, or reengineering effort that has recently occurred.
4. When an organization decides to operate facilities in other countries, how can HRM practices support this change?
5. Why do organizations outsource HRM functions? How does outsourcing affect the role of human resource professionals? Would you be more attracted to the role of

HR professional in an organization that outsources many HR activities or in the outside firm that has the contract to provide the HR services? Why?
6. Suppose you have been hired to manage human resources for a small company that offers business services including customer service calls and business report preparation. The 20-person company has been preparing to expand from serving a few local clients that are well-known to the company's owners. The owners believe that their experience and reputation for quality will help them expand to serve more and larger clients. What challenges will you need to prepare the company to meet? How will you begin?
7. What e-HRM resources might you use to meet the challenges in Question 4?
8. What HRM functions could an organization provide through self-service? What are some advantages and disadvantages of using self-service for these functions?
9. How is the employment relationship typical of modern organizations different from the relationship of a generation ago?

WHAT'S YOUR HR IQ?

The text Web site offers two more ways to check what you've learned so far. Use the Self-Assessment exercise to test your knowledge of trends in human resource manage-

ment. Go online with the Web Exercise to see how HRM may be affected by new technologies.

BusinessWeek CASE

BusinessWeek The Future of Work

No low-wage worker in Shanghai, New Delhi, or Dublin will ever take Mark Ryan's job. No software will ever do what he does, either. That's because Ryan manages people—

specifically, 100 technicians who serve half a million customers of Verizon Communications out of an office in Santa Fe Springs, California. A telephone lineman before moving up the corporate ladder, Ryan is earning a master's degree in organizational management at Verizon's expense. In the master's degree program he's studying topics like conflict resolution.

That's heady stuff for a guy who used to climb poles. "The technical side of the business is important," says Ryan, "but managing people and rewarding and recognizing the people who do an outstanding job is how we are going to succeed."

Sab Maglione is more vulnerable. The computer programmer from Somerville, New Jersey, was hired by an insurance company as an independent contractor in 2000 for good money but soon found himself training the representatives of Tata Consulting who would eventually move his work to India. His next contract in New York City paid half as much—but even that soon ended when he found himself out of work in December 2003. Maglione, who has an associate's degree in computer science, is studying hard and remains optimistic about getting a job but says he's been stymied by the "barrelful" of recent experience in the latest programming languages prospective employers demand. "If you don't have it, they say, 'Let's outsource it.'"

Ryan, the happy manager, and Maglione, the worried programmer, exemplify two powerful crosscurrents in the American job market. Changes in the economy in recent years have made some people more valuable and secure than ever, while pushing others—even those with skills that were recently regarded as highly valuable—to the margins.

What makes the difference? Research by economists at Massachusetts Institute of Technology and Harvard University concludes that the key factor is whether a job can be "routinized," or broken down into repeatable steps that vary little from day to day. Such a job is easier to replace with a clever piece of software or to hand over to a lower-paid worker outside the United States. By comparison, the jobs that will pay well in the future will be ones that are hard to reduce to a recipe. These attractive jobs—from factory floor management to sales to teaching to the professions—require flexibility, creativity, and lifelong learning. They generally also require subtle and frequent interactions with other people, often face to face.

Nor do you need an advanced degree to have a nonroutine job. You just need to do something that requires a lot of human interaction or that can't be boiled down to a repeatable procedure. The surviving secretaries, for example, have moved up from typing and answering phones to planning meetings and keeping books. Bank tellers handle special requests while ATMs take deposits and dispense cash. The factory workers most likely to keep their jobs will be those who make themselves experts on a variety of computer-controlled machines or who excel at quick turnaround of custom orders.

As the economy evolves, two kinds of jobs will remain impossible to routinize. One kind involves complex pattern recognition, such as spotting business opportunities or repairing a complex machine. The other relies on complex communication skills, such as those required to manage people or sell big-ticket items. At the same time, some jobs that are well paid could soon be routinized. Powerful computers, advanced software, and speedy communications have made routine work vulnerable. Well-paid legal researchers, tax preparers, and accountants are seeing their jobs outsourced abroad. Stock traders could eventually be replaced by automated trading systems; computer programming has been partly taken over by clever software, and part has been exported to lower-wage nations.

Clearly, the importance of nonroutine work increases the value of education. College graduates have steadily broadened their lead over the less-educated in earnings. As valuable as education is, technical knowledge alone won't cut it, because workers in other countries read the same textbooks. For many good jobs, in fact, education isn't as useful as specialized local knowledge. Demand is hot for plant managers who can improve a factory's efficiency. Also, there's plenty of demand for people who combine technical skills with industry-specific knowledge and people skills. Companies are looking for technical experts who also can work with others, can change direction quickly, and understand their organization's business.

SOURCE: Peter Coy, "The Future of Work," *BusinessWeek*, March 22, 2004, pp. 50–52.

QUESTIONS

1. How can HRM ensure that a company's employees are flexible, and creative and provide good customer service?
2. How might modern technology help with the activities you described in Question 1?
3. Which human resource functions are routine? Which are likely to be part of the "future of work" as described in this case?

CASE: Fostering Innovation at IBM

In a typical bureaucratic company, managers measure their success by the number of people who report to them and the size of their budgets (or, better yet, their earnings). By those measures, Rod Adkins was a star at IBM when he managed its Unix computing division, which boasted 35,000 employees and sales of $4 billion a year. And by those same measures, Adkins's next assignment was an embarrassment: heading the new pervasive-computing division, with zero employees.

In fact, IBM was depending on Adkins to help transform the company. IBM's name once symbolized modern technology, but the giant company had become too stodgy for the Internet age. Its research labs were still making discoveries and earning patents, but other companies more often developed the ideas into successful business enterprises. Managers were reluctant to take risks, preferring to preserve their existing businesses. IBM's executives decided the solution was to encourage innovative employees to create new businesses with applications expected to be winners a few years in the future. They wanted the best managers to be in charge of IBM's new great ideas, not just to preserve the old ones.

Adkins's new assignment, pervasive computing, was to extend the business of computers beyond machines on home and office desks. Pervasive computing uses wireless technology to bring computer power practically everywhere—for example, in the voice-command navigation systems installed in automobiles. Under Adkins's leadership, the pervasive-computing business grew from an idea to a division with sales of $2.4 billion in just three years.

That performance helped IBM surpass its goal for transformation. The pervasive-computing division is part of a larger effort to develop emerging-business opportunities (EBOs) under the leadership of IBM's senior vice president for strategy, J. Bruce Harreld. Harreld's objective was for the EBOs to generate about $2 billion in new revenue each year. In the program's first four years, IBM launched 25 EBOs. Three failed, and the remaining EBOs bring in $15 billion a year and rising.

The money is only part of the story. Successful new ventures at IBM are changing the way employees think of their company. According to Caroline Kovac, whose EBO involves computing for clients in the life sciences (for example, pharmaceuticals and biotechnology), "We've become more willing to experiment, more willing to accept failure, learn from it, and move on." Kovac adds that leading an EBO is now a coveted position at IBM.

To develop an EBO, its leader starts with as little as one employee and begins planning how to transform an idea into a business. Harreld meets regularly with the leader, guiding him or her away from the cautious thinking that is rewarded in an established bureaucracy. Harreld encourages the EBO leaders to take risks and continue learning and adjusting. Harreld ensures the group has the money it needs but forbids empire building. He also encourages the EBO leaders to draw upon the expertise of other IBM employees. The EBO leaders develop pilot projects with major customers; if they meet their objectives, IBM generously funds and staffs the project. If the initiative is not

bearing fruit in the pilot phase, Harreld ends the project and assigns its leader to another important job at the company. Harreld explains that it is important not to punish the leaders for failing when they take a risk, because even the failures are learning opportunities.

One of the successes, the pervasive-computing project, now operates the Pervasive Computing Advanced Technology Lab in Austin, Texas. There, researchers and engineers are investigating a wealth of high-tech ideas. Early on, Bill Bodin, who manages research at the lab, decided they needed a "digital home," and the group transformed their bare research environment into a mockup of a house that applies the technologies his group is researching. The home includes a kitchen and living room updated with the latest ideas in broadband, sensor, database, communication, and voice recognition technologies. With a flat-panel display in the living room, Bodin can open a control portal that uses voice recognition to operate all the devices in the living room, as well as the kitchen appliances, home security system, the lawn's sprinkler system, and the heating and air conditioning for the entire house. In the kitchen, appliances are programmable and can be controlled from anywhere via cell phone.

The EBOs are part of IBM's strategy to grow by developing high-profit products and services. Some of the company's past products, notably personal computers, are now commodities that compete on price. For IBM, profitability depends on finding new products by which the company can distinguish itself. In many cases, that means solving problems for customers, rather than just selling products. Salespeople and even researchers like Bodin must be able to work closely with customers to define needs and develop solutions.

SOURCE: Alan Deutschman, "Building a Better Skunk Works," *Fast Company*, March 2005; Brian Bergstein, "Palmisano Era in Full Swing," *Information Week*, August 23, 2004; and Jeff O'Heir, "The Future Is Now," *Computer Reseller News*, October 11, 2004, all downloaded from Infotrac at http://web7.infotrac.galegroup.com.

QUESTIONS

1. What kinds of employees does IBM need to meet the goals described in this case?
2. What challenges are involved in finding, motivating, and keeping these employees in today's business environment?
3. Suggest a few ways HRM can help IBM meet those challenges.

NOTES

1. Christopher Palmeri, Brian Grow, and Stan Crock, "Served in Iraq? Come Work for Us," *BusinessWeek*, December 13, 2004; and Peter Weaver, "Returning U.S. Troops: Handle with Care," *HR Magazine*, October 2004, both downloaded from Infotrac at http://web5.infotrac.galegroup.com.

2. Anne Fisher, "How to Battle the Coming Brain Drain," *Fortune*, March 21, 2005, downloaded from Infotrac at http://web7.infotrac.galegroup.com.

3. Martha Frase-Blunt, "Short-Term Executives," *HR Magazine*, June 2004, downloaded from Infotrac at http://web4.infotrac.galegroup.com.

4. Bureau of Labor Statistics, "Labor Force," *Occupational Outlook Quarterly*, Winter 2003–2004, pp. 42–48, downloaded at www.bls.gov.

5. Fisher, "How to Battle the Coming Brain Drain."

6. C. M. Solomon, "Managing the Baby Busters," *Personnel Journal*, March 1992, pp. 52–59; J. Wallace, "After X Comes Y," HR Magazine, April 2001, p. 192; and C. Solomon, "Ready or Not, Here Come the Net Kids," *Workforce*, February 2000, pp. 62–68.

7. B. Wooldridge and J. Wester, "The Turbulent Environment of Public Personnel Administration: Responding to the Challenge of the Changing Workplace of the Twenty-First Century," *Public Personnel Management* 20 (1991), pp. 207–24; J. Laabs, "The New Loyalty: Grasp It. Earn It. Keep It," *Workforce*, November 1998, pp. 34–39.

8. "Employee Dissatisfaction on Rise in Last 10 Years, New Report Says," *Employee Relations Weekly* (Washington, DC: Bureau of National Affairs, 1986).

9. Catherine Saillant, "A New Wrinkle in Workforce," *Los Angeles Times*, February 24, 2005, downloaded at www.latimes.com; and Barbara Rose, "Retirees Preparing to Step Back, Not Away," *Chicago Tribune*, January 16, 2005, sec. 1, pp. 1, 19.

10. Richard W. Johnson, "Trends in Job Demands among Older Workers, 1992–2002," *Monthly Labor Review* (July 2004), pp. 48–56, downloaded at www.bls.gov.

11. BLS, "Labor Force," p. 45.

12. T. H. Cox and S. Blake, "Managing Cultural Diversity: Implications for Organizational Competitiveness," *The Executive* 5 (1991), pp. 45–56.

13. "Impact of Diversity Initiatives on the Bottom Line Survey," *SHRM/Fortune*, June 2001.

14. Harry R. Weber, "Home Depot Wants Spanish-Speaking Workers," *Yahoo News*, February 14, 2005, http://story.news.yahoo.com.

15. T. Singer, "Comeback Markets," *Inc.*, May 2001, pp. 53–57+.

16. "Industry Report 2002," *Training*, October 2002, p. 51.

17. National Association of Manufacturers (NAM), "Center for Workforce Success," NAM Web site, www.nam.org, downloaded March 22, 2005; and Eric Heisler, "U.S. Factories Struggle to Attract Well-Trained Young Workers," *St. Louis Post-Dispatch*, September 17, 2004, downloaded at NAM Web site, www.nam.org.

18. J. A. Neal and C. L. Tromley, "From Incremental Change to Retrofit: Creating High-Performance Work Systems," *Academy of Management Executive* 9 (1995), pp. 42–54.

19. Bureau of Labor Statistics, "Occupational Employment." *Occupational Outlook Quarterly*, Winter 2003–2004, pp. 6–27; and BLS, "Tomorrow's Jobs," *Occupational Outlook Handbook*, last modified June 2, 2004, both downloaded at www.bls.gov.

20. "CIO Panel: Knowledge-Sharing Roundtable," *Information Week Online*, News in Review, April 26, 1999, www.informationweek.com; Buckman Laboratories Web site, www.buckman.com.

21. A. Carnevale and D. Desrochers, "Training in the Dilbert Economy," *Training & Development*, December 1999, pp. 32–36.

22. Conseco Web site, June 2001, www.conseco.com.

23. John S. McClenahen, "Bearing Necessities," *Industry Week*, October 2004, downloaded from Infotrac at http://web4.infotrac.galegroup.com.

24. Steve Bates, "Facing the Future," *HR Magazine*, July 2002, downloaded from Infotrac at http://web2.infotrac.galegroup.com.

25. Ibid.

26. J. R. Jablonski, *Implementing Total Quality Management: An Overview* (San Diego: Pfeiffer, 1991).

27. R. Hodgetts, F. Luthans, and S. Lee, "New Paradigm Organizations: From Total Quality to Learning to World-Class," *Organizational Dynamics*, Winter 1994, pp. 5–19.

28. William H. Miller, "Instability? Not a Problem," *Industry Week*, October 2004, downloaded from Infotrac at http://web4.infotrac.galegroup.com.

29. G. Fairclough, "Business Bulletin," *The Wall Street Journal*, March 5, 1998, p. A1.

30. P. Sebastian, "Business Bulletin," *The Wall Street Journal*, October 2, 1997, p. A1.

31. C. O'Reilly and J. Pfeffer, *Hidden Value: How Great Companies Achieve Extraordinary Results with Ordinary People* (Cambridge, MA: Harvard Business School Press, 2000).

32. J. Laabs, "Has Downsizing Missed Its Mark?" *Workforce*, April 1999, pp. 31–38.

33. N. Templin, "UAW to Unveil Pact on Slashing GM's Payroll," *The Wall Street Journal*, December 15, 1992, p. A3.

34. J. Lopez, "Managing: Early-Retirement Offers Lead to Renewed Hiring," *The Wall Street Journal*, January 26, 1993, p. B1.

35. A. Church, "Organizational Downsizing: What Is the Role of the Practitioner?" *Industrial-Organizational Psychologist* 33, no. 1 (1995), pp. 63–74.

36. S. Caudron, "HR Is Dead, Long Live HR," *Workforce*, January 2003, pp. 26–29.

37. E. Zimmerman, "B of A and Big-Time Outsourcing," *Workforce*, April 2001, pp. 50–54.

38. J. Kahn, "The World's Most Admired Companies," Fortune, October 26, 1998, pp. 206–26; A. Fisher, "The World's Most Admired Companies," *Fortune*, October 27, 1997, p. 232.

39. Jim Hopkins, "To Start Up Here, Companies Hire over There," *USA Today*, February 10, 2005, downloaded at www.usatoday.com.

40. Ibid.

41. Jay Solomon and Kathryn Kranhold, "In India's Outsourcing Boom, GE Played a Starring Role," *The Wall Street Journal*, March 23, 2005, downloaded at http://online.wsj.com.

42. J. L. Young, "Starbucks Expansion into China Is Slated," *The Wall Street Journal*, October 5, 1998, p. B13C.

43. M. Horrigan, "Employment Projections to 2012: Concepts and Context," *Monthly Labor Review* 127, no. 2 (February 2004), pp. 3–22.

44. "The People Problem," *Inc.*, State of Small Business 2001 issue, May 29, 2001, pp. 84–85.

45. National Association of Colleges and Employers, "Job Outlook 2002," www.jobweb.com.

46. R. L. Tung, "Expatriate Assignments: Enhancing Success and Minimizing Failure," *Academy of Management Executive* 12, no. 4 (1988), pp. 93–106.

47. M. J. Kavanaugh, H. G. Guetal, and S. I. Tannenbaum, *Human Resource Information Systems: Development and Application* (Boston: PWS-Kent, 1990).

48. Bill Roberts, "Empowerment or Imposition?" *HR Magazine*, June 2004, downloaded from Infotrac at http://web7.infotrac.galegroup.com.

49. Miniwatts International, "Internet Usage Stats for the Americas," *Internet World Stats*, www.internetworldstats.com, downloaded March 22, 2005.

50. This section is based on L. Grensing-Pophal, "Are You Suited for a Dot-Com?" *HR Magazine*, November 2000, pp. 75–80; and Leslie A. Weatherly, "HR Technology: Leveraging the Shift to Self-Service," *HR Magazine*, March 2005, downloaded from Infotrac at http://web7.infotrac.galegroup.com; and Roberts, "Empowerment or Imposition?"

51. Pui-Wing Tam and Nick Wingfield, "As Tech Matures, Workers File a Spate of Salary Complaints," *The Wall Street Journal*, February 24, 2005, pp. A1, A11.

52. See Weatherly, "HR Technology."

53. Pui-Wing Tam, Erin White, Nick Wingfield, and Kris Maher, "Snooping E-Mail by Software Is Now a Workplace Norm," *The Wall Street Journal*, March 9, 2005, downloaded at http://online.wsj.com.

54. Roberts, "Empowerment or Imposition?"

55. Weatherly, "HR Technology."

56. C. Tejada, "For Many, Taking Work Home Is Often a Job without Reward," *The Wall Street Journal*, Interactive Edition, March 5, 2002.

57. D. M. Rousseau, "Psychological and Implied Contracts in Organizations," *Employee Rights and Responsibilities Journal* 2 (1989), pp. 121–29.

58. D. Rousseau, "Changing the Deal While Keeping the People," *Academy of Management Executive* 11 (1996), pp. 50–61; M. A. Cavanaugh and R. Noe, "Antecedents and Consequences of the New Psychological Contract," *Journal of Organizational Behavior* 20 (1999), pp. 323–40.

59. Tejada, "For Many, Taking Work Home Is Often a Job without Reward."

60. E. O. Welles, "Great Expectations," *Inc.*, March 2001, pp. 68–70, 72–73.

61. M. DiNatale, "Characteristics of and Preferences for Alternative Work Arrangements, 1999," *Monthly Labor Review*, March 2001, pp. 28–49; and "Data Bank Annual," table, "Free Agent Workforce," *Workforce Management* 82, no. 13 (December 2003), p. 96.

62. A. Freedman, "Staffing Up," *Human Resource Executive*, January 2004, pp. 24–31.

63. Sue Shellenbarger, "Workin' 9 to 2," *The Wall Street Journal*, February 17, 2005, downloaded at http://online.wsj.com.

64. Bureau of Labor Statistics, "America Time-Use Survey Summary," news release, September 14, 2004, downloaded at www.bls.gov.

65. M. Hammers, "Family-Friendly Benefits Prompt Non-Parent Backlash," *Workforce Management* 82, no. 8 (2003), pp. 77–79.

66. J. Cook, "Keeping Work at Work," *Human Resource Executive*, July 2001, pp. 68–71.

67. Ibid.

68. C. Ansberry, "Old Industries Adopt Flex Staffing to Adapt to Rapid Pace of Change," *The Wall Street Journal*, Interactive Edition, March 22, 2002.

If you are using the Manager's Hot Seat DVD with this book, consider finishing case 4: Privacy: Burned by the Firewall? for this chapter.

CHAPTER 3

PROVIDING EQUAL EMPLOYMENT OPPORTUNITY AND A SAFE WORKPLACE

After reading this chapter, you should be able to:

What Do I Need to Know?

1. Explain how the three branches of government regulate human resource management.

2. Summarize the major federal laws requiring equal employment opportunity.

3. Identify the federal agencies that enforce equal employment opportunity, and describe the role of each.

4. Describe ways employers can avoid illegal discrimination and provide reasonable accommodation.

5. Define sexual harassment and tell how employers can eliminate or minimize it.

6. Explain employers' duties under the Occupational Safety and Health Act.

7. Describe the role of the Occupational Safety and Health Administration.

8. Discuss ways employers promote worker safety and health.

⬤ INTRODUCTION

Learning about employees and customers guided Weyerhaeuser Company as it developed a human resource policy suitable for a diverse business environment. From an employee survey, Weyerhaeuser, which produces forest products such as paper, lumber, and cardboard and paper packaging, learned that it needed to improve recruitment and retention of talented men and women from diverse ethnic groups. The company observed its markets and determined that growing populations of Hispanic and other ethnic groups could be better served by a workforce that represented these groups. For instance, Hispanic employees might be aware of new product ideas that would meet a demand unfamiliar to the company's majority non-Hispanic management team.

To cultivate a diverse workforce, human resource management at Weyerhaeuser cast a wider net to recruit through organizations like the National Society of Hispanic MBAs, the National Society of Black Engineers, Women in Construction, and similar groups. The company added hiring and retention of minorities to the goals for which bonuses are awarded to managers. These efforts apply lessons Weyerhaeuser learned from a safety program in which it combined training, communication, and rewards to reduce accident rates. The safety program cultivated a broad definition of safety, including a work environment that feels emotionally as well as physically safe for employees. That program paved the way for the diversity program—to create an environment in which no employee should be harassed because of race or gender. Although the company's jobs in forestry and paper mills are outside fields that have traditionally drawn women and members of racial and ethnic minorities, Weyerhaeuser has begun to see progress in the first years of the program. Effenus Henderson, Weyerhaeuser's director of recruiting, staffing and diversity, says building a workforce that understands and reflects the company's diverse markets is the "real challenge" that is critical for success.[1]

As we saw in Chapter 1, human resource management takes place in the context of the company's goals and society's expectations for how a company should operate. In the United States, the federal government has set some limits on how an organization can practice human resource management. Among these limits are requirements intended to prevent discrimination in hiring and employment practices and to protect the health and safety of workers while they are on the job. Questions about a company's compliance with these requirements can result in lawsuits and negative publicity that often cause serious problems for a company's success and survival. Conversely, a company that skillfully navigates the maze of regulations can gain an advantage over its competitors. A further advantage may go to companies that, like Weyerhaeuser, go beyond mere legal compliance to find ways of linking fair employment and worker safety to business goals such as building a workforce that is highly motivated and attuned to customers.

This chapter provides an overview of the ways government bodies regulate equal employment opportunity and workplace safety and health. It introduces you to major laws affecting employers in these areas, as well as the agencies charged with enforcing those laws. The chapter also discusses ways organizations can develop practices that ensure they are in compliance with the laws.

One point to make at the outset is that managers often want a list of do's and don'ts that will keep them out of legal trouble. Some managers rely on strict rules such as "Don't ever ask a female applicant if she is married," rather than learning the reasons behind those rules. Clearly, certain practices are illegal or at least inadvisable, and this chapter will provide guidance on avoiding such practices. However, managers who merely focus on how to avoid breaking the law are not thinking about how to be ethical or how to acquire and use human resources in the best way to carry out the company's mission. This chapter introduces ways to think more creatively and constructively about fair employment and workplace safety.

❧ REGULATION OF HUMAN RESOURCE MANAGEMENT

LO1
Explain how the three branches of government regulate human resource management.

All three branches of the U.S. government—legislative, executive, and judicial—play an important role in creating a legal environment for human resource management. The legislative branch, which consists of the two houses of Congress, has enacted a number of laws governing human resource activities. Senators and U.S. Representatives generally develop these laws in response to perceived societal needs. For example, during the civil rights movement of the early 1960s, Congress enacted Title VII of the Civil Rights Act to ensure that various minority groups received equal opportunities in many areas of life.

One way the executive branch communicates information about laws is through Web sites like Youth2Work. This site is designed to provide young workers with a safe workplace by making them aware of laws that, for example, restrict the amount of work they can do and the machinery they can operate.

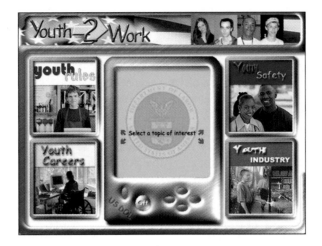

The executive branch, including the many regulatory agencies that the president oversees, is responsible for enforcing the laws passed by Congress. Agencies do this through a variety of actions, from drawing up regulations detailing how to abide by the laws to filing suit against alleged violators. Some federal agencies involved in regulating human resource management include the Equal Employment Opportunity Commission and the Occupational Safety and Health Administration. In addition, the president may issue executive orders, which are directives issued solely by the president, without requiring congressional approval. Some executive orders regulate the activities of organizations that have contracts with the federal government. For example, President Lyndon Johnson signed Executive Order 11246, which requires all federal contractors and subcontractors to engage in affirmative-action programs designed to hire and promote women and minorities. (We will explore the topic of affirmative action later in this chapter.)

The judicial branch, the federal court system, influences employment law by interpreting the law and holding trials concerning violations of the law. The U.S. Supreme Court, at the head of the judicial branch, is the court of final appeal. Decisions made by the Supreme Court are binding; they can be overturned only through laws passed by Congress. The Civil Rights Act of 1991 was partly designed to overturn Supreme Court decisions.

LO2
Summarize the major federal laws requiring equal employment opportunity.

equal employment opportunity (EEO)
The condition in which all individuals have an equal chance for employment, regardless of their race, color, religion, sex, age, disability, or national origin.

◈ EQUAL EMPLOYMENT OPPORTUNITY

Among the most significant efforts to regulate human resource management are those aimed at achieving **equal employment opportunity (EEO)**—the condition in which all individuals have an equal chance for employment, regardless of their race, color, religion, sex, age, disability, or national origin. The federal government's efforts to create equal employment opportunity include constitutional amendments, legislation, and executive orders, as well as court decisions that interpret the laws. Table 3.1 summarizes major EEO laws discussed in this chapter. These are U.S. laws; equal employment laws in other countries may differ.

Constitutional Amendments

Two amendments to the U.S. Constitution—the Thirteenth and Fourteenth—have implications for human resource management. The Thirteenth Amendment abolished slavery in the United States. Though you might be hard-pressed to cite an

TABLE 3.1

Summary of Major EEO Laws and Regulations

ACT	REQUIREMENTS	COVERS	ENFORCEMENT AGENCY
Thirteenth Amendment	Abolished slavery	All individuals	Court system
Fourteenth Amendment	Provides equal protection for all citizens and requires due process in state action	State actions (e.g., decisions of government organizations)	Court system
Civil Rights Acts (CRAs) of 1866 and 1871 (as amended)	Grant all citizens the right to make, perform, modify, and terminate contracts and enjoy all benefits, terms, and conditions of the contractual relationship	All individuals	Court system
Equal Pay Act of 1963	Requires that men and women performing equal jobs receive equal pay	Employers engaged in interstate commerce	EEOC
Title VII of CRA	Forbids discrimination based on race, color, religion, sex, or national origin	Employers with 15 or more employees working 20 or more weeks per year; labor unions; and employment agencies	EEOC
Age Discrimination in Employment Act of 1967	Prohibits discrimination in employment against individuals 40 years of age and older	Employers with 15 or more employees working 20 or more weeks per year; labor unions; employment agencies; federal government	EEOC
Rehabilitation Act of 1973	Requires affirmative action in the employment of individuals with disabilities	Government agencies; federal contractors and subcontractors with contracts greater than $2,500	OFCCP
Pregnancy Discrimination Act of 1978	Treats discrimination based on pregnancy-related conditions as illegal sex discrimination	All employees covered by Title VII	EEOC
Americans with Disabilities Act of 1990	Prohibits discrimination against individuals with disabilities	Employers with more than 15 employees	EEOC
Executive Order 11246	Requires affirmative action in hiring women and minorities	Federal contractors and subcontractors with contracts greater than $10,000	OFCCP
Civil Rights Act of 1991	Prohibits discrimination (same as Title VII)	Same as Title VII, plus applies Section 1981 to employment discrimination cases	EEOC
Uniformed Services Employment and Reemployment Rights Act of 1994	Requires rehiring of employees who are absent for military service, with training and accommodations as needed	Veterans and members of reserve components	Veterans' Employment and Training Service

example of race-based slavery in the United States today, the Thirteenth Amendment has been applied in cases where discrimination involved the "badges" (symbols) and "incidents" of slavery.

The Fourteenth Amendment forbids the states from taking life, liberty, or property without due process of law and prevents the states from denying equal protection of the laws. Recently it has been applied to the protection of whites in charges of reverse discrimination. In a case that marked the early stages of a move away from race-based quotas, Alan Bakke alleged that as a white man he had been discriminated against in the selection of entrants to the University of California at Davis medical school.[2] The university had set aside 16 of the available 100 places for "disadvantaged" applicants who were members of racial minority groups. Under this quota system, Bakke was able to compete for only 84 positions, whereas a minority applicant was able to compete for all 100. The federal court ruled in favor of Bakke, noting that this quota system had violated white individuals' right to equal protection under the law.

An important point regarding the Fourteenth Amendment is that it applies only to the decisions or actions of the government or of private groups whose activities are deemed government actions. Thus, a person could file a claim under the Fourteenth Amendment if he or she had been fired from a state university (a government organization) but not if the person had been fired by a private employer.

Legislation

The periods following the Civil War and during the civil rights movement of the 1960s were times when many voices in society pressed for equal rights for all without regard to a person's race or sex. In response, Congress passed laws designed to provide for equal opportunity. In later years, Congress has passed additional laws that have extended EEO protection more broadly.

Civil Rights Acts of 1866 and 1871

During Reconstruction, Congress passed two Civil Rights Acts to further the Thirteenth Amendment's goal of abolishing slavery. The Civil Rights Act of 1866 granted all persons the same property rights as white citizens, as well as the right to enter into and enforce contracts. Courts have interpreted the latter right as including employment contracts. The Civil Rights Act of 1871 granted all citizens the right to sue in federal court if they feel they have been deprived of some civil right. Although these laws might seem outdated, they are still used because they allow the plaintiff to recover both compensatory and punitive damages (that is, payment to compensate them for their loss plus additional damages to punish the offender).

Equal Pay Act of 1963

Under the Equal Pay Act of 1963, if men and women in an organization are doing equal work, the employer must pay them equally. The act defines *equal* in terms of skill, effort, responsibility, and working conditions. However, the act allows for reasons why men and women performing the same job might be paid differently. If the pay differences result from differences in seniority, merit, quantity or quality of production, or any factor other than sex (such as participating in a training program or working the night shift), then the differences are legal.

A former employee of Outback Steakhouse was recently awarded $2.2 million by a federal district court when she demonstrated that she had not received equal pay.

Dena Zechella worked for Outback's construction department, and as the company grew, Zechella assumed more and more responsibility until she was handling the acquisition and development of about 100 new restaurant sites a year. About a year and a half after Zechella's hiring, Outback hired a male employee to perform the same job functions. After Zechella trained the man, he took over most of Zechella's duties. Zechella complained, and the company transferred her to a clerical job. Zechella later learned that the man had been hired at almost twice her salary. After she complained again, the company fired her. The court awarded Zechella back wages plus $50,000 in compensatory damages for her emotional pain and suffering and $2.1 million in punitive damages.[3]

Title VII of the Civil Rights Act of 1964

The major law regulating equal employment opportunity in the United States is Title VII of the Civil Rights Act of 1964. Title VII directly resulted from the civil rights movement of the early 1960s, led by such individuals as Dr. Martin Luther King Jr. To ensure that employment opportunities would be based on character or ability rather than on race, Congress wrote and passed Title VII, and President Lyndon Johnson signed it into law in 1964. The law is enforced by the **Equal Employment Opportunity Commission (EEOC),** an agency of the Department of Justice.

Equal Employment Opportunity Commission (EEOC)
Agency of the Department of Justice charged with enforcing Title VII of the Civil Rights Act of 1964 and other antidiscrimination laws.

Title VII prohibits employers from discriminating against individuals because of their race, color, religion, sex, or national origin. An employer may not use these characteristics as the basis for not hiring someone, for firing someone, or for discriminating against them in the terms of their pay, conditions of employment, or privileges of employment. In addition, an employer may not use these characteristics to limit, segregate, or classify employees or job applicants in any way that would deprive any individual of employment opportunities or otherwise adversely affect his or her status as an employee. The act applies to organizations that employ 15 or more persons working 20 or more weeks a year and that are involved in interstate commerce, as well as state and local governments, employment agencies, and labor organizations.

Title VII also states that employers may not retaliate against employees for either "opposing" a perceived illegal employment practice or "participating in a proceeding" related to an alleged illegal employment practice. *Opposition* refers to expressing to someone through proper channels that you believe an illegal employment act has taken place or is taking place. *Participation in a proceeding* refers to testifying in an investigation, hearing, or court proceeding regarding an illegal employment act. The purpose of this provision is to protect employees from employers' threats and other forms of intimidation aimed at discouraging employees from bringing to light acts they believe to be illegal. Companies that violate this prohibition may be liable for punitive damages, as in the earlier mentioned case involving Outback Steakhouse.

Age Discrimination in Employment Act (ADEA)

One category of employees not covered by Title VII is older workers. Older workers sometimes are concerned that they will be the targets of discrimination, especially when a company is downsizing. Older workers tend to be paid more, so a company that wants to cut labor costs may save by laying off its oldest workers. To counter such discrimination, Congress in 1967 passed the Age Discrimination in Employment Act (ADEA), which prohibits discrimination against workers who are over the age of 40. Similar to Title VII, the ADEA outlaws hiring, firing, setting compensation rates, or other employment decisions based on a person's age being over 40.

Many firms have offered early-retirement incentives as an alternative or supplement to involuntary layoffs. Because this approach to workforce reduction focuses on older employees, who would be eligible for early retirement, it may be in violation of the ADEA. Early-retirement incentives require that participating employees sign an agreement waiving their rights to sue under the ADEA. Courts have tended to uphold the use of early-retirement incentives and waivers as long as the individuals were not coerced into signing the agreements, the agreements were presented in a way the employees could understand, and the employees had enough time to make a decision.[4] However, the Equal Employment Opportunity Commission recently expanded the interpretation of discriminatory retirement policies when it charged a law firm with having an illegal "age-based retirement policy." According to the charges, Sidley Austin Brown & Wood, based in Chicago, gave more than 30 lawyers older than age 40 notice that their status was being lowered from partner to special counsel or counsel and that they would be expected to leave the firm in a few years. The firm described the action as a way to provide more opportunities for young lawyers, but lawyers who were pressured to retire contended they were forced out as a way to boost profits by replacing highly paid partners with less-experienced, lower-paid lawyers—a charge Sidley has disputed. It will be up to the courts to determine whether Sidley's action violates the ADEA.[5]

Age discrimination complaints make up a large percentage of the complaints filed with the Equal Employment Opportunity Commission, and whenever the economy is slow, the number of complaints grows. For example, as shown in Figure 3.1, the number of age discrimination cases increased during the early 1990s, when many firms were downsizing. Another increase in age discrimination claims accompanied the economic slowdown at the beginning of this decade.[6] In addition, a recent ruling by the U.S. Supreme Court may open the door to more age discrimination lawsuits in the future. Under that ruling, workers who are 40 and older may sue employers for employment decisions that affect them differently than younger workers, whether or not the employers intended any harm (a topic we will return to in the later discussion of the employer's role). In that case, police officers and dispatchers of the Jackson, Mississippi, police department complained about decisions in which young workers received pay increases

Figure 3.1

Age Discrimination Complaints, 1991–2004

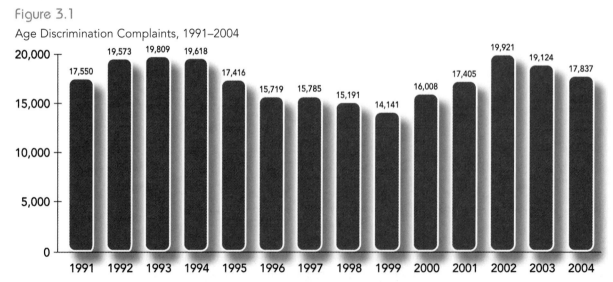

SOURCE: Equal Employment Opportunity Commission.

representing a larger percentage increase than older workers received. Although the Supreme Court found that these employees had a right to sue, it also found that the police department had a valid reason for the distribution of pay increases. It was trying to bring starting pay into line with pay received for similar positions at other police departments in the region, which would help it recruit new employees.[7]

In today's environment, in which firms are seeking talented individuals to achieve the company's goals, older employees can be a tremendous pool of potential resources. Baptist Health South Florida addresses the worker shortage in health care by making it easier for employees to stick around when they reach the usual retirement age. At Baptist, under a policy it calls Bridgement of Service, employees who have retired but want to return within five years are able to come back with the same level of seniority and benefits they had earned before leaving. Some of these employees work part-time and use their retirement savings to make up the difference in pay. Another policy that makes it easier to stay with Baptist allows workers to accumulate up to 1,000 hours of paid time off. As workers near retirement age, they can save up time and take an extended vacation to see if they really want to be away from work. Two of Baptist's recruiters specialize in transferring employees within the company, and they spend a large share of their time helping older workers change to jobs that are less physically demanding. The company also modifies jobs; for example, spring lifts in laundry containers permit housekeepers to move loads without bending over. Efforts such as these have helped to keep employee turnover, especially among older employees, far below the industry average.[8]

Vocational Rehabilitation Act of 1973

In 1973, Congress passed the Vocational Rehabilitation Act to enhance employment opportunity for individuals with disabilities. This act covers executive agencies and contractors and subcontractors that receive more than $2,500 annually from the federal government. These organizations must engage in affirmative action for individuals with disabilities. **Affirmative action** is an organization's active effort to find opportunities to hire or promote people in a particular group. Thus, Congress intended this act to encourage employers to recruit qualified individuals with disabilities and to make reasonable accommodations to all those people to become active members of the labor market. The Department of Labor's Employment Standards Administration enforces this act.

affirmative action
An organization's active effort to find opportunities to hire or promote people in a particular group.

Vietnam Era Veteran's Readjustment Act of 1974

Similar to the Rehabilitation Act, the Vietnam Era Veteran's Readjustment Act of 1974 requires federal contractors and subcontractors to take affirmative action toward employing veterans of the Vietnam War (those serving between August 5, 1964, and May 7, 1975). The Office of Federal Contract Compliance Procedures, discussed later in this chapter, has authority to enforce this act.

Pregnancy Discrimination Act of 1978

An amendment to Title VII of the Civil Rights Act of 1964, the Pregnancy Discrimination Act of 1978 defines discrimination on the basis of pregnancy, childbirth, or related medical conditions to be a form of illegal sex discrimination. According to the EEOC, this means that employers must treat "women who are pregnant or affected by related conditions . . . in the same manner as other applicants or employees with similar abilities or limitations."[9] For example, an employer may not refuse to hire a

BEST PRACTICES

PREGNANCY NO BARRIER AT PLANTE & MORAN

Even though the U.S. birth rate has fallen in recent years, the number of complaints about pregnancy discrimination has been rising faster than most other discrimination complaints. Reasons may include a greater share of women remaining on the job after pregnancy and competitive pressure for companies to get work done with fewer people, so there is no slack employers can use to help out a pregnant worker who needs time off. But in spite of these challenges, Plante & Moran has succeeded in helping employees balance work demands with the requirements of pregnancy, parenting, and other personal needs.

Not only does Plante & Moran assign new hires to a mentor to learn their way around the firm; it assigns new *mothers* (that is, pregnant workers) to a mentor: a colleague who is also a parent. This "parenting buddy" helps the new

mother plan a successful transition, including how to smoothly transfer clients to other employees during her leave and how to make arrangements for returning to work. When associate Tracey Ewing took a leave, partner Sue Perlin helped her plan a request to return on a part-time basis, enabling Ewing to work 30 hours a week.

During the tax season leading up to April 15 each year, many accountants work extraordinarily long hours to prepare clients' tax returns. The firm helps out with Saturday day care services, even on site at company offices.

Of course, motherhood is not the only reason employees need time for family matters. When Stacey Reeves was in her first year with Plante & Moran, her husband injured his back and required months of bed rest. Worse, the injury occurred at the beginning of tax season. Reeves went to her boss, dis-

traught about how to get her work done while caring for her husband. Her boss unhesitatingly counseled, "Family comes first." Not surprisingly, Reeves has since become a loyal employee, moving up to a position as associate with the firm.

Keeping talented professionals on board even part-time is less costly than replacing employees who become frustrated and leave. According to Plante & Moran's human resource director, Bill Bufe, the firm spends $75,000 to replace an employee earning that salary. And flexibility does not seem to hurt the company's business performance. While other big accounting firms' revenues have recently declined, Plante & Moran enjoyed a healthy increase.

SOURCE: Jena McGregor, "Balance and Balance Sheets," *Fast Company*, May 2004, pp. 96–97; and Stephanie Armour, "Pregnant Workers Report Growing Discrimination," *USA Today*, February 18, 2005, www.usatoday.com.

woman because she is pregnant. Decisions about work absences or accommodations must be based on the same policies as the organization uses for other disabilities. Benefits, including health insurance, should cover pregnancy and related medical conditions in the same way that it covers other medical conditions. Especially at small companies, the challenges of accommodating an employee's pregnancy may be difficult, but some companies are finding creative solutions. An example is accounting firm Plante & Moran, described in "Best Practices."

Americans with Disabilities Act (ADA) of 1990

One of the farthest-reaching acts concerning the management of human resources is the Americans with Disabilities Act. This 1990 law protects individuals with disabilities from being discriminated against in the workplace. It prohibits discrimination based on disability in all employment practices such as job application procedures, hiring, firing, promotions, compensation, and training. Other employment activities covered by the ADA are employment advertising, recruitment, tenure, layoff, leave, and fringe benefits.

The ADA defines **disability** as a physical or mental impairment that substantially limits one or more major life activities, a record of having such an impairment, or being regarded as having such an impairment. The first part of the definition refers to individuals who have serious disabilities—such as epilepsy, blindness, deafness, or paralysis—that affect their ability to perform major life activities such as walking, seeing, performing manual tasks, learning, caring for oneself, and working. The second part refers to individuals who have a history of disability, such as someone who has had cancer but is currently in remission, someone with a history of mental illness, and someone with a history of heart disease. The third part of the definition, "being regarded as having a disability," refers to people's subjective reactions, as in the case of someone who is severely disfigured; an employer might hesitate to hire such a person on the grounds that people will react negatively to such an employee.[10]

The ADA covers specific physiological disabilities such as cosmetic disfigurement and anatomical loss affecting the body's systems. In addition, it covers mental and psychological disorders such as mental retardation, organic brain syndrome, emotional or mental illness, and learning disabilities. Conditions not covered include obesity, substance abuse, eye and hair color, and lefthandedness.[11] Also, if a person uses mitigating measures (for example, medicine or equipment) that enable him or her to perform each major life activity with little or no difficulty, the person is not considered disabled under the ADA. Figure 3.2 shows the types of disabilities associated with complaints filed under the ADA.

In contrast to other EEO laws, the ADA goes beyond prohibiting discrimination to require that employers take steps to accommodate individuals covered under the act. If a disabled person is selected to perform a job, the employer (perhaps in consultation with the disabled employee) determines what accommodations are necessary for the

disability
Under the Americans with Disabilities Act, a physical or mental impairment that substantially limits one or more major life activities, a record of having such an impairment, or being regarded as having such an impairment.

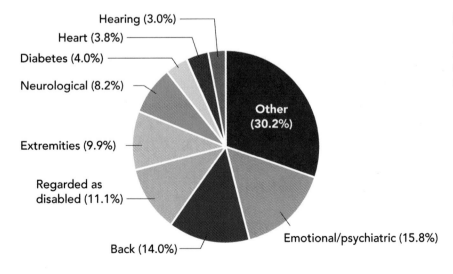

Figure 3.2

Disabilities Associated with Complaints Filed under ADA

Total complaints: 204,997

SOURCE: Equal Employment Opportunity Commission, "ADA Charge Data by Impairments/Bases: Receipts," www.eeoc.gov, cumulative data for July 26, 1992–September 30, 2004.

TABLE 3.2

Maximum Punitive Damages Allowed under the Civil Rights Act of 1991

EMPLOYER SIZE	DAMAGE LIMIT
14 to 100 employees	$ 50,000
101 to 200 employees	100,000
201 to 500 employees	200,000
More than 500 employees	300,000

employee to perform the job. Examples include using ramps and lifts to make facilities accessible, redesigning job procedures, and providing technology such as TDD lines for hearing-impaired employees. Some employers have feared that accommodations under the ADA would be expensive. However, in the years since the ADA went into effect, the Equal Employment Opportunity Commission has determined that the median cost of an accommodation is only $240, and one-fifth of accommodations cost nothing.[12] As technology advances, the cost of many technologies has been falling.

Civil Rights Act of 1991

In 1991 Congress broadened the relief available to victims of discrimination by passing a Civil Rights Act (CRA 1991). CRA 1991 amends Title VII of the Civil Rights Act of 1964, as well as the Civil Rights Act of 1866, the Americans with Disabilities Act, and the Age Discrimination in Employment Act of 1967. One major change in EEO law under CRA 1991 has been the addition of compensatory and punitive damages in cases of discrimination under Title VII and the Americans with Disabilities Act. Before CRA 1991, Title VII limited damage claims to *equitable relief,* which courts have defined to include back pay, lost benefits, front pay in some cases, and attorney's fees and costs. CRA 1991 allows judges to award compensatory and punitive damages when the plaintiff proves the discrimination was intentional or reckless. Compensatory damages include such things as future monetary loss, emotional pain, suffering, and loss of enjoyment of life. Punitive damages are a punishment; by requiring violators to pay the plaintiff an amount beyond the actual losses suffered, the courts try to discourage employers from discriminating.

Recognizing that one or a few discrimination cases could put an organization out of business, and so harm many innocent employees, Congress has limited the amount of punitive damages. As shown in Table 3.2, the amount of damages depends on the size of the organization charged with discrimination. The limits range from $50,000 per violation at a small company (14 to 100 employees) to $300,000 at a company with more than 500 employees. A company has to pay punitive damages only if it discriminated intentionally or with malice or reckless indifference to the employee's federally protected rights.

Uniformed Services Employment and Reemployment Rights Act of 1994

When members of the armed services were called up following the terrorist attacks of September 2001, a 1994 employment law—the Uniformed Services Employment and Reemployment Rights Act (USERRA)—assumed new significance. Under this law, employers must reemploy workers who left jobs to fulfill military duties for up to five years. When service members return from active duty, the employer must reemploy them in the job they would have held if they had not left to serve in the military, including the same seniority, status, and pay. Disabled veterans also have up to two years

Aric Miller, an Army reservist sergeant, was deployed for service with the 363rd military police unit in Iraq in February 2003. When he returned to the states in April 2004 he was able to resume his job as an elementary school teacher thanks to the 1994 Uniformed Services Employment and Reemployment Rights Act. The act states that the employer must reemploy them in the job they would have held if they had not left to serve in the military. Why is this act so important?

to recover from injuries received during their service or training, and employers must make reasonable accommodations for a remaining disability.

Service members also have duties under USERRA. Before leaving for duty, they are to give their employers notice, if possible. After their service, the law sets time limits for applying to be reemployed. Depending on the length of service, these limits range from approximately 2 to 90 days. Veterans with complaints under USERRA can obtain assistance from the Veterans' Employment and Training Service of the Department of Labor.

Executive Orders

Two executive orders that directly affect human resource management are Executive Order 11246, issued by Lyndon Johnson, and Executive Order 11478, issued by Richard Nixon. Executive Order 11246 prohibits federal contractors and subcontractors from discriminating based on race, color, religion, sex, or national origin. In addition, employers whose contracts meet minimum size requirements must engage in affirmative action to ensure against discrimination. Those receiving more than $10,000 from the federal government must take affirmative action, and those with contracts exceeding $50,000 must develop a written affirmative-action plan for each of their establishments. This plan must be in place within 120 days of the beginning of the contract. This executive order is enforced by the Office of Federal Contract Compliance Procedures.

Executive Order 11478 requires the federal government to base all its employment policies on merit and fitness. It specifies that race, color, sex, religion, and national origin may not be considered. Along with the government, the act covers all contractors and subcontractors doing at least $10,000 worth of business with the federal government. The U.S. Office of Personnel Management is in charge of ensuring that the government is in compliance, and the relevant government agencies are responsible for ensuring the compliance of contractors and subcontractors.

⬚ THE GOVERNMENT'S ROLE IN PROVIDING FOR EQUAL EMPLOYMENT OPPORTUNITY

LO3
Identify the federal agencies that enforce equal employment opportunity, and describe the role of each.

At a minimum, equal employment opportunity requires that employers comply with EEO laws. To enforce those laws, the executive branch of the federal government uses the Equal Employment Opportunity Commission and the Office of Federal Contract Compliance Procedures.

Equal Employment Opportunity Commission (EEOC)

The Equal Employment Opportunity Commission (EEOC) is responsible for enforcing most of the EEO laws, including Title VII, the Equal Pay Act, and the Americans with Disabilities Act. To do this, the EEOC investigates and resolves complaints about discrimination, gathers information, and issues guidelines.

When individuals believe they have been discriminated against, they may file a complaint with the EEOC or a similar state agency. They must file the complaint within 180 days of the incident. Figure 3.3 illustrates the number of charges filed with the EEOC for different types of discrimination in 2004. Many individuals file more than one type of charge (for instance, both race discrimination and retaliation), so the total number of complaints filed with the EEOC is less than the total of the amounts in each category.

After the EEOC receives a charge of discrimination, it has 60 days to investigate the complaint. If the EEOC either does not believe the complaint to be valid or fails to complete the investigation within 60 days, the individual has the right to sue in federal court. If the EEOC determines that discrimination has taken place, its representatives will attempt to work with the individual and the employer to try to achieve a reconciliation without a lawsuit. Sometimes the EEOC enters into a consent decree with the discriminating organization. This decree is an agreement between the agency and the organization that the organization will cease certain discriminatory practices and possibly institute additional affirmative-action practices to rectify its history of discrimination. A settlement with the EEOC can be costly, including such remedies as back pay, reinstatement of the employee, and promotions.

If the attempt at a settlement fails, the EEOC has two options. It may issue a "right to sue" letter to the alleged victim. This letter certifies that the agency has investigated the victim's allegations and found them to be valid. The EEOC's other option, which it uses less often, is to aid the alleged victim in bringing suit in federal court.

The EEOC also monitors organizations' hiring practices. Each year organizations that are government contractors or subcontractors or have 100 or more employees must file an Employer Information Report (EEO-1) with the EEOC. The **EEO-1 report,** shown in Figure 3.4, details the number of women and minorities employed in

EEO-1 report
The EEOC's Employer Information Report, which details the number of women and minorities employed in nine different job categories.

Figure 3.3

Types of Charges Filed with the EEOC

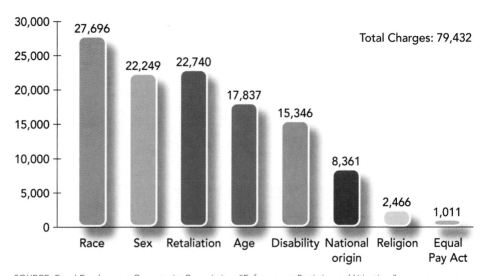

SOURCE: Equal Employment Opportunity Commission, "Enforcement Statistics and Litigation," www.eeoc.gov, modified February 15, 2005.

Figure 3.4

EEOC Form 100: Employer Information Report

Joint Reporting
Committee

• **Equal Employment
Opportunity Com-
mission**
• **Office of Federal
Contract Compli-
ance Programs (Labor)**

EQUAL EMPLOYMENT OPPORTUNITY

EMPLOYER INFORMATION REPORT EEO—1

Standard Form 100
(Rev. 3/97)

O.M.B. No. 3046-0007
EXPIRES 10/31/99
100-214

Section A—TYPE OF REPORT
Refer to instructions for number and types of reports to be filed.

1. Indicate by marking in the appropriate box the type of reporting unit for which this copy of the form is submitted (MARK ONLY ONE BOX).

    (1) ☐ Single-establishment Employer Report

    Multi-establishment Employer:
    (2) ☐ Consolidated Report (Required)
    (3) ☐ Headquarters Unit Report (Required)
    (4) ☐ Individual Establishment Report (submit one for each
           establishment with 50 or more employees)
    (5) ☐ Special Report

2. Total number of reports being filed by this Company (Answer on Consolidated Report only) _____

Section B—COMPANY IDENTIFICATION (*To be answered by all employers*)	OFFICE USE ONLY
1. Parent Company	
a. Name of parent company (owns or controls establishment in item 2) omit if same as label	a.
Address (Number and street)	b.
City or town State ZIP code	c.
2. Establishment for which this report is filed. (Omit if same as label)	
a. Name of establishment	d.
Address (Number and street) City or Town County State ZIP code	e.
b. Employer Identification No. (IRS 9-DIGIT TAX NUMBER)	f.

c. Was an EEO–1 report filed for this establishment last year? ☐ Yes ☐ No

Section C—EMPLOYERS WHO ARE REQUIRED TO FILE (*To be answered by all employers*)

☐ Yes ☐ No 1. Does the entire company have at least 100 employees in the payroll period for which you are reporting?

☐ Yes ☐ No 2. Is your company affiliated through common ownership and /or centralized management with other entities in an enterprise with a total employment of 100 or more?

☐ Yes ☐ No 3. Does the company or any of its establishments (a) have 50 or more employees AND (b) is not exempt as provided by 41 CFR 60-1.5, AND either (1) is a prime government contractor or first-tier subcontractor and has a contract, subcontract, or purchase order amounting to $50,000 or more, or (2) serves as a depository of Government funds in any amount or is a financial institution which is an issuing and paying agent for U.S. Savings Bonds and Savings Notes?
If the response to question C-3 is yes, please enter your Dun and Bradstreet identification number (it you have one): ☐☐☐☐☐☐☐☐☐

NOTE: If the answer is yes to questions 1, 2, or 3, complete the entire form, otherwise skip to Section G.

(continued)

Figure 3.4

EEOC Form 100: Employer Information Report (continued)

SF 100 Page 2

Section D—EMPLOYMENT DATA

Employment at this establishment—Report all permanent full-time and part-time employees including apprentices and on-the-job trainees unless specifically excluded as set forth in the instructions. Enter the appropriate figures on all lines and in all columns. Blank spaces will be considered as zeros.

JOB CATEGORIES		OVERALL TOTALS (SUM OF COL. B THRU K)	MALE					FEMALE				
			WHITE (NOT OF HISPANIC ORIGIN)	BLACK (NOT OF HISPANIC ORIGIN)	HISPANIC	ASIAN OR PACIFIC ISLANDER	AMERICAN INDIAN OR ALASKAN NATIVE	WHITE (NOT OF HISPANIC ORIGIN)	BLACK (NOT OF HISPANIC ORIGIN)	HISPANIC	ASIAN OR PACIFIC ISLANDER	AMERICAN INDIAN OR ALASKAN NATIVE
		A	B	C	D	E	F	G	H	I	J	K
Officials and Managers	1											
Professionals	2											
Technicians	3											
Sales Workers	4											
Office and Clerical	5											
Craft Workers (Skilled)	6											
Operatives (Semi-Skilled)	7											
Laborers (Unskilled)	8											
Service Workers	9											
TOTAL	10											
Total employment reported in previous EEO–1 report	11											

NOTE: Omit questions 1 and 2 on the Consolidated Report.

1. Date(s) of payroll period used: 2. Does this establishment employ apprentices?
                                                  1 ☐ Yes   2 ☐ No

Section E—ESTABLISHMENT INFORMATION *(Omit on the Consolidated Report)*

1. What is the major activity of this establishment? (Be specific, i.e., manufacturing steel castings, retail grocer, wholesale plumbing supplies, title insurance, etc. Include the specific type of product or type of service provided, as well as the principal business or industrial activity.)

OFFICE USE ONLY

g.

Section F—REMARKS

Use this item to give any identification data appearing on last report which differs from that given above, explain major changes in composition of reporting units and other pertinent information.

Section G—CERTIFICATION *(See Instructions G)*

Check one
1 ☐   All reports are accurate and were prepared in accordance with the instructions (check on consolidated only).
2 ☐   This report is accurate and was prepared in accordance with the instructions.

Name of Certifying Official	Title	Signature	Date
Name of person to contact regarding this report (Type or print)	Address (Number and Street)		
Title	City and State	ZIP Code	Telephone Number (including Area Code) / Extension

All reports and information obtained from individual reports will be kept confidential as required by Section 709(e) of Title VII.
WILLFULLY FALSE STATEMENTS ON THIS REPORT ARE PUNISHABLE BY LAW, U.S. CODE, TITLE 18, SECTION 1001.

nine different job categories. The EEOC computer analyzes those reports to identify patterns of discrimination, which the agency can then attack through class-action lawsuits. Employers must display EEOC posters detailing employment rights. These posters must be in prominent and accessible locations—for example, in a company's cafeteria or near its time clock. Also, employers should retain copies of documents related to employment decisions—recruitment letters, announcements of jobs, completed job applications, selections for training, and so on. Employers must keep these records for at least six months or until a complaint is resolved, whichever is later.

Besides resolving complaints and suing alleged violators, the EEOC issues guidelines designed to help employers determine when their decisions violate the laws enforced by the EEOC. These guidelines are not laws themselves. However, the courts give great consideration to them when hearing employment discrimination cases. For example, the *Uniform Guidelines on Employee Selection Procedures* is a set of guidelines issued by the EEOC and other government agencies. The guidelines identify ways an organization should develop and administer its system for selecting employees so as not to violate Title VII. The courts often refer to the *Uniform Guidelines* to determine whether a company has engaged in discriminatory conduct. Similarly, in the *Federal Register,* the EEOC has published guidelines providing details about what the agency will consider illegal and legal in the treatment of disabled individuals under the Americans with Disabilities Act.

Office of Federal Contract Compliance Procedures (OFCCP)

The **Office of Federal Contract Compliance Procedures (OFCCP)** is the agency responsible for enforcing the executive orders that cover companies doing business with the federal government. As we stated earlier in the chapter, businesses with contracts for more than $50,000 may not discriminate in employment based on race, color, religion, national origin, or sex, and they must have a written affirmative-action plan on file. This plan must include three basic components:

1. *Utilization analysis*—A comparison of the race, sex, and ethnic composition of the employer's workforce with that of the available labor supply. The percentages in the employer's workforce should not be greatly lower than the percentages in the labor supply.
2. *Goals and timetables*—The percentages of women and minorities the organization seeks to employ in each job group, and the dates by which the percentages are to be attained. These are meant to be more flexible than quotas, requiring only that the employer have goals and be seeking to achieve the goals.
3. *Action steps*—A plan for how the organization will meet its goals. Besides working toward its goals for hiring women and minorities, the company must take affirmative steps toward hiring Vietnam veterans and individuals with disabilities.

Each year, the OFCCP audits government contractors to ensure they are actively pursuing the goals in their plans. The OFCCP examines the plan and conducts on-site visits to examine how individual employees perceive the company's affirmative-action policies. If the agency finds that a contractor or subcontractor is not complying with the requirements, it has several options. It may notify the EEOC (if there is evidence of a violation of Title VII), advise the Department of Justice to begin criminal proceedings, request that the Secretary of Labor cancel or suspend any current contracts with the company, and forbid the firm from bidding on future contracts. For a company that depends on the federal government for a sizable share of its business, that last penalty is severe.

Uniform Guidelines on Employee Selection Procedures
Guidelines issued by the EEOC and other agencies to identify how an organization should develop and administer its system for selecting employees so as not to violate antidiscrimination laws.

Office of Federal Contract Compliance Procedures (OFCCP)
The agency responsible for enforcing the executive orders that cover companies doing business with the federal government.

LO4
Describe ways
employers can avoid
illegal discrimination
and provide
reasonable
accommodation.

❧ BUSINESSES' ROLE IN PROVIDING FOR EQUAL EMPLOYMENT OPPORTUNITY

Rare is the business owner or manager who wants to wait for the government to identify that the business has failed to provide for equal employment opportunity. Instead, out of motives ranging from concern for fairness to the desire to avoid costly lawsuits and settlements, most companies recognize the importance of complying with these laws. Often, management depends on the expertise of human resource professionals to help in identifying how to comply. These professionals can help organizations take steps to avoid discrimination and provide reasonable accommodation.

Avoiding Discrimination

How would you know if you had been discriminated against? Decisions about human resources are so complex that discrimination is often difficult to identify and prove. However, legal scholars and court rulings have arrived at some ways to show evidence of discrimination.

Disparate Treatment

disparate treatment
Differing treatment of individuals, where the differences are based on the individuals' race, color, religion, sex, national origin, age, or disability status.

One sign of discrimination is **disparate treatment**—differing treatment of individuals, where the differences are based on the individuals' race, color, religion, sex, national origin, age, or disability status. For example, disparate treatment would include hiring or promoting one person over an equally qualified person because of the individual's race. Another instance of disparate treatment is the Outback Steakhouse example we saw earlier in which a man was paid twice as much as a woman to perform the same job. Or suppose a company fails to hire women with school-age children (claiming the women will be frequently absent) but hires men with school-age children. In that situation, the women are victims of disparate treatment, because they are being treated differently based on their sex. To sustain a claim of discrimination based on disparate treatment, the women would have to prove that the employer intended to discriminate.

To avoid disparate treatment, companies can evaluate the questions and investigations they use in making employment decisions. These should be applied equally. For example, if the company investigates conviction records of job applicants, it should investigate them for all applicants, not just for applicants from certain racial groups. Companies may want to avoid some types of questions altogether. For example, questions about marital status can cause problems, because interviewers may unfairly make different assumptions about men and women. (Common stereotypes about women have been that a married woman is less flexible or more likely to get pregnant than a single woman, in contrast to the assumption that a married man is more stable and committed to his work.)

Sometimes a company can develop a more appropriate approach by focusing on the job requirement behind or implied by a question it would rather not ask. At the Teachers' College of Columbia University in New York, interviewers avoid questions about candidates' child care arrangements. Instead, says Diane Dobry, director of communications for the college, the interviewers discuss the work schedule. Dobry explains, "We say there are evening hours and weekend hours, but we don't ask [candidates] how they'll manage it. It's up to them."[13]

Is disparate treatment ever legal? The courts have held that in some situations, a factor such as sex or race may be a **bona fide occupational qualification (BFOQ),** that is, a necessary (not merely preferred) qualification for performing a job. A typical example is a job that includes handing out towels in a locker room. Requiring that employees who perform this job in the women's locker room be female is a BFOQ. However, it is very difficult to think of many jobs where criteria such as sex and race are BFOQs. In a widely publicized case from the 1990s, Johnson Controls, a manufacturer of car batteries, instituted a "fetal protection" policy that excluded women of childbearing age from jobs that would expose them to lead, which can cause birth defects. Johnson Controls argued that the policy was intended to provide a safe workplace and that sex was a BFOQ for jobs that involved exposure to lead. However, the Supreme Court disagreed, ruling that BFOQs are limited to policies directly related to a worker's ability to do the job.[14]

bona fide occupational qualification (BFOQ)
A necessary (not merely preferred) qualification for performing a job.

Disparate Impact

Another way to measure discrimination is by identifying **disparate impact**—a condition in which employment practices are seemingly neutral yet disproportionately exclude a protected group from employment opportunities. In other words, the company's employment practices lack obvious discriminatory content, but they affect one group differently than others. The earlier example of the Jackson police officers' claim of age discrimination is an example of disparate impact; the officers claimed that the police department's pay policy unfairly excluded the older officers from pay raises. A commonly used test of disparate impact is the **four-fifths rule,** which finds evidence of discrimination if the hiring rate for a minority group is less than four-fifths the hiring rate for the majority group. Keep in mind that this rule of thumb compares *rates* of hiring, not numbers of employees hired. Figure 3.5 illustrates how to apply the four-fifths rule.

disparate impact
A condition in which employment practices are seemingly neutral yet disproportionately exclude a protected group from employment opportunities.

An important distinction between disparate treatment and disparate impact is the role of the employer's intent. Proving disparate treatment in court requires showing that the employer intended the disparate treatment, but a plaintiff need not show intent in the case of disparate impact. It is enough to show that the result of the treatment was unequal. For example, the requirements for some jobs, such as firefighters or pilots, have sometimes included a minimum height. Although the intent may be to identify people who can perform the jobs, an unintended result may be disparate impact on groups that are shorter than average. Women, for example, tend to be shorter than men, and people of Asian ancestry tend to be shorter than people of European ancestry.

four-fifths rule
Rule of thumb that finds evidence of discrimination if an organization's hiring rate for a minority group is less than four-fifths the hiring rate for the majority group.

One way employers can avoid disparate impact is to be sure that employment decisions are really based on relevant, valid measurements. If a job requires a certain amount of strength and stamina, the employer would want measures of strength and stamina, not simply individuals' height and weight. The latter numbers are easier to obtain but more likely to result in charges of discrimination. Assessing validity of a measure can be a highly technical exercise requiring the use of statistics. The essence of such an assessment is to show that test scores or other measurements are significantly related to job performance. In the case of age discrimination, the Supreme Court's recent ruling allows a somewhat easier standard: To justify disparate impact on older employees, the employer must be able to show that the impact results from "reasonable factors other than age."[15] The Jackson police department set up a pay policy to help it recruit new officers, and the Supreme Court considered this plan reasonable.

Figure 3.5

Applying the Four-Fifths Rule

Example: A new hotel has to hire employees to fill 100 positions. Out of 300 total applicants, 200 are black, and the remaining 100 are white. The hotel hires 40 of the black applicants and 60 of the white applicants.

Step 1: Find the Rates

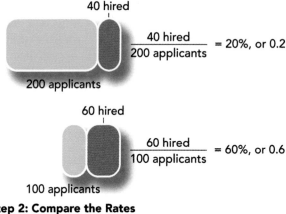

$$\frac{40 \text{ hired}}{200 \text{ applicants}} = 20\%, \text{ or } 0.2$$

$$\frac{60 \text{ hired}}{100 \text{ applicants}} = 60\%, \text{ or } 0.6$$

Step 2: Compare the Rates

$$\frac{0.2}{0.6} = 0.33 \qquad \frac{4}{5} = 0.8$$

$$0.33 < 0.8$$

The four-fifths requirement is not satisfied, and thus discrimination is proved.

EEO Policy

Employers can also avoid discrimination and defend against claims of discrimination by establishing and enforcing an EEO policy. The policy should define and prohibit un-lawful behaviors, as well as provide procedures for making and investigating complaints. The policy also should require that employees at all levels engage in fair conduct and respectful language. Derogatory language can support a court claim of discrimination.

Affirmative Action and Reverse Discrimination

In the search for ways to avoid discrimination, some organizations have used affirmative-action programs, usually to increase the representation of minorities. In its original form, affirmative action was meant as taking extra effort to attract and retain minority employees. These efforts have included extensively recruiting minority candidates on college campuses, advertising in minority-oriented publications, and providing educational and training opportunities to minorities. However, over the years, many organizations have resorted to quotas, or numerical goals for the proportion of certain minority groups, to ensure that their workforce mirrors the proportions of the labor market. Sometimes these organizations act voluntarily; in other cases, the quotas are imposed by the courts or the EEOC.

Whatever the reasons for these hiring programs, by increasing the proportion of minority or female candidates hired or promoted, they necessarily reduce the proportion of white or male candidates hired or promoted. In many cases, white and/or male individuals have fought against affirmative action and quotas, alleging what is called *reverse discrimination*. In other words, the organizations are allegedly discriminating

Regina Genwright talks to a voice-activated copier at the American Foundation for the Blind. The copier has a Braille keyboard and wheelchair-accessible height. Equipment like this can help employers make reasonable accommodation for their disabled employees.

against white males by preferring women and minorities. Affirmative action remains a controversial issue in the United States. Surveys have found that Americans are least likely to favor affirmative action when programs use quotas.[16]

Providing Reasonable Accommodation

Especially in situations involving religion and individuals with disabilities, equal employment opportunity may require that an employer make **reasonable accommodation.** In employment law, this term refers to an employer's obligation to do something to enable an otherwise qualified person to perform a job. Electrolux Group recently settled a case in which Muslim workers from Somalia complained they were disciplined for using an unscheduled break as prayer time. Observant Muslims pray five times a day, with two of the prayers offered within restricted time periods (early morning and at sunset). The Electrolux employees observed the sunset prayer by taking an unscheduled break traditionally offered to line employees on an as-needed basis. In the settlement, Electrolux arranged to allow the sunset prayer so that it could accommodate the religious practices of its Muslim workers without creating a business hardship.[17]

In the context of religion, this principle recognizes that for some individuals, religious observations and practices may present a conflict with work duties, dress codes, or company practices. For example, some religions require head coverings, or individuals might need time off to observe the sabbath or other holy days, when the company might have them scheduled to work. When the employee has a legitimate religious belief requiring accommodation, the employee should demonstrate this need to the employer. Assuming that it would not present an undue hardship, employers are required to accommodate such religious practices. They may have to adjust schedules so that employees do not have to work on days when their religion forbids it, or they may have to alter dress or grooming requirements.

For employees with disabilities, reasonable accommodations also vary according to the individuals' needs. As shown in Figure 3.6, employers may restructure jobs, make facilities in the workplace more accessible, modify equipment, or reassign an employee to a job that the person can perform. In some situations, a disabled individual may provide his or her own accommodation, which the employer allows, as in the case of a blind worker who brings a guide dog to work.

If accommodating a disability would require significant expense or difficulty, however, the employer may be exempt from the reasonable accommodation requirement (although the employer may have to defend this position in court). An accommodation is considered "reasonable" if it does not impose an undue hardship on the employer, such as an expense that is large in relation to a company's resources.

reasonable accommodation
An employer's obligation to do something to enable an otherwise qualified person to perform a job.

Figure 3.6
Examples of Reasonable Accommodations under the ADA

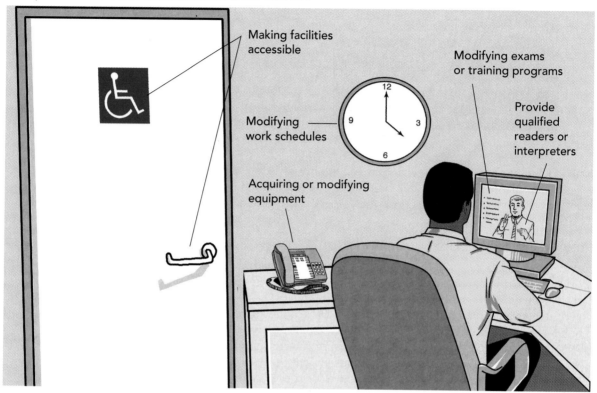

Note: Reasonable accommodations do *not* include hiring an unqualified person, lowering quality standards, or compromising coworkers' safety.

SOURCE: Based on Equal Employment Opportunity Commission, "The ADA: Your Responsibilities as an Employer," www.eeoc.gov, modified March 21, 2005.

LO5
Define sexual harassment and tell how employers can eliminate or minimize it.

sexual harassment
Unwelcome sexual advances as defined by the EEOC.

Preventing Sexual Harassment

Based on Title VII's prohibition of sex discrimination, the EEOC defines sexual harassment of employees as unlawful employment discrimination. **Sexual harassment** refers to unwelcome sexual advances. The EEOC has defined the types of behavior and the situations under which this behavior constitutes sexual harassment:

Unwelcome sexual advances, requests for sexual favors, and other verbal or physical contact of a sexual nature constitute sexual harassment when

1. Submission to such conduct is made either explicitly or implicitly a term of condition of an individual's employment,
2. Submission to or rejection of such conduct by an individual is used as the basis for employment decisions affecting such individual, or
3. Such conduct has the purpose or effect of unreasonably interfering with an individual's work performance or creating an intimidating, hostile, or offensive working environment.[18]

Under these guidelines, preventing sexual discrimination includes managing the workplace in a way that does not tolerate anybody's threatening or intimidating employees through sexual behavior.

In general, the most obvious examples of sexual harassment involve *quid pro quo harassment*, meaning that a person makes a benefit (or punishment) contingent on an employee's submitting to (or rejecting) sexual advances. For example, a manager who promises a raise to an employee who will participate in sexual activities is engaging in quid pro quo harassment. Likewise, it would be sexual harassment to threaten to reassign someone to a less desirable job if that person refuses sexual favors.

A more subtle, and possibly more pervasive, form of sexual harassment is to create or permit a "hostile working environment." This occurs when someone's behavior in the workplace creates an environment in which it is difficult for someone of a particular sex to work. Common complaints in sexual harassment lawsuits include claims that harassers ran their fingers through the plaintiffs' hair, made suggestive remarks, touched intimate body parts, posted pictures with sexual content in the workplace, and used sexually explicit language or told sex-related jokes. The reason that these behaviors are considered discrimination is that they treat individuals differently based on their sex.

Although a large majority of sexual harassment complaints received by the EEOC involve women being harassed by men, a growing share of sexual harassment claims have been filed by men. Some of the men claimed that they were harassed by women, but same-sex harassment also occurs and is illegal. Male employees of an Amarillo, Texas, car dealership won a lawsuit claiming that they were subjected to a sexually hostile work environment and disparate treatment by their male managers. The managers failed in their argument that behavior such as lewd comments and grabbing workers' genitals and buttocks was "harmless horseplay."[19]

To ensure a workplace free from sexual harassment, organizations can follow some important steps. First, the organization can develop a policy statement making it very clear that sexual harassment will not be tolerated in the workplace. Second, all employees, new and old, can be trained to identify inappropriate workplace behavior. In addition, the organization can develop a mechanism for reporting sexual harassment in a way that encourages people to speak out. Finally, management can prepare to act promptly to discipline those who engage in sexual harassment, as well as to protect the victims of sexual harassment.

Valuing Diversity

As we mentioned in Chapter 2, the United States is a diverse nation, and becoming more so. In addition, many U.S. companies have customers and operations in more than one country. Managers differ in how they approach the challenges related to this diversity. Some define a diverse workforce as a competitive advantage that brings them a wider pool of talent and greater insight into the needs and behaviors of their diverse customers. These organizations say they have a policy of *valuing diversity*.

The practice of valuing diversity has no single form; it is not written into law or business theory. Organizations that value diversity may practice some form of affirmative action, discussed earlier. They may have policies stating their value of understanding and respecting differences. Organizations may try to hire, reward, and promote employees who demonstrate respect for others. They may sponsor training programs designed to teach employees about differences among groups. Whatever their form, these efforts are intended to make each individual feel respected. Also, these actions can support equal employment opportunity by cultivating an environment in which individuals feel welcome and able to do their best.

LO6
Explain employers' duties under the Occupational Safety and Health Act.

Occupational Safety and Health Act (OSH Act)
U.S. law authorizing the federal government to establish and enforce occupational safety and health standards for all places of employment engaging in interstate commerce.

🔖 OCCUPATIONAL SAFETY AND HEALTH ACT (OSH ACT)

Like equal employment opportunity, the protection of employee safety and health is regulated by the government. Through the 1960s, workplace safety was primarily an issue between workers and employers. By 1970, however, roughly 15,000 work-related fatalities occurred every year. That year, Congress enacted the **Occupational Safety and Health Act (OSH Act),** the most comprehensive U.S. law regarding worker safety. The OSH Act authorized the federal government to establish and enforce occupational safety and health standards for all places of employment engaging in interstate commerce.

The OSH Act divided enforcement responsibilities between the Department of Labor and the Department of Health. Under the Department of Labor, the **Occupational Safety and Health Administration (OSHA)** is responsible for inspecting employers, applying safety and health standards, and levying fines for violation. The Department of Health is responsible for conducting research to determine the criteria for specific operations or occupations and for training employers to comply with the act. Much of the research is conducted by the National Institute for Occupational Safety and Health (NIOSH).

LO7
Describe the role of the Occupational Safety and Health Administration.

Occupational Safety and Health Administration (OSHA)
Labor Department agency responsible for inspecting employers, applying safety and health standards, and levying fines for violation.

General and Specific Duties

The main provision of the OSH Act states that each employer has a general duty to furnish each employee a place of employment free from recognized hazards that cause or are likely to cause death or serious physical harm. This is called the act's *general-duty clause.* Employers also must keep records of work-related injuries and illnesses and post an annual summary of these records from February 1 to April 30 in the following year. Figure 3.7 shows a sample of OSHA's Form 300A, the annual summary that must be posted, even if no injuries or illnesses occurred.

The act also grants specific rights; for example, employees have the right to:

- Request an inspection.
- Have a representative present at an inspection.
- Have dangerous substances identified.
- Be promptly informed about exposure to hazards and be given access to accurate records regarding exposure.
- Have employer violations posted at the work site.

The nearby "HR How To" box summarizes key points from OSHA's guidance on how new companies can ensure that they follow these requirements.

The Department of Labor recognizes many specific types of hazards, and employers must comply with all the occupational safety and health standards published by NIOSH. NIOSH has, for instance, determined that a noise level of 85 decibels (comparable to the noise of heavy city traffic) is potentially dangerous. A person exposed to this much noise over a long enough period of time could experience hearing loss as a result. Researchers in San Francisco measured noise levels at five local restaurants and found that the levels reached 85 decibels and often reached 105 decibels. Such levels could be a health risk for waiters working in the restaurant for eight hours at a time. Employers could respond in a number of ways, from permitting ear plugs to educating workers to reconsidering restaurant design (large bars, open kitchens, and high ceilings are a number of features that intensify noise levels).[20]

Figure 3.7

OSHA Form 300A: Summary of Work-Related Injuries and Illnesses

OSHA's Form 300A

Summary of Work-Related Injuries and Illnesses

Year 20____

U.S. Department of Labor
Occupational Safety and Health Administration

Form approved OMB no. 1218-0176

All establishments covered by Part 1904 must complete this Summary page, even if no work-related injuries or illnesses occurred during the year. Remember to review the Log to verify that the entries are complete and accurate before completing this summary.

Using the Log, count the individual entries you made for each category. Then write the totals below, making sure you've added the entries from every page of the Log. If you had no cases, write "0."

Employees, former employees, and their representatives have the right to review the OSHA Form 300 in its entirety. They also have limited access to the OSHA Form 301 or its equivalent. See 29 CFR Part 1904.35, in OSHA's recordkeeping rule, for further details on the access provisions for these forms.

Number of Cases

Total number of deaths	Total number of cases with days away from work	Total number of cases with job transfer or restriction	Total number of other recordable cases
(G) ____	(H) ____	(I) ____	(J) ____

Number of Days

Total number of days of job transfer or restriction	Total number of days away from work
(K) ____	(L) ____

Injury and Illness Types

Total number of . . .
(M)
(1) Injuries ____
(2) Skin disorders ____
(3) Respiratory conditions ____

(4) Poisonings ____
(5) All other illnesses ____

Establishment information

Your establishment name ____

Street ____

City ____ State ____ ZIP ____

Industry description (e.g., Manufacture of motor truck trailers) ____

Standard Industrial Classification (SIC), if known (e.g., SIC 3715) ____

Employment information (If you don't have these figures, see the Worksheet on the back of this page to estimate.)

Annual average number of employees ____

Total hours worked by all employees last year ____

Sign here

Knowingly falsifying this document may result in a fine.

I certify that I have examined this document and that to the best of my knowledge the entries are true, accurate, and complete.

Company executive ____ Title ____

(____) Phone ____ Date __/__/__

Post this Summary page from February 1 to April 30 of the year following the year covered by the form.

Public reporting burden for this collection of information is estimated to average 50 minutes per response, including time to review the instructions, search and gather the data needed, and complete and review the collection of information. Persons are not required to respond to the collection of information unless it displays a currently valid OMB control number. If you have any comments about these estimates or any other aspects of this data collection, contact: US Department of Labor, OSHA Office of Statistics, Room N-3644, 200 Constitution Avenue, NW, Washington, DC 20210. Do not send the completed forms to this office.

HR HOW TO

OFF TO A SAFE START

Starting a new business usually entails long hours for the owners and managers. It's no wonder, when you think of all the issues involved—raising money, finding a place to work, crafting the details of a business plan, hiring all the employees. And regardless of whether the business will manufacture goods or consist entirely of office workers, the government expects that the owners will address health and safety issues from the very start.

OSHA regulations have a (sometimes justifiable) reputation for being complex and difficult to follow. Fortunately, the agency has prepared materials designed to help businesses, including start-ups, succeed. A good place to begin is to call the local OSHA office or visit the agency's Web site (www.osha.gov). At the Web site, you can find helpful links, the 56-page *Small Business Handbook,* and a step-by-step guide called Compliance Assistance Quick Start. The General Industry Quick Start leads new-business owners step by step through the basics of

OSHA requirements, including links to the necessary forms.

When planning the setup of operations, new-business owners should also be planning how to keep their employees safe. According to OSHA, employers should have an Emergency Action Plan that describes what workers should do in case of a fire or other emergency. The workplace must have exit routes, and workers should know the routes. Employers also must identify any hazardous chemicals used in the workplace in order to provide information about those chemicals. This planning step should also identify potential hazards and determine whether any can be eliminated. Avoiding hazards may be as simple as arranging rooms so that electrical cords do not cause accidents.

Employers also must display OSHA's Safe and Healthful Workplaces poster in a location where it is conspicuous to employees and job candidates. The poster provides information about employees' rights and responsibilities under the OSH Act.

New-business owners must obtain copies of OSHA's Log of Work-Related Injuries and Illnesses. Recording any work-related injuries and illnesses on the log is another duty under the OSH Act. (Some businesses, such as employers in many services industries, are exempt, however.)

Employers can get guidance and training at OSHA area offices. They may request free and confidential on-site consultations to help them identify and correct hazards. Several OSHA training centers conduct courses related to worker safety and health. At the OSHA Web site, employers can also download interactive training materials on general and specific topics related to occupational safety and health.

By getting off to a safe start, employers help to create an environment in which employees recognize safety and health as important values of the organization.

SOURCE: Occupational Safety and Health Administration, "Compliance Assistance Quick Start," www.osha.gov, updated March 18, 2005.

Although NIOSH publishes numerous standards, it is clearly impossible for regulators to anticipate all possible hazards that could occur in the workplace. Thus, the general-duty clause requires employers to be constantly alert for potential sources of harm in the workplace (as defined by the standard of what a reasonably prudent person would do) and to correct them. Information about hazards can come from em-

You Have a Right to a Safe and Healthful Workplace.

IT'S THE LAW!

- You have the right to notify your employer or OSHA about workplace hazards. You may ask OSHA to keep your name confidential.
- You have the right to request an OSHA inspection if you believe that there are unsafe and unhealthful conditions in your workplace. You or your representative may participate in the inspection.
- You can file a complaint with OSHA within 30 days of discrimination by your employer for making safety and health complaints or for exercising your rights under the OSH Act.
- You have a right to see OSHA citations issued to your employer. Your employer must post the citations at or near the place of the alleged violation.
- Your employer must correct workplace hazards by the date indicated on the citation and must certify that these hazards have been reduced or eliminated.
- You have the right to copies of your medical records or records of your exposure to toxic and harmful substances or conditions.
- Your employer must post this notice in your workplace.

The *Occupational Safety and Health Act of 1970 (OSH Act)*, P.L. 91-596, assures safe and healthful working conditions for working men and women throughout the Nation. The Occupational Safety and Health Administration, in the U.S. Department of Labor, has the primary responsibility for administering the *OSH Act*. The rights listed here may vary depending on the particular circumstances. To file a complaint, report an emergency, or seek OSHA advice, assistance, or products, call 1-800-321-OSHA or your nearest OSHA office: • Atlanta (404) 562-2300 • Boston (617) 565-9860 • Chicago (312) 353-2220 • Dallas (214) 767-4731 • Denver (303) 844-1600 • Kansas City (816) 426-5861 • New York (212) 337-2378 • Philadelphia (215) 861-4900 • San Francisco (415) 975-4310 • Seattle (206) 553-5930. Teletypewriter (TTY) number is 1-877-889-5627. To file a complaint online or obtain more information on OSHA federal and state programs, visit OSHA's website at www.osha.gov. If your workplace is in a state operating under an OSHA-approved plan, your employer must post the required state equivalent of this poster.

1-800-321-OSHA
www.osha.gov

U.S. Department of Labor • Occupational Safety and Health Administration • OSHA 3165

OSHA is responsible for inspecting businesses, applying safety and health standards, and levying fines for violations. OSHA regulations prohibit notifying employers of inspections in advance.

ployees or from outside researchers. A recent study found that health care workers are unusually likely to develop work-related asthma. The researchers found that the disease occurred because the workers were frequently exposed to latex and disinfectants known to cause asthma. They also worked around asthma-aggravating materials, including cleaning products and materials used in renovating buildings. Hospitals and other health care providers can protect their workers from asthma by substituting nonlatex or powder-free gloves for powdered latex gloves. They also can be more selective in their use of disinfectants.[21]

Enforcement of the OSH Act

To enforce the OSH Act, the Occupational Safety and Health Administration conducts inspections. OSHA compliance officers typically arrive at a workplace unannounced; for obvious reasons, OSHA regulations prohibit notifying employers of inspections in advance. After presenting credentials, the compliance officer tells the employer the reasons for the inspection and describes, in a general way, the procedures necessary to conduct the investigation.

An OSHA inspection has four major components. First, the compliance officer reviews the company's records of deaths, injuries, and illnesses. OSHA requires this kind of record keeping at all firms with 11 or more full- or part-time employees. Next, the officer—typically accompanied by a representative of the employer (and perhaps by a representative of the employees)—conducts a "walkaround" tour of the employer's premises. On this tour, the officer notes any conditions that may violate specific published standards or the less specific general-duty clause. The third component of the inspection, employee interviews, may take place during the tour. At this time, anyone who is aware of a violation can bring it to the officer's attention. Finally, in a closing conference, the compliance officer discusses the findings with the employer, noting any violations.

Following an inspection, OSHA gives the employer a reasonable time frame within which to correct the violations identified. If a violation could cause serious injury or death, the officer may seek a restraining order from a U.S. District Court. The restraining order compels the employer to correct the problem immediately. In addition, if an OSHA violation results in citations, the employer must post each citation in a prominent place near the location of the violation.

Besides correcting violations identified during the inspection, employers may have to pay fines. These fines range from $20,000 for violations that result in death of an employee to $1,000 for less serious violations. Other penalties include criminal charges for falsifying records that are subject to OSHA inspection or for warning an employer of an OSHA inspection without permission from the Department of Labor.

Employee Rights and Responsibilities

Although the OSH Act makes employers responsible for protecting workers from safety and health hazards, employees have responsibilities as well. They have to follow OSHA's safety rules and regulations governing employee behavior. Employees also have a duty to report hazardous conditions.

right-to-know laws
State laws that require employers to provide employees with information about the health risks associated with exposure to substances considered hazardous.

Along with those responsibilities go certain rights. Employees may file a complaint and request an OSHA inspection of the workplace, and their employers may not retaliate against them for complaining. Employees also have a right to receive information about any hazardous chemicals they handle in the course of their jobs. OSHA's Hazard Communication Standard and many states' **right-to-know laws** require employers to provide employees with information about the health risks associated with exposure to substances considered hazardous. State right-to-know laws may be more stringent than federal standards, so organizations should obtain requirements from their state's health and safety agency, as well as from OSHA.

material safety data sheets (MSDSs)
Forms on which chemical manufacturers and importers identify the hazards of their chemicals.

Under OSHA's Hazard Communication Standard, organizations must have **material safety data sheets (MSDSs)** for chemicals that employees are exposed to. An MSDS is a form that details the hazards associated with a chemical; the chemical's producer or importer is responsible for identifying these hazards and detailing them on the form. Employers must also ensure that all containers of hazardous chemicals are labeled with information about the hazards, and they must train employees in safe handling of the chemicals. Office workers who encounter a chemical infrequently (such as a secretary who occasionally changes the toner in a copier) are not covered by these requirements. In the case of a copy machine, the Hazard Communication

Incidences per 100 Full-Time Workers

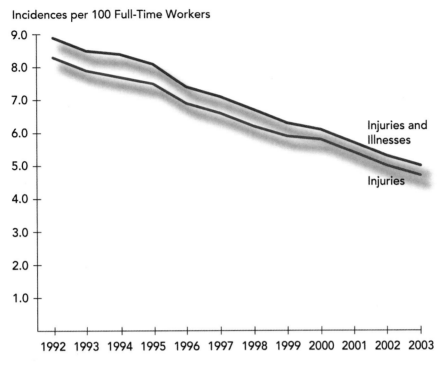

Figure 3.8

Rates of
Occupational
Injuries and Illnesses

Note: Data do not include fatal work-related injuries and illnesses.

SOURCE: Bureau of Labor Statistics, "Industry, Injury, and Illness Data," www.bls.gov, accessed March 31, 2005.

Standard would apply to someone whose job involves spending a large part of the day servicing or operating such equipment.

Impact of the OSH Act

The OSH Act has unquestionably succeeded in raising the level of awareness of occupational safety. Yet legislation alone cannot solve all the problems of work site safety. Indeed, the rate of occupational illnesses more than doubled between 1985 and 1990, according to the Bureau of Labor Statistics, while the rate of injuries rose by about 8 percent. However, as depicted in Figure 3.8, both rates have shown an overall downward trend since then.[22] The "Did You Know . . . ?" box shows the leading cases of injuries at work in 2002.

Many industrial accidents are a product of unsafe behaviors, not unsafe working conditions. Because the act does not directly regulate employee behavior, little behavior change can be expected unless employees are convinced of the standards' importance.[23] This principle has been recognized by labor leaders. For example, Lynn Williams, president of the United Steelworkers of America, has noted, "We can't count on government. We can't count on employers. We must rely on ourselves to bring about the safety and health of our workers."[24]

Because conforming to the law alone does not necessarily guarantee their employees will be safe, many employers go beyond the letter of the law. In the next section we examine various kinds of employer-initiated safety awareness programs that comply with OSHA requirements and, in some cases, exceed them.

TOP 10 CAUSES OF WORKPLACE INJURIES

Every year, Liberty Mutual conducts research it calls the Workplace Safety Index. In 2002, serious work-related injuries cost employers $49.6 billion. The leading cause was overexertion (for example, excessive lifting, pushing, carrying, or throwing), followed by falls on the same level (rather than from a height, such as a ladder), and bodily reaction (injury from movements such as bending, climbing, or slipping).

The 10 leading causes of workplace injuries in 2002

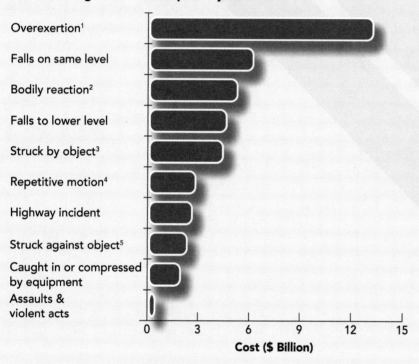

[1] Overexertion – Injuries caused from excessive lifting, pushing, pulling, holding, carrying, or throwing of an object.
[2] Bodily Reaction – Injuries from bending, climbing, slipping, or tripping without falling.
[3] Struck by Object – Such as a tool falling on a worker from above.
[4] Repetitive Motion – Injuries due to repeated stress or strain.
[5] Struck Against Object – Such as a worker walking into a door frame.

SOURCE: Liberty Mutual, "2004 Liberty Mutual Workplace Safety Index," www.libertymutual.com.

⬥ EMPLOYER-SPONSORED SAFETY AND HEALTH PROGRAMS

Many employers establish safety awareness programs to go beyond mere compliance with the OSH Act and attempt to instill an emphasis on safety. A safety awareness program has three primary components: identifying and communicating hazards, reinforcing safe practices, and promoting safety internationally.

Identifying and Communicating Job Hazards

Employees, supervisors, and other knowledgeable sources need to sit down and discuss potential problems related to safety. One method for doing this is the **job hazard analysis technique.**[25] With this technique, each job is broken down into basic elements, and each of these is rated for its potential for harm or injury. If there is agreement that some job element has high hazard potential, the group isolates the element and considers possible technological or behavior changes to reduce or eliminate the hazard.

Another means of isolating unsafe job elements is to study past accidents. The **technic of operations review (TOR)** is an analysis method for determining which specific element of a job led to a past accident.[26] The first step in a TOR analysis is to establish the facts surrounding the incident. To accomplish this, all members of the work group involved in the accident give their initial impressions of what happened. The group must then, through discussion, come to an agreement on the single, systematic failure that most likely contributed to the incident, as well as two or three major secondary factors that contributed to it.

United Parcel Service combined job analysis with employee empowerment to reduce injury rates dramatically. Concerned about the many sprains, strains, and other injuries experienced by its workers, UPS set up Comprehensive Health and Safety Process (CHSP) committees that bring together management and nonmanagement employees. Each committee investigates and reports on accidents, conducts audits of facilities and equipment, and advises employees on how to perform their jobs more safely. For example, the committees make sure delivery people know safe practices for lifting packages and backing up trucks. Whenever committee members see someone behaving unsafely, they are required to intervene. Since the CHSP committees began their work, the injury rate at UPS has fallen from over 27 injuries per 200,000 hours worked to just 10.2 injuries per 200,000, well on the way to the company's target injury rate of 3.2.[27]

To communicate with employees about job hazards, managers should talk directly with their employees about safety. Memos also are important, because the written communication helps establish a "paper trail" that can later document a history of the employer's concern regarding the job hazard. Posters, especially if placed near the hazard, serve as a constant reminder, reinforcing other messages.

In communicating risk, managers should recognize that different groups of individuals may constitute different audiences. Women and immigrants may be vulnerable in some situations, but for different reasons.[28] Certain jobs that are highly repetitive—for example, cashiers and administrative support—are dominated by women, who are therefore vulnerable to repetitive-strain injuries such as carpal tunnel syndrome. In addition, until recently, most of the personal protective equipment available for workers was designed to fit male bodies. When equipment does not fit properly, workers are less motivated to wear it, and they may have difficulty performing their jobs safely and accurately. Immigrants are vulnerable to safety problems when there are language or cultural barriers that make it difficult for them to learn safety

LO8
Discuss ways employers promote worker safety and health.

job hazard analysis technique
Safety promotion technique that involves breaking down a job into basic elements, then rating each element for its potential for harm or injury.

technic of operations review (TOR)
Method of promoting safety by determining which specific element of a job led to a past accident.

procedures, question situations that sound unsafe, or ask about tasks they don't understand fully. On a supplemental form to OSHA Form 300, the agency has begun asking whether language was a barrier to safety; according to Joe Reina of OSHA's Hispanic Task Force, "We [OSHA representatives] are finding out that the language barrier was a factor in many fatalities of immigrant workers." Because of this danger, efforts to improve communication in organizations benefit safety as well as motivation and productivity.

Other workers who may be at higher risk are at each end of the age spectrum.[29] Older workers are more likely than others to submit disability claims, and if they are injured, they tend to be absent longer than their younger colleagues. Conditions that may put older workers at risk include vision and hearing changes and decreases in co-ordination and balance. Organizations may need to make reasonable accommodations in response to such changes, both to protect their employees and to meet the challenges of an aging workforce, described in Chapter 2. With young workers, the safety challenge is to protect them from risk taking. Young workers may be especially eager to please the adults they work with, and they may be more fearful than their older colleagues when safety requires challenging authority. Employees who are new to the workforce may not be aware of the health and safety laws that are supposed to protect them. Research by the National Safety Council indicates that 40 percent of accidents happen to individuals in the 20-to-29 age group and that 48 percent of accidents happen to workers during their first year on the job.[30]

Reinforcing Safe Practices

To ensure safe behaviors, employers should not only define how to work safely but reinforce the desired behavior. One common technique for reinforcing safe practices is implementing a safety incentive program to reward workers for their support of and commitment to safety goals. Such programs start by focusing on monthly or quarterly goals or by encouraging suggestions for improving safety. Possible goals might include good housekeeping practices, adherence to safety rules, and proper use of protective equipment. Later, the program expands to include more wide-ranging, long-term goals. Typically, the employer distributes prizes in highly public forums, such as company or department meetings. Using merchandise for prizes, instead of cash, provides a lasting symbol of achievement. A good deal of evidence suggests that such incentive programs are effective in reducing the number and cost of injuries.[31]

Besides focusing on specific jobs, organizations can target particular types of injuries or disabilities, especially those for which employees may be at risk. For example, Prevent Blindness America estimates that 2,000 eye injuries occur every day in occupational settings.[32] Organizations can prevent such injuries through a combination of job analysis, written policies, safety training, protective eyewear, rewards and sanctions for safe and unsafe behavior, and management support for the safety effort. Similar practices for preventing other types of injuries are available in trade publications, through the National Safety Council, and on the Web site of the Occupational Safety and Health Administration (www.osha.gov).

Promoting Safety Internationally

Given the increasing focus on international management, organizations also need to consider how to ensure the safety of their employees regardless of the nation in which they operate. Cultural differences may make this more difficult than it seems. For example, a study examined the impact of one standardized corporationwide safety pol-

E-HRM

REEBOK APPLICATION TO SHED LIGHT ON WORKING CONDITIONS

As U.S. marketers of clothing and other products have arranged to have more and more goods produced in Asia, critics have charged that the employees who produce these goods often work in unsafe, unhealthful conditions. But even companies that want higher standards have difficulty ensuring that the factories comply. Under the leadership of chief technology officer Peter Burrows, Reebok created a solution: what it calls the Human Rights Tracking System. This software collects information about the factories supplying Reebok, ranging from their use of child labor to their air quality and number of fire escapes.

Managers can compare the data against their standards to make sure they are using contractors that at least meet minimal standards.

Other businesses have been interested in the software, so Burrows set up a nonprofit organization, the Fair Factories Clearinghouse. Reebok donated the software to the project, and other companies pay a subscription fee to use it. An advantage of using the clearinghouse is that garment makers often sign contracts with the same factories, so they can pool their information to avoid suppliers with a record of violating safety standards or human rights. In addition, under differ-

ent company programs, inspectors sometimes visit a factory repeatedly for different buyers. Sharing information online is more efficient. With regard to protecting human rights, says Burrows, "In this area of our business, we should collaborate, not compete." Ideally, the factories would be the ones competing to show that they can meet safety standards.

SOURCE: Scott Kirsner, "Reebok Offers Help Fighting Overseas Abuse," *Boston Globe*, January 17, 2005, www.boston. com; and Fair Factories Clearinghouse, "Fair Factories Clearinghouse Created to Support Compliance with Workplace Conditions in Factories," news release, January 13, 2005, www.fairfactories.org.

icy on employees in three different countries: the United States, France, and Argentina. The results of this study indicate that employees in the three countries interpreted the policy differently because of cultural differences. The individualistic, control-oriented culture of the United States stressed the role of top management in ensuring safety in a top-down fashion. However, this policy failed to work in Argentina, where the culture is more "collectivist" (emphasizing the group). Argentine employees tend to feel that safety is everyone's joint concern, so the safety programs needed to be defined from the bottom of the organization up.[33]

Another challenge in promoting safety internationally is that laws, enforcement practices, and political climates vary from country to country. With the increasing use of offshoring, described in Chapter 2, more companies have operations in countries where labor standards are far less strict than U.S. standards. Managers and employees in these countries may not think the company is serious about protecting workers' health and safety. In that case, strong communication and oversight will be necessary if the company intends to adhere to the ethical principle of valuing its foreign workers' safety as much as the safety of its U.S. workers. (The "e-HRM" box describes an innovation that may help with such efforts.) In an extreme example, Unocal Corporation recently settled a lawsuit in which people near a natural-gas pipeline in Myanmar (formerly Burma) said they were forced into slave labor and victimized by other crimes, including rape by soldiers guarding the pipeline. Unocal—which has since been acquired by ChevronTexaco—was one partner in the pipeline venture and agreed it would compensate those who sued and also contribute to aid programs providing health care and education in the region.[34] Although this type of situation might be unthinkable in North America, companies that wish to operate globally have to consider the extent to which they have ethical as well as legal obligations toward their workers and communities.

thinking ETHICALLY

Gays and Lesbians in the Picture at Eastman Kodak

Companies that promote diversity emphasize hiring, training, and retention of people in the classes protected by laws providing for equal employment opportunity. Some companies take diversity efforts further. For example, Eastman Kodak Company has made efforts to provide a harassment-free workplace for gay, lesbian, bisexual, and transgender employees (called GLBT employees for short). The company determined that GLBT employees often felt uncomfortable, so it provides diversity training and other efforts to make sure that these employees feel safe and respected. The programs are voluntary and part of the company's broader strategy called Winning and Inclusive Culture, which promotes teamwork and respect.

A recent survey by marketing firm Witeck-Combs Communications and pollster Harris Interactive found that 40 percent of those who identified themselves as GLBT employees felt fairly treated, but almost one-fourth of heterosexuals said they would be uncomfortable working with GLBT coworkers. In addition, some consumer groups boycott companies that have domestic-partner benefits or other diversity programs promoting tolerance of homosexual employees. However, Kodak executives maintain that fair treatment of gay employees makes the company more appealing to 15 million gay consumers. According to David Kassnoff, Kodak's manager of communications and public relations, praise for the company's efforts has "far outweighed" the few negative e-mails and limited public criticism generated by extending diversity programs to GLBT employees.

Source: Todd Henneman, "Acceptance of Gays, Lesbians Is a Big Part of Kodak's Diversity Picture," *Workforce Management*, December 2004, pp. 68–70.

Questions

1. How does including GLBT employees in Kodak's diversity program affect Kodak's customers? Its investors? Its workforce?
2. Is Kodak's policy toward GLBT employees good business? Is it good ethics? Should a company pursue a diversity policy that goes beyond legal requirements?

SUMMARY

1. Explain how the three branches of government regulate human resource management.
   The legislative branch develops laws such as those governing equal employment opportunity and worker safety and health. The executive branch establishes agencies such as the Equal Employment Opportunity Commission and Occupational Safety and Health Administration to enforce the laws by publishing regu-

lations, filing lawsuits, and other activities. The president may also issue executive orders, such as requirements for federal contractors. The judicial branch hears cases related to employment law and interprets the law.

2. Summarize the major federal laws requiring equal employment opportunity.
The Civil Rights Acts of 1866 and 1871 granted all persons equal property rights, contract rights, and the right to sue in federal court if they have been deprived of civil rights. The Equal Pay Act of 1963 requires equal pay for men and women who are doing work that is equal in terms of skill, effort, responsibility, and working conditions. Title VII of the Civil Rights Act of 1964 prohibits employment discrimination on the basis of race, color, religion, sex, or national origin. The Age Discrimination in Employment Act prohibits employment discrimination against persons older than 40. The Vocational Rehabilitation Act of 1973 requires that federal contractors engage in affirmative action in the employment of persons with disabilities. The Vietnam Era Veteran's Readjustment Act of 1974 requires affirmative action in employment of veterans who served during the Vietnam War. The Pregnancy Discrimination Act of 1978 treats discrimination based on pregnancy-related conditions as illegal sex discrimination. The Americans with Disabilities Act requires reasonable accommodations for qualified workers with disabilities. The Civil Rights Act of 1991 provides for compensatory and punitive damages in cases of discrimination. The Uniformed Services Employment and Reemployment Rights Act of 1994 requires that employers reemploy service members who left jobs to fulfill military duties.

3. Identify the federal agencies that enforce equal employment opportunity, and describe the role of each.
The Equal Employment Opportunity Commission is responsible for enforcing most of the EEO laws, including Title VII and the Americans with Disabilities Act. It investigates and resolves complaints, gathers information, and issues guidelines. The Office of Federal Contract Compliance Procedures is responsible for enforcing executive orders that call for affirmative action by companies that do business with the federal government. It monitors affirmative-action plans and takes action against companies that fail to comply.

4. Describe ways employers can avoid illegal discrimination and provide reasonable accommodation.
Employers can avoid discrimination by avoiding disparate treatment of job applicants and employees, as well as policies that result in disparate impact.

Companies can develop and enforce an EEO policy coupled with policies and practices that demonstrate a high value placed on diversity. Affirmative action may correct past discrimination, but quota-based activities can result in charges of reverse discrimination. To provide reasonable accommodation, companies should recognize needs based on individuals' religion or disabilities. Employees may need to make such accommodations as adjusting schedules or dress codes, making the workplace more accessible, or restructuring jobs.

5. Define sexual harassment and tell how employers can eliminate or minimize it.
Sexual harassment is unwelcome sexual advances and related behavior that makes submitting to the conduct a term of employment or the basis for employment decisions, or that interferes with an individual's work performance or creates a work environment that is intimidating, hostile, or offensive. Organizations can prevent sexual harassment by developing a policy that defines and forbids it, training employees to recognize and avoid this behavior, and providing a means for employees to complain and be protected.

6. Explain employers' duties under the Occupational Safety and Health Act.
Under the Occupational Safety and Health Act, employers have a general duty to provide employees a place of employment free from recognized safety and health hazards. They must inform employees about hazardous substances, maintain and post records of accidents and illnesses, and comply with NIOSH standards about specific occupational hazards.

7. Describe the role of the Occupational Safety and Health Administration.
The Occupational Safety and Health Administration publishes regulations and conducts inspections. If OSHA finds violations, it discusses them with the employer and monitors the employer's response in correcting the violation.

8. Discuss ways employers promote worker safety and health.
Besides complying with OSHA regulations, employers often establish safety awareness programs designed to instill an emphasis on safety. They may identify and communicate hazards through the job hazard analysis technique or the technic of operations review. They may adapt communications and training to the needs of different employees, such as differences in experience levels or cultural differences from one country to another. Employers may also establish incentive programs to reward safe behavior.

REVIEW AND DISCUSSION QUESTIONS

1. What is the role of each branch of the federal government with regard to equal employment opportunity?
2. For each of the following situations, identify one or more constitutional amendments, laws, or executive orders that might apply.
   a. A veteran of the Vietnam conflict experiences lower-back pain after sitting for extended periods of time. He has applied for promotion to a supervisory position that has traditionally involved spending most of the workday behind a desk.
   b. One of two female workers on a road construction crew complains to her supervisor that she feels uncomfortable during breaks, because the other employees routinely tell off-color jokes.
   c. A manager at an architectural firm receives a call from the local newspaper. The reporter wonders how the firm wishes to respond to calls from two of its employees alleging racial discrimination. About half of the firm's employees (including all of its partners and most of its architects) are white. One of the firm's clients is the federal government.
3. For each situation in the preceding question, what actions, if any, should the organization take?
4. The Americans with Disabilities Act requires that employers make reasonable accommodations for individuals with disabilities. How might this requirement affect law enforcement officers and fire fighters?
5. To identify instances of sexual harassment, the courts may use a "reasonable woman" standard of what constitutes offensive behavior. This standard is based on the idea that women and men have different ideas of what behavior is appropriate. What are the implications of this distinction? Do you think this distinction is helpful or harmful? Why?
6. Given that the "reasonable woman" standard referred to in Question 5 is based on women's ideas of what is appropriate, how might an organization with mostly male employees identify and avoid behavior that could be found to be sexual harassment?
7. What are an organization's basic duties under the Occupational Safety and Health Act?
8. OSHA penalties are aimed at employers, rather than employees. How does this affect employee safety?
9. How can organizations motivate employees to promote safety and health in the workplace?
10. For each of the following occupations, identify at least one possible hazard and at least one action employers could take to minimize the risk of an injury or illness related to that hazard.
   a. Worker in a fast-food restaurant
   b. Computer programmer
   c. Truck driver
   d. House painter

WHAT'S YOUR HR IQ?

The text Web site offers two more ways to check what you've learned so far. Use the Self-Assessment exercise to test your knowledge of equal employment opportunity. Go online with the Web Exercise to review the descriptions of employees' rights.

BusinessWeek CASE

BusinessWeek How Nissan Laps Detroit

Jonathan Gates slaps a wide slab of tan-colored, hard foam rubber on his workbench. He fastens a numbered tag in one corner and attaches black foam insulation at the edges. As soon as he puts a number on the piece of foam, which will become the top of a dashboard for a Nissan Quest minivan, the vehicle has an identity. All of the parts for a big chunk of the minivan's interior, decked out with the customer's choice of colors, fabrics, and options, will come together in the next 42 minutes.

Gates and his coworkers fill a crucial role at Nissan Motor Company's new Canton, Mississippi, assembly plant: Almost everything a driver touches inside a new Quest, Titan pickup, or Armada sport-utility vehicle is put together in a single module, starting at Gates's workbench. "This is the most important job," he says. And yet, amazingly, Gates doesn't even work for Nissan. He works for Lextron/Visteon Automotive Systems, a parts supplier that also builds the center console between the front seats and a subassembly of the car's front end. The finished modules pass over a wall to be bolted onto a car or truck body rolling down the assembly line. Lextron/Visteon does the work faster than Nissan could and pays $3 an hour less than the car maker pays assembly workers. Nissan is using a similar strategy for its vehicle frames, seats, electrical systems, and completed doors.

The Canton plant was designed with the same flexibility, shop-floor smarts, and management-dominated work rules that made Nissan's 20-year-old plant in Smyrna, Tennessee, the most productive factory in North America year after year. The Smyrna plant builds a car in just under 16 labor hours—6 fewer than the average Honda or Toyota plant, 8 fewer than GM, and 10 fewer than Ford. Its profit per vehicle is the best in North America.

The Canton plant, which opened in 2003, will almost certainly top that. Nissan's secret? Sure, its plants use cheaper, nonunion labor. Besides lower wages and benefits, outsourcing offers huge savings. And Nissan's plants are far more flexible in adjusting to market twists and turns. Canton can send a minivan, pickup truck, or sport-utility vehicle down the same assembly line, one after the other, without interruption.

At first glance, a Nissan factory does not look much different from one you would see in Detroit or St. Louis. But talk to the workers, and it soon becomes clear how relentlessly the company squeezes mere seconds out of the assembly process. "There's no silver bullet," says Emil E. Hassan, Nissan's senior vice president of manufacturing. "It's really just following up every day with improvements."

On the Smyrna passenger-car line, for instance, a worker stands on a moving platform, called a lineside limo, that inches along the body of an Xterra SUV. The limo carries all the tools and parts he needs. The assembler grabs a seat belt from a bin next to him, bolts it in, then moves along and installs the rear struts—all without having to make what used to be a 20-foot walk back and forth, three times per car.

Nissan runs a tight ship and works its employees harder than Detroit's Big Three auto companies. During the United Auto Workers' failed attempt to organize Smyrna in 2001, workers told the union that line speeds were too fast and people were getting injured, says Bob King, the UAW's vice president of organizing. The union says that in 2001, Nissan reported 31 injuries per 1,000 workers—twice the average at Big Three plants—according to logs reported to the Occupational Safety and Health Administration.

Nissan does not dispute the OSHA figures, but it denies its assembly lines are any less safe than Detroit's. Although the company won't release current numbers, executives do say that they have taken steps to reduce injuries. For instance, the company has workers do four different jobs during a typical eight-hour shift, to try to cut down on repetitive-motion injuries. Nissan claims that injury rates have fallen 60 percent in the past two years.

As for the finished product, the real test is still to come for Nissan. The company has yet to prove that the popularity of its Altima and G35 Infiniti sedans can carry over to minivans, big pickups, and big SUVs. But at least in terms of efficiency, each new Nissan is rolling off the line with a huge head start.

Source: David Welch, "How Nissan Laps Detroit," *BusinessWeek*, December 22, 2003, downloaded from Infotrac at http://web5.infotrac.galegroup.com.

QUESTIONS

1. Why are fast assembly lines important for achieving Nissan's goals? Can a company that cares about speed also care about safety?
2. If you worked in the human resource department for the Canton factory, how could you encourage the company to improve its safety record? What kinds of information would you want to present to back up your ideas?
3. Suggest a few general ways the company could improve safety at the Canton facility.

CASE: Did Marubeni America Discriminate in Reverse?

Recently, two white managers sued their employer, Marubeni America Corporation, for racial discrimination. The managers, Kevin Long and Ludvic Presto, claimed that the company paid higher salaries and bonuses to its Japanese and Asian executives. Marubeni, a subsidiary of a Japanese company that brokers international trades, denied the charges. The company, headquartered in New York City, sets up and carries out trade deals for industrial, agricultural, and consumer goods.

According to the lawsuit, Marubeni discriminated against Americans, non-Asian minorities, and women by paying them less, promoting them less often, and terminating them more readily than Asians. Numbers offered in support of this argument showed that out of the 121 top officers and managers of the 200-worker company, Marubeni has no African Americans or females and one Hispanic manager. Of the total employees, three are black. Besides these numbers, the lawsuit complains about the work environment. Allegedly, weekly management meetings were conducted in Japanese, which prevented employees from participating if they did not know the language. Also, the suit complains that some executives often used ethnic and racial slurs and that Presto was once denied permission to hire an African American woman because "we cannot hire a black person."

Long and Presto further contend that they were victims of retaliation. They say that when Long, a human resource manager, and Presto, the company's top auditor, complained about fraud, discrimination, and violations of immigration laws, the company placed them on administrative leave. Their lawyers assert that this response amounted to illegal retaliation for complaining about discrimination. The lawsuit requests millions in severance pay, pension and other benefits, and damages and legal costs. The company responded that it believes the lawsuit is merely a way for Long and Presto to obtain generous severance packages.

Evidence that may make the defense more difficult includes e-mail messages with guidelines that seem to be at odds with equal-employment opportunity requirements. For example, Long received a request from the vice president of the company's U.S. textile unit to hire a bright, aggressive salesperson, stating, "We prefer male and 25–30 years old, Asian like Chinese, Japanese, of course American or others is fine." The vice president elaborated, "As you know, in case of American guy, once reach income, all of a sudden stop working." Long also received a message about the possibility of replacing a pregnant employee because of concerns "about her unstable situation after the delivery." Long replied that such grounds for dismissal were inappropriate and illegal in the United States.

In the past, when Japanese companies operating in the United States have been sued for discrimination, the companies have argued they are exempt because of a 1953 treaty in which the United States and Japan gave the corporations of each other's country immunity from the other country's employment discrimination laws. In 1982, the Supreme Court rejected this argument because the company, Sumitomo, was a U.S. subsidiary, meaning it operated as a U.S. company owned by another company, which was Japanese. But in a later case, which the Supreme Court declined to hear, an appeals court exempted Uniden America Corporation, a U.S. subsidiary, because the discrimination favored Japanese citizens originally hired by the Japanese parent company.

Commenting on the Marubeni lawsuit, Sarah Crawford of the nonpartisan Lawyers Committee for Civil Rights under Law said it was unusual but such claims could become more common: "From what I've seen, it's a growing concern because of the increasing presence of multinational corporations" in the United States. Whatever the outcome of this lawsuit, it raises important issues for human resource management in our global economy.

Source: Kara Scannell, "Lawsuit Charges U.S. Unit of Japanese Company with Bias," *The Wall Street Journal*, January 20, 2005, pp. B1–B2; Seana K. Magee, "Caucasian Employees Sue Marubeni for Bias, Seek $65 Million," *Kyodo News International*, January 20, 2005, downloaded from Infotrac at http://web4.infotrac.galegroup.com; and Marubeni America Corporation, "About Us," www.marubeni-usa.com, accessed April 6, 2005.

QUESTIONS

1. Based on the evidence described in this case, what legal and ethical problems at Marubeni America can you identify related to equal-employment opportunity? Name specific laws that might apply.

2. In today's global economy, you are more likely to work for a company based in another country. Imagine that you work in the human resource department of a foreign-owned company, and describe how you might explain to foreign management why they should avoid discrimination.

3. The case quotes a Marubeni vice president's request to hire a salesperson with particular qualities. Pretend that the memo was written to you, and write an e-mail response that addresses the vice president's concerns and explains what you can legally do. Can you think of a legal course of action that would also meet this executive's business interests?

NOTES

1. Frank Jossi, "Cultivating Diversity," *Human Resource Executive*, December 2004, pp. 37–40.

2. *Bakke v. Regents of the University of California*, 17 F.E.P.C. 1000 (1978).

3. Equal Employment Opportunity Commission, "Jury Finds Outback Steakhouse Guilty of Sex Discrimination and Illegal Retaliation; Awards Victim $2.2 Million," news release, September 19, 2001.

4. "Labor Letter," *The Wall Street Journal*, August 25, 1987, p. 1.

5. Henry Weinstein, "U.S. Charges Law Partnership with Age Bias," *Los Angeles Times*, January 20, 2005, downloaded at Yahoo News, http://story.news.yahoo.com.

6. Equal Employment Opportunity Commission, "Enforcement Statistics and Litigation," www.eeoc.gov, modified February 15, 2005.

7. Jan Crawford Greenburg, "Age-Bias Law Expanded," *Chicago Tribune*, March 31, 2005, sec. 1, pp. 1, 17; and Jess Bravin, "Court Expands Age Bias Claims for Work Force," *The Wall Street Journal*, March 31, 2005, http://online.wsj.com.

8. Joe Mullich, "New Ideas Draw Older Workers," *Workforce Management*, March 2004, www.workforce.com.

9. Equal Employment Opportunity Commission, "Pregnancy Discrimination," *Discrimination by Type: Facts and Guidance*, www.eeoc.gov, modified March 2, 2005.

10. "ADA: The Final Regulations (Title I): A Lawyer's Dream/An Employer's Nightmare," *Employment Law Update* 16, no. 9 (1991), p. 1; and Equal Employment Opportunity Commission, "The Americans with Disabilities Act: A Primer for Small Business," www.eeoc.gov, modified February 4, 2004.

11. "ADA Supervisor Training Program: A Must for Any Supervisor Conducting a Legal Job Interview," *Employment Law Update* 7, no. 6 (1992), pp. 1–6; and Equal Employment Opportunity Commission, "The ADA: Your Responsibilities as an Employer," www.eeoc.gov, modified March 21, 2005.

12. EEOC, "The Americans with Disabilities Act: A Primer for Small Business."

13. Jacqueline Fitzgerald, "Drawing the Line in Interviews," *Chicago Tribune*, February 20, 2002, sec. 8, p. 2.

14. *UAW v. Johnson Controls, Inc.*, 499 U.S. 187 (1991).

15. Greenburg, "Age-Bias Law Expanded"; and Bravin, "Court Expands Age Bias Claims."

16. D. Kravitz and J. Platania, "Attitudes and Beliefs about Affirmative Action: Effects of Target and of Respondent Sex and Ethnicity," *Journal of Applied Psychology* 78 (1993), pp. 928–38.

17. Equal Employment Opportunity Commission, "EEOC and Electrolux Reach Voluntary Resolution in Class Religious Accommodation Case," news release, September 24, 2003, www.eeoc.gov.

18. EEOC guideline based on the Civil Rights Act of 1964, Title VII.

19. Equal Employment Opportunity Commission, "Texas Car Dealership to Pay $140,000 to Settle Same-Sex Harassment Suit by EEOC," news release, October 28, 2002, www.eeoc.gov.

20. National Safety Council, "Waiters' Work Is Risky Business," *Safety and Health Magazine*, NSC Web site, www.nsc.org, September 2000.

21. Reuters Limited, "Healthcare Workers Risk Getting Asthma on the Job," *Yahoo News*, March 24, 2005, http://news.yahoo.com.

22. Bureau of Labor Statistics, "Injuries, Illnesses, and Fatalities," www.bls.gov/iif/, accessed April 4, 2005; and Occupational Health and Safety Administration, "Statement of Labor Secretary Elaine L. Chao on Historic Lows in Workplace Injury and Illness," OSHA Web site, www.osha.gov, December 18, 2001.

23. J. Roughton, "Managing a Safety Program through Job Hazard Analysis," *Professional Safety* 37 (1992), pp. 28–31.

24. M. A. Verespec, "OSHA Reform Fails Again," *Industry Week*, November 2, 1992, p. 36.

25. Roughton, "Managing a Safety Program."

26. R. G. Hallock and D. A. Weaver, "Controlling Losses and Enhancing Management Systems with TOR Analysis," *Professional Safety* 35 (1990), pp. 24–26.

27. Douglas P. Shuit, "A Left Turn for Safety," *Workforce Management*, March 2005, pp. 49–50.

28. Sandy Smith, "Protecting Vulnerable Workers," *Occupational Hazards*, April 2004, downloaded from Infotrac at http://web5.infotrac.galegroup.com.

29. Ibid.

30. J. F. Mangan, "Hazard Communications: Safety in Knowledge," *Best's Review* 92 (1991), pp. 84–88.

31. R. King, "Active Safety Programs, Education Can Help Prevent Back Injuries," *Occupational Health and Safety* 60 (1991), pp. 49–52.

32. Prevent Blindness America, "2,000 Employees Suffer Work-Related Eye Injuries Every Day in the United States," news release, March 1, 2005, downloaded at www.preventblindness.org.

33. M. Janssens, J. M. Brett, and F. J. Smith, "Confirmatory Cross-Cultural Research: Testing the Viability of a Corporation-wide Safety Policy," *Academy of Management Journal* 38 (1995), pp. 364–82.

34. "Unocal Settles Four Lawsuits over Alleged Myanmar Abuses," *The Wall Street Journal*, March 21, 2005, http://online.wsj.com; and Marc Lifsher, "Unocal Settles Human Rights Lawsuit over Alleged Abuses at Myanmar Pipeline," *Los Angeles Times*, March 22, 2005, http://news.yahoo.com.

If you are using the Manager's Hot Seat DVD with this book, consider finishing case 1: Office Romance: Groping for Answers, for this chapter.

CHAPTER 4

ANALYZING WORK AND DESIGNING JOBS

After reading this chapter, you should be able to:

What Do I Need to Know?

1. Summarize the elements of work flow analysis.

2. Describe how work flow is related to an organization's structure.

3. Define the elements of a job analysis, and discuss their significance for human resource management.

4. Tell how to obtain information for a job analysis.

5. Summarize recent trends in job analysis.

6. Describe methods for designing a job so that it can be done efficiently.

7. Identify approaches to designing a job to make it motivating.

8. Explain how organizations apply ergonomics to design safe jobs.

9. Discuss how organizations can plan for the mental demands of a job.

❋ INTRODUCTION

Teach for America, a national organization that encourages college graduates to take teaching jobs in inner-city schools, received three times as many applications in 2001 as in the year before. Since then, the number of applications has continued to grow, reaching a record 17,000 applicants for the 2005 program. Elissa Clapp, the organization's vice president of recruitment and selection, says that one reason is a teacher's ability to make a difference in the lives of others: "People are seeking to ensure that all parts of their lives—professional as well as personal—are fulfilling and meaningful." Kay McElroy, a high school teacher and mother, sees another attraction: a work schedule that matches her children's school schedule. Along with the academic schedule and the ability to make a difference in children's lives comes a job that combines great responsibility with an administrative trend toward greater oversight of school performance. Teachers must plan lessons that meet wide differences in skill levels and learning styles, and their success is regularly evaluated with a battery of standardized tests administered to their students. Typically, the result is a workload that extends beyond classroom hours and walls. For Carrie McGill, who teaches in Albuquerque, New Mexico, "There are so many rules and so many guidelines these days, I don't feel like I can just walk in and know it." The paperwork piled in the back of her 10-year-old Saab makes the car an extension of her workplace.[1]

Heavy responsibility, duties that range from planning to paperwork to inspiring children, and a work schedule that runs from September to June-all these are elements of the teacher's job. These elements give rise to the types of skills and personalities required for success, and they in turn help to narrow the field of people who will succeed at teaching. Consideration of such elements is at the heart of analyzing work, whether in a school district or a multinational corporation.

This chapter discusses the analysis and design of work and, in doing so, lays out some considerations that go into making informed decisions about how to create and link jobs. The chapter begins with a look at the big-picture issues related to analyzing work flow and organizational structure. The discussion then turns to the more specific issues of analyzing and designing jobs. Traditionally, job analysis has emphasized the study of existing jobs in order to make decisions such as employee selection, training, and compensation. In contrast, job design has emphasized making jobs more efficient or more motivating. However, as this chapter shows, the two activities are interrelated.

⬧ WORK FLOW IN ORGANIZATIONS

Informed decisions about jobs take place in the context of the organization's overall work flow. Through the process of **work flow design,** managers analyze the tasks needed to produce a product or service. With this information, they assign these tasks to specific jobs and positions. (A **job** is a set of related duties. A **position** is the set of duties performed by one person. A school has many teaching *positions*; the person filling each of those positions is performing the *job* of teacher.) Basing these decisions on work flow design can lead to better results than the more traditional practice of looking at jobs individually.

work flow design
The process of analyzing the tasks necessary for the production of a product or service.

position
The set of duties (job) performed by a particular person.

job
A set of related duties.

Work Flow Analysis

Before designing its work flow, the organization's planners need to analyze what work needs to be done. Figure 4.1 shows the elements of a work flow analysis. For each type of work, such as producing a product line or providing a support service (accounting, legal support, and so on), the analysis identifies the output of the process, the activities involved, and three categories of inputs: raw inputs (materials and information), equipment, and human resources.

Outputs are the products of any work unit, whether a department, team, or individual. An output can be as readily identifiable as a completed purchase order, an employment test, or a hot, juicy hamburger. An output can also be a service, such as transportation, cleaning, or answering questions about employee benefits. Even at an organization that produces tangible goods, such as computers, many employees produce other outputs, such as components of the computers, marketing plans, and building security. Work flow analysis identifies the outputs of particular work units. The analysis considers not only the amount of output but also quality standards. This attention to outputs has only recently gained attention among HRM professionals. However, it gives a clearer view of how to increase the effectiveness of each work unit.

For the outputs identified, work flow analysis then examines the work processes used to generate those outputs. Work processes are the activities that members of a work unit engage in to produce a given output. Every process consists of operating procedures that specify how things should be done at each stage of developing the output. These procedures include all the tasks that must be performed in producing

LO1
Summarize the elements of work flow analysis.

figure 4.1

Developing a Work-
Unit Activity Analysis

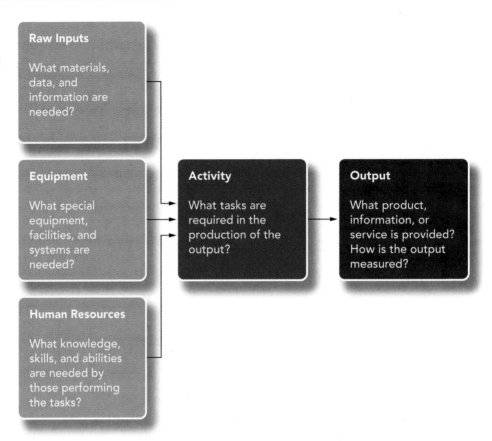

the output. Usually, the analysis breaks down the tasks into those performed by each person in the work unit. This analysis helps with design of efficient work systems by clarifying which tasks are necessary. Typically, when a unit's work load increases, the unit adds people, and when the work load decreases, some members of the unit may busy themselves with unrelated tasks in an effort to appear busy. Without knowledge of work processes, it is more difficult to identify whether the work unit is properly staffed. Knowledge of work processes also can guide staffing changes when work is automated or outsourced. At Unifi, a textile producer, high-speed data lines send shop-floor data in real time to analysts at the company's headquarters. Unifi no longer requires supervisors to carry out the tasks of monitoring and reporting on production.[2]

The final stage in work flow analysis is to identify the inputs used in the development of the work unit's product. As shown in Figure 4.1, these inputs can be broken down into the raw inputs (materials and knowledge), equipment, and human skills needed to perform the tasks. Makers of athletic shoes need nylon and leather, shoe-making machinery, and workers to operate the machinery, among other inputs. Nike and Reebok minimize the cost of inputs by subcontracting manufacturing to factories in countries where wages are low. In contrast, New Balance Athletic Shoes operates a factory in Norridgewock, Maine, where modern technology and worker training enable the company to afford U.S. workers. Teams of employees use automated equipment that operates over 20 sewing machines simultaneously. The employees are cross-trained in all tasks. The highly efficient factory produces shoes much faster than a typical Chinese shoe factory.[3]

Firefighters work as a team. They and their equipment are the "inputs" (they do the work), and the "output" is an extinguished fire and the rescue of people and pets. In any organization or team, workers need to be cross-trained in several skills to create an effective team. If these firefighters are trained to do any part of the job, the chief can deploy them rapidly as needed.

Work Flow Design and Organization's Structure

Besides looking at the work flow of each process, it is important to see how the work fits within the context of the organization's structure. Within an organization, units and individuals must cooperate to create outputs. Ideally, the organization's structure brings together the people who must collaborate in order to efficiently produce the desired outputs. The structure may do this in a way that is highly centralized (that is, with authority concentrated in a few people at the top of the organizaton) or decentralized (with authority spread among many people). The organization may group jobs according to functions (for example, welding, painting, packaging), or it may set up divisions to focus on products or customer groups.

Although there are an infinite number of ways to combine the elements of an organization's structure, we can make some general observations about structure and work design. If the structure is strongly based on function, workers tend to have low authority and to work alone at highly specialized jobs. Jobs that involve teamwork or broad responsibility tend to require a structure based on divisions other than functions. When the goal is to empower employees, companies therefore need to set up structures and jobs that enable broad responsibility, such as jobs that involve employees in serving a particular group of customers or producing a particular product, rather than performing a narrowly defined function. An extreme example would be W. L. Gore, described in the "Best Practices" box. The organization's structure also affects managers' jobs. Managing a division responsible for a product or customer group tends to require more experience and cognitive (thinking) ability than managing a department that handles a particular function.[4]

Work design often emphasizes the analysis and design of jobs, as described in the remainder of this chapter. Although all of these approaches can succeed, each focuses on one isolated job at a time. These approaches do not necessarily consider how that single job fits into the overall work flow or structure of the organization. To use these techniques effectively, human resources personnel should also understand their organization as a whole. Without this big-picture appreciation, they might redesign a job in a way that makes sense for the particular job but is out of line with the organization's work flow, structure, or strategy.

❧ JOB ANALYSIS

To achieve high-quality performance, organizations have to understand and match job requirements and people. This understanding requires **job analysis,** the process of getting detailed information about jobs. Analyzing jobs and understanding what is required to carry out a job provide essential knowledge for staffing, training, performance

LO2
Describe how work flow is related to an organization's structure.

LO3
Define the elements of a job analysis, and discuss their significance for human resource management.

job analysis
The process of getting detailed information about jobs.

JOBS WITHOUT TITLES PROMOTE INNOVATION AT W. L. GORE

When *Fast Company* magazine set out to find an innovative company, they eliminated some of the biggest contenders and settled on W. L. Gore & Associates, best known for creating Gore-Tex fabrics. Besides Gore-Tex, the company makes fabrics for such tough applications as clothing for soldiers and astronauts. It also makes medical products, air pollution filters, and hundreds of other items as diverse as dental floss and guitar strings. In fact, the company thrives on innovation: Gore employees are urged to look everywhere for opportunities to make something better than what is currently on the market.

How do you structure work when the commitment is to creativity? Structure might seem to stifle creativity, but Gore's work design is actually extremely flexible. The organizational structure is remarkably flat, with communication rather than formal authority as the basis for getting work done. Gore is organized into four broad product divisions, each with a division leader, but most employees don't have job titles. The only way to know who is doing what is to learn what

everyone does. The company keeps facilities small (factories contain up to 200 people) so that people can learn each other's skills and knowledge.

The experience of Diane Davidson illustrates how this type of work design affects people. The company hired her for its Citywear project, applying Gore-Tex fabrics to clothing designs suitable for office or party wear. From her experience in the hierarchical men's-shoe business, Davidson found the freedom of Gore confusing at first. She was assigned to a mentor, who discouraged her repeated questions about who her boss was. Eventually, Davidson concluded, "Your team is your boss, because you don't want to let them down." She figured out that people didn't need strict titles and job descriptions because their work was guided by whatever commitment they had made to their team— commitments that might bring together several functions, such as sales and product design.

Davidson and others find that this work design requires patience to learn team members' skills and roles. John

Mongan, who has participated in several Gore teams, says the first job on a new team is to spend a few months getting to know the team. He adds, "It takes 18 months to build credibility. Early on, it's really frustrating. In hindsight, it makes sense."

This flat structure with limited formal job design could stop a routine company in its tracks. But Gore is far from routine. It hires talented people and then enables them to draw on the best of each other's skills to produce one high-value product after another. As they gain skills, employees are expected to find new roles in which they can apply their additional skills. Because Gore is a privately held company (not traded on the stock market), it doesn't publish the financial statements used to compare businesses' success. But its growing product line, increasing payroll, and satisfied customers and employees testify to the company's success.

SOURCE: Alan Deutschman, "The Fabric of Creativity," *Fast Company,* December 2004, pp. 54–55, 58–62.

appraisal, and many other HR activities. For instance, a supervisor's evaluation of an employee's work should be based on performance relative to job requirements. In very small organizations, line managers may perform a job analysis, but usually the work is done by a human resource professional. A large company may have a compensation management department that includes job analysts (also called personnel analysts). Organizations may also contract with firms that provide this service.

Job Descriptions

An essential part of job analysis is the creation of job descriptions. A **job description** is a list of the tasks, duties, and responsibilities (TDRs) that a job entails. TDRs are observable actions. For example, a news photographer's job requires the jobholder to use a camera to take photographs. If you were to observe someone in that position for a day, you would almost certainly see some pictures being taken. When a manager attempts to evaluate job performance, it is most important to have detailed information about the work performed in the job (that is, the TDRs). This information makes it possible to determine how well an individual is meeting each job requirement.

A job description typically has the format shown in Figure 4.2. It includes the job title, a brief description of the TDRs, and a list of the essential duties with detailed specifications of the tasks involved in carrying out each duty. Although organizations may modify this format according to their particular needs, all job descriptions within an organization should follow the same format. This helps the organization make consistent decisions about such matters as pay and promotions. It also helps the organization show that it makes human resource decisions fairly.

Whenever the organization creates a new job, it needs to prepare a job description, using a process such as the one detailed in the "HR How To" box nearby. Job descriptions should then be reviewed periodically (say, once a year) and updated if necessary. Performance appraisals can provide a good opportunity for updating job descriptions, as the employee and supervisor compare what the employee has been doing against the details of the job description.

When organizations prepare many job descriptions, the process can become repetitive and time consuming. To address this challenge, a number of companies have devel-

job description
A list of the tasks, duties, and responsibilities (TDRs) that a particular job entails.

Figure 4.2

Sample Job Description

Sales Associate

Customer service and interaction with customers are key responsibilities of this position. A sales associate must work effectively with customers and other store associates and provide information about products and/or projects. This position also involves stocking merchandise, using tools and equipment, and maintenance duties (e.g., sweeping aisles, down-stocking shelves, etc.).

Major Tasks and Responsibilities
- Presenting a consistent, pleasant, and service-oriented image to customers
- Listening and asking appropriate questions to assist customers in completing projects
- Assisting and working with other store associates in order to complete job tasks
- Using computers, phones, and other equipment
- Cleaning and maintaining shelves, end caps, and aisles

SOURCE: "Retail Careers by Title," Home Depot Web site, www.homedepot.com, April 2, 2002.

HR HOW TO

WRITING A JOB DESCRIPTION

Preparing a job description begins with gathering information from sources who can identify the details of performing a task. These sources may include persons already performing the job and the supervisor, team leader, or, if the job is new, managers who are creating the new position. Asking the purpose of the new position can provide insight into what the company expects this person to accomplish. Besides people, sources of information may include the company's human resource files, such as past job advertisements and job descriptions, as well as general sources of information about similar jobs, such as O*NET (http://online. onetcenter.org).

There are several ways to gather information about the duties of a job:

- Employees can fill out a questionnaire that asks about what they do or complete a diary that details their activities over several days.

- A job analyst can visit the workplace and watch or videotape an employee performing the job. This method is most appropriate for jobs that are repetitive and involve physical activity.
- A job analyst can visit the workplace and ask an employee to show what the job entails. This method is most appropriate for clerical and technical jobs.
- A manager or supervisor can describe what a person holding the job must do to be successful. What would the job holder's outputs be? Would customers have clear answers to their questions? Would decision makers in the organization have accurate and timely data from this person? The analyst can identify the activities necessary to create these outputs.
- A supervisor or job analyst can review company records related to performing the job—for example, work

orders or summaries of customer calls. These records can show the kinds of problems a person solves in the course of doing a job.

After gathering information, the next step is to list all the activities and evaluate which are essential duties. One way to do this is to rate all the duties on a scale of 1 to 5, where 1 is most important. A rating scale also could rank the tasks according to how much time the person spends on them. Perhaps the ratings will show that some tasks are desirable but not essential.

Gathering information from many sources helps to verify which tasks are essential. Perhaps the job holder is aware of some activities that others do not notice. In other cases, the job holder might perform activities that are merely habits or holdovers from a time when they were essential. When people analyzing a job come to different conclusions about which

oped software that provides forms into which the job analyst can insert details about the specific job. Typically, the job analyst would use a library of basic descriptions, selecting one that is for a similar type of job and then modifying it to fit the organization's needs.

Organizations should give each newly hired employee a copy of his or her job description. This helps the employee to understand what is expected, but it shouldn't be presented as limiting the employee's commitment to quality and customer satisfaction. Ideally, employees will want to go above and beyond the listed duties when the situation and their abilities call for that. Many job descriptions include the phrase activities are essential, the person writing the job description should compare the listed activities with the company's goals and work flow to see which are essential. A group discussion also may help categorize tasks as essential, ideal, and unnecessary.

From these sources, the writer of the job description obtains the important elements of the description:

- *Title of the job*—The title should be descriptive and, if appropriate, indicate the job's level in the organization by using terms such as *junior, senior, assistant,* and *executive.*
- *Administrative information about the job*—Depending on the company's size and requirements, the job description may identify a division, department, supervisor's title, date of the analysis, name of the analyst, and other information for administering the company's human resource activities.
- *Summary of the job, focusing on its purpose and duties*— This summary should be brief and as specific as possible, including types of responsibilities, tools and equipment used, and level of authority (for example, the degree of authority and responsibility of the job holder—how much the person is supervised and how much the person supervises others or participates in teamwork).
- *Essential duties of the job*— These should be listed in order of importance to successful performance of the job and should include details such as physical requirements (for example, the amount of weight to be lifted), the persons with whom an employee in this job interacts, and the results to be accomplished. This section should include only duties that the job analysis identified as essential.
- *Additional responsibilities*— The job description may have a section stating that the position requires additional responsibilities as requested by the supervisor.
- *Job specifications*—The specifications cover the knowledge, skills, abilities, and other characteristics required for a person to be qualified to perform the job successfully. These may appear at the end of the job description or as a separate document.

SOURCE: D. B. Bordeaux, "Writing Job Descriptions," *Motor Age,* November 2001, downloaded from Findarticles.com; "Job Descriptions and the ADA," HRNext, www.hrnext.com, downloaded March 7, 2002; "Simple Job Analysis," HRNext, www.hrnext.com, downloaded March 7, 2002; C. Joinson, "Refocusing Job Descriptions," *HR Magazine,* January 2001, downloaded from Findarticles.com; and Lou Adler, "Know What You're Looking For," *Inc.com,* March 2005, www.inc.com.

and other duties as requested as a way to remind employees not to tell their supervisor, "But that's not part of my job."

Job Specifications

Whereas the job description focuses on the activities involved in carrying out a job, a **job specification** looks at the qualities of the person performing the job. It is a list of the knowledge, skills, abilities, and other characteristics (KSAOs) that an individual must have to perform the job. *Knowledge* refers to factual or procedural information

job specification
A list of the knowledge, skills, abilities, and other characteristics (KSAOs) that an individual must have to perform a particular job.

that is necessary for successfully performing a task. For example, this course is providing you with knowledge in how to manage human resources. A *skill* is an individual's level of proficiency at performing a particular task—that is, the capability to perform it well. With knowledge and experience, you could acquire skill in the task of preparing job specifications. *Ability*, in contrast to skill, refers to a more general enduring capability that an individual possesses. A person might have the ability to cooperate with others or to write clearly and precisely. Finally, *other characteristics* might be personality traits such as someone's persistence or motivation to achieve. Some jobs also have legal requirements, such as licensing or certification. Figure 4.3 is a set of sample job specifications for the job description in Figure 4.2.

In developing job specifications, it is important to consider all of the elements of KSAOs. As with writing a job description, the information can come from a combination of people performing the job, people supervising or planning for the job, and trained job analysts. At Acxiom Corporation, job specifications are based on an analysis of employees' roles and competencies (what they must be able to do), stated in terms of behaviors. To reach these definitions, groups studied what the company's good performers were doing and looked for the underlying abilities. For example, according to Jeff Standridge, Acxiom's organizational development leader, they might ask a panel about a high-performing software developer, and panel members might identify the employee's knowledge of the Java and C++ programming languages. Then, Standridge says, the job analysts would probe for the abilities behind this knowledge: "When we asked, 'If Java becomes obsolete in five years, will this person no longer be successful?' the panel responded, 'Oh no, he'll update his skills and be

Figure 4.3

Sample Job Specifications

> **Sales Associate**
>
> Major Skills and Competencies
> * Customer Focus: Ability to maintain a positive customer service orientation when dealing with customers on the phone and in person
> * Stress Tolerance: Ability to work effectively under stressful work conditions (e.g., dealing with multiple customers who need help quickly)
> * Teamwork: Ability to work well with others to achieve common goals
> * Listening/Communicating: Ability to listen attentively to others, ask appropriate questions, and speak in a clear and understandable manner
>
> Minimum Job Requirements
> * 18 years or older
> * Pass a drug test
> * Be able to work a flexible schedule including weekends, evenings, and holidays
> * Pass a sales associate test

SOURCE: "Retail Careers by Title," Home Depot Web site, www.homedepot.com, April 2, 2002.

figure 4.4

Does This Player Have the Right KSAOs to Succeed?

great in the new language.' . . . The employee's strength was not just in his specific skills but in his ability to learn."[5] On a less serious level, the cartoon in Figure 4.4 shows a young team member who seems to have an abundance of basketball skills but a limited supply of other desirable characteristics, such as an orientation toward teamwork.

In contrast to tasks, duties, and responsibilities, KSAOs are characteristics of people and are not directly observable. They are observable only when individuals are carrying out the TDRs of the job—and afterward, if they can show the product of their labor. Thus, if someone applied for a job as a news photographer, you could not simply look at the individual to determine whether he or she can spot and take effective photographs. However, you could draw conclusions later about the person's skills by looking at examples of his or her photographs.

Accurate information about KSAOs is especially important for making decisions about who will fill a job. A manager attempting to fill a position needs information about the characteristics required, and about the characteristics of each applicant. Interviews and selection decisions should therefore focus on KSAOs. In the earlier example of computer programming at Acxiom, the company would look for someone who knows the computer languages currently used, but also has a track record of taking the initiative to learn new computer languages as they are developed.

Operations that need to run 24 hours a day have special job requirements. For example, shutting down certain equipment at night may be inefficient or may cause production problems, or some industries, such as security and health care, may have customers who demand services around the clock. Globalization often means that operations take place across many time zones, requiring management at all hours. When a job entails working night shifts, job specifications should reflect this requirement. For most people, working at night disrupts their normal functioning and may cause disorders such as fatigue, depression, and obesity. However, people show wide variability in how well they respond to working at night. Research has found that people who work well at night tend to prefer sleeping late in the morning and staying up late. They also tend to sleep easily at different times of day, like to take naps, and exercise regularly. When job specifications call for nighttime work, a person's ability to handle a nocturnal work life may be the most critical KSAO.[6]

Sources of Job Information

Information for analyzing an existing job often comes from incumbents, that is, people who currently hold that position in the organization. They are a logical source of information, because they are most acquainted with the details of the job. Incumbents should be able to provide very accurate information.

A drawback of relying solely on incumbents' information is that they may have an incentive to exaggerate what they do, to appear more valuable to the organization. Information from incumbents should therefore be supplemented with information from observers, such as supervisors. Supervisors should review the information provided by incumbents, looking for a match between what incumbents are doing and what they are supposed to do. Research suggests that incumbents may provide the most accurate estimates of the actual time spent performing job tasks, while supervisors may be more accurate in reporting information about the importance of job duties.[7]

Dictionary of Occupational Titles
Created by the Department of Labor in the 1930s, the DOT listed over 12,000 jobs and requirements.

The government also provides background information for analyzing jobs. In the 1930s, the U.S. Department of Labor created the ***Dictionary of Occupational Titles (DOT)*** as a vehicle for helping the new public employment system link the demand for skills and the supply of skills in the U.S. workforce. The government perceived a need to lower the high unemployment rate by helping to match workers and employers. The *DOT* described over 12,000 jobs, as well as some of the requirements of successful job holders. Employment agencies and private employers used the *DOT* to help them staff jobs efficiently. It was also a valuable resource for workers because it listed the skills and educational requirements they would need for certain occupations.

This system served the United States well for over 60 years, but it became clear to Labor Department officials that jobs in the new economy were so different that the *DOT* no longer served its purpose. Technological change, global competition, and greater emphasis on flexibility were making the system obsolete. The Labor Department therefore abandoned the *DOT* in 1998 and introduced a new system, called the Occupational Information Network (O*NET). Instead of relying on fixed job titles and narrow task descriptions, O*NET uses a common language that generalizes across jobs to describe the abilities, work styles, work activities, and work context required for 1,000 broadly defined occupations. Users can visit O*NET OnLine (http://online.onetcenter.org) to review jobs' tasks, work styles and context, and requirements including skills, training, and experience. In Oklahoma City, Workforce Oklahoma's Eastside Career Connection Center

Manpower, a temporary services agency, uses O*Net to match its 2 million workers to particular jobs and it helps Manpower track demand nationwide.

used O*NET to guide small employers in listing job vacancies. For example, a metal fabrication company was having difficulty finding knowledgeable welders, so it decided to set up its own training program. The Eastside center worked with the company to define the desired skills, prepare job descriptions, and set up training aimed to fill the jobs described. On a larger scale, Manpower, a temporary-services agency, uses O*NET to match its 2 million workers to particular jobs. Using the O*NET classification system to define clients' jobs helps the company track demand nationwide.[8]

Position Analysis Questionnaire

After gathering information, the job analyst uses the information to analyze the job. One of the broadest and best-researched instruments for analyzing jobs is the **Position Analysis Questionnaire (PAQ).** This is a standardized job analysis questionnaire containing 194 items that represent work behaviors, work conditions, and job characteristics that apply to a wide variety of jobs. The questionnaire organizes these items into six sections concerning different aspects of the job:

1. *Information input*—Where and how a worker gets information needed to perform the job.
2. *Mental processes*—The reasoning, decision making, planning, and information-processing activities involved in performing the job.
3. *Work output*—The physical activities, tools, and devices used by the worker to perform the job.
4. *Relationships with other persons*—The relationships with other people required in performing the job.
5. *Job context*—The physical and social contexts where the work is performed.
6. *Other characteristics*—The activities, conditions, and characteristics other than those previously described that are relevant to the job.

The person analyzing a job determines whether each item on the questionnaire applies to the job being analyzed. The analyst rates each item on six scales: extent of use, amount of time, importance to the job, possibility of occurrence, applicability, and special code (special rating scales used with a particular item). The PAQ headquarters uses a computer to score the questionnaire and generate a report that describes the scores on the job dimensions.

Using the PAQ provides an organization with information that helps in comparing jobs, even when they are dissimilar. The PAQ also has the advantage that it considers the whole work process, from inputs through outputs. However, the person who fills out the questionnaire must have college-level reading skills, and the PAQ is meant to be completed only by job analysts trained in this method. In fact, the ratings of job incumbents tend to be less reliable than ratings by supervisors and trained analysts.[9] Also, the descriptions in the PAQ reports are rather abstract, so the reports may not be useful for writing job descriptions or redesigning jobs.

Task Analysis Inventory

Another type of job analysis method, the **task analysis inventory,** focuses on the tasks performed in a particular job. This method has several variations. In one, the task inventory-CODAP method, subject-matter experts such as job incumbents generate a list of the tasks performed in a job. Then they rate each task in terms of time

Position Analysis Questionnaire (PAQ)
A standardized job analysis questionnaire containing 194 questions about work behaviors, work conditions, and job characteristics that apply to a wide variety of jobs.

task analysis inventory
Job analysis method that involves listing the tasks performed in a particular job and rating each task according to a defined set of criteria.

spent on the task, frequency of task performance, relative importance, relative difficulty, and length of time required to learn the job. Because the tasks are measured in terms that are concrete and specific to the job, the people rating the job tend to agree with one another. The CODAP computer program organizes the responses into dimensions of similar tasks.[10]

Task analysis inventories can be very detailed, including 100 or more tasks. This level of detail can be helpful for developing employment tests and criteria for performance appraisal. However, they do not directly identify KSAOs needed for success in a job.

Fleishman Job Analysis System

To gather information about worker requirements, the **Fleishman Job Analysis System** asks subject-matter experts (typically job incumbents) to evaluate a job in terms of the abilities required to perform the job.[11] The survey is based on 52 categories of abilities, ranging from written comprehension to deductive reasoning, manual dexterity, stamina, and originality. As in the example in Figure 4.5, the survey items are arranged into a scale for each ability. Each begins with a description of the ability and a comparison to related abilities. Below this is a seven-point scale with phrases describing extemely high and low levels of the ability. The person completing the survey indicates which point on the scale represents the level of the ability required for performing the job being analyzed.

When the survey has been completed in all 52 categories, the results provide a picture of the ability requirements of a job. Such information is especially useful for employee selection, training, and career development.

Importance of Job Analysis

Job analysis is so important to HR managers that it has been called the building block of everything that personnel does.[12] The fact is that almost every human resource management program requires some type of information that is gleaned from job analysis:[13]

- *Work redesign*—Often an organization seeks to redesign work to make it more efficient or to improve quality. The redesign requires detailed information about the existing job(s). In addition, preparing the redesign is similar to analyzing a job that does not yet exist.
- *Human resource planning*—As planners analyze human resource needs and how to meet those needs, they must have accurate information about the levels of skill required in various jobs, so that they can tell what kinds of human resources will be needed.
- *Selection*—To identify the most qualified applicants for various positions, decision makers need to know what tasks the individuals must perform, as well as the necessary knowledge, skills, and abilities.
- *Training*—Almost every employee hired by an organization will require training. Any training program requires knowledge of the tasks performed in a job, so that the training is related to the necessary knowledge and skills.
- *Performance appraisal*—An accurate performance appraisal requires information about how well each employee is performing in order to reward employees who perform well and to improve their performance if it is below standard. Job analysis helps in identifying the behaviors and the results associated with effective performance.

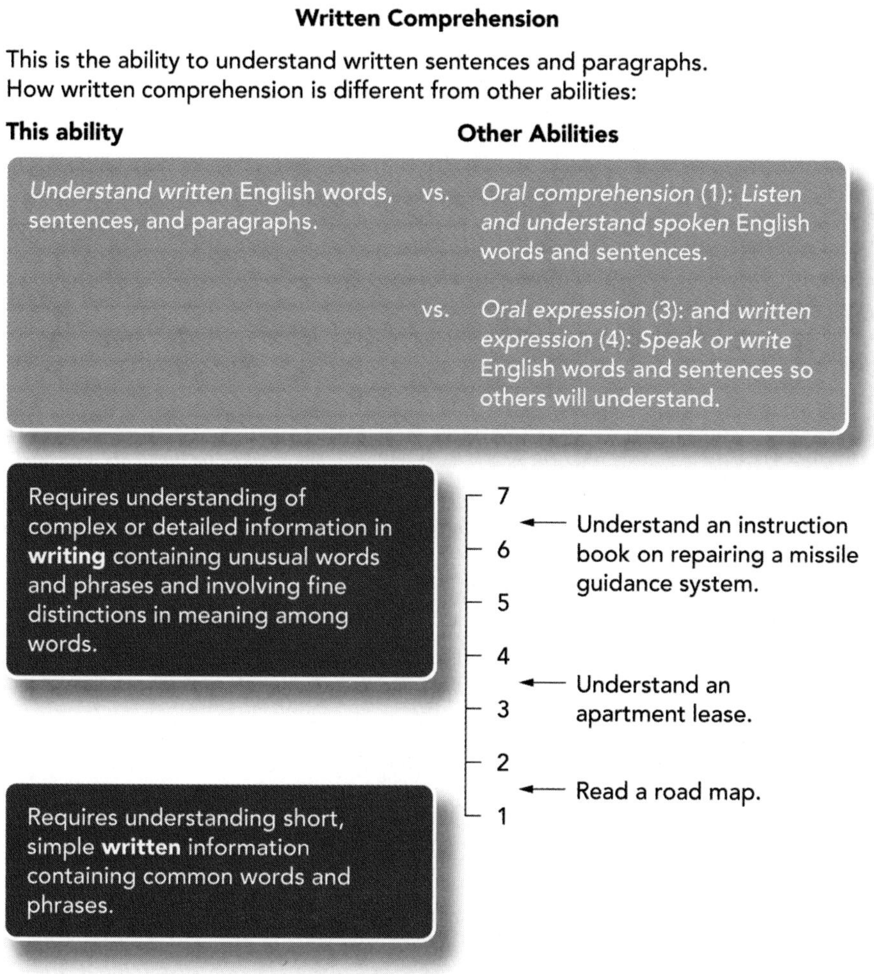

Written Comprehension

This is the ability to understand written sentences and paragraphs.
How written comprehension is different from other abilities:

This ability		Other Abilities
Understand written English words, sentences, and paragraphs.	vs.	Oral comprehension (1): Listen and understand spoken English words and sentences.
	vs.	Oral expression (3): and written expression (4): Speak or write English words and sentences so others will understand.

Requires understanding of complex or detailed information in **writing** containing unusual words and phrases and involving fine distinctions in meaning among words.

7

6 ← Understand an instruction book on repairing a missile guidance system.

5

4

3 ← Understand an apartment lease.

2

1 ← Read a road map.

Requires understanding short, simple **written** information containing common words and phrases.

SOURCE: From E. A. Fleishman and M. D. Mumford, "Evaluating Classifications of Job Behavior: A Construct Validation of the Ability Requirements Scales," *Personnel Psychology* 44 (1991), pp. 423–576. Copyright © 1991 by Blackwell Publishing. Reproduced with permission of Blackwell Publishing via Copyright Clearance Center.

Figure 4.5

Example of an Ability from the Fleishman Job Analysis System

- *Career planning*—Matching an individual's skills and aspirations with career opportunities requires that those in charge of career planning know the skill requirements of the various jobs. This allows them to guide individuals into jobs in which they will succeed and be satisfied.
- *Job evaluation*—The process of job evaluation involves assessing the relative dollar value of each job to the organization in order to set up fair pay structures. If employees do not believe pay structures are fair, they will become dissatisfied and may quit, or they will not see much benefit in striving for promotions. To put dollar values on jobs, it is necessary to get information about different jobs and compare them.

Job analysis supports several of these activities when it comes to automating major job duties, as described in the "e-HRM" box.

IHS Help Desk, which provides computer-related advice to companies, found out the importance of job descriptions by trying to operate without them. When the company

E-HRM

KIOSKS MAKE WORK DIFFERENT AT AIRPORT TERMINALS

Airport ticket agents once had jobs that were largely repetitive. One by one, passengers approached them, tickets in hand, to check in, receive seat assignments and boarding passes, and check their baggage. Today, however, airline passengers are more likely to bypass the ticket agent.

The technology behind the change is the Internet coupled with the airport kiosk. Travelers today go online to make reservations. Instead of a printed ticket, they are likely to receive an e-ticket, or confirmation of their online reservation. Then, when travelers arrive at the airport, hundreds of thousands of them head for kiosks, such as those built by Kinetics, based in Florida. These travelers would rather do much of the check-in work themselves instead of waiting in line for an agent. By swiping a credit card and touching a screen, they can obtain their boarding passes and find out which gate they should go to.

More and more airline passengers are checking themselves in. At Northwest Airlines, for example, use of the kiosks has grown from 20 percent of passengers in 2001 to half of the passengers in May 2003—and more than two-thirds checked themselves in during the following December. About two-thirds of Continental Airlines passengers use kiosks made by Kinetics. The main attraction is saving time. According to Continental's Scott O'Leary, kiosks have essentially eliminated waiting lines; the check-in time at a kiosk is only about one minute. Passengers also like the direct access to information. Instead of discussing seat assignments with an agent, hoping to be clear about what they want, they can look at a seating chart and choose an available seat that suits them best. Airport kiosks also offer information in 12 languages, an option that few agents can match.

When Kinetics began selling its airport kiosks, some people worried that ticket agents' jobs would be phased out. In fact, airlines have been making cuts in recent years but not primarily among ticket agents. The main impact on ticket agents is that their jobs have *changed*, rather than being eliminated. Instead of processing a steady stream of routine check-ins, the agents now handle special problems and requests. Instead of needing people who simply have the stamina to, in O'Leary's words, "punch the same combination of 122 keys over and over," the airlines need agents who can respond to unusual concerns and develop solutions aimed at satisfying travelers. This change must affect the recruiting, selection, training, and performance evaluation of ticket agents.

SOURCE: Based on Charles Fishman, "The Toll of a New Machine," *Fast Company,* May 2004, pp. 90–95.

started, management thought employees would be more flexible in assisting customers if they weren't limited by detailed descriptions of their jobs. However, when employees left the company, they expressed confusion during their exit interviews, according to Jean Rall, IHS's chief operating officer: "We started hearing employees say . . . , 'I got hired to do this and I do it well, but you haven't provided me with any vision about what I'm doing next.' Employees didn't see a professional identity or career path, and we couldn't manage employee expectations." Preparing job descriptions helped the company end such confusion and keep employees longer. Rall says job descriptions haven't limited employees, but have helped supervisors and employees with career development.[14]

Job analysis is also important from a legal standpoint. As we saw in Chapter 3, the government imposes requirements related to equal employment opportunity.

Detailed, accurate, objective job specifications help decision makers comply with these regulations by keeping the focus on tasks and abilities. These documents also provide evidence of efforts made to engage in fair employment practices. For example, to enforce the Americans with Disabilities Act, the Equal Employment Opportunity Commission may look at job descriptions to identify the essential functions of a job and determine whether a disabled person could have performed those functions with reasonable accommodations. Likewise, lists of duties in different jobs could be compared to evaluate claims under the Equal Pay Act. However, job descriptions and job specifications are not a substitute for fair employment practices.

Besides helping human resource professionals, job analysis helps supervisors and other managers carry out their duties. Data from job analysis can help managers identify the types of work in their units, as well as provide information about the work flow process, so that managers can evaluate whether work is done in the most efficient way. Job analysis information also supports managers as they make hiring decisions, review performance, and recommend rewards.

Trends in Job Analysis

As we noted in the earlier discussion of work flow analysis, organizations are beginning to appreciate the need to analyze jobs in the context of the organization's structure and strategy. In addition, organizations are recognizing that today's workplace must be adaptable and is constantly subject to change. Thus, although we tend to think of "jobs" as something stable, they actually tend to change and evolve over time. Those who occupy or manage jobs often make minor adjustments to match personal preferences or changing conditions.[15] Indeed, although errors in job analysis can have many sources, most inaccuracy is likely to result from job descriptions being outdated. For this reason, job analysis must not only define jobs when they are created, but also detect changes in jobs as time passes.

In today's world of rapidly changing products and markets, some observers have even begun to suggest that the concept of a "job" is obsolete. Some researchers and businesspeople have observed a trend they call *dejobbing*—viewing organizations as a field of work needing to be done, rather than as a set or series of jobs held by individuals. For example, at Amazon.com, HR director Scott Pitasky notes, "Here, a person might be in the same 'job,' but three months later be doing completely different work."[16] This means Amazon.com puts more emphasis on broad worker specifications ("entrepreneurial and customer-focused") than on detailed job descriptions ("HTML programming"), which may not be descriptive one year down the road.

These changes in the nature of work and the expanded use of "project-based" organizational structures require the type of broader understanding that comes from an

LO5
Summarize recent trends in job analysis.

Amazon.com practices "dejobbing," or designing work by project rather than by jobs. What would appeal to you about working for a company organized like this?

analysis of work flows. Because the work can change rapidly and it is impossible to rewrite job descriptions every week, job descriptions and specifications need to be flexible. At the same time, legal requirements (as discussed in Chapter 3) may discourage organizations from writing flexible job descriptions. So, organizations must balance the need for flexibility with the need for legal documentation. This presents one of the major challenges to be faced by HRM departments in the next decade. Many professionals are meeting this challenge with a greater emphasis on careful job design.

☰ JOB DESIGN

Although job analysis, as just described, is important for an understanding of existing jobs, organizations also must plan for new jobs and periodically consider whether they should revise existing jobs. When an organization is expanding, supervisors and human resource professionals must help plan for new or growing work units. When an organization is trying to improve quality or efficiency, a review of work units and processes may require a fresh look at how jobs are designed.

These situations call for **job design,** the process of defining how work will be performed and what tasks will be required in a given job, or *job redesign,* a similar process that involves changing an existing job design. To design jobs effectively, a person must thoroughly understand the job itself (through job analysis) and its place in the larger work unit's work flow process (through work flow analysis). Having a detailed knowledge of the tasks performed in the work unit and in the job, a manager then has many alternative ways to design a job. As shown in Figure 4.6, the available approaches emphasize different aspects of the job: the mechanics of doing a job efficiently, the job's impact on motivation, the use of safe work practices, and the mental demands of the job.

Designing Efficient Jobs

If workers perform tasks as efficiently as possible, not only does the organization benefit from lower costs and greater output per worker, but workers should be less fatigued. This point of view has for years formed the basis of classical **industrial engineering,** which looks for the simplest way to structure work in order to maximize

job design
The process of defining how work will be performed and what tasks will be required in a given job.

LO6
Describe methods for designing a job so that it can be done efficiently.

industrial engineering
The study of jobs to find the simplest way to structure work in order to maximize efficiency.

Figure 4.6

Approaches to Job Design

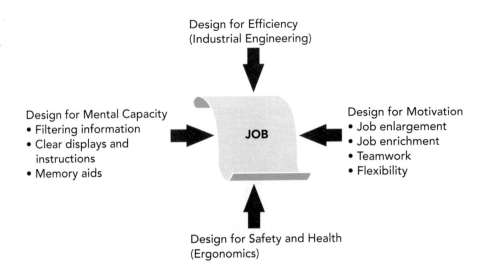

Design for Efficiency
(Industrial Engineering)

Design for Mental Capacity
• Filtering information
• Clear displays and instructions
• Memory aids

JOB

Design for Motivation
• Job enlargement
• Job enrichment
• Teamwork
• Flexibility

Design for Safety and Health
(Ergonomics)

WHAT COMPANIES WANT FROM HUMAN RESOURCE MANAGEMENT

According to a study by consulting giant Accenture, most senior executives want their human resource professionals to help them improve productivity. The following HRM initiatives were rated important by the most executives:

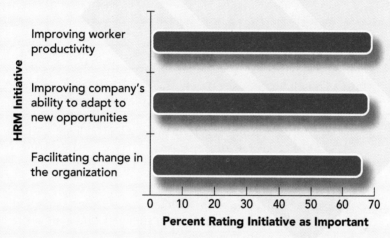

SOURCE: Mary Brandel, "HR Gets Strategic," *Computerworld*, January 24, 2005, www.computerworld.com.

efficiency. Typically, applying industrial engineering to a job reduces the complexity of the work, making it so simple that almost anyone can be trained quickly and easily to perform the job. Such jobs tend to be highly specialized and repetitive.

In practice, the scientific method traditionally seeks the "one best way" to perform a job by performing time-and-motion studies to identify the most efficient movements for workers to make. Once the engineers have identified the most efficient sequence of motions, the organization should select workers based on their ability to do the job, then train them in the details of the "one best way" to perform that job. The company also should offer pay structured to motivate workers to do their best. (Chapters 11 and 12 discuss pay and pay structures.)

Industrial engineering provides logical benefits, which as described in the "Did You Know . . . ?" box are among the benefits companies most desire from human resource management. However, a focus on efficiency alone can create jobs that are so simple and repetitive that workers get bored. Workers performing these jobs may feel their work is meaningless. Hence, most organizations combine industrial engineering with other approaches to job design.

Designing Jobs That Motivate

Especially when organizations must compete for employees, depend on skilled knowledge workers, or need a workforce that cares about customer satisfaction, a pure focus on efficiency will not achieve human resource objectives. These organizations need

LO7
Identify approaches to designing a job to make it motivating.

121

jobs that employees find interesting and satisfying, and job design should take into account factors that make jobs motivating to employees.

Following a merger with another hospital, Beth Israel Deaconess Medical Center was experiencing widespread dissatisfaction among its nurses. Turnover was high, and the hospital had difficulty replacing the nurses who left. In one year alone, more than 200 nurses left the hospital, which was spending $35,000 to replace each one. Beth Israel hired Dianne Anderson to be vice president of patient services, and she immediately addressed the problem by redesigning jobs and advertising the changes. Anderson worked with teams to rewrite the job descriptions so that nurses had more autonomy and authority to make decisions. Clerical workers were hired to handle much of the paperwork that had consumed nurses' time, so the nurses were free to spend more time with patients—tasks that attract people to nursing in the first place. The hospital set up a tuition reimbursement program and explained the career paths available to nurses who took certain courses. Two years after Beth Israel launched and advertised the changes, turnover fell by more than half, and most vacant positions were filled.[17]

A model that shows how to make jobs more motivating is the Job Characteristics Model, developed by Richard Hackman and Greg Oldham. This model describes jobs in terms of five characteristics:[18]

1. *Skill variety*—The extent to which a job requires a variety of skills to carry out the tasks involved.
2. *Task identity*—The degree to which a job requires completing a "whole" piece of work from beginning to end (for example, building an entire component or resolving a customer's complaint).
3. *Task significance*—The extent to which the job has an important impact on the lives of other people.
4. *Autonomy*—The degree to which the job allows an individual to make decisions about the way the work will be carried out.
5. *Feedback*—The extent to which a person receives clear information about performance effectiveness from the work itself.

As shown in Figure 4.7, the more of each of these characteristics a job has, the more motivating the job will be, according to the Job Characteristics Model. The model pre-

Figure 4.7

Characteristics of a Motivating Job

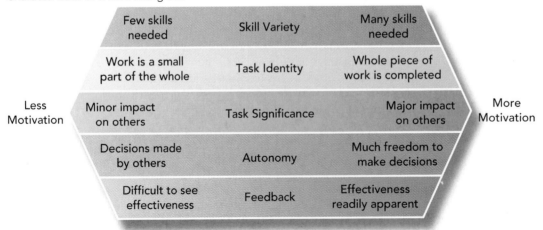

dicts that a person with such a job will be more satisfied and will produce more and better work. This approach to designing jobs includes such techniques as job enlargement, job enrichment, self-managing work teams, flexible work schedules, and telework.

Job Enlargement

In a job design, **job enlargement** refers to broadening the types of tasks performed. The objective of job enlargement is to make jobs less repetitive and more interesting. Methods of job enlargement include job extension and job rotation.

Job extension is enlarging jobs by combining several relatively simple jobs to form a job with a wider range of tasks. An example might be combining the jobs of receptionist, typist, and file clerk into jobs containing all three kinds of work. This approach to job enlargement is relatively simple, but if all the tasks are dull, workers will not necessarily be more motivated by the redesigned job.

Job rotation does not actually redesign the jobs themselves, but moves employees among several different jobs. This approach to job enlargement is common among production teams. During the course of a week, a team member may carry out each of the jobs handled by the team. Team members might assemble components one day and pack products into cases another day. As with job extension, the enlarged jobs may still consist of repetitious activities, but with greater variation among those activities.

job enlargement
Broadening the types of tasks performed in a job.

job extension
Enlarging jobs by combining several relatively simple jobs to form a job with a wider range of tasks.

job rotation
Enlarging jobs by moving employees among several different jobs.

Job Enrichment

The idea of **job enrichment,** or empowering workers by adding more decision-making authority to their jobs, comes from the work of Frederick Herzberg. According to Herzberg's two-factor theory, individuals are motivated more by the intrinsic aspects of work (for example, the meaningfulness of a job) than by extrinsic rewards such as pay. Herzberg identified five factors he associated with motivating jobs: achievement, recognition, growth, responsibility, and performance of the entire job. Thus, ways to enrich a manufacturing job might include giving employees authority to stop production when quality standards are not being met and having each employee perform several tasks to complete a particular stage of the process, rather than dividing up the tasks among the employees. For a salesperson in a store, job enrichment might involve the authority to resolve customer problems, including the authority to decide whether to issue refunds or replace merchandise.

job enrichment
Empowering workers by adding more decision-making authority to jobs.

Self-Managing Work Teams

Instead of merely enriching individual jobs, some organizations empower employees by designing work to be done by self-managing work teams. As described in Chapter 2, these teams have authority for an entire work process or segment. Team members typically have authority to schedule work, hire team members, resolve problems related to the team's performance, and perform other duties traditionally handled by management. Teamwork can give a job such motivating characteristics as autonomy, skill variety, and task identity.

Because team members' responsibilities are great, their jobs usually are defined broadly and include sharing of work assignments. Team members may, at one time or another, perform every duty of the team. The challenge for the organization is to provide enough training so that the team members can learn the necessary skills. Another approach, when teams are responsible for particular work processes or customers, is to assign the team responsibility for the process or customer, then let the team decide which members will carry out which tasks.

Teamwork can certainly make jobs more interesting, but teamwork's effectiveness is not guaranteed. Self-managing teams are most likely to accomplish their goals if they involve 6 to 18 employees who share the same technology (tools or ideas), location, and work hours. Such teams can be especially beneficial when a group's skills are relatively easy to learn (so that employees can readily learn one another's jobs) and demand for particular activities shifts from day to day (requiring flexibility). In addition, the job specifications should help the organization identify employees who will be willing and able to cooperate for the team's success. Such employees likely will have good problem-solving skills and be able to communicate well.

A study of work teams at a large financial services company found that the right job design was associated with effective teamwork.[19] In particular, when teams are self-managed and team members are highly involved in decision making, teams are more productive, employees more satisfied, and managers more pleased with performance. Teams also tend to do better when each team member performs a variety of tasks and when team members view their effort as significant.

Flexible Work Schedules

One way in which an organization can give employees some say in how their work is structured is to offer flexible work schedules. Depending on the requirements of the organization and the individual jobs, organizations may be able to be flexible in terms of when employees work. As introduced in Chapter 2, types of flexibility include flextime and job sharing. Figure 4.8 illustrates alternatives to the traditional 40-hour workweek.

flextime
A scheduling policy in which full-time employees may choose starting and ending times within guidelines specified by the organization.

Flextime is a scheduling policy in which full-time employees may choose starting and ending times within guidelines specified by the organization. The flextime policy may require that employees be at work between certain hours, say, 10:00 AM and 3:00 PM. Employees work additional hours before or after this period in order to work the full day. One employee might arrive early in the morning in order to leave at 3:00 PM to pick up children after school. Another employee might be a night owl who prefers to arrive at 10:00 AM and work until 6:00, 7:00, or even later in the evening. A flextime policy also may enable workers to adjust a particular day's hours in order to make time for doctor's appointments, children's activities, hobbies, or volunteer work. A work schedule that allows time for community and family interests can be extremely motivating for some employees.

job sharing
A work option in which two part-time employees carry out the tasks associated with a single job.

Job sharing is a work option in which two part-time employees carry out the tasks associated with a single job. Such arrangements can enable an organization to attract or retain valued employees who want more time to attend school or to care for family members. The job requirements in such an arrangement include the ability to work cooperatively and coordinate the details of one's job with another person.

Although not strictly a form of flexibility on the level of individual employees, another scheduling alternative is the *compressed workweek*. A compressed workweek is a schedule in which full-time workers complete their weekly hours in fewer than five days. For example, instead of working eight hours a day for five days, the employees could complete 40 hours of work in four 10-hour days. This alternative is most common, but some companies use other alternatives, such as scheduling 80 hours over nine days (with a three-day weekend every other week) or reducing the workweek from 40 to 38 or 36 hours. Employees may appreciate the extra days available for leisure, family, or volunteer activities. An organization might even use this schedule to offer a kind of flexibility—for example, letting workers vote whether they want a compressed workweek during the summer months. This type of schedule has a couple

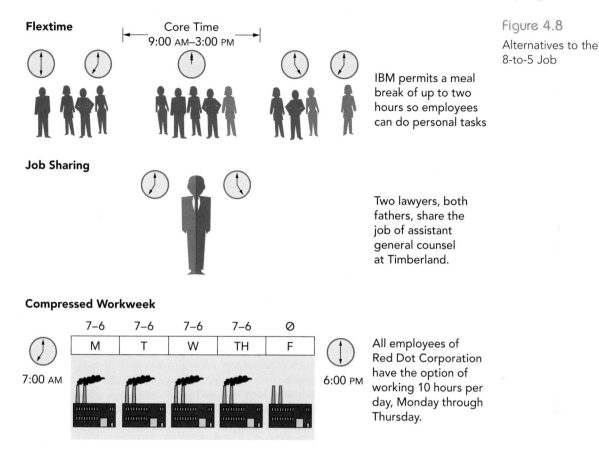

Figure 4.8

Alternatives to the
8-to-5 Job

Flextime

Core Time
9:00 AM–3:00 PM

IBM permits a meal
break of up to two
hours so employees
can do personal tasks

Job Sharing

Two lawyers, both
fathers, share the
job of assistant
general counsel
at Timberland.

Compressed Workweek

7–6	7–6	7–6	7–6	∅
M	T	W	TH	F

7:00 AM

6:00 PM

All employees of
Red Dot Corporation
have the option of
working 10 hours per
day, Monday through
Thursday.

of drawbacks, however. One is that employees may become exhausted on the longer workdays. Another is that if the arrangement involves working more than 40 hours during a week, the Fair Labor Standards Act requires the payment of overtime wages to nonsupervisory employees.

Atlanta law firm Alston & Bird combined flexibility with the use of work teams to make paralegals' jobs more motivating. In the high pressure of a law firm, paralegals often put in long hours. At Alston & Bird, paralegals are assigned to teams, and each team develops its own work schedules for members, using flexible work hours and job sharing as needed. Turnover is far below the industry average, and one employee notes, "I can't imagine a more interesting job or a better place to work."[20]

Telework

Flexibility can extend to work locations as well as work schedules. Before the Industrial Revolution, most people worked either close to or inside their own homes. Mass production technologies changed all this, separating work life from home life, as people began to travel to centrally located factories and offices. Today, however, skyrocketing prices for office space, combined with drastically reduced prices for portable communication and computing devices, seem ready to reverse this trend. The broad term for doing one's work away from a centrally located office is *telework* or telecommuting. Studies reveal that the cost savings from telework programs can top $8,000 per employee annually.

For employers, advantages of telework include less need for office space and the ability to offer greater flexibility to employees who are disabled or need to be available for children or elderly relatives. The employees using telework arrangements may be absent less often than employees with similar demands who must commute to work. Also, a recent study found that the majority of teleworkers say they are at least as productive working from home rather than from a central office.[21] Telework is easiest to implement for people in managerial, professional, or sales jobs, especially those that involve working and communicating on a computer. A telework arrangement is generally difficult to set up for manufacturing workers.

Given the possible benefits, it is not surprising that telework is a growing trend. According to the Institute for the Study of Distributed Work, the number of corporate employees who work outside the office at least two days a week has risen from 6.3 million in 1995 to 10.4 million in 2002. Bob Long, a global field-sales support manager for Dow Chemical, spends only 10 percent of his time at headquarters in Michigan, and the rest is divided between his New Jersey home office and trips to his customers. At microchip giant Intel, four out of 10 employees telecommute, and at Fannie Mae, a government-established buyer of home mortgages, half of the workforce has a telework arrangement.[22]

Designing Ergonomic Jobs

LO8
Explain how organizations apply ergonomics to design safe jobs.

ergonomics
The study of the interface between individuals' physiology and the characteristics of the physical work environment.

The way people use their bodies when they work—whether toting heavy furniture onto a moving van or sitting quietly before a computer screen—affects their physical well-being and may affect how well and how long they can work. The study of the interface between individuals' physiology and the characteristics of the physical work environment is called **ergonomics.** The goal of ergonomics is to minimize physical strain on the worker by structuring the physical work environment around the way the human body works. Ergonomics therefore focuses on outcomes such as reducing physical fatigue, aches and pains, and health complaints.

Ergonomic job design has been applied in redesigning equipment used in jobs that are physically demanding. Such redesign is often aimed at reducing the physical demands of certain jobs so that anyone can perform them. In addition, many interventions focus on redesigning machines and technology—for instance, adjusting the height of a computer keyboard to minimize occupational illnesses, such as carpal tunnel syndrome. The design of chairs and desks to fit posture requirements is very important in many office jobs. One study found that having employees participate in an ergonomic redesign effort significantly reduced the number and severity of cumulative trauma disorders (injuries that result from performing the same movement over and over), lost production time, and restricted-duty days.[23]

Often, redesigning work to make it more worker-friendly also leads to increased efficiencies. For example, at International Truck and Engine Corporation, one of the most difficult aspects of truck production was pinning the axles to the truck frame. Traditionally, the frame was lowered onto the axle and a crew of six people, armed with oversized hammers and crowbars, forced the frame onto the axle. Because the workers could not see the bolts they had to tighten under the frame, the bolts were often fastened improperly, and many workers injured themselves in the process. After a brainstorming session, the workers and engineers concluded that it would be better to flip the frame upside down and attach the axles from above. The result was a job that could be done twice as fast by half as many workers, who were much less likely to make mistakes or get injured.[24]

Although employers in all industries are supposed to protect workers under the "general duty" clause, nursing homes, grocery stores and poultry-processing plants are the only three industries for which OSHA has published ergonomic standards.

In 2002 the Occupational Safety and Health Administration moved away from an earlier plan to issue ergonomic regulations and instead launched what it calls a "four-pronged" strategy. The first prong is to issue guidelines (rather than regulations) for specific industries. As of the beginning of 2005, these guidelines have been issued for the nursing home, grocery store, and poultry-processing industries. Second, OSHA enforces violations of its requirement that employers have a general duty to protect workers from hazards, including ergonomic hazards. Third, OSHA works with industry groups to advise employers in those industries. And finally, OSHA established a National Advisory Committee on Ergonomics to define needs for further research. Overall, the emphasis is on providing employers with information, rather than specific requirements. Employers wondering how to begin protecting their workers from ergonomic hazards might also consider the regulations that OSHA had proposed in 2001; these direct employers to avoid five specific high-risk work practices:[25]

1. Using a keyboard for four hours straight without a break.
2. Lifting more than 75 pounds.
3. Kneeling or squatting for more than two hours a day.
4. Working with the back, neck, or wrists bent more than two hours a day.
5. Using large vibrating equipment such as chainsaws or jackhammers more than 30 minutes a day.

Although these regulations did not take effect, they do identify characteristics of jobs that may pose problems for employees. When jobs have these characteristics, employers should be vigilant about opportunities to improve work design, for the benefit of both workers and the organization.

Designing Jobs That Meet Mental Capabilities and Limitations

Just as the human body has capabilities and limitations, addressed by ergonomics, the mind, too, has capabilities and limitations. Besides hiring people with certain mental skills, organizations can design jobs so that they can be accurately and safely performed given the way the brain processes information. Generally, this means reducing

LO9
Discuss how organizations can plan for the mental demands of a job.

the information-processing requirements of a job. In these simpler jobs, workers may be less likely to make mistakes or have accidents. Of course, the simpler jobs also may be less motivating. Research has found that challenging jobs tend to fatigue and dissatisfy workers when they feel little control over their situation, lack social support, and feel motivated mainly to avoid errors. In contrast, they may enjoy the challenges of a difficult job where they have some control and social support, especially if they enjoy learning and are unafraid of making mistakes.[26]

There are several ways to simplify a job's mental demands. One is to limit the amount of information and memorization that the job requires. Organizations can also provide adequate lighting, easy-to-understand gauges and displays, simple-to-operate equipment, and clear instructions. Often, employees try to simplify some of the mental demands of their own jobs by creating checklists, charts, or other aids. Finally, every job requires some degree of thinking, remembering, and paying attention, so for every job, organizations need to evaluate whether their employees can handle the job's mental demands.

Applying the perceptual approach to the job of cashier, electronic cash registers have simplified some aspects of this job. In the past, a cashier read the total price displayed by a cash register, received payment, then calculated any change due the customer. Today, most stores have cash registers that compute the change due and display that amount. The cash register display makes the job easier. However, some cashiers may have been proud of their ability to figure change due, and for these people, the introduction of electronic cash registers may have reduced their job satisfaction. In this way, simplifying the mental demands of a job can also make it less interesting.

Because of this drawback to simplifying jobs, it can be most beneficial to simplify jobs where employees will most appreciate having the mental demands reduced (as in a job that is extremely challenging) or where the costs of errors are severe (as in the job of a surgeon or air-traffic controller). A relatively recent source of complexity in

Figure 4.9

Number of E-Mail Messages Sent from North American Businesses

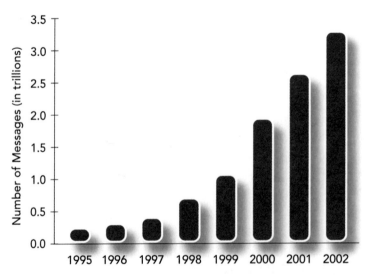

SOURCE: From Wall Street Journal. Online by E. Weinstein, "Rising Flood of Office E-Mail Messages Threatens to Drown the Unorganized," February 7, 2002. Copyright © 2002 by Dow Jones & Co., Inc. Reproduced with permission of Dow Jones & Co., Inc. via Copyright Clearance Center.

many jobs is the need to process a daily flood of e-mail messages. As shown in Figure 4.9, business sources alone are sending well over 2 trillion messages every day. Although the total from all sources is difficult to count, it is clear that e-mail has taken over a significant share of an eight-hour workday. Various studies estimate that office workers spend nearly an hour a day handling e-mail, and top managers may spend four times that much handling their messages.

Organizations take various steps to manage this challenge. Many have established policies—for example, limiting personal use of company e-mail and restricting the number of Internet discussion groups to which employees may subscribe. Some companies delete e-mail messages once a month. Another alternative is to install software that filters spam (electronic "junk mail"). Programs such as SpamKiller, Spam Buster, and Brightmail look for and block messages that match spam databases or have characteristics of spam. Of course, generators of spam continuously look for ways to evade these filters, so individual employees must develop ways of managing e-mail, just as they have simplified other aspects of their jobs in the past.[27]

thinking ETHICALLY

Who's Responsible When Workers Get Hurt?

One of the considerations of job design is ergonomics, but which measures are effective is still being debated. Without universal standards and with little history from which to learn, many employers worry that they will be expected to spend heavily on changes that will make little real difference to their workers' safety. Others are forging ahead and seeing benefits. Xerox has an ergonomics program for two reasons: a "moral imperative" to protect workers and a way to minimize the costs associated with injured workers.

Maple Landmark Woodcraft, a Vermont maker of wooden toys, asked OSHA regulators and its insurance company's loss-control experts for advice on how to make the factory safer after employees reported repetitive-motion injuries. The solution was to rotate workers among jobs. The company spent $7,000 but cut injury-related costs by $8,000.

Rockwell Automation, based in Milwaukee, applied ergonomic principles to combat a rise in shoulder injuries. Punch-press operators fed heavy sheets of metal into a stamping machine by shoving them in. Rockwell spent $56,000 for equipment to move the metal on and off the racks. It also evaluated office jobs, adjusting workstations to minimize injuries. Since then, motion-related injuries have tumbled.

According to Rockwell's manager of safety and environmental services, Brett Jorgenson, ergonomic studies also have disadvantages. Workers sometimes request new furniture or equipment, whether or not it is really needed. So, his policy is to treat purchases as a "last resort," but he responds to injury complaints whether or not the company concludes the injury really is job related.

Identifying the root cause of a repetitive-motion injury and the most effective solution can be difficult. Workplace and health consultant Richard Rossiter says sometimes after a factory spends millions of dollars to change a production line to prevent elbow injuries, workers begin to experience wrist and shoulder problems.

A more appropriate response might have been less-costly "in-house stretching programs," because the workers simply needed to become more fit.

SOURCE: Based on Eve Tahmincioglu, "Ergonomics Is Back on the Radar Screen for Both Business and Regulators," *Workforce Management,* July 2004, downloaded from Infotrac at http://web1. infotrac.galegroup.com.

Questions

1. What obligations, if any, do employers have when workers experience fatigue, soreness, or injury from physically demanding jobs?
2. If you worked in a human resource department and workers complained to you about pain associated with repetitive motions, what would you recommend that the company do?

SUMMARY

1. Summarize the elements of work flow analysis.
   The analysis identifies the amount and quality of a work unit's outputs, which may be products, parts of products, or services. Next, the analyst determines the work processes required to produce these outputs, breaking down tasks into those performed by each person in the work unit. Finally, the work flow analysis identifies the inputs used to carry out the processes and produce the outputs.

2. Describe how work flow is related to an organization's structure.
   Within an organization, units and individuals must cooperate to create outputs, and the organization's structure brings people together for this purpose. The structure may be centralized or decentralized, and people may be grouped according to function or into divisions focusing on particular products or customer groups. A functional structure is most appropriate for people who perform highly specialized jobs and hold relatively little authority. Employee empowerment and teamwork succeed best in a divisional structure. Because of these links between structure and types of jobs, considering such issues improves the success of job design.

3. Define the elements of a job analysis, and discuss their significance for human resource management.
   Job analysis is the process of getting detailed information about jobs. It includes preparation of job descriptions and job specifications. A job description lists the tasks, duties, and responsibilities of a job. Job specifications look at the qualities needed in a person performing the job. They list the knowledge, skills, abilities, and other characteristics that are required for successful performance of a job. Job analysis provides a foundation for carrying out many HRM responsibilities, including work redesign, human resource planning, employee selection and training, performance appraisal, career planning, and job evaluation to determine pay scales.

4. Tell how to obtain information for a job analysis.
   Information for analyzing an existing job often comes from incumbents and their supervisors. The Labor Department publishes general background information about jobs in the *Dictionary of Occupational Titles* and Occupational Information Network (O*NET). Job analysts, employees, and managers may complete a Position Analysis Questionnaire or task analysis inventory, or fill out a survey for the Fleishman Job Analysis System.

5. Summarize recent trends in job analysis.
   Some organizations are "dejobbing," or viewing organizations in terms of a field of work needing to be done, rather than as a set or series of jobs. These organizations look for employees who can take on different responsibilities as the field of work changes. Organizations are also adopting project-based structures and teamwork, which also require flexibility and the ability to handle broad responsibilities.

6. Describe methods for designing a job so that it can be done efficiently.
   The basic technique for designing efficient jobs is industrial engineering, which looks for the simplest way to structure work in order to maximize efficiency. Through methods such as time-and-motion studies, the industrial engineer creates jobs that are relatively simple and typically repetitive. These jobs may bore workers because they are so simple.

7. Identify approaches to designing a job to make it motivating.

   According to the Job Characteristics Model, jobs are more motivating if they have greater skill variety, task identity, task significance, autonomy, and feedback about performance effectiveness. Ways to create such jobs include job enlargement (through job extension or job rotation) and job enrichment. In addition, self-managing work teams offer greater skill variety and task identity. Flexible work schedules and telework offer greater autonomy.

8. Explain how organizations apply ergonomics to design safe jobs.

   The goal of ergonomics is to minimize physical strain on the worker by structuring the physical work environment around the way the human body works. Ergonomic design may involve modifying equipment to reduce the physical demands of performing certain jobs or redesign-ing the jobs themselves to reduce strain. Ergonomic design may target work practices associated with injuries, including using a keyboard for hours at a time, lifting heavy weights, extensive kneeling or squatting, using large vibrating equipment, and working with back, neck, or wrists bent for several hours a day.

9. Discuss how organizations can plan for the mental demands of a job.

   Employers may seek to reduce mental as well as physical strain. The job design may limit the amount of information and memorization involved. Adequate lighting, easy-to-read gauges and displays, simple-to-operate equipment, and clear instructions also can minimize mental strain. Computer software can simplify jobs—for example, by performing calculations or filtering out spam from important e-mail. Finally, organizations can select employees with the necessary abilities to handle a job's mental demands.

REVIEW AND DISCUSSION QUESTIONS

1. Assume you are the manager of a fast-food restaurant. What are the outputs of your work unit? What are the activities required to produce those outputs? What are the inputs?

2. Based on Question 1, consider the cashier's job in the restaurant. What are the outputs, activities, and inputs for that job?

3. Consider the "job" of college student. Perform a job analysis on this job. What tasks are required in the job? What knowledge, skills, and abilities are necessary to perform those tasks? Prepare a job description based on your analysis.

4. Discuss how the following trends are changing the skill requirements for managerial jobs in the United States:
   a. Increasing use of computers and the Internet.
   b. Increasing international competition.
   c. Increasing work-family conflicts.

5. How can a job analysis of each job in the work unit help a supervisor to do his or her job?

6. Consider the job of a customer service representative who fields telephone calls from customers of a retailer that sells online and through catalogs. What measures can an employer take to design this job to make it efficient? What might be some drawbacks or challenges of designing this job for efficiency?

7. How might the job in Question 6 be designed to make it more motivating? How well would these considerations apply to the cashier's job in Question 1?

8. What ergonomic considerations might apply to each of the following jobs? For each job, what kinds of costs would result from addressing ergonomics? What costs might result from failing to address ergonomics?
   a. A computer programmer.
   b. A UPS delivery person.
   c. A child care worker.

9. The chapter said that modern electronics have elimi-nated the need for a store's cashiers to calculate change due on a purchase. How does this development modify the job description for a cashier? If you were a store manager, how would it affect the skills and qualities of job candidates you would want to hire? Does this change in mental processing requirements affect what you would expect from a cashier? How?

10. Consider a job you hold now or have held recently. Would you want this job to be redesigned to place more emphasis on efficiency, motivation, ergonomics, or mental processing? What changes would you want, and why? (Or why do you not want the job to be re-designed?)

WHAT'S YOUR HR IQ?

The text Web site offers two more ways to check what you've learned so far. Use the Self-Assessment exercise to learn more about the Department of Labor's Occupational Information Network (O*NET). Go online with the Web Exercise to learn more about job analysis.

BusinessWeek CASE

BusinessWeek Why the "Laptop-on-a-Stick" Is a Hard-Pressed RN's Best Friend

When Melanie Weigeshoff joined Hackensack University Medical Center in 1998 as a nursing assistant, the hospital was still in the dark ages. Most medication orders, lab test results, and doctors' instructions for patient care were recorded on paper, in giant three-ring binders. Weigeshoff was constantly on the phone clarifying doctors' quickly scribbled notes, and she spent hours chronicling her patients' progress by hand. "We were always flipping, flipping, flipping through pages," she recalls, reenacting the frustration with frantic waves of her arms.

Today that primitive hospital is just a memory for Weigeshoff, now a staff nurse. Although she still uses paper on occasion, her primary tool since 2003 has been a laptop-on-a-stick, a PC that rolls around on what looks like an IV stand. As she greets patients at the start of each shift, she logs in to their electronic records through a wireless connection. She reviews vital signs—temperature, heart rate—which had been [typed] into the computer by a nurse's aide earlier. Then she clicks over to the medication orders, making note of each dose on the computer after she delivers it. "Charting is more accurate now," she says, "because we're right there, doing everything in real time." Best of all, she has shaved an hour of overtime off her day.

As the hospital industry grapples with an unrelenting nursing shortage, technology has taken a leading role in keeping employees like Weigeshoff happy. Many of the demands of managed care have been heaped onto nurses, burdening them with more patients to care for in less time and an endless flood of paperwork. The pressures have driven so many out of the profession that the supply of nurses is expected to fall 20 percent below the demand by 2010. Surveys reveal that one out of every three nurses under 30 plans to leave the job within a year. Technology that makes nurses' jobs easier won't be a panacea, but "it's an important consideration in making the hospital a better work environment," says Carol J. Bickford, senior policy fellow at the American Nurses Association.

Technology is lightening Weigeshoff's administrative load in all kinds of ways. As she prepares to visit patient Alvest Williams, she grabs the laptop and wheels it into his room. Earlier that day, a roboticized sorting machine in the pharmacy downstairs had read Alvest's prescriptions on his electronic chart and sent them to Weigeshoff's unit. As she checks each prescription on the screen, Williams calls out the names of the drugs in her basket to make sure Weigeshoff has everything, gesturing toward the laptop as if it were another person there to help him feel better. "Protonix?" asks the 60-year-old, who is recovering from pneumonia. "Yep," says Weigeshoff. In the past, she would have had to collect handwritten prescriptions, enter them into paper charts, and fax them to the pharmacy.

For Weigeshoff, the laptop-on-a-stick frees her to be the nurse she dreamed about being when she was a little girl growing up in northern New Jersey. As a teen, she relished the job of big sister, coddling her toddler brother and sister when they needed a Band-Aid on a scraped knee or a kiss on a bumped head. "I love taking care of people," says the ebullient nurse.

But when she first started in nursing, she often struggled to find time for the caregiving part of her job. She was always on the phone with the pharmacy, pressing them for medication refills, or with doctors, trying to decipher handwriting. Now the system ensures that the pharmacy gets drugs to nurses on schedule and that almost every piece of information she needs is at her fingertips, from what insurance plan her patients are on to what tests they've had in the hospital.

Weaning the nurses off traditional paper charts isn't always easy, though. "On the first day we go live [with the computer system] on a unit, everyone wants to kill me," says Teresa C. Moore, the hospital's manager of clinical informatics. "It's a drastic change." Unlike most of the doctors at Hackensack, the nurses are hospital employees and are required to use technology in their jobs. Moore runs weekly user groups to gather feedback.

Weigeshoff welcomes any technology that will make her job easier. Paper charts won't go away anytime soon—the hospital still requires printed copies of everything entered in the computer, and some notes can't be made digitally yet. "I would love to never have to write again," she says. A dream? Maybe. But at Hackensack, it's getting closer to reality.

SOURCE: "The Nurse: Melanie Weigeshoff," *BusinessWeek*, March 28, 2005, downloaded from Infotrac at http://web1.infotrac.galegroup.com.

Questions

1. Based on the information given in the case, identify as many tasks, duties, and responsibilities of Weigeshoff's original job at Hackensack as you can. Then identify tasks, duties, and responsibilities of her job after the new technology was introduced.
2. Based on the given information, identify knowledge, skills, abilities, and other characteristics required for successfully performing Weigeshoff's original job. Then do the same for her job with the new technology.
3. To complete a job description and job specifications for Weigeshoff's new job, what additional information would you need? How could you gather that information if you worked in Hackensack's human resource department?

CASE: GE Healthcare Needs High-Tech Workers to Build High-Tech Equipment

In a global economy where millions of manufacturing jobs have shifted from the United States to other countries, GE Healthcare has held its domestic manufacturing payroll steady. It makes its MRI machines, CT scanners, portable x-ray machines, and other sophisticated medical-imaging products in U.S. factories because of its people. These top-notch engineers, designers, and production workers know the products and processes necessary to make sophisticated equipment in an innovative industry. And GE constantly provides training to keep its people knowledgeable about what's new.

One practical reason for using U.S. facilities to make GE Healthcare's most advanced equipment is productivity. Production teams work closely with design engineers, both geographically and in terms of work design. When a new product is being developed, the company brings together a team from several functions including engineering, manufacturing, marketing, and service. Together, they consider whether the product meets customer demands, whether it will be produced as efficiently as possible, and whether it will be economical to service after it has been sold. When the new product is in production, the efforts to improve efficiency continue with input from manufacturing workers. For example, workers producing a CT machine suggested that it would be more efficient to attach the heavy machine's base at the beginning of the assembly process, rather than at the end. This change shortened assembly time and reduced the space needed on the factory floor.

Production technology contributes to efficiency. GE Healthcare's plant in Waukesha, Wisconsin, keeps track of parts with radio-frequency identification tags, which it calls e-tags. The e-tags are attached to carts used to carry parts around the huge (several hundred thousand square feet) facility. Each e-tag carries information identifying the items on the cart. Several times a day, a warehouse employee drives a cart around the factory, stopping at many points along the assembly lines to supply employees with the parts they need. As the cart travels, an antenna relays data about the parts to GE warehouse computers, which is recorded with tracking software. In this way, the warehouse knows just what assemblers need, and the assemblers don't have to wait around or go to the warehouse for more parts.

Finding workers who can handle the sophisticated manufacturing processes and constant innovation can be difficult. GE Healthcare builds relationships with technical colleges near its facilities. It guides them in providing courses that will deliver graduates who understand software and have skills in electromechanical troubleshooting. New hires get company-provided on-the-job training as well. Beyond that, the company provides two hours of monthly training in manufacturing techniques and in health and safety.

Ergonomics plays a role in job design, too. Whenever the company is developing a new product, it considers the ergonomic factors involved in assembling that product. For example, engineers look at the number of times an assembly worker must lift above the shoulders or below the hips. When possible, they reduce strain by altering the design of the product or manufacturing processes.

GE Healthcare also has production facilities outside the United States, which make the less-advanced products and components. For example, a Salt Lake City plant makes complicated x-ray machines that assemble mechanical components made in Monterrey, Mexico, generators built in Bangalore, India, and display screens imported from its Beijing factory. Explains Diane Mellor, who is responsible for managing GE Healthcare's supply chain, "No one has the luxury not to play in the global marketplace." However, she adds that efficient operations on a global scale give the company the revenues it needs to invest in the innovative products it makes in the United States. She adds that success depends on more than keeping labor costs down: "This is about speed to market, the right product, and operational efficiencies." Together, these advantages equip GE Healthcare to serve a sizable and fast-growing market.

SOURCE: Adapted from Kerry A. Dolan, "Made in America," *Forbes*, April 12, 2004, downloaded from Infotrac at http://web1.infotrac.galegroup.com.

Questions

1. Based on the information in the case, what knowledge, skills, abilities, and other characteristics are required for production workers at GE Healthcare?
2. Of the approaches to job design described in this chapter (see Figure 4.6), which has GE Healthcare applied to its production jobs?
3. For GE Healthcare to continue manufacturing in the United States, what principles of work design will continue to be significant?

NOTES

1. C. Tejada, "Home Office: Millions Don't Leave Work at Work," *The Wall Street Journal*, Interactive Edition, March 5, 2002; Teach for America, "Record Number of Applicants Answer Teach for America's Call to Civic Leadership," news release, March 1, 2005, www.teachforamerica.org; and C. Richards, "'Pink-Collar' Pressure," *Chicago Tribune*, March 6, 2002, sec. 8, pp. 1, 7.
2. D. Little, "Even the Supervisor Is Expendable: The Internet Allows Factories to Be Managed from Anywhere," *BusinessWeek*, July 23, 2001, p. 78.

3. D. Shook, "Why Nike Is Dragging Its Feet," *BusinessWeek Online*, March 19, 2001; A. Bernstein, "Backlash: Behind the Anxiety over Globalization," *BusinessWeek*, April 20, 2000, pp. 38-43; A. Bernstein, "Low Skilled Jobs: Do They Have to Move?" *BusinessWeek*, February 26, 2001.

4. J. R. Hollenbeck, H. Moon, A. Ellis, et al., "Structural Contingency Theory and Individual Differences: Examination of External and Internal Person-Team Fit," *Journal of Applied Psychology* 87 (2002), pp. 599–606.

5. C. Joinson, "Refocusing Job Descriptions," *HR Magazine*, January 2001, downloaded from Findarticles.com.

6. G. Koretz, "Perils of the Graveyard Shift: Poor Health and Low Productivity," *BusinessWeek*, March 10, 1997, p. 22; C. R. Maiwald, J. L. Pierce, and J. W. Newstrom, "Workin' 8 P.M. to 8 A.M. and Lovin' Every Minute of It," *Workforce*, July 1997, pp. 30–36.

7. A. O'Reilly, "Skill Requirements: Supervisor-Subordinate Conflict," *Personnel Psychology* 26 (1973), pp. 75–80; J. Hazel, J. Madden, and R. Christal, "Agreement between Worker-Supervisor Descriptions of the Worker's Job," *Journal of Industrial Psychology* 2 (1964), pp. 71–79.

8. U.S. Department of Labor, Employment and Training Administration, "O*NET in Action: Oklahoma," and "O*NET in Action: Manpower, Inc.," both accessed April 8, 2004, at www.doleta.gov/programs/onet/.

9. *PAQ Newsletter*, August 1989; and E. C. Dierdorff and M. A. Wilson, "A Meta-analysis of Job Analysis Reliability," *Journal of Applied Psychology* 88 (2003), pp. 635–46.

10. E. Primhoff, *How to Prepare and Conduct Job Element Examinations* (Washington, DC: U.S. Government Printing Office, 1975); and T. M. Manson, E. L. Levine, and M. T. Brannick, "The Construct Validity of Task Inventory Ratings: A Multitrait-Multimethod Analysis," *Human Performance* 13 (2000), pp. 1–22.

11. E. Fleishman and M. Reilly, *Handbook of Human Abilities* (Palo Alto, CA: Consulting Psychologists Press, 1992); E. Fleishman and M. Mumford, "Ability Requirements Scales," in *The Job Analysis Handbook for Business, Industry, and Government*, edited by S. Gael (New York: Wiley, 1988), pp. 917–35.

12. W. Cascio, *Applied Psychology in Personnel Management*, 4th ed. (Englewood Cliffs, NJ: Prentice Hall, 1991).

13. P. Wright and K. Wexley, "How to Choose the Kind of Job Analysis You Really Need," *Personnel*, May 1985, pp. 51–55.

14. C. Joinson, "Refocusing Job Descriptions."

15. M. K. Lindell, C. S. Clause, C. J. Brandt, and R. S. Landis, "Relationship between Organizational Context and Job Analysis Ratings," *Journal of Applied Psychology* 83 (1998), pp. 769–76.

16. S. Caudron, "Jobs Disappear when Work Becomes More Important," *Workforce*, January 2000, pp. 30–32.

17. G. Koprowski, "A Boston Hospital Finds a Cure for the Turnover Disease," *Workforce*, October 2003, pp. 77–78.

18. R. Hackman and G. Oldham, *Work Redesign* (Boston: Addison-Wesley, 1980).

19. M. A. Campion, G. J. Medsker, and A. C. Higgs, "Relations between Work Group Characteristics and Effectiveness: Implications for Designing Effective Work Groups," *Personnel Psychology* 46 (1993), pp. 823–50.

20. S. Greengard, "The Five-Alarm Job," *Workforce*, February 2004, pp. 43–48.

21. Karyn-Siobhan Robinson, "Where Did Everybody Go?" *HR Magazine*, May 2004, downloaded from Infotrac at http://web4.infotrac.galegroup.com.

22. Ibid.; S. Shellenbarger, "Workers Get Creative Finding Places to Sit and 'Telework,'" *The Wall Street Journal*, Interactive Edition, January 23, 2002; and Michelle Conlin, "Extreme Commuting," *BusinessWeek*, February 21, 2005, downloaded from Infotrac at http://web4.infotrac.galegroup.com.

23. D. May and C. Schwoerer, "Employee Health by Design: Using Employee Involvement Teams in Ergonomic Job Redesign," *Personnel Psychology* 47 (1994), pp. 861–86.

24. S. F. Brown, "International's Better Way to Build Trucks," *Fortune*, February 19, 2001, pp. 210k–210v.

25. Occupational Safety and Health Administration, "A Four-Pronged, Comprehensive Approach," Safety and Health Topics, OSHA Web site, www.osha.gov, last updated March 4, 2005; and G. Flynn, "Now Is the Time to Prepare for OSHA's Sweeping New Ergonomics Standard," *Workforce*, March 2001, pp. 76–77.

26. N. W. Van Yperen and M. Hagerdoorn, "Do High Job Demands Increase Intrinsic Motivation or Fatigue or Both? The Role of Job Support and Social Control," *Academy of Management Journal* 46 (2003), pp. 339–48; and N. W. Van Yperen and O. Janssen, "Fatigued and Dissatisfied or Fatigued but Satisfied? Goal Orientations and Responses to High Job Demands," *Academy of Management Journal* 45 (2002), pp. 1161–71.

27. E. Weinstein, "Rising Flood of Office E-Mail Messages Threatens to Drown the Unorganized," *The Wall Street Journal*, Interactive Edition, January 10, 2002; Associated Press, "With Mountain of Junk Mail Set to Grow, Companies Promote Tools to Reduce 'Spam,'" *The Wall Street Journal*, Interactive Edition, December 17, 2001.

If you are using the Manager's Hot Seat DVD with this book, consider finishing case 12: Virtual Workplace: Out of Office Reply, for this chapter.

2

ACQUIRING AND PREPARING HUMAN RESOURCES

PLANNING FOR AND RECRUITING HUMAN RESOURCES

❧ INTRODUCTION

Business news often contains stories of layoffs, as organizations seek cost savings or react to falling demand by cutting their workforce. Others go out of their way to find alternatives. Stacey Scott, founder and chief executive of Elgia, a provider of Web conferencing services, had trouble getting enough financing, so she kept her start-up afloat by moving away from high-cost Silicon Valley. At Elgia's new location in Roswell, Georgia, rents and salaries are far cheaper. Moving didn't require layoffs. Elgia's sales representative stayed in California and continued working there until she found another job. Since then, Scott has hired three employees in Georgia.[1]

With a bigger workforce, an established company needs more creativity to avoid layoffs. At Lincoln Electric, an Ohio-based manufacturer of welding equipment, demand for its products is not uniform, but the company is committed to avoiding layoffs during slow periods. Often, when orders slow down, workers move from one job to another, perhaps accepting a cut in pay. Rick Willard, a veteran employee in his fifties, is typical. He has worked at over a dozen different jobs during the past five years. At one point, he was part of a division that produced electric motors, then he built circuit boards for electric welding machines, followed by a stint manufacturing the harnesses that hold wires together in welding machines, and so on. Each job paid a different rate, and Willard has liked some assignments but hated others. However, he appreciates being able to remain employed and retain his health care and retirement benefits.[2]

As these two examples show, trends and events that affect the economy also create opportunities and problems in obtaining human resources. When customer demand rises (or falls), organizations may need more (or fewer) employees. When the labor market changes—say, when more people go to college or when a sizable share of the population retires—the supply of qualified workers may grow, shrink, or change in nature. Organizations recently have had difficulty filling information technology jobs because the demand for people with these skills outstrips the supply. To prepare for and respond to these challenges, organizations engage in *human resource planning*—defined in Chapter 1 as identifying the numbers and types of employees the organization will require to meet its objectives.

This chapter describes how organizations carry out human resource planning. In the first part of the chapter, we lay out the steps that go into developing and implementing a human resource plan. Throughout each section, we focus especially on recent trends and practices, including downsizing, employing temporary workers, and outsourcing. The remainder of the chapter explores the process of recruiting. We describe the process by which organizations look for people to fill job vacancies and the usual sources of job candidates. Finally, we discuss the role of recruiters.

THE PROCESS OF HUMAN RESOURCE PLANNING

LO1
Discuss how to plan for human resources needed to carry out the organization's strategy.

Organizations should carry out human resource planning so as to meet business objectives and gain an advantage over competitors. To do this, organizations need a clear idea of the strengths and weaknesses of their existing internal labor force. They also must know what they want to be doing in the future—what size they want the organization to be, what products and services it should be producing, and so on. This knowledge helps them define the number and kinds of employees they will need. Human resource planning compares the present state of the organization with its goals for the future, then identifies what changes it must make in its human resources to meet those goals. The changes may include downsizing, training existing employees in new skills, or hiring new employees.

These activities give a general view of HR planning. They take place in the human resource planning process shown in Figure 5.1. The process consists of three stages: forecasting, goal setting and strategic planning, and program implementation and evaluation.

Forecasting

The first step in human resource planning is **forecasting,** as shown in the top portion of Figure 5.1. In personnel forecasting, the HR professional tries to determine the supply of and demand for various types of human resources. The primary goal is to predict which areas of the organization will experience labor shortages or surpluses.

Forecasting supply and demand can use statistical methods or judgment. Statistical methods capture historic trends in a company's demand for labor. Under the right conditions, these methods predict demand and supply more precisely than a human forecaster can using subjective judgment. But many important events in the labor market have no precedent. When such events occur, statistical methods are of little use. To

forecasting
The attempts to determine the supply of and demand for various types of human resources to predict areas within the organization where there will be labor shortages or surpluses.

Figure 5.1

Overview of the Human Resource Planning Process

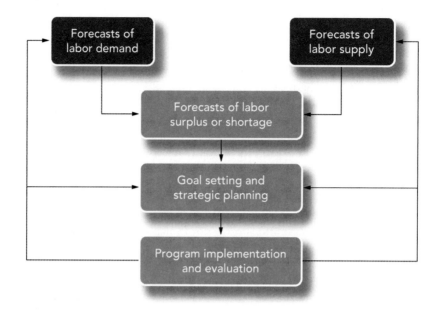

prepare for these situations, the organization must rely on the subjective judgments of experts. Pooling their "best guesses" is an important source of ideas about the future.

Forecasting the Demand for Labor

Usually, an organization forecasts demand for specific job categories or skill areas. After identifying the relevant job categories or skills, the planner investigates the likely demand for each. The planner must forecast whether the need for people with the necessary skills and experience will increase or decrease. There are several ways of making such forecasts.

At the most sophisticated level, an organization might use **trend analysis,** constructing and applying statistical models that predict labor demand for the next year, given relatively objective statistics from the previous year. These statistics are called **leading indicators**—objective measures that accurately predict future labor demand. They might include measures of the economy (such as sales or inventory levels), actions of competitors, changes in technology, and trends in the composition of the workforce. For example, a manufacturer of automobile parts that sells its product primarily to the Big Three automakers would use statistics on the Big Three automakers, using the numbers from recent time periods to predict the demand for the company's product in a later time period.

Statistical planning models are useful when there is a long, stable history that can be used to reliably detect relationships among variables. However, these models almost always have to be complemented with subjective judgments of experts. There are simply too many "once-in-a-lifetime" changes to consider, and statistical models cannot capture them.

Determining Labor Supply

Once a company has forecast the demand for labor, it needs an indication of the firm's labor supply. Determining the internal labor supply calls for a detailed analysis of how many people are currently in various job categories or have specific skills within the

LO2

Determine the labor demand for workers in various job categories.

trend analysis
Constructing and applying statistical models that predict labor demand for the next year, given relatively objective statistics from the previous year.

leading indicators
Objective measures that accurately predict future labor demand.

organization. The planner then modifies this analysis to reflect changes expected in the near future as a result of retirements, promotions, transfers, voluntary turnover, and terminations.

One type of statistical procedure that can be used for this purpose is the analysis of a **transitional matrix.** This is a chart that lists job categories held in one period and shows the proportion of employees in each of those job categories in a future period. It answers two questions: "Where did people who were in each job category go?" and "Where did people now in each job category come from?" Table 5.1 is an example of a transitional matrix.

This example lists job categories for an auto parts manufacturer. The jobs listed at the left were held in 2002; the numbers at the right show what happened to the people in 2005. The numbers represent proportions. For example, .95 means 95 percent of the people represented by a row in the matrix. The column headings under 2005 refer to the row numbers. The first row is sales managers, so the numbers under column (1) represent people who became sales managers. Reading across the first row, we see that 95 of the people who were sales managers in 2002 are still sales managers in 2005. The other 5 percent correspond to position (8), "Not in organization," meaning the 5 percent of employees who are not still sales managers have left the organization. In the second row are sales representatives. Of those who were sales reps in 2002, 5 percent were promoted to sales manager, 60 percent are still sales reps, and 35 percent have left the organization. In row (3), half (50 percent) of sales apprentices are still in that job, but 20 percent are now sales reps, and 30 percent have left the organization. This pattern of jobs shows a career path from sales apprentice to sales representative to sales manager. Of course, not everyone is promoted, and some of the people leave instead.

Reading down the columns provides another kind of information: the sources of employees holding the positions in 2005. In the first column, we see that most sales managers (95 percent) held that same job three years earlier. The other 5 percent were promoted from sales representative positions. Skipping over to column (3), half the sales apprentices on the payroll in 2005 held the same job three years before, and the other half were hired from outside the organization. This suggests that the organization fills sales manager positions primarily through promotions, so planning for this job would focus on preparing sales representatives. In contrast, planning to meet the organization's needs for sales apprentices would emphasize recruitment and selection of new employees.

transitional matrix A chart that lists job categories held in one period and shows the proportion of employees in each of those job categories in a future period.

2002	2005							
	(1)	(2)	(3)	(4)	(5)	(6)	(7)	(8)
(1) Sales manager	.95							.05
(2) Sales representative	.05	.60						.35
(3) Sales apprentice		.20	.50					.30
(4) Assistant plant manager				.90	.05			.05
(5) Production manager				.10	.75			.15
(6) Production assembler					.10	.80		.10
(7) Clerical							.70	.30
(8) Not in organization	.00	.20	.50	.00	.10	.20	.30	

TABLE 5.1

Transitional Matrix: Example for an Auto Parts Manufacturer

Matrices such as this one are extremely useful for charting historical trends in the company's supply of labor. More important, if conditions remain somewhat constant, they can also be used to plan for the future. For example, if we believe that that we are going to have a surplus of labor in the production assembler job category in the next three years, we can plan to avoid layoffs. Still, historical data may not always reliably indicate future trends. Planners need to combine statistical forecasts of labor supply with expert judgments. For example, managers in the organization may see that a new training program will likely increase the number of employees qualified for new openings. Forecasts of labor supply also should take into account the organization's pool of skills. Many organizations include inventories of employees' skills in an HR database. When the organization forecasts that it will need new skills in the future, planners can consult the database to see how many existing employees have those skills.

Besides looking at the labor supply within the organization, the planner should examine trends in the external labor market. The planner should keep abreast of labor market forecasts, including the size of the labor market, the unemployment rate, and the kinds of people who will be in the labor market. For example, we saw in Chapter 2 that the U.S. labor market is aging and that immigration is an important source of new workers. Important sources of data on the external labor market include the *Occupational Outlook Quarterly* and the *Monthly Labor Review*, published by the Labor Department's Bureau of Labor Statistics. Details and news releases are available at the Web site of the Bureau of Labor Statistics (**www.bls.gov**).

LO3
Summarize the advantages and disadvantages of ways to eliminate a labor surplus and avoid a labor shortage.

Determining Labor Surplus or Shortage

Based on the forecasts for labor demand and supply, the planner can compare the figures to determine whether there will be a shortage or surplus of labor for each job category. Determining expected shortages and surpluses allows the organization to plan how to address these challenges. The "Best Practices" box tells how one company has matched labor supply—in particular, the aging workforce—with its need for management talent in China.

Issues related to a labor surplus or shortage can pose serious challenges for the organization. General Motors Corporation has addressed a labor surplus by instituting several hiring freezes over the last few years. One consequence is that the average age of its labor force is relatively old, estimated at age 48 for 2005, with fully half of GM workers eligible to retire within the next few years. At the same time, GM has estimated that it needs to reduce its workforce by close to 20 percent, so its aging workforce offers an advantage. GM can wait and let retirement and natural attrition (people choosing to leave) take care of the needed downsizing. In terms of numbers, this solves the labor surplus problem, but it does not give the company control over which workers leave. The company has to make sure that the remaining employees have the necessary skills and are prepared to handle work that had been performed by the retiring employees. Also, GM spends more than most companies to pay pension and health care benefits for retirees. This substantial expense requires management as well.[3]

Goal Setting and Strategic Planning

The second step in human resource planning is goal setting and strategic planning, as shown in the middle of Figure 5.1. The purpose of setting specific numerical goals is to focus attention on the problem and provide a basis for measuring the organization's

AT ROCKWELL AUTOMATION, AGING WORKFORCE EQUALS VALUABLE EXPERIENCE

Many employers are wondering how they will cope as the U.S. workforce ages. Some are preparing to replace older workers, but many are adopting flexible work arrangements to encourage their older workers to stick around. And some companies are finding that certain assignments are just right for an older worker. Perhaps surprisingly, some of those assignments are far from the employee's home.

Rockwell Automation, for example, found that an older employee fit the bill for a management post in China. Rockwell was building a factory in Shanghai, and it needed someone to manage the project. Its choice for the job was Gene Allison, an employee in his sixties with a solid career in manufacturing. While the stereotype of someone Allison's age might be of someone who is set in his ways, that stereotype is unfair to open-minded employees like Allison. He was not tied down with family responsibilities, and his wife was eager to explore a country that had always fascinated her.

Allison's generation brings some particular advantages to the job. For one thing, they are likely to be familiar with older technologies that sometimes are still in use at foreign facilities. For example, at facilities supervised by Allison, machining might be done on equipment whose controls have to be set manually, while a U.S. factory might have computer-controlled equipment using laser-guided drills. In addition, the older workers are less likely to require some of the overseas perks a younger employee might require, such as tuition for his or her children to attend an international school. Some employees might be concerned about overseas health care, but Allison was satisfied with the care his wife received at Chinese hospitals after she was diagnosed with cancer.

Older workers' willingness to locate to Asia is a well-timed discovery. As China's economy develops, the huge nation is providing a major opportunity for companies in the United States and elsewhere. So in this case, a growing labor supply of older workers matches up with a growing demand for management talent in China.

SOURCE: James T. Areddy, "Older Workers from U.S. Take Jobs in China," *The Wall Street Journal*, June 22, 2004, pp. B1, B6; and Kathy Chu, "Older Workers Find New Favor among Employers," *The Wall Street Journal*, September 1, 2004, p. D3.

success in addressing labor shortages and surpluses. The goals should come directly from the analysis of labor supply and demand. They should include a specific figure indicating what should happen with the job category or skill area and a specific timetable for when the results should be achieved.

For each goal, the organization must choose one or more human resource strategies. A variety of strategies is available for handling expected shortages and surpluses of labor. The top of Table 5.2 shows major options for reducing an expected labor surplus, and the bottom of the table lists options for avoiding an expected labor shortage.

This planning stage is critical. The options differ widely in their expense, speed, and effectiveness. Options for reducing a labor surplus cause differing amounts of human suffering. The options for avoiding a labor shortage differ in terms of how easily the organization can undo the change if it no longer faces a labor shortage. For example, an organization probably would not want to handle every expected labor shortage by hiring new employees. The process is relatively slow and involves expenses to find and

TABLE 5.2

HR Strategies for
Addressing a Labor
Shortage or Surplus

OPTIONS FOR REDUCING A SURPLUS		
OPTION	SPEED OF RESULTS	AMOUNT OF SUFFERING CAUSED
Downsizing	Fast	High
Pay reductions	Fast	High
Demotions	Fast	High
Transfers	Fast	Moderate
Work sharing	Fast	Moderate
Hiring freeze	Slow	Low
Natural attrition	Slow	Low
Early retirement	Slow	Low
Retraining	Slow	Low

OPTIONS FOR AVOIDING A SHORTAGE		
OPTION	SPEED OF RESULTS	ABILITY TO CHANGE LATER
Overtime	Fast	High
Temporary employees	Fast	High
Outsourcing	Fast	High
Retrained transfers	Slow	High
Turnover reductions	Slow	Moderate
New external hires	Slow	Low
Technological innovation	Slow	Low

train new employees. Also, if the shortage becomes a surplus, the organization will have to consider laying off some of the employees. Layoffs involve another set of expenses, such as severance pay, and they are costly in terms of human suffering.

Another consideration in choosing an HR strategy is whether the employees needed will contribute directly to the organization's success. Organizations are most likely to benefit from hiring and retaining employees who provide a **core competency**—that is, a set of knowledges and skills that make the organization superior to competitors and create value for customers. At a store, for example, core competencies include choosing merchandise that shoppers want and providing shoppers with excellent service. For other work that is not a core competency—say, cleaning the store and providing security—the organization may benefit from using HR strategies other than hiring full-time employees.

Organizations try to anticipate labor surpluses far enough ahead that they can freeze hiring and let natural attrition (people leaving on their own) reduce the labor force. Unfortunately for many workers, in the past decade, the typical way organizations have responded to a surplus of labor has been downsizing, which delivers fast results. Beyond the obvious economic impact, downsizing has a psychological impact that spills over and affects families, increasing the rates of divorce, child abuse, and drug and alcohol addiction.[4] To handle a labor shortage, organizations typically hire temporary employees or use outsourcing. Because downsizing, using temporary employees, and outsourcing are most common, we will look at each of these in greater detail in the following sections.

core competency
A set of knowledges
and skills that make
the organization
superior to
competitors and
create value for
customers.

Cold Stone Creamery employees give their company the competitive advantage with their "entertainment factor." The company is known to seek out employees who like to perform and "audition" rather than interview potential employees.

Downsizing

As we discussed in Chapter 2, **downsizing** is the planned elimination of large numbers of personnel with the goal of enhancing the organization's competitiveness. Many organizations adopted this option in the late 1980s and early 1990s, especially in the United States. Over 85 percent of the Fortune 1000 firms downsized between 1987 and 2001, resulting in more than 8 million permanent layoffs—an unprecedented figure in U.S. economic history. The jobs eliminated were not temporary losses due to downturns in the business cycle, but permanent losses resulting from changes in the competitive pressures faced by businesses today. In fact, 8 out of every 10 companies that underwent downsizing were earning a profit at the same time.[5]

downsizing
The planned elimination of large numbers of personnel with the goal of enhancing the organization's competitiveness.

The primary reason organizations engage in downsizing is to promote future competitiveness. According to surveys, they do this by meeting four objectives:

1. *Reducing costs*—Labor is a large part of a company's total costs, so downsizing is an attractive place to start cutting costs.
2. *Replacing labor with technology*—Closing outdated factories, automating, or introducing other technological changes reduces the need for labor. Often, the labor savings outweigh the cost of the new technology.
3. *Mergers and acquisitions*—When organizations combine, they often need less bureaucratic overhead, so they lay off managers and some professional staff members. After software maker Oracle Corporation acquired PeopleSoft, it laid off about 5,000 employees, almost one out of 10. It kept most of PeopleSoft's technical employees so that the company could continue meeting plans for product development and support, meaning the vulnerable positions were those involving administrative functions.[6]
4. *Moving to more economical locations*—Some organizations move from one area of the United States to another, especially from the Northeast, Midwest, and California to the South and the mountain regions of the West. Such moves are one reason that recent job growth has been strongest in Florida and Arizona. In contrast, Michigan, a state in which it is relatively expensive to operate, actually lost jobs during 2004, a period of national economic growth.[7] Other moves have

shifted jobs to other countries. Electronic Data Systems, a computer-services company based in Plano, Texas, plans to double the number of employees in low-wage countries to 20,000 at the same time it is planning to cut 20,000 higher-wage workers such as those in the United States. At least one-fourth of the new EDS jobs will be in India.[8]

Although the jury is still out on whether these downsizing efforts have enhanced performance, some indications are that the results have not lived up to expectations. According to a study of 52 Fortune 100 firms, most firms that announced a downsizing campaign showed worse, rather than better, financial performance in the years that followed.[9]

Why do so many downsizing efforts fail to meet expectations? There seem to be several reasons. First, although the initial cost savings give a temporary boost to profits, the long-term effects of an improperly managed downsizing effort can be negative. Downsizing leads to a loss of talent, and it often disrupts the social networks through which people are creative and flexible.[10] In one study of hospitals that cut costs by eliminating jobs across the board, the downsizing was followed by an increase in patient mortality rates. And within a year and a half, the costs had climbed to pre-downsizing levels.[11]

Also, many companies wind up rehiring. Downsizing campaigns often eliminate people who turn out to be irreplaceable. In one survey, 80 percent of the firms that had downsized wound up replacing some of the very people they had laid off. One senior manager of a Fortune 100 firm described a situation in which a bookkeeper making $9 an hour was let go. Later, the company realized she knew many things about the company that no one else knew, so she was hired back as a consultant—for $42 an hour.[12] Hiring back formerly laid-off workers has become so routine that many organizations track their laid-off employees, using software formerly used for tracking job applicants. If the organization ever faces a labor shortage, it can quickly contact these former workers and restore them to the payroll.[13]

Finally, downsizing efforts often fail because employees who survive the purge become self-absorbed and afraid to take risks. Motivation drops because any hope of future promotions—or any future—with the company dies. Many employees start looking for other employment opportunities. The negative publicity associated with a downsizing campaign can also hurt the company's image in the labor market, so it is harder to recruit employees later. (The "Did You Know . . . ?" box gives an example of the importance of job security to workers.) The key to avoiding this kind of damage is to ensure that the need for the layoff is well explained and that procedures for carrying out the layoff are fair.[14] Although this advice may sound like common sense, organizations are often reluctant to provide complete information, especially when a layoff results from top-level mismanagement.[15]

Many problems with downsizing can be reduced with better planning. A good example is Marlow Industries, a Dallas-based manufacturer of temperature-control instruments. Because of lower-priced foreign competition, Marlow's revenues recently plummeted 60 percent. The company responded with a three-part strategy to keep it alive: (1) moving routine, low-profit work to China, (2) automating processes, and (3) eliminating middle managers. The remaining U.S. workforce was one-fourth its original size. Marlow's leadership understood that the changes could demoralize the remaining workers, so executives communicated extensively with the employees. The company's president, Barry Nickerson, explained the company's finances and its plans to operate more profitably in the future, including its commitment to keeping the high-end manufac-

TECH WORKERS MOST CONCERNED ABOUT JOB SECURITY

According to a recent survey of information technology workers, lack of job security is their major source of stress. The graph shows the sources of stress the workers cited most often.

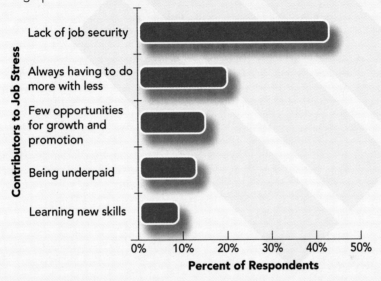

SOURCE: Ed Frauenheim, "Survey: Techies Stressed over Job Insecurity," CNet News.com, March 17, 2005, www.news.com.

turing work in the United States. Within a few years, Marlow had survived the business downturn.[16] The "HR How To" box offers guidelines for carrying out downsizing.

Still, downsizing hardly guarantees an increase in an organization's competitiveness. Organizations should more carefully consider using all the other avenues for eliminating a labor surplus (shown in Table 5.2). Many of these take effect slowly, so organizations must improve their forecasting or be stuck with downsizing as their only viable option.

Early-Retirement Programs

Another popular way to reduce a labor surplus is with an early-retirement program. As we discussed in Chapter 2, the average age of the U.S. workforce is increasing. But even though many baby boomers are approaching traditional retirement age, early indications are that this group has no intention of retiring soon.[17] Several forces fuel the drawing out of older workers' careers. First, the improved health of older people in general, combined with the decreased physical labor required by many jobs, has made working longer a viable option. Also, many workers fear Social Security will be cut and have skimpy employer-sponsored pensions that may not cover their expenses. Finally, age discrimination laws and the outlawing of mandatory retirement ages have limited organizations' ability to induce older workers to retire. Under the pressures associated with an aging labor force, many employers try to encourage older workers to leave voluntarily by offering a variety of early-retirement incentives. The more lucrative of

HR HOW TO

MINIMIZING THE PAIN OF LAYOFFS

Although layoffs are always painful, handling the task well can maintain employees' dignity and improve the organization's long-term health. When layoffs increased in 2001, *Inc.* magazine asked Helen Drinan, chief executive officer of the Society for Human Resource Management, to offer advice on minimizing the pain of layoffs. Here's what she recommended:

- *Communicate fully.* As soon as you know about layoffs, tell employees the news, in detail. First tell the people who will be laid off. Then tell the whole group what you are doing and why. If there's information you *don't* know, disclose that, too.
- *Empower managers to make choices.* The company's executives shouldn't decide precisely which people to lay off. People who are closer to

the situation should be involved in such decisions.
- *Ask laid-off employees to leave immediately, but be humane about it.* It's probably unwise to let employees hang around for days, using the company's phones and computers. Still, you don't have to send over a security guard to usher the employees out of the building. Ways to be humane include offering to stay late and help pack personal belongings, providing an outplacement service, and offering to be a reference in the laid-off employee's job hunt.
- *Budget for layoffs.* Plan to give laid-off employees at least two weeks' severance pay, plus more based on years of employment. If possible, include outplacement services in the layoff budget.

- *Plan ahead.* Even when times are good, managers know that downsizing is often part of an organization's strategy. Drinan recommends the mental exercise of asking what you would do if the organization had to reduce its staff by 10 percent.

Why go to all this trouble for a change that is essentially about cutting costs? Quite simply, because even after layoffs, an organization still needs dedicated, talented people. In Drinan's words, "You want to treat [laid-off] people well, because this becomes an object lesson for everyone in your organization about how you treat employees."

SOURCE: Mike Hofman, "Five Rules for Making Layoffs Less Painful," *Inc.*, April 2001, pp. 97–98.

these programs succeed by some measures. Research suggests that these programs encourage lower-performing older workers to retire.[18] Sometimes they work so well that too many workers retire.

Many organizations are moving from early-retirement programs to phased-retirement programs. In a *phased-retirement program*, the organization can continue to enjoy the experience of older workers while reducing the number of hours that these employees work, as well as the cost of those employees. This option also can give older employees the psychological benefit of easing into retirement, rather than being thrust entirely into a new way of life.[19]

Employing Temporary and Contract Workers

While downsizing has been a popular way to reduce a labor surplus, the most widespread methods for eliminating a labor shortage are hiring temporary and contract workers and outsourcing work. Employers may arrange to hire a temporary worker through an agency that specializes in linking employers with people who have the necessary skills. The employer pays the agency, which in turn pays the temporary worker. Employers also may contract directly with individuals, often professionals, to provide a particular service.

Temporary Workers

As we saw in Chapter 2, the federal government estimated that organizations are using over a million temporary workers. Temporary employment is popular with employers because it gives them flexibility they need to operate efficiently when demand for their products changes rapidly.

In addition to flexibility, temporary employment offers lower costs. Using temporary workers frees the employer from many administrative tasks and financial burdens associated with being the "employer of record." The cost of employee benefits, including health care, pension, life insurance, workers' compensation, and unemployment insurance, can account for 40 percent of payroll expenses for permanent employees. Assuming the agency pays for these benefits, a company using temporary workers may save money even if it pays the agency a higher rate for that worker than the usual wage paid to a permanent employee.

Agencies that provide temporary employees also may handle some of the tasks associated with hiring. Small companies that cannot afford their own testing programs often get employees who have been tested by a temporary agency. Many temporary agencies also train employees before sending them to employers. This reduces employers' training costs and eases the transition for the temporary worker and employer.

Key Resources, an agency in Greensboro, North Carolina, gives employers access to a segment of the workforce they otherwise might not be able to use: immigrants. The company has found reliable, hardworking employees in the local Hispanic and Vietnamese immigrant communities. Because many of these workers are unable to speak English, the agency also hires translators. For simple jobs, the agency can provide a translator for a day or two at no charge. For more complex jobs, the agency charges the client for a translator who stays on for the entire project and also performs other duties.[20]

Finally, temporary workers may offer value not available from permanent employees. Because the temporary worker has little experience at the employer's organization, this person brings an objective point of view to the organization's problems and procedures. Also, a temporary worker may have a great deal of experience in other organizations. A temporary worker at Lord, Abbett and Company, an investment firm in New York, suggested an efficient software program for managing investment portfolios. The worker had been trained with that program at a different firm.

Employee or Contractor?

Besides using a temporary-employment agency, a company can obtain workers for limited assignments by entering into contracts with them. If the person providing the services is an independent contractor, rather than an employee, the company does not pay employee benefits, such as health insurance and vacations. As with using temporary employees, the savings can be significant, even if the contractor works at a higher rate of pay. The "e-HRM" box describes how technology can further improve the efficiency of using contractors.

FedEx Ground recently built up an efficient delivery system by signing on drivers to work as independent contractors. These contract drivers lease vans and buy uniforms

E-HRM

ONLINE SYSTEM LETS SHELL OIL PLAN FOR CONTRACT WORKERS

Shell Oil Products U.S., a subsidiary of Shell Oil Company, spends about $100 million a year for contract workers. They handle short-term assignments as varied as accounting and information technology consulting. Planning the most efficient way to hire and use these workers has been a massive challenge for the Houston company. Each department had its own forms and procedures to find contractors, set rates, and keep track of the work. The company was using workers from more than 20 contracting firms for administrative employees alone. Shell decided to use technology to reduce the costs.

Shell found help in Web-based software developed by IQNavigator. The software qualifies suppliers, gathers and publishes requests for proposals from contract firms, collects time and expense data from the contractors, and prepares invoices. These tasks are all handled online. In addition, the software lets Shell managers compare current and past spending and performance to help them choose suppliers and negotiate contract terms. They can also go online to check the status of ongoing projects.

As a Shell team worked with IQNavigator to set up the system, they streamlined the process of planning and contracting for workers, and they reduced the number of contracting firms so that they could negotiate better rates with their preferred suppliers. Although the company is getting better rates, the suppliers are happy because of their larger, steadier stream of business from Shell.

The biggest challenge in setting up the new system was getting the Shell employees used to the new process. Some were reluctant to use a shorter list of suppliers. Shell handles this obstacle by educating its people about the business benefits of the new system. Still, Kim Chapman, the project's team leader, admits, "People don't like that kind of scrutiny and aren't always accepting of that level of change." Convincing them is easier, however, because the company's chief executive officer and chief financial officer both have given the project their support. No wonder, considering that the project's goal is to reduce spending on contract workers by an impressive 8 percent a year. With human resource goals, as with other business goals, a bottom-line benefit is the way to win an executive's heart.

SOURCE: Thomas Hoffman, "Contingent Workforce: Managing the Temporary Players," *Computerworld*, June 30, 2003, www.computerworld.com; and IQNavigator, "IQNavigator Selected by Shell Oil Products U.S. to Automate Services Procurement and Spend Management," news release, April 1, 2003, www.iqnavigator.com.

from FedEx and take responsibility for the deliveries along a particular route. They are responsible for their business expenses, including gasoline and maintenance of their trucks. FedEx pays them according to the number of packages they deliver plus a bonus based on its own information about customer satisfaction. The payment method provides an incentive for the contractors to work hard and drum up new business. Some successful drivers have hired their own employees and leased additional trucks.[21]

This strategy carries risks, however. If the person providing the service is a contractor and not an employee, the company is not supposed to directly supervise the worker. The company can tell the contractor what criteria the finished assignment should meet but not, for example, where or what hours to work. This distinction is significant, because under federal law, if the company treats the contractor as an employee, the company has certain legal obligations, described in Part 4, related to matters such as overtime pay and withholding taxes. With regard to FedEx Ground, some drivers have become dissatisfied with their working arrangement and complained that they are actually employees. In courts in California, Montana, and New Jersey, judges found FedEx Ground drivers with contracts to be employees (the company appealed those rulings). The Internal Revenue Service has begun investigating these arrangements, to see whether FedEx management is exerting too much control. For FedEx, the challenge is to figure out whether it can continue an arrangement it says many drivers prefer, exert enough influence to ensure contractors meet its standards, and also meet the legal requirements for independent contractor status.[22]

When an organization wants to consider using independent contractors as a way to expand its labor force temporarily, human resource professionals can help by alerting the company to the need to verify that the arrangement will meet the legal requirements. A good place to start is with the advice to small businesses at the Internal Revenue Service Web site (**www.irs.gov**); search for "independent contractor" to find links to information and guidance. In addition, the organization may need to obtain professional legal advice.

Guidelines for Using Temporary Employees and Contractors

To benefit from using contract or temporary workers, organizations must overcome the disadvantages associated with this type of labor force. One drawback is that tension often exists between temporary and permanent employees. According to surveys, one-third of full-time employees perceive temporary workers as a threat to their own job security. Such an attitude can interfere with cooperation and, in some cases, lead to outright sabotage if the situation is not well managed.

One way organizations should manage this situation is to complete any downsizing efforts before bringing in temporary or contract workers. Surviving a downsizing is almost like experiencing a death in the family. In this context, a decent time interval needs to occur before new temporary workers are introduced. Without the delay, the surviving employees will associate the downsizing effort (which was a threat) with the new temporary employees (who could be perceived as outsiders brought in to replace old friends). If an upswing in demand follows a downsizing effort, the organization should probably begin meeting its expanded demand for labor by granting overtime to core employees. If the demand persists, the organization will be more certain that the upswing will last and future layoffs will be unnecessary. The extended stretches of overtime will eventually tax the full-time employees, so they will accept using temporary workers to help lessen their load.

Organizations that use temporary or contract workers must avoid treating them as second-class citizens. One way to do this is to ensure that the temporary agency provides temporaries with benefits that are comparable with those enjoyed by the organization's permanent workers. For example, one temporary agency, MacTemps, gives its workers long-term health coverage, full disability insurance, and complete dental coverage. This not only reduces the benefit gap between the temporary and permanent workers but also helps attract the best temporary workers in the first place.

Outsourcing

Instead of using a temporary or contract employee to fill a single job, an organization might want a broader set of services. Contracting with another organization to perform a broad set of services is called **outsourcing.** Organizations use outsourcing as a way to operate more efficiently and save money. They choose outsourcing firms that promise to deliver the same or better quality at a lower cost. One reason they can do

outsourcing
Contracting with another organization to perform a broad set of services.

this is that the outside company specializes in the service and can benefit from economies of scale (the economic principle that producing something in large volume tends to cost less for each additional unit than producing in small volume). This efficiency is often the attraction for outsourcing human resource functions such as payroll. Costs also are lower when the outsourcing firm is located in a part of the world where wages are relatively low. The labor forces of countries such as China, India, Jamaica, and those in Eastern Europe have been creating an abundant supply of labor for unskilled and low-skilled work.

The first uses of outsourcing emphasized manufacturing and routine tasks. However, technological advances in computer networks and transmission have speeded up the outsourcing process and have helped it spread beyond manufacturing areas and low-skilled jobs. For example, Xpitax provides for the outsourcing of income tax preparation. Accounting firms send the company electronic files of clients' data, and Xpitax puts the data on a secure Internet server. In India, Xpitax accountants retrieve the data and prepare the tax returns.[23]

In the case of manufacturing, outsourcing may make good sense in the short term but may hurt U.S. firms' competitiveness. Outsourcing reduces manufacturing costs, but companies eventually will have more and more difficulty designing products that apply innovations in technology. According to this argument, unrestrained outsourcing starts a downward spiral of more and more outsourcing until the organization no longer produces anything of value. Companies that manufacture goods develop their own design teams and compete directly and with a substantial competitive advantage.

Organizations that are interested in outsourcing should plan how they will avoid problems. Outsourcing an operation means giving up direct control, particularly when outsourcing to another country. Some companies that have tried offshoring have been disappointed by the results. Sometimes cost savings have been lost to quality-control problems, security violations, and poor customer service. To prevent such problems, organizations should use outsourcing primarily for repetitive, predictable tasks. For example, Dell Computer sends almost all of its call center service work for home computers to India. But the problems of Dell's business users tend to be more complex and unpredictable, so Dell uses a U.S. call center for those customers.[24]

Overtime and Expanded Hours

Organizations facing a labor shortage may be reluctant to hire employees, even temporary workers, or to commit to an outsourcing arrangement. Especially if the organization expects the shortage to be temporary, it may prefer an arrangement that is simpler and less costly. Under some conditions, these organizations may try to garner more hours from the existing labor force. Many employers opted for this strategy during the 1990s. As a result, 6 percent of the automobiles assembled in North America in 1997 resulted from overtime production—equivalent to the output of an additional four auto plants running on straight time (no overtime).[25]

A major downside of overtime is that the employer must pay nonmanagement employees one-and-a-half times their normal wages for work done overtime. Even so, employers see overtime pay as preferable to the costs of hiring and training new employees. The preference is especially strong if the organization doubts that the current higher level of demand for its products will last long.

For a short time at least, many workers appreciate the added compensation for working overtime. Over extended periods, however, employees feel stress and frustration from working long hours. Overtime therefore is best suited for short-term labor shortages.

Implementing and Evaluating the HR Plan

For whatever HR strategies are selected, the final stage of human resource planning involves implementing the strategies and evaluating the outcomes. This stage is represented by the bottom part of Figure 5.1. When implementing the HR strategy, the organization must hold some individual accountable for achieving the goals. That person also must have the authority and resources needed to accomplish those goals. It is also important that this person issue regular progress reports, so the organization can be sure that all activities occur on schedule and that the early results are as expected.

Implementation at Electronic Data Systems involves using technology to make HR professionals aware of what skills the organization will need in the future, giving them time to prepare for change. The company has a database detailing employees' work histories and skills; over two-thirds of the 120,000 employees are in the database so far. Employees enter the data themselves, using a Web-based system that allows them to select from pull-down menus and offers places to enter additional information. The information in the database includes knowledge of computer languages and certifications, as well as other education and work assignments completed. HR professionals compare information in the database against the company's five-year plan to identify any skills gaps. For example, EDS determined that 22,000 employees can program using COBOL, far more than the company expects to need. To solve this labor surplus, the company is preparing training programs in newer languages where the company has a labor shortage. Thus, the HR planning process is tied to the company's training activities.[26]

In evaluating the results, the most obvious step is checking whether the organization has succeeded in avoiding labor shortages or surpluses. Along with measuring these numbers, the evaluation should identify which parts of the planning process contributed to success or failure. In EDS's case, evaluation would include whether the company has a close match between the number of programmers who know each language and the number needed to program in that language. If there is a skills gap, the evaluation should consider whether the problem lies with the forecasts used to plan training or with the implementation. For example, are programmers signing up for training, do they know about the training, and is enough of the right kind of training available?

Applying HR Planning to Affirmative Action

As we discussed in Chapter 3, many organizations have a human resource strategy that includes affirmative action to manage diversity or meet government requirements. Meeting affirmative-action goals requires that employers carry out an additional level of human resource planning aimed at those goals. In other words, besides looking at its overall workforce and needs, the organization looks at the representation of subgroups in its labor force—for example, the proportion of women and minorities.

Affirmative-action plans forecast and monitor the proportion of employees who are members of various protected groups (typically, women and racial or ethnic minorities). The planning looks at the representation of these employees in the organization's job categories and career tracks. The planner can compare the proportion of employees who are in each group with the proportion each group represents in the labor market. For example, the organization might note that in a labor market that is 25 percent Hispanic, 60 percent of its customer service personnel are Hispanic. This type of comparison is called a **workforce utilization review.** The organization can use this process to determine whether there is any subgroup whose proportion in the relevant labor market differs substantially from the proportion in the job category.

workforce utilization review A comparison of the proportion of employees in protected groups with the proportion that each group represents in the relevant labor market.

If the workforce utilization review indicates that some group—for example, African Americans—makes up 35 percent of the relevant labor market for a job category but that this same group constitutes only 5 percent of the employees actually in the job category at the organization, this is evidence of underutilization. That situation could result from problems in selection or from problems in internal movement (promotions or other movement along a career path). One way to diagnose the situation would be to use transitional matrices, such as the matrix shown in Table 5.1 earlier in this chapter.

The steps in a workforce utilization review are identical to the steps in the HR planning process that were shown in Figure 5.1. The organization must assess current utilization patterns, then forecast how these are likely to change in the near future. If these analyses suggest the organization is underutilizing certain groups and if forecasts suggest this pattern is likely to continue, the organization may need to set goals and timetables for changing. The planning process may identify new strategies for recruitment or selection. The organization carries out these HR strategies and evaluates their success.

◈ RECRUITING HUMAN RESOURCES

LO4
Describe recruitment policies organizations use to make job vacancies more attractive.

recruiting
Any activity carried on by the organization with the primary purpose of identifying and attracting potential employees.

As the first part of this chapter shows, it is difficult to always predict exactly how many (if any) new employees the organization will have to hire in a given year in a given job category. The role of human resource recruitment is to build a supply of potential new hires that the organization can draw on if the need arises. In human resource management, **recruiting** consists of any practice or activity carried on by the organization with the primary purpose of identifying and attracting potential employees.[27] It thus creates a buffer between planning and the actual selection of new employees (the topic of the next chapter).

Because of differences in companies' strategies, they may assign different degrees of importance to recruiting.[28] In general, however, all companies have to make decisions in three areas of recruiting: personnel policies, recruitment sources, and the characteristics and behavior of the recruiter. As shown in Figure 5.2, these aspects of recruiting have different effects on whom the organization ultimately hires. Personnel policies influence the characteristics of the positions to be filled. Recruitment sources influence the kinds of job applicants an organization reaches. And the nature and behavior of the recruiter affect the characteristics of both the vacancies and the applicants. Ultimately, an applicant's decision to accept a job offer—and the organization's decision to make the offer—depend on the match between vacancy characteristics and applicant characteristics.

Kelsey August has experienced the impact of this principle as she has struggled to find entry-level employees, including packers, shippers, and production workers, for her direct-marketing company, Lone Star Direct. Unskilled workers were just as happy to work for McDonald's and Wendy's, which were paying wages of $10 to $12 per hour in Austin, Texas, where Lone Star is located. After such desperate efforts as hiring away the cashiers in stores where she shopped, August tried running a newspaper ad for part-time jobs. To August's surprise, a flood of applications poured in, mostly from women with children. Lone Star revised its personnel policies to suit this new group of employees, with benefits emphasizing flexible work hours and perks that appeal to young mothers. Many of these employees are high school dropouts, so Lone Star brings in instructors to help them prepare for their high school equivalency diplomas. The company also started paying a $200 bonus to employees who refer candidates—which enabled the company to cut its budget for job advertising.[29]

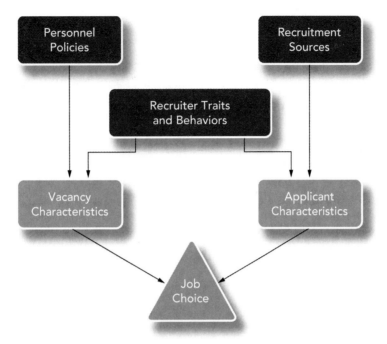

Figure 5.2

Three Aspects of Recruiting

The remainder of this chapter explores these three aspects of recruiting: personnel policies, recruitment sources, and recruiter traits and behaviors.

PERSONNEL POLICIES

An organization's *personnel policies* are its decisions about how it will carry out human resource management, including how it will fill job vacancies. These policies influence the nature of the positions that are vacant. According to the research on recruitment, it is clear that characteristics of the vacancy are more important than recruiters or recruiting sources for predicting job choice.[30] Several personnel policies are especially relevant to recruitment:

- Recruiting existing employees to fill vacancies or hiring from outside the organization.
- Meeting or exceeding the market rate of pay.
- Emphasizing job security or the right to terminate employees.
- Images of the organization conveyed in its advertising.

Let's explore the impact of each of these policy areas.

Internal versus External Recruiting

Opportunities for advancement make a job more attractive to applicants and employees. Organizations with policies to "promote from within" try to fill upper-level vacancies by recruiting candidates internally—that is, finding candidates who already work for the organization. In a 2001 survey of students pursuing a master's degree in business administration (MBA), a policy of promotion from within was the students' top consideration when they were evaluating jobs at a company.[31]

As personnel policies, decisions about internal versus external recruiting affect the nature of jobs. As we will discuss later in the chapter, they also influence recruitment sources and the nature of applicants. For now, we will focus on the impact of these

Retailers tend to promote from within their organizations, a policy that is attractive to many workers.

decisions as personnel policies. Promote-from-within policies signal to job applicants that the company provides opportunities for advancement, both for the present vacancy and for later vacancies created when people are promoted to fill higher-level vacancies.

Besides providing a career path, internal recruiting can help prevent layoffs during a labor surplus, signaling a policy of retaining valued employees whenever possible. Wachovia Corporation experienced a surplus of investment bankers after stock market slumps in 2003 lowered the demand for their services. Many of Wachovia's investment bankers risked being laid off. However, the company used technology to promote from within. It had a database containing all its open positions and résumés of its employees. Human resource personnel were able to search the databases to find matches between skills sets and job requirements. In this way, Wachovia was able to find new positions for half the investment bankers whose jobs were eliminated.[32]

Lead-the-Market Pay Strategies

Pay is an important job characteristic for almost all applicants. Organizations have a recruiting advantage if their policy is to take a "lead-the-market" approach to pay— that is, pay more than the current market wages for a job. Higher pay can also make up for a job's less desirable features. For example, many organizations pay employees more for working midnight shifts than daytime shifts. (This practice is called paying a *shift differential*; we will take a closer look at these and other decisions about pay in Chapters 11 and 12.)

Organizations that compete for applicants based on pay can do so using forms of pay other than wages or salary. During the 1990s, many employers offered stock option plans (the right to buy company stock at a set price at a specified time). At that time, stock options were attractive because stock prices in general were rising rapidly. However, when stock prices fell sharply in 2001, the appeal of stock options as a form of pay also declined. More traditional forms of pay have currently regained their importance. As Figure 5.3 shows, the share of students who listed stock options as their most important incentive fell by more than half between January 2000 and January 2001. At the same time, the share of students who most valued flexible hours increased substantially.[33]

Employment-at-Will Policies

employment at will Employment principle that if there is no specific employment contract saying otherwise, the employer or employee may end an employment relationship at any time, regardless of cause.

Within the laws of the state where they are operating, employers have latitude to set policies about their rights in an employment relationship. A widespread policy follows the principle of **employment at will,** which holds that if there is no specific employment contract saying otherwise, the employer or employee may end an employment relationship at any time, regardless of cause. An alternative to employment at

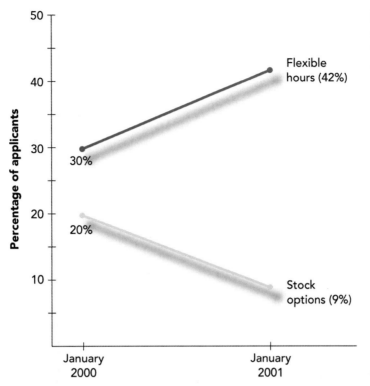

Figure 5.3

Changing Nature of the "Most Important Benefit" among New Job Applicants

will is to establish extensive **due-process policies,** which formally lay out the steps an employee may take to appeal an employer's decision to terminate that employee. When employees have sued on the grounds that employers discharged them wrongfully, court decisions of the last few decades have eroded employers' rights to terminate employees with impunity.[34] To protect organizations from being sued on the grounds of wrongful discharge, their lawyers have sometimes recommended that they make sure all their recruitment documents say the employment is "at will." Organizations have been advised to avoid any mention of due process in company handbooks, personnel manuals, and recruiting brochures.[35]

In decisions about employment-at-will policies, organizations should consider not only the legal advantages of employment at will but also the effect of such policies on recruitment. For many applicants, job security is important. If the organization's recruiting materials emphasize due process, rights of appeal, and mechanisms for filing grievances, the message is that the company is concerned about protecting employees, and job security is high. Materials that emphasize employment at will send a message that job security is minimal. Job applicants are more attracted to organizations with due-process policies than to organizations with employment-at-will policies.[36]

due-process policies
Policies that formally lay out the steps an employee may take to appeal the employer's decision to terminate that employee.

Image Advertising

Besides advertising specific job openings, as discussed in the next section, organizations may advertise themselves as a good place to work in general.[37] Advertising designed to create a generally favorable impression of the organization is called *image advertising.* Image advertising is particularly important for organizations in highly competitive labor markets that perceive themselves as having a bad image.[38]

Image advertising, such as in this campaign to recruit nurses, promotes a whole profession or organization as opposed to a specific job opening. This ad is designed to create a positive impression of the profession, which is now facing a shortage of workers.

Research suggests that the image of an organization's brand—for example, innovative, dynamic, or fun—influences the degree to which a person feels attracted to the organization.[39] This attraction is especially true if the person's own traits seem to match those of the organization. Also, job applicants seem to be particularly sensitive to issues of diversity and inclusion in image advertising. So, organizations should ensure that their image advertisements depict the broad nature of the labor market from which they intend to recruit.[40]

One organization that has used image advertising creatively is the U.S. Army. As the insurgency has persisted in Iraq, recruitment targets have become more difficult to meet, so these efforts are crucial for that organization to fulfill its mission. Besides print and broadcast advertising, the army has a recruiting Web site (**www.goarmy. com**). The site features video clips profiling a theme of strength: "Strength for now. Strength for later. Army training strengthens you for life." It provides information about what is involved in being a soldier and what pay and benefits the Army provides. To build involvement, there is even a game called America's Army, which simulates training missions. In contrast to peacetime recruitment, when it might be enough to emphasize opportunities to see the world and receive educational benefits, wartime recruiting requires capturing the interest of people who can be inspired literally to fight for freedom.

Whether the goal is to influence the perception of the public in general or specific segments of the labor market, job seekers form beliefs about the nature of the organizations well before they have any direct interviewing experience with these companies. Thus, organizations must assess their reputation in the labor market and correct any shortcomings they detect in people's actual image of them.[41]

LO5
List and compare sources of job applicants.

❧ RECRUITMENT SOURCES

Another critical element of an organization's recruitment strategy is its decisions about where to look for applicants. The total labor market is enormous and spread over the entire globe. As a practical matter, an organization will draw from a small fraction of that total market. The methods the organization chooses for communicating its labor needs and the audiences it targets will determine the size and nature of the labor market the organization taps to fill its vacant positions.[42] A person who responds to a job advertisement on the Internet is likely to be different from a person responding to a sign hanging outside a factory. Figure 5.4 summarizes major sources from which organizations draw recruits. Each source has advantages and disadvantages.

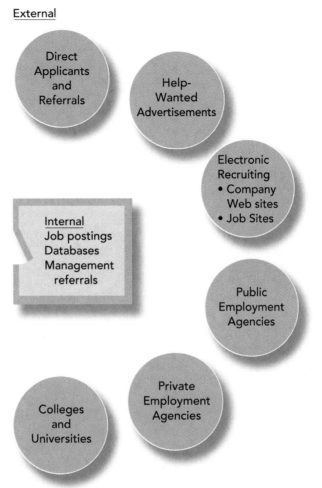

Figure 5.4
Recruitment Sources

Internal Sources

As we discussed with regard to personnel policies, an organization may emphasize internal or external sources of job applicants. Internal sources are employees who currently hold other positions in the organization. Organizations recruit existing employees through **job posting,** or communicating information about the vacancy on company bulletin boards, in employee publications, on corporate intranets, and anywhere else the organization communicates with employees. Managers also may identify candidates to recommend for vacancies. Policies that emphasize promotions and even lateral moves to achieve broader career experience can give applicants a favorable impression of the organization's jobs. The use of internal sources also affects what kinds of people the organization recruits.

For the employer, relying on internal sources offers several advantages.[43] First, it generates applicants who are well known to the organization. In addition, these applicants are relatively knowledgeable about the organization's vacancies, which minimizes the possibility they will have unrealistic expectations about the job. Finally, filling vacancies through internal recruiting is generally cheaper and faster than looking outside the organization.

job posting
The process of communicating information about a job vacancy on company bulletin boards, in employee publications, on corporate intranets, and anywhere else the organization communicates with employees.

The value of a strong internal hiring system can be seen in the experience of Whirlpool. In 2001, it was difficult for someone inside the company to know what jobs were available within the huge manufacturing conglomerate. The job-posting system was a paper-and-pencil process, organized regionally, so it was difficult and time-consuming to obtain information about positions out of state. The company replaced this ineffective system with a Web-based system that allows managers to enter information about open positions and lets employees enter their résumés. Both use a standardized format, so the software can search for key terms and locate matches. In 2003, Whirlpool filled over half of its open positions with internal hires, cutting costs for recruiting and training by $1 million. The system also satisfies employees, who can use it for planning their careers.[44]

External Sources

Despite the advantages of internal recruitment, organizations often have good reasons to recruit externally.[45] For entry-level positions and perhaps for specialized upper-level positions, the organization has no internal recruits from which to draw. Also, bringing in outsiders may expose the organization to new ideas or new ways of doing business. An organization that uses only internal recruitment can wind up with a workforce whose members all think alike and therefore may be poorly suited to innovation.[46] So organizations often recruit through direct applicants and referrals, advertisements, employment agencies, schools, and Web sites.

Direct Applicants and Referrals

direct applicants
People who apply for a vacancy without prompting from the organization.

referrals
People who apply for a vacancy because someone in the organization prompted them to do so.

Even without a formal effort to reach job applicants, an organization may hear from candidates through direct applicants and referrals. **Direct applicants** are people who apply for a vacancy without prompting from the organization. **Referrals** are people who apply because someone in the organization prompted them to do so. According to a recent survey of large companies, the largest share of new employees hired (about one-third) came from referrals, and the next largest share (30 percent) came from on-line applications, about half of which were direct applications made at the employer's Web site.[47] These two sources of recruits share some characteristics that make them excellent pools from which to draw.

One advantage is that many direct applicants are to some extent already "sold" on the organization. Most have done some research and concluded there is enough fit between themselves and the vacant position to warrant submitting an application, a process called *self-selection*, which, when it works, eases the pressure on the organization's recruiting and selection systems. A form of aided self-selection occurs with referrals. Many job seekers look to friends, relatives, and acquaintances to help find employment. Using these social networks not only helps the job seeker, but also simplifies recruitment for employers.[48] Current employees (who are familiar with the vacancy as well as the person they are referring) decide that there is a fit between the person and the vacancy, so they convince the person to apply for the job.

An additional benefit of using such sources is that it costs much less than formal recruiting efforts. Considering these combined benefits, referrals and direct applications are among the best sources of new hires. Some employers offer current employees financial incentives for referring applicants who are hired and perform acceptably on the job (for example, if they stay 180 days). Other companies play off their good reputations in the labor market to generate direct applications. Caterpillar, which makes construction and mining equipment, takes a long-term approach to cultivating community relationships in order to attract applications from qualified Hispanic workers. In general, Hispanic professionals are more likely to seek jobs through personal networks, rather than through formal channels. The company has partnered with Texas A & M University and the Hispanic Alliance for Career Enhancement (HACE). Caterpillar established a career center at Texas A & M, which has a reputation for excellent engineering students and a significant Hispanic population. HACE has helped the company develop ties to community leaders and campus organizations. Together, these partnerships give the company a positive reputation and have helped the company recruit Hispanic professionals. Their presence in the company's management ranks further enhance Caterpillar's reputation as a place that welcomes talented Hispanic people and rewards them based on their contributions, not their background.[49]

The major downside of referrals is that they limit the likelihood of exposing the organization to fresh viewpoints. People tend to refer others who are like themselves. Furthermore, sometimes referrals contribute to hiring practices that are or that appear unfair, an example being **nepotism,** or the hiring of relatives. Employees may resent the hiring and rapid promotion of "the boss's son" or "the boss's daughter," or even the boss's friend.

nepotism
The practice of hiring relatives.

Advertisements in Newspapers and Magazines

Open almost any newspaper or magazine and you can find advertisements of job openings. These ads typically generate a less desirable group of applicants than direct applications or referrals, and do so at greater expense. However, few employers can fill all their vacancies purely through direct applications and referrals, so they usually need to advertise. Also, an employer can take many steps to increase the effectiveness of recruitment through advertising.

The person designing a job advertisement needs to answer two questions:

What do we need to say?
To whom do we need to say it?

With respect to the first question, an ad should give readers enough information to evaluate the job and its requirements, so they can make a well-informed judgment about their qualifications. Providing enough information may require long advertisements, which cost more. The employer should evaluate the additional costs against the costs of providing too little information: Vague ads generate a huge number of applicants, including many who are not reasonably qualified or would not accept the job if they learned more about it. Reviewing all these applications to eliminate unsuitable applicants is expensive.

Specifying whom to reach with the message helps the advertiser decide where to place the ad. The most common medium for advertising jobs is the classified section of local newspapers. These ads are relatively inexpensive yet reach many people in a specific geographic area who are currently looking for work (or at least interested enough to be reading the classifieds). On the downside, this medium offers little ability to target skill levels. Typically, many of the people reading classified ads are either over- or underqualified for the position. Also, people who are not looking for work rarely read the classifieds. These people may include candidates the organization could lure from their current employers. For reaching a specific part of the labor market, including certain skill levels and more people who are employed, the organization may get better results from advertising in professional or industry journals. Some employers also advertise on television—particularly cable television.[50]

Figure 5.5

Sources of Recruits

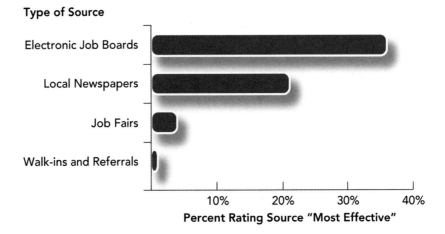

Type of Source

Electronic Job Boards

Local Newspapers

Job Fairs

Walk-ins and Referrals

Percent Rating Source "Most Effective"

Electronic Recruiting

The Internet has opened up new vistas for organizations trying to recruit talent. Increasingly, organizations are refining their use of this medium. As shown in Figure 5.5, over one-third of HR executives responding to a 2001 survey indicated that electronic job boards were the most effective source of recruits for their organization.[51] According to CareerXRoads, 10 times as many employees are hired in response to Internet postings as in response to newspaper ads.[52] Their numbers are not limited to tech-savvy computer programmers. To fill jobs at the new Wynn Las Vegas hotel and casino, human resource officer Arte Nathan used newspaper ads, a Web site, and an employment center staffed with bilingual workers. To Nathan's surprise, most of the applications came in via the Internet. For service workers, Nathan had expected "there would be some percentage who either didn't have access to a computer or didn't speak English." Apparently, computer access was not an issue for most workers around Las Vegas.[53]

There are many ways to employ the Internet for recruiting. One of the easiest ways to get into "e-cruiting" is simply to use the organization's own Web site to solicit applications. Although most large corporations have this capability, not all of them have learned to recruit effectively. Some provide only generalities about careers at the company, but today's job seekers expect to find descriptions of open positions and an easy way to submit a résumé. A user-friendly career site is not complicated. Basics include a prominent link to career information from the company's home page and additional links to career information for categories of candidates, such as college graduates, returning military personnel, or people in a particular profession. The user also should be able to link to information about the company, to evaluate whether it will be a good fit with the candidates' interests and strengths. Candidates also appreciate an e-mail response that the company has received the résumé—especially a response that gives a timetable about further communications from the company.[54]

Providing a way to submit applications at the company Web site is not so successful for smaller and less well-known organizations, because fewer people are likely to visit the Web site. These organizations may get better results by going to the Web sites that are set up to attract job seekers, such as Monster, HotJobs, and CareerBuilder, which attract a vast array of applicants. At these sites, job seekers submit standardized résumés. Employers can search the site's database for résumés that include specified key terms, and they can also submit information about their job opportunities, so that job seekers can search that information by key term. With both employers and job seekers submitting information to and conducting searches on them, these sites offer an efficient way to find matches between job seekers and job vacancies. However, a drawback is that the big job Web sites can provide too many leads of inferior quality because they are so huge and serve all job seekers and employers, not a select segment.

Because of this limitation of the large Web sites, smaller, more tailored Web sites called "niche boards" focus on certain industries, occupations, or geographic areas. Telecommcareers.net, for example, is a site devoted to, as the name implies, the telecommunications industry. CIO.com, a companion site to *CIO Magazine*, specializes in openings for chief information officers. In addition, some blogs cover jobs in particular industries. Written informally, blogs attract job seekers who want to read firsthand comments and news about jobs in their specialty. Several recruiters at Microsoft write blogs about careers at that company. Other blogs are related to industries, rather than particular companies. From the company's perspective, blogs can reach people who are serious about researching a job. The downside is that the company may have little control about the information in the blog itself or in the sources to which the blog is linked.[55]

In the end, with so many information resources readily available online, recruiters have to gain experience in what works for the particular organization and the types of positions it must fill. Diana Meisenhelter, vice president of staffing and talent acquisition at Wyndham International, has found that she needs to visit different sites to fill different kinds of positions at the hotel chain. According to Meisenhelter, Monster gives her the most candidates for general positions such as accounting and administrative support. To fill management jobs, she gets the best leads on the company's own recruiting Web page. And when she needs candidates with work experience in the hotels, she uses HCareers.com, a Web site that specializes in jobs in the hospitality industry.[56]

Public Employment Agencies

The Social Security Act of 1935 requires that everyone receiving unemployment compensation be registered with a local state employment office. These state employment offices work with the U.S. Employment Service (USES) to try to ensure that unemployed individuals eventually get off state aid and back on employer payrolls. To accomplish this, agencies collect information from the unemployed people about their skills and experience.

Employers can register their job vacancies with their local state employment office, and the agency will try to find someone suitable, using its computerized inventory of local unemployed individuals. The agency refers candidates to the employer at no charge. The organization can interview or test them to see if they are suitable for its vacancies. Besides offering access to job candidates at low cost, public employment agencies can be a useful resource for meeting certain diversity objectives. Laws often mandate that the agencies maintain specialized "desks" for minorities, disabled individuals, and Vietnam War veterans. Employers that feel they currently are underutilizing any of these subgroups of the labor force may find the agencies to be an excellent source.

The government also provides funding to a variety of local employment agencies. For example, in Virginia, the Frederick County Job Training Agency receives funding from the federal, state, and county governments to help unemployed workers find and prepare for new jobs. When the Von Hoffmann Corporation closed its Frederick plant to consolidate operations in Missouri and Iowa, the 165 employees didn't want to move. A career consultant at the Job Training Agency met with each of them to record their work history and goals. The laid-off workers also can use the agency to visit online job sites, mail résumés at no charge, and participate in classes on writing résumés and interviewing for a job. The Job Training Agency shares a building with the county's Office of Economic Development, in the hope that the development agency, which encourages businesses to locate in the county, can work with it to match employers and workers.[57]

Private Employment Agencies

In contrast to public employment agencies, which primarily serve the blue-collar labor market, private employment agencies provide much the same service for the white-collar labor market. Workers interested in finding a job can sign up with a private employment agency whether or not they are currently unemployed. Another difference between the two types of agencies is that private agencies charge the employers for providing referrals. Therefore, using a private employment agency is more expensive than using a public agency, but the private agency is a more suitable source for certain kinds of applicants.

For managers or professionals, an employer may use the services of a type of private agency called an *executive search firm (ESF)*. People often call these agencies "head-hunters" because, unlike other employment agencies, they find new jobs for people almost exclusively already employed. For job candidates, dealing with executive search firms can be sensitive. Typically, executives do not want to advertise their availability, because it could trigger a negative reaction from their current employer. ESFs serve as a buffer, providing confidentiality between the employer and the recruit. That benefit may give an employer access to candidates it cannot recruit in other, more direct ways.

Colleges and Universities

Most colleges and universities have placement services that seek to help their graduates obtain employment. On-campus interviewing is the most important source of recruits for entry-level professional and managerial vacancies.[58] Organizations tend to focus especially on colleges that have strong reputations in areas for which they have critical needs—say, chemical engineering or public accounting.[59] The recruiting strategy at 3M includes concentrating on 25 to 30 selected universities. The company has a commitment to those selected universities and returns to them each year with

One of the best ways for a company to establish a stronger presence on a campus is with a college internship program. Embassy Suites is one company that participates in such a program. How does this benefit the company and the students at the same time?

new job openings. HR professionals make sure that the same person works with the same university year in and year out, to achieve "continuity of contact."[60]

Many employers have found that successfully competing for the best students requires more than just signing up prospective graduates for interview slots. One of the best ways to establish a stronger presence on a campus is with a college internship program. Dun & Bradstreet funds a summer intern program for minority MBA students. D&B often hires these interns for full-time positions when they graduate.[61] Internship programs give an organization early access to potential applicants and let the organization assess their capabilities directly.

Another way of increasing the employer's presence on campus is to participate in university job fairs. In general, a job fair is an event where many employers gather for a short time to meet large numbers of potential job applicants. Although job fairs can be held anywhere (such as at a hotel or convention center), campuses are ideal locations because of the many well-educated, yet unemployed, individuals who are there. Job fairs are an inexpensive means of generating an on-campus presence. They can even provide one-on-one dialogue with potential recruits—dialogue that would be impossible through less interactive media, such as newspaper ads.

Evaluating the Quality of a Source

In general, there are few rules that say what recruitment source is best for a given job vacancy. Therefore, it is wise for employers to monitor the quality of all their recruitment sources. One way to do this is to develop and compare **yield ratios** for each source.[62] A yield ratio expresses the percentage of applicants who successfully move from one stage of the recruitment and selection process to the next. For example, the organization could find the number of candidates interviewed as a percentage of the total number of résumés generated by a given source (that is, number of interviews divided by number of résumés). A high yield ratio (large percentage) means that the source is an effective way to find candidates to interview. By comparing the yield ratios of different recruitment sources, HR professionals can determine which source is the best or most efficient for the type of vacancy.

yield ratio
A ratio that expresses the percentage of applicants who successfully move from one stage of the recruitment and selection process to the next.

Another measure of recruitment success is the *cost per hire*. To compute this amount, find the cost of using a particular recruitment source for a particular type of vacancy. Then divide that cost by the number of people hired to fill that type of vacancy. A low cost per hire means that the recruitment source is efficient; it delivers qualified candidates at minimal cost.

To see how HR professionals use these measures, look at the examples in Table 5.3. This table shows the results for a hypothetical organization that used five kinds of recruitment sources to fill a number of vacancies. For each recruitment source, the table shows four yield ratios and the cost per hire. To fill these jobs, the best two sources of recruits were local universities and employee referral programs. Newspaper ads generated the largest number of recruits (500 résumés). However, only 50 were judged acceptable, of which only half accepted employment offers, for a cumulative yield ratio of 25/500, or 5 percent. Recruiting at renowned universities generated highly qualified applicants, but relatively few of them ultimately accepted positions with the organization. Executive search firms produced the highest cumulative yield ratio. These generated only 20 applicants, but all of them accepted interview offers, most were judged acceptable, and 79 percent of these acceptable candidates took jobs with the organization. However, notice the cost per hire. The executive search firms charged $90,000 for finding these 15 employees, resulting in the largest cost per hire. In

TABLE 5.3

Results of a Hypothetical Recruiting Effort

	RECRUITING SOURCE					
	LOCAL UNIVERSITY	RENOWNED UNIVERSITY	EMPLOYEE REFERRALS	NEWSPAPER AD	ONLINE JOB BOARD AD	EXECUTIVE SEARCH FIRMS
Résumés generated	200	400	50	500	7000	20
Interview offers accepted	175	100	45	400	500	20
Yield ratio	**87%**	**25%**	**90%**	**80%**	**7%**	**100%**
Applicants judged acceptable	100	95	40	50	350	19
Yield ratio	**57%**	**95%**	**89%**	**12%**	**70%**	**95%**
Accept employment offers	90	10	35	25	200	15
Yield ratio	**90%**	**11%**	**88%**	**50%**	**57%**	**79%**
Cumulative yield ratio	90/200 **45%**	10/400 **3%**	35/50 **70%**	25/500 **5%**	200/7,000 **3%**	15/20 **75%**
Cost	$30,000	$50,000	$15,000	$20,000	$5,000	$90,000
Cost per hire	**$333**	**$5,000**	**$428**	**$800**	**$25**	**$6,000**

contrast, local universities provided modest yield ratios at the lowest cost per hire. Employee referrals provided excellent yield ratios at a slightly higher cost.

LO6
Describe the recruiter's role in the recruitment process, including limits and opportunities.

RECRUITER TRAITS AND BEHAVIORS

As we showed in Figure 5.2, the third influence on recruitment outcomes is the recruiter, including this person's characteristics and the way he or she behaves. The recruiter affects the nature of both the job vacancy and the applicants generated. However, the recruiter often becomes involved late in the recruitment process. In many cases, by the time a recruiter meets some applicants, they have already made up their minds about what they desire in a job, what the vacant job has to offer, and their likelihood of receiving a job offer.[63]

Many applicants approach the recruiter with some skepticism. Knowing it is the recruiter's job to sell them on a vacancy, some applicants discount what the recruiter says, in light of what they have heard from other sources, such as friends, magazine articles, and professors. For these and other reasons, recruiters' characteristics and behaviors seem to have limited impact on applicants' job choices.

Characteristics of the Recruiter

Most organizations must choose whether their recruiters are specialists in human resources or are experts at particular jobs (that is, those who currently hold the same kinds of jobs or supervise people who hold the jobs). According to some studies, applicants perceive HR specialists as less credible and are less attracted to jobs when re-

figure 5.6

Recruits Who Were Offended by Recruiters

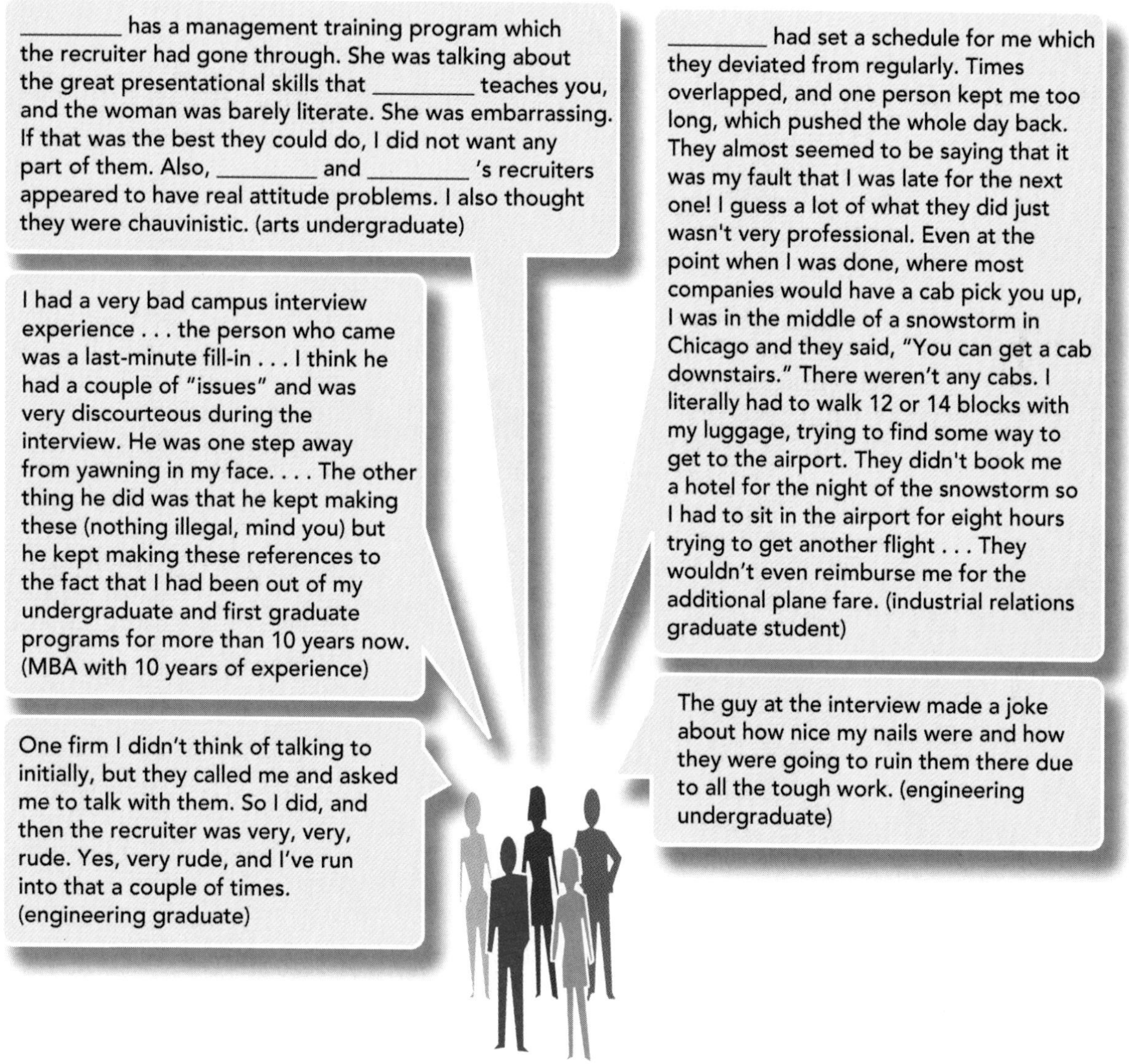

> _____ has a management training program which the recruiter had gone through. She was talking about the great presentational skills that _____ teaches you, and the woman was barely literate. She was embarrassing. If that was the best they could do, I did not want any part of them. Also, _____ and _____ 's recruiters appeared to have real attitude problems. I also thought they were chauvinistic. (arts undergraduate)

> I had a very bad campus interview experience . . . the person who came was a last-minute fill-in . . . I think he had a couple of "issues" and was very discourteous during the interview. He was one step away from yawning in my face. . . . The other thing he did was that he kept making these (nothing illegal, mind you) but he kept making these references to the fact that I had been out of my undergraduate and first graduate programs for more than 10 years now. (MBA with 10 years of experience)

> One firm I didn't think of talking to initially, but they called me and asked me to talk with them. So I did, and then the recruiter was very, very, rude. Yes, very rude, and I've run into that a couple of times. (engineering graduate)

> _____ had set a schedule for me which they deviated from regularly. Times overlapped, and one person kept me too long, which pushed the whole day back. They almost seemed to be saying that it was my fault that I was late for the next one! I guess a lot of what they did just wasn't very professional. Even at the point when I was done, where most companies would have a cab pick you up, I was in the middle of a snowstorm in Chicago and they said, "You can get a cab downstairs." There weren't any cabs. I literally had to walk 12 or 14 blocks with my luggage, trying to find some way to get to the airport. They didn't book me a hotel for the night of the snowstorm so I had to sit in the airport for eight hours trying to get another flight . . . They wouldn't even reimburse me for the additional plane fare. (industrial relations graduate student)

> The guy at the interview made a joke about how nice my nails were and how they were going to ruin them there due to all the tough work. (engineering undergraduate)

cruiters are HR specialists.[64] The evidence does not completely discount a positive role for personnel specialists in recruiting. It does indicate, however, that these specialists need to take extra steps to ensure that applicants perceive them as knowledgeable and credible.

In general, applicants respond positively to recruiters whom they perceive as warm and informative. "Warm" means the recruiter seems to care about the applicant and to be enthusiastic about the applicant's potential to contribute to the organization. "Informative" means the recruiter provides the kind of information the applicant is seeking. The evidence of impact of other characteristics of recruiters—including their age, sex, and race—is complex and inconsistent.[65]

Behavior of the Recruiter

Recruiters affect results not only by providing plenty of information, but by providing the right kind of information. Perhaps the most-researched aspect of recruiting is the level of realism in the recruiter's message. Because the recruiter's job is to attract candidates, recruiters may feel pressure to exaggerate the positive qualities of the vacancy and to downplay its negative qualities. Applicants are highly sensitive to negative information. The highest-quality applicants may be less willing to pursue jobs when this type of information comes out.[66] But if the recruiter goes too far in a positive direction, the candidate can be misled and lured into taking a job that has been misrepresented. Then unmet expectations can contribute to a high turnover rate. When recruiters describe jobs unrealistically, people who take those jobs may come to believe that the employer is deceitful.[67]

realistic job preview
Background information about a job's positive and negative qualities.

Many studies have looked at how well **realistic job previews**—background information about jobs' positive and negative qualities—can get around this problem and help organizations minimize turnover among new employees. On the whole, the research suggests that realistic job previews have a weak and inconsistent effect on turnover.[68] Although recruiters can go overboard in selling applicants on the desirability of a job vacancy, there is little support for the belief that informing people about the negative characteristics of a job will "inoculate" them so that the negative features don't cause them to quit.[69]

Finally, for affecting whether people choose to take a job, but even more so, whether they stick with a job, the recruiter seems less important than an organization's personnel policies that directly affect the job's features (pay, security, advancement opportunities, and so on).

Enhancing the Recruiter's Impact

Nevertheless, although recruiters are probably not the most important influence on people's job choices, this does not mean recruiters cannot have an impact. Most recruiters receive little training.[70] If we were to determine what does matter to job candidates, perhaps recruiters could be trained in those areas.

Researchers have tried to find the conditions in which recruiters do make a difference. Such research suggests that an organization can take several steps to increase the positive impact that recruiters have on job candidates:

- Recruiters should provide timely feedback. Applicants dislike delays in feedback. They may draw negative conclusions about the organization (for starters, that the organization doesn't care about their application).
- Recruiters should avoid offensive behavior. They should avoid behaving in ways that might convey the wrong impression about the organization.[71] Figure 5.6 quotes applicants who felt they had extremely bad experiences with recruiters. Their statements provide examples of behaviors to avoid.
- The organization can recruit with teams rather than individual recruiters. Applicants view job experts as more credible than HR specialists, and a team can include both kinds of recruiters. HR specialists on the team provide knowledge about company policies and procedures.

Through such positive behavior, recruiters can give organizations a better chance of competing for talented human resources. In the next chapter, we will describe how an organization selects the candidates that best meet its needs.

thinking ETHICALLY

When Employees Leave

The chapter described ways organizations can manage a labor surplus by downsizing or using temporary and contract workers. Layoffs are just one reason the average U.S. worker has an estimated 9.2 jobs between the ages of 18 and 34. Employees also leave voluntarily, especially when the demand for their skills is strong.

Just as there is advice for organizations laying off workers, some people offer advice to employees who leave voluntarily. Deborah Keary, a director at the Society for Human Resource Management, cautions employees to continue making a good impression: "You never know when your boss will be a good reference." She suggests giving the employer as much notice as possible, even as much as a month's notice so that the employer has more time to find a replacement. However, some employers do become upset when an employee quits, so a wise precaution might be for the employee to collect any personal documents (including computer files) before telling his or her boss. Marc Karasu of HotJobs suggests that the departing employee help out as much as possible with hiring a replacement—for example, writing a job ad or instructions for performing the job. In addition, employees should continue to work hard during the period before they leave.

Despite all advice and good intentions, some employees do fumble their career decisions. Early in her career, an attorney in New York looked for a job for several months. Eventually a law firm made an offer. Although the firm was not the lawyer's first choice, the pay was better than the lawyer's current pay. Afraid to wait any longer for offers from other companies, the lawyer accepted the position. She gave her boss notice but had second thoughts. Her boss let her change her mind, but a month later, the lawyer received another, more appealing offer and resigned again.

SOURCE: Adelle Waldman, "Making a Good Last Impression," *The Wall Street Journal*, March 24, 2005, http://online.wsj.com.

Questions

1. What ethical obligations does an organization have when downsizing?
2. Compare those obligations with the ethical obligations of an employee who leaves an organization voluntarily.
3. Consider the example of the New York lawyer. How would you have advised the lawyer to handle this situation? How would you have wanted to handle it if you were the employer?

SUMMARY

1. Discuss how to plan for human resources needed to carry out the organization's strategy.
   The first step in human resource planning is personnel forecasting. Through trend analysis and good judgment, the planner tries to determine the supply of and demand for various human resources. Based on whether a surplus or a shortage is expected, the planner sets goals and creates a strategy for achieving those goals. The organization then implements its HR strategy and evaluates the results.

2. Determine the labor demand for workers in various job categories.
   The planner can look at leading indicators, assuming trends will continue in the future. Multiple regression can convert several leading indicators into a single

prediction of labor needs. Analysis of a transitional matrix can help the planner identify which job categories can be filled internally and where high turnover is likely.

3. Summarize the advantages and disadvantages of ways to eliminate a labor surplus and avoid a labor shortage.
To reduce a surplus, downsizing, pay reductions, and demotions deliver fast results but at a high cost in human suffering that may hurt surviving employees' motivation and future recruiting. Also, the organization may lose some of its best employees. Transferring employees and requiring them to share work are also fast methods and the consequences in human suffering are less severe. A hiring freeze or natural attrition is slow to take effect but avoids the pain of layoffs. Early-retirement packages may unfortunately induce the best employees to leave and may be slow to implement; however, they, too, are less painful than layoffs. Retraining can improve the organization's overall pool of human resources and maintain high morale, but it is relatively slow and costly.

   To avoid a labor shortage, requiring overtime is the easiest and fastest strategy, which can easily be changed if conditions change. However, overtime may exhaust workers and can hurt morale. Using temporary employees and outsourcing do not build an in-house pool of talent, but by these means staffing levels can be quickly and easily modified. Transferring and retraining employees require investment of time and money, but can enhance the quality of the organization's human resources; however, this may backfire if a labor surplus develops. Hiring new employees is slow and expensive but strengthens the organization if labor needs are expected to expand for the long term. Using technology as a substitute for labor can be slow to implement and costly, but it may improve the organization's long-term performance. New technology and hiring are difficult to reverse if conditions change.

4. Describe recruitment policies organizations use to make job vacancies more attractive.
Internal recruiting (promotions from within) generally makes job vacancies more attractive because candidates see opportunities for growth and advancement.

Lead-the-market pay strategies make jobs economically desirable. Due-process policies signal that employers are concerned about employee rights. Image advertising can give candidates the impression that the organization is a good place to work.

5. List and compare sources of job applicants.
Internal sources, promoted through job postings, generate applicants who are familiar to the organization and motivate other employees by demonstrating opportunities for advancement. However, internal sources are usually insufficient for all of an organization's labor needs. Direct applicants and referrals tend to be inexpensive and to generate applicants who have self-selected; this source risks charges of unfairness, especially in cases of nepotism. Newspaper and magazine advertising reaches a wide audience and may generate many applications, although many are likely to be unsuitable. Electronic recruiting gives organizations access to a global labor market, tends to be inexpensive, and allows convenient searching of databases. Public employment agencies are inexpensive and typically have screened applicants. Private employment agencies charge fees but may provide many services. Another inexpensive channel is schools and colleges, which may give the employer access to top-notch entrants to the labor market.

6. Describe the recruiter's role in the recruitment process, including limits and opportunities.
Through their behavior and other characteristics, recruiters influence the nature of the job vacancy and the kinds of applicants generated. Applicants tend to perceive job experts as more credible than recruiters who are HR specialists. They tend to react more favorably to recruiters who are warm and informative. Recruiters should not mislead candidates. Realistic job previews are helpful, but have a weak and inconsistent effect on job turnover compared to personnel policies and actual job conditions. Recruiters can improve their impact by providing timely feedback, avoiding behavior that contributes to a negative impression of the organization, and teaming up with job experts.

REVIEW AND DISCUSSION QUESTIONS

1. Suppose an organization expects a labor shortage to develop in key job areas over the next few years. Recommend general responses the organization could make in each of the following areas:
   a. Recruitment.
   b. Training.
   c. Compensation (pay and employee benefits).
2. Review the sample transitional matrix shown in Table 5.1. What jobs experience the greatest turnover

(employees leaving the organization)? How might an organization with this combination of jobs reduce the turnover?
3. In the same transitional matrix, which jobs seem to rely the most on internal recruitment? Which seem to rely most on external recruitment? Why?
4. Why do organizations combine statistical and judgmental forecasts of labor demand, rather than relying on statistics or judgment alone? Give an example of a

situation in which each type of forecast would be inaccurate.

5. Some organizations have detailed affirmative-action plans, complete with goals and timetables, for women and minorities, yet have no formal human resource plan for the organization as a whole. Why might this be the case? What does this practice suggest about the role of human resource management in these organizations?

6. Give an example of a personnel policy that would help attract a larger pool of job candidates. Give an example of a personnel policy that would likely reduce the pool of candidates. Would you expect these policies to influence the quality as well as the number of applicants? Why or why not?

7. Discuss the relative merits of internal versus external recruitment. Give an example of a situation in which each of these approaches might be particularly effective.

8. List the jobs you have held. How were you recruited for each of these? From the organization's perspective, what were some pros and cons of recruiting you through these methods?

9. Recruiting people for jobs that require international assignments is increasingly important for many organizations. Where might an organization go to recruit people interested in such assignments?

10. A large share of HR professionals have rated e-cruiting as their best source of new talent. What qualities of electronic recruiting do you think contribute to this opinion?

11. How can organizations improve the effectiveness of their recruiters?

WHAT'S YOUR HR IQ?

The text Web site offers two more ways to check what you've learned so far. Use the Self-Assessment exercise to test your knowledge of HR planning and recruiting. Go online with the Web Exercise to take a sample questionnaire for job applicants.

BusinessWeek CASE

BusinessWeek Good Help Is So Hard to Find

When Indian software services giant Wipro Ltd. hires middle managers these days, it doesn't just negotiate pay and benefits. Instead, the company engages in an elaborate mating ritual that includes helping a new hire find a home, providing compensation for lost salary to recruits who don't give enough notice when leaving their previous jobs, and even easing school admissions for their children. "We have to offer a virtual valet service for them," says Sudip Banerjee, president of enterprise solutions at Wipro.

It's no wonder Wipro has to be more aggressive in wooing staffers these days. The Indian outsourcing industry grew by a sizzling 35 percent in 2004 as big multinationals and smaller U.S. and European companies handed over to Indian firms everything from software development and computer help desks to financial analysts. That growth has boosted competition for workers, as employment in the sector jumped by 20 percent in 2004. Entry-level wages have climbed by as much as 15 percent annually over the past two years, while salaries for midlevel managers have clocked 30 percent annual growth during the same period, to a median of $31,131.

The quest for workers is creating a talent crunch that some believe might dull India's competitive edge in outsourcing. "With rising wages, many companies are just not making money here in India, especially in call centers," says Chiranjit Banerjee, a director for human resource firm Quest Research. The industry employs 1 million people in India, but that number is expected to double by 2008, says Nasscom, India's software industry association. Although India produces 2 million college graduates a year, the services industry has a shortage of seasoned professionals. On-the-job training can fill the gap, but it's pricey: Educating a new recruit takes months and costs up to 40 percent of a rookie's annual salary. Worse, once the newbies get some experience, they're often lured away by rivals offering higher pay.

To some extent, the rising wages faced by the services industry are offset by falling costs in other areas. But at least one company is scaling back in Bangalore. In January 2005, Tampa-based Sykes Enterprises—a call center operator that has been in India since 2002—said it would shift much of the work handled by its Indian operators to centers in Manila, Philippines, and Shanghai, China. "We moved calls to other facilities in Asia to get a higher rate of return," says Dan Hernandez, Sykes's vice president for global strategies.

The biggest worry for most in the business is the shortage of managers. The industry needs 15 to 20 percent more midlevel execs than it can muster, Nasscom and company officials say. Without these professionals, teams of software writers, analysts, or call center operators can drift, hurting productivity. "The shortage has worsened as employees cash in stock options granted in the past few years and start looking for a better deal," says Ajit Isaac, chief executive of Bangalore headhunter Adecco Peopleone Consulting. After options granted by Infosys in 1999 vested in 2004, Isaac says more than 25 middle managers contacted him about finding new jobs.

The crunch is serious enough that companies are doing everything they can to keep talented veterans from jumping ship. At Accenture, top managers spend at least an hour every couple of weeks with software coders and call center operators to make sure they understand shop floor issues, and every quarter, teams and their leaders head to a nearby resort to review operations and relax. At Wipro, CEO Vivek Paul often chats with midlevel hires. And Infosys in 2004 marked a milestone—reaching $1 billion in revenues—with celebrations featuring Indian pop singers and gala dinners. The company also handed out $25 million in bonuses—between $500 and $5,000 for each worker.

For favored employees, there are lavish perks and opportunities for advancement. Wipro, for example, attempts to identify leaders early, putting top performers into an accelerated training program, and sometimes pays for a certification in project management. Call center operator 24/7 Customer pays half the $2,900 annual tuition for employees to earn a business certificate from the Indian Institute of Management in Bangalore. Cincinnati-based Convergys Corporation, the world's largest call center company, initially had trouble finding managers for its Indian operation. "We hired almost from the street: from hotels, airlines, and even manufacturing and the railways," says Maneesh Goswami, a senior manager at Convergys. Today, though, it has beefed up its in-house training and hires 10 percent of project managers from outside, down from 75 percent three years ago. Some companies are even looking to Indian expatriates to fill the management gap. In the past three years, about 20,000 tech professionals returned to India from abroad, says Nasscom.

Most insiders expect the talent crunch to be relatively short-lived. Although wages for midlevel managers will continue to rise, many Indian execs say their companies have enough of a profit cushion to absorb increased labor costs. They also say wage inflation in the United States and Europe will raise costs for rivals overseas, helping the Indians remain competitive. Indian colleges have begun offering courses in tech project management and back-office processing, so within a few years, companies should have an easier time finding qualified recruits.

SOURCE: Josey Puliyenthuruthel and Manjeet Kripalani, "Good Help Is So Hard to Find," *BusinessWeek*, February 14, 2005, downloaded from Infotrac at http://web6.infotrac.galegroup.com.

Questions

1. Based on the information given in this case, do tech services companies in India face a labor shortage or a labor surplus? Explain in terms of factors related to the labor supply and demand.
2. What have the companies done to meet their human resource needs under these conditions?
3. What else could the companies do to align their human resources with the expected needs?

CASE: Where John H. Daniel Company Finds Tailors

Most Americans buy clothes made overseas in low-wage countries. There are some exceptions to foreign manufacturing, however. One is John H. Daniel Company, which makes high-end custom suits in Knoxville, Tennessee. The suits, priced between $800 and $2,900, are made from premium fabrics and tailored to fit each buyer. Such fine items require a labor-intensive process using expert tailors.

Competing in this industry is challenging. In the 1970s, about 30 companies made custom suits in the United States, but only a handful survived. Suits are worn less often today, and men who do buy a suit are often satisfied with one made inexpensively overseas and sold off the rack. Other buyers want a suit made to order, but supplying them is difficult because there is a shortage of master tailors in the United States. In the words of Benton Bryan, the company's chief operating officer, "You can find someone who can mend pants, but master tailors who can make a collar or set a sleeve or baste canvas is a whole other story."

In the past, the supply of master tailors consisted mainly of immigrants from countries that no longer meet that demand. For example, skilled tailors from Italy once came to America to earn better wages than Europe could pay. But today Italians can prosper in their home country. And few Americans are drawn toward learning this craft.

Benton Bryan and his father, Richard, the company's chief executive officer, considered options for addressing this labor shortage. One possibility was to outsource tailoring to a foreign supplier, but the Bryans rejected that idea. They wanted to avoid moving themselves or their employees, many of whom had been loyal to the company for years. Instead, they hired several tailors away from a competitor in New York.

Those hiring decisions provided the inspiration for the Bryans' solution to their labor shortage. The tailors hired from the competitor were Turkish immigrants. These employees could serve as translators and recruiting guides to hire more tailors from Turkey, which has a large supply of master tailors. In that country, wages are low enough that John H. Daniel's starting wage of $11.50 is a significant incentive to move. In addition, large companies in Turkey are competing with the independent tailors, making their future there more difficult.

Benton Bryan and one of his Turkish employees traveled to Turkey to begin recruiting. They traveled around Istanbul, stopping at market stalls and upscale stores where tailors worked. When the two met tailors, they invited them to stop by their hotel and apply to work in America. Each night about 100 tailors would come to the hotel. They had a half hour to demonstrate such tailoring skills as sewing a sleeve and a buttonhole into a jacket. During that first trip, Bryan and his employee identified 13 prospective employees, and their success provided the basis for future recruiting trips.

After identifying recruits, the next step is to get government permission to bring the employees into the United States. The company's general counsel (the lawyer on its payroll), Jackson L. Case IV, originally expected to work mainly on issues like workers' compensation. Instead, he has devoted much of his time to working with the federal departments of Labor, State, and Homeland Security, obtaining visas for new employees and their families. To get the visas, he has to demonstrate that no Americans are available to do the work, so he runs want ads for master tailors and shows the lack of qualified responses.

Case is also responsible for welcoming the new arrivals. When John H. Daniel hired Yusuf Okuyucu, Case and a group of three dozen Turkish people, including employees and their families, met Okuyucu, his wife, and their daughter at the airport in Knoxville. They all drove to an apartment complex in West Knoxville, where the company had rented an apartment for the new family. (After a few months, the family pays the rent.) Case had ensured that the apartment was prepared with basic furniture, dishes, and a television. The next day, Case and Benton Bryan returned to deliver an envelope containing $1,000 in cash to help the new arrivals get started in America. Through an interpreter, Bryan told them, "The most important thing you can do is ask us if you need anything. The worst thing you can do is not to ask for help."

Help is something the company realizes immigrants will need. When tailors bring school-age children, the company takes them to the health department to receive vaccinations and then to school to register. They may issue no-interest loans so that their new employees can buy cars, repaid at $25 per month. Case estimates that hiring a Turkish worker and bringing the family to Knoxville costs the company $12,000 in time and cash. When it comes to helping his new employees settle in, Richard Bryan says, "If they've got nobody to do it, we've got to do it for them. I mean, we brought 'em here."

SOURCE: Michael M. Phillips, "Why Turkish Tailors Seem So Well-Suited to Work in Tennessee," *The Wall Street Journal,* April 12, 2005, http://online. wsj.com.

Questions

1. What options did John H. Daniel Company's executives identify for meeting its need for tailors?
2. What are the advantages and drawbacks of relying on Turkey as a source of tailors?
3. Could the Internet improve the company's ability to recruit tailors? Explain.

NOTES

1. Stacy Forster, "New Ventures Meet the Challenges of a Struggling Start-up Climate," *The Wall Street Journal Online,* March 27, 2002, http://online.wsj.com.
2. C. Ansberty, "Old Industries Adopt Flex Staffing to Adapt to Rapid Pace of Change," *The Wall Street Journal,* March 22, 2002, pp. A1–A2.
3. D. Welch, "A Contract the Big Three Can Take to the Bank," *BusinessWeek,* September 29, 2003, p. 46.
4. M. Conlin, "Savaged by the Slowdown," *BusinessWeek,* September 17, 2001, pp. 74–77.
5. W. F. Cascio, "Whither Industrial and Organizational Psychology in a Changing World of Work?" *American Psychologist* 50 (1995), pp. 928–39.
6. John Pallatto and Lisa Vaas, "Oracle Firings Bring Black Friday for PeopleSoft Staffers," *eWeek,* January 14, 2005, www.eweek.com.
7. Matthew Benjamin, "Career Guide 2005," *U.S. News & World Report,* March 21, 2005, pp. 34–42.
8. Neil King Jr., "A Whole New World," *The Wall Street Journal,* September 27, 2004, pp. R1, R3.
9. K. P. DeMeuse, P. A. Vanderheiden, and T. J. Bergmann, "Announced Layoffs: Their Effect on Corporate Financial Performance," *Human Resource Management* 33 (1994), pp. 509–30.
10. P. P. Shaw, "Network Destruction: The Structural Implications of Downsizing," *Academy of Management Journal* 43 (2000), pp. 101–12.
11. Jon E. Hilsenrath, "Adventures in Cost Cutting," *The Wall Street Journal,* May 10, 2004, pp. R1, R3.
12. W. F. Cascio, "Downsizing: What Do We Know? What Have We Learned?" *Academy of Management Executive* 7 (1993), pp. 95–104.
13. J. Schu, "Internet Helps Keep Goodwill of Downsized Employees," *Workforce,* July 2001, p. 15.
14. D. Skatlicki, J. H. Ellard, and B. R. C. Kellin, "Third Party Perceptions of a Layoff: Procedural, Derogation,

and Retributive Aspects of Justice," *Journal of Applied Psychology* 83 (1998), pp. 119–27.

15. R. Folger and D. P. Skarlicki, "When Tough Times Make Tough Bosses: Managerial Distancing as a Function of Layoff Blame," *Academy of Management Journal* 41 (1998), pp. 79–87.

16. Hilsenrath, "Adventures in Cost Cutting," p. R3.

17. Kathy Chu, "Older Workers Find New Favor among Employers," *The Wall Street Journal*, September 1, 2004, p. D3.

18. S. Kim and D. Feldman, "Healthy, Wealthy, or Wise: Predicting Actual Acceptances of Early Retirement Incentives at Three Points in Time," *Personnel Psychology* 51 (1998), pp. 623–42.

19. D. Fandray, "Gray Matters," *Workforce*, July 2000, pp. 27–32.

20. Rifka Rosenwein, "Help (Still) Wanted," *Inc.*, April 2001, pp. 51–52, 54–55.

21. Irwin Speizer, "Going to Ground," *Workforce Management*, December 2004, pp. 39–44.

22. Ibid.; and Monica Langley, "Drivers Deliver Trouble to FedEx by Seeking Employee Benefits," *The Wall Street Journal*, January 7, 2005, pp. A1, A8.

23. Kris Maher, "Next on the Outsourcing List," *The Wall Street Journal*, March 23, 2004, pp. B1, B8.

24. L. D. Tyson, "Outsourcing: Who's Safe Anymore?" *BusinessWeek*, February 23, 2004, p. 26.

25. G. Koretz, "Overtime versus New Factories," *BusinessWeek*, May 4, 1998, p. 34.

26. Anne Freedman, "Filling the Gap," *Human Resource Executive*, January 2005, pp. 1, 22–30.

27. A. E. Barber, *Recruiting Employees* (Thousand Oaks, CA: Sage, 1998).

28. J. D. Olian and S. L. Rynes, "Organizational Staffing: Integrating Practice with Strategy," *Industrial Relations* 23 (1984), pp. 170–83.

29. Rosenwein, "Help (Still) Wanted."

30. G. T. Milkovich and J. M. Newman, *Compensation* (Homewood, IL.: Richard D. Irwin, 1990).

31. S. J. Marks, "After School," *Human Resources Executive*, June 15, 2001, pp. 49–51.

32. P. J. Kiger, "The Center of Attention," *Workforce*, March 2004, pp. 51–52.

33. Jobtrack.com, "Changing Views on Valued Benefits," June 30, 2001, p. 1.

34. M. Leonard, "Challenges to the Termination-at-Will Doctrine," *Personnel Administrator* 28 (1983), pp. 49–56.

35. C. Schowerer and B. Rosen, "Effects of Employment-at-Will Policies and Compensation Policies on Corporate Image and Job Pursuit Intentions," *Journal of Applied Psychology* 74 (1989), pp. 653–56.

36. Ibid.

37. M. Magnus, "Recruitment Ads at Work," *Personnel Journal* 64 (1985), pp. 42–63.

38. S. L. Rynes and A. E. Barber, "Applicant Attraction Strategies: An Organizational Perspective," *Academy of Management Review* 15 (1990), pp. 286–310; J. A. Breaugh, *Recruitment: Science and Practice* (Boston: PWS-Kent, 1992), p. 34.

39. J. E. Slaughter, M. J. Zickar, S. Highhouse, and D. C. Mohr, "Personality Trait Inferences about Organizations: Development of a Measure and Assessment of Construct Validity," *Journal of Applied Psychology* 89 (2004), pp. 85–103.

40. D. R. Avery, "Reactions to Diversity in Recruitment Advertising-Are Differences in Black and White?" *Journal of Applied Psychology* 88 (2003), pp. 672–79.

41. D. M. Cable, L. Aiman-Smith, P. Mulvey, and J. R. Edwards, "The Sources and Accuracy of Job Applicants' Beliefs about Organizational Culture," *Academy of Management Journal* 43 (2000), pp. 1076–85.

42. M. A. Conrad and S. D. Ashworth, "Recruiting Source Effectiveness: A Meta-Analysis and Re-examination of Two Rival Hypotheses," paper presented at the annual meeting of the Society of Industrial/Organizational Psychology, Chicago, 1986.

43. Breaugh, *Recruitment*.

44. L. G. Klaff, "New Internal Hiring Systems Reduce Cost and Boost Morale," *Workforce*, March 2004, pp. 76–78.

45. Breaugh, *Recruitment*, pp. 113–14.

46. R. S. Schuler and S. E. Jackson, "Linking Competitive Strategies with Human Resource Management Practices," *Academy of Management Executive* 1 (1987), pp. 207–19.

47. Jessica Mintz, "Large Firms Increasingly Rely on Employees for Job Referrals," *The Wall Street Journal*, March 1, 2005, p. B4.

48. C. R. Wanberg, R. Kanfer, and J. T. Banas, "Predictors and Outcomes of Networking Intensity among Job Seekers," *Journal of Applied Psychology* 85 (2000), pp. 491–503.

49. Robert Rodriguez, "Tapping the Hispanic Labor Pool," *HR Magazine*, April 2004, downloaded from Infotrac at http://web2.infotrac.galegroup.com.

50. Breaugh, *Recruitment*, p. 87.

51. J. Smith, "Is Online Recruiting Getting Easier?" *Workforce*, September 2, 2001, p. 1.

52. Allan Schweyer, "Does Internet Recruiting Work?" *Inc.com*, Resources, March 1, 2005, www.inc.com.

53. Jennifer C. Berkshire, "For Massive Hiring Effort, Vegas Resort Wagers on High-Tech, Tried-and-True," *Workforce Management*, March 2005, pp. 65–67.

54. Martha Frase-Blunt, "Make a Good First Impression," *HR Magazine*, April 2004, downloaded from Infotrac at http://web2.infotrac.galegroup.com.

55. Kris Maher, "Blogs Catch On as Online Tool for Job Seekers and Recruiters," *The Wall Street Journal*, September 28, 2004, p. B10.

56. Stacy Forster, "The Best Way to Recruit New Workers," *The Wall Street Journal*, September 15, 2003, p. R8.

57. Amy Joyce, "When a Plant Closes, Job Agency Steps In," *Washington Post*, January 24, 2005, www.washingtonpost.com.

58. P. Smith, "Sources Used by Employers When Hiring College Grads," *Personnel Journal*, February 1995, p. 25.

59. J. W. Boudreau and S. L. Rynes, "Role of Recruitment in Staffing Utility Analysis," *Journal of Applied Psychology* 70 (1985), pp. 354–66.

60. D. Anfuso, "3M's Staffing Strategy Promotes Productivity and Pride," *Personnel Journal*, February 1995, pp. 28–34.

61. L. Winter, "Employers Go to School on Minority Recruiting," *The Wall Street Journal*, December 15, 1992, p. B1.

62. R. Hawk, *The Recruitment Function* (New York: American Management Association, 1967).

63. C. K. Stevens, "Effects of Preinterview Beliefs on Applicants' Reactions to Campus Interviews," *Academy of Management Journal* 40 (1997), pp. 947–66.

64. M. S. Taylor and T. J. Bergman, "Organizational Recruitment Activities and Applicants' Reactions at Different Stages of the Recruitment Process," *Personnel Psychology* 40 (1984), pp. 261–85; C. D. Fisher, D. R. Ilgen, and W. D. Hoyer, "Source Credibility, Information Favorability, and Job Offer Acceptance," *Academy of Management Journal* 22 (1979), pp. 94–103.

65. L. M. Graves and G. N. Powell, "The Effect of Sex Similarity on Recruiters' Evaluation of Actual Applicants: A Test of the Similarity-Attraction Paradigm," *Personnel Psychology* 48 (1995), pp. 85–98.

66. R. D. Tretz and T. A. Judge, "Realistic Job Previews: A Test of the Adverse Self-Selection Hypothesis," *Journal of Applied Psychology* 83 (1998), pp. 330–37.

67. P. Hom, R. W. Griffeth, L. E. Palich, and J. S. Bracker, "An Exploratory Investigation into Theoretical Mechanisms Underlying Realistic Job Previews," *Personnel Psychology* 51 (1998), pp. 421–51.

68. G. M. McEvoy and W. F. Cascio, "Strategies for Reducing Employee Turnover: A Meta-Analysis," *Journal of Applied Psychology* 70 (1985), pp. 342–53; S. L. Premack and J. P. Wanous, "A Meta-Analysis of Realistic Job Preview Experiments," *Journal of Applied Psychology* 70 (1985), pp. 706–19.

69. P. G. Irving and J. P. Meyer, "Reexamination of the Met-Expectations Hypothesis: A Longitudinal Analysis," *Journal of Applied Psychology* 79 (1995), pp. 937–49.

70. R. W. Walters, "It's Time We Become Pros," *Journal of College Placement* 12 (1985), pp. 30–33.

71. S. L. Rynes, R. D. Bretz, and B. Gerhart, "The Importance of Recruitment in Job Choice: A Different Way of Looking," *Personnel Psychology* 44 (1991), pp. 487–522.

If you are using the Manager's Hot Seat DVD with this book, consider finishing case 10: Diversity: Mediating Morality, for this chapter.

CHAPTER 6

SELECTING EMPLOYEES AND PLACING THEM IN JOBS

What Do I Need to Know?

After reading this chapter, you should be able to:

1. Identify the elements of the selection process.

2. Define ways to measure the success of a selection method.

3. Summarize the government's requirements for employee selection.

4. Compare the common methods used for selecting human resources.

5. Describe major types of employment tests.

6. Discuss how to conduct effective interviews.

7. Explain how employers carry out the process of making a selection decision.

❧ INTRODUCTION

Unlike a lot of entrepreneurs, Jeff Soderberg specifically avoids hiring workaholics. He knows better, because he once was one himself. Soderberg cofounded a software business, and as he devoted every waking hour to the company, he sacrificed his marriage along with his leisure time, only to be fired one day. Later, when Soderberg started Software Technology Group (STG), he decided he needed a new style that would keep him in business for the long run. STG provides information technology experts on a contract basis, helping clients with their software projects. Client companies want to get their software running as fast as possible, and STG insists that clients hire enough staff, rather than forcing programmers to work around the clock. According to Soderberg, "We have to make sure that our consultants don't burn out. We have to think long-term. . . . We can't afford to think only about the finish line of the current software project." With regard to hiring, that means Soderberg asks prospective employees about their hobbies. Applicants who call themselves workaholics don't get a job offer. Soderberg explains, "To put a workaholic on the staff would be like trying to mix oil and water. You have to create a team that shares the same values, and having a healthy lifestyle is one of our values."[1]

As Jeff Soderberg knows, hiring decisions are about finding the people who will be a good fit with the job and the organization. Any organization that appreciates the competitive edge provided by good people must take the utmost care in choosing its members. The organization's decisions about selecting personnel are central to its ability to survive, adapt, and grow. Selection decisions become especially critical when organizations face tight labor markets or must compete for talent with other organizations in the same industry. If a competitor keeps getting the best applicants, the remaining companies must make do with who is left.

This chapter will familiarize you with ways to minimize errors in employee selection and placement. The chapter starts by describing the selection process and how to evaluate possible methods for carrying out that process. It then takes an in-depth look at the most widely used methods: applications and résumés, employment tests, and interviews. The chapter ends by describing the process by which organizations arrive at a final selection decision.

◈ SELECTION PROCESS

Through **personnel selection,** organizations make decisions about who will or will not be allowed to join the organization. Selection begins with the candidates identified through recruitment and attempts to reduce their number to the individuals best qualified to perform the available jobs. At the end of the process, the selected individuals are placed in jobs with the organization.

The process of selecting employees varies considerably from organization to organization and from job to job. At most organizations, however, selection includes the steps illustrated in Figure 6.1. First, a human resource professional reviews the applications received to see which meet the basic requirements of the job. For candidates who meet the basic requirements, the organization administers tests and reviews work samples to rate the candidates' abilities. Those with the best abilities are invited to the organization for one or more interviews. Often, supervisors and team members are involved in this stage of the process. By this point, the decision makers are beginning to form opinions about which candidates are most desirable. For the top few candidates, the organization should check references and conduct background checks to verify that the organization's information is correct. Then supervisors, teams, and other decision makers select a person to receive a job offer. In some cases, the candidate may negotiate with the organization regarding salary, benefits, and the like. If the candidate accepts the job, the organization places him or her in that job.

How does an organization decide which of these elements to use, and in what order? Some organizations simply repeat a selection process that is familiar. If members

LO1
Identify the elements of the selection process.

personnel selection
The process through which organizations make decisions about who will or will not be allowed to join the organization.

Figure 6.1

Steps in the Selection Process

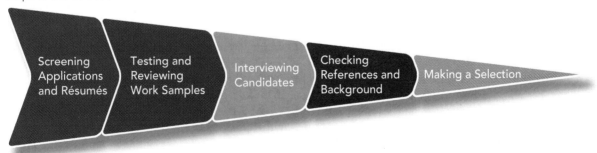

Figure 6.2

Criteria for
Evaluating Selection
Methods

of the organization underwent job interviews, they conduct job interviews, asking familiar questions. However, what organizations *should* do is to create a selection process in support of its job descriptions. In Chapter 3, we explained that a job description identifies the knowledge, skills, abilities, and other characteristics required for successfully performing a job. The selection process should be set up in such a way that it lets the organization identify people who have the necessary KSAOs. The Federal Aviation Administration (FAA) has recently been studying this issue to address an expected labor shortage in air-traffic controllers. In the past, up to half of the controllers originally hired by the FAA failed to receive their certification; the agency was in effect wasting $10 million a year to hire and train those people. To improve its selection process, the FAA researched which tests would identify the people with the skills associated with success in this demanding job. The agency determined that it needs to fill the positions with individuals who are skillful at spatial (three-dimensional) thinking, have strong memories, and work well under time pressure. It has been identifying tests that select people with those strengths.[2]

LO2
Define ways to
measure the success
of a selection
method.

This kind of strategic approach to selection requires ways to measure the effectiveness of selection tools. From science, we have basic standards for this. The best selection methods will provide information that is reliable and valid and can be generalized to apply to the organization's group of candidates. In addition, selection should measure characteristics that have practical benefits for the organization. Finally, selection criteria must meet the legal requirements in effect where the organization operates. Figure 6.2 summarizes these criteria.

Reliability

reliability
The extent to which
a measurement is
free from random
error.

The **reliability** of a type of measurement indicates how free that measurement is from random error.[3] A reliable measurement therefore generates consistent results. Assuming that a person's intelligence is fairly stable over time, a reliable test of intelligence should generate consistent results if the same person takes the test several times. Organizations that construct intelligence tests therefore should be able to provide (and explain) information about the reliability of their tests.

Usually, this information involves statistics such as *correlation coefficients*. These statistics measure the degree to which two sets of numbers are related. A higher correlation coefficient signifies a stronger relationship. At one extreme, a correlation co-efficient of 1.0 means a perfect positive relationship—as one set of numbers goes up, so does the other. If you took the same vision test three days in a row, those scores would probably have nearly a perfect correlation. At the other extreme, a correlation of –1.0 means a perfect negative correlation—when one set of numbers goes up, the other goes down. In the middle, a correlation of 0 means there is no correlation at all. For example, the correlation between weather and intelligence would be at or near 0. A reliable test would be one for which scores by the same person (or people with sim-ilar attributes) have a correlation close to 1.0.

Validity

For a selection measure, **validity** describes the extent to which performance on the measure (such as a test score) is related to what the measure is designed to assess (such as job performance). Although we can reliably measure such characteristics as weight and height, these measurements do not provide much information about how a per-son will perform most kinds of jobs. Thus, for most jobs height and weight provide lit-tle validity as selection criteria. One way to determine whether a measure is valid is to compare many people's scores on that measure with their job performance. For ex-ample, suppose people who score above 60 words per minute on a keyboarding test consistently get high marks for their performance in data-entry jobs. This observation suggests the keyboarding test is valid for predicting success in that job.

As with reliability, information about the validity of selection methods often uses correlation coefficients. A strong positive (or negative) correlation between a mea-sure and job performance means the measure should be a valid basis for selecting (or rejecting) a candidate. This information is important, not only because it helps or-ganizations identify the best employees, but also because organizations can demon-strate fair employment practices by showing that their selection process is valid. The federal government's *Uniform Guidelines on Employee Selection Procedures* accept three ways of measuring validity: criterion-related, content, and construct validity.

Criterion-Related Validity

The first category, **criterion-related validity,** is a measure of validity based on showing a substantial correlation between test scores and job performance scores. In the exam-ple in Figure 6.3, a company compares two measures—an intelligence test and college grade point average—with performance as sales representative. In the left graph, which shows the relationship between the intelligence test scores and job perfor-mance, the points for the 20 sales reps fall near the 45-degree line. The correlation co-efficient is near .90 (for a perfect 1.0, all the points would be on the 45-degree line). In the graph at the right, the points are scattered more widely. The correlation be-tween college GPA and sales reps' performance is much lower. In this hypothetical ex-ample, the intelligence test is more valid than GPA for predicting success at this job.

Two kinds of research are possible for arriving at criterion-related validity:

1. **Predictive validation**—This research uses the test scores of all applicants and looks for a relationship between the scores and future performance. The re-searcher administers the tests, waits a set period of time, and then measures the performance of the applicants who were hired.
2. **Concurrent validation**—This type of research administers a test to people who currently hold a job, then compares their scores to existing measures of job

validity
The extent to which performance on a measure (such as a test score) is related to what the measure is designed to assess (such as job performance).

criterion-related validity
A measure of validity based on showing a substantial correlation between test scores and job performance scores.

predictive validation
Research that uses the test scores of all applicants and looks for a relationship between the scores and future performance of the applicants who were hired.

concurrent validation
Research that consists of administering a test to people who currently hold a job, then comparing their scores to existing measures of job performance.

figure 6.3

Criterion-Related Measurements of a Student's Aptitude

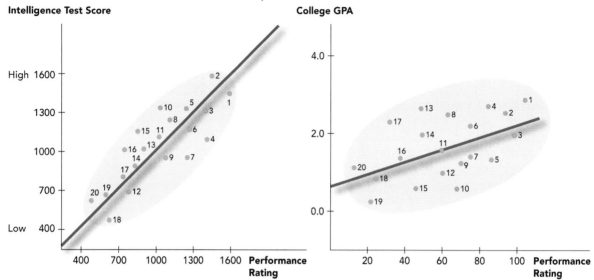

performance. If the people who score highest on the test also do better on the job, the test is assumed to be valid.

Predictive validation is more time consuming and difficult, but it is the best measure of validity. Job applicants tend to be more motivated to do well on the tests, and their performance on the tests is not influenced by their firsthand experience with the job. Also, the group studied is more likely to include people who perform poorly on the test—a necessary ingredient to accurately validate a test.[4]

Content and Construct Validity

content validity
Consistency between the test items or problems and the kinds of situations or problems that occur on the job.

Another way to show validity is to establish **content validity**—that is, consistency between the test items or problems and the kinds of situations or problems that occur on the job.[5] A test that is "content valid" exposes the job applicant to situations that are likely to occur on the job. It tests whether the applicant has the knowledge, skills, or ability to handle such situations.

For example, a general contracting firm that constructs tract housing needed to hire a construction superintendent.[6] This job involved organizing, supervising, and inspecting the work of many subcontractors. The tests developed for this position attempted to mirror the job. One test was a scrambled subcontractor test. The applicant had to take a random list of subcontractors (roofing, plumbing, electrical, and so on) and put them in the order that each firm should appear on the construction site. A second test measured recognition of construction errors. In this test, the applicant went into a shed that was specially constructed to have 25 common and expensive errors, including faulty wiring and upside-down windows. The applicant was supposed to record all the problems he or she could detect. The content of these tests so closely parallels the content of the job that it was safe to use test performance as the basis for predicting job performance.

The usual basis for deciding that a test has content validity is through expert judgment. Experts can rate the test items according to whether they mirror essential functions of the job. Because establishing validity is based on the experts' subjective judgments, content validity is most suitable for measuring behavior that is concrete and observable.

For tests that measure abstract qualities such as intelligence or leadership ability, establishment of validity may have to rely on **construct validity.** This involves establishing that tests really do measure intelligence, leadership ability, or other such "constructs," as well as showing that mastery of this construct is associated with successful performance of the job. For example, if you could show that a test measures something called "mechanical ability," and that people with superior mechanical ability perform well as assemblers, then the test has construct validity for the assembler job. Tests that measure a construct usually measure a combination of behaviors thought to be associated with the construct.

construct validity Consistency between a high score on a test and high level of a construct such as intelligence or leadership ability, as well as between mastery of this construct and successful performance of the job.

Ability to Generalize

Along with validity in general, we need to know whether a selection method is valid in the context in which the organization wants to use it. A **generalizable** method applies not only to the conditions in which the method was originally developed—job, organization, people, time period, and so on. It also applies to other organizations, jobs, applicants, and so on. In other words, is a selection method that was valid in one context also valid in other contexts?

Researchers have studied whether tests of intelligence and thinking skills (called *cognitive ability*) can be generalized. The research has supported the idea that these tests are generalizable across many jobs. However, as jobs become more complex, the validity of many of these tests increases. In other words, they are most valid for complex jobs.[7]

generalizable Valid in other contexts beyond the context in which the selection method was developed.

Practical Value

Not only should selection methods such as tests and interview responses accurately predict how well individuals will perform, they should produce information that actually benefits the organization. Being valid, reliable, and generalizable adds value to a method. Another consideration is the cost of using the selection method. Selection procedures such as testing and interviewing cost money. They should cost significantly

Launched in July 2005, Discovery was the first space shuttle to be launched since the space shuttle Columbia burned up upon launch in 2003. NASA invested a lot in selecting Discovery's Crew Commander Eileen Marie Collins because a good hiring decision could yield a big benefit but a bad one could be costly for NASA.

utility
The extent to which something provides economic value greater than its cost.

less than the benefits of hiring the new employees. Methods that provide economic value greater than the cost of using them are said to have **utility.**

The choice of a selection method may differ according to the job being filled. If the job involves providing a product or service of high value to the organization, it is worthwhile to spend more to find a top performer. At a company where salespeople are responsible for closing million-dollar deals, the company will be willing to invest more in selection decisions. At a fast-food restaurant, such an investment will not be worthwhile; the employer will prefer faster, simpler ways to select workers who ring up orders, prepare food, and keep the facility clean.

The utility of drug tests has been an issue recently. Employers want their workers to behave safely and be on the right side of the law, so they want to hire people who do not abuse drugs. Few would dispute the reliability and validity of a properly conducted drug test. However, drug tests can be expensive, and in most situations, they rarely identify hard-core drug abusers. In a study of a test used in a department of the federal government, the total spending on drug testing divided by the number of users who were identified yielded a cost of $77,000 to detect each drug addict. Thus, utility may be a reason that the percentage of companies using drug tests has been declining.[8]

New technology has improved the utility of many selection methods, especially employment testing. However, as described in the "e-HRM" box, these high-tech selection procedures also raise new legal issues.

LO3
Summarize the government's requirements for employee selection.

Legal Standards for Selection

As we discussed in Chapter 3, the U.S. government imposes legal limits on selection decisions. The government requires that the selection process be conducted in a way that avoids discrimination and provides access to employees with disabilities. The laws described in Chapter 3 have many applications to the selection process:

- The Civil Rights Act of 1991 places requirements on the choice of selection methods. An employer that uses a neutral-appearing selection method that damages a protected group is obligated to show that there is a business necessity for using that method. For example, if an organization uses a test that eliminates many candidates from minority groups, the organization must show that the test is valid for predicting performance of that job. In this context, good performance does not include "customer preference" or "brand image" as a justification for adverse impact. For example, Abercrombie & Fitch was not able to justify its low rate of hiring nonwhite applicants on the basis that certain managers thought they lacked an "A&F look."[9]
- The Civil Rights Act of 1991 also prohibits preferential treatment in favor of minority groups. In the case of an organization using a test that tends to reject members of minority groups, the organization may not simply adjust minority applicants' scores upward. Such practices, besides being illegal, can interfere with motivation. According to research, when employees perceive selection decisions to be based partially on membership in some group (minority group or women), this perception undermines the confidence of members of the supposedly protected group. Their job performance suffers as well.[10]
- Equal employment opportunity laws affect the kinds of information an organization may gather on application forms and in interviews. As summarized in Table 6.1, the organization may not ask questions that gather information about a person's protected status, even indirectly. For example, requesting the dates a person attended high school and college could indirectly gather information about an applicant's age.

E-HRM

NEW TECHNOLOGY REDEFINES PERSONNEL SELECTION

As companies have moved more of their selection process online, questions have arisen about the meaning of such standard terms as *applicant, test,* and *test taker.*

The term *applicant* seems straightforward. In a paper-based selection system, a job seeker became an applicant when he or she turned in an application form to the employment office or when a recruiter opened an envelope containing a résumé from that person. However, today individuals can spam organizations with unsolicited résumés for positions that are not even open or for which the person is not remotely qualified. Does the employer have to open these résumés and treat them with the same careful record-keeping that is associated with printed résumés mailed in response to an advertisement? The answer matters for demonstrating that the company is complying with equal employment opportunity laws. The Equal Employment Opportunity Commission has been developing rules that would allow organizations to treat spammers differently from more serious applicants so the task of documenting résumés will be more manageable.

The term *test* also had a relatively clear traditional meaning, bringing to mind paper and No. 2 pencils. On most paper-and-pencil tests, applicants respond to all the items in the same order, and the answers are scored with the same answer sheets. With a standardized test, everyone can understand that a person who scores two points higher has outperformed the lower-scoring person. But electronic testing is more flexible and so less standard. An electronic test may adjust questions according to earlier responses.

For example, with computer adaptive testing, a test does not have one set of questions, but instead questions are drawn from a giant pool of items based in part on how well the applicant is performing. The test begins with items of average difficulty, and if the respondent answers correctly, the test sends more difficult items, continuing to raise the difficulty until it reaches a point at which it has the necessary information to assess the level at which the applicant gets about half the answers right. Conversely, if the applicant provides wrong answers, the testing system makes the questions easier until the applicant gets about half of

them correct. This testing method is complex, but if done properly, it provides an extremely reliable and efficient evaluation of the applicant's skills. However, different people are answering different questions, so some may think this method is unfair.

Finally, defining a *test taker* was more obvious in the days when testing usually took place face-to-face so that the employer could readily observe a person's identity. However, when an organization offers a test online, it becomes more difficult to establish who is actually entering information at the computer. Although technologies are being developed to handle this problem, many organizations use Internet tests only as an initial screen to weed out masses of unqualified applicants. Then the employer can conduct face-to-face testing to uncover any cheaters.

SOURCE: D. P. Shuit, "Employers Beset by Résumé Spam Might Get Break from the EEOC," *Workforce,* April 2004, pp. 54–55; D. Weichmann and A. M. Ryan, "Reactions to Computerized Testing in Selection Contexts," *International Journal of Selection and Assessment,* June–September 2003, pp. 215–29; and K. Kersting, "How Do You Test on the Web? Responsibly," *Monitor on Psychology,* March 2004, pp. 26–27.

- The Americans with Disabilities Act (ADA) of 1991 requires employers to make "reasonable accommodation" to disabled individuals and restricts many kinds of questions during the selection process.[11] Under the ADA, preemployment questions

TABLE 6.1

Permissible and
Impermissible
Questions for
Applications and
Interviews

PERMISSIBLE QUESTIONS	IMPERMISSIBLE QUESTIONS
What is your full name? Have you ever worked under a different name?	What was your maiden name? What's the nationality of your name?
Are you at least 18 years old?	How old are you?
Do you understand the job requirements? Are you able to perform this job, with or without reasonable accommodation?	What is your height? your weight? Do you have any disabilities? Have you been seriously ill? Please provide a photograph of yourself.
What languages do you speak? [Statement that employment is subject to verification of applicant's identity and employment eligibility under immigration laws]	What is your ancestry? Are you a citizen of the United States? Where were you born? How did you learn to speak that language?
What schools have you attended? What degrees have you earned? What was your major?	Is that school affiliated with [religious group]? When did you attend high school? [to learn applicant's age]
[No questions about religion]	What is your religion? What religious holidays do you observe?
Please provide the names of any relatives currently employed by this employer.	What is your marital status? Would you like to be addressed as Mrs., Ms., or Miss? Do you have any children?
Have you ever been convicted of a crime?	Have you ever been arrested?
Please give the name and address of a person we may contact in case of an emergency.	Please give the name and address of a relative we may contact in case of an emergency.
What organizations or groups do you belong to (excluding those that indicate members' race, religion, color, national origin, or ancestry)?	What organizations or groups do you belong to?

Note: This table provides examples and is not intended as a complete listing of permissible and impermissible questions. The examples are based on federal requirements; state laws vary and may affect these examples.

SOURCE: Examples based on "Legal and Illegal Preemployment Inquiries," *Inc.com*, Human Resources Advice pages, www.inc.com, downloaded March 7, 2002; S. Kahn, B. B. Brown, M. Lanzarone, *Legal Guide to Human Resources* (Boston, MA: Warren, Gorham & Lamont, 1995).

may not investigate disabilities, but must focus on job performance. An interviewer may ask, "Can you meet the attendance requirements for this job?" but may not ask, "How many days did you miss work last year because you were sick?" Also, the employer may not, in making hiring decisions, use employment physical exams or other tests that could reveal a psychological or physical disability.

Along with equal employment opportunity, organizations must be concerned about candidates' privacy rights. The information gathered during the selection process may include information that employees consider confidential. For some jobs, background checks look at candidates' credit history. The Fair Credit Reporting Act requires that employers obtain a candidate's consent before using a third party to check the candidate's credit history or references. If the employer then decides to take an adverse action (such as not hiring) based on the report, the employer must give the applicant a copy of the report and summary of the applicant's rights *before* taking the action.

Another legal requirement is that employers hiring people to work in the United States must ensure that anyone they hire is eligible for employment in this country. Under the Immigration Reform and Control Act of 1986, employers must verify and maintain records on the legal rights of applicants to work in the United States. They do this by having applicants fill out the Immigration and Naturalization Service's Form I-9 and present documents showing their identity and eligibility to work. Employers must complete their portion of each Form I-9, check the applicant's documents, and retain the Form I-9 for at least three years. At the same time, assuming a person is eligible to work under this law, the law prohibits the employer from discriminating against the person on the basis of national origin or citizenship status.

An important principle of selection is to combine several sources of information about candidates, rather than relying solely on interviews or a single type of testing. The sources should be chosen carefully to relate to the characteristics identified in the job description. When organizations do this, they are increasing the validity of the decision criteria. They are more likely to make hiring decisions that are fair and unbiased. They also are more likely to choose the best candidates.

▨ JOB APPLICATIONS AND RÉSUMÉS

LO4
Compare the common methods used for selecting human resources.

Nearly all employers gather background information on applicants at the beginning of the selection process. The usual ways of gathering background information are by asking applicants to fill out application forms and provide résumés. Organizations also verify the information by checking references and conducting background checks.

Asking job candidates to provide background information is inexpensive. The organization can get reasonably accurate information by combining applications and résumés with background checks and well-designed interviews.[12] A major challenge with applications and résumés is the sheer volume of work they generate for the organization. Especially considering how easy it is for candidates to submit applications or résumés online, human resource departments often are swamped with far more résumés than they can carefully review. The "Best Practices" box explains how one company has used technology to meet this challenge.

Application Forms

Asking each applicant to fill out an employment application is a low-cost way to gather basic data from many applicants. It also ensures that the organization has certain standard categories of information, such as mailing address and employment history, from each. Figure 6.4 is an example of an application form.

Employers can buy general-purpose application forms from an office supply store, or they can create their own forms to meet unique needs. Either way, employment applications include areas for applicants to provide several types of information:

- *Contact information*—The employee's name, address, phone number, and e-mail address.
- *Work experience*—Companies the applicant worked for, job titles, and dates of employment.

BEST PRACTICES

COMPUTERS CHANNEL FLOOD OF RÉSUMÉS AT SOUTHERN COMPANY

Southern Company, an energy company headquartered in Atlanta, needs to hire more than 2,000 full-time employees each year to meet personnel needs in the four southern states where the company operates. The company's recruiters do such a good job of drawing applicants that they have to sort through more than 100,000 applications to fill those positions. In the past, says Eric Muller, who is responsible for recruiting at Southern, the recruiters felt overwhelmed: "They were victims of their own successful sourcing efforts."

Going online didn't help, because the company simply added e-mail as another source, not automation, to the process. The Web site made it easy to send résumés to Southern, but they just added to what the company's recruiters called the "résu-mess." Some candidates replied to every job advertisement on the site—those they qualified for and those requiring different experience.

To improve its selection process, Southern Company contracted to use electronic recruiting software from a suite called HireEnterprise. (The suite also includes software for applicant tracking and staffing analysis.) Since Southern was using software through application services provider Hire.com, rather than creating or buying a program, it had the system running in little more than a month. Hire.com provided training in how to use the system. Muller says learning the system was easy because the tools resembled those for shopping online: "If you can use [Amazon.com], you can use this software."

The system works by leading applicants through a process that gives the company the information it needs for screening applicants. When job seekers visit Southern Company's Web site and click on the link to jobs, the link takes them to a server operated by Hire.com. There they can search for positions and, if they wish, set up an account in which they indicate their education, job preferences, location, and other information about themselves. They can sign up to receive alerts if a position that matches their criteria opens up.

The system helps Southern narrow its pool of applicants. The system asks applicants a series of screening questions, tailored to the type of applicant and job. For example, it might ask, "In which subject do you have a master's degree?" or, "Are you used to functioning independently with minimum supervision?" The company sets up the software to weight certain questions more heavily than others. The software screens out applicants who do not qualify based on these criteria. This automation reduces one of the most time-consuming aspects of reviewing résumés: screening out unqualified applicants. When Southern Company started using the HireEnterprise system, it screened out about 40 percent of applicants. As the company improved the questions, the system has increased the percentage screened out to 65 percent. This automation frees recruiters to spend more time learning about the applicants who are qualified.

SOURCE: Drew Robb, "Screening for Speedier Selection," *HR Magazine*, September 2004, downloaded from Infotrac at http://web7.infotrac.galegroup.com.

- *Educational background*—High school, college, and universities attended and degree(s) awarded.
- *Applicant's signature*—Signature following a statement that the applicant has provided true and complete information.

Figure 6.4
Sample Job Application Form

APPLICATION FOR EMPLOYMENT
An Equal Opportunity Employer

FIRST NAME	MIDDLE NAME	LAST NAME		SOCIAL SECURITY NUMBER
LOCAL	STREET ADDRESS	CITY AND STATE	ZIP CODE	TELEPHONE
PERMANENT	STREET ADDRESS	CITY AND STATE	ZIP CODE	TELEPHONE
ELECTRONIC MAIL ADDRESS				

PLEASE ANSWER ALL ITEMS. IF NOT APPLICABLE, WRITE N/A.

ARE YOU A U.S. CITIZEN OR AUTHORIZED TO BE LEGALLY EMPLOYED ON AN ONGOING BASIS IN THE U.S. BASED ON YOUR VISA OR IMMIGRATION STATUS? ☐ YES ☐ NO | ARE YOU OVER 18 YEARS OF AGE? YES ☐ NO ☐

DO YOU CURRENTLY HAVE A NONIMMIGRANT U.S. VISA? ☐ YES ☐ NO IF YES, PLEASE SPECIFY:

DO YOU HAVE ANY RELATIVES EMPLOYED HERE? ☐ NO ☐ YES
IF YES, GIVE NAME, RELATIONSHIP AND LOCATION WHERE THEY WORK

DO YOU HAVE ANY RELATIVES EMPLOYED BY THE COMPETITION? ☐ NO ☐ YES WHAT COMPANY?

ARE YOU ABLE TO TRAVEL AS REQUIRED FOR THE POSITION SOUGHT? ☐ YES ☐ NO | ARE YOU WILLING TO RELOCATE? ☐ YES ☐ NO

ARE THERE GEOGRAPHICAL AREAS WHICH YOU WOULD PREFER OR REFUSE? ☐ NO ☐ YES IF YES, PLEASE SPECIFY:

HAVE YOU EVER BEEN CONVICTED OR PLED GUILTY TO ANY FELONY OR MISDEMEANOR OTHER THAN FOR A MINOR TRAFFIC VIOLATION? ☐ NO ☐ YES
IF YES, STATE THE DATE(S) AND LOCATION(S):

WHEN	WHERE	NATURE OF OFFENSE(S)

WORK PREFERENCE

SPECIFIC POSITION FOR WHICH YOU ARE APPLYING		NUMBER OF YEARS OF RELATED EXPERIENCE
LIST COMPUTER SOFTWARE PACKAGES OR PROGRAMMING LANGUAGE SKILLS		
STARTING SALARY EXPECTED	DATE AVAILABLE TO START WORK	HOW DID YOU HAPPEN TO APPLY FOR A POSITION HERE?

HAVE YOU EVER WORKED AT, OR APPLIED FOR WORK HERE BEFORE? ☐ NO ☐ YES
IF YES: WHEN? WHERE?

LIST EMPLOYMENT REFERENCES HERE, IF NOT INCLUDED ON ATTACHED RESUME

TURN OVER

COMPLETE THIS SECTION IF INFORMATION IS NOT INCLUDED ON ATTACHED RESUME

EDUCATION CIRCLE THE HIGHEST GRADE COMPLETED: ELEMENTARY 6 7 8 HIGH SCHOOL 1 2 3 4 COLLEGE 1 2 3 4 5 6 7 8

HIGH SCHOOL NAME(S)	LOCATION(S)		GRADUATED ☐ YES ☐ NO	GRADE AVERAGE	CLASS RANK ____ OUT OF ____
COLLEGE NAME(S)	LOCATION(S)	MAJOR FIELD(S) OF STUDY AND PRINCIPAL PROFESSOR (OR ADVISOR)		DEGREE(S) RECEIVED	OVERALL AND MAJOR GPA'S

ACADEMIC HONORS OR OTHER SPECIAL RECOGNITION

FOREIGN LANGUAGES READ FOREIGN LANGUAGES SPOKEN

HAVE YOU TAKEN THE GMAT, GRE, SAT OR OTHER ACADEMIC ENTRANCE TEST(S) WITHIN THE LAST TEN YEARS? ☐ YES ☐ NO
IF YES, LIST TEST(S), DATE(S) AND HIGHEST SCORE(S).

	DATE TAKEN	SCORE(S)			
SAT		TOTAL: ____	VERBAL:		MATHEMATICAL: ____
ACT		TOTAL: ____	ENGLISH: ____	MATHEMATICS: ____	READING: ____ SCIENCE: ____
GRE (GENERAL TEST)		TOTAL: ____	VERBAL: ____	QUANTITATIVE: ____	ANALYTICAL: ____
GMAT		TOTAL: ____	VERBAL: ____	MATH: ____	AWA: ____
OTHER		TOTAL: ____			

EMPLOYMENT AND MILITARY RECORD

LIST MOST RECENT FIRST. I AGREE TO FURNISH VERIFICATION IF REQUESTED.
ATTACH RESUME. RESPOND BELOW IF INFORMATION IS NOT INCLUDED ON RESUME.

NAME AND ADDRESS OF EMPLOYER	POSITION HELD	PRIMARY RESPONSIBILITIES AND ACCOUNTABILITIES	SALARY		DATES		REASON FOR LEAVING
			START	FINISH	FROM	TO	

ENCIRCLE THOSE EMPLOYERS YOU DO NOT WANT US TO CONTACT
TURN OVER

The application form may include other areas for the applicant to provide additional information, such as specific work experiences, technical skills, or memberships in professional or trade groups. Also, including the date on an application is useful for keeping up-to-date records of job applicants. The application form should not request information that could violate equal employment opportunity standards. For example, questions about an applicant's race, marital status, or number of children would be inappropriate.

By reviewing application forms, HR personnel can identify which candidates meet minimum requirements for education and experience. They may be able to rank applicants—for example, giving applicants with 10 years' experience a higher ranking than applicants with 2 years' experience. In this way, the applications enable the organization to narrow the pool of candidates to a number it can afford to test and interview.

Résumés

The usual way that applicants introduce themselves to a potential employer is to submit a résumé. An obvious drawback of this information source is that applicants control the content of the information, as well as the way it is presented. This type of information is therefore biased in favor of the applicant and (although this is unethical) may not even be accurate. However, this inexpensive way to gather information does provide employers with a starting point. Organizations typically use résumés as a basis for deciding which candidates to investigate further.

Organizations like Home Depot are using technology to make the selection process more efficient by gathering information electronically rather than on paper. By electronically accepting applications Home Depot can weed out the good candidates from the bad easier than physically reading through every single application they receive.

As with employment applications, an HR staff member reviews the résumés to identify candidates meeting such basic requirements as educational background, related work performed, and types of equipment the person has used. Because résumés are created by the job applicants (or the applicants have at least approved résumés created by someone they hire), they also may provide some insight into how candidates communicate and present themselves. Employers tend to decide against applicants whose résumés are unclear, sloppy, or full of mistakes. On the positive side, résumés may enable applicants to highlight accomplishments that might not show up in the format of an employment application. Review of résumés is most valid when the content of the résumés is evaluated in terms of the elements of a job description.

References

Application forms often ask that applicants provide the names of several references. Applicants provide the names and phone numbers of former employers or others who can vouch for their abilities and past job performance. In some situations, the applicant may provide letters of reference written by those people. It is then up to organization to have someone contact the references to gather information or verify the accuracy of the information provided by the applicant.

As you might expect, references are not an unbiased source of information. Most applicants are careful to choose references who will say something positive. In addition, former employers and others may be afraid that if they express negative opinions, they will be sued. Their fear is understandable. In 2003, a jury awarded $283,000 to a truck driver whose past employer told a would-be employer that he "was late most of the time, regularly missed two days a week, had a problem with authority and a poor work ethic."[13] A company called BadReferences.com will check an employee's references on the employee's behalf and document what information the former employers are providing. That documentation places an unhappy former employee in a strong legal position.[14]

Usually the organization checks references after it has determined that the applicant is a finalist for the job. Contacting references for all applicants would be time-consuming, and it does pose some burden on the people contacted. Part of that burden is the risk of giving information that is seen as too negative or too positive. If the person who is a reference gives negative information, there is a chance the candidate will claim *defamation,* meaning the person damaged the applicant's reputation by making statements that cannot be proved truthful.[15] At the other extreme, if the person gives a glowing statement about a candidate, and the new employer later learns of misdeeds such as sexual misconduct or workplace violence, the new employer might sue the former employer for misrepresentation.[16]

Because such situations occasionally arise, often with much publicity, people who give references tend to give as little information as possible. Most organizations have policies that the human resource department will handle all requests for references and that they will only verify employment dates and sometimes the employee's final salary. In organizations without such a policy, HR professionals should be careful— and train managers to be careful—to stick to observable, job-related behaviors and to avoid broad opinions that may be misinterpreted. In spite of these drawbacks of references, the risks of not learning about significant problems in a candidate's past outweigh the possibility of getting only a little information. Potential employers should check references.

Figure 6.5

A Job Candidate
Who Inspires a
Background Check

MISTER BOFFO

Background Checks

A background check is a way to verify that applicants are as they represent themselves to be. Unfortunately, as humorously illustrated in Figure 6.5, not all candidates are open and honest. About 8 out of 10 large companies and over two-thirds of smaller organizations say they conduct criminal background checks. One of those businesses is Wal-Mart stores, which employs more U.S. workers than any other company. Wal-Mart uses private services, which check their databases to look for records of criminal offenses. The background checks are performed on applicants Wal-Mart has screened and identified as qualified for a position. If the background check shows a candidate has lied on his or her job application, the company will not hire that person. If the background check turns up a criminal conviction, Wal-Mart's policy is to evaluate each candidate individually, considering the nature and date of the offense and the responsibilities of the job for which the person is being considered.[17]

Avert Inc. provides HR services, including background checks on prospective employees. In its experience, nearly one-fourth of candidates misrepresented something in their employment or educational background, more than one in eight had employers who said they would not rehire them if given the chance, and about 1 out of 16 had records of criminal behavior within recent years. Numbers like these make a lot of employers think background checks are a wise investment. Caution has become even more the watchword following the terrorist attacks of September 2001. Avert, for example, experienced a major jump in requests for background checks in the months following the attacks.[18]

Verifying credentials and conducting background checks are more complicated when candidates are not U.S. citizens. Their education may include degrees from schools outside the United States. In such cases, the organization has to determine how the institution and the degree awarded compare with schools and degrees in the United States. Some companies, including Mobil Corporation, get around this issue by conducting their own screening tests for basic skills in reading and math. Other companies, such as the Knowledge Company in Fairfax, Virginia, use work sample tests. For example, an applicant for an engineering job would have to submit designs for a certain product, and experts evaluate the drawings. Criminal background checks also are difficult. Except for serious crimes, U.S. records contain little about crimes committed outside the United States. These and other hurdles can discourage U.S. employers from hiring foreign nationals. Organizations that overcome the hurdles therefore can gain an advantage in hiring the best of this talent.[19]

❧ EMPLOYMENT TESTS AND WORK SAMPLES

When the organization has identified candidates whose applications or résumés indicate they meet basic requirements, the organization continues the selection process with this narrower pool of candidates. Often, the next step is to gather objective data through one or more employment tests. These tests fall into two broad categories:

1. **Aptitude tests** assess how well a person can learn or acquire skills and abilities. In the realm of employment testing, the best-known aptitude test is the General Aptitude Test Battery (GATB), used by the U.S. Employment Service.
2. **Achievement tests** measure a person's existing knowledge and skills. For example, government agencies conduct civil service examinations to see whether applicants are qualified to perform certain jobs.

Employment tests may assess general abilities, such as physical strength, or specific skills, such as keyboarding speed. Some organizations also use personality tests to find applicants who have personality traits associated with successful job performance, as well as integrity tests to weed out dishonest candidates. In addition, drug testing and medical examinations try to ensure that candidates meet physical job requirements and will not be impaired on the job. Before using any test, organizations should investigate the test's validity and reliability. Besides asking the testing service to provide this information, it is wise to consult more impartial sources of information, such as the ones identified in Table 6.2.

Physical Ability Tests

Physical strength and endurance play less of a role in the modern workplace than in the past, thanks to the use of automation and modern technology. Even so, many jobs still require certain physical abilities or psychomotor abilities (those connecting brain

LO5
Describe major types of employment tests.

aptitude tests
Tests that assess how well a person can learn or acquire skills and abilities.

achievement tests
Tests that measure a person's existing knowledge and skills.

TABLE 6.2

Sources of Information about Employment Tests

Mental Measurements Yearbook	Descriptions and reviews of tests that are commercially available
Principles for the Validation and Use of Personnel Selection Procedures Society for Industrial and (Organizational Psychology)	Guide to help organizations evaluate tests
Standards for Educational and Psychological Tests (American Psychological Association)	Description of standards for testing programs
Tests: A Comprehensive Reference for Assessments in Psychology, Education, and Business	Descriptions of thousands of tests
Test Critiques	Reviews of tests, written by professionals in the field

and body, as in the case of eye-hand coordination). When these abilities are essential to job performance or avoidance of injury, the organization may use physical ability tests. These evaluate one or more of the following areas of physical ability: muscular tension, muscular power, muscular endurance, cardiovascular endurance, flexibility, balance, and coordination.[20]

Although these tests can accurately predict success at certain kinds of jobs, they also tend to exclude women and people with disabilities. As a result, use of physical ability tests can make the organization vulnerable to charges of discrimination. It is therefore important to be certain that the abilities tested for really are essential to job performance or that the absence of these abilities really does create a safety hazard.

Cognitive Ability Tests

cognitive ability tests
Tests designed to measure such mental abilities as verbal skills, quantitative skills, and reasoning ability.

Although fewer jobs require muscle power today, brainpower is essential for most jobs. Organizations therefore benefit from people who have strong mental abilities. **Cognitive ability tests**—sometimes called "intelligence tests"—are designed to measure such mental abilities as verbal skills (skill in using written and spoken language), quantitative skills (skill in working with numbers), and reasoning ability (skill in thinking through the answer to a problem). Many jobs require all of these cognitive skills, so employers often get valid information from general tests. Many reliable tests are commercially available. The tests are especially valid for complex jobs and for those requiring adaptability in changing circumstances.[21]

The evidence of validity, coupled with the relatively low cost of these tests, makes them appealing, except for one problem: concern about legal issues. These concerns arise from a historical pattern in which use of the tests has had an adverse impact on African Americans. Some organizations responded with *race norming*, establishing different norms for hiring members of different racial groups. Race norming poses its own problems, not the least of which is the negative reputation it bestows on the minority employees selected using a lower standard. In addition, the Civil Rights Act of 1991 forbids the use of race or sex norming. Organizations that want to base selection decisions on cognitive ability therefore must make difficult decisions about how to measure this ability while avoiding legal problems. One possibility is a concept called *banding*. This concept treats a range of scores as being similar, as when an instructor gives the grade of A to any student whose average test score is at least 90. All applicants within a range of scores, or band, are treated as having the same score. Then within the set of "tied" scores, employers give preference to underrepresented groups. This is a controversial practice, and some have questioned its legality.[22]

Pilots require high cognitive ability. Cognitive ability tests may be used to select individuals for such positions. What other positions might require some measure of an individual's ability to handle their complexities?

Job Performance Tests and Work Samples

Many kinds of jobs require candidates that excel at performing specialized tasks, such as operating a certain machine, handling phone calls from customers, or designing advertising materials. To evaluate candidates for such jobs, the organization may administer tests of the necessary skills. Sometimes the candidates take tests that involve a sample of work, or they may show existing samples of their work. Examples of job performance tests include tests of keyboarding speed and *in-basket tests*. An in-basket test measures the ability to juggle a variety of demands, as in a manager's job. The candidate is presented with simulated memos and phone messages describing the kinds of problems that confront a person in the job. The candidate has to decide how to respond to these messages, and in what order. Examples of jobs for which candidates provide work samples include graphic designers and writers.

Tests for selecting managers may take the form of an **assessment center**—a wide variety of specific selection programs that use multiple selection methods to rate applicants or job incumbents on their management potential. An assessment center typically includes in-basket tests, tests of more general abilities, and personality tests. Combining several assessment methods increases the validity of this approach.

Job performance tests have the advantage of being job specific—that is, tailored to the kind of work done in a specific job. These tests therefore have a high level of validity, especially when combined with cognitive ability tests and a highly structured interview.[23] This advantage can become a disadvantage, however, if the organization wants to generalize the results of a test for one job to candidates for other jobs. The tests are more appropriate for identifying candidates who are generally able to solve the problems associated with a job, rather than for identifying which particular skills or traits the individual possesses.[24] Developing different tests for different jobs can become expensive. One way to save money is to prepare computerized tests that can be delivered online to various locations.

assessment center A wide variety of specific selection programs that use multiple selection methods to rate applicants or job incumbents on their management potential.

Personality Inventories

In some situations, employers may also want to know about candidates' personalities. For example, one way that psychologists think about personality is in terms of the "Big Five" traits: extroversion, adjustment, agreeableness, conscientiousness, and inquisitiveness (explained in Table 6.3). There is evidence that people who score high on conscientiousness tend to excel at work, especially when they also have high cognitive ability.[25] For people-related jobs like sales and management, extroversion and agreeableness also seem to be associated with success.[26] Strong social skills help conscientious people ensure that they get positive recognition for their hard work.[27]

1. Extroversion	Sociable, gregarious, assertive, talkative, expressive
2. Adjustment	Emotionally stable, nondepressed, secure, content
3. Agreeableness	Courteous, trusting, good-natured, tolerant, cooperative, forgiving
4. Conscientiousness	Dependable, organized, persevering, thorough, achievement-oriented
5. Inquisitiveness	Curious, imaginative, artistically sensitive, broadminded, playful

TABLE 6.3

Five Major Personality Dimensions Measured by Personality Inventories

The usual way to identify a candidate's personality traits is to administer one of the personality tests that are commercially available. The employer pays for the use of the test, and the organization that owns the test then scores the responses and provides a report about the test taker's personality. An organization that provides such tests should be able to discuss the test's validity and reliability. Assuming the tests are valid for the organization's jobs, they have advantages. Administering commercially available personality tests is simple, and these tests have generally not violated equal opportunity employment requirements.[28]

According to surveys, 30 to 40 percent of U.S. companies are using personality tests, and about 2,500 companies offer versions of these tests. With so much availability, it is important for employers to ask test providers about research demonstrating their tests' reliability and validity. Employers should also evaluate whether using the tests improves their own hiring decisions. Universal Studios says the quality of its workers at its Hollywood theme park has improved since it began using personality tests. Customer satisfaction and employee retention have risen, and absenteeism and theft have declined. Universal varies the tests according to the type of job the applicant is applying for. The company considers the test scores but doesn't rule out employees just because they have a low score. However, according to recruiter Nathan Giles, "In almost every case, the results of the test are what we see in their interviews." At sporting goods retailer the Finish Line, managers may not hire candidates who score poorly on personality tests. The Finish Line uses the tests to identify individuals with qualities such as sociability and initiative. Bank of America uses personality tests that measure behaviors with questions such as "Were you most comfortable working with a large team, or one or two others, or on your own?" The bank says retention and productivity have improved since it started using the tests.[29]

Honesty Tests and Drug Tests

No matter what employees' personalities may be like, organizations want employees to be honest and to behave safely. Some organizations are satisfied to assess these qualities based on judgments from reference checks and interviews. Others investigate these characteristics more directly through the use of honesty tests and drug tests.

The most famous kind of honesty test is the polygraph, the so-called lie detector test. However, in 1988 the passage of the Polygraph Act banned the use of polygraphs for screening job candidates. As a result, testing services have developed paper-and-pencil honesty (or integrity) tests. Generally these tests ask applicants directly about their attitudes toward theft and their own experiences with theft. Table 6.4 shows a sample of the items on such a test. Most of the research into the validity of these tests has been conducted by the testing companies, but evidence suggests they do have some ability to predict such behavior as theft of the employer's property.[30]

As concerns about substance abuse have grown during recent decades, so has the use of drug testing. As a measure of a person's exposure to drugs, chemical testing has high reliability and validity. However, these tests are controversial for several reasons. Some people are concerned that they invade individuals' privacy. Others object from a legal perspective. When all applicants or employees are subject to testing, whether or not they have shown evidence of drug use, the tests might be an unreasonable search and seizure or a violation of due process. Taking urine and blood samples involves invasive procedures, and accusing someone of drug use is a serious matter.

Employers considering the use of drug tests should ensure that their drug-testing programs conform to some general rules. First, the tests should be administered sys-

TABLE 6.4

Sample Items from a
Typical Honesty Test

1. It's OK to take something from a company that is making too much profit.
2. Stealing is just a way of getting your fair share.
3. When a store overcharges its customers, it's OK to change price tags on merchandise.
4. If you could get into a movie without paying and not get caught, would you do it?
5. Is it OK to go around the law if you don't actually break it?

SOURCE: "T or F? Honesty Tests," *Inc.* magazine, 1992, p. 104. Reprinted with permission.

tematically to all applicants for the same job. If some applicants for a machinist's job are tested, then all applicants for that job should take the same test. Second, testing seems most defensible for jobs that involve safety hazards when not performed properly. For example, it is easier to justify drug testing for a roofer's job than for the job of answering the telephone at the roofing company. In addition, the applicant should receive a report of the test results and should know how to appeal those results (and perhaps be retested). The organization also should respect applicants' privacy. As far as possible, the tests should be conducted in an environment that is not intrusive, and the results should be strictly confidential. Finally, when the organization tests current employees, the testing program should be part of a wider organizational program that provides rehabilitation counseling.[31]

Another way organizations can avoid some of the problems with drug testing is to replace those tests with impairment testing of employees, also called *fitness-for-duty testing*. These testing programs measure whether a worker is alert and mentally able to perform critical tasks at the time of the test. The test does not investigate the cause of any impairment—whether the employee scores poorly because of illegal drugs, alcohol, prescription drugs, over-the-counter medicines, or simple fatigue. A typical impairment test looks like a video game. The employee looks into a dark viewport and tries to follow a randomly moving point of light with his or her eyes. The equipment analyzes the person's performance and compares it with a baseline to see whether the person is fit for duty at that moment. Results are available in as little as two minutes. Because the test measures involuntary physical response, employees cannot cheat (as some have done on urine or blood tests). These tests are expensive, so they are most appropriate for high-stakes industries, such as building aircraft, spacecraft, or making surgical equipment.[32]

Medical Examinations

Especially for physically demanding jobs, organizations may wish to conduct medical examinations to see that the applicant can meet the job's requirements. Employers may also wish to establish an employee's physical condition at the beginning of employment, so that there is a basis for measuring whether the employee has suffered a work-related disability later on. At the same time, as described in Chapter 3, organizations may not discriminate against individuals with disabilities who could perform a job with reasonable accommodations. Likewise, they may not use a measure of size or strength that discriminates against women, unless those requirements are valid in predicting the ability to perform a job. Furthermore, to protect candidates' privacy, medical exams must be related to job requirements and may not be given until the candidate has received a job offer. Therefore, organizations must be careful in how they use medical examinations. Many organizations make selection decisions first, then conduct the exams to confirm that the employee can handle the job, with any reasonable accommodations required. Limiting the use of medical exams in this way also holds down the cost of what tends to be an expensive process.

❧ INTERVIEWS

LO6
Discuss how to conduct effective interviews.

Supervisors and team members most often get involved in the selection process at the stage of employment interviews. These interviews bring together job applicants and representatives of the employer to obtain information and evaluate the applicant's qualifications. While the applicant is providing information, he or she is also forming opinions about what it is like to work for the organization. Most organizations use interviewing as part of the selection process. In fact, this method is used more than any other.

Interviewing Techniques

nondirective interview
A selection interview in which the interviewer has great discretion in choosing questions to ask each candidate.

structured interview
A selection interview that consists of a predetermined set of questions for the interviewer to ask.

situational interviews
A structured interview in which the interviewer describes a situation likely to arise on the job, then asks the candidate what he or she would do in that situation.

behavior description interview (BDI)
A structured interview in which the interviewer asks the candidate to describe how he or she handled a type of situation in the past.

An interview may be nondirective or structured. In a **nondirective interview,** the interviewer has great discretion in choosing questions to ask each candidate. For example, the interviewer might ask, "What is your greatest accomplishment in your current position?" The candidate's reply might suggest to the interviewer what other questions to ask. Often, these interviews include open-ended questions about the candidate's strengths, weaknesses, career goals, and work experience. Because nondirective interviews give the interviewer wide latitude, their reliability is not great. Also, interviewers do not necessarily ask valid questions. Inexperienced or poorly informed interviewers may ask questions that are irrelevant or even illegal.

To manage the risks of a nondirective interview, many organizations substitute the use of a **structured interview,** which establishes a set of questions for the interviewer to ask. Ideally, these questions are related to the requirements set out in the job description. They should cover the candidate's knowledge required to perform this type of job, his or her experience in handling job-related situations, and other job-related personal requirements such as willingness to travel, work overtime, or learn new skills. The interviewer asks questions from the list and is supposed to avoid asking questions that are not on the list. Some interviewers object to being limited in this way, but a list of well-written questions can provide more valid and reliable results.

Some of the best results of interviewing come from the use of **situational interviews.** In this type of structured interview, the interviewer describes a situation likely to arise on the job, then asks the candidate what he or she would do in that situation. Situational interviews have been shown to have high validity in predicting job performance.[33] A variation is the **behavior description interview (BDI),** in which the interviewer asks the candidate to describe how he or she handled a type of situation in the past. Questions about the candidates' actual experiences tend to have the highest validity.[34]

When Andrew Kindler was a hiring manager, he used open-ended BDI-style questions to good effect. When interviewing candidates for management positions, he would ask them to describe the most difficult ethical dilemma they had to solve at work. Kindler's objective was to learn about each candidate's ethics and problem-solving style. In one instance, a candidate for a position as the corporation's general counsel (an important legal position) said he had never encountered an ethical dilemma. Kindler quickly eliminated that candidate from consideration, on the grounds that "a lawyer who has never encountered an ethical dilemma doesn't have ethics."[35]

When interviewing candidates, it's valid to ask about willingness to travel if that is part of the job. Interviewers might ask questions about previous business travel experiences and/or how interviewees handled situations requiring flexibility and self-motivation (qualities that would be an asset in someone who is traveling alone and solving business problems on the road).

The common setup for either a nondirected or structured interview is for an individual (an HR professional or the supervisor for the vacant position) to interview each candidate face to face. However, variations on this approach are possible. In a **panel interview,** several members of the organization meet to interview each candidate. A panel interview gives the candidate a chance to meet more people and see how people interact in that organization. It provides the organization with the judgments of more than one person, to reduce the effect of personal biases in selection decisions. Panel interviews can be especially appropriate in organizations that use teamwork. At the other extreme, some organizations conduct interviews without any interviewers; they use a computerized interviewing process. The candidate sits at a computer and enters replies to the questions presented by the computer. Such a format eliminates a lot of personal bias—along with the opportunity to see how people interact. Therefore, computer interviews are useful for gathering objective data, rather than assessing people skills.

panel interview
Selection interview in which several members of the organization meet to interview each candidate.

Advantages and Disadvantages of Interviewing

The wide use of interviewing is not surprising. People naturally want to see prospective employees firsthand. As we noted in Chapter 1, the top qualities that employers seek in new hires include communication skills and interpersonal skills. Talking face to face can provide evidence of these skills. Interviews can give insights into candidates' personalities and interpersonal styles. They are more valid, however, when they focus on job knowledge and skill. Interviews also provide a means to check the accuracy of information on the applicant's résumé or job application. Asking applicants to elaborate about their experiences and offer details reduces the likelihood of a candidate being able to invent a work history.[36] Container Store effectively uses interviews to identify employees who "encourage one another," in the words of Kevin Fuller, the retailer's director of training and recruiting. To assess applicants' ability and commitment to teamwork, the company conducts interviews in groups of up to 10 applicants. The applicants carry out challenges such as helping someone use a product to solve a problem. Interviewers observe the sales pitch to measure the applicants' selling skills and enthusiasm.[37]

Despite these benefits, interviewing is not necessarily the most accurate basis for making a selection decision. Research has shown that interviews can be unreliable, low in validity,[38] and biased against a number of different groups.[39] Interviews are also costly. They require that at least one person devote time to interviewing each candidate, and the applicants typically have to be brought to one geographic location. Interviews are also subjective, so they place the organization at greater risk of discrimination complaints by applicants who were not hired, especially if those individuals were asked questions not entirely related to the job. The Supreme Court has held that subjective selection methods like interviews must be validated, using methods that provide criterion-related or content validation.[40]

Organizations can avoid some of these pitfalls.[41] Human resource staff should keep the interviews narrow, structured, and standardized. The interview should focus on accomplishing a few goals, so that at the end of the interview, the organization has ratings on several observable measures, such as ability to express ideas. The interview should not try to measure abilities and skills—for example, intelligence—that tests can measure better. As noted earlier, situational interviews are especially effective for doing this. Organizations can prevent problems related to subjectivity by training interviewers and using more than one person to conduct interviews. Training typically includes focusing on the recording of observable facts, rather than on making subjective judgments, as well as developing interviewers' awareness of their biases.[42] Using a structured system for taking notes is helpful for limiting subjectivity and helping the interviewer remember and justify an evaluation later.[43] Finally, to address costs of interviewing, many organizations videotape interviews and send the tapes (rather than the applicants) from department to department. The nearby "HR How To" box provides more specific guidelines for successful interviewing.

Preparing to Interview

Organizations can reap the greatest benefits from interviewing if they prepare carefully. A well-planned interview should be standardized, comfortable for the participants, and focused on the job and the organization. The interviewer should have a quiet place in which to conduct interviews without interruption. This person should be trained in how to ask objective questions, what subject matter to avoid, and how to detect and handle his or her own personal biases or other distractions in order to fairly evaluate candidates.

The interviewer should have enough documents to conduct a complete interview. These should include a list of the questions to be asked in a structured interview, with plenty of space for recording the responses. When the questions are prepared, it is also helpful to determine how the answers will be scored. For example, if questions ask how interviewees would handle certain situations, consider what responses are best in terms of meeting job requirements. If the job requires someone who motivates others, then a response that shows motivating behavior would receive a higher score. The interviewer also should have a copy of the interviewee's employment application and résumé, to review before the interview and refer to during the interview. If possible, the interviewer should also have printed information about the organization and the

HR HOW TO

INTERVIEWING EFFECTIVELY

Interviewing is one HR function that almost all managers become involved with at some point. Most managers and team leaders want a role in interviewing candidates for the positions that report to them. Therefore, HR professionals need to teach as well as learn effective interviewing skills. Here are some ways to conduct interviews that identify the best candidates:

- *Decide what you're looking for.* Review the job description for the vacant position, and identify the qualifications, motivations, behaviors, and values of a successful employee in that position.
- *Plan the interview.* Write questions that relate to the qualifications, motivations, behaviors, and values you are looking for. Make sure the questions are legally permissible (if you aren't sure, get legal advice). Also, prepare the information you will be giving the candidates: description of job duties and background about the organization.
- *Put the applicant at ease.* Often, people who interview for a job are nervous, or at least cautious. Spend the first

few minutes of the interview making the applicant comfortable. Chat about casual matters—the weather, the traffic, the fishing trophy on your wall—and wait for the candidate to relax. You can't learn much about someone who is tense.

- *Work from a list.* If you prepared well, you have a list of job-related questions to cover with each candidate. These should include behavior-based questions that meet the objectives you defined during the planning phase. Let candidates know that everyone is answering the same questions. If you cover all the questions on your list with each candidate, you will have a more valid basis for comparison.
- *Listen and follow up.* As the candidate is speaking, concentrate on the answers, not on your next question. Try to let the candidate do most of the talking, even if that means you are silent while the candidate thinks. Your list of questions should include follow-up questions that emphasize the qualities you are looking for. If the desired quality is high ethical standards, you might ask,

"Describe what you would do if a coworker asked you to lie for him or her?" and then probe for more detail with, "What would you say?"

- *Take notes.* Explain ahead of time that you are taking notes so that you will have accurate information to refer to later. Record answers and behaviors, not your impressions and judgments.
- *Close the interview gracefully.* A good final question is, "Is there anything we haven't discussed that you'd like me to know?" Then give the candidate general information about what stage the selection process is in and when the candidate can expect to hear from you.

SOURCE: University of Michigan, Recruiting and Employment Services, "Behavior/Skill-Based Interviewing," *Conducting a Successful Employee Selection Process*, http://www.umich.edu/~hraa/empserv/deptinfo/empsel.htm, accessed April 15, 2005; G. P. Smith, "Improve Your Interviewing Techniques," *BLR Online HR Newsletter* (Business & Legal Reports), www.blr.com, downloaded March 20, 2002; and G. Gabriel, "Pick the Super Performers," *Job Resources*, National Association for Female Executives Web site, http://nafe.com, downloaded March 19, 2002.

job. Near the beginning of the interview, it is a good idea to go over the job specifications, organizational policies, and so on, so that the interviewee has a clearer understanding of the organization's needs.

The interviewer should schedule enough time to review the job requirements, discuss the interview questions, and give the interviewee a chance to ask questions. To close, the interviewer should thank the candidate for coming and provide information about what to expect—for example, that the organization will contact a few finalists within the next two weeks or that a decision will be made by the end of the week.

❦ SELECTION DECISIONS

LO7
Explain how employers carry out the process of making a selection decision.

After reviewing applications, scoring tests, conducting interviews, and checking references, the organization needs to make decisions about which candidates to place in which jobs. In practice, most organizations find more than one qualified candidate to fill an open position. The selection decision typically combines ranking based on objective criteria along with subjective judgments about which candidate will make the greatest contribution.

How Organizations Select Employees

The selection decision should not be a simple matter of whom the supervisor likes best or which candidate will take the lowest offer. Rather, the people making the selection should look for the best fit between candidate and position. In general, the person's performance will result from a combination of ability and motivation. Often, the selection is a choice among a few people who possess the basic qualifications. The decision makers therefore have to decide which of those people have the best combination of ability and motivation to fit in the position and in the organization as a whole.

multiple-hurdle model
Process of arriving at a selection decision by eliminating some candidates at each stage of the selection process.

The usual process for arriving at a selection decision is to gradually narrow the pool of candidates for each job. This approach, called the **multiple-hurdle model,** is based on a process such as the one shown earlier in Figure 6.1. Each stage of the process is a hurdle, and candidates who overcome a hurdle continue to the next stage of the process. For example, the organization reviews applications and/or résumés of all candidates, conducts some tests on those who meet minimum requirements, conducts initial interviews with those who had the highest test scores, follows up with additional interviews or testing, and then selects a candidate from the few who survived this process. The "Did You Know . . . ?" box describes the thinking of an interviewer who applies the multiple-hurdle model. Another, more expensive alternative is to take most applicants through all steps of the process and then to review all the scores to find the most desirable candidates. With this alternative, decision makers may use a **compensatory model,** in which a very high score on one type of assessment can make up for a low score on another.

compensatory model
Process of arriving at a selection decision in which a very high score on one type of assessment can make up for a low score on another.

Whether the organization uses a multiple-hurdle model or conducts the same assessments on all candidates, the decision maker(s) needs criteria for choosing among qualified candidates. An obvious strategy is to select the candidates who score highest on tests and interviews. However, employee performance depends on motivation as well as ability. It is possible that a candidate who scores very high on an ability test might be "overqualified"—that is, the employee might be bored by the job the organization needs to fill, and a less-able employee might actually be a better fit. Similarly, a highly motivated person might learn some kinds of jobs very quickly, potentially outperforming someone who has the necessary skills. Furthermore, some organizations have policies of developing employees for career paths in the organization. Such organizations might place less emphasis on the skills needed for a

FIRST IMPRESSIONS MATTER

Hiring manager Brian Krueger says that although a typical initial interview lasts 30 minutes to an hour, he screens out most candidates in the first five minutes of the interview. He says candidates who don't impress the interviewer in the first five minutes of an interview rarely recover from that missed opportunity. What can an interviewer learn in five minutes? Most interviewers already know

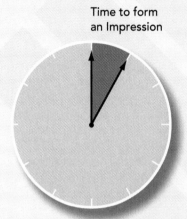

Time to form an Impression

what's on the résumé. Krueger says he responds positively to candidates who are articulate, maintain eye contact, have a pleasant manner, and present themselves professionally with neat and professional attire and good posture.

SOURCE: Brian Krueger, "The Truth about Interviewing," and "The Most Important Interview Non-verbals," CollegeGrad.com E-Zine, www.collegegrad.com, accessed April 22, 2005.

particular job and more emphasis on hiring candidates who share the organization's values, show that they have the people skills to work with others in the organization, and are able to learn the skills needed for advancement.

Finally, organizations have choices about who will make the decision. Usually a supervisor makes the final decision, often alone. This person may couple knowledge of the job with a judgment about who will fit in best with others in the department. The decision could also be made by a human resource professional using standardized, objective criteria. Especially in organizations that use teamwork, selection decisions may be made by a work team or other panel of decision makers.

Communicating the Decision

The human resource department is often responsible for notifying applicants about the results of the selection process. When a candidate has been selected, the organization should communicate the offer to the candidate. The offer should include the job responsibilities, work schedule, rate of pay, starting date, and other relevant details. If placement in a job requires that the applicant pass a physical examination, the offer should state that contingency. The person communicating the offer should also indicate a date by which the candidate should reply with an acceptance or rejection of the offer. For some jobs, such as management and professional positions, the candidate and organization may negotiate pay, benefits, and work arrangements before they arrive at a final employment agreement.

The person who communicates this decision should keep accurate records of who was contacted, when, and for which position, as well as of the candidate's reply. The HR department and the supervisor also should be in close communication about the job offer. When an applicant accepts a job offer, the HR department must notify the supervisor, so that he or she can be prepared for the new employee's arrival.

thinking ETHICALLY

Background Checks: Restraint Needed?

The discussion of background checks earlier in the chapter mentioned that a majority of companies check the backgrounds of at least some applicants. The use of background checks is prompted by concerns for security and safety. But background checks also pose concerns related to false information, as well as the possibility that job seekers with problems in their past can never get a fresh start.

Johnnie Ulrigg is one employee who was victimized by a mistake. Four days after he was hired to make deliveries for a department store in Missoula, Montana, his supervisor told him that a background check had generated a list of convictions for violating probation. He hadn't reported these on his job application, so he was fired. But Ulrigg hadn't lied; the report was misleading. Several Montana counties had been recording the failure to pay a traffic ticket as a probation violation. It took Ulrigg about two years to clear his record, during which time he could find only part-time jobs. He never convinced the department store to rehire him. In California, a laid-off man named Ron Peterson was uncertain why he had difficulty finding a new job. He did a background check on himself and turned up a report of a man with a similar name and the same birth date who had pleaded guilty to a misdemeanor. Now Peterson is trying to figure out how to clear his name.

Ex-convicts might have a harder time winning sympathy for their dilemma. One of them, Peter Demain, was sentenced to six years in prison for possession of 21 pounds of marijuana. During his incarceration, he worked in the prison kitchen, eventually achieving a promotion to head baker. After his release, Demain tried to find work as a baker, but all the local stores and bakeries turned him down, some even ordering him to leave the premises immediately upon learning of his prior conviction. According to Lewis Maltby, president of the National WorkRights Institute, "Forty-six million people in this country have been convicted of something sometime in their lives, and our economy would collapse if none of them could get jobs." Others worry that if ex-cons cannot find employment, they may see crime as their only alternative.

Of course, the flip side is that employers have to be concerned about their hiring decisions. Wal-Mart recently instituted background checks on job applicants. That policy followed reports of two incidents at Wal-Mart stores in South Carolina in which different employees were accused of sexually assaulting young female shoppers; both men had criminal convictions for sexually related crimes.

SOURCE: Kris Maher, "The Jungle," *The Wall Street Journal*, January 20, 2004, p. A8; Ann Zimmerman and Kortney Stringer, "As Background Checks Proliferate, Ex-Cons Face Jobs Lock," *The Wall Street Journal*, August 26, 2004, pp. B1, B3; and Amy Joyce, "Checking Job Applicants' Backgrounds Easy but Dicey," *Columbus Dispatch*, August 30, 2004.

Questions

1. When an employer is deciding whether to use background checks of job applicants, who may be affected by that decision?
2. Suppose you are a recruiter and have identified an applicant who possesses excellent knowledge, skills, ability, and other characteristics required for a po-

sition in your organization. Then you learn from a background check that this applicant was once convicted of a crime. What would you do? Would you need further information, and if so, what information?

3. Would your answer to Question 2 be different if you identified two qualified candidates, and only one candidate's background check turned up a problem? Could there ever be a valid reason to hire the candidate with the problem in his or her past?

SUMMARY

1. Identify the elements of the selection process.
   Selection typically begins with a review of candidates' employment applications and résumés. The organization administers tests to candidates who meet basic requirements, and qualified candidates undergo one or more interviews. Organizations check references and conduct background checks to verify the accuracy of information provided by candidates. A candidate is selected to fill each vacant position. Candidates who accept offers are placed in the positions for which they were selected.

2. Define ways to measure the success of a selection method.
   One criterion is reliability, which indicates the method is free from random error, so that measurements are consistent. A selection method should also be valid, meaning that performance on the measure (such as a test score) is related to what the measure is designed to assess (such as job performance). Criterion-related validity shows a correlation between test scores and job performance scores. Content validity shows consistency between the test items or problems and the kinds of situations or problems that occur on the job. Construct validity establishes that the test actually measures a specified construct, such as intelligence or leadership ability, which is presumed to be associated with success on the job. A selection method also should be generalizable, so that it applies to more than one specific situation. Each selection method should have utility, meaning it provides economic value greater than its cost. Finally, selection methods should meet the legal requirements for employment decisions.

3. Summarize the government's requirements for employee selection.
   The selection process must be conducted in a way that avoids discrimination and provides access to persons with disabilities. This means selection methods must be valid for job performance, and scores may not be adjusted to discriminate against or give preference to any group. Questions may not gather information about a person's membership in a protected class, such as race, sex, or religion, nor may the employer investigate a person's disability status. Employers must respect candidates' privacy rights and ensure that they keep personal information confidential. They must obtain consent before conducting background checks and notify candidates about adverse decisions made as a result of background checks.

4. Compare the common methods used for selecting human resources.
   Nearly all organizations gather information through employment applications and résumés. These methods are inexpensive, and an application form standardizes basic information received from all applicants. The information is not necessarily reliable, because each applicant provides the information. These methods are most valid when evaluated in terms of the criteria in a job description. References and background checks help to verify the accuracy of the information. Employment tests and work samples are more objective. To be legal, any test must measure abilities that actually are associated with successful job performance. Employment tests range from general to specific. General-purpose tests are relatively inexpensive and simple to administer. Tests should be selected to be related to successful job performance and avoid charges of discrimination. Interviews are widely used to obtain information about a candidate's interpersonal and communication skills and to gather more detailed information about a candidate's background. Structured interviews are more valid than unstructured ones. Situational interviews provide greater validity than general questions. Interviews are costly and may introduce bias into the selection process. Organizations can minimize the drawbacks through preparation and training.

5. Describe major types of employment tests.
   Physical ability tests measure strength, endurance, psychomotor abilities, and other physical abilities. They can be accurate but can discriminate and are not always job related. Cognitive ability tests, or intelligence tests, tend to be valid, especially for complex jobs and those requiring adaptability. They are a relatively low-cost way to predict job performance but have been

challenged as discriminatory. Job performance tests tend to be valid but are not always generalizable. Using a wide variety of job performance tests can be expensive. Personality tests measure personality traits such as extroversion and adjustment. Research supports their validity for appropriate job situations, especially for individuals who score high on conscientiousness, extroversion, and agreeableness. These tests are relatively simple to administer and generally meet legal requirements. Organizations may use paper-and-pencil honesty tests, which can predict certain behaviors, including employee theft. Organizations may not use polygraphs to screen job candidates. Organizations may also administer drug tests (if all candidates are tested and drug use can be an on-the-job safety hazard). A more job-related approach is to use impairment testing. Passing a medical examination may be a condition of employment, but to avoid discrimination against persons with disabilities, organizations usually administer a medical exam only after making a job offer.

6. Discuss how to conduct effective interviews.
   Interviews should be narrow, structured, and standardized. Interviewers should identify job requirements and create a list of questions related to the requirements.

Interviewers should be trained to recognize their own personal biases and conduct objective interviews. Panel interviews can reduce problems related to interviewer bias. Interviewers should put candidates at ease in a comfortable place that is free of distractions. Questions should ask for descriptions of relevant experiences and job-related behaviors. The interviewers also should be prepared to provide information about the job and the organization.

7. Explain how employers carry out the process of making a selection decision.
   The organization should focus on the objective of finding the person who will be the best fit with the job and organization. This includes an assessment of ability and motivation. Decision makers may use a multiple-hurdle model in which each stage of the selection process eliminates some of the candidates from consideration at the following stages. At the final stage, only a few candidates remain, and the selection decision determines which of these few is the best fit. An alternative is a compensatory model, in which all candidates are evaluated with all methods. A candidate who scores poorly with one method may be selected if he or she scores very high on another measure.

REVIEW AND DISCUSSION QUESTIONS

1. What activities are involved in the selection process? Think of the last time you were hired for a job. Which of those activities were used in selecting you? Should the organization that hired you have used other methods as well?

2. Why should the selection process be adapted to fit the organization's job descriptions?

3. Choose two of the selection methods identified in this chapter. Describe how you can compare them in terms of reliability, validity, ability to generalize, utility, and compliance with the law.

4. Why does predictive validation provide better information than concurrent validation? Why is this type of validation more difficult?

5. How do U.S. laws affect organizations' use of each of the employment tests? Interviews?

6. Suppose your organization needs to hire several computer programmers, and you are reviewing résumés you obtained from an online service. What kinds of information will you want to gather from the "work experience" portion of these résumés? What kinds of information will you want to gather from the "education" portion of these résumés? What methods would you use for verifying or exploring this information? Why would you use those methods?

7. For each of the following jobs, select the two kinds of tests you think would be most important to include in the selection process. Explain why you chose those tests.
   a. City bus driver.
   b. Insurance salesperson.
   c. Member of a team that sells complex high-tech equipment to manufacturers.
   d. Member of a team that makes a component of the equipment in (c).

8. Suppose you are a human resource professional at a large retail chain. You want to improve the company's hiring process by creating standard designs for interviews, so that every time someone is interviewed for a particular job category, that person answers the same questions. You also want to make sure the questions asked are relevant to the job and maintain equal employment opportunity. Think of three questions to include in interviews for each of the following jobs. For each question, state why you think it should be included.
   a. Cashier at one of the company's stores.
   b. Buyer of the stores' teen clothing line.
   c. Accounts payable clerk at company headquarters.

9. How can organizations improve the quality of their interviewing so that interviews provide valid information?

10. Some organizations set up a selection process that is long and complex. In some people's opinion, this kind of selection process not only is more valid but also has symbolic value. What can the use of a long, complex selection process symbolize to job seekers? How do you think this would affect the organization's ability to attract the best employees?

WHAT'S YOUR HR IQ?

The text Web site offers two more ways to check what you've learned so far. Use the Self-Assessment exercise to practice behavioral interview questions. Go online with the Web Exercise to analyze a selection tool used by some convenience stores.

BusinessWeek CASE

BusinessWeek How Google Searches for Talent

March 26, 2005, heralds the opening of the spring season in India, a day celebrated with riotous color and revelry. But in one corner of Bangalore, India's info tech hub, the sunny Saturday is heavy with tension. At an Internet café, a group of engineers and math majors, all in their twenties, hunch over terminals, ready to write some killer code—and, with luck, launch careers with one of the world's premier tech companies, Google Inc.

It's the Google India Code Jam, a contest to find the most brilliant coder in South and Southeast Asia. The fastest will win $6,900—and more important, the offer of a coveted job at one of Google's research and development centers. At the stroke of 10:30 A.M., the contestants begin, emerging exhausted three hours later. "It's been incredibly difficult and awesome," says Nitin Gupta, a computer science undergrad at the Indian Institute of Technology at Bombay.

Google has staged Code Jams in the United States, but this is its first such bakeoff in Asia, and the response is huge. Some 14,000 aspirants registered from all over South and Southeast Asia for the first round in February. The top 50 were selected for the finals in Bangalore: 39 from India, 8 from Singapore, and 3 from Indonesia. "It's a dog-eat-dog world," says Robert Hughes, president of TopCoder Inc., the Glastonbury, Connecticut, testing company that runs the Code Jams. "Wherever the best talent is, Google wants them."

And the winner is . . . one of these clever IIT grads from India, right? Surprisingly, no. Ardian Poernomo, a third-year undergrad computer engineering student at Singapore's Nanyang Technological University, lands in first place. The number two finisher, Pascal Alfadian, a second-year student at the Universitas Katolik Parahyangan in West Java, is Indonesian, too. Poernomo didn't commit to taking a job with Google, however. He may go for a doctorate degree in computer science in the United States.

Still, Google now has a new pool of Asian talent to choose from. According to Krishna Bharat, head of Google's India research and development center, all the finalists will be offered jobs. And Google needs them. The search company has been frustrated by its inability to find top-notch engineers for its year-old Indian center, according to industry insiders. Its Bangalore staff now totals 25, but it was hoping to have signed up at least 100 engineers by December 2004.

Google's frustrations in India stem from two factors. One is the red-hot job market in Indian tech. Engineering students are assured of a job a year before they graduate. But Google makes things hard for itself by having some of the most exacting hiring standards going. The contest is an example. Participants are tested on aptitude in problem solving, on designing and writing code, and on testing peer-written work. Finalists are asked to create and test software for unique Web searches and to get from point A to B in a city with a minimum number of turns. The final challenge is programming a war-based board game, a task so complex that only winner Poernomo completed it.

For Google, the Code Jam will serve as a shortcut through its hiring regime. Candidates normally go through a seven-stage process that can last months—and, at the end of it, they're more likely to be rejected than hired. Much of that screening can be set aside for Code Jam winners.

For Wunderkinder like Poernomo, Google can be patient. Stanford grad Jon McAlister was the 2001 winner of TopCoder's U.S. Collegiate Code Jam but didn't sign up with Google until 2004. He eventually rejected competing offers from Goldman, Sachs & Company and Microsoft. "Google is the genuine engineering company," says McAlister. Google hopes its India finalists think so, too.

SOURCE: Josey Puliyenthuruthel, "How Google Searches—for Talent," *BusinessWeek*, April 11, 2005, downloaded from Infotrac at http://web6.infotrac.galegroup.com.

Questions

1. Google's product is the Internet search engine of the same name. Why do you think the company uses a contest (the Code Jam) as one of its selection methods? What are some benefits of this method?
2. What knowledge, skills, abilities, or other characteristics of computer programmers would the Code Jam *not* evaluate?
3. Would you predict that the Code Jam is a valid and reliable selection method for Google programmers? Would you advise Google to use similar methods for other positions at the company? Explain.

CASE: Should Wal-Mart Standardize Selection?

The process for securing a management position at Wal-Mart has seemed arbitrary to some. One observer called it "a tap-on-the shoulder process, where Wal-Mart would reach down and anoint somebody and invite them into upper management." One reason it looked this way was Wal-Mart's practice of decentralized decision making, meaning the company left many decisions up to the managers of individual stores or departments. This decentralization has allowed the company to be creative and quick thinking in terms of purchasing and merchandising. But in terms of human resource management, more centralized control might have prevented some problems.

Wal-Mart has recently been in legal hot water because women statistically have been selected for promotion less often than men. Many female workers who served Wal-Mart for years and received glowing yearly performance evaluations watched in frustration as they were passed over for management jobs that went to men who seemed to be less qualified. Because the company lacked standard, centralized practices for promoting employees into management, it is hard for outsiders (and even corporate management) to say exactly what motives were behind these selection decisions. However, it is easier to track the outcomes of those decisions. According to numbers in the discrimination filing, women made up more than two-thirds of Wal-Mart's hourly employees but less than one-third of the management positions. (Wal-Mart says the numbers are closer to 60 percent and 40 percent.) Recently, 1.5 million current and former female employees of Wal-Mart filed a class-action lawsuit charging that Wal-Mart discriminated against women in its promotion practices—the largest such lawsuit in history.

Two practices contributed to the problem. First, Wal-Mart did not have a policy of posting job openings so that all employees could see what positions were available. Often, the local store manager simply filled an opening without notifying employees that there was an open position. Second, each store manager made selection decisions according to his or her own methods. The company didn't require managers to detail or justify their criteria for accepting or rejecting candidates. So, when it became apparent that the decision-making process was adversely affecting women—in terms of pay as well as advancement—Wal-Mart had difficulty pointing to any legitimate criteria that could justify the hiring decisions.

Wal-Mart may also have contributed to the problem through its broad approach to human resource management. The company generally recruited human resource staffers from the ranks of line workers, rather than from professional HR programs or colleges whose graduates specialize in human resource management. Wal-Mart emphasized cost cutting, and since human resource management does not directly generate sales, the function was treated as an unfortunate cost of doing business.

Wal-Mart's deemphasis of human resource management may have made the company vulnerable to Costco, a direct competitor that seems more dedicated to human resource management. Costco, like Wal-Mart, emphasizes low costs, but it pays workers higher wages and has more-formal systems to offer opportunities to be promoted. At Costco stores, turnover among employees is only half that of Wal-Mart stores. In addition, promotion policies that emphasize competence and experience help Costco build a more effective managerial staff. These differences may help explain why, on average, a Costco store generates nearly double the revenue of a Wal-Mart store the same size.

As Wal-Mart defends the lawsuit, it also has to weigh decisions about whether to change its selection process so that discrimination lawsuits are less likely in the future. Huge changes could be interpreted as an admission of having done something wrong, and decentralized decision making has helped the company grow into a huge, widely admired corporation. However, the company has made some adjustments. One change is to begin rewarding managers for diversity in selection decisions. Now 15 percent of a manager's bonus is tied to diversity goals such as achieving a close match between the percentage of women and minorities who apply for a position and the percentage who are accepted. Also, the company has begun requiring that hourly workers with the same experience be hired at the same level of starting pay, regardless of their pay history.

SOURCE: D. P. Shuit, "People Problems on Every Aisle," *Workforce,* February 2004, pp. 26–34; J. Useem, "Should We Admire Wal-Mart?" *Fortune,* March 8, 2004, pp. 118–20; W. Zellner, "A New Pay Scheme for Wal-Mart Workers," *BusinessWeek,* June 14, 2004, p. 39; J. Helyer, "The Only Company That Wal-Mart Fears," *Fortune,* November 24, 2003, pp. 158–66; and B. Morris, "How Corporate America Is Betraying Women," *Fortune,* January 10, 2005, downloaded from Infotrac at http://web2.infotrac. galegroup.com.

Questions

1. Wal-Mart has a tradition of leaving many decisions up to store managers. In this type of organization, how can HRM professionals help managers make effective selection decisions?
2. Suppose you have been asked to improve selection procedures at Wal-Mart to avoid discrimination charges in the future. What methods from this chapter would improve the current system? Keeping in mind that store managers might not be eager to give up their decision-making authority, what single change would you advise as a first step?
3. How would you explain to the company's management that this step would benefit them? Create an argument for your position.

NOTES

1. E. Watters, "*Inc.* 500 Balancing Act: 'Come Here, Work, and Get Out of Here. You Don't Live Here. You Live Someplace Else,'" *Inc.,* October 30, 2001, pp. 56–58, 60–61.
2. Scott McCartney, "The Air-Traffic Cops Go to School," *The Wall Street Journal,* March 29, 2005, http://online.wsj.com.
3. J. C. Nunnally, *Psychometric Theory* (New York: McGraw-Hill, 1978).
4. N. Schmitt, R. Z. Gooding, R. A. Noe, and M. Kirsch, "Meta-Analysis of Validity Studies Published between 1964 and 1982 and the Investigation of Study Characteristics," *Personnel Psychology* 37 (1984), pp. 407–22.
5. C. H. Lawshe, "Inferences from Personnel Tests and Their Validity," *Journal of Applied Psychology* 70 (1985), pp. 237–38.
6. D. D. Robinson, "Content-Oriented Personnel Selection in a Small Business Setting," *Personnel Psychology* 34 (1981), pp. 77–87.
7. F. L. Schmidt and J. E. Hunter, "The Future of Criterion-Related Validity," *Personnel Psychology* 33 (1980), pp. 41–60; F. L. Schmidt, J. E. Hunter, and K. Pearlman, "Task Differences as Moderators of Aptitude Test Validity: A Red Herring," *Journal of Applied Psychology* 66 (1982), pp. 166–85; and R. L. Gutenberg, R. D. Arvey, H. G. Osburn, and R. P. Jeanneret, "Moderating Effects of Decision-Making/Information Processing Dimensions on Test Validities," *Journal of Applied Psychology* 68 (1983), pp. 600–8.
8. A. Meisler, "Negative Results," *Workforce,* October 2003, pp. 35–40.
9. A. Meisler, "When Bad Things Happen to Hot Brands," *Workforce,* July 2003, pp. 20–21.
10. G. Flynn, "The Reverse Discrimination Trap," *Workforce,* June 2003, pp. 106–7; and M. E. Heilman, W. S. Battle, C. E. Keller, and R. A. Lee, "Type of Affirmative Action Policy: A Determinant of Reactions to Sex-Based Preferential Selection," *Journal of Applied Psychology* 83 (1998), pp. 190–205.
11. B. S. Murphy, "EEOC Gives Guidance on Legal and Illegal Inquiries under ADA," *Personnel Journal,* August 1994, p. 26.
12. T. W. Dougherty, D. B. Turban, and J. C. Callender, "Confirming First Impressions in the Employment Interview: A Field Study of Interviewer Behavior," *Journal of Applied Psychology* 79 (1994), pp. 659–65.
13. D. D. Hatch, "Bad Reference for Ex-employee Judged Defamatory," *Workforce,* December 2003, p. 20.
14. E. Zimmerman, "A Subtle Reference Trap for Unwary Employers," *Workforce,* April 2003, p. 22.
15. A. Ryan and M. Lasek, "Negligent Hiring and Defamation: Areas of Liability Related to Pre-employment Inquiries," *Personnel Psychology* 44 (1991), pp. 293–319.
16. A. Long, "Addressing the Cloud over Employee References: A Survey of Recently Enacted State Legislation," *William and Mary Law Review* 39 (October 1997), pp. 177–228.
17. Ann Zimmerman, "Wal-Mart to Probe Job Applicants," *The Wall Street Journal,* August 12, 2004, pp. A3, A6.
18. R. Theim, "Psychometric Testing," *Chicago Tribune,* March 6, 2002, sec. 6, pp. 1, 4.
19. C. J. Bachler, "Global Inpats—Don't Let Them Surprise You," *Personnel Journal,* June 1996, pp. 54–65; R. Horn, "Give Me Your Huddled . . . High-Tech Ph.D.s: Are High Skilled Foreigners Displacing U.S. Workers?" *BusinessWeek,* November 6, 1995, pp. 161–62; S. Greengard, "Gain the Edge in the

Knowledge Race," *Personnel Journal,* August 1996, pp. 52–56.

20. L. C. Buffardi, E. A. Fleishman, R. A. Morath, and P. M. McCarthy, "Relationships between Ability Requirements and Human Errors in Job Tasks," *Journal of Applied Psychology* 85 (2000), pp. 551–64; J. Hogan, "Structure of Physical Performance in Occupational Tasks," *Journal of Applied Psychology* 76 (1991), pp. 495–507.

21. J. F. Salagado, N. Anderson, S. Moscoso, C. Bertuas, and F. De Fruyt, "International Validity Generalization of GMA and Cognitive Abilities: A European Community Meta-analysis," *Personnel Psychology* 56 (2003), pp. 573–605; M. J. Ree, J. A. Earles, and M. S. Teachout, "Predicting Job Performance: Not Much More than *g*," *Journal of Applied Psychology* 79 (1994), pp. 518–24; L. S. Gottfredson, "The *g* Factor in Employment," *Journal of Vocational Behavior* 29 (1986), pp. 293–96; J. E. Hunter and R. H. Hunter, "Validity and Utility of Alternative Predictors of Job Performance," *Psychological Bulletin* 96 (1984), pp. 72–98; Gutenberg et al., "Moderating Effects of Decision-Making/Information Processing Dimensions on Test Validities"; F. L. Schmidt, J. G. Berner, and J. E. Hunter, "Racial Differences in Validity of Employment Tests: Reality or Illusion," *Journal of Applied Psychology* 58 (1974), pp. 5–6; and J. A. LePine, J. A. Colquitt, and A. Erez, "Adaptability to Changing Task Contexts: Effects of General Cognitive Ability, Conscientiousness, and Openness to Experience," *Personnel Psychology* 53 (2000), pp. 563–93.

22. D. A. Kravitz and S. L. Klineberg, "Reactions to Versions of Affirmative Action among Whites, Blacks, and Hispanics," *Journal of Applied Psychology* (2000), pp. 597–611.

23. F. L. Schmidt and J. E. Hunter, "The Validity and Utility of Selection Methods in Personnel Psychology: Practical and Theoretical Implications of 85 Years of Research Findings," *Psychological Bulletin* 124 (1998), pp. 262–74.

24. W. Arthur, E. A. Day, T. L. McNelly, and P. S. Edens, "Meta-Analysis of the Criterion-Related Validity of Assessment Center Dimensions," *Personnel Psychology* 56 (2003), pp. 125–54; and C. E. Lance, T. A. Lambert, A. G. Gewin, F. Lievens, and J. M. Conway, "Revised Estimates of Dimension and Exercise Variance Components in Assessment Center Postexercise Dimension Ratings," *Journal of Applied Psychology* 89 (2004), pp. 377–85.

25. W. S. Dunn, M. K. Mount, M. R. Barrick, and D. S. Ones, "Relative Importance of Personality and General Mental Ability on Managers' Judgments of Applicant Qualifications," *Journal of Applied Psychology* 79 (1995), pp. 500–9; P. M. Wright, K. M. Kacmar, G. C. McMahan, and K. Deleeuw, "*P* = *f*(M × A): Cognitive Ability as a Moderator of the Relationship between Personality and Job Performance," *Journal of Management* 21 (1995), pp. 1129–39.

26. M. Mount, M. R. Barrick, and J. P. Strauss, "Validity of Observer Ratings of the Big Five Personality Factors," *Journal of Applied Psychology* 79 (1994), pp. 272–80.

27. L. A. Witt and G. R. Ferris, "Social Skill as Moderator of the Conscientiousness–Performance Relationship: Convergent Results across Four Studies," *Journal of Applied Psychology* 88 (2003), pp. 809–20.

28. L. Joel, *Every Employee's Guide to the Law* (New York: Pantheon, 1993).

29. Ariana Eunjung Cha, "Employers Relying on Personality Tests to Screen Applicants," *Washington Post*, March 27, 2005, www.washingtonpost.com; and Barbara Rose, "Critics Wary as More Jobs Hinge on Personality Tests," *Chicago Tribune*, October 31, 2004, sec. 1, pp. 1, 15.

30. D. S. Ones, C. Viswesvaran, and F. L. Schmidt, "Comprehensive Meta-Analysis of Integrity Test Validities: Findings and Implications for Personnel Selection and Theories of Job Performance," *Journal of Applied Psychology* 78 (1993), pp. 679–703; and H. J. Bernardin and D. K. Cooke, "Validity of an Honesty Test in Predicting Theft among Convenience Store Employees," *Academy of Management Journal* 36 (1993), pp. 1079–1106.

31. K. R. Murphy, G. C. Thornton, and D. H. Reynolds, "College Students' Attitudes toward Drug Test Programs," *Personnel Psychology* 43 (1990), pp. 615–31; and M. E. Paronto, D. M. Truxillo, T. N. Bauer, and M. C. Leo, "Drug Testing, Drug Treatment, and Marijuana Use: A Fairness Perspective," *Journal of Applied Psychology* 87 (2002), pp. 1159–66.

32. E. Beck, "Is the Time Right for Impairment Testing?" *Workforce*, February 2001, pp. 69–71; J. Farley, "Better than Caffeine," *USA Today*, March 9, 2001, p. C1; J. Hamilton, "A Video Game That Tells if Employees Are Fit for Work," *BusinessWeek*, June 3, 1991, pp. 34–35.

33. M. A. McDaniel, F. P. Morgeson, E. G. Finnegan, M. A. Campion, and E. P. Braverman, "Use of Situational Judgment Tests to Predict Job Performance: A Clarification of the Literature," *Journal of Applied Psychology* 86 (2001), pp. 730–40; J. Clavenger, G. M. Perreira, D. Weichmann, N. Schmitt, and V. S. Harvey, "Incremental Validity of Situational Judgment Tests," *Journal of Applied Psychology* 86 (2001), pp. 410–17.

34. M. A. Campion, J. E. Campion, and J. P. Hudson, "Structured Interviewing: A Note of Incremental

Validity and Alternative Question Types," *Journal of Applied Psychology* 79 (1994), pp. 998–1002; E. D. Pulakos and N. Schmitt, "Experience-Based and Situational Interview Questions: Studies of Validity," *Personnel Psychology* 48 (1995), pp. 289–308; and A. P. J. Ellis, B. J. West, A. M. Ryan, and R. P. DeShon, "The Use of Impression Management Tactics in Structured Interviews: A Function of Question Type?" *Journal of Applied Psychology* 87 (2002), pp. 1200–8.

35. J. Cleaver, "What Kind of Question Is That?" *Chicago Tribune*, April 24, 2002, sec. 6, pp. 1, 4.

36. N. Schmitt, F. L. Oswald, B. H. Kim, M. A. Gillespie, L. J. Ramsey, and T. Y Yoo, "The Impact of Elaboration on Socially Desirable Responding and the Validity of Biodata Measures," *Journal of Applied Psychology* 88 (2003), pp. 979–88; and N. Schmitt and C. Kunce, "The Effects of Required Elaboration of Answers to Biodata Questions," *Personnel Psychology* 55 (2002), pp. 569–87.

37. Vicki Powers, "Finding Workers Who Fit," *Business 2.0*, November 2004, p. 74.

38. Hunter and Hunter, "Validity and Utility of Alternative Predictors of Job Performance."

39. R. Pingitore, B. L. Dugoni, R. S. Tindale, and B. Spring, "Bias against Overweight Job Applicants in a Simulated Interview," *Journal of Applied Psychology* 79 (1994), pp. 184–90.

40. *Watson v. Fort Worth Bank and Trust*, 108 Supreme Court 2791 (1988).

41. M. A. McDaniel, D. L. Whetzel, F. L. Schmidt, and S. D. Maurer, "The Validity of Employment Interviews: A Comprehensive Review and Meta-Analysis," *Journal of Applied Psychology* 79 (1994), pp. 599–616; A. I. Huffcutt and W. A. Arthur, "Hunter and Hunter (1984) Revisited: Interview Validity for Entry-Level Jobs," *Journal of Applied Psychology* 79 (1994), pp. 184–90.

42. Y. Ganzach, A. N. Kluger, and N. Klayman, "Making Decisions from an Interview: Expert Measurement and Mechanical Combination," *Personnel Psychology* 53 (2000), pp. 1–21; G. Stasser and W. Titus, "Effects of Information Load and Percentage of Shared Information on the Dissemination of Unshared Information during Group Discussion," *Journal of Personality and Social Psychology* 53 (1987), pp. 81–93.

43. C. H. Middendorf and T. H. Macan, "Note-Taking in the Interview: Effects on Recall and Judgments," *Journal of Applied Psychology* 87 (2002), pp. 293–303.

If you are using the Manager's Hot Seat DVD with this book, consider finishing case 14: Diversity in Hiring: Candidate Conundrum, for this chapter.

TRAINING EMPLOYEES

≫ INTRODUCTION

The problem facing Espresso Connection was that sales were flat. The chain of drive-through coffee stands, based in Everett, Washington, used a variety of advertising media, but the customers attracted by the ads simply weren't coming back. Espresso Connection's owner, Christian Kar, identified the source of this problem as poor customer service. He decided he needed to teach employees how to impress customers.

Espresso Connection hired several part-time trainers and set up a practice facility. Newly hired employees no longer rely on their coworkers to teach them what to do. Instead, they spend a week in the practice facility, learning to use the equipment, followed by another week of on-the-job training at a store. The first week prepares employees to work fast, a goal that quickly affects Espresso Connection's bottom line. Says Kar, "Our locations are really, really small. Unless our staff really focuses on getting customers through there more efficiently, we quickly would hit a brick wall in terms of revenues." Moving fast also cuts the waiting time for Espresso Connection's customers. The other major goal of the training is to teach employees specific skills related to customer service—for example, keeping the window open while serving customers. A few years after Espresso Connection started the training, the company saw its sales nearly double.[1]

Training consists of an organization's planned efforts to help employees acquire job-related knowledge, skills, abilities, and behaviors, with the goal of applying these on the job. A training program may range from formal classes to one-on-one mentoring, and it may take place on the job or at remote locations. No matter what its form, training can benefit the organization when it is linked to organizational needs and when it motivates employees.

This chapter describes how to plan and carry out an effective training program. We begin by discussing how to develop effective training in the context of the organization's strategy. Next, we discuss how organizations assess employees' training needs. We then review training methods and the process of evaluating a training program. The chapter concludes by discussing some special applications of training: orientation of new employees and the management of diversity.

training
An organization's planned efforts to help employees acquire job-related knowledge, skills, abilities, and behaviors, with the goal of applying these on the job.

⬥ TRAINING LINKED TO ORGANIZATIONAL NEEDS

The nature of the modern business environment makes training more important today than it ever has been. Rapid change, especially in the area of technology, requires that employees continually learn new skills, from the use of robots to collaboration on the Internet. The new psychological contract, described in Chapter 2, has created the expectation that employees invest in their own career development. Employees with this expectation will value employment at an organization that provides learning opportunities. Growing reliance on teamwork creates a demand for the ability to solve problems in teams, an ability that often requires formal training. Finally, the diversity of the U.S. population, coupled with the globalization of business, requires

LO1
Discuss how to link training programs to organizational needs.

Figure 7.1

Stages of Instructional Design

Assess needs for training

Ensure readiness for training

Plan training program
• Objectives
• Trainers
• Methods

Feedback

Implement training program

Evaluate results of training

that employees be able to work well with people who are different from them. Successful organizations often take the lead in developing this ability.

With training so essential in modern organizations, it is important to provide training that is effective. An effective training program actually teaches what it is designed to teach, and it teaches skills and behaviors that will help the organization achieve its goals. Training programs may prepare employees for future positions in the organization, enable the organization to respond to change, reduce turnover, enhance worker safety, improve customer service and product design, and meet many other goals. To achieve those goals, HR professionals approach training through **instructional design**—a process of systematically developing training to meet specified needs.

instructional design
A process of systematically developing training to meet specified needs.

A complete instructional design process includes the steps shown in Figure 7.1. It begins with an assessment of the needs for training—what the organization requires that its people learn. Next, the organization ensures that employees are ready for training in terms of their attitudes, motivation, basic skills, and work environment. The third step is to plan the training program, including the program's objectives, instructors, and methods. The organization then implements the program. Finally, evaluating the results of the training provides feedback for planning future training programs.

❧ NEEDS ASSESSMENT

Instructional design logically should begin with a **needs assessment,** the process of evaluating the organization, individual employees, and employees' tasks to determine what kinds of training, if any, are necessary. As this definition indicates, the needs assessment answers questions in the three broad areas shown in Figure 7.2:[2]

needs assessment
The process of evaluating the organization, individual employees, and employees' tasks to determine what kinds of training, if any, are necessary.

1. *Organization*—What is the context in which training will occur?
2. *Person*—Who needs training?
3. *Task*—What subjects should the training cover?

The answers to these questions provide the basis for planning an effective training program.

A variety of conditions may prompt an organization to conduct a needs assessment. Management may observe that some employees lack basic skills or are performing poorly. Decisions to produce new products, apply new technology, or design new jobs should prompt a needs assessment, because these changes tend to require new skills. The decision to conduct a needs assessment also may be prompted by outside forces, such as customer requests or legal requirements.

figure 7.2

Needs Assessment

Pfizer employees go through a representative training phase which teaches them about different Pfizer products and how to market them. Workers typically need to be trained in several processes to work in flexible manufacturing.

The outcome of the needs assessment is a set of decisions about how to address the issues that prompted the needs assessment. These decisions do not necessarily include a training program, because some issues should be resolved through methods other than training. For example, suppose a company uses delivery trucks to transport anesthetic gases to medical facilities, and a driver of one of these trucks mistakenly hooks up the supply line of a mild anesthetic from the truck to the hospital's oxygen system, contaminating the hospital's oxygen supply. This performance problem prompts a needs assessment. Whether or not the hospital decides to provide more training will depend partly on the reasons the driver erred. The driver may have hooked up the supply lines incorrectly because of a lack of knowledge about the appropriate line hookup, anger over a request for a pay raise being denied, or mislabeled valves for connecting the supply lines. Out of these three possibilities, only the lack of knowledge can be corrected through training. Other outcomes of a needs assessment might include plans for better rewards to improve motivation, better hiring decisions, and better safety precautions.

The remainder of this chapter discusses needs assessment and then what the organization should do when assessment indicates a need for training. The possibilities for action include offering existing training programs to more employees; buying or developing new training programs; and improving existing training programs. Before we consider the available training options, let's examine the elements of the needs assessment in more detail.

Organization Analysis

Usually, the needs assessment begins with the **organization analysis.** This is a process for determining the appropriateness of training by evaluating the characteristics of the organization. The organization analysis looks at training needs in light of the organization's strategy, resources available for training, and management's support for training activities.

organization analysis
A process for determining the appropriateness of training by evaluating the characteristics of the organization.

Training needs will vary depending on whether the organization's strategy is based on growing or shrinking its personnel, whether it is seeking to serve a broad customer base or focusing on the specific needs of a narrow market segment, and various other strategic scenarios. An organization that concentrates on serving a niche market may need to continually update its workforce on a specialized skills set. A company that is cutting costs with a downsizing strategy may need to train employees who will be laid off in job search skills. The employees who remain following the downsizing may need cross-training so that they can handle a wider variety of responsibilities. Recently, this was the situation at Saint Paul, Minnesota, check printer Deluxe Corporation, which had reduced the number of account managers by almost two-thirds after downsizing. Most of those who remained were either new employees or employees who had been with the company for more than 20 years; among both groups, morale was poor. The company decided to combine sales training with efforts to restore employee morale. Two trainers worked with three of the company's top-performing account managers to develop and deliver the training program. Besides learning to shift their focus from selling products to building customer relationships, the account managers learned time management skills. In addition, sales managers and directors learned how to better coach their account managers in the field.[3]

Anyone planning a training program must consider whether the organization has the budget, time, and expertise for training. For example, if the company is installing computer-based manufacturing equipment in one of its plants, it can ensure that it has the necessary computer-literate employees in one of three ways. If it has the technical experts on its staff, they can train the employees affected by the change. Or the company may use testing to determine which of its employees are already computer literate and then replace or reassign employees who lack the necessary skills. The third choice is to purchase training from an outside individual or organization.

Even if training fits the organization's strategy and budget, it can be viable only if the organization is willing to support the investment in training. Managers increase the success of training when they support it through such actions as helping trainees see how they can use their newly learned knowledge, skills, and behaviors on the job.[4] Conversely, the managers will be most likely to support training if the people planning it can show that it will solve a significant problem or result in a significant improvement, relative to its cost. Managers appreciate training proposals with specific goals, timetables, budgets, and methods for measuring success.

Person Analysis

person analysis
A process of determining individuals' needs and readiness for training.

Following the organizational assessment, needs assessment turns to the remaining areas of analysis: person and task. The **person analysis** is a process for determining individuals' needs and readiness for training. It involves answering several questions:

- Do performance deficiencies result from a lack of knowledge, skill, or ability? (If so, training is appropriate; if not, other solutions are more relevant.)
- Who needs training?
- Are these employees ready for training?

The answers to these questions help the manager identify whether training is appropriate and which employees need training. In certain situations, such as the introduction of a new technology or service, all employees may need training. However, when needs assessment is conducted in response to a performance problem, training is not always the best solution.

The person analysis is therefore critical when training is considered in response to a performance problem. In assessing the need for training, the manager should identify all the variables that can influence performance. The primary variables are the person's ability and skills, his or her attitudes and motivation, the organization's input (including clear directions, necessary resources, and freedom from interference and distractions), performance feedback (including praise and performance standards), and positive consequences to motivate good performance. Of these variables, only ability and skills can be affected by training. Therefore, before planning a training program, it is important to be sure that any performance problem results from a deficiency in knowledge and skills. Otherwise, training dollars will be wasted, because the training is unlikely to have much effect on performance.

The person analysis also should determine whether employees are ready to undergo training. In other words, the employees to receive training not only should require additional knowledge and skill, but must be willing and able to learn. (After our discussion of the needs assessment, we will explore the topic of employee readiness in greater detail.)

Task Analysis

The third area of needs assessment is **task analysis,** the process of identifying the tasks, knowledge, skills, and behaviors that training should emphasize. Usually, task analysis is conducted along with person analysis. Understanding shortcomings in performance usually requires knowledge about the tasks and work environment as well as the employee.

> **task analysis**
> The process of identifying and analyzing tasks to be trained for.

To carry out the task analysis, the HR professional looks at the conditions in which tasks are performed. These conditions include the equipment and environment of the job, time constraints (for example, deadlines), safety considerations, and performance standards. These observations form the basis for a description of work activities, or the tasks required by the person's job. For a selected job, the analyst interviews employees and their supervisors to prepare a list of tasks performed in that job. Then the analyst validates the list by showing it to employees, supervisors, and other subject-matter experts and asking them to complete a questionnaire about the importance, frequency, and difficulty of the tasks. Figure 7.3 is an example of a task statement questionnaire. In this example, the questionnaire begins by defining categories that specify a task's importance, frequency, and difficulty. Then, for a production supervisor's job, the questionnaire lists five tasks. For each task, the subject-matter expert uses the scales to rate the task's importance, frequency, and difficulty.

The information from these questionnaires is the basis for determining which tasks will be the focus of the training. The person or committee conducting the needs assessment must decide what levels of importance, frequency, and difficulty signal a need for training. Logically, training is most needed for tasks that are important, frequent, and at least moderately difficult. For each of these tasks, the analysts must identify the knowledge, skills, and abilities required to perform the task. This information usually comes from interviews with subject-matter experts, such as employees who currently hold the job.

> **LO3**
> Explain how to assess employees' readiness for training.

❧ READINESS FOR TRAINING

Effective training requires not only a program that addresses real needs, but also a condition of employee readiness. **Readiness for training** is a combination of employee characteristics and positive work environment that permit training. The

> **readiness for training**
> A combination of employee characteristics and positive work environment that permit training.

Figure 7.3

Sample Task Statement Questionnaire

Name _____ Date _____
Position _____

Instructions: Please rate each of the task statements according to three factors: the **importance** of the task for effective performance, how **frequently** the task is performed, and the degree of **difficulty** required to become effective in the task.

Use the following three scales in making your ratings.

Importance	*Frequency*
4 = Task is critical for effective performance.	4 = Task is performed once a day.
3 = Task is important but not critical for effective performance.	3 = Task is performed once a week.
2 = Task is of some importance for effective performance.	2 = Task is performed once every few months.
1 = Task is of no importance for effective performance.	1 = Task is performed once or twice a year.
0 = Task is not performed.	0 = Task is not performed.

Difficulty

4 = Effective performance of the task requires extensive prior experience and/or training (12-18 months or longer).

3 = Effective performance of the task requires minimal prior experience and training (6-12 months).

2 = Effective performance of the task requires a brief period of prior training and experience (1-6 months).

1 = Effective performance of the task does not require specific prior training and/or experience.

0 = Task is not performed.

Task (circle the number from the scales above)	*Importance*	*Frequency*	*Difficulty*
1. Ensuring maintenance on equipment, tools, and safety controls	0 1 2 3 4	0 1 2 3 4	0 1 2 3 4
2. Monitoring employee performance	0 1 2 3 4	0 1 2 3 4	0 1 2 3 4
3. Scheduling employees	0 1 2 3 4	0 1 2 3 4	0 1 2 3 4
4. Using statistical software on the computer	0 1 2 3 4	0 1 2 3 4	0 1 2 3 4
5. Monitoring changes made in processes using statistical methods	0 1 2 3 4	0 1 2 3 4	0 1 2 3 4

necessary employee characteristics include ability to learn the subject matter, favorable attitudes toward the training, and motivation to learn. A positive work environment is one that encourages learning and avoids interfering with the training program.

Employee Readiness Characteristics

Employees learn more from training programs when they are highly motivated to learn—that is, when they really want to learn the content of the training program.[5] Employees tend to feel this way if they believe they are able to learn, see potential benefits from the training program, are aware of their need to learn, see a fit between the training and their career goals, and have the basic skills needed for participating in the program. Managers can influence a ready attitude in a variety of ways. For example, they can provide feedback that encourages employees, establish rewards for learning, and communicate with employees about the organization's career paths and future needs.

Work Environment

Readiness for training also depends on two broad characteristics of the work environment: situational constraints and social support.[6] *Situational constraints* are the limits on training's effectiveness that arise from the situation or the conditions within the organization. Constraints can include a lack of money for training, lack of time for training or practicing, and failure to provide proper tools and materials for learning or applying the lessons of training. Conversely, trainees are likely to apply what they learn if the organization gives them opportunities to use their new skills and if it rewards them for doing so.[7]

Social support refers to the ways the organization's people encourage training, including giving trainees praise and encouraging words, sharing information about participating in training programs, and expressing positive attitudes toward the organization's training programs. Managers play an especially important role in providing social support. Besides offering positive feedback, they can emphasize the importance of training, show how training programs relate to employees' jobs, and provide opportunities for employees to apply what they learn. Table 7.1 summarizes some ways in which managers can support training. At the minimum, they should allow trainees to participate in training programs. At the other extreme, managers who not only encourage training but conduct the training sessions themselves are most likely to back up training by reinforcing new skills, providing feedback on progress, and giving trainees opportunities to practice.

Support can come from employees' peers as well as from supervisors and managers. The organization can formally provide peer support by establishing groups of employees who meet regularly to discuss their progress. Such a group might hold face-to-face meetings or communicate by e-mail or over the organization's intranet, sharing ideas as well as encouragement. For example, group members can share how they coped with challenges related to what they have learned and how they obtained resources they needed for applying their training. Another way to encourage peer support is for the human resource department or others in the organization to publish a newsletter with articles relevant to training. The newsletter might include interviews with employees who successfully applied new skills. Finally, the organization can assign experienced employees as mentors to trainees, providing advice and support related to the training.

Understand the content of the training.
Know how training relates to what you need employees to do.
In performance appraisals, evaluate employees on how they apply training to their jobs.
Support employees' use of training when they return to work.
Ensure that employees have the equipment and technology needed to use training.
Prior to training, discuss with employees how they plan to use training.
Recognize newly trained employees who use training content.
Give employees release time from their work to attend training.
Explain to employees why they have been asked to attend training.
Give employees feedback related to skills or behavior they are trying to develop.

TABLE 7.1

What Managers Should Do to Support Training

SOURCE: Based on A. Rossett, "That Was a Great Class, but . . . " *Training and Development,* July 1997, p. 21.

TRAINING DECISIONS ARE OFTEN HR'S JOB

In a survey of U.S. companies, about half said their training or human resource department controls training purchases. Most others leave the decision up to a senior manager or the department receiving training.

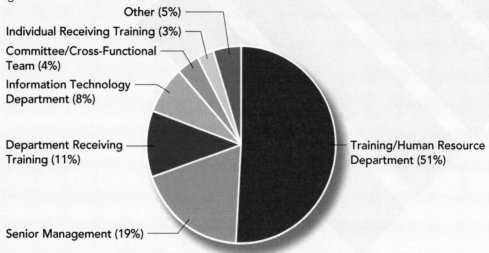

Other (5%)
Individual Receiving Training (3%)
Committee/Cross-Functional Team (4%)
Information Technology Department (8%)
Department Receiving Training (11%)
Training/Human Resource Department (51%)
Senior Management (19%)

Who Controls Spending on Training

SOURCE: Based on Holly Dolezalek, "*Training* Magazine's 23rd Annual Comprehensive Analysis of Employer-Sponsored Training in the United States," *Training*, October 2004, downloaded from Infotrac at http://web5.infotrac.galegroup.com.

LO4
Describe how to plan an effective training program.

PLANNING THE TRAINING PROGRAM

As described in the "Did You Know . . . ?" box, decisions about training are often the responsibility of a specialist in the organization's training or human resources department. When the needs assessment indicates a need for training and employees are ready to learn, the person responsible for training should plan a training program that directly relates to the needs identified. Planning begins with establishing objectives for the training program. Based on those objectives, the planner decides who will provide the training, what topics the training will cover, what training methods to use, and how to evaluate the training.

Objectives of the Program

Formally establishing objectives for the training program has several benefits. First, a training program based on clear objectives will be more focused and more likely to succeed. In addition, when trainers know the objectives, they can communicate them to the employees participating in the program. Employees learn best when they know what the training is supposed to accomplish. Finally, down the road, establishing objectives provides a basis for measuring whether the program succeeded, as we will discuss later in this chapter.

Companies such as Tires Plus provide intensive training and educational programs for their employees. This company supports training by making resources available. Management has a favorable attitude toward training, which motivates employees to stay with the company and work toward advancement.

Effective training objectives have three components:

1. A statement of what the employee is expected to do (performance or outcome).
2. A statement of the quality or level of performance that is acceptable.
3. A statement of the conditions under which the trainee is expected to apply what he or she learned (for instance, physical conditions, mental stresses, or equipment failure).[8]

If possible, the objectives should include measurable performance standards. Suppose a training objective for a store's customer service training program is: "After training, the employee will be able to express concern to all irate customers with a brief (fewer than 10 words) apology, only after the customer has stopped talking, and no matter how upset the customer is." Here, measures include the length and timing of the apology.

Finally, training objectives should identify any resources required to carry out the desired performance or outcome. This helps the organization ensure that employees will be able to apply what they have learned.

A related issue at the outset is who will participate in the training program. Some training programs are developed for all employees of the organization or all members of a team. Other training programs identify individuals who lack desirable skills or have potential to be promoted, then provide training in the areas of need that are identified for the particular employees. When deciding whom to include in training, the organization has to avoid illegal discrimination. The organization should not—intentionally or unintentionally—exclude members of protected groups, such as women, minorities, and older employees. During the training, all participants should receive equal treatment, such as equal opportunities for practice. In addition, the training program should provide reasonable accommodation for trainees with disabilities. The kinds of accommodations that are appropriate will vary according to the type of training and type of disability. One employee might need an interpreter, whereas another might need to have classroom instruction provided in a location accessible to wheelchairs.

In-House or Contracted Out?

An organization can provide an effective training program, even if it lacks expertise in training. The "Best Practices" box describes how Intel uses its own program, staffed with contract teachers, to provide language training that meets the objective of better

INTEL BRIDGES THE LANGUAGE GAP WITH TRAINING

Computer-chip maker Intel has a huge workforce: 78,000 employees in 294 offices in 48 countries. Teams at Intel regularly include employees from different cultures working in different locations. At multinational companies, English tends to be the common language that all can use to communicate. But Intel's management knows that even if all employees can use English, misunderstandings can arise, especially among people who usually speak a different language.

At Intel, employees with a business need can take classes in Mandarin (a Chinese language), Japanese, and Spanish at various offices throughout the United States, free of charge. The courses are not designed to prepare employees to work in foreign countries. Instead, they target employees who, through technology, work directly with foreign clients or work on teams with employees from other countries. The classwork is also designed to help minimize the culture gaps within international teams.

The company contracted with an outside firm to provide the optional 12-week courses, taught at three levels. The courses meet for two hours a week and cost the company approximately $300 per person. Employees are allowed to repeat courses.

Marcos Garciaacosta, a business alliance manager at Intel who is based in Arizona, has been taking Japanese classes since he joined the company seven years ago. He says the "ease and flexibility of on-site classes" keep him motivated to continue to learn. And while he says he is far from fluent, he is now proficient enough to communicate better with his business contacts and customers in Japan.

The in-house training approach is not new to Intel. Company spokeswoman Tracy Koon says Intel offered its first language programs in Japanese in the 1980s. But the program remains relatively small. In the first two years of the program, Intel spent $54,000 to train 180 employees in the three languages, a tiny fraction of the workforce. But although the program is small, Intel is receiving some positive results. Kathy Powell, the foundational development manager for Intel University, the division of the company that manages training, says the demand for foreign-language courses is increasing. Intel plans to expand the language-training program to overseas offices and to train hundreds more employees.

The language classes are part of a larger in-house cultural-training curriculum for Intel employees. The company also offers optional one-day classes with titles such as "Working with Russia" and "Doing Business with the Japanese," which are designed to give employees basic information about how to work with people from other cultures. Classes of about 15 students explore the culture, history, and business practices of companies with which Intel does business. Koon explains, "By having these language and cultural tools at your disposal . . . , you can understand the do's and don'ts of the cultures." She adds, "You're not going to be an effective team if you are constantly offending the other members without knowing it."

SOURCE: Based on G. Weber, "Intel's Internal Approach," *Workforce Management* 83 (2004), p. 49; and K. Kranhold, D. Bileklan, M. Karnitschnig, and G. Parker, "Lost in Translation," *The Wall Street Journal*, May 18, 2004, pp. B1, B6.

communication among its employees and customers. Many companies and consultants provide training services to organizations. Community colleges often work with employers to train employees in a variety of skills. PepsiCo needs highly skilled maintenance workers to take care of the sophisticated machinery at the Gatorade factory

TABLE 7.2

Questions to Ask Vendors and Consultants

How much and what type of experience does your company have in designing and delivering training?

What are the qualifications and experiences of your staff?

Can you provide demonstrations or examples of training programs you have developed?

Would you provide references of clients for whom you worked?

What evidence do you have that your programs work?

SOURCE: Based on R. Zemke and J. Armstrong, "Evaluating Multimedia Developers," *Training*, November 1996, pp. 33–38. Adapted with permission. Lakewood Publications, Minneapolis, MN.

in Tolleson, Arizona. So PepsiCo and a neighboring manufacturer arranged for Maricopa Community College to provide courses in topics such as math and electricity. The college provides the instructor, and PepsiCo company provides the equipment to practice on.[9]

To select a training service, an organization can mail several vendors a *request for proposal (RFP)*, which is a document outlining the type of service needed, the type and number of references needed, the number of employees to be trained, the date by which the training is to be completed, and the date by which proposals should be received. A complete RFP also indicates funding for the project and the process by which the organization will determine its level of satisfaction. Putting together a request for proposal is time-consuming but worthwhile because it helps the organization clarify its objectives, compare vendors, and measure results.

Vendors that believe they are able to provide the services outlined in the RFP submit proposals that provide the types of information requested. The organization reviews the proposals to eliminate any vendors that do not meet requirements and to compare the vendors that do qualify. They check references and select a candidate, based on the proposal and the vendor's answers to questions such as those listed in Table 7.2.

The cost of purchasing training from a contractor can vary substantially. In general, it is much costlier to purchase specialized training that is tailored to the organization's unique requirements than to participate in a seminar or training course that teaches general skills or knowledge. According to estimates by consultants, preparing a training program can take 10 to 20 hours for each hour of instruction. Highly technical content that requires the developer to meet often with experts in the subject can take 50 percent longer.[10]

Even in organizations that send employees to outside training programs, someone in the organization may be responsible for coordinating the overall training program. Called *training administration*, this is typically the responsibility of a human resources professional. Training administration includes activities before, during, and after training sessions.

Choice of Training Methods

Whether the organization prepares its own training programs or buys training from other organizations, it is important to verify that the content of the training relates directly to the training objectives. Such relevance to the organization's needs and objectives ensures that training money is well spent. Tying training content closely to objectives also improves trainees' learning, because it increases the likelihood that the training will be meaningful and helpful.

After deciding on the goals and content of the training program, planners must decide how the training will be conducted. As we will describe in the next section, a wide variety of methods is available. Training methods fall into the broad categories of presentation methods, hands-on methods, and group-building methods.[11]

With **presentation methods,** trainees receive information provided by instructors or via computers or other media. Trainees may assemble in a classroom to hear a lecture, or the material may be presented on videotapes, CD-ROMs, Web sites, or in workbooks. Presentations are appropriate for conveying facts or comparing alternative processes. Computer-based training methods tend to be less expensive than bringing trainees together in a classroom.

In contrast to presentation methods, **hands-on methods** actively involve the trainee in learning by trying out the behaviors being taught. Someone may help the trainee learn skills while on the job. Hands-on methods away from the job include simulations, games, role-plays, and interactive learning on computers. Hands-on training is appropriate for teaching specific skills and helping trainees understand how skills and behaviors apply to their jobs. These methods also help trainees learn to handle interpersonal issues, such as handling problems with customers.

Group-building methods help trainees share ideas and experiences, build group or team identity, understand how interpersonal relationships work, and get to know their own strengths and weaknesses and those of their coworkers. The various techniques available involve examining feelings, perceptions, and beliefs about the trainees' group. Participants discuss how to apply what they learn in the training program to the group's performance at work. Group-building methods are appropriate for establishing teams or work groups, or for improving their performance.

Training programs may use these methods alone or in combination. An organization that has blended its training approaches is CAN, a Chicago-based company with employees located across the United States and Canada. Live seminars kick off a course and conclude it. In between are online case studies, question-and-answer sessions, and simulations. Trainees work in teams of 10 people. They communicate with each other through chat rooms, threaded discussions, and virtual meetings. The instructor is available to answer questions online. Trainees may be asked to put ideas into practice and then submit updates and questions using message rooms. Coaches and mentors guide the trainees to additional reference materials as needed. The trainees complete an accountability plan summarizing actions they will take to show their managers they have met their objectives for the course.[12] In general, the methods used should be suitable for the course content and the learning abilities of the participants. The following section explores the options in greater detail.

❧ TRAINING METHODS

A wide variety of methods is available for conducting training. Figure 7.4 shows the percentages of companies using various training methods: classroom instruction, seminars (face-to-face and remote), self-study, role-plays, case studies, learning games, experiential programs. Of these methods, the most widely used are traditional classroom training, public seminars, self-study online, and case studies.

Classroom Instruction

At school, we tend to associate learning with classroom instruction, and that type of training is most widely used in the workplace, too. Classroom instruction typically involves a trainer lecturing a group. Trainers often supplement lectures with slides, dis-

Figure 7.4

Overview of Use of Instructional Methods

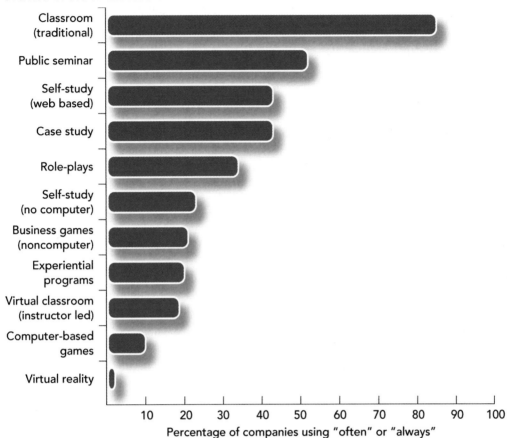

cussions, case studies, question-and-answer sessions, and role playing. Actively involving trainees enhances learning.

When the course objectives call for presenting information on a specific topic to many trainees, classroom instruction is one of the least expensive and least time-consuming ways to accomplish that goal. Learning will be more effective if trainers enhance lectures with job-related examples and opportunities for hands-on learning.

Modern technology has expanded the notion of the classroom to classes of trainees scattered in various locations. With *distance learning*, trainees at different locations attend programs over phone and computer lines. Through audio- and videoconferencing, they can hear and see lectures and participate in discussions. Computers can enable participants to share documents as well. FileNeT Corporation uses distance learning to help its sales force keep up with new software products. The salespeople disliked the company's early efforts to get them to read about new products on the Web; instead of enrolling for these online self-study courses, they flooded the company with requests for one-on-one assistance. The company had more success with Webcasting, providing classroom instruction through live broadcasts, allowing them to submit questions. As FileNeT has replaced some of its classroom training with

Webcasting, it has saved $500,000 a year.[13] Distance learning provides many of the benefits of classroom training without the cost and time of travel to a shared classroom. The major disadvantage of distance learning is that interaction between the trainer and audience may be limited. To overcome this hurdle, distance learning usually provides a communications link between trainees and trainer. Also, on-site instructors or facilitators should be available to answer questions and moderate question-and-answer sessions.

Audiovisual Training

Presentation methods need not require that trainees attend a class. Trainees can also work independently, using course material prepared on audiotapes and videotapes or in workbooks. Audiovisual techniques such as overhead transparencies, slides, and videos can also supplement classroom instruction.

Training with videotapes has been used for improving communications skills, interviewing skills, and customer service skills. Videotapes can also be effective for demonstrating how to follow procedures, such as welding methods. Morse-Brothers provides training to the drivers of its ready-mix trucks with a series of videos. A mentor-driver selects a weekly video, schedules viewing sessions, keeps attendance records, and guides a wrap-up discussion. The short (10 minutes or less) videos cover topics such as safe driving, avoidance of excessive idling, and observing product tests at job sites. The mentor-drivers are trained in leading the discussion that follows the video, including how to call attention to key learning points and relate the topics to issues the drivers encounter on the job.[14]

Users of audiovisual training often have some control over the presentation. They can review material and may be able to slow down or speed up the lesson. Videotapes and video clips on CD-ROM can show situations and equipment that cannot be easily demonstrated in a classroom. Another advantage of audiovisual presentations is that they give trainees a consistent presentation, not affected by an individual trainer's goals and skills. The problems associated with these methods may include their trying to present too much material, poorly written dialogue, overuse of features such as humor or music, and drama that distracts from the key points. A well-written and carefully produced video can overcome these problems.

Computer-Based Training

Although almost all organizations use classroom training, new technologies are gaining in popularity as technology improves and becomes cheaper. With computer-based training, participants receive course materials and instruction distributed over the Internet or on CD-ROM. Often, these materials are interactive, so participants can answer questions and try out techniques, with course materials adjusted according to participants' responses. Online training programs may allow trainees to submit questions via e-mail and to participate in online discussions. Multimedia capabilities enable computers to provide sounds, images, and video presentations, along with text.

Computer-based training is generally less expensive than putting an instructor in a classroom of trainees. The low cost to deliver information gives the company flexibility in scheduling training, so that it can fit around work requirements. Training can be delivered in smaller doses, so material is easier to remember.[15] Finally, it is easier to customize computer-based training for individual learners.

The Shoney's and Captain D's restaurant chains must train more than 8,000 employees each year on the basics of operating the business, including how to make french fries, hush puppies, and coleslaw, while managers need training in business issues and back-office operations. The biggest challenge was how to train employees spread over 20 states. Shoney's solution was called OneTouch, which allows users to send and receive video, voice, data, and live Web pages, so that team members can interact with trainers. The OneTouch system is available on desktop PCs positioned anywhere in the restaurant, as well as on computers stationed in warehouses and at repair bays. The training sessions cover topics related to new-employee orientation, kitchen operations, and dining room services. Each module introduces topics and follows up with quizzes. For example, one kitchen program shows trainees what the coleslaw ingredients are and where they are located in the restaurant. Trainees watch a video and practice along with it. After practicing, they take a quiz, and the manager verifies that they have completed the topic. The training is consistent, easy to update, and enables employees to learn each other's skills.[16]

Electronic Performance Support Systems

Computers can support trainees in applying training content to their jobs. *Electronic performance support systems (EPSSs)* are computer applications that provide access to skills training, information, and expert advice when a problem occurs on the job.[17] An EPSS gives trainees an electronic information source that they can refer to as they try applying new skills on the job. For example, Atlanta-based poultry processor Cagle's uses an EPSS for employees who maintain the chicken-processing machines.[18] The makers of machines that measure and cut chickens are continually improving this equipment, so that companies have no practical way to train technicians in the equipment's details. Instead, companies train technicians in the basic procedures for maintaining the machinery. When a problem occurs, the technicians combine the basic training with the EPSS to obtain enough information to fix the problem. On the EPSS, the technicians can look up detailed instructions for repairs, check parts availability, and find replacement parts in inventory.

E-Learning

Receiving training via the Internet or the organization's intranet is called **e-learning** or online learning. E-learning may bring together Web-based training, distance learning, virtual classrooms, and the use of CD-ROMs. Course content is presented with a combination of text, video, graphics, and sound. E-learning has three important characteristics. First, it involves electronic networks that enable the delivery, sharing, and updating of information and instruction. Second, e-learning is delivered to the trainee via computers with Internet access. Finally, it goes beyond traditional training objectives to offer tools and information that will help trainees improve performance. The system also may handle course enrollment, testing and evaluation of participants, and monitoring of progress.

e-learning
Receiving training via the Internet or the organization's intranet.

With e-learning, trainees have a great deal of control. They determine what they learn, how fast they progress through the program, how much time they practice, and when they learn. E-learners also may choose to collaborate or interact with other trainees and experts. They may use the training system's links to other learning resources such as reference materials, company Web sites, and other training programs. The "e-HRM" box describes how the advantages of e-learning have improved sales-force training at Cisco Systems.

Like other forms of computer-based learning, e-learning can reduce training costs and time. Trainees often appreciate the multimedia capabilities, which appeal to several

CISCO SYSTEMS SOLD ON E-LEARNING

Cisco Systems of San Jose, California, is a leading company that develops networking systems for the Internet. But after growth throughout the 1990s, Cisco fell on hard times during the 2001 economic downturn, and the company had to lay off more than 4,000 employees. Still, Cisco did not cut back on its commitment to employee learning. Chief executive John Chambers believed training in the form of e-learning would help Cisco recover from its economic woes and create stronger ties with information technology.

A team consisting of the company's Internet Learning Solutions Group, the Information Technology Unit, and Chambers developed the Cisco Media Network. They collaborated to ensure a match between the company's tools and technology, its business purpose, and effective learning principles. The Cisco Media Network is a large, private broadcasting network linked via satellite to a worldwide grid of computer servers. The network serves about 1,000 users. The content comes from the company's business units, technology groups, and product marketing groups. The network broadcasts include the company's annual meeting, video briefings by executives, and learning portals for employees and customers.

The Media Network has been useful for developing e-learning for Cisco's account managers, who are the company's front-line sales force. To determine the account managers' needs, Cisco carried out a needs assessment that included interviews with them to identify what they needed to learn and how much time they had available for learning. Many of the account managers said learning content was not being delivered to them in a way that fit their work patterns or learning styles. Account managers spend a lot of time traveling, so they wanted to get on the Internet, find out what they needed to know, and get out again. They preferred not to sit in front of a personal computer for a long e-learning course.

Responding to these preferences, Cisco began offering the Account Manager Learning Environment (AMLE). The AMLE is based on four business objectives: increase sales, shrink time from closing a deal to receiving revenue, lower time required for account managers to become competent in a topic, and reduce travel and costs.

The learning goals for the AMLE also include creating a learning environment that motivates account managers to use it. To achieve these objectives, the AMLE consists of a suite of learning tools—everything from small chunks of information and short skill-building sessions, to a simulator that presents various scenarios of sales calls to give account managers practice in handling difficult questions that come up in real-world situations. In the simulator, the questions arrive through a realistic audio feed. The account manager selects a response, and the program delivers immediate and specific feedback for improvement.

Account managers using the AMLE can choose remote access or download lessons to the hard drive of their computer. While traveling, they can access a "talk show" and save it to their laptop or to an MP3 player. The talk show discusses issues related to their work. In addition, Cisco offers a magazine with fast facts and advice.

SOURCE: Based on M. Delahoussaye and R. Zemke, "Ten Things We Know for Sure about On-Line Learning," *Training,* September 2001, pp. 48–59; and P. Galagan, "Delta Force," *T&D,* July 2002, pp. 21–28.

senses, and the opportunity to actively participate in learning and apply it to situations on the job. The best e-learning combines the advantages of the Internet with the principles of a good learning environment. It takes advantage of the Web's dynamic nature and ability to use many positive learning features, including hyperlinks to other training sites and content, control by the trainee, and ability for trainees to collaborate.

On-the-Job Training

Although people often associate training with classrooms, much learning occurs while employees are performing their jobs. **On-the-job training (OJT)** refers to training methods in which a person with job experience and skill guides trainees in practicing job skills at the workplace. This type of training takes various forms, including apprenticeships and internships.

An **apprenticeship** is a work-study training method that teaches job skills through a combination of structured on-the-job training and classroom training. The OJT component of an apprenticeship involves the apprentice assisting a certified tradesperson (a journeyman) at the work site. Typically, the classroom training is provided by local trade schools, high schools, and community colleges. Under state and federal guidelines, apprenticeship programs must require at least 144 hours of classroom instruction plus 2,000 hours (one year) of on-the-job experience.[19] Some apprenticeship programs are sponsored by individual companies, others by employee unions. As shown in the left column of Table 7.3, most apprenticeship programs are in the skilled trades, such as plumbing, carpentry, and electrical work. For trainees, a major advantage of apprenticeship is the ability to earn an income while learning a trade. In addition, training through an apprenticeship is usually effective because it involves hands-on learning and extensive practice. Will-Burt Corporation of Orrville, Ohio, started an apprenticeship program for machinists and brake press set-up operators. Each session combines classroom studies with hours of on-the-job training. After they have completed their apprentice training, employees who want to become journeymen must take additional training in classes taught on-site through a partnership between Will-Burt and Wayne College, University of Akron.[20]

An **internship** is on-the-job learning sponsored by an educational institution as a component of an academic program. The sponsoring school works with local employers to place students in positions where they can gain experience related to their area of study. For example, in Cedar Rapids, Iowa, Kirkwood Community College participates in an organization called Workplace Learning Connection, which finds students internships at hundreds of local companies.[21] High school students who pass a screening by the Workplace Learning Connection participate in semester-long internships. Many interns hope the internship will not only teach them about a workplace but also lead to a job offer. Brian Whitlatch interned at the Iowa 80 Truck Stop, where he helped mechanics work on trucks. He worked without pay as an intern, but he received course credit and, three weeks before graduation, a job offer. Many internships prepare students for professions such as those listed in the right column of Table 7.3.

on-the-job training (OJT)
Training methods in which a person with job experience and skill guides trainees in practicing job skills at the workplace.

apprenticeship
A work-study training method that teaches job skills through a combination of on-the-job training and classroom training.

internship
On-the-job learning sponsored by an educational institution as a component of an academic program.

TABLE 7.3

Typical Jobs for Apprentices and Interns

APPRENTICESHIP	INTERNSHIP
Bricklayer	Accountant
Carpenter	Doctor
Electrician	Journalist
Plumber	Lawyer
Printer	Nurse
Welder	

To be effective, OJT programs should include several characteristics:

- The organization should issue a policy statement describing the purpose of OJT and emphasizing the organization's support for it.
- The organization should specify who is accountable for conducting OJT. This accountability should be included in the relevant job descriptions.
- The organization should review OJT practices at companies in similar industries.
- Managers and peers should be trained in OJT principles.
- Employees who conduct OJT should have access to lesson plans, checklists, procedure manuals, training manuals, learning contracts, and progress report forms.
- Before conducting OJT with an employee, the organization should assess the employees' level of basic skills.[22]

The OJT program at Borden's North American Pasta Division has many of these characteristics.[23] Borden's carefully selects, trains, and rewards the managers and peers who act as trainers. The train-the-trainer course involves classroom training as well as time on the manufacturing floor to learn how to operate machinery such as pasta machines and correctly teach other employees how to use the equipment. Trainees in the OJT program complete a checklist in which they verify that the trainer helped them learn the skills needed and used effective teaching techniques.

Simulations

simulation
A training method that represents a real-life situation, with trainees making decisions resulting in outcomes that mirror what would happen on the job.

A **simulation** is a training method that represents a real-life situation, with trainees making decisions resulting in outcomes that mirror what would happen on the job. Simulations enable trainees to see the impact of their decisions in an artificial, risk-free environment. They are used to teaching production and process skills as well as management and interpersonal skills. Time Warner cable installers learn how to correctly install cable and high-speed Internet connections by crawling into two-story houses that have been built inside the company's training center. Trainees drill through the walls and crawl around inside these simulated houses, learning how to work in different types of homes.[24]

Simulators must have elements identical to those found in the work environment. The simulator needs to respond exactly as equipment would under the conditions and response given by the trainee. For this reason, simulators are expensive to develop and need constant updating as new information about the work environment becomes available. Still, they are an excellent training method when the risks of a mistake on the job are great. Trainees do not have to be afraid of the impact of wrong decisions when using the simulator, as they would be with on-the-job training.

virtual reality
A computer-based technology that provides an interactive, three-dimensional learning experience.

A recent development in simulations is the use of virtual reality technology. **Virtual reality** is a computer-based technology that provides an interactive, three-dimensional learning experience. Using specialized equipment or viewing the virtual model on a computer screen, trainees move through the simulated environment and interact with its components.[25] Devices relay information from the environment to the trainees' senses. For example, audio interfaces, gloves that provide a sense of touch, treadmills, or motion platforms create a realistic but artificial environment. Devices also communicate information about the trainee's movements to a computer. Virtual reality is a feature of the simulated environment of the advanced manufacturing courses in Motorola's Pager Robotic Assembly facility. Employees wear a head-mounted display that lets them view a virtual world of lab space, robots, tools, and the assembly operation. The trainees hear the sounds of using the real equipment. The equipment responds as if trainees were actually using it in the factory.[26]

Business Games and Case Studies

Training programs use business games and case studies to develop employees' management skills. A case study is a detailed description of a situation that trainees study and discuss. Cases are designed to develop higher-order thinking skills, such as the ability to analyze and evaluate information. They also can be a safe way to encourage trainees to take appropriate risks, by giving them practice in weighing and acting on uncertain outcomes. There are many sources of case studies, including Harvard Business School, the Darden Business School at the University of Virginia, and McGraw-Hill publishing company.

With business games, trainees gather information, analyze it, and make decisions that influence the outcome of the game. For instance, legendary motorcycle maker Harley-Davidson uses a business game to help prospective dealers understand how dealerships make money. The game involves 15 to 35 people working in teams. Each of the five rounds of the game challenges teams to manage a Harley dealership and compete against each other. In each round, the teams face a different business situation—new products, a change in interest rates, or a crisis such as a fire at the business. Between rounds, participants attend lectures and discuss case studies that teach the concepts reinforced by the game.[27] Games stimulate learning because they actively involve participants and mimic the competitive nature of business. A realistic game may be more meaningful to trainees than presentation techniques such as classroom instruction.

Training with case studies and games requires that participants come together to discuss the cases or the progress of the game. This requires face-to-face or electronic meetings. Also, participants must be willing to be actively involved in analyzing the situation and defending their decisions.

Behavior Modeling

Research suggests that one of the most effective ways to teach interpersonal skills is through behavior modeling.[28] This involves training sessions in which participants observe other people demonstrating the desired behavior, then have opportunities to practice the behavior themselves. For example, a training program could involve four-hour sessions, each focusing on one interpersonal skill, such as communicating or coaching. At the beginning of each session, participants hear the reasons for using the key behaviors, then they watch a videotape of a model performing the key behaviors. They practice through role-playing and receive feedback about their performance. In addition, they evaluate the performance of the model in the videotape and discuss how they can apply the behavior on the job.

Experiential Programs

To develop teamwork and leadership skills, some organizations enroll their employees in a form of training called **experiential programs.** In experiential programs, participants learn concepts and then apply them by simulating the behaviors involved and analyzing the activity, connecting it with real-life situations.[29] In France, some businesses are signing up their managers to attend cooking schools, where they whip up a gourmet meal together. Jacques Bally, who works for a school run by one of France's top chefs, says cooking is a great way to learn teamwork: "It's like in any squad, everyone is responsible for playing their part; they have their own tasks but a common objective—and if they want to eat in the end, then they have to get the meal ready."[30]

experiential programs Training programs in which participants learn concepts and apply them by simulating behaviors involved and analyzing the activity, connecting it with real-life situations.

One of the most important features of organizations today is teamwork. Experiential programs include team-building exercises like wall climbing and rafting to help build trust and cooperation among employees.

Experiential training programs should follow several guidelines. A program should be related to a specific business problem. Participants should feel challenged and move outside their comfort zones but within limits that keep their motivation strong and help them understand the purpose of the program. California-based Quantum Corporation used experiential learning to build the teamwork it needed to carry out a project to overhaul the company's infrastructure. The project would bring together employees who were not used to working with each other. They came from the company's information technology, engineering, marketing, and graphic design departments and worked in locations dispersed across several countries. In the experiential training, a group of actors led the team through a series of improvisational activities designed to get the team members to share personal stories. The actors interpreted those stories, and sometimes team members played the parts. Following this training, the team members reported greater understanding of one another, a condition that later helped the team meet deadlines and complete projects.[31]

adventure learning
A teamwork and leadership training program based on the use of challenging, structured outdoor activities.

One form of experiential program, called **adventure learning,** uses challenging, structured outdoor activities, which may include difficult sports such as dogsledding or mountain climbing. Other activities may be structured tasks like climbing walls, completing rope courses, climbing ladders, or making "trust falls" (in which each trainee stands on a table and falls backward into the arms of other group members).

Does adventure learning work? The impact of these programs has not been rigorously tested, but participants report they gained a greater understanding of themselves and the ways they interact with their coworkers. One key to the success of such programs may be that the organization insist that entire work groups participate together. This encourages people to see, discuss, and correct the kinds of behavior that keep the group from performing well.

Before requiring employees to participate in experiential programs, the organization should consider the possible drawbacks. Because these programs are usually physically demanding and often require participants to touch each other, companies face certain risks. Some employees may be injured or may feel that they were sexually harassed or that their privacy was invaded. Also, the Americans with Disabilities Act (discussed in Chapter 3) raises questions about requiring employees with disabilities to participate in physically demanding training experiences.

Team Training

A possible alternative to experiential programs is team training, which coordinates the performance of individuals who work together to achieve a common goal. An organization may benefit from providing such training to groups when group members must share information and group performance depends on the performance of the individual group members. Examples include the military, nuclear power plants, and commercial airlines. In those work settings, much work is performed by crews, groups, or teams. Success depends on individuals' coordinating their activities to make decisions, perhaps in dangerous situations.

Ways to conduct team training include cross-training and coordination training.[32] In **cross-training,** team members understand and practice each other's skills so that they are prepared to step in and take another member's place. In a factory, for example, production workers could be cross-trained to handle all phases of assembly. This enables the company to move them to the positions where they are most needed to complete an order on time.

Coordination training trains the team in how to share information and decisions to obtain the best team performance. This type of training is especially important for commercial aviation and surgical teams. Both of these kinds of teams must monitor different aspects of equipment and the environment at the same time sharing information to make the most effective decisions regarding patient care or aircraft safety and performance.

For both kinds of team training, the training program usually brings together several training methods. To teach communication skills, training could begin with a lecture about communicating, followed by an opportunity for team members to role-play scenarios related to communication on the team. Boeing combined a number of methods in a team training program designed to improve the effectiveness of the 250 teams designing the Boeing 777.[33] Teams include members from a variety of specialties, from design engineers to marketing professionals. These team members had to understand how the process or product they were designing would fit with the rest of the finished jet. Boeing's training started with an extensive orientation emphasizing how team members were supposed to work together. Then the teams received their work assignments. Trainers helped the teams work through problems as needed, with assistance in communication skills, conflict resolution, and leadership.

Training may also target the skills needed by the teams' leaders. **Team leader training** refers to training people in the skills necessary for team leadership. For example, the training may be aimed at helping team leaders learn to resolve conflicts or coordinate activities.

Action Learning

Another form of group building is **action learning.** In this type of training, teams or work groups get an actual problem, work on solving it and commit to an action plan, and are accountable for carrying out the plan.[34] Typically, 6 to 30 employees participate in action learning; sometimes the participants include customers and vendors.

cross-training
Team training in which team members understand and practice each other's skills so that they are prepared to step in and take another member's place.

coordination training
Team training that teaches the team how to share information and make decisions to obtain the best team performance.

team leader training
Training in the skills necessary for effectively leading the organization's teams.

action learning
Training in which teams get an actual problem, work on solving it and commit to an action plan, and are accountable for carrying it out.

For instance, a group might include a customer that buys the product involved in the problem to be solved. Another arrangement is to bring together employees from various functions affected by the problem. ATC, a public transportation services management company in Illinois, used action learning to help boost profitability by reducing operating costs. Employees were divided into Action Workout Teams to identify ways of reducing costs and to brainstorm effective solutions. The process assumed that employees closest to where the work gets done have the best ideas about how to solve problems. Teams of five to seven employees met once a week for a couple of hours for up to two months. The teams studied problems and issues such as overtime, preventive maintenance, absenteeism, parts inventory, and inefficient safety-inspection procedures. The teams assigned priorities to their ideas, developed action plans, tried their ideas, and measured the outcomes, eventually saving the company more than $1.8 million.[35]

The effectiveness of action learning has not been formally evaluated. This type of training seems to result in a great deal of learning, however, and employees are able to apply what they learn because action learning involves actual problems the organization is facing. The group approach also helps teams identify behaviors that interfere with problem solving.

LO6
Summarize how to implement a successful training program.

◈ IMPLEMENTING THE TRAINING PROGRAM: PRINCIPLES OF LEARNING

Learning permanently changes behavior. For employees to acquire knowledge and skills in the training program and apply what they have learned in their jobs, the training program must be implemented in a way that applies what we know about how people learn. Researchers have identified a number of ways employees learn best.[36] Table 7.4 summarizes ways that training can best encourage learning. In general, effective training communicates learning objectives clearly, presents information in distinctive and memorable ways, and helps trainees link the subject matter to their jobs.

Employees are most likely to learn when training is linked to their current job experiences and tasks.[37] There are a number of ways trainers can make this link. Training sessions should present material using familiar concepts, terms, and examples. As far as possible, the training context—such as the physical setting or the images presented on a computer—should mirror the work environment. Along with physical elements, the context should include emotional elements. In the earlier example of training store personnel to handle upset customers, the physical context is more relevant if it includes trainees acting out scenarios of personnel dealing with unhappy customers. The role-play interaction between trainees adds emotional realism and further enhances learning.

To fully understand and remember the content of the training, employees need a chance to demonstrate and practice what they have learned. Trainers should provide ways to actively involve the trainees, have them practice repeatedly, and have them complete tasks within a time that is appropriate in light of the learning objectives. Practice requires physically carrying out the desired behaviors, not just describing them. Practice sessions could include role-playing interactions, filling out relevant forms, or operating machinery or equipment to be used on the job. The more the trainee practices these activities, the more comfortable he or she will be in applying the skills on the job. People tend to benefit most from practice that occurs over several sessions, rather than one long practice session.[38] For complex tasks, it may be

TABLE 7.4

Ways That Training
Helps Employees
Learn

TRAINING ACTIVITY	WAYS TO PROVIDE TRAINING ACTIVITY
Communicate the learning objective.	Demonstrate the performance to be expected. Give examples of questions to be answered.
Use distinctive, attention-getting messages.	Emphasize key points. Use pictures, not just words.
Limit the content of training.	Group lengthy material into chunks. Provide a visual image of the course material. Provide opportunities to repeat and practice material.
Guide trainees as they learn.	Use words as reminders about sequence of activities. Use words and pictures to relate concepts to one another and to their context.
Elaborate on the subject.	Present the material in different contexts and settings. Relate new ideas to previously learned concepts. Practice in a variety of contexts and settings.
Provide memory cues.	Suggest memory aids. Use familiar sounds or rhymes as memory cues.
Transfer course content to the workplace.	Design the learning environment so that it has elements in common with the workplace. Require learners to develop action plans that apply training content to their jobs. Use words that link the course to the workplace.
Provide feedback about performance.	Tell trainees how accurately and quickly they are performing their new skill. Show how trainees have met the objectives of the training.

SOURCE: Adapted from R. M. Gagne, "Learning Processes and Instruction," *Training Research Journal* 1 (1995/96), pp. 17–28.

most effective to practice a few skills or behaviors at a time, then combine them in later practice sessions.

Trainees need to understand whether or not they are succeeding. Therefore, training sessions should offer feedback. Effective feedback focuses on specific behaviors and is delivered as soon as possible after the trainees practice or demonstrate what they have learned.[39] One way to do this is to videotape trainees, then show the video while indicating specific behaviors that do or do not match the desired outcomes of the training. Feedback should include praise when trainees show they have learned material, as well as guidance on how to improve.

Well-designed training helps people remember the content. Training programs need to break information into chunks that people can remember. Research suggests that people can attend to no more than four to five items at a time. If a concept or procedure involves more than five items, the training program should deliver information in shorter sessions or chunks.[40] Other ways to make information more memorable include presenting it with visual images and practicing some tasks enough that they become automatic.

Written materials should have an appropriate reading level. A simple way to assess **readability**—the difficulty level of written materials—is to look at the words being used and at the length of sentences. In general, it is easiest to read short sentences and simple, standard words. If training materials are too difficult to understand, several adjustments can help. The basic approach is to rewrite the material looking for ways to simplify it.

readability
The difficulty level of written materials.

GETTING EMPLOYEES INVOLVED IN LEARNING

Employees will get the most out of training that is well designed to get them involved in learning. Generating interest is especially important in today's work environment, where most employees feel pressed for time. They need to know that the training program will help them achieve their objectives. Whether online or in person, the goal for the organization is to create an effective learning environment.

The obvious starting point is to make sure the learning site is comfortable and any needed equipment is working. Trainers also need to ensure that any materials have been distributed to employees. The content of the training must also be relevant to the people being trained, so it is important to talk to employees during the planning phase. Trainers need to know what employees think about the topic, or they may later find themselves fighting to sell its relevance. Trainer Dennis Stevenson makes a point of visiting job sites to gather information. He walks around and asks people about the problems they're facing. Then, says Stevenson, "When I go back [later] and tell them what the benefits of the training are going to be, I can tie those to the problem they told me about, rather than something I invent." Training course enrollment should be easy for employees, and their records should be kept up to date.

Relevance also includes the elements of timing and practice. Training programs should be offered at a time in employees' careers when they can really use the information. They should also be allowed to practice new skills and obtain immediate feedback through on-the-job observation, tests, and quizzes.

Training will seem most relevant in an organization that clearly values and rewards learning. Supervisors should model this behavior by participating in opportunities to learn. Supervisors who interact directly with their employees during training can provide specific feedback for improvement and praise. They can also demonstrate a correct behavior or skill.

- Substitute simple, concrete words for unfamiliar or abstract words.
- Divide long sentences into two or more short sentences.
- Divide long paragraphs into two or more short paragraphs.
- Add checklists (like this one) and illustrations to clarify the text.

Another approach is to substitute videotapes, hands-on learning, or other non-written methods for some of the written material. A longer-term solution is to use tests to identify employees who need training to improve their reading levels and to provide that training first.

The "HR How To" box provides further ideas for implementing training in a way that motivates employees and enables them to learn.

LO7
Evaluate the success of a training program.

MEASURING RESULTS OF TRAINING

After a training program ends, or at intervals during an ongoing training program, organizations should ensure that the training is meeting objectives. The stage to prepare for evaluating a training program is when the program is being developed. Along with designing course objectives and content, the planner should identify how to measure achievement of objectives. Depending on the objectives, the evaluation can use one or more of the measures shown in Figure 7.5 on page 234—trainee satisfaction with

The organization might also offer rewards for completing educational programs—including prestige, not just money. Southern California Water Company offers a 40-hour Train-the-Trainer Program in which employees learn how to teach what they have learned. These employees conduct most of the company's training, bringing their firsthand experience to the subject matter.

People often want training to be fun, and the right kind of fun can in fact enhance learning. But the entertaining elements of the training should not be merely silly; that kind of fun is distracting. Instead, the trainer should look for ways to engage the trainees in the course's content.

That's what Stevenson did when he was conducting training for dockworkers at an organization that was having trouble with sexual harassment. Female workers had been filing and winning lawsuits, and the company decided it needed to conduct sensitivity training. Stevenson realized that most dockworkers would not be enthusiastic about being asked to learn "sensitivity." Instead, he opened the program by introducing himself and pulling out a mousetrap. He invited participants to stick their finger in the trap. When no one volunteered, Stevenson showed how to spring the trap without injury, letting a few volunteers try his method. Then Stevenson pulled out a rat trap and again asked for volunteers. Again, no one stepped forward, although they enjoyed watching the trap smash pencils. Finally, to everyone's entertainment, he brought out a man-sized trap, 30 by 48 inches. Throughout this demonstration, Stevenson brought home his main point: Some "traps" hurt a little but are bearable, while others are dangerous and can break a person. This method engaged his audience and opened them up to thinking about more constructive ways to work with female employees.

SOURCE: Based on Dianne Molvig, "Yearning for Learning," *HR Magazine*, March 2002, downloaded from Find-Articles at http://www.findarticles.com.

the program, knowledge or abilities gained, use of new skills and behavior on the job (transfer of training), and improvements in individual and organizational performance. The usual way to measure whether participants have acquired information is to administer tests on paper or electronically. Trainers or supervisors can observe whether participants demonstrate the desired skills and behaviors. Surveys measure changes in attitude. Changes in company performance have a variety of measures, many of which organizations keep track of for preparing performance appraisals, annual reports, and other routine documents in order to demonstrate the final measure of success shown in Figure 7.5—return on investment.

Evaluation Methods

Evaluation of training should look for **transfer of training,** or on-the-job use of knowledge, skills, and behaviors learned in training. Transfer of training requires that employees actually learn the content of the training program and that the necessary conditions are in place for employees to apply what they learned. Thus, the assessment can look at whether employees have an opportunity to perform the skills related to the training. The organization can measure this by asking employees three questions about specific training-related tasks:

transfer of training
On-the-job use of knowledge, skills, and behaviors learned in training.

Figure 7.5

Measures of Training
Success

1. Do you perform the task?
2. How many times do you perform the task?
3. To what extent do you perform difficult and challenging learned tasks?

Frequent performance of difficult training-related tasks would signal great opportunity to perform. If there is low opportunity to perform, the organization should conduct further needs assessment and reevaluate readiness to learn. Perhaps the organization does not fully support the training activities in general or the employee's supervisor does not provide opportunities to apply new skills. Lack of transfer can also mean that employees have not learned the course material. The organization might offer a refresher course to give trainees more practice. Another reason for poor transfer of training is that the content of the training may not be important for the employee's job.

Assessment of training also should evaluate training *outcomes*, that is, what (if anything) has changed as a result of the training. The relevant training outcomes are the ones related to the organization's goals for the training and its overall performance. Possible outcomes include the following:

- Information such as facts, techniques, and procedures that trainees can recall after the training.
- Skills that trainees can demonstrate in tests or on the job.
- Trainee and supervisor satisfaction with the training program.
- Changes in attitude related to the content of the training (for example, concern for safety or tolerance of diversity).
- Improvements in individual, group, or company performance (for example, greater customer satisfaction, more sales, fewer defects).

Training is a significant part of many organizations' budgets. Therefore, economic measures are an important way to evaluate the success of a training program. Businesses that invest in training want to achieve a high *return on investment*—the monetary benefits of the investment compared to the amount invested, expressed as a percentage. For example, IBM's e-learning program for new managers, Basic Blue, costs $8,708 per manager.[41] The company has measured an improvement in each new manager's performance worth $415,000. That gives IBM a benefit of $415,000 − $8,708 = $406,292 for each manager. This is an extremely large return on investment: $406,292/$8,708 = 46.65, or 4,665 percent! In other words, for every $1 IBM invests in Basic Blue, it receives almost $47.

For any of these methods, the most accurate but most costly way to evaluate the training program is to measure performance, knowledge, or attitudes among all employees before the training, then to train only part of the employees. After the training is complete, the performance, knowledge, or attitudes are again measured, and the trained group is compared with the untrained group. A simpler but less accurate way to assess the training is to conduct the pretest and posttest on all trainees, comparing their performance, knowledge, or attitudes before and after the training. This form of measurement does not rule out the possibility that change resulted from something other than training (for example, a change in the compensation system). The simplest approach is to use only a posttest. Of course, this type of measurement does not enable accurate comparisons, but it may be sufficient, depending on the cost and purpose of the training.

Applying the Evaluation

The purpose of evaluating training is to help with future decisions about the organization's training programs. Using the evaluation, the organization may identify a need to modify the training and gain information about the kinds of changes needed. The organization may decide to expand on successful areas of training and cut back on training that has not delivered significant benefits.

At Walgreens, evaluation of training for pharmacy technicians convinced the company that formal training was economically beneficial. The drugstore chain developed a training course as an alternative to on-the-job training from pharmacists. Some of the newly hired technicians participated in the test of the program, taking part in 20 hours of classroom training and 20 hours of supervision on the job. Other technicians relied on the old method of being informally trained by the pharmacists who had hired them. After the training had ended, pharmacists who supervised the technicians completed surveys about the technicians' performance. The surveys indicated that formally trained technicians were more efficient and wasted less of the pharmacists' time. Also, sales in pharmacies with formally trained technicians exceeded sales in pharmacies with technicians trained on the job by an average of $9,500 each year.[42]

APPLICATIONS OF TRAINING

Two categories of training that have become widespread among U.S. companies are orientation of new employees and training in how to manage workforce diversity.

Orientation of New Employees

Many employees receive their first training during their first days on the job. This training is the organization's **orientation** program—its training designed to prepare employees to perform their job effectively, learn about the organization, and establish work relationships. Organizations provide for orientation because, no matter how realistic the information provided during employment interviews and site visits, people feel shock and surprise when they start a new job.[43] Also, employees need to become familiar with job tasks and learn the details of the organization's practices, policies, and procedures.

The objectives of orientation programs include making new employees familiar with the organization's rules, policies, and procedures. Table 7.5 summarizes the content of a typical orientation program. Such a program provides information about the overall

LO8
Describe training methods for employee orientation and diversity management.

orientation
Training designed to prepare employees to perform their jobs effectively, learn about their organization, and establish work relationships.

TABLE 7.5

Content of a Typical
Orientation Program

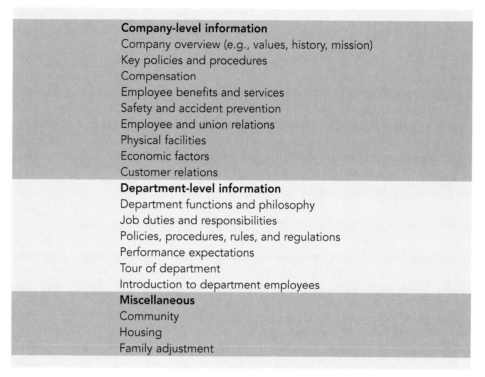

Company-level information
Company overview (e.g., values, history, mission)
Key policies and procedures
Compensation
Employee benefits and services
Safety and accident prevention
Employee and union relations
Physical facilities
Economic factors
Customer relations
Department-level information
Department functions and philosophy
Job duties and responsibilities
Policies, procedures, rules, and regulations
Performance expectations
Tour of department
Introduction to department employees
Miscellaneous
Community
Housing
Family adjustment

SOURCE: J. L. Schwarz and M. A. Weslowski, "Employee Orientation: What Employers Should Know," *Journal of Contemporary Business Issues*, Fall 1995, p. 48. Used with permission.

company and about the department in which the new employee will be working. The topics include social as well as technical aspects of the job. Miscellaneous information helps employees from out of town learn about the surrounding community.

Orientation at National City Corporation, a bank and financial services company based in Cleveland, includes several courses. The Early Success program offers new hires a comfortable environment, support network, and series of classes about products and customer service. The program includes an overview of National City's corporate objectives, employee benefits, and information about the brand. Another course, called People, Policies, and Practices, covers the material in the employee handbook. Top-Notch Customer Care focuses on how to provide service and work in teams. Each new employee is matched with a peer (called a *buddy*) who is available to answer the new employee's questions. Since National City launched its orientation program, its employees are far less likely to quit within the first three months on the job, an improvement that has saved the company about $1.35 million a year.[44]

At The Container Store, orientation is about more than job skills.[45] The company also wants employees to care about what they are doing and to be committed to the organization. New employees at The Container Store participate in a one-week training program called Foundation Week. During the first day of Foundation Week, employees learn the company's philosophy, and they spend most of the day with the store manager. On the following days, they learn about the way merchandise is arranged in the stores, various selling techniques, roles of employees in different positions, and ways to provide customer service. Only after completing the entire week of training do employees receive the apron they wear while at work. The manager presents the apron during a ceremony intended to encourage the new hires. According to Barbara Anderson, The Container Store's director of community services and staff development, "The psychological effect of having to wait for that apron is incredible." Anderson says that since the company started its Foundation Week program, newly hired employees are more self-confident and productive, and they tend to stay with the company longer.

Orientation programs may combine various training methods such as printed and audiovisual materials, classroom instruction, on-the-job training, and e-learning. Decisions about how to conduct the orientation depend on the type of material to be covered and the number of new employees, among other factors.

Diversity Training

In response to Equal Employment Opportunity laws and market forces, many organizations today are concerned about managing diversity—creating an environment that allows all employees to contribute to organizational goals and experience personal growth. This kind of environment includes access to jobs as well as fair and positive treatment of all employees. Chapter 3 described how organizations manage diversity by complying with the law. Besides these efforts, many organizations provide training designed to teach employees attitudes and behaviors that support the management of diversity. Such training may have some or all of the following goals:

- Employees should understand how their values and stereotypes influence their behavior toward others of different gender and ethnic, racial, and religious backgrounds.
- Employees should gain an appreciation of cultural differences among themselves.
- Employees should avoid and correct behaviors that isolate and intimidate minority group members.

Diversity training programs, like the one conducted by Harvard Pilgrim Health Care, are designed to teach employees attitudes and behaviors that support the management of diversity. Why is it important for companies to provide this type of training?

diversity training
Training designed to change employee attitudes about diversity and/or develop skills needed to work with a diverse workforce.

Training designed to change employee attitudes about diversity and/or develop skills needed to work with a diverse workforce is called **diversity training.** These programs generally emphasize either attitude awareness and change or behavior change.

Programs that focus on attitudes have objectives to increase participants' awareness of cultural and ethnic differences, as well as differences in personal characteristics and physical characteristics (such as disabilities). These programs are based on the assumption that people who become aware of differences and their stereotypes about those differences will be able to avoid letting stereotypes influence their interactions with people. Many of these programs use videotapes and experiential exercises to increase employees' awareness of the negative emotional and performance effects of stereotypes and resulting behaviors on members of minority groups. A risk of these programs is that they may actually reinforce stereotypes by focusing on differences rather than similarities among coworkers.[46] But it is generally held that greater awareness has a positive effect.

Programs that focus on behavior aim at changing the organizational policies and individual behaviors that inhibit employees' personal growth and productivity. Sometimes these programs identify incidents that discourage employees from working up to their potential. Employees work in groups to discuss specific promotion opportunities or management practices that they believe were handled unfairly. Another approach is to teach managers and employees basic rules of behavior in the workplace.[47] Trainees may be more positive about receiving this type of training than other kinds of diversity training. Finally, some organizations provide diversity training in the form of *cultural immersion*, sending employees directly into communities where they have to interact with persons from different cultures, races, and nationalities. Participants might talk with community members, work in community organizations, or learn about events that are significant to the community they visit. For example, the United Parcel Service (UPS) Community Internship Program is designed to help UPS senior managers understand the needs of diverse customers and a diverse workforce through exposure to poverty and inequality. In projects that typically last four weeks, managers travel to cities throughout the United States, where they work on problems facing local populations. They may serve meals to the homeless, work in AIDS centers, help migrant farm workers, build temporary housing and schools, and manage children in a Head Start program. UPS managers report that the program helps them look for unconventional solutions to problems. One manager, after being impressed by the creative and practical ideas that addicts in a halfway house suggested for keeping teens away from drugs, realized she needed to capitalize more on the creativity of the employees she supervised. When she returned to her job, she began involving her full staff more in problem solving.[48]

Although many organizations have used diversity training, few have provided programs lasting more than a day, and few have researched their long-term effectiveness.[49] The little research that exists on the subject has provided no support for a direct link between diversity programs and business success, but there is evidence that some characteristics make diversity training more effective.[50] Most important, the training should be tied to business objectives, such as understanding customers. The support and involvement of top management, and the involvement of managers at all levels, also are important. Diversity training should emphasize learning behaviors and skills, not blaming employees. Finally, the program should be well structured, connected to the organization's rewards for performance, and include a way to measure the success of the training.

thinking ETHICALLY

Can You Teach People to Be Ethical?

This chapter looked at training as a way to ensure that employees have a variety of skills and abilities, such as knowing how to perform the tasks involved in a particular trade and being able to work constructively with a diverse group of people. Some organizations also provide training to help their employees make ethical decisions.

Molson Coors Brewing Company offers its employees several resources related to ethics, including interactive e-learning, ethics leadership training, and a visual "map" to guide ethical decision making. These training resources support detailed ethics policies and supplement a company help line to call for guidance in specific situations. According to Warren Malmquist, who developed the ethics training for Adolph Coors Company before its 2005 acquisition of Molson, "The goal of the program is to step beyond rules and guidelines and teach employees how to think, clarify, and analyze situations." The e-learning program presents scenarios and provides feedback to help employees see the ethical principles related to their decisions. The program includes a series of modules presented as an "expedition" from a base camp to the top of the mountain. As the employee ascends through the modules, the topics become more complex and the choices less obvious. All new hires must complete this course within 90 days, and existing employees must take refresher courses.

SOURCE: Based on Samuel Greengard, "Golden Values," *Workforce Management*, March 2005, pp. 52–53.

Questions

1. To make ethical decisions, what skills and abilities do you need? What else do you need besides skills and abilities?
2. Do you think the ethics training described here will help make Molson Coors employees more ethical? Explain.
3. Suppose you became responsible for providing ethics training at Molson Coors. What additional ideas from the chapter or your own experience would you want to apply to the program described here?

SUMMARY

1. Discuss how to link training programs to organizational needs.
   Organizations need to establish training programs that are effective. In other words, they teach what they are designed to teach, and they teach skills and behaviors that will help the organization achieve its goals. Organizations create such programs through instructional design. This process begins with a needs assessment. The organization then ensures readiness for training, including employee characteristics and organizational support. Next, the organization plans a training program, implements the program, and evaluates the results.

2. Explain how to assess the need for training.
   Needs assessment consists of an organization analysis, person analysis, and task analysis. The organization analysis determines the appropriateness of training by

evaluating the characteristics of the organization, including its strategy, resources, and management support. The person analysis determines individuals' needs and readiness for training. The task analysis identifies the tasks, knowledge, skills, and behaviors that training should emphasize. It is based on examination of the conditions in which tasks are performed, including equipment and environment of the job, time constraints, safety considerations, and performance standards.

3. Explain how to assess employees' readiness for training.
Readiness for training is a combination of employee characteristics and positive work environment that permit training. The necessary employee characteristics include ability to learn the subject matter, favorable attitudes toward the training, and motivation to learn. A positive work environment avoids situational constraints such as lack of money and time. In a positive environment, both peers and management support training.

4. Describe how to plan an effective training program.
Planning begins with establishing objectives for the training program. These should define an expected performance or outcome, the desired level of performance, and the conditions under which the performance should occur. Based on the objectives, the planner decides who will provide the training, what topics the training will cover, what training methods to use, and how to evaluate the training. Even when organizations purchase outside training, someone in the organization, usually a member of the HR department, often is responsible for training administration. The training methods selected should be related to the objectives and content of the training program. Training methods may include presentation methods, hands-on methods, or group-building methods.

5. Compare widely used training methods.
Classroom instruction is most widely used and is one of the least expensive and least time-consuming ways to present information on a specific topic to many trainees. It also allows for group interaction and may include hands-on practice. Audiovisual and computer-based training need not require that trainees attend a class, so organizations can reduce time and money spent on training. Computer-based training may be interactive and may provide for group interaction. On-the-job training methods such as apprenticeships and internships give trainees first-hand experiences. A simulation represents a real-life situation, enabling trainees to see the effects of their decisions without dangerous or expensive consequences. Business games and case studies are other methods for practicing decision-making skills. Participants need to come together in one location or collaborate online. Behavior modeling gives trainees a chance to observe desired behaviors, so this technique can be effective for teaching interpersonal skills. Experiential and adventure learning programs provide an opportunity for group members to interact in challenging circumstances but may exclude members with disabilities. Team training focuses a team on achievement of a common goal. Action learning offers relevance, because the training focuses on an actual work-related problem.

6. Summarize how to implement a successful training program.
Implementation should apply principles of learning. In general, effective training communicates learning objectives, presents information in distinctive and memorable ways, and helps trainees link the subject matter to their jobs. Employees are most likely to learn when training is linked to job experiences and tasks. Employees learn best when they demonstrate or practice what they have learned and when they receive feedback that helps them improve. Trainees remember information better when it is broken into small chunks, presented with visual images, and practiced many times. Written materials should be easily readable by trainees.

7. Evaluate the success of a training program.
Evaluation of training should look for transfer of training by measuring whether employees are performing the tasks taught in the training program. Assessment of training also should evaluate training outcomes, such as change in attitude, ability to perform a new skill, and recall of facts or behaviors taught in the training program. Training should result in improvement in the group's or organization's outcomes, such as customer satisfaction or sales. An economic measure of training success is return on investment.

8. Describe training methods for employee orientation and diversity management.
Employee orientation is training designed to prepare employees to perform their job effectively, learn about the organization, and establish work relationships. Organizations provide for orientation because, no matter how realistic the information provided during employment interviews and site visits, people feel shock and surprise when they start a new job, and they need to learn the details of how to perform the job. A typical orientation program includes information about the overall company and the department in which the new employee will be working, covering social as well as technical aspects of the job. Orientation programs may combine several training methods, from printed materials to on-the-job training to e-learning. Diversity

training is designed to change employee attitudes about diversity and/or develop skills needed to work with a diverse workforce. Evidence regarding these programs suggests that diversity training is most effec-

tive if it is tied to business objectives, has management support, emphasizes behaviors and skills, and is well structured with a way to measure success.

REVIEW AND DISCUSSION QUESTIONS

1. "Melinda!" bellowed Toran to the company's HR specialist, "I've got a problem, and you've got to solve it. I can't get people in this plant to work together as a team. As if I don't have enough trouble with our competitors and our past-due accounts, now I have to put up with running a zoo. You're responsible for seeing that the staff gets along. I want a training proposal on my desk by Monday." Assume you are Melinda.
    a. Is training the solution to this problem? How can you determine the need for training?
    b. Summarize how you would conduct a needs assessment.
2. How should an organization assess readiness for learning? In Question 1, how do Toran's comments suggest readiness (or lack of readiness) for learning?
3. Assume you are the human resource manager of a small seafood company. The general manager has told you that customers have begun complaining about the quality of your company's fresh fish. Currently, training consists of senior fish cleaners showing new employees how to perform the job. Assuming your needs assessment indicates a need for training, how would you plan a training program? What steps should you take in planning the program?
4. Many organizations turn to e-learning as a less expensive alternative to classroom training. What are some other advantages of substituting e-learning for classroom training? What are some disadvantages?
5. Suppose the managers in your organization tend to avoid delegating projects to the people in their groups. As a result, they rarely meet their goals. A training needs analysis indicates that an appropriate solution is training in management skills. You have identified two outside training programs that are consistent with your goals. One program involves experiential programs, and the other is an interactive computer program. What are the strengths and weak-

nesses of each technique? Which would you choose? Why?
6. Consider your current job or a job you recently held. What types of training did you receive for the job? What types of training would you like to receive? Why?
7. A manufacturing company employs several maintenance employees. When a problem occurs with the equipment, a maintenance employee receives a description of the symptoms and is supposed to locate and fix the source of the problem. The company recently installed a new, complex electronics system. To prepare its maintenance workers, the company provided classroom training. The trainer displayed electrical drawings of system components and posed problems about the system. The trainer would point to a component in a drawing and ask, "What would happen if this component were faulty?" Trainees would study the diagrams, describe the likely symptoms, and discuss how to repair the problem. If you were responsible for this company's training, how would you evaluate the success of this training program?
8. In Question 7, suppose the maintenance supervisor has complained that trainees are having difficulty troubleshooting problems with the new electronics system. They are spending a great deal of time on problems with the system and coming to the supervisor with frequent questions that show a lack of understanding. The supervisor is convinced that the employees are motivated to learn the system, and they are well qualified. What do you think might be the problems with the current training program? What recommendations can you make for improving the program?
9. Who should be involved in orientation of new employees? Why would it not be appropriate to provide employee orientation purely online?
10. Why do organizations provide diversity training? What kinds of goals are most suitable for such training?

WHAT'S YOUR HR IQ?

The text Web site offers two more ways to check what you've learned so far. Use the Self-Assessment exercise to evaluate your own training needs. Go online with the Web Exercise to see a demo of an online learning course.

BusinessWeek CASE

BusinessWeek The Learning Environment at United Technologies

Even to his closest friends, George David of United Technologies Corporation (UTC) comes off as a study in contrasts. He will speak passionately about the problem of the country's growing income gap between rich and poor before a crowd of factory workers at UTC's Carrier air-conditioner plant in Collierville, Tennessee—though he himself took home a pay packet worth $70 million last year. Before anyone can write off their leader as heartless, David's eyes tear up while recalling Yuzuru Ito, the late quality guru who helped him formulate his guiding principles of leadership.

Getting a handle on George David isn't easy. An ardent student of both history and management, he has the air of an academic and talks like some modern-day Plato in a production plant. But David, 62, is more than a head-in-the-clouds theorist. He has transformed his old-line industrial conglomerate into a $31 billion powerhouse of productivity with relentless attention to detail. He has taken commodity products such as elevators and air conditioners and, thanks to a constant innovation and superior technology, turned them into high-margin businesses that dominate worldwide. And while he can terminate thousands of workers at a stroke in the name of efficiency, he also has crafted one of the most progressive employee education programs in the world—even extending benefits to laid-off workers.

Together, these disparate impulses have yielded big results. In David's decade at the helm, this philosopher king of manufacturing has more than quadrupled earnings per share and outperformed even the mythic General Electric Company in returns to investors (stock price performance). Profitability measures, too, have improved significantly.

David has racked up these results despite his penchant for controversial investments that don't directly benefit the bottom line, at least not within any normal time horizon. His Employee Scholar Program costs $60 million a year, and workers don't even have to tie their studies to the job. Anything goes, from medieval poetry to medical training, with UTC picking up the tab. David also likes to move early to fund new technologies, such as fuel cells. David believes these initiatives are the seed corn that will grow into businesses that can sustain the company long after he has left office. UTC spends more than $2.5 billion a year on research and development, spawning more than 350 patents a year.

When asked how much new technology has contributed to the productivity revolution at UTC, David puts his thumb and index finger together in a circle and says "zero." He adds that technology has been critical to product innovation and improved communication, but most gains in the plant come from better processes, not better machines.

As business ebbs and flows, it's workers who often pay a dreadful price. David is achingly blunt about the need for employees to control their destinies in everything from health care to job security. But perhaps more than any other leader in Corporate America today, he is also deeply committed to giving them the tools to do this. His Employee Scholar Program gives workers up to three paid hours off a week to study and pays up front for the entire cost of books, tuition, and fees for any education program—except, perhaps, the kind found on matchbook covers or pricey pilot training. The program covers every employee, from the elevator technician in Zimbabwe to the office assistant in Tyler, Texas, with some education benefits even extending to laid-off workers. And, for each degree earned, employees get up to $10,000 in UTC stock or stock options.

That commitment has helped a relatively low-profile company draw some of the best in business. What's more, once workers bag the degree and take home the stock, they tend to stay. Retention among employee scholars is about 20 percent higher than for regular U.S. workers. Lance Bartosz, a 30-year-old engineering manager, joined the company after learning about the program from a friend. So far, he has completed an MBA and is now getting a master's degree in engineering. "This has made me feel a stronger allegiance to UTC."

One of David's first tasks as president was to persuade a retiree named Yuzuru Ito to work on improving the productivity of UTC's businesses. David first encountered Ito in 1989, after he was brought in by the unit's Japanese joint venture partner, Matsushita Industrial, to figure out why Otis's fancy new Elevonic 401 elevators were such clunkers. Their callback rates—the number of times per year a building owner has to call mechanics for service—were as high as 40 per unit a year, versus an average of 0.5 for rival Mitsubishi Electric. Under Ito, engineers analyzed the cause of the problem, and the work they did changed the fundamental design of the elevator line worldwide.

David leaned on Ito, first as a consultant and then as a full-time adviser, to make the techniques he used to analyze the elevators adaptable and accessible to every person in the plant. The program evolved and became known as ACE, or Achieving Competitive Excellence. "ACE pilots" are production line workers who learn the quality process in a matter of days. They learn to pinpoint problems ranging from fundamental design flaws to a coworker's fatigue from staying up with a newborn all night. One recent result: more logical placement of elevator parts that trims $300 off the cost of each elevator.

David extended the teachings all the way down through the organization. In 1998, he launched an "Ito University" where anyone—not just a bunch of bright young management wannabes—can analyze and share UTC case studies in quality. Lecturers are as likely to be accomplished production line workers as ambitious execs. ACE bulletin boards, documenting every inch of accomplishment on a particular site, became staples in UTC plants.

SOURCE: Excerpted from Diane Brady, "The Unsung CEO," *BusinessWeek*, November 1, 2004, downloaded from Infotrac at http://web5.infotrac.galegroup.com.

Questions

1. Briefly summarize the training methods used by United Technologies Corporation. What corporate goals do these methods seem intended to support?
2. What are the advantages of offering tuition reimbursement to all employees, rather than targeting training to particular job-related skills? What are the disadvantages?
3. What are the advantages of opening Ito University to all employees? What are the disadvantages?

CASE: Learning Is Business at Nokia

Nokia Corporation, the world leader in mobile communications, has over 50,000 employees and net sales of $30 billion. Nokia consists of two business groups: Nokia Networks and Nokia Mobile Phones. The company also includes the separate Nokia Ventures Organization and a corporate research unit, Nokia Research Center. Nokia's goal is to strengthen the company's position as the leading communications and systems provider by offering personalized communication technology and entering new business segments that the company predicts will experience fast growth. As the demand for wireless access to services increases, Nokia plans to lead the development and commercialization of networks and systems required to make wireless content more accessible and rewarding for customers.

The management approach at Nokia, known as the "Nokia way," consists of the Nokia values, its organizational competencies, and its operations and processes used to maintain efficiency. The company has built its current and future strength on the Nokia way. The company has a flat, decentralized structure, and it emphasizes networking, speed, and flexibility in decision making. Nokia's values include customer satisfaction, respect for the individual, achievement, and continuous learning.

Continuous learning provides employees with the opportunity to develop themselves and to stay technologically current. Employees are encouraged to share experiences, take risks, and learn together. Continuous learning goes beyond formal training classes. At Nokia, continuous learning means employees support each other's growth, developing and improving relationships by exchanging and developing ideas. The company uses e-learning to give employees the freedom to choose the best possible time and place for personal development.

Nokia's top management is committed to continuous learning. The business group presidents are "owners" of all global management and leadership programs for senior managers. They provide input into the development of these programs and appoint "godfathers" from their management teams to participate throughout each program and design the program's content. Together with the training and development staff, the godfathers help the learning processes. Most of the programs involve active learning in the form of strategic projects the participants must complete. Top managers review the projects and have authority to take action based on recommendations from the project team.

The value Nokia places on continuous learning translates into opportunities for personal and professional growth. Employees are encouraged to create their own development plan and use available learning methods. Highly skilled employees serve as coaches to help other employees develop and share ideas with one another. Nokia employees have access to a wide variety of training and development opportunities including learning centers and the Learning Marketplace Internet, which has information on all the available learning opportunities such as e-learning and classroom courses. These programs bring together employees from all of Nokia's business groups. Nokia believes that this creates knowledge as employees share their different traditions and experiences.

In addition to formal programs, Nokia emphasizes on-the-job learning through job rotation and challenging work assignments. Managers also have a wide range of opportunities to improve their management and leadership skills. Some of these result from the performance management process, during which employees and their managers set goals and review performance.

Nokia emphasizes that learning should result in improved operations and better business results. So, the company uses a combination of measures to evaluate the results of training. After employees have completed a program, Nokia asks them for their immediate reactions. Other measures include whether the employees have attained the expected level of competence. Nokia's top managers believe that the main benefits of its learning programs are the sharing of knowledge, the reinforcement of continuous learning, and the commitment of employees to the company.

SOURCE: Based on the Nokia Corporation Web site, www.nokia.com, August 22, 2003; and L. Masalin, "Nokia Leads Change through Continuous Learning," *Academy of Management Learning and Education* 2 (2003), pp. 68–72.

Questions

1. Nokia's commitment to continuous learning emphasizes a belief that the organization benefits when employees share their knowledge with each other. Which of the training methods and ideas in this chapter would contribute to this kind of knowledge sharing?

2. How might the company's training department promote the sharing of knowledge?

3. Is there a difference between support for learning (which Nokia expresses) and support for training? Explain.

NOTES

1. E. Barker, "High-Test Education," *Inc.*, July 2001, pp. 81–82.

2. I. L. Goldstein, E. P. Braverman, and H. Goldstein, "Needs Assessment," in *Developing Human Resources*, ed. K. N. Wexley (Washington, DC: Bureau of National Affairs, 1991), pp. 5-35–5-75.

3. K. Ellis, "Smarter, Faster, Better," *Training*, April 2003, pp. 27–31.

4. J. Z. Rouillier and I. L. Goldstein, "Determinants of the Climate for Transfer of Training" (presented at Society of Industrial/Organizational Psychology meetings, St. Louis, MO, 1991); J. S. Russell, J. R. Terborg, and M. L. Powers, "Organizational Performance and Organizational Level Training and Support," *Personnel Psychology* 38 (1985), pp. 849–63; H. Baumgartel, G. J. Sullivan, and L. E. Dunn, "How Organizational Climate and Personality Affect the Payoff from Advanced Management Training Sessions," *Kansas Business Review* 5 (1978), pp. 1–10.

5. R. A. Noe, "Trainees' Attributes and Attitudes: Neglected Influences on Training Effectiveness," *Academy of Management Review* 11 (1986), pp. 736–49; T. T. Baldwin, R. T. Magjuka, and B. T. Loher, "The Perils of Participation: Effects of Choice on Trainee Motivation and Learning," *Personnel Psychology* 44 (1991), pp. 51–66; S. I. Tannenbaum, J. E. Mathieu, E. Salas, and J. A. Cannon-Bowers, "Meeting Trainees' Expectations: The Influence of Training Fulfillment on the Development of Commitment, Self-Efficacy, and Motivation," *Journal of Applied Psychology* 76 (1991), pp. 759–69.

6. L. H. Peters, E. J. O'Connor, and J. R. Eulberg, "Situational Constraints: Sources, Consequences, and Future Considerations," in *Research in Personnel and Human Resource Management*, ed. K. M. Rowland and G. R. Ferris (Greenwich, CT: JAI Press, 1985), vol. 3, pp. 79–114; E. J. O'Connor, L. H. Peters, A. Pooyan, J. Weekley, B. Frank, and B. Erenkranz, "Situational Constraints' Effects on Performance, Affective Reactions, and Turnover: A Field Replication and Extension," *Journal of Applied Psychology* 69 (1984), pp. 663–72; D. J. Cohen, "What Motivates Trainees?" *Training and Development Journal*, November 1990, pp. 91–93; Russell, Terborg, and Powers, "Organizational Performance."

7. J. B. Tracey, S. I. Trannenbaum, and M. J. Kavanaugh, "Applying Trade Skills on the Job: The Importance of the Work Environment," *Journal of Applied Psychology* 80 (1995), pp. 239–52; P. E. Tesluk, J. L. Farr, J. E. Mathieu, and R. J. Vance, "Generalization of Employee Involvement Training to the Job Setting: Individuals and Situational Effects," *Personnel Psychology* 48 (1995), pp. 607–32; J. K. Ford, M. A. Quinones, D. J. Sego, and J. S. Sorra, "Factors Affecting the Opportunity to Perform Trained Tasks on the Job," *Personnel Psychology* 45 (1992), pp. 511–27.

8. B. Mager, *Preparing Instructional Objectives*, 2nd ed. (Belmont, CA: Lake, 1984); B. J. Smith and B. L. Delahaye, *How to Be an Effective Trainer*, 2nd ed. (New York: Wiley, 1987).

9. J. Bailey, "Community Colleges Can Help Small Firms with Job Training," *The Wall Street Journal Online*, http://online.wsj.com, February 19, 2002.

10. R. Zemke and J. Armstrong, "How Long Does It Take? (The Sequel)," *Training*, May 1997, pp. 69–79.

11. C. Lee, "Who Gets Trained in What?" *Training*, October 1991, pp. 47–59; W. Hannum, *The Application of Emerging Training Technology* (San Diego, CA: University Associates, 1990); B. Filipczak, "Make Room for Training," *Training*, October 1991, pp. 76–82; A. P. Carnevale, L. J. Gainer, and A. S. Meltzer, *Workplace Basics Training Manual* (San Francisco: Jossey-Bass, 1990).

12. G. Yohe, "The E-Collaborators," *Human Resource Executive*, August 2002, pp. 41–44.

13. S. Alexander, "Reducing the Learning Burden," *Training*, September 2002, pp. 32–34.

14. T. Skylar, "When Training Collides with a 35-Ton Truck," *Training*, March 1996, pp. 32–38.

15. G. Yohe, "The Best of Both?" *Human Resource Executive*, March 6, 2002, pp. 35, 38–39.

16. E. Hollis, "Shoney's Workforce: Development on the Side," *Chief Learning Officer*, March 2003, pp. 32–34.

17. G. Stevens and E. Stevens, "The Truth about EPSS," *Training and Development* 50 (1996), pp. 59–61.

18. "In Your Face EPSSs," *Training*, April 1996, pp. 101–2.

19. Olivia Crosby, "Apprenticeships: Career Training, Credentials—and a Paycheck in Your Pocket," *Occu-*

pational Outlook Quarterly, Summer 2002, downloaded from FindArticles at www.findarticles.com.

20. K. Ellis, "More than an Assembly Line," *Training*, January 2002, p. 33.
21. Bailey, "Community College Can Help Small Firms with Job Training."
22. W. J. Rothwell and H. C. Kanzanas, "Planned OJT Is Productive OJT," *Training and Development Journal*, October 1990, pp. 53–56.
23. B. Filipczak, "Who Owns Your OJT?" *Training*, December 1996, pp. 44–49.
24. M. Pramik, "Installers Learn on Practice Dwellings," *Columbus Dispatch*, February 7, 2003, p. F1.
25. N. Adams, "Lessons from the Virtual World," *Training*, June 1995, pp. 45–48.
26. Ibid.
27. "Business War Games," *Training*, December 2002, p. 18.
28. G. P. Latham and L. M. Saari, "Application of Social Learning Theory to Training Supervisors through Behavior Modeling," *Journal of Applied Psychology* 64 (1979), pp. 239–46.
29. D. Brown and D. Harvey, *An Experiential Approach to Organizational Development* (Englewood Cliffs, NJ: Prentice Hall, 2000); and J. Schettler, "Learning by Doing," *Training*, April 2002, pp. 38–43.
30. Kim Willsher, "French Firms Drop Bungee for Bouillon," *Guardian Unlimited*, February 25, 2005, www.guardian.co.uk.
31. Schettler, "Learning by Doing."
32. C. Clements, R. J. Wagner, C. C. Roland, "The Ins and Outs of Experiential Training," *Training and Development*, February 1995, pp. 52–56.
33. P. Froiland, "Action Learning," *Training*, January 1994, pp. 27–34.
34. Ibid.
35. "A Team Effort," *Training*, September 2002, p. 18.
36. C. E. Schneier, "Training and Development Programs: What Learning Theory and Research Have to Offer," *Personnel Journal*, April 1974, pp. 288–93; M. Knowles, "Adult Learning," in *Training and Development Handbook*, 3rd ed., ed. R. L. Craig (New York: McGraw-Hill, 1987), pp. 168–79; R. Zemke and S. Zemke, "30 Things We Know for Sure about Adult Learning," *Training*, June 1981, pp. 45–52; B. J. Smith and B. L. Delahaye, *How to Be an Effective Trainer*, 2nd ed. (New York: Wiley, 1987).
37. K. A. Smith-Jentsch, F. G. Jentsch, S. C. Payne, and E. Salas, "Can Pretraining Experiences Explain Individual Differences in Learning?" *Journal of Applied Psychology* 81 (1996), pp. 110–16.
38. W. McGehee and P. W. Thayer, *Training in Business and Industry* (New York: Wiley, 1961).
39. R. M. Gagne and K. L. Medsker, *The Condition of Learning* (Fort Worth, TX: Harcourt-Brace, 1996).
40. J. C. Naylor and G. D. Briggs, "The Effects of Task Complexity and Task Organization on the Relative Efficiency of Part and Whole Training Methods," *Journal of Experimental Psychology* 65 (1963), pp. 217–24.
41. K. Mantyla, *Blended E-Learning* (Alexandria, VA: ASTD, 2001).
42. B. Gerber, "Does Your Training Make a Difference? Prove It!" *Training*, March 1995, pp. 27–34.
43. M. R. Louis, "Surprise and Sense Making: What Newcomers Experience in Entering Unfamiliar Organizational Settings," *Administrative Science Quarterly* 25 (1980), pp. 226–51.
44. M. Hammers, "Quashing Quick Quits," *Workforce*, May 2003, p. 50.
45. C. Joinson, "Hit the Floor Running, Start the Cart . . . and Other Neat Ways to Train New Employees," *HR Magazine* 6, no. 1 (Winter 2001), downloaded from the Society for Human Resource Management Web site, www.shrm.org.
46. S. M. Paskoff, "Ending the Workplace Diversity Wars," *Training*, August 1996, pp. 43–47; H. B. Karp and N. Sutton, "Where Diversity Training Goes Wrong," *Training*, July 1993, pp. 30–34.
47. Paskoff, "Ending the Workplace Diversity Wars."
48. L. Lavelle, "For UPS Managers, a School of Hard Knocks," *BusinessWeek*, July 22, 2002, pp. 58–59; and M. Berkley, *UPS Community Internship Program (CIP) Fact Sheet* (Atlanta, GA: United Parcel Service, 2003).
49. S. Rynes and B. Rosen, "A Field Study of Factors Affecting the Adoption and Perceived Success of Diversity Training," *Personnel Psychology* 48 (1995), pp. 247–70.
50. S. Rynes and B. Rosen, "What Makes Diversity Programs Work?" *HR Magazine*, October 1994, pp. 67–73; Rynes and Rosen, "A Field Survey of Factors Affecting the Adoption and Perceived Success of Diversity Training"; J. Gordon, "Different from What? Diversity as a Performance Issue," *Training*, May 1995, pp. 25–33; T. Kochan, K. Bezrukova, R. Ely, S. Jackson, A. Joshi, K. Jehn, J. Leonard, D. Levine, and D. Thomas, "The Effects of Diversity on Business Performance: Report of the Diversity Research Network," *Human Resource Management* 42 (2003), pp. 8–21; and F. Hansen, "Diversity's Business Case Just Doesn't Add Up," *Workforce*, June 2003, pp. 29–32.

If you are using the Manager's Hot Seat DVD with this book, consider finishing case 15: Working in Teams: Cross-Functional Dysfunction, for this chapter.

ASSESSING PERFORMANCE AND DEVELOPING EMPLOYEES

MANAGING EMPLOYEES' PERFORMANCE

❧ INTRODUCTION

When Synergy, a Philadelphia-based software company, was a start-up, its seven employees would regularly meet to discuss performance issues. Sitting around a table, they would informally discuss what changes to make in order to help the company meet its goals. Now that the company has more than 250 employees, that approach to improving performance is no longer practical. Synergy has developed a formal process for giving each employee feedback about his or her performance. That process includes a rating system used by an employee's manager, colleagues, and employees, as well as employees in other departments, to score the employee's performance four times a year. Employees also rate their own performance. This system lets employees compare their impressions of their work with other people's impressions. The regular feedback helps employees improve by focusing on what is important for the success of their careers and for Synergy as a whole.[1]

Rating employees' performance, as Synergy does, is a central part of performance management. **Performance management** is the process through which managers ensure that employees' activities and outputs contribute to the organization's goals. This process requires knowing what activities and outputs are desired, observing whether they occur, and providing feedback to help employees meet expectations. In the course of providing feedback, managers and employees may identify performance problems and establish ways to resolve those problems.

In this chapter we examine a variety of approaches to performance management. We begin by describing the activities involved in managing performance, then discuss the purpose of carrying out this process. Next, we discuss specific approaches to performance management, including the strengths and weaknesses of each approach. We also look at various sources of performance information. The next section explores the kinds of errors that commonly occur during the assessment of performance, as well as ways to reduce those errors. Then we describe ways of giving performance feedback effectively and intervening when performance must improve. Finally, we summarize legal and ethical issues affecting performance management.

performance management
The process through which managers ensure that employees' activities and outputs contribute to the organization's goals.

THE PROCESS OF PERFORMANCE MANAGEMENT

Traditional approaches to management have viewed **performance appraisal,** or the measurement of specified areas of an employee's performance, as the primary means of performance management. In the traditional approaches, the human resource department is responsible for setting up and managing a performance appraisal system. Managers conduct performance appraisals as one of their administrative duties. They tend to view the appraisals as a yearly ritual in which they quickly fill out forms and present the information to their employees, one by one. Appraisals include negative information (areas needing improvement), so the meetings for discussing performance appraisals tend to be uncomfortable for managers and employees alike. Often, managers feel they do not know how to evaluate performance effectively, and employees feel they are excluded from the process and that their contributions are not recognized.[2] The left side of Table 8.1 lists some of the criticisms that have been leveled against this style of performance management.

performance appraisal
The measurement of specified areas of an employee's performance.

As indicated on the right side of Table 8.1, these problems can be solved through a more effective approach to performance management. Appraising performance need not cause the problems listed in the table. If done correctly, the process can provide valuable benefits to employees and the organization alike. For example, a performance

PROBLEM	SOLUTION
Discourages teamwork	Make collaboration a criterion on which employees will be evaluated.
Evaluators are inconsistent or use different criterion and standards	Provide training for managers; have the HR department look for patterns on appraisals that suggest bias or over- or underevaluation.
Only valuable for very good or very poor employees	Evaluate specific behaviors or results to show specifically what employees need to improve.
Encourages employees to achieve short-term goals	Include both long-term and short-term goals in the appraisal process.
Manager has complete power over the employee	Managers should be appraised for how they appraise their employees.
Too subjective	Evaluate specific behavior or results.
Produces emotional anguish	Focus on behavior; do not criticize employees; conduct appraisal on time.

TABLE 8.1

Performance Appraisal Problems and Performance Management Solutions

SOURCE: Based on J. A. Siegel, "86 Your Appraisal Process?" *HR Magazine,* October 2000, pp. 199–202.

management system can tell top performers that they are valued, encourage communication between managers and their employees, establish uniform standards for evaluating employees, and help the organization identify its strongest and weakest performers. According to the Hay Group, companies on its Global Most Admired list, which it prepares for *Fortune* magazine, have chief executive officers who understand that performance measurement helps the organization motivate people and link performance to rewards.[3] Many of these executives report that performance measurement encourages employees to cooperate and helps the company focus on smooth operations, customer loyalty, and employee development.

LO1
Identify the activities involved in performance management.

To meet these objectives, performance management extends beyond mere appraisals to include several activities. As shown in Figure 8.1, these are defining performance, measuring performance, and feeding back performance information. First, the organization specifies which aspects of performance are relevant to the organization. These decisions are based on the job analysis, described in Chapter 4. Next, the organization measures the relevant aspects of performance by conducting performance appraisals. Finally, through performance feedback sessions, managers give employees information about their performance so they can adjust their behavior to meet the organization's goals. When there are performance problems, the feedback session should include efforts to identify and resolve the underlying problems. In addition, performance feedback can come through the organization's rewards, as described in Chapter 12.

Using this performance management process in place of the traditional performance appraisal routine helps managers and employees focus on the organization's goals. Unfortunately, as described in the "Did You Know . . . ?" box, this is an area in which many organizations need to improve.

Computer software is available to help managers at various stages of performance management. Software can help managers customize performance measurement forms. The manager uses the software to establish a set of performance standards for each job. The manager rates each employee according to the predetermined standards, and the software provides a report that compares the employee's performance to the standards and identifies the employee's strengths and weaknesses. Other software offers help with diagnosing performance problems. This type of software asks questions—for example, Does the employee work under time pressure? The answers suggest reasons for performance problems and ways the manager can help the employee improve.

Figure 8.1
Stages of the Performance Management Process

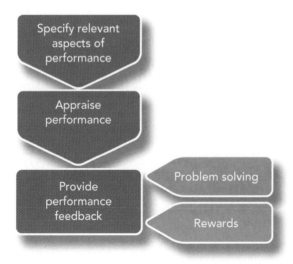

FEW COMPANIES KNOW BUSINESS IMPACT OF PERFORMANCE MANAGEMENT

Almost one-third of companies don't evaluate their performance management systems at all, and many that do evaluate don't consider the effect of the system on their bottom line. Hewitt Associates, which provides human resources outsourcing and consulting services, conducted a survey of major U.S. companies. It found that many evaluations measure "success" of a performance plan in terms of whether paperwork is turned in on time or employees are satisfied with the system.

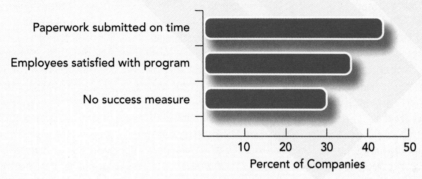

Measure of Performance Management System's Success

SOURCE: Hewitt Associates, "Hewitt Study Reveals Companies Measure Employees, Not Themselves, with Performance Plans," news release, April 6, 2005, www.hewitt.com.

⬙ PURPOSES OF PERFORMANCE MANAGEMENT

LO2
Discuss the purposes of performance management systems.

Organizations establish performance management systems to meet three broad purposes: strategic, administrative, and developmental. *Strategic purpose* means effective performance management helps the organization achieve its business objectives. It does this by helping to link employees' behavior with the organization's goals. Performance management starts with defining what the organization expects from each employee. It measures each employee's performance to identify where those expectations are and are not being met. This enables the organization to take corrective action, such as training, incentives, or discipline. Performance management can achieve its strategic purpose only when measurements are truly linked to the organization's goals and when the goals and feedback about performance are communicated to employees.

The strategic priorities of aerospace and electronics giant Lockheed Martin include meeting ethical standards by establishing what those standards are, making sure employees know them, and enforcing them. Performance management supports that strategy. Each year, every Lockheed Martin senior manager is expected to identify an employee who has set a good example of ethical behavior and to recommend that person for the company's Chairman's Award. The company selects one of the nominated employees to receive the award for meeting "the highest standards for integrity and business conduct," which is presented by the chairman at a special ceremony. Success

HR HOW TO

SETTING UP A PERFORMANCE MANAGEMENT SYSTEM TO MEET GOALS

No single performance management system is ideal for all organizations. But the system is most likely to fulfill its purposes if it follows several guidelines.

The system should support the organization's values and beliefs. For example, if employee involvement is an important value, then performance measurement should include self- or peer appraisals.

The organization's top management must show that it supports the system. In most companies, senior management is involved in designing and implementing the performance management system. Their positive involvement encourages others in the organization to take responsibility for ensuring that evaluations are completed on time and that the system is used consistently.

Those planning the system should identify the most important measures of company per-

formance. These should measure how well the company is doing relative to its business goals and strategy. Goals for individual employees should support the overall company goals.

Job descriptions should be linked to the performance management system. This helps employees see that the activities they are supposed to do, the goals for which they are rewarded, and the goals of the organization are all related.

Verify that the performance management system assesses employees fairly and objectively based on clearly understood standards of performance or in terms of their contribution relative to that of other employees. Employees should understand what constitutes poor, good, and excellent performance.

Managers must be trained how to use the performance measurement system and how to give performance feedback

daily, not just in annual reviews. For employees, training programs should be related to the skills and behaviors necessary for meeting performance goals.

The performance management system should be linked to financial rewards. For this connection to work as intended, the organization must communicate with employees about how the program works.

The performance management system needs to be evaluated. The organization should verify that it meets company goals. Based on the evaluation, the organization should adjust the system.

SOURCE: Based on L. Weatherly, *Performance Management: Getting It Right from the Start* (Alexandria, VA: Society for Human Resource Management, 2004); and E. Lawler and M. McDermott, "Current Performance Management Practices," *World at Work Journal* 12, no. 2 (2003), pp. 49–60.

in finding an ethical employee to nominate is one of the outcomes measured on the managers' performance evaluations.[4]

The *administrative purpose* of a performance management system refers to the ways in which organizations use the system to provide information for day-to-day decisions about salary, benefits, and recognition programs. Performance management can also support decision making related to employee retention, termination for poor behavior, and hiring or layoffs. Because performance management supports these administrative decisions, the information in a performance appraisal can have a great impact on the future of individual employees. Managers recognize this, which is the reason they may feel uncomfortable conducting performance appraisals when the appraisal information is negative and, therefore, likely to lead to a layoff, disappointing pay increase, or other negative outcome.

Finally, performance management has a *developmental purpose*, meaning that it serves as a basis for developing employees' knowledge and skills. Even employees who are meeting expectations can become more valuable when they hear and discuss performance feedback. Effective performance feedback makes employees aware of their strengths and of the areas in which they can improve. Discussing areas in which employees fall short can help the employees and their manager uncover the source of problems and identify steps for improvement. Although discussing weaknesses may feel uncomfortable, it is necessary when performance management has a developmental purpose.

The "HR How To" box recommends ways to develop a performance management system that can meet its strategic, administrative, and developmental purposes.

♦ CRITERIA FOR EFFECTIVE PERFORMANCE MANAGEMENT

LO3
Define five criteria for measuring the effectiveness of a performance management system.

In Chapter 6, we saw that there are many ways to predict performance of a job candidate. Similarly, there are many ways to measure the performance of an employee. For performance management to achieve its goals, its methods for measuring performance must be good. Selecting these measures is a critical part of planning a performance management system. Criteria that determine the effectiveness of performance measures include each measure's fit with the organization's strategy, its validity, its reliability, the degree to which it is acceptable to the organization, and the extent to which it gives employees specific feedback. These criteria are summarized in Figure 8.2.

A performance management system should aim at achieving employee behavior and attitudes that support the organization's strategy, goals, and culture. If a company emphasizes customer service, then its performance management system should define the kinds of behavior that contribute to good customer service. Performance appraisals should measure whether employees are engaging in those behaviors. Feedback should help employees improve in those areas. When an organization's strategy changes, human resource personnel should help managers assess how the performance management system should change to serve the new strategy.

As we discussed in Chapter 6, *validity* is the extent to which a measurement tool actually measures what it is intended to measure. In the case of performance appraisal,

Figure 8.2

Criteria for Effective Performance Measures

validity refers to whether the appraisal measures all the relevant aspects of performance and omits irrelevant aspects of performance. Figure 8.3 shows two sets of information. The circle on the left represents all the information in a performance appraisal; the circle on the right represents all relevant measures of job performance. The overlap of the circles contains the valid information. Information that is gathered but irrelevant is "contamination." Comparing salespeople based on how many calls they make to customers could be a contaminated measure. Making a lot of calls does not necessarily improve sales or customer satisfaction, unless every salesperson makes only well-planned calls. Information that is not gathered but is relevant represents a deficiency of the performance measure. For example, suppose a company measures whether employees have good attendance records but not whether they work efficiently. This limited performance appraisal is unlikely to provide a full picture of employees' contribution to the company. Performance measures should minimize both contamination and deficiency.

With regard to a performance measure, reliability describes the consistency of the results that the performance measure will deliver. *Interrater reliability* is consistency of results when more than one person measures performance. Simply asking a supervisor to rate an employee's performance on a scale of 1 to 5 would likely have low interrater reliability; the rating will differ depending on who is scoring the employees. *Test-retest reliability* refers to consistency of results over time. If a performance measure lacks test-retest reliability, determining whether an employee's performance has truly changed over time will be impossible.

Whether or not a measure is valid and reliable, it must meet the practical standard of being acceptable to the people who use it. For example, the people who use a performance measure must believe that it is not too time-consuming. Likewise, if employees believe the measure is unfair, they will not use the feedback as a basis for improving their performance.

Finally, a performance measure should specifically tell employees what is expected of them and how they can meet those expectations. Being specific helps performance management meet the goals of supporting strategy and developing employees. If a measure does not specify what an employee must do to help the organization achieve its goals, it does not support the strategy. If the measure fails to point out employees' performance problems, they will not know how to improve.

The "Best Practices" box describes how the performance management system at Children's Hospital in Boston meets some of these criteria of effective performance measures. The system supports the company's strategy, is valid and acceptable, and delivers specific goals and feedback.

Figure 8.3

Contamination and Deficiency of a Job Performance Measure

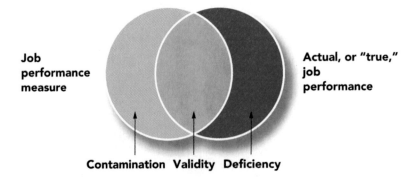

| 1 line short |

CHILDREN'S HOSPITAL MEASURES TEAM PERFORMANCE

Children's Hospital in Boston was determined to improve cash flow and shorten the billing cycle (the time to receive payment of a bill). The hospital's accounts receivable department was taking more than 100 days to receive payment. The hospital wanted to show employees the relationship between quarterly cash flow and the number of days a bill awaited payment. To do this, the hospital decided to evaluate and reward team performance.

Managers determine who will be rewarded and on what basis, and they have to communicate the plan and its benefits to employees. Team members have a set of three goals. In order of difficulty from least to greatest, they are threshold, target, and optimal goals. These categories are defined in terms of how long a bill remains in accounts receivable. Teams receive a quarterly payment of $500 for meeting the threshold goal, $1,000 for meeting the target goal, or $1,500 for meeting the optimal goal. The payment is divided among the team members according to the number of scheduled hours they worked. To earn the incentive, team members must work together, bill by bill, to process the paperwork faster.

To make sure employees understood the plan, the hospital held a series of meetings that presented information about what the dollar value is of each day a bill spends in accounts receivable and how the hospital is affected by poor cash flow. After employees understood how their work affects cash flow and how their efforts could improve it, they began working as a team. Employees started to take the initiative to follow up with patients, insurers, and medical records personnel. If any team members were not carrying their weight, peer pressure persuaded them to contribute more. Employees receive weekly progress reports so they can monitor their performance.

The teamwork has netted positive results. At the end of the program's first year, employees reduced the average number of days a bill spent in accounts receivable to just under 76. The plan also helped the hospital recruit and retain employees for its accounts payable team.

SOURCE: Based on D. Cadrain, "Put Success in Sight," *HR Magazine*, May 2003, pp. 85–92.

METHODS FOR MEASURING PERFORMANCE

Organizations have developed a wide variety of methods for measuring performance. Some methods rank each employee to compare employees' performance. Other methods break down the evaluation into ratings of individual attributes, behaviors, or results. Many organizations use a measurement system that includes a variety of the preceding measures, as in the case of applying total quality management to performance management. Table 8.2 compares these methods in terms of our criteria for effective performance management.

LO4
Compare the major methods for measuring performance.

Making Comparisons

The performance appraisal method may require the rater to compare one individual's performance with that of others. This method involves some form of ranking, in which some employees are best, some are average, and others are worst. The usual

TABLE 8.2

Basic Approaches to Performance Measurement

APPROACH	CRITERIA				
	FIT WITH STRATEGY	**VALIDITY**	**RELIABILITY**	**ACCEPTABILITY**	**SPECIFICITY**
Comparative	Poor, unless manager takes time to make link	Can be high if ratings are done carefully	Depends on rater, but usually no measure of agreement used	Moderate; easy to develop and use but resistant to normative standard	Very low
Attribute	Usually low; requires manager to make link	Usually low; can be fine if developed carefully	Usually low; can be improved by specific definitions of attributes	High; easy to develop and use	Very low
Behavioral	Can be quite high	Usually high; minimizes contamination and deficiency	Usually high	Moderate; difficult to develop, but accepted well for use	Very high
Results	Very high	Usually high; can be both contaminated and deficient	High; main problem can be test–retest—depends on timing of measure	High; usually developed with input from those to be evaluated	High regarding results, but low regarding behaviors necessary to achieve them
Quality	Very high	High, but can be both contaminated and deficient	High	High; usually developed with input from those to be evaluated	High regarding results, but low regarding behaviors necessary to achieve them

techniques for making comparisons are simple ranking, forced distribution, and paired comparison.

Simple ranking requires managers to rank employees in their group from the highest performer to the poorest performer. In a variation of this approach, *alternation ranking*, the manager works from a list of employees. First, the manager decides which employee is best and crosses that person's name off the list. From the remaining names, the manager selects the worst employee and crosses off that name. The process continues with the manager selecting the second best, second worst, third best, and so on until all the employees have been ranked. The major downside of ranking involves validity. To state a performance measure as broadly as "best" or "worst" doesn't define what exactly is good or bad about the person's contribution to the organization. Ranking therefore raises questions about fairness.

Another way to compare employees' performance is with the **forced-distribution method.** This type of performance measurement assigns a certain percentage of employees to each category in a set of categories. For example, the organization might establish the following percentages and categories:

simple ranking
Method of performance measurement that requires managers to rank employees in their group from the highest performer to the poorest performer.

- Exceptional—5 percent
- Exceeds standards—25 percent
- Meets standards—55 percent
- Room for improvement—10 percent
- Not acceptable—5 percent

The manager completing the performance appraisal would rate 5 percent of his or her employees as exceptional, 25 percent as exceeding standards, and so on. A forced-distribution approach works best if the members of a group really do vary this much in terms of their performance. It overcomes the temptation to rate everyone high in order to avoid conflict. However, a manager who does very well at selecting, motivating, and training employees will have a group of high performers. This manager would have difficulty assigning employees to the bottom categories. In that situation, saying that some employees require improvement or are "not acceptable" not only will be inaccurate, but will hurt morale.

Another variation on rankings is the **paired-comparison method.** This approach involves comparing each employee with each other employee to establish rankings. Suppose a manager has five employees, Allen, Barbara, Caitlin, David, and Edgar. The manager compares Allen's performance to Barbara's and assigns one point to whichever employer is the higher performer. Then the manager compares Allen's performance to Caitlin's, then to David's, and finally to Edgar's. The manager repeats this process with Barbara, comparing her performance to Caitlin's, David's, and Edgar's. When the manager has compared every pair of employees, the manager counts the number of points for each employee. The employee with the most points is considered the top-ranked employee. Clearly, this method is time-consuming if a group has more than a handful of employees. For a group of 15, the manager must make 105 comparisons.

In spite of the drawbacks, ranking employees offers some benefits. It counteracts the tendency to avoid controversy by rating everyone favorably or near the center of the scale. Also, if some managers tend to evaluate behavior more strictly (or more leniently) than others, a ranking system can erase that tendency from performance scores. Therefore, ranking systems can be useful for supporting decisions about how to distribute pay raises or layoffs. Some ranking systems are easy to use, which makes them acceptable to the managers who use them. A major drawback of rankings is that they often are not linked to the organization's goals. Also, a simple ranking system leaves the basis for the ranking open to interpretation. In that case, the rankings are not helpful for employee development and may hurt morale or result in legal challenges.

Rating Individuals

Instead of focusing on arranging a group of employees from best to worst, performance measurement can look at each employee's performance relative to a uniform set of standards. The measurement may evaluate employees in terms of attributes (characteristics or traits) believed desirable. Or the measurements may identify whether employees have *behaved* in desirable ways, such as closing sales or completing assignments. For both approaches, the performance management system must identify the desired attributes or behaviors, then provide a form on which the manager can rate the employee in terms of those attributes or behaviors. Typically, the form includes a rating scale, such as a scale from 1 to 5, where 1 is the worst performance and 5 is the best.

Rating Attributes

graphic rating scale
Method of performance measurement that lists traits and provides a rating scale for each trait; the employer uses the scale to indicate the extent to which an employee displays each trait.

The most widely used method for rating attributes is the **graphic rating scale.** This method lists traits and provides a rating scale for each trait. The employer uses the scale to indicate the extent to which the employee being rated displays the traits. The rating scale may provide points to circle (as on a scale going from 1 for poor to 5 for excellent), or it may provide a line representing a range of scores, with the manager marking a place along the line. Figure 8.4 shows an example of a graphic rating scale that uses a set of ratings from 1 to 5. A drawback of this approach is that it leaves to the particular manager the decisions about what is "excellent knowledge" or "commendable judgment" or "poor interpersonal skills." The result is low reliability, because managers are likely to arrive at different judgments.

mixed-standard scales
Method of performance measurement that uses several statements describing each trait to produce a final score for that trait.

To get around this problem, some organizations use **mixed-standard scales,** which use several statements describing each trait to produce a final score for that trait. The manager scores the employee in terms of how the employee compares to each statement. Consider the sample mixed-standard scale in Figure 8.5. To create this scale, the organization determined that the relevant traits are initiative, intelligence, and relations with others. For each trait, sentences were written to describe a person having a high level of that trait, a medium level, and a low level. The sentences for the traits were rearranged so that the nine statements about the three traits are mixed together. The manager who uses this scale reads each sentence, then indicates whether the employee performs above (+), at (0), or below (−) the level described. The key in the middle section of Figure 8.5 tells how to use the pluses, zeros, and minuses to score performance. Someone who excels at every level of performance (pluses for high, medium, and low performance) receives a score of 7 for that trait. Someone who fails to live up to every description of performance (minuses for high, medium, and low) receives a score of 1 for that trait. The bottom of Figure 8.5 calculates the scores for the ratings used in this example.

Figure 8.4

Example of a Graphic Rating Scale

The following areas of performance are significant to most positions. Indicate your assessment of performance on each dimension by circling the appropriate rating.

PERFORMANCE DIMENSION	RATING				
	DISTINGUISHED	EXCELLENT	COMMENDABLE	ADEQUATE	POOR
Knowledge	5	4	3	2	1
Communication	5	4	3	2	1
Judgment	5	4	3	2	1
Managerial skill	5	4	3	2	1
Quality performance	5	4	3	2	1
Teamwork	5	4	3	2	1
Interpersonal skills	5	4	3	2	1
Initiative	5	4	3	2	1
Creativity	5	4	3	2	1
Problem solving	5	4	3	2	1

Figure 8.5

Example of a Mixed-Standard Scale

Three traits being assessed:	Levels of performance in statements:
Initiative (INTV)	High (H)
Intelligence (INTG)	Medium (M)
Relations with others (RWO)	Low (L)

Instructions: Please indicate next to each statement whether the employee's performance is above (+), equal to (0), or below (–) the statement.

INTV	H	1. This employee is a real self-starter. The employee always takes the initiative and his/her superior never has to prod this individual.	+
INTG	M	2. While perhaps this employee is not a genius, s/he is a lot more intelligent than many people I know.	+
RWO	L	3. This employee has a tendency to get into unnecessary conflicts with other people.	0
INTV	M	4. While generally this employee shows initiative, occasionally his/her superior must prod him/her to complete work.	+
INTG	L	5. Although this employee is slower than some in understanding things, and may take a bit longer in learning new things, s/he is of average intelligence.	+
RWO	H	6. This employee is on good terms with everyone. S/he can get along with people even when s/he does not agree with them.	–
INTV	L	7. This employee has a bit of a tendency to sit around and wait for directions.	+
INTG	H	8. This employee is extremely intelligent, and s/he learns very rapidly.	–
RWO	M	9. This employee gets along with most people. Only very occasionally does s/he have conflicts with others on the job, and these are likely to be minor.	–

Scoring Key:

STATEMENTS			SCORE
HIGH	MEDIUM	LOW	
+	+	+	7
0	+	+	6
–	+	+	5
–	0	+	4
–	–	+	3
–	–	0	2
–	–	–	1

Example score from preceding ratings:

	STATEMENTS			SCORE
	HIGH	MEDIUM	LOW	
Initiative	+	+	+	7
Intelligence	0	+	+	6
Relations with others	–	–	0	2

Rating attributes is the most popular way to measure performance in organizations. In general, attribute-based performance methods are easy to develop and can be applied to a wide variety of jobs and organizations. If the organization is careful to identify which attributes are associated with high performance, and to define them carefully on the appraisal form, these methods can be reliable and valid. However, appraisal forms

An employee's performance measurement differs from job to job. For example, a car dealer's performance is measured by the dollar amount of sales, the number of new customers and customer satisfaction surveys. How would the performance measurements of a car dealer differ from those of a company CEO?

often fail to meet this standard. In addition, measurement of attributes is rarely linked to the organization's strategy. Furthermore, employees tend perhaps rightly to be defensive about receiving a mere numerical rating on some attribute. How would you feel if you were told you scored 2 on a 5-point scale of initiative or communication skill? The number might seem arbitrary, and it doesn't tell you how to improve.

Rating Behaviors

One way to overcome the drawbacks of rating attributes is to measure employees' behavior. To rate behaviors, the organization begins by defining which behaviors are associated with success on the job. Which kinds of employee behavior help the organization achieve its goals? The appraisal form asks the manager to rate an employee in terms of each of the identified behaviors.

One way to rate behaviors is with the **critical-incident method.** This approach requires managers to keep a record of specific examples of the employee acting in ways that are either effective or ineffective. Here's an example of a critical incident in the performance evaluation of an appliance repairperson:

> A customer called in about a refrigerator that was not cooling and was making a clicking noise every few minutes. The technician prediagnosed the cause of the problem and checked his truck for the necessary parts. When he found he did not have them, he checked the parts out from inventory so that the customer's refrigerator would be repaired on his first visit and the customer would be satisfied promptly.

This incident provides evidence of the employee's knowledge of refrigerator repair and concern for efficiency and customer satisfaction. Evaluating performance in this specific way gives employees feedback about what they do well and what they do poorly. The manager can also relate the incidents to how the employee is helping the company achieve its goals. Keeping a daily or weekly log of critical incidents requires significant effort, however, and managers may resist this requirement. Also, critical incidents may be unique, so they may not support comparisons among employees.

A **behaviorally anchored rating scale (BARS)** builds on the critical-incidents approach. The BARS method is intended to define performance dimensions specifically, using statements of behavior that describe different levels of performance.[5] (The statements are "anchors" of the performance levels.) The scale in Figure 8.6 shows various performance levels for the behavior of "preparing for duty." The statement at the top (rating 7) describes the highest level of preparing for duty. The statement at the bottom describes behavior associated with poor performance. These statements are based on data about past performance. The organization gathers many critical incidents representing effective and ineffective performance, then classifies them from most to least effective.

critical-incident method
Method of performance measurement based on managers' records of specific examples of the employee acting in ways that are either effective or ineffective.

behaviorally anchored rating scale (BARS)
Method of performance measurement that rates behavior in terms of a scale showing specific statements of behavior that describe different levels of performance.

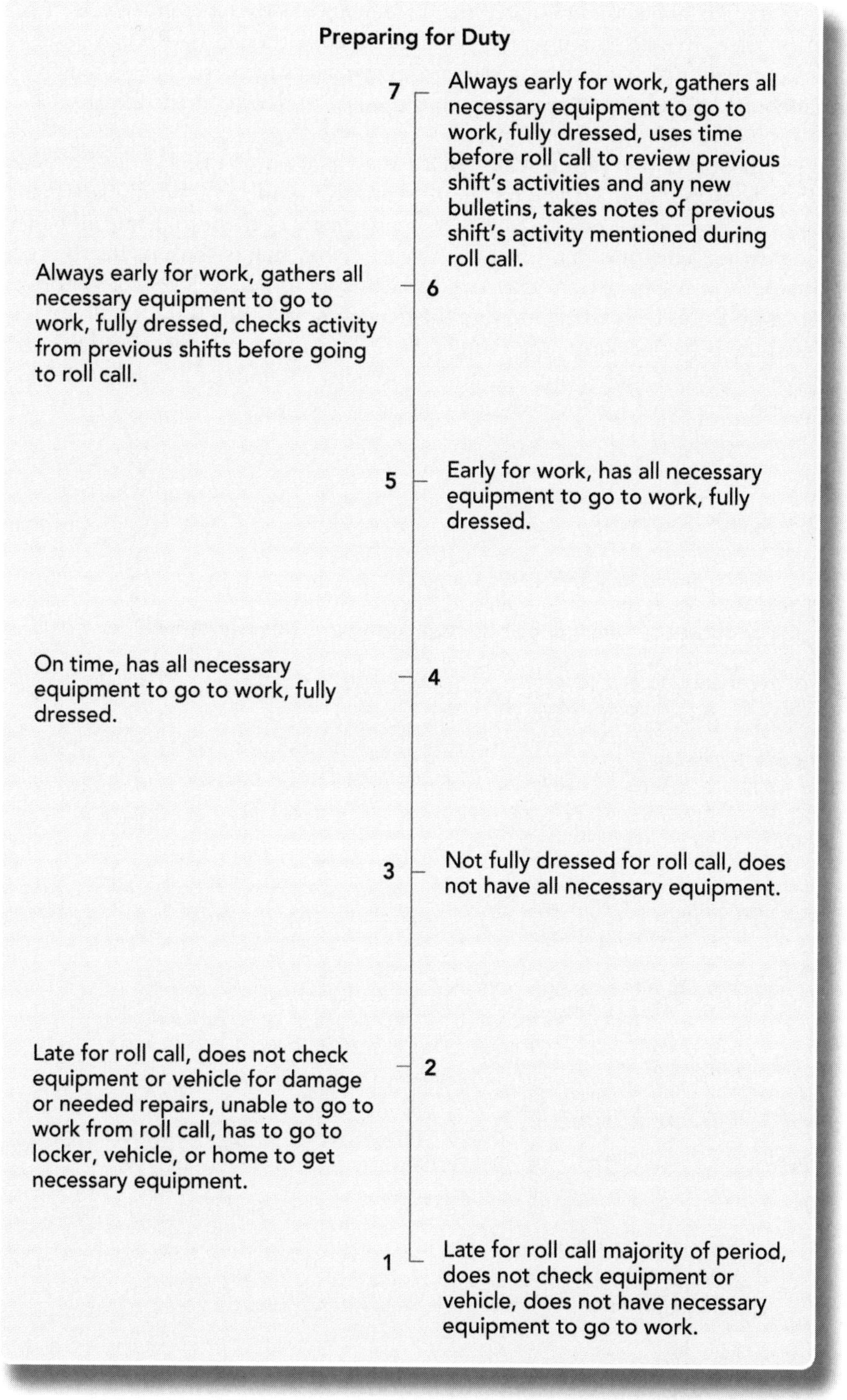

Preparing for Duty

Figure 8.6

Task-BARS Rating
Dimension: Patrol
Officer

7 — Always early for work, gathers all necessary equipment to go to work, fully dressed, uses time before roll call to review previous shift's activities and any new bulletins, takes notes of previous shift's activity mentioned during roll call.

Always early for work, gathers all necessary equipment to go to work, fully dressed, checks activity from previous shifts before going to roll call.

6

5 — Early for work, has all necessary equipment to go to work, fully dressed.

On time, has all necessary equipment to go to work, fully dressed.

4

3 — Not fully dressed for roll call, does not have all necessary equipment.

Late for roll call, does not check equipment or vehicle for damage or needed repairs, unable to go to work from roll call, has to go to locker, vehicle, or home to get necessary equipment.

2

1 — Late for roll call majority of period, does not check equipment or vehicle, does not have necessary equipment to go to work.

SOURCE: Adapted from R. Harvey, "Job Analysis," in *Handbook of Industrial & Organizational Psychology,* 2nd ed., ed. M. Dunnette and L. Hough (Palo Alto, CA: Consulting Psychologists Press, 1991), p. 138.

When experts about the job agree the statements clearly represent levels of performance, they are used as anchors to guide the rater. Although BARS can improve interrater reliability, this method can bias the manager's memory. The statements used as anchors can help managers remember similar behaviors, at the expense of other critical incidents.[6]

behavioral observation scale (BOS)
A variation of a BARS which uses all behaviors necessary for effective performance to rate performance at a task.

A **behavioral observation scale (BOS)** is a variation of a BARS. Like a BARS, a BOS is developed from critical incidents.[7] However, while a BARS discards many examples in creating the rating scale, a BOS uses many of them to define all behaviors necessary for effective performance (or behaviors that signal ineffective performance). As a result, a BOS may use 15 behaviors to define levels of performance. Also, a BOS asks the manager to rate the frequency with which the employee has exhibited the behavior during the rating period. These ratings are averaged to compute an overall performance rating. Figure 8.7 provides a simplified example of a BOS for measuring the behavior "overcoming resistance to change."

Figure 8.7
Example of a Behavioral Observation Scale

Overcoming Resistance to Change

Directions: Rate the frequency of each behavior from 1 (Almost Never) to 5 (Almost Always).

1. Describes the details of the change to employees.
   Almost Never 1 2 3 4 5 Almost Always

2. Explains why the change is necessary.
   Almost Never 1 2 3 4 5 Almost Always

3. Discusses how the change will affect the employee.
   Almost Never 1 2 3 4 5 Almost Always

4. Listens to the employee's concerns.
   Almost Never 1 2 3 4 5 Almost Always

5. Asks the employee for help in making the change work.
   Almost Never 1 2 3 4 5 Almost Always

6. If necessary, specifies the date for a follow-up meeting
   to respond to the employee's concerns.
   Almost Never 1 2 3 4 5 Almost Always

Score: Total number of points = _____

Performance

Points	Performance Rating
6–10	Below adequate
11–15	Adequate
16–20	Full
21–25	Excellent
26–30	Superior

Scores are set by management.

A major drawback of this method is the amount of information required. A BOS can have 80 or more behaviors, and the manager must remember how often the employee exhibited each behavior in a 6- to 12-month rating period. This is taxing enough for one employee, but managers often must rate 10 or more employees. Even so, compared to BARS and graphic rating scales, managers and employees have said they prefer BOS for ease of use, providing feedback, maintaining objectivity, and suggesting training needs.[8]

Another approach to assessment builds directly on a branch of psychology called *behaviorism*, which holds that individuals' future behavior is determined by their past experiences—specifically, the ways in which past behaviors have been reinforced. People tend to repeat behaviors that have been rewarded in the past. Providing feedback and reinforcement can therefore modify individuals' future behavior. Applied to behavior in organizations, **organizational behavior modification (OBM)** is a plan for managing the behavior of employees through a formal system of feedback and reinforcement. Specific OBM techniques vary, but most have four components:[9]

1. Define a set of key behaviors necessary for job performance.
2. Use a measurement system to assess whether the employee exhibits the key behaviors.
3. Inform employees of the key behaviors, perhaps in terms of goals for how often to exhibit the behaviors.
4. Provide feedback and reinforcement based on employees' behavior.

OBM techniques have been used in a variety of settings. For example, a community mental health agency used OBM to increase the rates and timeliness of critical job behaviors by showing employees the connection between job behaviors and the agency's accomplishments.[10] This process identified job behaviors related to administration, record keeping, and service provided to clients. Feedback and reinforcement improved staff performance. OBM also increased the frequency of safety behaviors in a processing plant.[11]

Behavioral approaches such as organizational behavior modification and rating scales can be very effective. These methods can link the company's goals to the specific behavior required to achieve those goals. Behavioral methods also can generate specific feedback, along with guidance in areas requiring improvements. As a result, these methods tend to be valid. The people to be measured often help in developing the measures, so acceptance tends to be high as well. When raters are well trained, reliability also tends to be high. However, behavioral methods do not work as well for complex jobs in which it is difficult to see a link between behavior and results or there is more than one good way to achieve success.[12]

> **organizational behavior modification (OBM)** A plan for managing the behavior of employees through a formal system of feedback and reinforcement.

Measuring Results

Performance measurement can focus on managing the objective, measurable results of a job or work group. Results might include sales, costs, or productivity (output per worker or per dollar spent on production), among many possible measures. Two of the most popular methods for measuring results are measurement of productivity and management by objectives.

Productivity is an important measure of success, because getting more done with a smaller amount of resources (money or people) increases the company's profits. Productivity usually refers to the output of production workers, but it can be used more generally as a performance measure. To do this, the organization identifies the products—set of activities or objectives—it expects a group or individual to accomplish. At a repair shop, for instance, a product might be something like "quality of repair." The next step is to define how to measure production of these products. For quality of repair, the repair shop could track the percentage of items returned because they still do not work after a repair and the percentage of quality-control inspections passed. For each measure, the organization decides what level of performance is desired. Finally, the organization sets up a system for tracking these measures and giving employees feedback about their performance in terms of these measures. This type of performance measurement can be time-consuming to set up, but research suggests it can improve productivity.[13]

Management by objectives (MBO) is a system in which people at each level of the organization set goals in a process that flows from top to bottom, so employees at all levels are contributing to the organization's overall goals. These goals become the standards for evaluating each employee's performance. An MBO system has three components:[14]

management by objectives (MBO)
A system in which people at each level of the organization set goals in a process that flows from top to bottom, so employees at all levels are contributing to the organization's overall goals; these goals become the standards for evaluating each employee's performance.

1. Goals are specific, difficult, and objective. The goals listed in the second column of Table 8.3 provide two examples for a bank.
2. Managers and their employees work together to set the goals.
3. The manager gives objective feedback through the rating period to monitor progress toward the goals. The two right-hand columns in Table 8.3 are examples of feedback given after one year.

MBO can have a very positive effect on an organization's performance. In 70 studies of MBO's performance, 68 showed that productivity improved.[15] The productivity gains tended to be greatest when top management was highly committed to MBO. Also, because staff members are involved in setting goals, it is likely that MBO systems effectively link individual employees' performance with the organization's overall goals.

In general, evaluation of results can be less subjective than other kinds of performance measurement. This makes measuring results highly acceptable to employees and managers alike. Results-oriented performance measurement is also relatively easy to link to the organization's goals. However, measuring results has problems with validity, because results may be affected by circumstances beyond each employee's performance. Also, if the organization measures only final results, it may fail to measure significant aspects of performance that are not directly related to those results. If individuals focus only on aspects of performance that are measured, they may neglect significant skills or behaviors. For example, if the organization measures only produc-

TABLE 8.3

Management by Objectives: Two Objectives for a Bank

KEY RESULT AREA	OBJECTIVE	% COMPLETE	ACTUAL PERFORMANCE
Loan portfolio management	Increase portfolio value by 10% over the next 12 months	90	Increased portfolio value by 9% over the past 12 months
Sales	Generate fee income of $30,000 over the next 12 months	150	Generated fee income of $45,000 over the past 12 months

Coaches provide feedback to their team just as managers provide feedback to their employees. Feedback is important so that individuals know what they are doing well and what areas they may need to work on.

tivity, employees may not be concerned enough with customer service. The outcome may be high efficiency (costs are low) but low effectiveness (sales are low, too).[16] Finally, focusing strictly on results does not provide guidance on how to improve. If baseball players are in a hitting slump, simply telling them that their batting average is .190 may not improve their hitting. The coach would help more by providing feedback about how or what to change (for instance, taking one's eye off the ball or dropping one's shoulder).[17]

Total Quality Management

The principles of *total quality management*, introduced in Chapter 2, provide methods for performance measurement and management. Total quality management (TQM) differs from traditional performance measurement in that it assesses both individual performance and the system within which the individual works. This assessment is a process through which employees and their customers work together to set standards and measure performance, with the overall goal being to improve customer satisfaction. In this sense, an employee's customers may be inside or outside the organization; a "customer" is whoever uses the goods or services produced by the employee. The feedback aims at helping employees continuously improve the satisfaction of their customers. The focus on continuously improving customer satisfaction is intended to avoid the pitfall of rating individuals on outcomes, such as sales or profits, over which they do not have complete control.

With TQM, performance measurement essentially combines measurements of attributes and results. The feedback in TQM is of two kinds: (1) subjective feedback from managers, peers, and customers about the employee's personal qualities such as cooperation and initiative; and (2) objective feedback based on the work process. The second kind of feedback comes from a variety of methods called *statistical quality control*. These methods use charts to detail causes of problems, measures of performance, or relationships between work-related variables. Employees are responsible for tracking these measures to identify areas where they can avoid or correct problems. Because of the focus on systems, this feedback may result in changes to a work process, rather than assuming that a performance problem is the fault of an employee. The TQM system's focus has practical benefits, but it does not serve as well to support decisions about work assignments, training, or compensation.

SOURCES OF PERFORMANCE INFORMATION

All the methods of performance measurement require decisions about who will collect and analyze the performance information. To qualify for this task, a person should have an understanding of the job requirements and the opportunity to see the employee doing the job. The traditional approach is for managers to gather information about their employees' performance and arrive at performance ratings. However, many sources are possible. As illustrated in Figure 8.8, possibilities of information sources include managers, peers, subordinates, self, and customers.

Using just one person as a source of information poses certain problems. People tend to like some people more than others, and those feelings can bias how an employee's efforts are perceived. Also, one person is likely to see an employee in a limited number of situations. A supervisor, for example, cannot see how an employee behaves when the supervisor is not watching—for example, when a service technician is at the customer's facility. To get as complete an assessment as possible, some organizations combine information from most or all of the possible sources, in what is called a **360-degree performance appraisal.**

Managers

The most-used source of performance information is the employee's manager. For example, Burlington Northern Santa Fe Corporation improved its performance management process by holding leaders accountable for setting annual goals, creating individual development plans, providing feedback and coaching to employees, and self-evaluation. An online performance management system supports the process. The

Figure 8.8
Sources of Performance Information

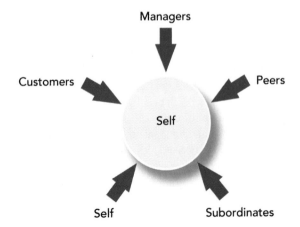

company's executive team creates the overall company objectives, which cascade down to each department and employee, so each employee can see how he or she contributes to the company's success. Managers and employees can go online to see how they and the department are progressing on the objectives. This system encourages managers to give their employees the communication, feedback, and coaching they need.[18]

It is usually safe for organizations to assume that supervisors have extensive knowledge of the job requirements and that they have enough opportunity to observe their employees. In other words, managers possess the basic qualifications for this responsibility. Another advantage of using managers to evaluate performance is that they have an incentive to provide accurate and helpful feedback, because their own success depends so much on their employees' performance.[19] Finally, when managers try to observe employee behavior or discuss performance issues in the feedback session, their feedback can improve performance, and employees tend to perceive the appraisal as accurate.[20]

Still, in some situations, problems can occur with using supervisors as the source of performance information. For employees in some jobs, the supervisor does not have enough opportunity to observe the employee performing job duties. A sales manager with many outside salespeople cannot be with the salespeople on many visits to customers. Even if the sales manager does make a point of traveling with salespeople for a few days, they are likely to be on their best behavior while the manager is there. The manager cannot observe how they perform at other times.

Peers

Another source of performance information is the employee's peers or coworkers. Peers are an excellent source of information about performance in a job where the supervisor does not often observe the employee. Examples include law enforcement and sales. For these and other jobs, peers may have the most opportunity to observe the employee in day-to-day activities. Peers have expert knowledge of job requirements. They also bring a different perspective to the evaluation and can provide extremely valid assessments of performance.[21]

Peer evaluations obviously have some potential disadvantages. Friendships (or rivalries) have the potential to bias ratings. Research, however, has provided little evidence that this is a problem.[22] Another disadvantage is that when the evaluations are done to support administrative decisions, peers are uncomfortable with rating employees for decisions that may affect themselves. Generally, peers are more favorable toward participating in reviews to be used for employee development.[23]

Subordinates

For evaluating the performance of managers, subordinates are an especially valuable source of information. Subordinates—the people reporting to the manager—often have the best chance to see how well a manager treats employees.

Subordinate evaluations have some potential problems because of the power relationships involved. Subordinates are reluctant to say negative things about the person to whom they report; they prefer to provide feedback anonymously. Managers, however, have a more positive reaction to this type of feedback when the subordinates are identified. When feedback forms require that the subordinates identify themselves, they tend to give the manager higher ratings.[24] Another problem is that when managers receive ratings from their subordinates, the employees have more power, so managers tend to emphasize employee satisfaction, even at the expense of productivity. This issue arises primarily when the evaluations are used for administrative decisions. Therefore, as with peer evaluations, subordinate evaluations are most appropriate for developmental purposes. To protect employees, the process should be anonymous and use at least three employees to rate each manager.

Self

No one has a greater chance to observe the employee's behavior on the job than does the employee himself or herself. Self-ratings are rarely used alone, but they can contribute valuable information. A common approach is to have employees evaluate their own performance before the feedback session. This activity gets employees thinking about their performance. Areas of disagreement between the self-appraisal and other evaluations can be fruitful topics for the feedback session.

The obvious problem with self-ratings is that individuals have a tendency to inflate assessments of their performance. Especially if the ratings will be used for administrative decisions, exaggerating one's contributions has practical benefits. Also, social psychologists have found that, in general, people tend to blame outside circumstances for their failures while taking a large part of the credit for their successes. Supervisors can soften this tendency by providing frequent feedback, but because people tend to perceive situations this way, self-appraisals are not appropriate as the basis for administrative decisions.[25]

Customers

According to the Bureau of Labor Statistics, service industries will account for a major portion of job growth between 2002 and 2012.[26] Services are often produced and consumed on the spot—so, the customer is often the only person who directly observes the service performance, and therefore, the customer may be the best source of performance information.

Many companies in service industries have introduced customer evaluations of employee performance. Marriott Corporation provides a customer satisfaction card in every room and mails surveys to a random sample of its hotel customers. Whirlpool's Consumer Services Division conducts both mail and telephone surveys of customers after factory technicians have serviced their appliances. These surveys allow the company to evaluate an individual technician's customer-service behaviors while in the customer's home.

Using customer evaluations of employee performance is appropriate in two situations.[27] The first is when an employee's job requires direct service to the customer or linking the customer to other services within the organization. Second, customer evaluations are appropriate when the organization is interested in gathering information to determine what products and services the customer wants. That is, customer evaluations contribute to the organization's goals by enabling HRM to support the organization's marketing activities. In this regard, customer evaluations are useful both for evaluating an employee's performance and for helping to determine whether the organization can improve customer service by making changes in HRM activities such as training or compensation.

The weakness of customer surveys for performance measurement is their expense. The expenses of a traditional survey, such as printing, postage, telephone, and labor, can add up to hundreds of dollars to evaluate one individual. Many organizations therefore limit the information gathering to short periods once a year.

❧ ERRORS IN PERFORMANCE MEASUREMENT

As we noted in the previous section, one reason for gathering information from several sources is that performance measurements are not completely objective, and errors can occur. People observe behavior, and they have no practical way of knowing all the circumstances, intentions, and outcomes related to that behavior, so they interpret what they see. In doing so, observers make a number of judgment calls, and in some situations may even distort information on purpose. Therefore, fairness in rating performance and interpreting performance appraisals requires that managers understand the kinds of distortions that commonly occur.

LO6
Define types of rating errors and explain how to minimize them.

Types of Rating Errors

Several kinds of errors and biases commonly influence performance measurements. Usually people make these errors unintentionally, especially when the criteria for measuring performance are not very specific.

Similar to Me

A common human tendency is to give a higher evaluation to people we consider similar to ourselves. Most of us tend to think of ourselves as effective. If others seem to be like us in some way—physical characteristics, family or economic background, attitudes, or beliefs—we expect them to be effective as well. Research has demonstrated that this effect, called the **similar-to-me error,** is strong. One unfortunate result (besides inaccuracy) is that when similarity is based on characteristics such as race or sex, the decisions may be discriminatory.[28]

similar-to-me error
Rating error of giving a higher evaluation to people who seem similar to oneself.

Contrast

Sometimes, instead of comparing an individual's performance against an objective standard, the rater compares that individual with other employees. Suppose an employee is completely competent and does exactly what the job requires. But that employee has several coworkers who are outstanding; they keep breaking sales records or thinking up clever ways to shave time off production processes. If the person rating the employee is contrasting the employee's performance with the exceptional coworkers and gives lower performance ratings than the employee deserves, this is **contrast error.** The lowered rating does not accurately reflect what the employee is doing.

contrast error
Rating error caused by comparing employee's performance to coworkers rather than to an objective standard.

Errors in Distribution

Raters often tend to use only one part of a rating scale—the low scores, the high scores, or the middle of the range. Sometimes a group of employees really do perform equally well (or poorly). In many cases, however, similar ratings for all members of a group are not an accurate description of performance, but an error in distribution. When a rater inaccurately assigns high ratings to all employees, this error is called **leniency.** When a rater incorrectly gives low ratings to all employees, holding them to unreasonably high standards, the resulting error is called **strictness.** Rating all employees as somehow "average" or in the middle of the scale is called the **central tendency.**

These errors pose two problems. First, they make it difficult to distinguish among employees rated by the same person. Decisions about promotions, job assignments, and so on are more difficult if employees all seem to be performing at the same level. Second, these errors create problems in comparing the performance of individuals

leniency error
Rating error of assigning inaccurately high ratings to all employees.

strictness error
Rating error of giving low ratings to all employees, holding them to unreasonably high standards.

central tendency
Incorrectly rating all employees at or near the middle of a rating scale.

rated by different raters. If one rater is lenient and the other is strict, employees of the strict rater will receive significantly fewer rewards than employees of the lenient rater. The rewards are not tied to actual performance but are to some degree erroneous.

Halo and Horns

Another common problem is that raters often fail to distinguish among different aspects of performance. Consider a research lab that hires chemists. A chemist who expresses herself very well may appear to have greater knowledge of chemistry than a chemist with poor communication skills. In this example, a rater could easily fail to distinguish between communication skills and scientific skills.

This type of error can make a person look better, or worse, overall. When the rater reacts to one positive performance aspect by rating the employee positively in all areas of performance, the bias is called the **halo error,** as in the example of the chemist who communicates well, giving the impression of overall intelligence. In contrast, when the rater responds to one negative aspect by rating an employee low in other aspects, the bias is called the **horns error.** Suppose an employee is sometimes tardy. The rater takes this as a sign of lack of motivation, lack of ambition, and inability to follow through with responsibility—an example of the horns error.

When raters make halo and horns errors, the performance measurements cannot provide the specific information needed for useful feedback. Halo error signals that no aspects of an employee's performance need improvement, possibly missing opportunities for employee development. Horns error tells the employee that the rater has a low opinion of the employee. The employee is likely to feel defensive and frustrated, rather than motivated to improve.

halo error
Rating error that occurs when the rater reacts to one positive performance aspect by rating the employee positively in all areas of performance.

horns error
Rating error that occurs when the rater responds to one negative aspect by rating an employee low in other aspects.

Ways to Reduce Errors

Training can reduce rating errors.[29] Raters can be trained how to avoid rating errors.[30] Prospective raters watch videotapes whose scripts or story-lines are designed to lead them to make specific rating errors. After rating the fictional employees in the videotapes, raters discuss their rating decisions and how such errors affected their rating decisions. Training programs offer tips for avoiding the errors in the future.

Another training method for raters focuses not on errors in rating, but on the complex nature of employee performance.[31] Raters learn to look at many aspects of performance that deserve their attention. Actual examples of performance are studied to bring out various performance dimensions and the standards for those dimensions. The objective of this training is to help raters evaluate employees' performance more thoroughly and accurately.

Political Behavior in Performance Appraisals

Unintentional errors are not the only cause of inaccurate performance measurement. Sometimes the people rating performance distort an evaluation on purpose, to advance their personal goals. This kind of appraisal politics is unhealthy especially because the resulting feedback does not focus on helping employees contribute to the organization's goals. High-performing employees who are rated unfairly will become frustrated, and low-performing employees who are overrated will be rewarded rather than encouraged to improve. Therefore, organizations try to identify and discourage appraisal politics.

Several characteristics of appraisal systems and company culture tend to encourage appraisal politics. Appraisal politics are most likely to occur when raters are account-

E-HRM

AT SEAGATE, PERFORMANCE MEASURES ARE ONLINE FOR ALL TO SEE

Seagate Technologies, which makes disk drives, has used computer technology to help employees understand its performance management system and ensure that employees and managers follow the performance management process as intended. To set up this process, Seagate's chief executive posted his top five goals for the company on the company's internal Web site. Over the weeks that followed, the company's top managers added their goals. To do this, they first reviewed the CEO's goals and then determined how they could contribute to achieving those goals. Professional employees at Seagate did the same, adding goals in support of their managers' goals.

Goal setting continued after those initial postings. Four times a year, employees work with their managers to update their goals. They can refer to a section of the Web site that offers coaching on how to support organizational goals through personal goal setting.

Besides setting their own goals, employees can see everyone else's goals. The 15,000 managerial and professional employees have posted their 56,000 goals on a site accessible to every employee in the company. An employee can see what his or her manager is trying to accomplish. And as managers adjust goals, others can adjust their own goals accordingly.

The computer system helps Seagate employees stay on track. It sends reminders to employees when they are nearing a due date for meeting a goal. It lets managers transfer goals among employees who might benefit the organization by working toward common goals.

Seagate's performance management system also supports the appraisal process. Performance data go into the computer system, and the software scores each employee's performance according to how well the employee is meeting goals. The overall appraisal rating is based 70 percent on how close the employee comes to meeting the goals and 30 percent on whether the employee engaged in the activities associated with achieving the goals. The company has a compensation system that uses the performance information to help determine pay increases.

SOURCE: Based on M. Hayes, "Goals Oriented," *Information Week*, March 10, 2003, www.informationweek.com.

able to the employee being rated, the goals of rating are not compatible with one another, performance appraisal is directly linked to highly desirable rewards, top executives tolerate or ignore distorted ratings, and senior employees tell newcomers company "folklore" that includes stories about distorted ratings.

Political behavior occurs in every organization. Organizations can minimize appraisal politics by establishing an appraisal system that is fair. Some ways to promote fairness are to involve managers and employees in developing the system, use consistent standards for evaluating different employees, require that feedback be timely and complete, allow employees to challenge their evaluation, and communicate expectations about performance standards, evaluations, and rewards.[32] The organization can also help managers give accurate and fair appraisals by training them to use the appraisal process, encouraging them to recognize accomplishments that the employees themselves have not identified, and fostering a climate of openness in which employees feel they can be honest about their weaknesses.[33] The "e-HRM" box describes how Seagate Technologies uses Internet technology to help it apply these principles.

LO7
Explain how
to provide
performance
feedback effectively.

◈ GIVING PERFORMANCE FEEDBACK

Once the manager and others have measured an employee's performance, this information must be given to the employee. Only after the employee has received feedback can he or she begin to plan how to correct any shortcomings. Although the feedback stage of performance management is essential, it is uncomfortable to managers and employees. Delivering feedback feels to the manager as if he or she is standing in judgment of others—a role few people enjoy. Receiving criticism feels even worse. Fortunately, managers can do much to smooth the feedback process and make it effective.

Scheduling Performance Feedback

Performance feedback should be a regular, expected management activity. The custom or policy at many organizations is to give formal performance feedback once a year. But annual feedback is not enough. One reason is that managers are responsible for correcting performance deficiencies as soon as they occur. If the manager notices a problem with an employee's behavior in June, but the annual appraisal is scheduled for November, the employee will miss months of opportunities for improvement.

Another reason for frequent performance feedback is that feedback is most effective when the information does not surprise the employee. If an employee has to wait for up to a year to learn what the manager thinks of his work, the employee will wonder whether he is meeting expectations. Employees should instead receive feedback so often that they know what the manager will say during their annual performance review.

Preparing for a Feedback Session

Managers should be well prepared for each formal feedback session. The manager should create the right context for the meeting. The location should be neutral. If the manager's office is the site of unpleasant conversations, a conference room may be

When giving
performance
feedback, do it in an
appropriate meeting
place. Meet in a
setting that is
neutral and free of
distractions. What
other factors are
important for a
feedback session?

more appropriate. In announcing the meeting to an employee, the manager should describe it as a chance to discuss the role of the employee, the role of the manager, and relationship between them. Managers should also say (and believe) that they would like the meeting to be an open dialogue.

Managers should also enable the employee to be well prepared. The manager should ask the employee to complete a self-assessment ahead of time. The self-assessment requires employees to think about their performance over the past rating period and to be aware of their strengths and weaknesses, so they can participate more fully in the discussion. Even though employees may tend to overstate their accomplishments, the self-assessment can help the manager and employee identify areas for discussion. When the purpose of the assessment is to define areas for development, employees may actually understate their performance. Also, differences between the manager's and the employee's rating may be fruitful areas for discussion.

Conducting the Feedback Session

During the feedback session, managers can take any of three approaches. In the "tell-and-sell" approach, managers tell the employees their ratings and then justify those ratings. In the "tell-and-listen" approach, managers tell employees their ratings and then let the employees explain their side of the story. In the "problem-solving" approach, managers and employees work together to solve performance problems in an atmosphere of respect and encouragement. Not surprisingly, research demonstrates that the problem-solving approach is superior. Perhaps surprisingly, most managers rely on the tell-and-sell approach.[34] Managers can improve employee satisfaction with the feedback process by letting employees voice their opinions and discuss performance goals.[35]

Applying some additional principles will also make performance feedback more effective: Feedback should include a balance of praise and criticism, reflecting an accurate assessment of what the employee is doing. Criticism is most effective if it is brief, however, leading to problem solving. The content of the feedback should emphasize behavior, not personalities. For example, "You did not meet the deadline" can open a conversation about what needs to change, but "You're not motivated" may make the employee feel defensive and angry. The feedback session should end with goal setting and a decision about when to follow up.

≫ FINDING SOLUTIONS TO PERFORMANCE PROBLEMS

LO8
Summarize ways to produce improvement in unsatisfactory performance.

When performance evaluation indicates that an employee's performance is below standard, the feedback process should launch an effort to correct the problem. Even when the employee is meeting current standards, the feedback session may identify areas in which the employee can improve in order to contribute more to the organization in a current or future job. In sum, the final, feedback stage of performance management involves identifying areas for improvement and ways to improve performance in those areas.

As shown in Figure 8.9, the most effective way to improve performance varies according to the employee's ability and motivation. In general, when employees have high levels of ability and motivation, they perform at or above standards. But when they lack ability, motivation, or both, corrective action is needed. The type of action called for depends on what the employee lacks.

Figure 8.9

Improving
Performance

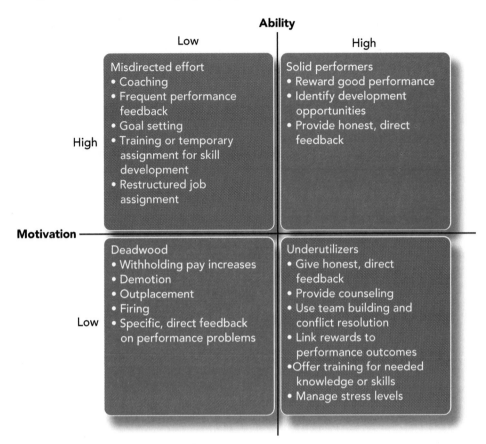

SOURCE: Based on M. London, *Job Feedback* (Mahwah, NJ: Lawrence Erlbaum Associates, 1997), pp. 96–97.
Used by permission.

To determine an employee's ability level, the manager should consider whether the employee has the knowledge, skills, and abilities needed to perform the job effectively. Sometimes lack of ability is an issue when an employee is new or the job has changed. When a motivated employee lacks knowledge, skills, or abilities in some area, there are a number of ways to help the employee improve. The manager may offer coaching, training, and more detailed feedback. Sometimes it is appropriate to restructure the job so that its demands no longer exceed the employee's abilities.

To determine an employee's level of motivation, managers need to consider whether the employee is holding a job he or she wants. A belief that pay and other rewards are too small can also hurt motivation. Sometimes personal problems are such a distraction that they interfere with motivation. Managers with an unmotivated employee can explore ways to demonstrate that the employee is being treated fairly and rewarded adequately. The solution may be as simple as delivering more positive feedback (praise). Employees may also benefit from a referral for counseling or help with stress management.

Employees whose performance is poor because they have neither the motivation nor the ability to perform the job may not be a good fit for the position. Performance may improve if the manager directs their attention to the significance of the problem by withholding rewards or by providing specific feedback. If employees do not respond by improving their performance, the organization may have to demote or terminate these underperformers.

As a rule, employees who combine high ability with high motivation are solid performers. As Figure 8.9 indicates, managers should by no means ignore these employees on the grounds of leaving well enough alone. Rather, such employees are likely to appreciate opportunities for further development. Rewards and direct feedback help to maintain these employees' high motivation levels.

◈ LEGAL AND ETHICAL ISSUES IN PERFORMANCE MANAGEMENT

LO9
Discuss legal and ethical issues that affect performance management.

In developing and using performance management systems, human resource professionals need to ensure that these systems meet legal requirements, such as the avoidance of discrimination. In addition, performance management systems should meet ethical standards, such as protection of employees' privacy.

Legal Requirements for Performance Management

Because performance measures play a central role in decisions about pay, promotions, and discipline, employment-related lawsuits often challenge an organization's performance management system. Lawsuits related to performance management usually involve charges of discrimination or unjust dismissal.

Discrimination claims often allege that the performance management system discriminated against employees on the basis of their race of sex. Many performance measures are subjective, and measurement errors, such as those described earlier in the chapter, can easily occur. The Supreme Court has held that the selection guidelines in the federal government's *Uniform Guidelines on Employee Selection Procedures* also apply to performance measurement.[36] (These guidelines were discussed in Chapters 3 and 6.) In general, these guidelines require that organizations avoid using criteria such as race and age as a basis for employment decisions. This requires overcoming widespread rating errors. A substantial body of evidence has shown that white and black raters tend to give higher ratings to members of their own racial group, even after rater training.[37] In addition, evidence suggests that this tendency is strongest when one group is only a small percentage of the total work group. When the vast majority of the group is male, females receive lower ratings; when the minority is male, males receive lower ratings.[38]

With regard to lawsuits filed on the grounds of unjust dismissal, the usual claim is that the person was dismissed for reasons besides the ones that the employer states. Suppose an employee who works for a defense contractor discloses that the company defrauded the government. If the company fires the employee, the employee might argue that the firing was a way to punish the employee for blowing the whistle. In this type of situation, courts generally focus on the employer's performance management system, looking to see whether the firing could have been based on poor performance. To defend itself, the employer would need a performance management system that provides evidence to support its employment decisions.

To protect against both kinds of lawsuits, it is important to have a legally defensible performance management system.[39] Such a system would be based on valid job analyses, as described in Chapter 4, with the requirements for job success clearly communicated

Getting ratings from a diverse group of employees and thus getting a variety of viewpoints could be a check on one person's rating errors. Other ways to avoid bias in performance management are to have a legally defensible rating system, to train raters in how to use the system, and to provide a way for employees to appeal an evaluation they think is inaccurate.

to employees. Performance measurement should evaluate behaviors or results, rather than traits. The organization should use multiple raters (including self-appraisals) and train raters in how to use the system. The organization should provide for a review of all performance ratings by upper-level managers and set up a system for employees to appeal when they believe they were evaluated unfairly. Along with feedback, the system should include a process for coaching or training employees to help them improve, rather than simply dismissing poor performers.

Electronic Monitoring and Employee Privacy

Computer technology now supports many performance management systems. Organizations often store records of employees' performance ratings, disciplinary actions, and work-rule violations in electronic databases. Many companies use computers to monitor productivity and other performance measures electronically. At a New York law firm, Akin & Smith, paralegals, receptionists, and clerks clock in by placing a finger on a sensor kept at a secretary's desk. The managing partners believe the system improves productivity and keeps everyone honest, holding them to their lunch times. At the Mitsubishi Motors North American plant in Normal, Illinois, accounting managers can check from their desktop computers how many of the plant's 500 white-collar employees have shown up for work. The employees sign in using a Web-based system on their computers. The 2,600 assembly-line workers are also tracked. They register their arrival at work with an identification badge that replaces the traditional paper time card.[40]

Congress has considered laws to regulate computer monitoring. In the meantime, organizations need to consider how employees react to this type of performance measurement. Electronic monitoring provides detailed, accurate information, but employees may find it demoralizing, degrading, and stressful. They are more likely to accept electronic monitoring if the organization explains its purpose and links it to help in improving performance. It is also essential that organizations protect the privacy of performance measurements, as they must do with other employee records.

thinking ETHICALLY

Do Financial Goals Get Managers in Trouble?

The owners of a corporation naturally expect the company's managers and employees to work to increase the company's value (often expressed in terms of its stock price). Other basic financial goals for a business are to increase profits through greater sales or lower costs. But can a company's people focus on those goals too much?

Susan Annunzio of the Hudson Highland Center for High Performance conducted a study in which she concluded that the main cause of employees' difficulties in improving profits and innovating was an excessive focus on short-term financial results. When she talked to employees about their group's performance, 10 percent said they worked in high-performing groups, and 38 percent said they worked in "nonperforming" groups. Of those in the nonperforming groups, one-third said their groups used to be high-performing, but they began to fail when managers started raising their standards at the same time they were reducing budgets and staff.

Why does that happen? One opinion is that managers feel pressured to keep cutting costs to deliver greater profits in each quarterly financial statement. They can eliminate valuable employees, and the remainder feel their jobs are becoming impossible. Organizational psychologist Richard Hagberg worked with a sales vice president who was urged to meet daily sales targets yet at the same time cut staff to meet profit goals. The vice president wanted to plan improvements to the product line and develop a new competitive strategy, but his time was spent figuring out how to squeeze more work from a shrinking staff.

Other employees fear that the only way to meet targets is through unethical practices such as faking their performance data. Annunzio interviewed a factory manager who was given a goal to reduce operating costs. The manager thought of ways to meet the target within a month, but he spread the improvements over a year so that his boss wouldn't immediately come back with a stiffer goal for him to meet.

SOURCE: Based on Carol Hymowitz, "When Meeting Targets Becomes the Strategy, CEO Is on Wrong Path," *The Wall Street Journal*, March 8, 2005, http://online.wsj.com.

Questions

1. Who benefits when a company's employees are focused on making the company more profitable?
2. Do goals related to short-term profits—for this month or this quarter—ever conflict with longer-term goals? Explain. Do these goals conflict with ethical standards? Explain.
3. Imagine that you are one of the managers described in this story or another manager who believes you cannot meet financial targets without deception or harm to the company. What should you do?

SUMMARY

1. Identify the activities involved in performance management.

   Performance management is the process through which managers ensure that employees' activities and outputs contribute to the organization's goals. The organization begins by specifying which aspects of performance are relevant to the organization. Next, the organization measures the relevant aspects of performance through performance appraisal. Finally, in performance feedback sessions, managers provide employees with information about their performance so they can adjust their behavior to meet the organization's goals. Feedback includes efforts to identify and solve problems.

2. Discuss the purposes of performance management systems.

   Organizations establish performance management systems to meet three broad purposes. Effective performance management helps the organization with strategic purposes, that is, meeting business objectives. It does this by helping to link employees' behavior with the organization's goals. The administrative purpose of performance management is to provide information for day-to-day decisions about salary, benefits, recognition, and retention or termination. The developmental purpose of performance management is using the system as a basis for developing employees' knowledge and skills.

3. Define five criteria for measuring the effectiveness of a performance management system.

   Performance measures should fit with the organization's strategy by supporting its goals and culture. Performance measures should be valid, so they measure all the relevant aspects of performance and do not measure irrelevant aspects of performance. These measures should also provide interrater and test-retest reliability, so that appraisals are consistent among raters and over time. Performance measurement systems should be acceptable to the people who use them or receive feedback from them. Finally, a performance measure should specifically tell employees what is expected of them and how they can meet those expectations.

4. Compare the major methods for measuring performance.

   Performance measurement may use ranking systems such as simple ranking, forced distribution, or paired comparisons to compare one individual's performance with that of other employees. These methods may be time-consuming, and they will be seen as unfair if actual performance is not distributed in the same way as the ranking system requires. However, ranking counteracts some forms of rater bias and helps distinguish employees for administrative decisions. Other approaches involve rating employees' attributes, behaviors, or outcomes. Rating attributes is relatively simple but not always valid, unless attributes are specifically defined. Rating behaviors requires a great deal of information, but these methods can be very effective. They can link behaviors to goals, and ratings by trained raters may be highly reliable. Rating results, such as productivity or achievement of objectives, tends to be less subjective than other kinds of rating, making this approach highly acceptable. Validity may be a problem because of factors outside the employee's control. This method also tends not to provide much basis for determining how to improve. Focusing on quality can provide practical benefits but is not as useful for administrative and developmental decisions.

5. Describe major sources of performance information in terms of their advantages and disadvantages.

   Performance information may come from an employee's self-appraisal and from appraisals by the employee's supervisor, employees, peers, and customers. Using only one source makes the appraisal more subjective. Organizations may combine many sources into a 360-degree performance appraisal. Gathering information from each employee's manager may produce accurate information, unless the supervisor has little opportunity to observe the employee. Peers are an excellent source of information about performance in a job where the supervisor does not often observe the employee. Disadvantages are that friendships (or rivalries) may bias ratings and peers may be uncomfortable with the role of rating a friend. Subordinates often have the best chance to see how a manager treats employees. Employees may be reluctant to contribute honest opinions about a supervisor unless they can provide information anonymously. Self-appraisals may be biased, but they do come from the person with the most knowledge of the employee's behavior on the job, and they provide a basis for discussion in feedback sessions, opening up fruitful comparisons and areas of disagreement between the self-appraisal and other appraisals. Customers may be an excellent source of performance information, although obtaining customer feedback tends to be expensive.

6. Define types of rating errors and explain how to minimize them.

   People observe behavior often without a practical way of knowing all the relevant circumstances and outcomes, so they necessarily interpret what they see. A common tendency is to give higher evaluations to people we consider similar to ourselves. Other errors involve using only part of the rating scale: Giving all employees ratings at the high end of the scale is called leniency error. Rating everyone at the low end of the scale is called strictness error. Rating all employees at or near the middle is called central tendency. The halo error refers to rating employees positively in all areas because of strong performance observed in one area. The horns error is rating employees negatively in all areas because of weak performance observed in one area. Ways to reduce rater error are training raters to be aware of their tendencies to make rating errors and training them to be sensitive to the complex nature of employee performance so they will consider many aspects of performance in greater depth. Politics also may influence ratings. Organizations can minimize appraisal politics by establishing a fair appraisal system, involving managers and employees in developing the system, allowing employees to challenge evaluations, communicating expectations, and fostering a climate of open discussion.

7. Explain how to provide performance feedback effectively.
   Performance feedback should be a regular, scheduled management activity, so that employees can correct problems as soon as they occur. Managers should prepare by establishing a neutral location, emphasizing that the feedback session will be a chance for discussion and asking the employee to prepare a self-assessment. During the feedback session, managers should strive for a problem-solving approach and encourage employees to voice their opinions and discuss performance goals. The manager should look for opportunities to praise and should limit criticism. The discussion should focus on behavior and results rather than on personalities.

8. Summarize ways to produce improvement in unsatisfactory performance.
   For an employee who is motivated but lacks ability, the manager should provide coaching and training, give detailed feedback about performance, and consider restructuring the job. For an employee who has ability but lacks motivation, the manager should investigate whether outside problems are a distraction and if so, refer the employee for help. If the problem has to do with the employee's not feeling appreciated or rewarded, the manager should try to deliver more praise and evaluate whether additional pay and other rewards are appropriate. For an employee lacking both ability and motivation, the manager should consider whether the employee is a good fit for the position. Specific feedback or withholding rewards may spur improvement, or the employee may have to be demoted or terminated. Solid employees who are high in ability and motivation will continue so and may be able to contribute even more if the manager provides appropriate direct feedback, rewards, and opportunities for development.

9. Discuss legal and ethical issues that affect performance management.
   Lawsuits related to performance management usually involve charges of discrimination or unjust dismissal. Managers must make sure that performance management systems and decisions treat employees equally, without regard to their race, sex, or other protected status. Organizations can do this by establishing and using valid performance measures and by training raters to evaluate performance accurately. A system is more likely to be legally defensible if it is based on behaviors and results, rather than on traits, and if multiple raters evaluate each person's performance. The system should include a process for coaching or training employees to help them improve, rather than simply dismissing poor performers. An ethical issue of performance management is the use of electronic monitoring. This type of performance measurement provides detailed, accurate information, but employees may find it demoralizing, degrading, and stressful. They are more likely to accept it if the organization explains its purpose, links it to help in improving performance, and keeps the performance data private.

REVIEW AND DISCUSSION QUESTIONS

1. How does a complete performance management system differ from the use of annual performance appraisals?
2. Give two examples of an administrative decision that would be based on performance management information. Give two examples of developmental decisions based on this type of information.
3. How can involving employees in the creation of performance standards improve the effectiveness of a performance management system? (Consider the criteria for effectiveness shown in Figure 8.2.)
4. Consider how you might rate the performance of three instructors from whom you are currently taking a course. (If you are currently taking only one or two courses, consider this course and two you recently completed.)
   a. Would it be harder to *rate* the instructors' performance or to *rank* their performance? Why?
   b. Write three items to use in rating the instructors—one each to rate them in terms of an attribute, a behavior, and an outcome.

c. Which measure in (b) do you think is most valid? Most reliable? Why?

d. Many colleges use questionnaires to gather data from students about their instructors' performance. Would it be appropriate to use the data for administrative decisions? Developmental decisions? Other decisions? Why or why not?

5. Imagine that a pet supply store is establishing a new performance management system to help employees provide better customer service. Management needs to decide who should participate in measuring the performance of each of the store's salespeople. From what sources should the store gather information? Why?

6. Would the same sources be appropriate if the store in Question 5 used the performance appraisals to support decisions about which employees to promote? Explain.

7. Suppose you were recently promoted to a supervisory job in a company where you have worked for two years. You genuinely like almost all your coworkers, who now report to you. The only exception is one employee, who dresses more formally than the others and frequently tells jokes that embarrass you and the other workers. Given your preexisting feelings for the employees, how can you measure their performance fairly and effectively?

8. Continuing the example in Question 7, imagine that you are preparing for your first performance feedback session. You want the feedback to be effective—that is, you want the feedback to result in improved performance. List five or six steps you can take to achieve your goal.

9. Besides giving employees feedback, what steps can a manager take to improve employees' performance?

10. Suppose you are a human resource professional helping to improve the performance management system of a company that sells and services office equipment. The company operates a call center that takes calls from customers who are having problems with their equipment. Call center employees are supposed to verify that the problem is not one the customer can easily handle (for example, equipment that will not operate because it has come unplugged). Then, if the problem is not resolved over the phone, the employees arrange for service technicians to visit the customer. The company can charge the customer only if a service technician visits, so performance management of the call center employees focuses on productivity—how quickly they can complete a call and move on to the next caller. To measure this performance efficiently and accurately, the company uses electronic monitoring.

a. How would you expect the employees to react to the electronic monitoring? How might the organization address the employees' concerns?

b. Besides productivity in terms of number of calls, what other performance measures should the performance management system include?

c. How should the organization gather information about the other performance measures?

WHAT'S YOUR HR IQ?

The text Web site offers two more ways to check what you've learned so far. Use the Self-Assessment exercise to conduct an assessment of your performance in a job or project. Go online with the Web Exercise to see what other HR professionals are saying about specific topics.

BusinessWeek CASE

BusinessWeek UnumProvident under Fire for Roster of Rejections

In 25 years as a public defender in Philadelphia, Michael J. Kelly juggled as many as 25 cases at once, spending hours meeting with criminal defendants inside prisons and cramming for thousands of court appearances. The years of stress took their toll: In 1999, Kelly was diagnosed with an enlarged heart—a condition that, as one doctor put it, turned him into a walking heart attack. "I don't think he can work," his cardiologist now says.

Kelly filed a disability claim with UnumProvident Corporation. That's when the stress really began. The Chattanooga, Tennessee, disability insurer turned him down repeatedly after he quit his job at his doctor's urging. Kelly struggled to get by on his savings and Social Security checks but was forced to file for bankruptcy. UnumProvident said Kelly was still capable of light work. But when asked about the claim recently, J. Christopher Collins, the insurer's deputy general counsel, said he "would like to look at [it] more closely."

UnumProvident is being forced to revisit many of its cases. A growing chorus of policyholders, plaintiffs' lawyers, former employees, and regulators charges that the company systematically rejects as many claims—legitimate or not—

as it feels it can get away with. If true, that's especially troubling because the $9.9 billion outfit is the nation's largest disability insurer.

Forty-five states are jointly investigating how UnumProvident handles claims. In a separate action in 2003, the state of Georgia fined the company $1 million and set up a system to scrutinize its handling of every rejected claim involving Georgia residents for two years. In an interview, Georgia Insurance Commissioner John W. Oxendine describes "a corporate culture built on finding every technical reason to deny claims." He says his study concluded that claims handlers routinely overruled doctors by rejecting payouts to policyholders. UnumProvident chief executive Thomas R. Watjen denies the allegations made by Georgia. He adds that he "very much endorsed" the multistate review in hopes that it will end the accusations dogging the insurer.

What has caught the eye of regulators is the avalanche of thousands of lawsuits and tens of millions in jury awards against UnumProvident over the past few years. In 2002, a California judge upheld a $7.67 million jury award to a former Berkeley chiropractor, Joan Hangarter, and sternly warned Unum against future violations, including "employing biased medical examiners, destroying medical records, and withholding from claimants information about their benefits." In 2003, a California jury awarded $31.7 million to a Novato eye surgeon, Randall Chapman. A phobia had given him the shakes, preventing him from performing operations. The company denied his claims, saying he failed to accept treatment recommended by its doctor. When a Superior Court judge, Lynn O'Malley Taylor, reduced that verdict to $6.1 million, she nonetheless rebuked UnumProvident for the "creation of a claims-handling procedure that appears designed to avoid performing a thorough, competent and objective investigation of [a] plaintiff's claim."

Former employees and plaintiffs' attorneys who have seen UnumProvident's files paint a picture of an aggressive corporate culture. They say managers kept a lid on costs by pushing claims handlers and investigators to find any reason to deny large payouts. In depositions, some company physicians said they felt pressured by managers to render the medical opinions needed to deny claims.

The culture was symbolized by the company's "Hungry Vulture" award for top performers, say former employees. The prize even carried the motto "Patience my foot . . . I'm gonna kill something." George A. Shell Jr., senior vice president of UnumProvident's benefits operations, says the award—which has been discontinued—was never given to workers for denying claims but simply to exemplary employees to recognize good performance.

UnumProvident officials in interviews dismiss any notion that they cultivated a milieu in which employees were pressured to reject claims. "You won't lose your job because you made a decision to pay a claim," says Shell. The officials also say less than one-half of 1 percent of

claims result in lawsuits. At the same time, the company has installed a new procedure in which a separate panel of reviewers—and not the original claims handlers—now examines appeals.

Insurance industry experts trace the company's problems to its decision in the early 1980s to target the market for lawyers, doctors, and other professionals who own their own practices. The policies weren't cheap, but they guaranteed annual payments that usually ranged well into six figures if policyholders could no longer practice their specialty. At first, the policies were a big profit center for the industry. Then claims started arriving in far greater numbers than expected. Other insurers scaled back, but Provident Companies, Inc., as it was then called, doubled its bet, acquiring rivals Paul Revere Corporation and Unum Corporation.

That's when Linda Nee, a veteran claims handler at Unum's head office in Portland, Maine, and other employees there say they started seeing a more ruthless approach to claims. The pressure peaked, they say, in the last month of each quarter, when managers looked for claims to terminate to get under budget. The company vigorously denies that it rejects claims for financial reasons.

Meanwhile, UnumProvident's fortunes were going into reverse. Its stock price plunged from $61.45 in 1999 to $6 a share in 2003. The combination of poor investments and a crush of big-dollar claims from policies written in the 1980s left investors wondering whether the insurer could raise enough capital to adequately build its reserves. Unum did raise $1 billion, but profits remain weighed down by the lawsuits and the growing number of claims from its old policies.

SOURCE: Excerpted from Dean Foust, "Disability Claim Denied!" *BusinessWeek,* December 22, 2003, downloaded from Infotrac at http://web5.infotrac.galegroup.com.

Questions

1. An insurer like UnumProvident sells policies and invests the revenues until it needs the money to pay claims. Its profits come from the earnings on its investments and from charging more for policies than it pays out for claims. How should the goals of Unum's claims handlers (the people who make decisions about paying claims) support the company's profit objectives? In what ways might boosting short-term profits by denying claims conflict with other company goals?

2. Suggest some performance measures for claims handlers that could help the company meet short-term and long-term goals. Could your suggestions help the company reduce its legal problems?

3. As described in this case, has UnumProvident behaved ethically? Explain. How can a performance management system help the company with its real or perceived ethics problems?

CASE: Forced Rankings Popular at Big Corporations

Many U.S. companies, including Ford Motor Company, General Electric, Microsoft, and Hewlett-Packard, use forced-ranking systems and forced-distribution systems. Their use of the systems has sometimes generated lawsuits and negative publicity and triggered poor employee morale.

At General Electric forced distribution was advocated by the company's former chief executive, Jack Welch. Welch insisted that GE annually identify and remove the bottom-performing 10 percent of the workforce. Such performance ranking takes several forms. Most commonly, employees are grouped into three, four, or five categories—usually of unequal size—indicating the best workers, the worst workers, and one to three categories in between. At General Electric, managers were required to place employees into the top 20 percent, middle 70 percent, and bottom 10 percent. The bottom 10 percent receive no bonuses and can be terminated.

Why are forced-distribution systems popular? Top-level managers at many companies have observed that despite corporate performance being flat or decreasing, compensation costs have continued to spiral upward, and performance ratings remain high. They question how there can be so little connection between corporate performance and employees' evaluations and compensation. Forced-distribution systems are a way to help match company and employee performance with compensation. Poor performers receive no salary increase, and average performers receive smaller increases than are given to top performers.

A forced-distribution system also helps managers tailor development activities to employees based on their performance. For example, poor performers are given specific feedback about what they need to improve and what the timetable is for making the changes. If they do not improve, they are dismissed. Top performers are encouraged to participate in development activities such as challenging job experiences and leadership programs to prepare them for top management positions. So, the use of a forced-distribution system is a way for companies to increase performance, motivate employees, and open the door for new talent to join the company in place of poor performers.

Still, the practice has problems. Forced distribution asks managers to differentiate between good, average, and poor performers, a distinction many managers find difficult to make. The systems have been difficult to implement, and some companies have gotten into trouble.

In 2002 Ford settled two class-action lawsuits for $10.5 million. Ford said it needed its forced-ranking system because its culture discouraged frankness in performance evaluations. The Ford Motors Performance Management System involved grading 1,800 middle managers as A, B, or C, with 10 percent receiving a C. Managers who received a C for one year received no bonus; two years at the

C level meant possible demotion and termination. Some employees claimed the system harmed older, white workers because they received a larger proportion of C grades. Eventually, Ford eliminated the forced-ranking system.

Dow Chemical Global had a forced-ranking system until the mid-1990s. The system caused a lot of problems. A study showed that the system took too much time and energy, and managers were focused on the appraisal instead of improving employee performance. The same employees consistently were evaluated in the top 15 percent, so other employees wondered how they could ever achieve a higher ranking. The company also found that the system was used to deny employees raises. In addition, it did not fit with Dow's philosophy of recruiting the best employees: If the company hired the best, how then could some be rated as poor performers? Dow replaced the system with one in which managers define performance expectations and then communicate them along with the company's values and the employee's role in maintaining those values. Employees are compared against performance standards, rather than against one another.

Goodyear Tire and Rubber used a system in which 10 percent of its staff would be rated as A performers and singled out for promotion. Another 10 percent would be rated as C performers and targeted for improvement or dismissal. After getting a second C rating in two years, a chemist at Goodyear was fired. He was fired a few days before he received a patent for a new kind of aircraft tire. The chemist and seven other Goodyear employees sued the company, claiming the forced-ranking system targeted older employees and not poor performers. Although Goodyear contested the lawsuit, it also abandoned the labeling of employees as A, B, or C. Its new categories are "exceeds expectations," "meets expectations," and "unsatisfactory." Employees in the bottom category are still expected to improve or to face reassignment or firing.

SOURCE: S. Bates, "Forced Ranking," *HR Magazine*, June 2003, pp. 63–68; A. Meisler, "Deadman's Curve," *Workforce Management*, July 2003, pp. 44–49; M. Lowery, "Forcing the Issue," *Human Resource Executive*, October 16, 2003, pp. 26–29; and M. Boyle, "Performance Reviews: Perilous Curves Ahead," *Fortune*, May 28, 2001, pp. 187–88.

Questions

1. What are the pros and cons of forced-distribution and forced-ranking systems?
2. Suppose Ford, Goodyear, or Dow Chemical contracted with you to modify its performance management system to avoid some of the problems it has experienced. What would you suggest the company do?
3. What advantages will your ideas have over the company's current system? How will you measure the success of your ideas?

NOTES

1. P. Kiger, "Frequent Employee Feedback Is Worth the Cost and Time," *Workforce*, March 2001, pp. 62–65.
2. C. Lee, "Performance Appraisal: Can We Manage Away the Curse?" *Training*, May 1996, pp. 44–49.
3. "Measuring People Power," *Fortune*, October 2, 2000.
4. Andy Meisler, "Lockheed Is Doing Right and Doing Well," *Workforce Management*, March 2004, www.workforce.com.
5. P. Smith and L. Kendall, "Retranslation of Expectations: An Approach to the Construction of Unambiguous Anchors for Rating Scales," *Journal of Applied Psychology* 47 (1963), pp. 149–55.
6. K. Murphy and J. Constans, "Behavioral Anchors as a Source of Bias in Rating," *Journal of Applied Psychology* 72 (1987), pp. 573–77; M. Piotrowski, J. Barnes-Farrel, and F. Estig, "Behaviorally Anchored Bias: A Replication and Extension of Murphy and Constans," *Journal of Applied Psychology* 74 (1989), pp. 823–26.
7. G. Latham and K. Wexley, *Increasing Productivity through Performance Appraisal* (Boston: Addison-Wesley, 1981).
8. U. Wiersma and G. Latham, "The Practicality of Behavioral Observation Scales, Behavioral Expectation Scales, and Trait Scales," *Personnel Psychology* 39 (1986), pp. 619–28.
9. D. C. Anderson, C. Crowell, J. Sucec, K. Gilligan, and M. Wikoff, "Behavior Management of Client Contacts in a Real Estate Brokerage: Getting Agents to Sell More," *Journal of Organizational Behavior Management* 4 (2001), pp. 580–90; F. Luthans and R. Kreitner, *Organizational Behavior Modification and Beyond* (Glenview, IL: Scott-Foresman, 1975).
10. K. L. Langeland, C. M. Jones, and T. C. Mawhinney, "Improving Staff Performance in a Community Mental Health Setting: Job Analysis, Training, Goal Setting, Feedback, and Years of Data," *Journal of Organizational Behavior Management* 18 (1998), pp. 21–43.
11. J. Komaki, R. Collins, and P. Penn, "The Role of Performance Antecedents and Consequences in Work Motivation," *Journal of Applied Psychology* 67 (1982), pp. 334–40.
12. S. Snell, "Control Theory in Strategic Human Resource Management: The Mediating Effect of Administrative Information," *Academy of Management Journal* 35 (1992), pp. 292–327.
13. R. Pritchard, S. Jones, P. Roth, K. Stuebing, and S. Ekeberg, "The Evaluation of an Integrated Approach to Measuring Organizational Productivity," *Personnel Psychology* 42 (1989), pp. 69–115.
14. G. Odiorne, *MOBII: A System of Managerial Leadership for the 80s* (Belmont, CA: Pitman, 1986).
15. R. Rodgers and J. Hunter, "Impact of Management by Objectives on Organizational Productivity," *Journal of Applied Psychology* 76 (1991), pp. 322–26.
16. P. Wright, J. George, S. Farnsworth, and G. McMahan, "Productivity and Extra-role Behavior: The Effects of Goals and Incentives on Spontaneous Helping," *Journal of Applied Psychology* 78, no. 3 (1993), pp. 374–81.
17. Latham and Wexley, *Increasing Productivity through Performance Appraisal*.
18. K. Ellis, "Developing for Dollars," *Training*, May 2003, pp. 34–39.
19. R. Heneman, K. Wexley, and M. Moore, "Performance Rating Accuracy: A Critical Review," *Journal of Business Research* 15 (1987), pp. 431–48.
20. T. Becker and R. Klimoski, "A Field Study of the Relationship between the Organizational Feedback Environment and Performance," *Personnel Psychology* 42 (1989), pp. 343–58; H. M. Findley, W. F. Giles, K. W. Mossholder, "Performance Appraisal and Systems Facets: Relationships with Contextual Performance," *Journal of Applied Psychology* 85 (2000), pp. 634–40.
21. K. Wexley and R. Klimoski, "Performance Appraisal: An Update," in *Research in Personnel and Human Resource Management*, vol. 2, ed. K. Rowland and G. Ferris (Greenwich, CT: JAI Press, 1984).
22. F. Landy and J. Farr, *The Measurement of Work Performance: Methods, Theory, and Applications* (New York: Academic Press, 1983).
23. G. McEvoy and P. Buller, "User Acceptance of Peer Appraisals in an Industrial Setting," *Personnel Psychology* 40 (1987), pp. 785–97.
24. D. Antonioni, "The Effects of Feedback Accountability on Upward Appraisal Ratings," *Personnel Psychology* 47 (1994), pp. 349–56.
25. R. Steel and N. Ovalle, "Self-Appraisal Based on Supervisor Feedback," *Personnel Psychology* 37 (1984), pp. 667–85; L. E. Atwater, "The Advantages and Pitfalls of Self-Assessment in Organizations," in *Performance Appraisal: State of the Art in Practice*, ed. J. W. Smither (San Francisco: Jossey-Bass, 1998), pp. 331–65.
26. M. W. Horrigan, "Employment Projections to 2012: Concepts and Context," *Monthly Labor Review* 127 (2004), pp. 3–11.
27. J. Bernardin, C. Hagan, J. Kane, and P. Villanova, "Effective Performance Management: A Focus on Precision, Customers, and Situational Constraints," in *Performance Appraisal: State of the Art in Practice*, pp. 3–48.
28. K. Wexley and W. Nemeroff, "Effects of Racial Prejudice, Race of Applicant, and Biographical Similarity

on Interviewer Evaluations of Job Applicants," *Journal of Social and Behavioral Sciences* 20 (1974), pp. 66–78.

29. D. Smith, "Training Programs for Performance Appraisal: A Review," *Academy of Management Review* 11 (1986), pp. 22–40.

30. G. Latham, K. Wexley, and E. Pursell, "Training Managers to Minimize Rating Errors in the Observation of Behavior," *Journal of Applied Psychology* 60 (1975), pp. 550–55.

31. E. Pulakos, "A Comparison of Rater Training Programs: Error Training and Accuracy Training," *Journal of Applied Psychology* 69 (1984), pp. 581–88.

32. S. W. Gilliland and J. C. Langdon, "Creating Performance Management Systems That Promote Perceptions of Fairness," in *Performance Appraisal: State of the Art in Practice*, pp. 209–43.

33. S. W. J. Kozlowski, G. T. Chao, and R. F. Morrison, "Games Raters Play: Politics, Strategies, and Impression Management in Performance Appraisal," in *Performance Appraisal: State of the Art in Practice*, pp. 163–205.

34. K. Wexley, V. Singh, and G. Yukl, "Subordinate Participation in Three Types of Appraisal Interviews," *Journal of Applied Psychology* 58 (1973), pp. 54–57; K. Wexley, "Appraisal Interview," in *Performance Assessment*, ed. R. A. Berk (Baltimore: Johns Hopkins University Press, 1986), pp. 167–85.

35. D. Cederblom, "The Performance Appraisal Interview: A Review, Implications, and Suggestions," *Academy of Management Review* 7 (1982), pp. 219–27; B. D. Cawley, L. M. Keeping, and P. E. Levy, "Participation in the Performance Appraisal Process and Employee Reactions: A Meta-analytic Review of Field Investigations," *Journal of Applied Psychology* 83, no. 3 (1998), pp. 615–63; W. Giles and K. Mossholder, "Employee Reactions to Contextual and Session Components of Performance Appraisal," *Journal of Applied Psychology* 75 (1990), pp. 371–77.

36. *Brito v. Zia Co.*, 478 F.2d 1200 (10th Cir. 1973).

37. K. Kraiger and J. Ford, "A Meta-Analysis of Ratee Race Effects in Performance Rating," *Journal of Applied Psychology* 70 (1985), pp. 56–65.

38. P. Sackett, C. DuBois, and A. Noe, "Tokenism in Performance Evaluation: The Effects of Work Group Representation on Male-Female and White-Black Differences in Performance Ratings," *Journal of Applied Psychology* 76 (1991), pp. 263–67.

39. G. Barrett and M. Kernan, "Performance Appraisal and Terminations: A Review of Court Decisions since *Brito v. Zia* with Implications for Personnel Practices," *Personnel Psychology* 40 (1987), pp. 489–503; H. Feild and W. Holley, "The Relationship of Performance Appraisal System Characteristics to Verdicts in Selected Employment Discrimination Cases," *Academy of Management Journal* 25 (1982), pp. 392–406; J. M. Werner and M. C. Bolino, "Explaining U.S. Courts of Appeals Decisions Involving Performance Appraisal: Accuracy, Fairness, and Validation," *Personnel Psychology* 50 (1997), pp. 1–24; J. A. Segal, "86 Your Performance Appraisal Process," *HR Magazine*, October 2000, pp. 199–202.

40. K. Maher, "Big Employer Is Watching," *The Wall Street Journal*, November 4, 2003, pp. B1, B6.

If you are using the Manager's Hot Seat DVD with this book, consider finishing case 9: Project Management: Steering the Committee, for this chapter.

DEVELOPING EMPLOYEES FOR FUTURE SUCCESS

INTRODUCTION

As we noted in Chapter 1, employees' commitment to their organization depends on how their managers treat them. To "win the war for talent" managers must be able to identify high-potential employees, make sure the organization uses the talents of these people, and reassure them of their value, so that they do not become dissatisfied and leave the organization. Managers also must be able to listen. Although new employees need strong direction, they expect to be able to think independently and be treated with respect. In all these ways, managers provide for **employee development**— the combination of formal education, job experiences, relationships, and assessment of personality and abilities to help employees prepare for the future of their careers. Human resource management establishes a process for employee development that prepares employees to help the organization meet its goals.

This chapter explores the purpose and activities of employee development. We begin by discussing the relationships among development, training, and career management. Next, we look at development approaches, including formal education, assessment, job experiences, and interpersonal relationships. The chapter emphasizes the types of skills, knowledge, and behaviors that are strengthened by each development method, so employees and their managers can choose appropriate methods when planning for development. The third section of the chapter describes the steps of

employee development
The combination of formal education, job experiences, relationships, and assessment of personality and abilities to help employees prepare for the future of their careers.

LO1
Discuss how development is related to training and careers.

the career management process, emphasizing the responsibilities of employee and employer at each step of the process. The chapter concludes with a discussion of special challenges related to employee development—the so-called glass ceiling, succession planning, and dysfunctional managers.

◈ TRAINING, DEVELOPMENT, AND CAREER MANAGEMENT

Organizations and their employees must constantly expand their knowledge, skills, and behavior to meet customer needs and compete in today's demanding and rapidly changing business environment. More and more companies operate internationally, requiring that employees understand different cultures and customs. More companies organize work in terms of projects or customers, rather than specialized functions, so employees need to acquire a broad range of technical and interpersonal skills. Many companies expect employees at all levels to perform roles once reserved for management. Modern organizations are expected to provide development opportunities to employees without regard to their sex, race, ethnic background, or age, so that they have equal opportunity for advancement. In this climate, organizations are placing greater emphasis on training and development. To do this, organizations must understand development's relationship to training and career management.

Development and Training

The definition of development indicates that it is future oriented. Development implies learning that is not necessarily related to the employee's current job.[1] Instead, it prepares employees for other positions in the organization and increases their ability to move into jobs that may not yet exist.[2] Development also may help employees prepare for changes in their current jobs, such as changes resulting from new technology, work designs, or customers. So development is about preparing for change in the form of new jobs, new responsibilities, or new requirements.

In contrast, training traditionally focuses on helping employees improve performance of their current jobs. Many organizations have focused on linking training programs to business goals. In these organizations, the distinction between training and development is more blurred. Table 9.1 summarizes the traditional differences.

Development for Careers

The concept of a career has changed in recent years. In the traditional view, a career consists of a sequence of positions within an occupation or organization.[3] For example, an academic career might begin with a position as a university's adjunct professor. It continues with appointment to faculty positions as assistant professor, then as-

TABLE 9.1

Training versus Development

	TRAINING	DEVELOPMENT
Focus	Current	Future
Use of work experiences	Low	High
Goal	Preparation for current job	Preparation for changes
Participation	Required	Voluntary

With changes such as downsizing, restructuring, bankruptcy and growth being the norm in the modern business environment, employees are finding that they need to continuously learn new skills in order to stay competitive.

sociate professor, and finally full professor. An engineer might start as a staff engineer, then with greater experience earn promotions to the positions of advisory engineer, senior engineer, and vice president of engineering. In these examples, the career resembles a set of stairs from the bottom of a profession or organization to the top.

Changes such as downsizing, restructuring, bankruptcy, and growth have become the norm in the modern business environment. As this has happened, the concept of career has become more fluid. The new concept of a career is often referred to as a **protean career**—that is, a career that frequently changes based on changes in the person's interests, abilities, and values and in the work environment. For example, an engineer might decide to take a sabbatical from her position to work in management at the United Way for a year. The purpose of this change could be to develop her managerial skills and evaluate whether she likes managerial work more than engineering. As in this example, the concept of a protean career assumes that employees will take major responsibility for managing their careers. This concept is consistent with the modern *psychological contract* we described in Chapter 2. In place of the traditional expectation of job security and advancement within a company, today's employees need to take control over their careers and personal responsibility for managing their careers. They look for organizations that will support them by providing development opportunities and flexible work arrangements so they can pursue their goals.

In this environment, employees need to develop new skills, rather than rely on an unchanging base of knowledge. This need results from employers' efforts to respond to customer demands. The extent and types of knowledge that an employee needs have changed.[4] For example, many traditional manufacturing jobs were repetitive and required little skill or education, but today's blue-collar workers need to operate computerized equipment and adjust processes for customized orders. Jobs are less likely to last a lifetime, so the workers frequently need to learn new skills to qualify for newly created positions. Also, the traditional career requires "knowing how," or having the appropriate skills and knowledge to provide a particular service or product. Such knowledge and skills remain important, but a protean career also requires that employees "know why" and "know whom." Knowing why means understanding the employer's business and culture in order to apply knowledge and skills in a way that contributes to the business. Knowing whom means developing relationships that contribute to the employer's success—for example, connections with vendors, suppliers, community members, customers, or industry experts. Learning these categories of knowledge requires more than formal courses and training programs. Rather, the employee must build relationships and obtain useful job experiences.

protean career
A career that frequently changes based on changes in the person's interests, abilities, and values and in the work environment.

These relationships and experiences often take an employee along a career path that is far different from the traditional steps upward through an organization or profession. Although such careers will not disappear, more employees will follow a spiral career path in which they cross the boundaries between specialties and organizations. As organizations provide for employee development (and as employees take control of their own careers), they will need a pair of opportunities. First, employees need to determine their interests, skills, and weaknesses. Second, based on that information, employees seek development experiences that will likely involve jobs and relationships as well as formal courses. As discussed later in the chapter, organizations can meet these needs through a system for *career management* or *development planning*. Career management helps employees select development activities that prepare them to meet their career goals. It helps employers select development activities in line with their human resource needs.

LO2
Identify the methods organizations use for employee development.

❧ APPROACHES TO EMPLOYEE DEVELOPMENT

Employee development is a huge job at Cardinal Health, the largest provider of health care products and services in the world. The company, headquartered in Dublin, Ohio, has 50,000 employees in 22 countries. To develop employees, the company assesses its managers and potential managers in its 10 core competencies of leadership: customer orientation, personal leadership, business acumen, teamwork, innovation and risk taking, results orientation, integrity, strategic thinking, interpersonal skills, and maturity. Based on their strengths and weaknesses in these areas, the employees then participate in training programs, job experiences, and mentoring programs designed to help them improve. The aim of the program is to develop leadership that is strong in all 10 core competencies.[5]

As at Cardinal Health, employee development often focuses on managers, but development is useful for all levels of employees. For example, a grocery store manager could give clerks feedback as part of their performance appraisals. At the same time, the manager could ask the clerks to think of ways to change their weaknesses and invite them to state goals, such as positions they desire to hold in the future. In this way, the performance management process can support employee development.

The many approaches to employee development fall into four broad categories: formal education, assessment, job experiences, and interpersonal relationships.[6] Figure 9.1 summarizes these four methods. Many organizations combine these approaches, as in the previous example of Cardinal Health.

Formal Education

Organizations may support employee development through a variety of formal educational programs, either at the workplace or off-site. These may include workshops designed specifically for the organization's employees, short courses offered by consultants or universities, university programs offered to employees who live on campus during the program, and executive MBA programs (which enroll managers to meet on weekends or evenings to earn a master's degree in business administration). These programs may involve lectures by business experts, business games and simulations, experiential programs, and meetings with customers. Chapter 7 described most of these training methods, including their pros and cons.

Many companies, including Motorola, IBM, General Electric, and Metropolitan Financial, operate training and development centers that offer one- or two-day sem-

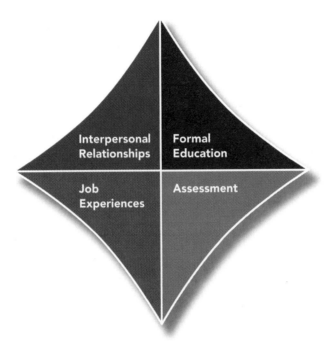

Figure 9.1

The Four
Approaches to
Employee
Development

inars and week-long programs. For example, GE's Management Development Institute in Crotonville, New York, teaches courses in manufacturing and sales, marketing, and advanced management training.[7] Some courses are available to all employees early in their careers, but advanced programs are limited to executives nominated by the CEO of their business division. Classroom training is presented by GE executives, project managers, and university professors. In addition, participants use e-learning to prepare for classroom sessions. The company also is setting up what it calls virtual learning communities, which are simulations in which a group of participants solve problems related to running a virtual business, competing against other groups. The group members must communicate via e-mail and phone calls, just as busy managers of a global corporation keep in touch today.

Independent institutions offering executive education include Harvard, the Wharton School of Business, the University of Michigan, and the Center for Creative Leadership. A growing number of companies and universities are using distance learning (discussed in Chapter 7) to reach executive audiences. For example, Duke University's Fuqua School of Business offers an electronic executive MBA program. Students use personal computers to view lectures on CD-ROM, download study aids, discuss lectures, and work on team projects using computer bulletin boards, e-mail, and live chat. They also use the Internet to research topics and companies.

Another trend in executive education is for employers and the education provider to create short courses with content designed specifically for the audience. An example of this type of customized learning is the Global Leadership Program run by Columbia University's business school. There, executives work on real problems they face in their jobs. One participant, a manager for window maker Pella Corporation, left the program with a plan for international sales.[8]

Executive education also may supplement formal courses with other types of development activities. Avon Products offers its Passport Program to employees thought to have potential to be general managers.[9] To learn Avon's global strategy, they meet for each session in a different country. The program brings a team of employees together for six-week periods spread over 18 months. University faculty and consultants give participants general background of a functional area. The team then works with Avon senior executives on a country project, such as how to enter a new market. The teams present their projects to Avon's top managers.

Assessment

Another way to provide for employee development is **assessment**—collecting information and providing feedback to employees about their behavior, communication style, or skills.[10] Information for assessment may come from the employees, their peers, managers, and customers. The most frequent uses of assessment are to identify employees with managerial potential to measure current managers' strengths and weaknesses. Organizations also use assessment to identify managers with potential to move into higher-level executive positions. Organizations that assign work to teams may use assessment to identify the strengths and weaknesses of individual team members and the effects of the team members' decision-making and communication styles on the team's productivity.

For assessment to support development, the information must be shared with the employee being assessed. Along with that assessment information, the employee needs suggestions for correcting skill weaknesses and for using skills already learned. The suggestions might be to participate in training courses or develop skills through new job experiences. Based on the assessment information and available development opportunities, employees should develop action plans to guide their efforts at self-improvement.

Organizations vary in the methods and sources of information they use in developmental assessment. Many organizations appraise performance. Organizations with sophisticated development systems use psychological tests to measure employees' skills, personality types, and communication styles. They may collect self, peer, and manager ratings of employees' behavior and style of working with others. The tools used for

One way to develop employees is to begin with an assessment which may consist of assigning an activity to a team and seeing who brings what skills and strengths to the team. How can this assessment help employees?

these assessment methods include the Myers-Briggs Type Indicator, assessment centers, the Benchmarks assessment, performance appraisal, and 360-degree feedback.

Myers-Briggs Type Indicator®

The most popular psychological test for employee development is the **Myers-Briggs Type Indicator (MBTI)®.** This assessment, taken by millions of people each year, identifies individuals' preferences for source of energy, means of information gathering, way of decision making, and lifestyle. The results of the assessment provide information for team building and leadership development. The assessment consists of more than 100 questions about how the person feels or prefers to behave in different situations (such as "Are you usually a good 'mixer' or rather quiet and reserved?" and so forth). The MBTI® is based on the work of Carl Jung, noted psychologist who believed that differences in individuals' behavior result from their degree of extroversion–introversion and from their psychological makeup across several other dimensions. The assessment described these differences and individuals' preferences in the four areas:

1. The *energy* dimension indicates where individuals gain interpersonal strength and vitality, measured as their degree of introversion or extroversion. Extroverted types (E) gain energy through interpersonal relationships. Introverted types (I) gain energy by focusing on inner thoughts and feelings.
2. The *information-gathering* dimension relates to the preparations individuals make before making decisions. Individuals with a Sensing (S) preference tend to gather the facts and details to prepare for a decision. Intuitive types (N) tend to focus less on the facts and more on possibilities and relationships among them.
3. In *decision making,* individuals differ in the amount of consideration they give to their own and others' values and feelings, as opposed to the hard facts of a situation. Individuals with a Thinking (T) preference try always to be objective in making decisions. Individuals with a Feeling (F) preference tend to evaluate the impact of the alternatives on others, as well as their own feelings; they are more subjective.
4. The *lifestyle* dimension describes an individual's tendency to be either flexible or structured. Individuals with a Judging (J) preference focus on goals, establish deadlines, and prefer to be conclusive. Individuals with a Perceiving (P) preference enjoy surprises, are comfortable with changing a decision, and dislike deadlines.

The alternatives for each of the four dichotomies result in 16 possible combinations, the personality types summarized in Table 9.2. Of course people are likely to be mixtures of these types; but the point of the assessment is that certain types predominate in individuals.

As a result of their psychological types, people develop strengths and weaknesses. For example, individuals who are Introverted, Sensing, Thinking, and Judging (known as ISTJs) tend to be serious, quiet, practical, orderly, and logical. They can organize tasks, be decisive, and follow through on plans and goals. As a consequence, however—that is, by not having the opposite preferences (Extroversion, Intuition, Feeling, and Perceiving)—ISTJs have several weaknesses. They may have difficulty responding to unexpected opportunities, appear to their colleagues to be too task-oriented or impersonal, and make decisions too fast.

Applying this kind of information about employees' preferences or tendencies helps organizations understand the communication, motivation, teamwork, work styles, and leadership of the people in their groups. For example, salespeople or executives who want to communicate better can apply what they learn about their own

Myers-Briggs Type Indicator (MBTI)® Psychological test that identifies individuals' preferences for source of energy, means of information gathering, way of decision making, and lifestyle, providing information for team building and leadership development.

TABLE 9.2

Personality Types Used in the Myers-Briggs Type Indicator Assessment

	SENSING TYPES (S)		INTUITIVE TYPES (N)	
	THINKING (T)	FEELING (F)	FEELING (F)	THINKING (T)
Introverts (I) Judging (J)	**ISTJ** Quiet, serious, earn success by thoroughness and dependability. Practical, matter-of-fact, realistic, and responsible. Decide logically what should be done and work toward it steadily, regardless of distractions. Take pleasure in making everything orderly and organized—their work, their home, their life. Value traditions and loyalty.	**ISFJ** Quiet, friendly, responsible, and conscientious. Committed and steady in meeting their obligations. Thorough, painstaking, and accurate. Loyal, considerate, notice and remember specifics about people who are important to them, concerned with how others feel. Strive to create an orderly and harmonious environment at work and at home.	**INFJ** Seek meaning and connection in ideas, relationships, and material possessions. Want to understand what motivates people and are insightful about others. Conscientious and committed to their firm values. Develop a clear vision about how best to serve the common good. Organized and decisive in implementing their vision.	**INTJ** Have original minds and great drive for implementing their ideas and achieving their goals. Quickly see patterns in external events and develop long-range explanatory perspectives. When committed, organize a job and carry it through. Skeptical and independent, have high standards of competence and performance—for themselves and others.
Perceiving (P)	**ISTP** Tolerant and flexible, quiet observers until a problem appears, then act quickly to find workable solutions. Analyze what makes things work and readily get through large amounts of data to isolate the core of practical problems. Interested in cause and effect, organize facts using logical principles, value efficiency.	**ISFP** Quiet, friendly, sensitive, and kind. Enjoy the present moment, what's going on around them. Like to have their own space and to work within their own time frame. Loyal and committed to their values and to people who are important to them. Dislike disagreements and conflicts, do not force their opinions or values on others.	**INFP** Idealistic, loyal to their values and to people who are important to them. Want an external life that is congruent with their values. Curious, quick to see possibilities, can be catalysts for implementing ideas. Seek to understand people and to help them fulfill their potential. Adaptable, flexible, and accepting unless a value is threatened.	**INTP** Seek to develop logical explanations for everything that interests them. Theoretical and abstract, interested more in ideas than in social interaction. Quiet, contained, flexible, and adaptable. Have unusual ability to focus in depth to solve problems in their area of interest. Skeptical, sometimes critical, always analytical.

personality styles and the way other people perceive them. For team development, the MBTI® can help teams match team members with assignments based on their preferences and thus improve problem solving.[11] The team could assign brainstorming (idea-generating) tasks to employees with an Intuitive preference and evaluation of the ideas to employees with a Sensing preference.

Research on the validity, reliability, and effectiveness of the MBTI® is inconclusive.[12] People who take the MBTI® find it a positive experience and say it helps them change their behavior. MBTI® scores appear to be related to one's occupation; that is, people in the same occupation tend to have the same or similar personality types. Analysis of managers' scores in the United States, England, Latin America, and Japan found that a large majority of managers are ISTJ, INTJ, ESTJ, or ENTJ. However, MBTI® scores are not necessarily stable over time. Studies in which the MBTI® was administered at two different times found that as few as one-fourth of those who took the assessment were classified as exactly the same type the second time. Still, the MBTI® is a valuable tool for understanding communication styles and the ways people prefer to interact with others. It is not appropriate for measuring job performance, however, or as the only means of evaluating promotion potential.

SENSING TYPES (S)		INTUITIVE TYPES (N)	
THINKING (T)	FEELING (F)	FEELING (F)	THINKING (T)

Extroverts (E) Perceiving (P)	**ESTP** Flexible and tolerant, they take a pragmatic approach focused on immediate results. Theories and conceptual explanations bore them—they want to act energetically to solve the problem. Focus on the here-and-now, spontaneous, enjoy each moment that they can be active with others. Enjoy material comforts and style. Learn best through doing.	**ESFP** Outgoing, friendly, and accepting. Exuberant lovers of life, people, and material comforts. Enjoy working with others to make things happen. Bring common sense and a realistic approach to their work, and make work fun. Flexible and spontaneous, adapt readily to new people and environments. Learn best by trying a new skill with other people.	**ENFP** Warmly enthusiastic and imaginative. See life as full of possibilities. Make connections between events and information very quickly, and confidently proceed based on the patterns they see. Want a lot of affirmation from others, and readily give appreciation and support. Spontaneous and flexible, often rely on their ability to improvise and their verbal fluency.	**ENTP** Quick, ingenious, stimulating, alert, and outspoken. Resourceful in solving new and challenging problems. Adept at generating conceptual possibilities and then analyzing them strategically. Good at reading other people. Bored by routine, will seldom do the same thing the same way, apt to turn to one new interest after another.
Judging (J)	**ESTJ** Practical, realistic, matter-of-fact. Decisive, quickly move to implement decisions. Organize projects and people to get things done, focus on getting results in the most efficient way possible. Take care of routine details. Have a clear set of logical standards, systematically follow them and want others to also. Forceful in implementing their plans.	**ESFJ** Warmhearted, conscientious, and cooperative. Want harmony in their environment, work with determination to establish it. Like to work with others to complete tasks accurately and on time. Loyal, follow through even in small matters. Notice what others need in their day-by-day lives and try to provide it. Want to be appreciated for who they are and for what they contribute.	**ENFJ** Warm, empathetic, responsive, and responsible. Highly attuned to the emotions, needs, and motivations of others. Find potential in everyone, want to help others fulfill their potential. May act as catalysts for individual and group growth. Loyal, responsive to praise and criticism. Sociable, facilitate others in a group, and provide inspiring leadership.	**ENTJ** Frank, decisive, assume leadership readily. Quickly see illogical and inefficient procedures and policies, develop and implement comprehensive systems to solve organizational problems. Enjoy long-term planning and goal setting. Usually well informed, well read, enjoy expanding their knowledge and passing it on to others. Forceful in presenting their ideas.

Assessment Centers

At an **assessment center,** multiple raters or evaluators (assessors) evaluate employees' performance on a number of exercises.[13] An assessment center is usually an off-site location such as a conference center. Usually 6 to 12 employees participate at one time. The primary use of assessment centers is to identify whether employees have the personality characteristics, administrative skills, and interpersonal skills needed for managerial jobs. Organizations also use them to determine whether employees have the skills needed for working in teams.

The types of exercises used in assessment centers include leaderless group discussions, interviews, in-baskets, and role plays.[14] In a **leaderless group discussion,** a team of five to seven employees is assigned a problem and must work together to solve it within a certain time period. The problem may involve buying and selling supplies, nominating a subordinate for an award, or assembling a product. Interview questions typically cover each employee's work and personal experiences, skill strengths and weaknesses, and career plans. In-basket exercises, discussed as a selection method in Chapter 6, simulate the administrative tasks of a manager's job, using a pile of documents for the employee to handle. In role plays, the participant takes the part of a manager or employee in a situation involving the skills to be assessed. For example, a participant might be given the role of a manager who must discuss performance problems with an employee, played by

assessment center
An assessment process in which multiple raters or evaluators (assessors) evaluate employees' performance on a number of exercises, usually as they work in a group at an off-site location.

leaderless group discussion
An assessment center exercise in which a team of five to seven employees is assigned a problem and must work together to solve it within a certain time period.

someone who works for the assessment center. Other exercises in assessment centers might include interest and aptitude tests to evaluate an employee's vocabulary, general mental ability, and reasoning skills. Personality tests may be used to determine employees' ability get along with others, tolerance for uncertainty, and other traits related to success as a manager or team member.

The assessors are usually managers who have been trained to look for employee behaviors that are related to the skills being assessed. Typically, each assessor observes and records one or two employees' behaviors in each exercise. The assessors review their notes and rate each employee's level of skills (for example, 5 = high level of leadership skills, 1 = low level of leadership skills). After all the employees have completed the exercises, the assessors discuss their observations of each employee. They compare their ratings and try to agree on each employee's rating for each of the skills.

As we mentioned in Chapter 6, research suggests that assessment center ratings are valid for predicting performance, salary level, and career advancement.[15] Assessment centers may also be useful for development because of the feedback that participants receive about their attitudes, skill strengths, and weaknesses.[16] Managers at Steelcase, which makes office furniture, participate in assessment center activities including an in-basket exercise, an interview simulation, a timed scheduling exercise in which participants fill positions created by absences, and a role play in which managers confront an employee with a performance problem and work out a solution. These exercises relate closely to what managers have to do at work, so the feedback they receive in the assessment center can target specific skills they need as managers.[17]

Benchmarks

Benchmarks
A measurement tool that gathers ratings of a manager's use of skills associated with success in managing.

A development method that focuses on measuring management skills is an instrument called **Benchmarks.** This measurement tool gathers ratings of a manager's use of skills associated with success in managing. The items measured by Benchmarks are based on research into the lessons that executives learn in critical events of their careers.[18] Items measure the 16 skills and perspectives listed in Table 9.3, including how well managers deal with subordinates, acquire resources, and create a productive work climate. Research has found that managers who have these skills are more likely to receive positive performance evaluations, be considered promotable, and be promoted.[19]

To provide a complete picture of managers' skills, the managers' supervisors, their peers, and the managers themselves all complete the instrument. The results include a summary report, which the organization provides to the manager so he or she can see the self-ratings in comparison to the ratings by others. Also available with this method is a development guide containing examples of experiences that enhance each skill and ways successful managers use the skill.

Performance Appraisals and 360-Degree Feedback

As we stated in Chapter 8, *performance appraisal* is the process of measuring employees' performance. This information can be useful for employee development under certain conditions.[20] The appraisal system must tell employees specifically about their performance problems and ways to improve their performance. Employees must gain a clear understanding of the differences between current performance and expected performance. The appraisal process must identify causes of the performance discrepancy and develop plans for improving performance. Managers must be trained to deliver frequent performance feedback and must monitor employees' progress in carrying out their action plans.

TABLE 9.3

Skills Related to Success as a Manager

Resourcefulness	Can think strategically, engage in flexible problem solving, and work effectively with higher management.
Doing whatever it takes	Has perseverance and focus in the face of obstacles.
Being a quick study	Quickly masters new technical and business knowledge.
Building and mending relationships	Knows how to build and maintain working relationships with coworkers and external parties.
Leading subordinates	Delegates to subordinates effectively, broadens their opportunities, and acts with fairness toward them.
Compassion and sensitivity	Shows genuine interest in others and sensitivity to subordinates' needs.
Straightforwardness and composure	Is honorable and steadfast.
Setting a developmental climate	Provides a challenging climate to encourage subordinates' development.
Confronting problem subordinates	Acts decisively and fairly when dealing with problem subordinates.
Team orientation	Accomplishes tasks through managing others.
Balance between personal life and work	Balances work priorities with personal life so that neither is neglected.
Decisiveness	Prefers quick and approximate actions to slow and precise ones in many management situations.
Self-awareness	Has an accurate picture of strengths and weaknesses and is willing to improve.
Hiring talented staff	Hires talented people for the team.
Putting people at ease	Displays warmth and a good sense of humor.
Acting with flexibility	Can behave in ways that are often seen as opposites.

SOURCE: Adapted with permission from C. D. McCauley, M. M. Lombardo, and C. J. Usher, "Diagnosing Management Development Needs: An Instrument Based on How Managers Develop," *Journal of Management* 15 (1989), pp. 389–403.

A recent trend in performance appraisals, also discussed in Chapter 8, is *360-degree feedback*—performance measurement by the employee's supervisor, peers, employees, and customers. Often the feedback involves rating the individual in terms of work-related behaviors. For development purposes, the rater would identify an area of behavior as a strength of that employee or an area requiring further development. The results presented to the employee show how he or she was rated on each item and how self-evaluations differ from other raters' evaluations. The individual reviews the results, seeks clarification from the raters, and sets specific development goals based on the strengths and weaknesses identified.[21]

Consider how Capital One, a consumer credit company, uses 360-degree feedback.[22] The company developed assessments based on specific competencies, so raters evaluate those areas of performance, concentrating on three or four strengths or areas requiring development. The questions seek comments, which often provide specific information about what aspect of the competency needs to be improved. Using the ratings and comments, the company can tailor coaching and training to fit each person's needs. In this way, the company links feedback from the 360-degree assessment to employee development plans.

There are several benefits of 360-degree feedback. Organizations collect multiple perspectives of managers' performance, allowing employees to compare their own personal evaluations with the views of others. This method also establishes formal communications about behaviors and skill ratings between employees and their internal and external customers. For example, in response to feedback from the employees in his group, a telecommunications executive learned to air his opinions more freely in meetings of the company's executive committee.[23] This method is most likely to be effective if the rating instrument enables reliable or consistent ratings, assesses behaviors or skills that are job related, and is easy to use. Also, the system should ensure raters' confidentiality, and managers should receive and act on the feedback.[24]

There are potential limitations of 360-degree feedback. This method demands a significant amount of time for raters to complete the evaluations. If raters, especially subordinates or peers, provide negative feedback, some managers might try to identify and punish them. A facilitator is needed to help interpret results. Finally, simply delivering ratings to a manager does not provide ways for the manager to act on the feedback (for example, development planning, meeting with raters, or taking courses). As noted earlier, any form of assessment should be accompanied by suggestions for improvement and development of an action plan.

Job Experiences

Most employee development occurs through **job experiences**[25]—the combination of relationships, problems, demands, tasks, and other features of an employee's jobs. Using job experiences for employee development assumes that development is most likely to occur when the employee's skills and experiences do not entirely match the skills required for the employee's current job. To succeed, employees must stretch their skills. In other words, they must learn new skills, apply their skills and knowledge in new ways, and master new experiences.[26] For example, companies that want to prepare employees to expand overseas markets are assigning them to a variety of international jobs.

LO4
Explain how job experiences can be used for developing skills.

job experiences
The combination of relationships, problems, demands, tasks, and other features of an employee's jobs.

Working outside one's home country is the most important job experience that can develop an employee for a career in the global economy.

Most of what we know about development through job experiences comes from a series of studies conducted by the Center for Creative Leadership.[27] These studies asked executives to identify key career events that made a difference in their managerial styles and the lessons they learned from these experiences. The key events included job assignments (such as fixing a failed operation), interpersonal relationships (getting along with supervisors), and types of transitions (situations in which the manager at first lacked the necessary background). Through job experiences like these, managers learn how to handle common challenges, prove themselves, lead change, handle pressure, and influence others.

The usefulness of job experiences for employee development varies depending on whether the employee views the experiences as positive or negative sources of stress. When employees view job experiences as positive stressors, the experiences challenge them and stimulate learning. When they view job experiences as negative stressors, employees may suffer from high levels of harmful stress. Of the job demands studied, managers were most likely to experience negative stress from creating change and overcoming obstacles (adverse business conditions, lack of management support, lack of personal support, or a difficult boss). Research suggests that all of the job demands except obstacles are related to learning.[28] Organizations should offer job experiences that are most likely to increase learning, and they should consider the consequences of situations that involve negative stress.

Although the research on development through job experiences has focused on managers, line employees also can learn through job experiences. Organizations may, for example, use job experiences to develop skills needed for teamwork, including conflict resolution, data analysis, and customer service. These experiences may occur when forming a team and when employees switch roles within a team.

Various job assignments can provide for employee development. The organization may enlarge the employee's current job or move the employee to different jobs. Lateral moves include job rotation, transfer, or temporary assignment to another organization. The organization may also use downward moves or promotions as a source of job experience. Figure 9.2 summarizes these alternatives.

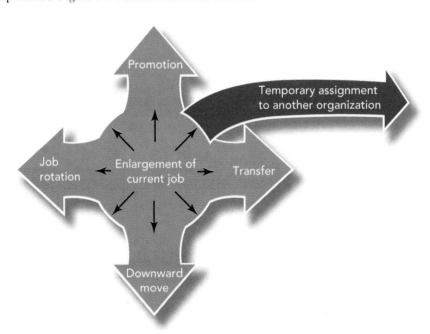

Figure 9.2

How Job Experiences Are Used for Employee Development

Job Enlargement

As Chapter 4 stated in the context of job design, *job enlargement* involves adding challenges or new responsibilities to employees' current jobs. Examples include completing a special project, switching roles within a work team, or researching new ways to serve customers. An engineering employee might join a task force developing new career paths for technical employees. The work on the project could give the engineer a leadership role through which the engineer learns about the company's career development system while also practicing leadership skills to help the task force reach its goals. In this way, job enlargement not only makes a job more interesting but also creates an opportunity for employees to develop new skills.

Job Rotation

Another job design technique that can be applied to employee development is *job rotation,* moving employees through a series of job assignments in one or more functional areas. W. W. Grainger, a distributor of business maintenance products, regularly moves employees across functions—for example, from marketing to information technology, from field-office work to corporate-office work, from regional sales offices to distribution centers—to help employees think strategically about different parts of the business. Each employee has a customized development plan, and employees are assigned new positions based on the skills they need. The length of time in each position depends on the skills and experience the employee needs. Some employees return to their original jobs, while others may move to another department.[29]

Job rotation helps employees gain an appreciation for the company's goals, increases their understanding of different company functions, develops a network of contacts, and improves problem-solving and decision-making skills.[30] Job rotation also helps employees increase their salary and earn promotions faster. However, job rotation poses some problems for employees and the organization. Knowing they will be rotated to another job may give the employees a short-term perspective on problems and their solutions. Employees may feel less satisfied and motivated because they have difficulty developing specialized skills and leave the position too soon to fulfill any challenging assignments. The rotation of employees through a department may hurt productivity and increase the workload of those who remain after employees are rotated out. Job rotation is most likely to succeed when it meets certain conditions:[31]

- Job rotation is used for developing skills as well as gaining experience for management careers.
- Employees understand specifically what skills rotation is to develop.
- The organization uses job rotation for all levels and types of employees.
- Job rotation is linked with the career management process so employees know what development needs each assignment addresses.
- The organization manages the timing of rotations to maximize their benefits and minimize their costs.
- All employees have equal opportunities for job rotation, regardless of their demographic group.

Transfers, Promotions, and Downward Moves

Most companies use upward, downward, and lateral moves as an option for employee development. In a **transfer,** the organization assigns an employee to a position in a different area of the company. Transfers do not necessarily increase job responsibili-

transfer
Assignment of an employee to a position in a different area of the company, usually in a lateral move.

ties or compensation. They are usually lateral moves, that is, moves to a job with a similar level of responsibility. They may involve relocation to another part of the country or even to another country.

Relocation can be stressful because of the demands of moving, especially when family members are affected. People have to find new housing, shopping, health care, and leisure facilities, and they often lack the support of nearby friends and family. These stresses come at the same time the employee must learn the expectations and responsibilities associated with the new position. Because transfers can provoke anxiety, many companies have difficulty getting employees to accept them. Employees most willing to accept transfers tend to be those with high career ambitions, a belief that the organization offers a promising future, and a belief that accepting the transfer will help the company succeed.[32]

A **downward move** occurs when an employee is given less responsibility and authority. The organization may demote an employee because of poor performance or move the employee to a lower-level position in another function so that the employee can develop different skills. The temporary cross-functional move is the most common way to use downward moves for employee development. For example, engineers who want to move into management often take lower-level positions, such as shift supervisor, to develop their management skills.

Many employees have difficulty associating transfers and downward moves with development; these changes may feel more like forms of punishment. Employees often decide to leave an organization rather than accept such a change, and then the organization must bear the costs of replacing those employees. Employees will be more likely to accept transfers and downward moves as development opportunities if the organization provides information about the change and its possible benefits and involves the employee in planning the change. Employees are also more likely to be positive about such a recommendation if the organization provides clear performance objectives and frequent feedback. Employers can encourage an employee to relocate by providing financial assistance with the move, information about the new location and job, and help for family members, such as identifying schools, child care and elder care options, and job search assistance for the employee's spouse.[33]

A **promotion** involves moving an employee into a position with greater challenges, more responsibility, and more authority than in the previous job. Usually promotions include pay increases. Because promotions improve the person's pay, status, and feelings of accomplishment, employees are more willing to accept promotions than lateral or downward moves. Even so, employers can increase the likelihood that employees will accept promotions by providing the same kind of information and assistance that are used to support transfers and downward moves. Organizations can more easily offer promotions if they are profitable and growing. In other conditions, opportunities for promoting employees may be limited.

Temporary Assignments with Other Organizations

In some cases, an employer may benefit from the skills an employee can learn at another organization. The employer may encourage the employee to participate in an **externship**—a full-time temporary position at another organization. Mercer Management, a consulting firm, uses externships to develop employees who want experience in a specific industry.[34] Mercer Management promises to employ the externs after their assignments end. One employee with several years' experience as a Mercer consultant became vice president of Internet services for Binney and Smith, the

downward move
Assignment of an employee to a position with less responsibility and authority.

promotion
Assignment of an employee to a position with greater challenges, more responsibility, and more authority than in the previous job, usually accompanied by a pay increase.

externship
Employee development through a full-time temporary position at another organization.

BEST PRACTICES

SABBATICALS FOSTER DEVELOPMENT AT INTEL AND XEROX

Sabbaticals are a part of the development opportunities available to all Intel employees after seven years with the company. Employees may take up to eight weeks off, and some add sabbaticals and vacation time together for a three-month break. But the time off presents a scheduling challenge for those who remain on the job. In 2004, over 4,000 Intel workers were gone at some point for their sabbaticals. So, managers and employees must work closely to schedule the time away and plan who will cover the work.

The effort is worth it for participants and the company, however. Employees like Clifton Corpus find that the time off changes their perspective for the better. Says Corpus, "Before my sabbatical, I wasn't proactive. I just wanted to do a good job. Now I want to take

more responsibility in order to advance." Not only does the employee on sabbatical receive the benefits of this program, but the employees who handle that person's work receive experience that Intel managers consider valuable cross-training.

Xerox spreads the benefits even further with Social Service Leave, a sabbatical program that encourages community service. Employees must apply to be selected for the program, in which they can serve a nonprofit organization for up to a year. One employee chosen, Steven Mueller, worked with Green Chimneys Children's Services in Brewster, New York, a residential program for troubled children. Mueller, a Xerox sales manager, worked with a group of boys on the facility's farm. Projects included restoring a worn-out old tractor—

a goal that took three months. Recalling the glee of the boys when the tractor finally started, Mueller says, "I gained a tremendous sense of satisfaction and purpose."

The boys weren't the only people who were pleased. Joseph Cahalan, Xerox's vice president of communications and social responsibility, sees the program as a way for employees to develop leadership skills. Because employees go to the nonprofit organizations as volunteers, not managers, they have to accomplish goals through interpersonal skills rather than management authority. Says Cahalan, "It makes them more effective managers when they get back."

SOURCE: Based on Christine Larson, "Time Out," *U.S. News & World Report*, February 28, 2005, pp. EE2–EE8.

maker of Crayola crayons. He had been consulting on an Internet project for Binney and Smith and wanted to implement his recommendations, rather than just give them to the client and move on to another project. He started working at Binney and Smith while remaining employed by Mercer Management, though his pay comes from Binney and Smith. Mercer believes that employees who participate in its externship program will remain committed to the consulting firm because they have a chance to learn and grow professionally without the demands of a job search.

sabbatical
A leave of absence from an organization to renew or develop skills.

Temporary assignments can include a **sabbatical**—a leave of absence from an organization to renew or develop skills. Employees on sabbatical often receive full pay and benefits. Sabbaticals let employees get away from the day-to-day stresses of their jobs and acquire new skills and perspectives. Sabbaticals also allow employees more time for personal pursuits such as writing a book or spending more time with family members. Fallon Worldwide, an advertising agency, offers a sabbatical program called Dreamcatchers to staff members who want to work on a project or travel. Dreamcatchers was developed to help the agency avoid employee burnout and loss of creative edge. Employees have taken time off to write novels, to kayak, and to motorcycle through the Alps. Fallon matches employee contributions of up to $1,000 annually for two years and offers up to two extra weeks of paid vacation. The agency's partners believe the program has helped them retain key employees and recruit new ones, as well as meet the goal of recharging creativity.[35] How employees spend their sabbaticals varies from company to company. Some employees may work for a nonprofit service agency; others may study at a college or university or travel and work on special projects in non-U.S. subsidiaries of the company. The "Best Practices" box describes how sabbaticals work at Intel and Xerox.

Interpersonal Relationships

Employees can also develop skills and increase their knowledge about the organization and its customers by interacting with a more experienced organization member. Two types of relationships used for employee development are mentoring and coaching.

Mentors

A **mentor** is an experienced, productive senior employee who helps develop a less experienced employee, called the *protégé*. Most mentoring relationships develop informally as a result of interests or values shared by the mentor and protégé. According to research, the employees most likely to seek and attract a mentor have certain personality characteristics: emotional stability, ability to adapt their behavior to the situation, and high needs for power and achievement.[36] Mentoring relationships also can develop as part of the organization's planned effort to bring together successful senior employees with less experienced employees.

One major advantage of formal mentoring programs is that they ensure access to mentors for all employees, regardless of gender or race. Another advantage is that participants in a company-sponsored mentoring program know what is expected of them.[37] However, in an artificially created relationship, mentors may have difficulty providing counseling and coaching.[38] Mentoring programs tend to be most successful when they are voluntary and participants understand the details of the program. Rewarding managers for employee development is also important, because it signals that mentoring and other development activities are worthwhile. In addition, the organization should carefully select mentors based on their interpersonal and technical skills, train them for the role, and evaluate whether the program has met its objectives. Information technology can help organizations meet some of these guidelines. The "e-HRM" box describes how computer software by Triple Creek Associates helps employees find and select their mentors and stay on track to meeting their development goals.

New York Hospital–Cornell Medical Center developed a well-planned mentoring program for its housekeeping employees. Each mentor has between 5 and 10 protégés to meet with once each quarter. To qualify as mentors, employees must receive outstanding performance evaluations, demonstrate strong interpersonal skills, and be able to perform basic cleaning tasks and essential duties of all housekeeping positions, including safety procedures. The mentors undergo a two-day training program that emphasizes communication skills. They also learn how to convey information about the job and give directions effectively without criticizing employees. The program helps new employees learn their duties more quickly, and it gives the mentors a chance to quickly identify and correct problems.[39]

LO5
Summarize principles of successful mentoring programs.

mentor
An experienced, productive senior employee who helps develop a less experienced employee (a protégé).

E-HRM

TRIPLE CREEK ASSOCIATES PUTS MENTORING ONLINE

One of the big challenges of mentoring is finding the right matches between employees with development needs and people with experience in the areas requiring development. If finding a match sounds a lot like a dating service, then the service offered by Triple Creek Associates is not surprising: an electronic matchmaking service for mentoring. In a typical arrangement, a Triple Creek client recruits people willing to serve as mentors, builds up a database in which these people provide information about their skills and work experience, and then begins offering the mentoring program to its employees. Triple Creek hosts the software for the process and usually tailors it to the company's human resource requirements.

To use the system, an employee completes a self-profile that indicates that employee's areas of development need. The system then searches the database, looking for potential mentors and rating them according to how well their strengths match the person's development needs. The employee can see which of these potential mentors rank as the closest matches and can select one or more to interview in person, over the phone, or online. When the employee has found a good match, the mentoring relationship begins, proceeding along the terms of a formal mentoring agreement established by the pair. During the process, the Triple Creek system provides meeting reminders and evaluation forms so that the participants can track their progress.

One of the companies that uses the Triple Creek system is Dow Chemical, which has 1,500 mentoring pairs enrolled in the system. With offices in 167 countries, the company's management knew it couldn't rely on employees to physically find the mentors with the necessary background—the best match for an employee in Midland, Texas, could be a manager in Germany.

When Dow employee Michael Witt wanted to deepen his management ability and knowledge of the corporation, he found a mentor through this system. Witt, whose title was products stewardship specialist, was surprised to find that the closest match was the company's chief information officer, David Kepler. Though Witt, in his words, "hadn't even been to the executive offices," he contacted Kepler, and they began meeting periodically to discuss Witt's career and the company's products. The mentoring relationship helped Witt serve on a team that oversees product development, and Witt is optimistic about his career prospects at Dow. Kepler, too, is pleased with the mentoring system. He praises the requirement that protégés do the work of establishing goals, choosing a mentor, and evaluating progress. Says Kepler, "That forces them to think about what they want out of the relationship."

SOURCE: Based on Eve Tahmincioglu, "Looking for a Mentor? Technology Can Help Make the Right Match," *Workforce Management*, December 2004, pp. 63–65; and Triple Creek Associates, "Tour," www.3creek.com, accessed May 12, 2005.

Mentors and protégés can both benefit from a mentoring relationship. Protégés receive career support, including coaching, protection, sponsorship, challenging assignments, and visibility among the organization's managers. They also receive benefits of a positive relationship—a friend and role model who accepts them, has a positive opinion toward them, and gives them a chance to talk about their worries. Employees with mentors are also more likely to be promoted, earn higher salaries, and have more influence within their organization.[40] Acting as a mentor gives managers a chance to develop their interpersonal skills and increase their feelings that they are

HR HOW TO

GUIDELINES FOR COACHING

Because employees are an essential, valuable resource, managers should be as involved in employee development as they are in other decisions about resources such as setting budgets, schedules, and sales targets. Managers often have not been formally trained in coaching and other development methods, however. A good starting point for managers is to meet the guidelines for coaching below. In addition, managers' own development plans probably should include some training in coaching and other aspects of employee development. By helping employees achieve more and be more effective, good manager-coaches help their entire team achieve.

- *The coach holds every team member accountable for development.* Managers should meet with each employee at least once a year to review the employee's career development. The employee should have specific goals and action plans to discuss at these meetings.

- *The coach inspires each team member to improve.* Each employee should prepare a written development plan. Some employees may be reluctant to prepare a plan because they are comfortable maintaining their current position in the organization, doing familiar tasks each day. However, the rate of change in today's business environment simply does not permit this view of work. Even staying in the same position requires continuous learning.

- *The coach uses experiences as teaching opportunities.* Managers should look beyond formal reviews to see day-to-day opportunities for coaching. How could the employee have handled the difficult customer or the flood of phone calls? What did someone do well that can be shared with the rest of the team?

- *The coach is committed to coaching.* Managers should support employees when they pursue development programs. If the employee will attend a workshop, the manager should support the effort to learn, not undermine it with comments such as, "The work will be piling up while you're gone."

- *The coach strengthens the whole team.* Managers should identify opportunities for job rotation. Part of coaching is noticing when employees might benefit the organization by trying new activities and learning new skills.

SOURCE: Based on Cliff F. Grimes, "Coaching Employees," Accel-Team, www.accel-team.com, accessed April 15, 2005.

---

contributing something important to the organization. Working with the protégé on technical matters such as new research in the field may also increase the mentor's technical knowledge. When General Electric became involved in e-commerce, it used younger employees with Web expertise to mentor older managers. As the veterans became more familiar with the Internet, their young mentors became more comfortable working with senior managers and developed their business expertise.[41]

So that more employees can benefit from mentoring, some organizations use *group mentoring programs*, which assign four to six protégés to a successful senior employee. A potential advantage of group mentoring is that protégés can learn from each other as well as from the mentor. The leader helps protégés understand the organization, guides them in analyzing their experiences, and helps them clarify career directions. Each member of the group may complete specific assignments, or the group may work together on a problem or issue.

LO6
Tell how managers
and peers develop
employees through
coaching.

Coaching

A **coach** is a peer or manager who works with an employee to motivate the employee, help him or her develop skills, and provide reinforcement and feedback. Coaches may play one or more of three roles:[42]

coach
A peer or manager who works with an employee to motivate the employee, help him or her develop skills, and provide reinforcement and feedback.

1. Working one-on-one with an employee, as when giving feedback.
2. Helping employees learn for themselves—for example, helping them find experts and teaching them to obtain feedback from others.
3. Providing resources such as mentors, courses, or job experiences.

The "HR How To" box on page 303 offers guidelines for effective coaching.

Best Buy, a consumer-electronics retailer, has invested nearly $10 million on coaches for all top managers.[43] Once a month, top executives spend a few hours with an industrial psychologist who helps them work through leadership issues. One manager discussed with his coach how to balance the needs of some of the managers who worked for him with the company's business needs. His managers were more comfortable focusing on traditional store retailing at a time when the company needed a focus on competition on the Internet. The manager being coached needed to learn how to lead his team and push new ideas without squelching team members.

LO7
Identify the steps in
the process of
career management.

❧ SYSTEMS FOR CAREER MANAGEMENT

Employee development is most likely to meet the organization's needs if it is part of a human resource system of career management. In practice, organizations' career management systems vary. Some rely heavily on informal relationships, while others are sophisticated programs. As shown in Figure 9.3, a basic career management system involves four steps: self-assessment, reality check, goal setting, and action planning. At each step, both the employee and the organization have responsibilities. The system is most likely to be beneficial if it is linked to the organization's objectives and needs, has support from top management, and is created with employee participation.[44] Human resource professionals can also contribute to the system's success by ensuring that it is linked to other HR practices such as performance management, training, and recruiting.

Figure 9.3

Steps and Responsibilities in the Career Management Process

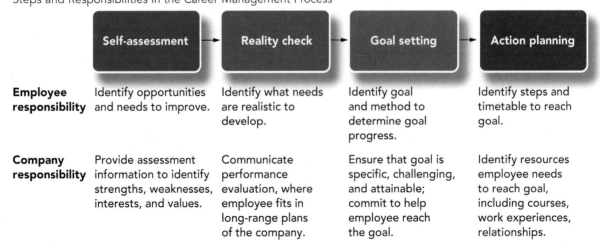

	Self-assessment	Reality check	Goal setting	Action planning
Employee responsibility	Identify opportunities and needs to improve.	Identify what needs are realistic to develop.	Identify goal and method to determine goal progress.	Identify steps and timetable to reach goal.
Company responsibility	Provide assessment information to identify strengths, weaknesses, interests, and values.	Communicate performance evaluation, where employee fits in long-range plans of the company.	Ensure that goal is specific, challenging, and attainable; commit to help employee reach the goal.	Identify resources employee needs to reach goal, including courses, work experiences, relationships.

Self-Assessment

In discussing the methods of employee development, we highlighted several assessment tools. Such tools may be applied to the first stage of career development, **self-assessment.** This is the use of information by employees to determine their career interests, values, aptitudes, and behavioral tendencies. The employee's responsibility is to identify opportunities and personal areas needing improvement. The organization's responsibility is to provide assessment information for identifying strengths, weaknesses, interests, and values.

Self-assessment tools often include psychological tests such as the Myers-Briggs Type Inventory (described earlier in the chapter), the Strong-Campbell Interest Inventory, and the Self-Directed Search. The Strong-Campbell inventory helps employees identify their occupational and job interests. The Self-Directed Search identifies employees' preferences for working in different kinds of environments—sales, counseling, and so on. Tests may also help employees identify the relative values they place on work and leisure activities. Self-assessment tools can include exercises such as the one in Figure 9.4. This type of exercise helps an employee consider his or her current career status, future plans, and the fit between the career and the employee's current situation and resources. Some organizations provide counselors to help employees in the self-assessment process and to interpret the results of psychological tests. Completing the self-assessment can help employees identify a development need. Such a need can result from gaps between current skills or interests and the type of work or position the employee has or wants.

These benefits are realized by the Opportunity Knocks development program established by First USA.[45] Following the bank's merger with Bank One, the company found that employees felt dissatisfied with the opportunities they perceived for professional growth, so First USA set up Opportunity Knocks to help employees take charge of their careers. The program's philosophy is what it calls the "five Ps": person, perspective, place, possibility, and plan. The first of these goals is related to self-assessment and the others relate to other steps in the career management process. The person (individual employee) is supposed to understand his or her own skills, values, and interests and communicate them. To help the employee do this, the company provides self-assessment tools.

self-assessment
The use of information by employees to determine their career interests, values, aptitudes, behavioral tendencies, and development needs.

Reality Check

In the next step of career management, the **reality check,** employees receive information about their skills and knowledge and where these assets fit into the organization's plans. The employee's responsibility is to identify what skills she or he could realistically develop in light of the opportunities available. The organization's responsibility is to communicate the performance evaluation and the opportunities available to the employee, given the organization's long-range plans. Opportunities might include promotions and transfers.

Usually the employer conducts the reality check as part of a performance appraisal or as the feedback stage of performance management. In well-developed career management systems, the manager may hold separate discussions for performance feedback and career development. In the philosophy of First USA's Opportunity Knocks program, the "perspective" aspect corresponds to the reality check. After completing the self-assessment, the First USA employee is expected to seek feedback (perspective) from his or her peers and manager. Along with this step, employees are supposed not only to understand their own jobs but also to develop a sense of First USA's goals and the developments in the industry, profession, and workplace that require new skills. This understanding is represented as "place" in the program's philosophy.

reality check
Information employers give employees about their skills and knowledge and where these assets fit into the organization's plans.

Figure 9.4

Sample Self-Assessment Exercise

Step 1: Where am I?
Examine current position of life and career.
Think about your life from past and present to the future. Draw a time line to represent important events.

Step 2: Who am I?
Examine different roles.
Using 3" × 5" cards, write down one answer per card to the question "Who am I?"

Step 3: Where would I like to be, and what would I like to happen?
Begin setting goals.
Consider your life from present to future. Write an autobiography answering these questions:
• What do you want to have accomplished?
• What milestones do you want to achieve?
• What do you want to be remembered for?

Step 4: An ideal year in the future
Identify resources needed.
Consider a one-year period in the future. Answer these questions:
• If you had unlimited resources, what would you do?
• What would the ideal environment look like?
• Does the ideal environment match Step 3?

Step 5: An ideal job
Create current goal.
In the present, think about an ideal job for you with your available resources. Describe your role, resources, and type of training or education needed.

Step 6: Career by objective inventory
Summarize current situation.
• What gets you excited each day?
• What do you do well? What are you known for?
• What do you need to achieve your goals?
• What could interfere with reaching your goals?
• What should you do now to move toward reaching your goals?
• What is your long-term career objective?

SOURCE: Based on J. E. McMahon and S. K. Merman, "Career Development," in *The ASTD Training and Development Handbook,* 4th ed., ed. R. L. Craig (New York:McGraw-Hill, 1996), pp. 679–97. Reproduced with permission.

Goal Setting

Based on the information from the self-assessment and reality check, the employee sets short- and long-term career objectives. These goals usually involve one or more of the following categories:

- Desired positions, such as becoming sales manager within three years.
- Level of skill to apply—for example, to use one's budgeting skills to improve the unit's cash flow problems.
- Work setting—for example, to move to corporate marketing within two years.

- Skill acquisition, such as learning how to use the company's human resource information system.

As in these examples, the goals should be specific, and they should include a date by which the goal is to be achieved. It is the employee's responsibility to identify the goal and the method of determining her or his progress toward that goal.

Usually the employee discusses the goals with his or her manager. The organization's responsibilities are to ensure that the goal is specific, challenging, and attainable and to help the employee reach the goal. At First USA, goal setting is the "possibility" part of the Opportunity Knocks philosophy. Employees are encouraged to consider a variety of possibilities: moving laterally or vertically or enriching their current job.

Action Planning

During the final step, employees prepare an action plan for how they will achieve their short- and long-term career goals. The employee is responsible for identifying the steps and timetable to reach the goals. The employer should identify resources needed, including courses, work experiences, and relationships.

Action plans may involve any one or a combination of the development methods discussed earlier in the chapter—training, assessment, job experiences, or the help of a mentor or coach. The approach used depends on the particular developmental needs and career objectives. For example, suppose the program manager in an information systems department uses feedback from performance appraisals to determine that he needs greater knowledge of project management software. The manager plans to increase that knowledge by reading articles (formal education), meeting with software vendors, and contacting the vendors' customers to ask them about the software they have used (job experiences). The manager and his supervisor agree that six months will be the target date for achieving the higher level of knowledge through these activities.

The outcome of action planning often takes the form of a career development plan. Figure 9.5 is an example of a development plan for a product manager. Development plans usually include descriptions of strengths and weaknesses, career goals, and development activities for reaching each goal. Action planning at First USA embodies the "plan" phase. Employees decide to develop particular skills and competencies that will help them reach specific career goals. To support this process, the company provides workshops and career resource centers offering business publications, career management literature, and computers. Employment development advisers are also available to counsel employees.

🎇 DEVELOPMENT-RELATED CHALLENGES

A well-designed system for employee development can help organizations face three widespread challenges: the glass ceiling, succession planning, and dysfunctional behavior by managers.

The Glass Ceiling

As we mentioned in Chapter 1, women and minorities are rare in the top level of U.S. corporations. Observers of this situation have noted that it looks as if an invisible barrier is keeping women and minorities from reaching the top jobs, a barrier that has come to be known as the **glass ceiling.** The "Did You Know . . . ?" box shows recent

LO8
Discuss how organizations are meeting the challenges of the "glass ceiling," succession planning, and dysfunctional managers.

glass ceiling
Circumstances resembling an invisible barrier that keep most women and minorities from attaining the top jobs in organizations.

Figure 9.5

Career Development Plan

| **Name:** | **Title:** Project Manager | **Immediate Manager:** |

Competencies

Please identify your three greatest strengths and areas for improvement.

Strengths

• Strategic thinking and execution (confidence, command skills, action orientation)
• Results orientation (competence, motivating others, perseverance)
• Spirit for winning (building team spirit, customer focus, respect colleagues)

Areas for Improvement

• Patience (tolerance of people or processes and sensitivity to pacing)
• Written communications (ability to write clearly and succinctly)
• Overly ambitious (too much focus on successful completion of projects rather than developing relationships with individuals involved in the projects)

Career Goals

Please describe your overall career goals.

• **Long-term:** Accept positions of increased responsibility to a level of general manager (or beyond). The areas of specific interest include but are not limited to product and brand management, technology and development, strategic planning, and marketing.
• **Short-term:** Continue to improve my skills in marketing and brand management while utilizing my skills in product management, strategic planning, and global relations.

Next Assignments

Identify potential next assignments (including timing) that would help you develop toward your career goals.

• Manager or director level in planning, development, product, or brand management. Timing estimated to be Spring 2007.

Training and Development Needs

List both training and development activities that will either help you develop in your current assignment or provide overall career development.

• Master's degree classes will allow me to practice and improve my written communications skills. The dynamics of my current position, teamwork, and reliance on other individuals allow me to practice patience and to focus on individual team members' needs along with the success of the project.

Employee _____ **Date** _____
Immediate Manager _____ **Date** _____
Mentor _____ **Date** _____

---

statistics indicating the low representation of women in the leadership of the largest U.S. corporations.

The glass ceiling is likely caused by a lack of access to training programs, appropriate developmental job experiences, and developmental relationships such as mentoring.[46] According to research, women and men have equal access to job experiences involving transitions or creating change.[47] But male managers receive significantly more assignments involving great responsibility (high stakes, managing business diversity, handling external pressure) than female managers of similar ability and man-

WOMEN ARE FAR OUTNUMBERED AT THE TOP

Although women are about half of the U.S. labor force and hold about half of management and professional jobs, their numbers remain small in the upper levels of corporate management. Less than 2 percent of Fortune 500 chief executive officers are females, and as shown, roughly 16 percent of corporate officers are female. When the highest-paid officers are counted, their representation shrinks. The reasons for the low numbers aren't always obvious. Company surveys have found that many high-contributing employees leave because they feel they aren't valued, lack opportunities for advancement, or struggle to develop a leadership style that subordinates are comfortable with (not weak but not bossy). These problems could all be addressed through more effective employee development.

SOURCE: Catalyst, "Women in the Fortune 500," news release, February 10, 2005, www.catalystwomen.org; Claudia H. Deutsch, "It's Boring at the Top for Female Executives," *International Herald Tribune*, May 3, 2005, www.iht.com; and Carol Hymowitz, "Carly Fiorina's Lesson in Equality," *The Wall Street Journal*, February 10, 2005, http://online.wsj.com.

Corporate Officers in the Fortune 500

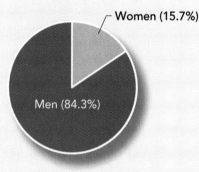

Women (15.7%)

Men (84.3%)

Top-Earning Corporate Officers in the Fortune 500

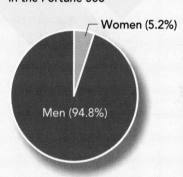

Women (5.2%)

Men (94.8%)

agerial level. Also, female managers report experiencing more challenge due to lack of personal support (which, as we saw earlier in the chapter, is related to harmful stress). With regard to developmental relationships, women and minorities often have trouble finding mentors. They may not participate in the organization's, profession's, or community's "old boys' network." Also, managers in the organization may prefer to interact with people who have similar status or may avoid interacting with certain people because of discomfort or negative stereotypes.[48]

Organizations can use development systems to help break through the glass ceiling. Managers making developmental assignments need to carefully consider whether stereotypes are influencing the types of assignments men and women receive. A formal process for regularly identifying development needs and creating action plans can make these decisions more objective.

An organization that is actively working to eliminate the glass ceiling is Deloitte & Touche, an accounting, tax, and consulting firm with offices throughout the United States.[49] Deloitte & Touche had been experiencing high turnover of talented women, so it set up a task force chaired by the company's chief executive officer to analyze the problem and develop recommendations. The task force gathered data by having every management professional in the company attend a workshop designed to explore how attitudes about gender affected the work environment. The workshops included discussions, videos, and case studies, such as one case in which two promising candidates, one male and one female, with identical skills were evaluated. The workshops also focused on how work assignments were allocated. The workshops found differences in the ways men and women were evaluated and in the kinds of assignments they were given, based on managers' assumptions about men and women. As a result, Deloitte & Touche began to rethink how assignments were given, to make sure women had opportunities for highly visible assignments. The company started a formal process for career planning for women and men and began offering networking events at which women could meet successful female partners and high-level managers. Deloitte & Touche began measuring turnover and promotion rates and linking rewards to meeting career development objectives. Through these changes, the company improved its retention of women, and reducing turnover has saved $250 million in hiring and training costs.

Succession Planning

Organizations have always had to prepare for the retirement of their leaders, but the need is more intense than ever. The aging of the workforce means that a greater share of employees are reaching retirement age. Many organizations are fueling the trend by downsizing through early-retirement programs. As positions at the top of organizations become vacant, many organizations have determined that their middle managers are fewer and often unprepared for top-level responsibility. This situation has raised awareness of the need for **succession planning**—the process of identifying and tracking high-potential employees who will be able to fill top management positions when they become vacant.

> **succession planning**
> The process of identifying and tracking high-potential employees who will be able to fill top management positions when they become vacant.

Succession planning offers several benefits.[50] It forces senior management to regularly and thoughtfully review the company's leadership talent. It assures that top-level management talent is available. It provides a set of development experiences that managers must complete to be considered for top management positions, so the organization does not promote managers before they are ready. Succession planning systems also help attract and retain ambitious managerial employees by providing development opportunities.

Succession planning focuses on *high-potential employees*, that is, employees the organization believes can succeed in higher-level business positions such as general manager of a business unit, director of a function (such as marketing or finance), or chief executive officer.[51] A typical approach to development of high-potential employees is to have them complete an individual development program including education, executive mentoring and coaching, and rotation through job assignments. Job assignments are based on the successful career paths of the managers whom the high-potential employees are preparing to replace. High-potential employees may also receive special assignments, such as making presentations and serving on committees and task forces.

Research shows that an effective program for developing high-potential employees has three stages:[52]

1. *Selection of high-potential employees*—Organizations may select outstanding performers and employees who have completed elite academic programs, such as earning a master's degree in business administration from a prestigious university. They may also use the results of psychological tests such as assessment centers.

GE knew that Jack Welch would be retiring, so the company planned for the succession. Welch is shown here with Jeffrey Immelt, the new CEO. What are the benefits of succession planning?

2. *Developmental experiences*—As employees participate in developmental experiences, the organization identifies those who succeed in the experiences. The organization looks for employees who continue to show qualities associated with success in top jobs, such as communication skills, leadership talent, and willingness to make sacrifices for the organization. Employees who display these qualities continue to be considered high-potential employees.

3. *Active involvement with the CEO*—High-potential employees seen by top management as fitting into the organization's culture and having personality characteristics necessary for representing the company become actively involved with the chief executive officer. The CEO exposes these employees to the organization's key people and gives them a greater understanding of the organization's culture. The development of high-potential employees is a slow process. Reaching stage 3 may take 15 to 20 years.

Figure 9.6 breaks this process into seven steps. It begins with identifying the positions to be planned for and the employees to be included in the plan. Planning should also include establishing position requirements and deciding how to measure employees' potential for being able to fill those requirements. The organization also needs to develop a process for reviewing the existing talent. The next step is to link succession planning with other human resource systems. Finally, the organization needs a way to provide employees with feedback about career paths available to them and how well they are progressing toward their goals.

A good example of succession planning is the system at WellPoint, a health care company headquartered in Thousand Oaks, California, with operations across the United States. WellPoint has a Web-based corporate database that identifies employees for management jobs throughout the company and tracks the development of employee talent. The succession-planning system includes 600 managers and executives, with detailed information on possible candidates, including performance evaluations, summaries of accomplishments at the company, self-evaluations and career goals, and personal information such as willingness to relocate. Standards are used to identify each candidate's strengths and identify the best candidates for promotion. Managers and the human resource team can use the system to identify and evaluate candidates for every management position in the company. They can also track the development of promising candidates and identify areas where further development is needed. In areas where development needs exceed management talent, WellPoint sets up additional training programs.[53]

At some organizations, succession planning systems identify a few potential managers for each position. This limited approach allows the organization to target development activities to the most talented managers, but it may not prepare enough

Figure 9.6

Process for
Developing a
Succession Plan

SOURCE: Based on B. Dowell, "Succession
Planning," in *Implementing Organizational
Interventions*, ed. J. Hedge and E. Pulaskos (San
Francisco: Jossey-Bass, 2002), pp. 78–109.

managers to fill vacant positions. High-potential employees who are not on the short
list for managerial jobs may leave. American Express's approach avoids this problem
by identifying many qualified leaders, which builds commitment to the company.

Dysfunctional Managers

A manager who is otherwise competent may engage in some behaviors that make him
or her ineffective or even "toxic"—someone who stifles good ideas and drives away employees. These dysfunctional behaviors include insensitivity to others, inability to be a
team player, arrogance, poor conflict management skills, inability to meet business objectives, and inability to adapt to change.[54] For example, suppose a manager has great
depth of technical knowledge and has excellent ability in keeping two steps ahead of
competitors. But the manager is abrasive and aggressive with employees and peers and

Figure 9.7
Dysfunctional Managers

DILBERT © Scott Adams/Dist. by United Feature Syndicate, Inc. Reprinted by permission.

has a leadership style that discourages employees from contributing their ideas. This manager is likely to have difficulty motivating employees and may alienate people inside and outside the organization. Some of these dysfunctional manager behaviors are illustrated humorously in the popular "Dilbert" comic strip, shown in Figure 9.7.

When a manager is an otherwise valuable employee and is willing to improve, the organization may try to help him or her change the dysfunctional behavior. The usual ways to provide this type of development include assessment, training, and counseling. The organization may enroll the manager in a program designed specifically to help managers with dysfunctional behavior, such as the Individual Coaching for Effectiveness (ICE) program. The ICE program includes diagnosis, coaching, and support activities, which are tailored to each manager's needs.[55] Psychologists conduct the diagnosis, coach and counsel the manager, and develop action plans for implementing new skills on the job.

During diagnosis, the psychologist collects information about the manager's personality, skills, and interests. The information comes from psychological tests and interviews with the manager, his or her supervisor, and colleagues. The psychological tests help the psychologist determine whether the manager will be able to change the dysfunctional behavior. For example, change will be difficult if the manager is extremely defensive. If the diagnosis indicates the manager can benefit from the program, the manager and supervisor work with the psychologist to set specific developmental objectives.

During the coaching phase of the program, the manager receives information about the target skills or behavior. This may include principles of effective communication or teamwork, tolerance of individual differences in the workplace, or conducting effective meetings. Next, the manager participates in behavior modeling training, described in Chapter 7. The manager also receives psychological counseling to overcome beliefs that may interfere with learning the desired behavior.

The support phase of the ICE program creates conditions to ensure that the manager can use the new behaviors and skills on the job. The manager's supervisor gives the manager and psychologist feedback about the manager's progress in using the new skills and behaviors. The psychologist and manager identify situations in which the manager may tend to rely on dysfunctional behavior. The coach and manager also develop action plans that outline how the manager should try to use new behaviors in daily work activities.

The effectiveness of this kind of program has not yet been thoroughly studied. Still, research suggests that managers who participate in programs like ICE improve their skills and are less likely to be terminated.[56] This suggests that organizations can benefit from offering development opportunities to valuable employees with performance problems, not just to star performers.

thinking ETHICALLY

Whom Do You Serve?

For some ambitious employees, the career path leads to their organization's top jobs. And as we saw in Chapter 1, those employees increasingly include HR professionals who identify ways they can contribute value to the organization. They learn to speak the numbers- and performance-oriented language of business, and they show they perform well when given top leadership roles. One example is Chuck Nielson, who until recently held the top HR job at Texas Instruments. Nielson, now a consultant, ensured his own career development by seeking out challenging assignments and demonstrating his success. He recalls a time when he felt excluded from the company's key decisions; he told his boss, "Play me or trade me." From then on, he was invited to participate in meetings where executives made decisions about strategy; he prepared himself to contribute and in that way established credibility.

But just as HR professionals are gaining this type of leadership role, they are encountering some role conflicts. On the one hand, especially at the level of a corporate officer, a manager is expected to serve the corporation's interests. On the other hand, HR professionals may have responsibilities to watch out for employees' interests, such as employee benefits. Ideally, the benefits plans would align with company goals, but occasionally interests collide.

Consider the situation faced by Cindy Olson, who was the executive vice president of human resources and community relations for Enron Corporation during the time that financial misdeeds caused the company to collapse. The benefits for Enron employees included 401(k) retirement savings plans, which were heavily invested in Enron stock. As the value of that stock plunged, the employees lost their retirement savings. Was Olson's responsibility to protect the employees who were supposed to benefit from the plan she administered, or was it to protect the corporation by maintaining the employees' investments in Enron stock? In court documents, Olson has said her role as a corporate officer was primary. The U.S. Labor Department has argued that her corporate responsibility was secondary to her role as plan fiduciary (a person legally required to act in the interests of another, in this case, the employees). The issue has not yet been resolved in the courts, but the ethical dimension is worth considering now, whatever the legal outcome.

SOURCE: Based on Richard F. Stolz, "What HR Will Stand For," *Human Resource Executive*, January 2003, pp. 1, 21–28.

Questions

1. Should Cindy Olson have made her first priority Enron or its employees? Explain your reasoning.
2. Does this sort of potential conflict make it impossible for HR professionals to serve as corporate officers? Explain.
3. How could employee development programs help address this type of ethical conflict before problems arise?

SUMMARY

1. Discuss how development is related to training and careers.

   Employee development is the combination of formal education, job experiences, relationships, and assessment of personality and abilities to help employees prepare for the future of their careers. Training is more focused on improving performance in the current job, but training programs may support employee development. In modern organizations, the concept of a career is fluid—a protean career that changes along with changes in a person's interests, abilities, and values and changes in the work environment. To plan and prepare for a protean career requires active career management, which includes planning for employee development.

2. Identify the methods organizations use for employee development.

   Organizations may use formal educational programs at the workplace or off-site, such as workshops, university courses and degree programs, company-sponsored training, or programs offered by independent institutions. Organizations may use the assessment process to help employees identify strengths and areas requiring further development. Assessment can help the organization identify employees with managerial potential or identify areas in which teams need to develop. Job experiences help employees develop by stretching their skills as they meet new challenges. Interpersonal relationships with a more experienced member of the organization—often in the role of mentor or coach—can help employees develop their understanding of the organization and its customers.

3. Describe how organizations use assessment of personality type, work behaviors, and job performance to plan employee development.

Organizations collect information and provide feedback to employees about their behavior, communication style, and skills. The information may come from the employees, their peers, managers, and customers. Many organizations use performance appraisals as a source of assessment information. Appraisals may take the form of 360-degree feedback. Some organizations use psychological tests designed for this purpose, including the Myers-Briggs Type Indicator and the Benchmarks assessment. Assessment centers combine a variety of methods to provide assessment information. Managers must share the assessments, along with suggestions for improvement.

4. Explain how job experiences can be used for developing skills.

Job experiences contribute to development through a combination of relationships, problems, demands, tasks, and other features of an employee's jobs. The assumption is that development is most likely to occur when the employee's skills and experiences do not entirely match the skills required for the employee's current job, so employees must stretch to meet the demands of the new assignment. The impact varies according to whether the employee views the experience as a positive or negative source of stress. Job experiences that support employee development may include job enlargement, job rotations, transfers, promotions, downward moves, and temporary assignments with other organizations.

5. Summarize principles of successful mentoring programs.

A mentor is an experienced, productive senior employee who helps develop a less experienced employee. Although most mentoring relationships develop informally, organizations can link mentoring to development goals by establishing a formal mentoring program. A formal program also provides a basis for ensuring that all eligible employees are included. Mentoring programs tend to be most successful when they are voluntary and participants understand the details of the program. The organization should reward managers for employee development, carefully select mentors based on interpersonal and technical skills, train them for the role, and evaluate whether the program has met its objectives.

6. Tell how managers and peers develop employees through coaching.

A coach is a peer or manager who works with an employee to motivate the employee, help him or her develop skills, and provide reinforcement and feedback. Coaches should be prepared to take on one or more of three roles: working one-on-one with an employee, helping employees learn for themselves, and providing resources, such as mentors, courses, or job experiences.

7. Identify the steps in the process of career management.

First, during self-assessment, employees use information to determine their career interests, values, aptitudes, and behavioral tendencies, looking for opportunities and areas needing improvement. Self-assessment tools often include psychological tests or exercises that ask about career status and plans. The second step is the reality check, during which the organization communicates information about the employee's skills and knowledge and how these fit into the organization's plan. The employee then sets goals and discusses them with his or her manager, who ensures that the goals are specific, challenging, and attainable. Finally, the employee works with his or her manager to create an action plan for development activities that will help the employee achieve the goals.

8. Discuss how organizations are meeting the challenges of the "glass ceiling," succession planning, and dysfunctional managers.

The glass ceiling is a barrier that has been observed preventing women and minorities from achieving top jobs in an organization. Development programs can ensure that these employees receive access to development resources such as coaches, mentors, and developmental job assignments. Succession planning ensures that the organization prepares qualified employees to fill management jobs as managers retire. It focuses on applying employee development to high-potential employees. Effective succession planning includes methods for selecting these employees, providing them with developmental experiences, and getting the CEO actively involved with employees who display qualities associated with success as they participate in the developmental activities. For dysfunctional managers who have the potential to contribute to the organization, the organization may offer development targeted at correcting the areas of dysfunction. Typically, the process includes collecting information about the manager's personality, skills, and interests; providing feedback, training, and counseling; and ensuring that the manager can apply new, functional behaviors on the job.

REVIEW AND DISCUSSION QUESTIONS

1. How does development differ from training? How does development support career management in modern organizations?
2. What are the four broad categories of development methods? Why might it be beneficial to combine all of these methods into a formal development program?
3. Recommend a development method for each of the following situations, and explain why you chose that method.
   a. An employee recently promoted to the job of plant supervisor is having difficulty motivating employees to meet quality standards.
   b. A sales manager annoys salespeople by dictating every detail of their work.
   c. An employee has excellent leadership skills but lacks knowledge of the financial side of business.
   d. An organization is planning to organize its production workers into teams for the first time.
4. A company that markets sophisticated business management software systems uses sales teams to help customers define needs and to create systems that meet those needs. The teams include programmers, salespeople who specialize in client industries, and software designers. Occasionally sales are lost as a result of conflict or communication problems among team members. The company wants to improve the effectiveness of these teams, and it wants to begin with assessment. How can the teams use 360-degree feedback and psychological tests to develop?
5. In an organization that wants to use work experiences as a method of employee development, what basic options are available? Which of these options would be most attractive to you as an employee? Why?
6. Many employees are unwilling to relocate because they like their current community and family members prefer not to move. Yet preparation for management requires that employees develop new skills, strengthen areas of weakness, and be exposed to new aspects of the organization's business. How can an organization change an employee's current job to develop management skills?
7. Many people feel that mentoring relationships should occur naturally, in situations where senior managers feel inclined to play that role. What are some advantages of setting up a formal mentoring program, rather than letting senior managers decide how and whom to help?
8. What are the three roles of a coach? How is a coach different from a mentor? What are some advantages of using someone outside the organization as a coach? Some disadvantages?
9. Why should organizations be interested in helping employees plan their careers? What benefits can companies gain? What are the risks?
10. What are the manager's roles in a career management system? Which role do you think is most difficult for the typical manager? Which is the easiest role? List reasons why managers might resist becoming involved in career management.
11. What is the glass ceiling? What are the possible consequences to an organization that has a glass ceiling? How can employee development break the glass ceiling? Can succession planning help? Explain.
12. Why might an organization benefit from giving employee development opportunities to a dysfunctional manager, rather than simply dismissing the manager? Do these reasons apply to nonmanagement employees as well?

WHAT'S YOUR HR IQ?

The text Web site offers two more ways to check what you've learned so far. Use the Self-Assessment exercise to test your knowledge of employee development. Go online with the Web Exercise to see how leadership programs at GE are structured.

BusinessWeek CASE

BusinessWeek **Grooming the Next Boss for Quest**

Of all the challenges confronting managers and directors, few are as difficult or as critical as finding and training a chief executive-in-waiting. But Kenneth W. Freeman, CEO of Quest Diagnostics, was determined not to leave his company in the lurch. He started grooming his hand-picked successor five years before he left. When he transferred management of the $4.7 billion medical-testing company to Surya N. Mohapatra at the annual meeting in

2004, it was the culmination of a meticulous succession process that experts say is a case study in how to choose a future CEO and prepare him or her for the job.

Freeman's search for a successor started in 1999. He was on the brink of an acquisition spree that would triple Quest's revenues in five years. But he knew the buying binge couldn't last and that Quest's next CEO would need a science background to exploit advances in medicine and technology to generate internal growth. To identify candidates, he put 200 executives from Quest and a recently acquired rival through an *Apprentice*-like challenge: day-long case assignments that allowed him to see their leadership skills in action. "This was his legacy," says Audrey B. Smith, a consultant with Development Dimensions International who worked with Freeman. "He felt huge pressure to make the right decision."

Of all the executives, one stood out: his new chief operating officer. Mohapatra came to Quest in February 1999 from Picker International, a maker of medical imaging systems. He had extensive experience in cardiovascular disease and information technology—areas that would be crucial to Quest's future. What's more, he was CEO material. Says Freeman: "Here was a guy who was incredibly smart, who could balance a whole bunch of priorities at the same time, who could be incredibly focused, and who did not know the meaning of failure."

Four months after Mohapatra's arrival, Freeman named him president, giving him a clear—but by no means guaranteed—shot at the top job. The two men could not be more different. Mohapatra, a scientist with several patents to his name, grew up in India. Freeman, a New Yorker, had a long finance career at Corning. When Corning Clinical Laboratories was spun off as Quest in 1996, Freeman became CEO, a position he says he had no intention of occupying for more than 10 years.

Front-runner or not, it quickly became clear that if Mohapatra was to be CEO, he would need basic leadership skills. During his first week, one of the most glaring deficiencies, poor public speaking skills, became apparent. At a "town meeting" with employees in Baltimore, Mohapatra told the crowd of 800 that he was glad to be there—then clammed up. Freeman decided the best way to coax Mohapatra out of his shell was trial by fire. In the months that followed, he had Mohapatra make unscripted comments to employees, meet with shareholders, and field questions from analysts on conference calls. He is now a more polished, confident speaker.

As a scientist, Mohapatra had come to Quest with habits that Freeman thought could undermine him as

CEO. A deep thinker, he took weeks to make decisions that should take only days. And he was far more "hands-on" than he needed to be, sometimes reopening interviews for jobs that his subordinates were ready to fill. Freeman challenged Mohapatra to make faster decisions and give his executive team more authority. Every Sunday afternoon for five years, the two engaged in lengthy telephone conversations during which Freeman would analyze Mohapatra's evolving management style and suggest further improvements. It was, Freeman now concedes, "pure browbeating." Perhaps, but it worked. "Am I more ready now than I was four years ago? Absolutely," says Mohapatra.

Fine-tuning Mohapatra's management skills was only part of the challenge. Making him an active board participant was equally important. When he arrived, Mohapatra deferred to Freeman in board debates, contributing little. Freeman forced him to be more assertive—at first surreptitiously, by leaving the room during discussions, and later by asking him to conduct formal board presentations. Even after joining the board in 2002, Mohapatra continued to strike some directors as aloof. By changing the seating chart, Freeman was able to increase Mohapatra's face time with other directors. "You want someone to be able to speak their mind and participate," says Gail R. Wilensky, an independent director. "It helped."

When his long incubation ends, Mohapatra's success will be far from assured. Maintaining double-digit growth won't be easy as takeover targets become scarce. That's the way it is in business; the future is never assured. But Freeman has done about as much to increase the odds as a CEO can.

SOURCE: L. Lavelle, "How to Groom the Next Boss," *BusinessWeek*, May 10, 2004, pp. 93–94.

Questions

1. What development activities did Kenneth Freeman use to prepare Surya Mohapatra for the position of CEO? What other development activities could he have used?
2. Would an outside coach have provided coaching as effective as the coaching Mohapatra received from Freeman? Explain.
3. Imagine you are an HR manager at Quest and the new CEO has asked you to set up systems that apply some of the development activities that prepared him for leadership. Mohapatra wants to prepare all of Quest's management team in similar ways. Suggest a few ways the company could develop its other managers along the lines Freeman used with Mohapatra.

CASE: Developing Employees at Booz Allen Hamilton

Booz Allen Hamilton, a consulting firm headquartered in McLean, Virginia, uses a program it calls the Development Framework to help managers and employees choose the right combination of development activities to strengthen skills and manage careers. Employee development is especially important at an organization like Booz Allen, whose business success is based on its people's ability to sell and deliver consulting and technology solutions. These solutions are only as good as the intellectual capital—knowledge, skills, competencies, and abilities—of the employees who create them.

The Development Framework consists of four sections:
1. *Development roles:* Managers, mentors, development staff, and other roles in the development process.
2. *Performance expectations:* A description of competencies, performance results, and major job experiences required to succeed at each level of the company.
3. *Development needs:* Needs that frequently occur at each career level, those that vary by individual, and the "derailers" that can stall career progress and hurt performance.
4. *Development road map:* Descriptions of development activities that should occur at each career level and that support development needs and prevent derailers.

The company provides ways to prevent or deal with derailers and support development needs. Activities include job experiences, training and education, coaching and mentoring, and self-directed experiences.

Employees can access the Development Framework online via the company's virtual campus and Web site. Managers can use the tool to discuss development needs in their departments.

The framework includes the competencies for each staff level and for each employee. This list allows employees to view their personal development needs online. For each of the competencies that employees want to strengthen, the framework provides a list of activities employees can use to develop those competencies. So, employees can use the

Development Framework to take charge of their own careers. For example, employees can ask, "I'm at this level, and this person is above me; how can I get there?"

Booz Allen provides the Development Framework to help employees better understand how to develop themselves. The firm views development as a shared responsibility between employees and the company. The framework helps employees realize that development can occur through activities other than training classes.

The Development Framework makes good business sense for Booz Allen. It ties employee development to the company's strategy and associates it with different levels of the organization. While it is helping employees build successful careers, it is also helping the company increase its intellectual capital. In addition, it guides the firm in preparing potential leaders. That challenge is significant, because Booz Allen is growing at a rate of 20 percent per year.

SOURCE: Based on G. Johnson, "The Development Framework," *Training,* February 2003, pp. 32–36.

Questions
1. How well does this description of employee development at Booz Allen Hamilton fit the model of career management in Figure 9.3?
2. What additional principles from the model of career management would you advise Booz Allen to add to its Development Framework?
3. If you were an employee of Booz Allen, what information and tools would you hope to find at the Development Framework page of the company's Web site?

NOTES

1. M. London, *Managing the Training Enterprise* (San Francisco: Jossey-Bass, 1989).
2. R. W. Pace, P. C. Smith, and G. E. Mills, *Human Resource Development* (Englewood Cliffs, NJ: Prentice Hall, 1991); W. Fitzgerald, "Training versus Development," *Training and Development Journal,* May 1992, pp. 81–84; R. A. Noe, S. L. Wilk, E. J. Mullen, and J. E. Wanek, "Employee Development: Issues in Construct Definition and Investigation of Antecedents," in *Improving Training Effectiveness in Work Organizations,* ed. J. K. Ford (Mahwah, NJ: Lawrence Erlbaum, 1997), pp. 153–89.
3. J. H. Greenhaus and G. A. Callanan, *Career Management,* 2nd ed. (Fort Worth, TX: Dryden Press, 1994); and D. Hall, *Careers in and out of Organizations* (Thousand Oaks, CA: Sage, 2002).
4. M. B. Arthur, P. H. Claman, and R. J. DeFillippi, "Intelligent Enterprise, Intelligent Careers," *Academy of Management Executive* 9 (1995), pp. 7–20; and

C. Ansberry, "A New Blue-Collar World," *The Wall Street Journal,* June 30, 2003, p. B1.
5. *Cardinal Health: A Tradition of Performance* (brochure) (Dublin, OH: Cardinal Health, 2003).
6. R. J. Campbell, "HR Development Strategies," in *Developing Human Resources,* ed. K. N. Wexley (Washington, DC: BNA Books, 1991), pp. 5-1–5-34; M. A. Sheppeck and C. A. Rhodes, "Management Development: Revised Thinking in Light of New Events of Strategic Importance," *Human Resource Planning* 11 (1988), pp. 159–72; B. Keys and J. Wolf, "Management Education: Current Issues and Emerging Trends," *Journal of Management* 14 (1988), pp. 205–29; L. M. Saari, T. R. Johnson, S. D. McLaughlin, and D. Zimmerle, "A Survey of Management Training and Education Practices in U.S. Companies," *Personnel Psychology* 41 (1988), pp. 731–44.
7. T. A. Stewart, "GE Keeps Those Ideas Coming," *Fortune,* August 12, 1991, pp. 41–49; N. M. Tichy,

"GE's Crotonville: A Staging Ground for a Corporate Revolution," *The Executive* 3 (1989), pp. 99–106; General Electric Web site, www.ge.com; and Sarah Murray, "Expanded Training Centre for the Best of General Electric," *Financial Times*, March 22, 2004, downloaded at www.ge.com.

8. J. Reingold, "Corporate America Goes to School," *BusinessWeek*, October 20, 1997, pp. 66–72.

9. Ibid.

10. A. Howard and D. W. Bray, *Managerial Lives in Transition: Advancing Age and Changing Times* (New York: Guilford, 1988); J. Bolt, *Executive Development* (New York: Harper Business, 1989); J. R. Hinrichs and G. P. Hollenbeck, "Leadership Development," in *Developing Human Resources*, pp. 5-221–5-237.

11. A. Thorne and H. Gough, *Portraits of Type* (Palo Alto, CA: Consulting Psychologists Press, 1993).

12. D. Druckman and R. A. Bjork, eds., *In the Mind's Eye: Enhancing Human Performance* (Washington, DC: National Academy Press, 1991); M. H. McCaulley, "The Myers-Briggs Type Indicator and Leadership," in *Measures of Leadership*, ed. K. E. Clark and M. B. Clark (West Orange, NJ: Leadership Library of America, 1990), pp. 381–418.

13. G. C. Thornton III and W. C. Byham, *Assessment Centers and Managerial Performance* (New York: Academic Press, 1982); L. F. Schoenfeldt and J. A. Steger, "Identification and Development of Management Talent," in *Research in Personnel and Human Resource Management*, vol. 7, ed. K. N. Rowland and G. Ferris (Greenwich, CT: JAI Press, 1989), pp. 151–81.

14. Thornton and Byham, *Assessment Centers and Managerial Performance*.

15. P. G. W. Jansen and B. A. M. Stoop, "The Dynamics of Assessment Center Validity: Results of a Seven-Year Study," *Journal of Applied Psychology* 86 (2001), pp. 741–53; D. Chan, "Criterion and Construct Validation of an Assessment Centre," *Journal of Occupational and Organizational Psychology* 69 (1996), pp. 167–81.

16. R. G. Jones and M. D. Whitmore, "Evaluating Developmental Assessment Centers as Interventions," *Personnel Psychology* 48 (1995), pp. 377–88.

17. J. Schettler, "Building Bench Strength," *Training*, June 2002, pp. 55–58.

18. C. D. McCauley and M. M. Lombardo, "Benchmarks: An Instrument for Diagnosing Managerial Strengths and Weaknesses," in *Measures of Leadership*, pp. 535–45.

19. C. D. McCauley, M. M. Lombardo, and C. J. Usher, "Diagnosing Management Development Needs: An Instrument Based on How Managers Develop," *Journal of Management* 15 (1989), pp. 389–403.

20. S. B. Silverman, "Individual Development through Performance Appraisal," in *Developing Human Resources*, pp. 5-120–5-151.

21. B. Pfau and I. Kay, "Does 360-Degree Feedback Negatively Affect Company Performance?" *HR Magazine* 47 (2002), pp. 54–59; J. F. Brett and L. E. Atwater, "360-Degree Feedback: Accuracy, Reactions, and Perceptions of Usefulness," *Journal of Applied Psychology* 86 (2001), pp. 930–42.

22. A. Freedman, "The Evolution of 360s," *Human Resource Executive*, December 2002, pp. 47–51.

23. L. Atwater, P. Roush, and A. Fischthal, "The Influence of Upward Feedback on Self- and Follower Ratings of Leadership," *Personnel Psychology* 48 (1995), pp. 35–59; J. F. Hazucha, S. A. Hezlett, and R. J. Schneider, "The Impact of 360-Degree Feedback on Management Skill Development," *Human Resource Management* 32 (1993), pp. 325–51; J. W. Smither, M. London, N. Vasilopoulos, R. R. Reilly, R. E. Millsap, and N. Salvemini, "An Examination of the Effects of an Upward Feedback Program over Time," *Personnel Psychology* 48 (1995), pp. 1–34.

24. D. Bracken, "Straight Talk about Multirater Feedback," *Training and Development*, September 1994, pp. 44–51.

25. M. W. McCall Jr., *High Flyers* (Boston: Harvard Business School Press, 1998).

26. R. S. Snell, "Congenial Ways of Learning: So Near yet So Far," *Journal of Management Development* 9 (1990), pp. 17–23.

27. M. McCall, M. Lombardo, and A. Morrison, *Lessons of Experience* (Lexington, MA: Lexington Books, 1988); M. W. McCall, "Developing Executives through Work Experiences," *Human Resource Planning* 11 (1988), pp. 1–11; M. N. Ruderman, P. J. Ohlott, and C. D. McCauley, "Assessing Opportunities for Leadership Development," in *Measures of Leadership*, pp. 547–62; C. D. McCauley, L. J. Estman, and P. J. Ohlott, "Linking Management Selection and Development through Stretch Assignments," *Human Resource Management* 34 (1995), pp. 93–115.

28. C. D. McCauley, M. N. Ruderman, P. J. Ohlott, and J. E. Morrow, "Assessing the Developmental Components of Managerial Jobs," *Journal of Applied Psychology* 79 (1994), pp. 544–60.

29. M. Solomon, "Trading Places," *ComputerWorld*, November 5, 2002, www.computerworld.com.

30. M. London, *Developing Managers* (San Francisco: Jossey-Bass, 1985); M. A. Camion, L. Cheraskin, and M. J. Stevens, "Career-Related Antecedents and Outcomes of Job Rotation," *Academy of Management Journal* 37 (1994), pp. 1518–42; London, *Managing the Training Enterprise*.

31. L. Cheraskin and M. Campion, "Study Clarifies Job Rotation Benefits," *Personnel Journal*, November 1996, pp. 31–38.

32. R. A. Noe, B. D. Steffy, and A. E. Barber, "An Investigation of the Factors Influencing Employees'

Willingness to Accept Mobility Opportunities," *Personnel Psychology* 41 (1988), pp. 559–80; S. Gould and L. E. Penley, "A Study of the Correlates of Willingness to Relocate," *Academy of Management Journal* 28 (1984), pp. 472–78; J. Landau and T. H. Hammer, "Clerical Employees' Perceptions of Intra-organizational Career Opportunities," *Academy of Management Journal* 29 (1986), pp. 385–405; J. M. Brett and A. H. Reilly, "On the Road Again: Predicting the Job Transfer Decision," *Journal of Applied Psychology* 73 (1988), pp. 614–20.

33. J. M. Brett, "Job Transfer and Well-Being," *Journal of Applied Psychology* 67 (1992), pp. 450–63; F. J. Minor, L. A. Slade, and R. A. Myers, "Career Transitions in Changing Times," in *Contemporary Career Development Issues*, ed. R. F. Morrison and J. Adams (Hillsdale, NJ: Lawrence Erlbaum, 1991), pp. 109–20; C. C. Pinder and K. G. Schroeder, "Time to Proficiency Following Job Transfers," *Academy of Management Journal* 30 (1987), pp. 336–53; G. Flynn, "Heck No-We Won't Go!" *Personnel Journal*, March 1996, pp. 37–43.

34. R. E. Silverman, "Mercer Tries to Keep Employees through Its 'Externship' Program," *The Wall Street Journal*, November 7, 2000, p. B18.

35. E. Jossi, "Taking Time Off from Advertising," *Workforce*, April 2002, p. 15.

36. D. B. Turban and T. W. Dougherty, "Role of Protégé Personality in Receipt of Mentoring and Career Success," *Academy of Management Journal* 37 (1994), pp. 688–702; E. A. Fagenson, "Mentoring: Who Needs It? A Comparison of Protégés' and Non-protégés' Needs for Power, Achievement, Affiliation, and Autonomy," *Journal of Vocational Behavior* 41 (1992), pp. 48–60.

37. A. H. Geiger, "Measures for Mentors," *Training and Development Journal*, February 1992, pp. 65–67.

38. K. E. Kram, *Mentoring at Work: Developmental Relationships in Organizational Life* (Glenview, IL: Scott-Foresman, 1985); L. L. Phillips-Jones, "Establishing a Formalized Mentoring Program," *Training and Development Journal* 2 (1983), pp. 38–42; K. Kram, "Phases of the Mentoring Relationship," *Academy of Managment Journal* 26 (1983), pp. 608–25; G. T. Chao, P. M. Walz, and P. D. Gardner, "Formal and Informal Mentorships: A Comparison of Mentoring Functions and Contrasts with Nonmentored Counterparts," *Personnel Psychology* 45 (1992), pp. 619–36; and C. Wanberg, E. Welsh, and S. Hezlett, "Mentoring Research: A Review and Dynamic Process Model," in *Research in Personnel and Human Resources Management*, ed. J. Martocchio and G. Ferris (New York: Elsevier Science, 2003), pp. 39–124.

39. C. M. Solomon, "Hotel Breathes Life into Hospital's Customer Service," *Personnel Journal*, October 1995, p. 120.

40. R. A. Noe, D. B. Greenberger, and S. Wang, "Mentoring: What We Know and Where We Might Go," in *Research in Personnel and Human Resources Management*, vol. 21, ed. G. Ferris and J. Martocchio (New York: Elsevier Science, 2002), pp. 129–74; and T. D. Allen, L. T. Eby, M. L. Poteet, E. Lentz, and L. Lima, "Career Benefits Associated with Mentoring for Protégés: A Meta-Analysis," *Journal of Applied Psychology* 89 (2004), pp. 127–36.

41. M. Murray, "GE Mentoring Program Turns Underlings into Teachers of the Web," *The Wall Street Journal*, February 15, 2000, pp. B1, B16.

42. D. B. Peterson and M. D. Hicks, *Leader as Coach* (Minneapolis: Personnel Decisions, 1996).

43. J. S. Lublin, "Building a Better CEO," *The Wall Street Journal*, April 14, 2000, pp. B1, B4.

44. B. Baumann, J. Duncan, S. E. Former, and Z. Leibowitz, "Amoco Primes the Talent Pump," *Personnel Journal*, February 1996, pp. 79–84.

45. P. Kiger, "At First USA Bank, Promotions and Job Satisfaction Are Up," *Workforce*, March 2001, pp. 54–56.

46. P. J. Ohlott, M. N. Ruderman, and C. D. McCauley, "Gender Differences in Managers' Developmental Job Experiences," *Academy of Management Journal* 37 (1994), pp. 46–67.

47. L. A. Mainiero, "Getting Anointed for Advancement: The Case of Executive Women," *Academy of Management Executive* 8 (1994), pp. 53–67; J. S. Lublin, "Women at Top Still Are Distant from CEO Jobs," *The Wall Street Journal*, February 28, 1995, pp. B1, B5; P. Tharenov, S. Latimer, and D. Conroy, "How Do You Make It to the Top? An Examination of Influences on Women's and Men's Managerial Advancements," *Academy of Management Journal* 37 (1994), pp. 899–931.

48. U.S. Department of Labor, *A Report on the Glass Ceiling Initiative* (Washington, DC: Labor Department, 1991); R. A. Noe, "Women and Mentoring: A Review and Research Agenda," *Academy of Management Review* 13 (1988), pp. 65–78; B. R. Ragins and J. L. Cotton, "Easier Said than Done: Gender Differences in Perceived Barriers to Gaining a Mentor," *Academy of Management Journal* 34 (1991), pp. 939–51.

49. D. McCracken, "Winning the Talent War for Women," *Harvard Business Review*, November–December 2000, pp. 159–67.

50. W. J. Rothwell, *Effective Succession Planning*, 2nd ed. (New York: AMACOM, 2001).

51. B. E. Dowell, "Succession Planning," in *Implementing Organizational Interventions*, ed. J. Hedge and E. D. Pulakos (San Francisco: Jossey-Bass, 2002), pp. 78–109.

52. C. B. Derr, C. Jones, and E. L. Toomey, "Managing High-Potential Employees: Current Practices in Thirty-Three U.S. Corporations," *Human Resource*

Management 27 (1988), pp. 273–90; K. M. Nowack, "The Secrets of Succession," *Training and Development* 48 (1994), pp. 49–54; J. S. Lublin, "An Overseas Stint Can Be a Ticket to the Top," *The Wall Street Journal*, January 29, 1996, pp. B1, B2.

53. P. Kiger, "Succession Planning Keeps WellPoint Competitive," *Workforce*, April 2002, pp. 50–54.

54. M. W. McCall Jr. and M. M. Lombardo, "Off the Track: Why and How Successful Executives Get Derailed," *Technical Report*, no. 21 (Greensboro, NC: Center for Creative Leadership, 1983); E. V. Veslo and J. B. Leslie, "Why Executives Derail: Perspectives across Time and Cultures," *Academy of Management Executive* 9 (1995), pp. 62–72.

55. L. W. Hellervik, J. F. Hazucha, and R. J. Schneider, "Behavior Change: Models, Methods, and a Review of Evidence," in *Handbook of Industrial and Organizational Psychology*, vol. 3, 2nd ed., ed. M. D. Dunnette and L. M. Hough (Palo Alto, CA: Consulting Psychologists Press, 1992), pp. 823–99.

56. D. B. Peterson, "Measuring and Evaluating Change in Executive and Managerial Development," paper presented at the annual conference of the Society for Industrial and Organizational Psychology, Miami, 1990.

If you are using the Manager's Hot Seat DVD with this book, consider finishing case 11: Personal Disclosure: Confession Coincidence? for this chapter.

SEPARATING AND RETAINING EMPLOYEES

What Do I Need to Know?

1. Distinguish between involuntary and voluntary turnover, and describe their effects on an organization.

2. Discuss how employees determine whether the organization treats them fairly.

3. Identify legal requirements for employee discipline.

4. Summarize ways in which organizations can fairly discipline employees.

5. Explain how job dissatisfaction affects employee behavior.

6. Describe how organizations contribute to employees' job satisfaction and retain key employees.

❧ INTRODUCTION

Manitowoc, Wisconsin, was once a center of boat-building activity, and Burger Boat developed a reputation for building high-quality yachts there. So it was a sad event in 1990 when Burger became the last of the shipbuilders to leave or close down. What Burger's absentee corporate ownership did not fully appreciate, however, was the commitment of Burger's people, many of whom were their families' third generation with the company. Some even sneaked into the closed shipyard to get their tools and finish a boat they had been working on. With the help of Chicago entrepreneur David Ross, who moved to Manitowoc, a group of employees were able to revive the company. Today, orders and revenues are flowing in, and Burger is again profitable. About his decision to invest in Burger, Ross says, "I determined that this company was zero without the people who made it famous."[1]

Every organization recognizes that it needs satisfied, loyal customers and satisfied, loyal investors. Customers and investors provide the financial resources that let an organization survive and grow. In addition, as David Ross appreciates, success requires satisfied, loyal employees. Research provides evidence that retaining employees helps retain customers and investors.[2] Organizations with low turnover and satisfied employees tend to perform better.[3] On the other side of the coin, organizations have to act when an employee's performance consistently falls short.

Sometimes terminating a poor performer is the only way to show fairness, ensure quality, and maintain customer satisfaction.

This chapter explores the dual challenges of separating and retaining employees. We begin by distinguishing involuntary and voluntary turnover, describing how each affects the organization. Next we explore the separation process, including ways to manage this process fairly. Finally, we discuss measures the organization can take to encourage employees to stay. These topics provide a transition between Parts 3 and 4. The previous chapters in Part 3 considered how to assess and improve performance, and this chapter describes measures to take depending on whether performance is high or low. Part 4 discusses pay and benefits, both of which play an important role in employee retention.

MANAGING VOLUNTARY AND INVOLUNTARY TURNOVER

Organizations must try to ensure that good performers want to stay with the organization and that employees whose performance is chronically low are encouraged—or forced—to leave. Both of these challenges involve *employee turnover*, that is, employees leaving the organization. When the organization initiates the turnover (often with employees who would prefer to stay), the result is **involuntary turnover.** Examples include terminating an employee for drug use or laying off employees during a downturn. Most organizations use the word *termination* to refer only to a discharge related to a discipline problem, but some organizations call any involuntary turnover a termination. When the employees initiate the turnover (often when the organization would prefer to keep them), it is **voluntary turnover.** Employees may leave to retire or to take a job with a different organization.

In general, organizations try to avoid the need for involuntary turnover and to minimize voluntary turnover, especially among top performers. Both kinds of turnover are costly, as summarized in Table 10.1. Replacing workers is expensive, and new employees need time to learn their jobs. In addition, people today are more ready to sue a former employer if they feel they were unfairly discharged. The prospect of workplace violence also raises the risk associated with discharging employees. Effective human resource management can help the organization minimize both kinds of turnover, as well as carry it out effectively when necessary. Despite a company's best efforts at personnel selection, training, and compensation, some employees will fail to meet performance requirements or will violate company policies. When this happens, organizations need to apply a discipline program that could ultimately lead to discharging the individual.

For a number of reasons, discharging employees can be very difficult. First, the decision has legal aspects that can affect the organization. Historically, if the organiza-

LO1
Distinguish between involuntary and voluntary turnover, and describe their effects on an organization.

involuntary turnover
Turnover initiated by an employer (often with employees who would prefer to stay).

voluntary turnover
Turnover initiated by employees (often when the organization would prefer to keep them).

TABLE 10.1
Costs Associated with Turnover

INVOLUNTARY TURNOVER	VOLUNTARY TURNOVER
Recruiting, selecting, and training replacements	Recruiting, selecting, and training replacements
Lost productivity	Lost productivity
Lawsuits	Loss of talented employees
Workplace violence	

tion and employee do not have a specific employment contract, the employer or employee may end the employment relationship at any time. This is the *employment-at-will doctrine*, described in Chapter 5. This doctrine has eroded significantly, however. Employees who have been terminated sometimes sue their employers for wrongful discharge. Some judges have considered that there could be an implied employment contract if employees meet certain criteria such as length of employment, promotions, raises, or favorable performance appraisals—even when the organization has a handbook that says there is an employment-at-will relationship.[4] In a typical lawsuit for wrongful discharge, the former employee tries to establish that the discharge violated either an implied agreement or public policy (for example, firing an employee for refusing to do something illegal). In cases of wrongful discharge, employees often win settlements of hundreds of thousands of dollars.

Along with the financial risks of dismissing an employee, there are issues of personal safety. Distressing as it is that some former employees go to the courts, far worse are the employees who react to a termination decision with violence. Violence in the workplace has become a major organizational problem. Although any number of organizational actions or decisions may incite violence among employees, the "nothing else to lose" aspect of an employee's dismissal makes the situation dangerous, especially when the nature of the work adds other risk factors.[5]

Retaining top performers is not always easy either, and recent trends have made this more difficult than ever. The rash of layoffs and downsizings of the early and mid-1990s reduced employees' loyalty to their organizations. This mistrust coupled with the tight labor markets of the 1990s created a workforce that is now both willing and able to leave on a moment's notice.

❧ EMPLOYEE SEPARATION

Because of the critical financial and personal risks associated with employee dismissal, it is easy to see why organizations must develop a standardized, systematic approach to discipline and discharge. These decisions should not be left solely to the discretion of individual managers or supervisors. Policies that can lead to employee separation should be based on principles of justice and law, and they should allow for various ways to intervene. The "HR How To" box compares these guidelines with Donald Trump's firings on the popular TV show "The Apprentice."

Principles of Justice

The sensitivity of a system for disciplining and possibly terminating employees is obvious, and it is critical that the system be seen as fair. Employees form conclusions about the system's fairness based on the system's outcomes and procedures and the way managers treat employees when carrying out those procedures. Figure 10.1 summarizes these principles as outcome fairness, procedural justice, and interactional justice. Outcome fairness involves the ends of a discipline process, while procedural and interactional justice focus on the means to those ends. Not only is behavior in accord with these principles ethical, but research has also linked the last two categories of justice with employee satisfaction and productivity.[6]

People's perception of **outcome fairness** depends on their judgment that the consequences of a decision to employees are just. As shown in Figure 10.1, one employee's consequences should be consistent with other employees' consequences. Suppose several employees went out to lunch, returned drunk, and were reprimanded.

LO2
Discuss how employees determine whether the organization treats them fairly.

outcome fairness
A judgment that the consequences given to employees are just.

HR HOW TO

IS "THE APPRENTICE" A GOOD MODEL FOR EMPLOYEE SEPARATION?

Beginning in 2003, employee terminations became a fixture in American living rooms, thanks to the television show "The Apprentice." In this reality TV show, several people compete in groups to win the approval of—and a job with—real estate magnate Donald Trump, who acts as their supervisor. Each week, Trump terminates one employee, using his signature declaration, "You're fired!" The show ends when only one employee remains to claim the prize: a six-figure position in one of Trump's real-world business organizations.

"The Apprentice" has been both popular and controversial. Some have debated whether the show is actually a "total lack of reality" show in terms of describing how the business world operates. Some people have said the show accurately portrays the scheming and backstabbing that takes place in high levels of corporate politics, but the overtly sexual nature of much of the show's action is more of a soap opera than a day at the office.

Still, a look at the way Trump terminates employees highlights negative and positive aspects of how to terminate employees:

- On the negative side, an obvious no-no is his use of sarcasm, humor, and humiliation. Although this behavior makes the TV show more entertaining, it violates standards of fair play. If anything, a termination calls for extra care in treating the employee with respect. Besides being a more just approach, it may protect the organization and its employees. Someone who has been humiliated is more likely to return later with a lawyer (or a gun). Juries that hear evidence of cruel intent during the termination process are more likely to favor the discharged employee in a lawsuit.
- On the positive side, Trump gets high marks for candor. Many real managers try to soothe hurt feelings by sugarcoating their message, but honesty makes the process of firing more just and acceptable. When Trump fires a contestant, he lays out the reasons, focusing on specific behaviors and incidents that support the decision. The person receives clear information about what aspects of his or her performance were not up to Trump's standards.

Perhaps the worst move a manager can make is to pretend the termination is unrelated to performance when, in fact, it is. If a terminated employee is told that a termination decision is based on a need to cut costs by eliminating the position, and the employee later learns someone was hired as a replacement, the employee has trapped the organization in a lie. If the employee can find grounds for a discrimination lawsuit, an organization that has lied once will have a hard time convincing jurors it is telling the truth about whether it discriminated.

SOURCE: J. Merritt, "What Trump Saw in Bill: The Donald," *BusinessWeek*, April 16, 2004, pp. 31–32; J. Merritt, "A Gut Course in Post-Grad Scheming," *BusinessWeek*, February 2, 2004, p. 41; A. L. Rupe, "Horrors from the Bad-Firing Files," *Workforce*, November 2003, pp. 16–18; and A. L. Rupe, "Plain and Simple: Liars Lose," *Workforce*, March 2004, pp. 14–16.

A few weeks later, another employee was fired for being drunk at work. Employees might well conclude that outcomes are not fair because they are inconsistent. Another basis for outcome fairness is that everyone should know what to expect. Organizations promote outcome fairness when they clearly communicate policies regarding the consequences of inappropriate behavior. Finally, the outcome should be proportionate to the behavior. Terminating an employee for being late to work, espe-

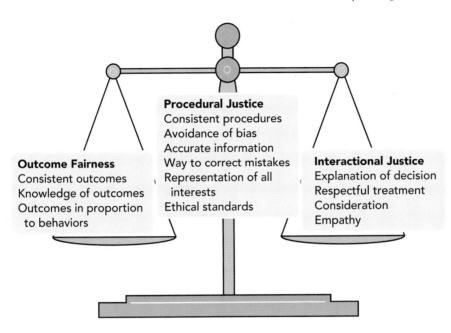

figure 10.1
Principles of Justice

cially if this is the first time the employee is late, would seem out of proportion to the offense in most situations. Employees' sense of outcome fairness usually would reserve loss of a job for the most serious offenses.

People's perception of **procedural justice** is their judgment that fair methods were used to determine the consequences an employee receives. Figure 10.1 shows six principles that determine whether people perceive procedures as fair. The procedures should be consistent from one person to another, and the manager using them should suppress any personal biases. The procedures should be based on accurate information, not rumors or falsehoods. The procedures should also be correctable, meaning the system includes safeguards, such as channels for appealing a decision or correcting errors. The procedures should take into account the concerns of all the groups affected—for example, by gathering information from employees, customers, and managers. Finally, the procedures should be consistent with prevailing ethical standards, such as concerns for privacy and honesty.

A perception of **interactional justice** is a judgment that the organization carried out its actions in a way that took the employee's feelings into account. It is a judgment about the ways that managers interact with their employees. A disciplinary action meets the standards of interactional justice if the manager explains to the employee how the action is procedurally just. The manager should listen to the employee. The manager should also treat the employee with dignity and respect and should empathize with the employee's feelings. Even when a manager discharges an employee for doing something wrong, the manager can speak politely and state the reasons for the action.

Meeting these standards can be difficult, because managers are as uncomfortable as anyone else when they have to deliver bad news. As a result, organizations sometimes handle separation and other negative actions in ways that employees find infuriating. For example, Inacom handled the layoff of 5,000 employees by directing them to call an 800 number. At that number, a recording told the employees they were off work, effective immediately. Chrysler workers didn't even make it inside the building to get the news. Workers figured out they were laid off when their ID badges no longer operated the security gates at the factory entrance. And in January 2000, Amazon.com

procedural justice
A judgment that fair methods were used to determine the consequences an employee receives.

interactional justice
A judgment that the organization carried out its actions in a way that took the employee's feelings into account.

announced job cuts by sending e-mails to employees at their homes, telling them they were no longer needed. None of these methods leaves room for such measures of interactional justice as listening to the employee. A better approach is for a direct supervisor to deliver the news, perhaps with the assistance of an HR specialist, who can answer questions about company policy.[7]

Justice issues also come into play in the use of *noncompete agreements*—contracts in which employees agree that in the future they will not take a job with a competitor of the employer. Some noncompete agreements limit this restriction by preventing future employment with competitors only in a certain geographic area or within a certain time period after leaving the employer. Outside that area or after that time period, the former employee may work for a competitor without violating the agreement. Employers see the agreements as fair because the employers have invested in training employees and providing them with the skills, information, personal contacts, and experiences that make them valuable in the workplace. From the employer's point of view, it would be unfair for an employee to obtain these advantages, then take them to a competitor in exchange for higher pay. From many employees' point of view, the agreements are unfair because they make it impractical to find another job if employees are dissatisfied—or even if they are laid off.

<table>
<tr><td>LO3
Identify legal
requirements for
employee discipline.</td><td>

Legal Requirements

The law gives employers wide latitude in hiring and firing, but employers must meet certain requirements. They must avoid wrongful discharge and illegal discrimination. They also must meet standards related to employees' privacy and adequate notice of layoffs.

</td></tr>
</table>

Wrongful Discharge

As we noted earlier in the chapter, discipline practices must avoid the charge of wrongful discharge. First, this means the discharge may not violate an implied agreement. For instance, terminating an employee may violate an implied agreement if the employer had promised the employee job security or if the action is inconsistent with company policies. Suppose an organization has stated that an employee with an unexcused absence will receive a warning for the first violation, but an angry supervisor fires an employee for being absent on the day of an important meeting. That employee may be able to claim violation of an implied agreement. Similarly, if an organization's employee handbook or intranet Web page includes statements of employment rights, such as "permanent" employment after 90 days' probation, a court might find those statements to be an implied employment agreement.[8]

Another reason a discharge may be considered wrongful is that it violates public policy. Violations of public policy include terminating the employee for refusing to do something illegal, unethical, or unsafe. Suppose an employee refuses to dump chemicals into the sewer system; firing that employee could be a violation of public policy. It is also a violation of public policy to terminate an employee for doing what the law requires—for example, cooperating with a government investigation, reporting illegal behavior by the employer, or reporting for jury duty.

HR professionals can help organizations avoid (and defend against) charges of wrongful discharge by establishing and communicating policies for handling misbehavior. They should define unacceptable behaviors and identify how the organization will respond to them. Managers should follow these procedures consistently and document precisely the reasons for disciplinary action. In addition, the organization should train managers to avoid making promises that imply job security (for example, "As long as you keep up that level of performance, you'll have a job with us"). Finally, in writing and reviewing employee handbooks, HR professionals should avoid any statements that could be interpreted as employment contracts. When there is any doubt about a statement, the organization should seek legal advice.

Discrimination

Another benefit of a formal discipline policy is that it helps the organization comply with equal employment opportunity requirements. As in other employment matters, employers must make decisions without regard to individuals' age, sex, race, or other protected status. If two employees steal from the employer but one is disciplined more harshly than the other, the employee who receives the harsher punishment could look for the cause in his or her being of a particular race, country of origin, or some other group. Evenhanded, carefully documented discipline can avoid such claims.

Employees' Privacy

The courts also have long protected individuals' privacy in many situations. At the same time, employers have legitimate reasons for learning about some personal matters, especially when behavior outside the workplace can affect productivity, workplace safety, and employee morale. Employers therefore need to ensure that the information they gather and use is relevant to these matters. For example, safety and security make it legitimate to require drug testing of all employees holding jobs such as police officer, firefighter, and airline flight crew.[9] (Governments at the federal, state, and local levels have many laws affecting drug-testing programs, so it is wise to get legal advice before planning such tests.) Likewise, an employee who has committed a violent crime outside the workplace may be prone to violent actions against coworkers or customers. Complicating this situation, an arrest does not prove a person's guilt; only a conviction does. Therefore, the organization might place an arrested employee on a leave of absence and then terminate the employee only if the arrest leads to a conviction.

Organizations such as day care facilities or schools must protect an employees' right to privacy in their lives and on the job while balancing the need to protect children from harm.

Privacy issues also surface when employers wish to search or monitor employees on the job. An employer that suspects theft by employees or drug use on the job may wish to search employees for evidence. In general, random searches of areas such as desks, lockers, and toolboxes are permissible, so long as the employer can justify that there is probable cause for the search and the organization has work rules that provide for searches.[10] Employers can act fairly and minimize the likelihood of a lawsuit by publicizing the search policy, applying it consistently, asking for the employee's consent before the search begins, and conducting the search discreetly. Also, when a search is a random check, it is important to clarify that no one has been accused of misdeeds.[11]

To prevent theft is also one reason employers use surveillance techniques such as security cameras and telephone recording to monitor employees. Widespread use of computers and the Internet makes it possible for surveillance to include reading employees' files and e-mail, logging their Internet use, and using global positioning devices to monitor their travels.[12] As with physical searches, employers should be certain that electronic surveillance serves a necessary business purpose and that employees know about the surveillance, are clear about what behavior is expected, and know the consequences for being caught in misbehavior. For example, employees should know that their e-mail messages are not private. Employees may legitimately forbid employees from using business time and computers for personal communications. Still, says Sandy Hughes, leader of Procter & Gamble's global privacy council, "At some level, you have to trust your employees are going to be doing the right things." Electronic monitoring is not a good substitute for careful hiring, thorough training, and positive leadership.

No matter how sensitively the organization gathers information leading to disciplinary actions, it should also consider privacy issues when deciding who will see the information.[13] In general, it is advisable to share the information only with people who have a business need to see it—for example, the employee's supervisor, union officials, and in some cases, coworkers. Letting outsiders know the reasons for terminating an employee can embarrass the employee, who might file a defamation lawsuit. HR professionals can help organizations avoid such lawsuits by working with managers to determine fact-based explanations and to decide who needs to see these explanations.

Figure 10.2 summarizes these measures for protecting employees' privacy.

Notification of Layoffs

LO4
Summarize ways in which organizations can fairly discipline employees.

Sometimes terminations are necessary not because of individuals' misdeeds, but because the organization determines that for economic reasons it must close a facility. An organization that plans such broad-scale layoffs may be subject to the Workers' Adjustment Retraining and Notification Act. This federal law requires that organizations with more than 100 employees give 60 days' notice before any closing or layoff that will affect at least 50 full-time employees. If employers covered by this law do not give notice to the employees (and their union, if applicable), they may have to provide back pay and fringe benefits and pay penalties as well. Several states and cities have similar laws, and the federal law contains a number of exemptions. Therefore, it is important to seek legal advice before implementing a plant closing.

Progressive Discipline

hot-stove rule
Principle of discipline that says discipline should be like a hot stove, giving clear warning and following up with consistent, objective, immediate consequences.

Organizations look for methods of handling problem behavior that are fair, legal, and effective. A popular principle for responding effectively is the **hot-stove rule.** According to this principle, discipline should be like a hot stove: The glowing or burning stove gives

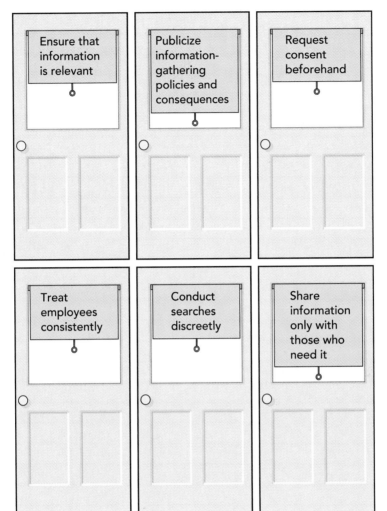

Figure 10.2

Measures for Protecting Employees' Privacy

warning not to touch. Anyone who ignores the warning will be burned. The stove has no feelings to influence which people it burns, and it delivers the same burn to any touch. Finally, the burn is immediate. Like the hot stove, an organization's discipline should give warning and have consequences that are consistent, objective, and immediate.

The principles of justice suggest that the organization prepare for problems by establishing a formal discipline process in which the consequences become more serious if the employee repeats the offense. Such a system is called **progressive discipline.** A typical progressive discipline system identifies and communicates unacceptable behaviors and responds to a series of offenses with the actions shown in Figure 10.3—spoken and then written warnings, temporary suspension, and finally, termination. This process fulfills the purpose of discipline by teaching employees what is expected of them and creating a situation in which employees must try to do what is expected. It seeks to prevent misbehavior (by publishing rules) and to correct, rather than merely punish, misbehavior.

Such procedures may seem exasperatingly slow, especially when the employee's misdeeds hurt the team's performance. In the end, however, if an employee must be discharged, careful use of the procedure increases other employees' belief that the organization is fair and reduces the likelihood that the problem employee will sue (or at

progressive discipline
A formal discipline process in which the consequences become more serious if the employee repeats the offense.

Figure 10.3

Progressive Discipline Responses

least that the employee will win in court). For situations in which misbehavior is dangerous, the organization may establish a stricter policy, even terminating an employee for the first offense. In that case, it is especially important to communicate the procedure—not only to ensure fairness but also to prevent the dangerous misbehavior.

Creating a formal discipline process is a primary responsibility of the human resource department. The HR professional should consult with supervisors and managers to identify unacceptable behaviors and establish rules and consequences for violating the rules. The rules should cover disciplinary problems such as the ones identified in Table 10.2. For each infraction, the HR professional would identify a series of responses, such as those in Figure 10.3. In addition, the organization must communicate these rules and consequences in writing to every employee. Ways of publishing rules include presenting them in an employee handbook, posting them on the company's intranet, and displaying them on a bulletin board. Supervisors should be familiar with the rules, so that they can discuss them with employees and apply them consistently.

Along with rules and a progression of consequences for violating the rules, a progressive discipline system should have requirements for documenting the rules, offenses, and responses. For issuing an unofficial warning about a less-serious offense, it may be enough to have a witness present. Even then, a written record would be helpful in case the employee repeats the offense in the future. The organization should provide a document for managers to file, recording the nature and date of the offense, the specific improvement expected, and the consequences of the offense. It is also helpful to indicate how the offense affects the performance of the individual employee, others in the group, or the organization as a whole. These documents are important for demonstrating to a problem employee why he or she has been suspended or terminated. They also back up the organization's actions if it should have to defend a lawsuit. Following the hot-stove rule, the supervisor should complete and discuss the documentation immediately after becoming aware of the offense. A copy of the

TABLE 10.2

Common Problems Requiring Discipline

Tardiness
Absenteeism
Unsafe work practices
Poor quantity or quality of work
Sexual harassment of coworkers
Coming to work impaired by alcohol or drugs
Theft of company property
Cyberslacking (surfing the Internet at work)

records should be placed in the employee's personnel file. The organization may have a policy of removing records of warnings after a period such as six months, on the grounds that the employee has learned from the experience.

As we noted in the earlier discussion of procedural justice, the discipline system should provide an opportunity to hear every point of view and to correct errors. Before discussing and filing records of misbehavior, it is important for the supervisor to investigate the incident. The employee should be made aware of what he or she is said to have done wrong and should have an opportunity to present his or her version of events. Anyone who witnessed the misdeed also should have a chance to describe what happened. In general, employees who belong to a union have a right to the presence of a union representative during a formal investigation interview if they request representation.[14]

Besides developing these policies, HR professionals have a role in carrying out progressive discipline.[15] In meetings to announce disciplinary actions, it is wise to include two representatives of the organization. Usually, the employee's supervisor presents the information, and a representative from the HR department acts as a witness. This person can help the meeting stay on track and, if necessary, can later confirm what happened during the meeting. Especially at the termination stage of the process, the employee may be angry, so it is helpful to be straightforward but polite. The supervisor should state the reason for the meeting, the nature of the problem behavior, and the consequences. Listening to the employee is important, but because an investigation was already conducted, there is no purpose to arguing. When an employee is suspended or terminated, the organization should designate a person to escort the employee from the building to protect the organization's people and property.

Alternative Dispute Resolution

Sometimes problems are easier to solve when an impartial person helps to create the solution. Therefore, at various points in the discipline process, the employee or organization might want to bring in someone to help with problem solving. Rather than turning to the courts every time an outsider is desired, more and more organizations are using **alternative dispute resolution (ADR).** A variety of ADR techniques show promise for resolving disputes in a timely, constructive, cost-effective manner.

In general, a system for alternative dispute resolution proceeds through the four stages shown in Figure 10.4:

1. **Open-door policy**—Based on the expectation that two people in conflict should first try to arrive at a settlement together, the organization has a policy of making managers available to hear complaints. Typically, the first "open door" is that of the employee's immediate supervisor, and if the employee does not get a resolution

alternative dispute resolution (ADR)
Methods of solving a problem by bringing in an impartial outsider but not using the court system.

open-door policy
An organization's policy of making managers available to hear complaints.

Figure 10.4

Typical Stages of Alternative Dispute Resolution

| Open-door policy | Peer review | Mediation | Arbitration |

peer review
Process for resolving disputes by taking them to a panel composed of representatives from the organization at the same levels as the people in the dispute.

mediation
Nonbinding process in which a neutral party from outside the organization hears the case and tries to help the people in conflict arrive at a settlement.

arbitration
Binding process in which a professional arbitrator from outside the organization (usually a lawyer or judge) hears the case and resolves it by making a decision.

from that person, the employee may appeal to managers at higher levels. This policy works only to the degree that managers who hear complaints listen and are able to act.

2. **Peer review**—If the people in conflict cannot reach an agreement, they take their conflict to a panel composed of representatives from the organization at the same levels as the people in the dispute. The panel hears the case and tries to help the parties arrive at a settlement. To set up a panel to hear disputes as they arise, the organization may assign managers to positions on the panel and have employees elect nonmanagement panel members.

3. **Mediation**—If the peer review does not lead to a settlement, a neutral party from outside the organization hears the case and tries to help the people in conflict arrive at a settlement. The process is not binding, meaning the mediator cannot force a solution.

4. **Arbitration**—If mediation fails, a professional arbitrator from outside the organization hears the case and resolves it by making a decision. Most arbitrators are experienced employment lawyers or retired judges. The employee and employer both have to accept this person's decision. Recently, an arbitrator required Dow Chemical Company to rehire a dozen workers it had fired.[16] Dow had discovered that over 250 workers were using the company's e-mail system to send sexually explicit and violent material, but it fired only 12 of them. The rest were reprimanded. Because the discipline was not consistent, it did not stand up in arbitration.

Each stage reflects a somewhat broader involvement of people outside the dispute. The hope is that the conflict will be resolved at earlier stages, where the costs, time, and embarrassing publicity are lowest. However, even the arbitration stage tends to be much faster, simpler, and more private than a lawsuit.[17]

Experience shows that ADR can effectively save time and money. Over a four-year period of using ADR, Houston-based Kellogg, Brown and Root experienced a 90 percent drop in its legal fees. Of 2,000 disputes, only 30 ever reached the stage of binding arbitration.[18]

Employee Assistance Programs

employee assistance program (EAP)
A referral service that employees can use to seek professional treatment for emotional problems or substance abuse.

While ADR is effective in dealing with problems related to performance and disputes between people at work, many of the problems that lead an organization to want to terminate an employee involve drug or alcohol abuse. In these cases, the organization's discipline program should also incorporate an **employee assistance program (EAP).** An EAP is a referral service that employees can use to seek professional treatment for emotional problems or substance abuse. EAPs began in the 1950s with a focus on treating alcoholism, and in the 1980s they expanded into drug treatment. Today, many are now fully integrated into employers' overall health benefits plans, where they refer employees to covered mental health services.

EAPs vary widely, but most share some basic elements. First, the programs are usually identified in official documents published by the employer, such as employee handbooks. Supervisors (and union representatives when workers belong to a union) are trained to use the referral service for employees whom they suspect of having health-related problems. The organization also trains employees to use the system to refer themselves when necessary. The organization regularly evaluates the costs and benefits of the program, usually once a year.

The Employee Assistance Program is an important support base for employees with emotional or substance abuse problems and some organizations are recognized for their success with this program. Kim Edens, the Democratic Senatorial Committee Campaign EAP manager, recently accepted the Secretary of Defense Community Drug Awareness Award for an unprecedented fourth year.

The variations among EAPs make evaluating these programs especially important. For example, the treatment for alcoholism varies widely, including hospitalization and participation in Alcoholics Anonymous (AA). General Electric performed an experiment to compare the outcomes of these treatments, and it found that employees who were hospitalized tended to fare the best in a two-year follow-up.[19] Other research has evaluated whether short-term, low-cost treatments wind up being more costly in terms of long-term health and health-care spending. In a study of drug dependency, the results were similar to those of the GE study, but in the case of depression, medications such as Prozac may offer promise for treatment by primary care physicians.[20]

Outplacement Counseling

An employee who has been discharged is likely to feel angry and confused about what to do next. If the person feels there is nothing to lose and nowhere else to turn, the potential for violence or a lawsuit is greater than most organizations are willing to tolerate. This concern is one reason many organizations provide **outplacement counseling,** which tries to help dismissed employees manage the transition from one job to another. Organizations also may address ongoing poor performance with discussion about whether the employee is a good fit for the current job. Rather than simply firing the poor performer, the supervisor may encourage this person to think about leaving. In this situation, the availability of outplacement counseling may help the employee decide to look for another job. This approach may protect the dignity of the employee who leaves and promote a sense of fairness.

Some organizations have their own staff for conducting outplacement counseling. Other organizations have contracts with outside providers to help with individual

outplacement counseling
A service in which professionals try to help dismissed employees manage the transition from one job to another.

cases. Either way, the goals for outplacement programs are to help the former employee address the psychological issues associated with losing a job—grief, depression, and fear—while at the same time helping the person find a new job.

Outplacement counseling tries to help people realize that losing a job is not the end of the world and that other opportunities exist. For many people, losing a job actually has benefits. The job loss can be a learning experience that plants the seed for future success. For example, when John Morgridge was fired from his job with Honeywell, he realized that he was so assertive and loved independence so much that he would never be comfortable in a large, bureaucratic organization. Instead of trying to land a job in another company like Honeywell, he applied his skills to building computer network maker Cisco Systems, which became an industry leader.[21]

Although this was a success story for Morgridge, letting this talented manager go certainly spelled a lost opportunity for Honeywell. Retaining people who can contribute knowledge and talent is essential to business success. Therefore, the remainder of this chapter explores issues related to retaining employees.

◈ JOB WITHDRAWAL

job withdrawal
A set of behaviors with which employees try to avoid the work situation physically, mentally, or emotionally.

Organizations need employees who are fully engaged and committed to their work. Therefore, retaining employees goes beyond preventing them from quitting. The organization needs to prevent a broader negative condition, called **job withdrawal**—or a set of behaviors with which employees try to avoid the work situation physically, mentally, or emotionally. Job withdrawal results when circumstances such as the nature of the job, supervisors and coworkers, pay levels, or the employee's own disposition cause the employee to become dissatisfied with the job. As shown in Figure 10.5, this job dissatisfaction produces job withdrawal. Job withdrawal may take the form of behavior change, physical job withdrawal, or psychological withdrawal. Some researchers believe employees engage in the three forms of withdrawal behavior in that order, while others think they select from these behaviors to address the particular sources of job dissatisfaction they experience.[22]

LO5
Explain how job dissatisfaction affects employee behavior.

Job Dissatisfaction

Many aspects of people and organizations can cause job dissatisfaction, and managers and HR professionals need to be aware of them because correcting them can increase job satisfaction and prevent job withdrawal. The causes of job dissatisfaction identified in Figure 10.5 fall into four categories: personal dispositions, tasks and roles, supervisors and coworkers, and pay and benefits.

Figure 10.5

Job Withdrawal Process

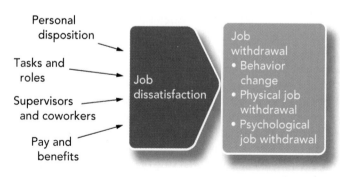

Personal Dispositions

Job dissatisfaction is a feeling experienced by individuals, so it is not surprising that many researchers have studied individual personality differences to see if some kinds of people are more disposed to be dissatisfied with their jobs. Several personal qualities have been found to be associated with job dissatisfaction, including negative affectivity and negative self-evaluations.

Negative affectivity means pervasive low levels of satisfaction with all aspects of life, compared with other people's feelings. People with negative affectivity experience feelings such as anger, contempt, disgust, guilt, fear, and nervousness more than other people do, at work and away.[23] They tend to focus on the negative aspects of themselves and others.[24] Not surprisingly, people with negative affectivity tend to be dissatisfied with their jobs, even after changing employers or occupations.[25]

Core self-evaluations are bottom-line opinions individuals have of themselves and may be positive or negative. People with a positive core self-evaluation have high self-esteem, believe in their ability to accomplish their goals, and are emotionally stable. They also tend to experience job satisfaction.[26] Part of the reason for their satisfaction is that they tend to seek out and obtain jobs with desirable characteristics, and when they are in a situation they dislike, they are more likely to seek change in socially acceptable ways.[27] In contrast, people with negative core self-evaluations tend to blame other people for their problems, including their dissatisfying jobs. They are less likely to work toward change; they either do nothing or act aggressively toward the people they blame.[28]

Tasks and Roles

As a predictor of job dissatisfaction, nothing surpasses the nature of the task itself.[29] Many aspects of a task have been linked to dissatisfaction. Of particular significance are the complexity of the task, the degree of physical strain and exertion required, and the value the employee places on the task.[30] In general, employees (especially women) are bored and dissatisfied with simple, repetitive jobs.[31] People also are more dissatisfied with jobs requiring a great deal of physical strain and exertion. Because automation has removed much of the physical strain associated with jobs, employers often overlook this consideration. Still, many jobs remain physically demanding. Finally, employees feel dissatisfied if their work is not related to something they value.

Employees not only perform specific tasks, but also have roles within the organization.[32] A person's **role** consists of the set of behaviors that people expect of a person in that job. These expected behaviors include the formally defined duties of the job but also much more. Sometimes things get complicated or confusing. Coworkers, supervisors, and customers have expectations for how the employee should behave often going far beyond a formal job description and having a large impact on the employee's work satisfaction. Several role-related sources of dissatisfaction are the following:

- **Role ambiguity** is uncertainty about what the organization and others expect from the employee in terms of what to do or how to do it. Employees suffer when they are unclear about work methods, scheduling, and performance criteria, perhaps because others hold different ideas about these. Employees particularly want to know how the organization will evaluate their performance. When they aren't sure, they become dissatisfied.[33]
- **Role conflict** is an employee's recognition that demands of the job are incompatible or contradictory; a person cannot meet all the demands. For example, a company

role
The set of behaviors that people expect of a person in a particular job.

role ambiguity
Uncertainty about what the organization expects from the employee in terms of what to do or how to do it.

role conflict
An employee's recognition that demands of the job are incompatible or contradictory.

Military reservists who are sent overseas often experience role conflict among *three* roles: soldier, family member, and civilian employee. Overseas assignments often intensify role conflicts.

might bring together employees from different functions to work on a team to develop a new product. Team members feel role conflict when they realize that their team leader and functional manager have conflicting expectations of them. Also, many employees may feel conflict between work roles and family roles. A role conflict may be triggered by an organization's request that an employee take an assignment overseas. Foreign assignments can be highly disruptive to family members, and the resulting role conflict is the top reason that people quit overseas assignments.[34]

role overload
A state in which too many expectations or demands are placed on a person.

- **Role overload** results when too many expectations or demands are placed on a person. (The opposite situation is *role underload*.) After an organization downsizes, it may expect so much of the remaining employees that they experience role overload. A recent study found that many middle- and upper-level managers were working more than 60 hours a week. Such heavy work requirements not only overload individuals but may lay a foundation for role conflict.[35]

Supervisors and Coworkers

Negative behavior by managers and peers in the workplace can produce tremendous dissatisfaction. Research by the Corporate Leadership Council found that employees who said they planned to leave their jobs most often said it was because managers acted as if they did not value the employees.[36] For instance, they said managers did not listen to the employees' opinions. Likewise, in their book *First Break All the Rules*, Marcus

Buckingham and Curt Coffman say people don't leave organizations; they leave managers.[37] In other cases, conflicts between employees left unaddressed by management may cause job dissatisfaction severe enough to lead to withdrawal or departure.

Pay and Benefits

For all the concern with positive relationships and interesting work, it is important to keep in mind that employees definitely care about their earnings. A job is the primary source of income and financial security for most people. Pay also is an indicator of status within the organization and in society at large, so it contributes to some people's self-worth. For all these reasons, satisfaction with pay is significant for retaining employees. Decisions about pay and benefits are so important and complex that the chapters of the next part of this book are devoted to this topic.

With regard to job satisfaction, the pay level—that is, the amount of income associated with each job—is especially important. Employers seeking to lure away another organization's employees often do so by offering higher pay. Benefits, such as insurance and vacation time, are also important, but employees often have difficulty measuring their worth. Therefore, although benefits influence job satisfaction, employees may not always consider them as much as pay itself.

Behavior Change

A reasonable expectation is that an employee's first response to dissatisfaction would be to try to change the conditions that generate the dissatisfaction. As the employee tries to bring about changes in policy or personnel, the efforts may involve confrontation and conflict with the employee's supervisor. In an organization where employees are represented by a union, as we will discuss in Chapter 14, more grievances may be filed.

From the manager's point of view, the complaints, confrontations, and grievances may feel threatening. On closer inspection, however, this is an opportunity for the manager to learn about and solve a potentially important problem. Don McAdams, a manager at Johnsonville Foods, recalls an incident in which one particular employee had been very critical of the company's incentive system. McAdams listened to the employee's concerns and asked him to head a committee charged with developing a better incentive system. The employee was at first taken aback but eventually accepted the challenge. He became so enthusiastic about the project that he was the one who presented the system to the employees. His history of criticizing the old system gave him great credibility with the other employees. In this way, the employee became a force for constructive change.[38]

In this example, the result was positive because the organization responded to legitimate concerns. When employees cannot work with management to make changes, they may look for help from outside the organization. Some employees may engage in *whistle-blowing*, taking their charges to the media in the hope that if the public learns about the situation, the organization will be forced to change. From the organization's point of view, whistle-blowing is harmful because of the negative publicity.

Another way employees may go outside the organization for help is to file a lawsuit. This way to force change is available if the employee is disputing policies on the grounds that they violate state and federal laws, such as those forbidding employment discrimination or requiring safe working conditions. Defending a lawsuit is costly, both financially and in terms of the employer's image, whether the organization wins or loses. Most employers would prefer to avoid lawsuits and whistle-blowing. Keeping employees satisfied is one way to do this.

Physical Job Withdrawal

If behavior change has failed or seems impossible, a dissatisfied worker may physically withdraw from the job. Options for physically leaving a job range from arriving late to calling in sick, requesting a transfer, or leaving the organization altogether. All these options are costly to the employer.

Finding a new job is rarely easy and can take months, so employees often are cautious about quitting. Employees who would like to quit may be late for work. Tardiness is costly because late employees are not contributing for part of the day. Especially when work is done by teams, the tardiness creates difficulties that spill over and affect the entire team's ability to work. Absenteeism is even more of a problem. According to a recent survey, employers spent 15 cents out of every payroll dollar to make up for absent workers.[39] The "Did You Know . . . ?" box summarizes reasons for employees' unplanned absences.

An employee who is dissatisfied because of circumstances related to the specific job—for example, an unpleasant workplace or unfair supervisor—may be able to resolve that problem with a job transfer. If the source of the dissatisfaction is organizational policies or practices, such as low pay scales, the employee may leave the organization altogether. These forms of physical job withdrawal contribute to high turnover rates for the department or organization. As a result, the organization faces the costs of replacing the employees, as well as lost productivity until replacement employees learn the jobs.

Organizations need to be concerned with their overall turnover rates as well as the nature of the turnover in terms of who is staying and who is leaving. For example, turnover rates among minorities at the managerial level are often two or three times the turnover among white males. One reason these managers give for leaving is that they see little opportunity for promotions. Chapter 9 discussed how organizations are addressing this problem through career management and efforts to break the glass ceiling.

Psychological Withdrawal

Employees need not leave the company in order to withdraw from their jobs. Especially if they have been unable to find another job, they may psychologically remove themselves. They are physically at work, but their minds are elsewhere.

Psychological withdrawal can take several forms. If an employee is primarily dissatisfied with the job itself, the employee may display a very low level of job involvement. **Job involvement** is the degree to which people identify themselves with their jobs. People with a high level of job involvement consider their work an important part of their life. Doing well at work contributes to their sense of who they are (their *self-concept*). For a dissatisfied employee with low job involvement, performing well or poorly does not affect the person's self-concept.

When an employee is dissatisfied with the organization as a whole, the person's organizational commitment may be low. **Organizational commitment** is the degree to which an employee identifies with the organization and is willing to put forth effort on its behalf.[40] Employees with high organizational commitment will stretch themselves to help the organization through difficult times. Employees with low organizational commitment are likely to leave at the first opportunity for a better job. They have a strong intention to leave, so like employees with low job involvement, they are hard to motivate.

job involvement
The degree to which people identify themselves with their jobs.

organizational commitment
The degree to which an employee identifies with the organization and is willing to put forth effort on its behalf.

? DID YOU KNOW?

ILLNESS IS NOT WHY MOST EMPLOYEES CALL IN SICK

According to data from a CCH survey of employers, less than 40 percent of unscheduled absences occur because the employee is sick. Employees also take time off to cope with family and personal needs, to relieve stress, and simply because they feel entitled to take a day off every now and then.

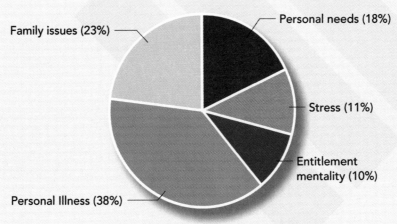

Reasons for Unscheduled Absences

- Personal needs (18%)
- Family issues (23%)
- Stress (11%)
- Entitlement mentality (10%)
- Personal Illness (38%)

SOURCE: Barbara Rose, "Absences Make the Firms Grow Tougher," *Chicago Tribune*, April 18, 2005, sec. 1, pp. 1, 16.

◈ JOB SATISFACTION

Clearly, organizations want to prevent the withdrawal behaviors discussed above. As we saw in Figure 10.5, the driving force behind job withdrawal is dissatisfaction. To prevent job withdrawal, organizations therefore need to promote **job satisfaction,** a pleasant feeling resulting from the perception that one's job fulfills or allows for the fulfillment of one's important job values.[41] Several aspects of job satisfaction are:

- Job satisfaction is related to a person's values, defined as "what a person consciously or unconsciously desires to obtain."
- Different employees have different views of which values are important, so the same circumstances can produce different levels of job satisfaction.
- Job satisfaction is based on perception, not always on an objective and complete measurement of the situation. Each person compares the job situation to his or her values, and people are likely to differ in what they perceive.

In sum, values, perceptions, and ideas of what is important are the three components of job satisfaction. People will be satisfied with their jobs as long as they perceive that their jobs meet their important values. As shown in Figure 10.6, organizations can contribute to job satisfaction by addressing the four sources of job dissatisfaction we identified earlier: personal dispositions, job tasks and roles, supervisors and coworkers, and pay and benefits. The "Best Practices" box describes how Applebee's improved employee retention by addressing these sources of dissatisfaction.

LO6
Describe how organizations contribute to employees' job satisfaction and retain key employees.

job satisfaction
A pleasant feeling resulting from the perception that one's job fulfills or allows for the fulfillment of one's important job values.

Figure 10.6

Increasing Job Satisfaction

Personal Dispositions

In our discussion of job withdrawal, we noted that sometimes personal qualities of the employee, such as negative affectivity and negative core self-evaluation, are associated with job dissatisfaction. This linkage suggests employee selection in the first instance plays a role in raising overall levels of employee satisfaction. People making the selection decisions should look for evidence of whether employees are predisposed to being satisfied. Interviews should explore employees' satisfaction with past jobs. If an applicant says he was dissatisfied with his past six jobs, what makes the employer think the person won't be dissatisfied with the organization's vacant position?

Employers also should recognize that dissatisfaction with other facets of life can spill over into the workplace. A worker who is having problems with a family member may attribute some of the negative feelings to the job or organization. Of course, managers should not try to become clinical psychologists for their employees and applicants. Still, when employees express negativity and dissatisfaction in many areas, managers should consider that the employee may be clinically depressed.[42] The manager should suggest that the employee contact the organization's employee assistance program or his or her physician. Depression is a common condition, but most cases can be managed with proper care. As a reasonable accommodation under the Americans with Disabilities Act, the employer may need to grant the employee time off or a flexible schedule to accommodate treatment.

Tasks and Roles

Organizations can improve job satisfaction by making jobs more complex and meaningful, as we discussed in Chapter 4. Some of the methods available for this approach to job design are job enrichment and job rotation. Organizations also can increase satisfaction by developing clear and appropriate job roles.

APPLEBEE'S FEATURES EMPLOYEE RETENTION ON ITS MENU

When HR professional Lou Kaucic switched from a manufacturing company to a fast-food company, he was astounded by the high turnover rates typical of the food-service industry. The company representative interviewing Kaucic for the job told him that employee turnover was so high the company wasn't sure how to measure it. Kaucic took the job anyway, and his commitment to retaining employees has persisted beyond that job to his current position as vice president of human resources for Applebee's Neighborhood Grill & Bar.

Applebee's, with 1,600 restaurants in 49 states and nine countries, has more than 100,000 employees and annual store management turnover of 14 percent—a challenging level but far lower than the industry average of 50 percent. Kaucic and the company's chief executive planned a future in which success hinges on what Kaucic sums up as "people, not just people, but noticeably better people." In other words, the company focuses on retaining the employees identified as its top and middle performers.

This effort includes helping store managers identify which candidates to bring into the company in the first place. Careful hiring decisions can prevent turnover later, when an employee turns out to be a poor fit for a job, yet many restaurant managers lack a strong background in interviewing. So, Applebee's created a set of assessments to help managers measure job candidates in terms of punctuality, stamina, cooperation, and appearance. Kaucic says the managers initially thought the process was troublesome but eventually saw that they were hiring better people.

Once the right people are on board, Applebee's focuses on keeping them. The company identified a pattern of employees quitting after one month or before the end of three months on the job. To keep these new employees committed, Kaucic developed a contest called "Block Party," in which teams of employees receive prizes for knowing aspects of their job, such as safe cooking temperatures and techniques for handling problems with customers.

The company communicates its goals and rewards efforts to meet those goals. Kaucic invented the acronym *BIG Fun TRIP* for the principles of Balance, Innovation, Guest-driven, Fun, Teamwork, Results, Integrity, and Passion for service. Employees can nominate one another for living up to these principles in their work.

For managers, retention efforts begin with identifying the skills of successful managers and identifying which of the managers are meeting and exceeding standards. Retention efforts focus on the top-performing 80 percent. For these managers, Applebee's set up a compensation system that rewards them with bonuses and deferred compensation (a retirement program). The best managers may be recognized through appointment to two leadership councils.

Applebee's strengthens coworker relationships among its regional HR managers and staff using quarterly phone calls. During the calls, group members present goals for hiring and retention. Those listening rate their perception of the goals as "bullish," "bearish," or "neutral," imitating the language of investors. The HR employees are motivated by the conversation with their peers.

SOURCE: Frank Jossi, "Turning Turnover Around," *Human Resource Executive*, October 16, 2004, p. 28.

Job Complexity

Not only can job design add to enriching complexity, but employees themselves sometimes take measures to make their work more interesting. Some employees bring personal stereo headsets to work, so they can listen to music or radio shows while they are working. Many supervisors disapprove, worrying that the headsets will interfere with the employees' ability to provide good customer service. However, in simple jobs with minimal customer contact (like processing paperwork or entering data into computers), research suggests that personal stereo headsets can improve performance. One study examined the use of stereo headsets by workers in 32 jobs at a large retailing company. The stereo-using group outperformed the no-stereo group on simple jobs (like invoice processor) but performed worse than the stereo-free group on complex jobs (such as accountant).[43]

Meaningful Work

Through work design and communications with employees, organizations can make work more meaningful. After all, over a million volunteer workers in the United States perform their jobs almost exclusively because of the meaning they attach to the work. Some of these jobs are even low in complexity and high in physical exertion. The volunteers see themselves as performing a worthwhile service, and this overrides the other two factors and makes the job satisfying. Similarly, several low-paying occupations (such as social services and religious orders) explicitly try to make up for low pay by appealing to workers' nonfinancial values. The Peace Corps, for example, tries to recruit applicants by describing the work as "the toughest job you will ever love."

Clear and Appropriate Roles

Organizations can do much to avoid role-related sources of dissatisfaction. They can define roles, clearly spelling out work methods, schedules, and performance measures. They can be realistic about the number of hours required to complete job requirements. When jobs require overtime hours, the employer must be prepared to comply with laws requiring overtime pay, as well as to help employees manage the conflict between work and family roles.

To help employees manage role conflict, employers have turned to a number of family-friendly policies. These policies may include provisions for child care, elder care, flexible work schedules, job sharing, telecommuting, and extended parental leaves.[44] Although these programs create some headaches for managers in terms of scheduling work and reporting requirements, they increase employees' commitment to the organization.[45] Organizations with family-friendly policies also have enjoyed improvements in performance, especially those that employ a large percentage of women.[46] Chapter 13 discusses such benefits in greater detail.

Organizations should also pay attention to the fit between job titles and roles, especially as more and more Americans feel overworked. A 2001 survey of U.S. workers indicated that almost half felt they were working too many hours, and roughly one-fourth worked six days and over 50 hours a week.[47] One consequence of this perception is an increase in the number of lawsuits filed by people who are suing for overtime pay. The Fair Labor Standards Act exempts managers and professionals from its requirement that the company pay overtime to employees who work more than a 40-hour week. Increasingly, employees are complaining that they have been misclassified as managers and should be treated as nonexempt workers. Their job titles sound like managerial jobs, but their day-to-day activities involve no supervision. Companies that have defended against such lawsuits include U-Haul, Taco Bell, PepsiCo, Auto Zone, and Wal-Mart.[48]

role analysis technique
A process of formally identifying expectations associated with a role.

Because role problems rank just behind job problems in creating job dissatisfaction, some interventions aim directly at role elements. One of these is the **role analysis technique,** a process of formally identifying expectations associated with a role. The technique follows the steps shown in Figure 10.7. The *role occupant* (the person who

Figure 10.7

Steps in the Role Analysis Technique

fills a role) and each member of the person's *role set* (people who directly interact with this employee) each write down their expectations for the role. They meet to discuss their expectations and develop a preliminary list of the role's duties and behaviors, trying to resolve any conflicts among expectations. Next, the role occupant lists what he or she expects of others in the set, and the group meets again to reach a consensus on these expectations. Finally, the group modifies its preliminary list and reaches a consensus on the occupant's role. This process may uncover instances of overload and underload, and the group tries to trade off requirements to develop more balanced roles.

Supervisors and Coworkers

The two primary sets of people in an organization who affect job satisfaction are coworkers and supervisors. A person may be satisfied with these people for one of three reasons:

1. The people share the same values, attitudes, and philosophies. Most individuals find this very important, and many organizations try to foster a culture of shared values. Even when this does not occur across the whole organization, values shared between workers and their supervisor can increase satisfaction.[49]

Coworker relationships can contribute to job satisfaction, and organizations therefore try to provide opportunities to build positive relationships. Would a strong sense of teamwork and friendship help you enjoy your work more?

2. The coworkers and supervisor may provide social support, meaning they are sympathetic and caring. Social support greatly increases job satisfaction, whether the support comes from supervisors or coworkers.[50] Turnover is also lower among employees who experience support from other members of the organization.[51]
3. The coworkers or supervisor may help the person attain some valued outcome. For example, they can help a new employee figure out what goals to pursue and how to achieve them.[52]

Because a supportive environment reduces dissatisfaction, many organizations foster team building both on and off the job (such as with softball or bowling leagues). The idea is that playing together as a team will strengthen ties among group members and develop relationships in which individuals feel supported by one another. Of course, management cannot ensure that each employee will develop friendships, but the team-building activities can make it easier for employees to interact, which is a necessary first step toward building a relationship.

Pay and Benefits

Organizations recognize the importance of pay in their negotiations with job candidates. HR professionals can support their organizations in this area by repeatedly monitoring pay levels in their industry and for the professions or trades they employ. As we noted in Chapter 5 and will discuss further in Chapter 11, organizations make decisions about whether to match or exceed the industry averages. Also, HR professionals can increase job satisfaction by communicating to employees the value of their benefits.

Two other aspects of pay satisfaction influence job satisfaction. One is satisfaction with pay structure—the way the organization assigns different pay levels to different levels and job categories. A manager of a sales force, for example, might be satisfied with her pay level until she discovers that some of the sales representatives she supervises are earning more than she is. The other important aspect of pay satisfaction is pay raises. People generally expect that their pay will increase over time. They will be satisfied if their expectations are met or dissatisfied if raises fall short of expectations. HR professionals can contribute to these sources of job satisfaction by helping to communicate the reasoning behind the organization's pay structure and pay raises. For example, sometimes economic conditions force an organization to limit pay raises. If employees understand the circumstances (and recognize that the same conditions are likely to be affecting other employers), they may feel less dissatisfied.

E-HRM

TECHNOLOGY MAKES SURVEYS PART OF THE ROUTINE

Assessing employee attitudes is important, but most organizations treat it more like an annual checkup than a day-to-day activity. In the past, this limited approach was necessary because of the effort required to prepare and process interviews on paper. Paper-and-pencil surveys typically generated not only paperwork but also travel, mailing expense, and time to enter information into computers and prepare reports.

Today, Internet access and easy-to-use software have allowed organizations to conduct surveys on the Web. Putting a survey online saves the expenses of printing, travel, and data entry, significantly reducing the costs of employee surveys. Online employee surveys offer additional benefits as well.

Internet surveys shorten the time between asking a question and receiving the results. SAP, a software company that conducts computer-administered surveys, can deliver results to employers in four days. If managers set aside time to review the results when they arrive, the organization can act on them quickly, demonstrating to employees that their opinions matter to their employer.

Online surveys also free the organization from the limits of the once-a-year survey schedule. The employer can set up its system to deliver questions and tabulate responses much more frequently. This way, the organization can ask just a few targeted questions each time or repeat questions over time to follow trends in opinions. For example, eePulse, a survey firm, provides its clients with weekly survey results that provide detailed data on opinion changes. The timeliness of the data makes it easier for the employer to link specific actions to employees' attitudes or opinions. In organizations where the employer is making many changes over the course of a year, it would otherwise be hard to attribute changes in attitudes to any single employer action.

Software for analyzing survey responses addresses the common complaint that annual survey data is "a mile wide and an inch thick," mentioning a lot of topics but offering little meaningful insight into any of them. Ratings of "leadership" or "pay" may signal a general problem but give little insight into what solutions would be most meaningful. Those insights often are sparked by open-ended questions seeking comments from employees. Until recently, comments were hard to tabulate and review in a large company with many survey responses. Modern software handles this problem by applying search tools to identify key words and phrases that occur frequently. The software can categorize the comments according to themes, generating reports that are more concise and meaningful.

SOURCE: N. Eason, "Tech Lends an Ear to the Workplace," *CNN.com*, September 8, 2003, p. 1; K. Thomas, "Ticking the Right Boxes," *Financial Times*, April 28, 2004, pp. 2–4; S. Raphael, "Employers Start to Listen as eePulse Delivers," *Business Direct Weekly*, July 24, 2003, pp. 1–2; and S. Jones, "Ever Sharp Eyes Are Watching You," *BusinessWeek*, July 22, 2003, pp. 22–23.

Monitoring Job Satisfaction

Employers can better retain employees if they are aware of satisfaction levels, so they can make changes if employees are dissatisfied. The usual way to measure job satisfaction is with some kind of survey. A systematic, ongoing program of employee surveys should be part of the organization's human resource strategy. This program allows the organization to monitor trends and prevent voluntary turnover. For example, if satisfaction with promotion opportunities has been falling over several years, the trend may signal a need for better career management (a topic of Chapter 9). An organizational change, such as a merger, also might have important consequences for job satisfaction. In addition, ongoing surveys give the organization a way to measure whether policies adopted to improve job satisfaction and employee retention are working. Organizations can also compare results from different departments to identify groups with successful practices that may apply elsewhere in the organization. Another benefit is that some scales provide data that organizations can use to compare themselves to others in the same industry. This information will be valuable for creating and reviewing human resource policies that enable organizations to attract and retain employees in a competitive job market. Finally, conducting surveys gives employees a chance to be heard, so the practice itself can contribute to employee satisfaction. The "e-HRM" box describes how technology is helping organizations improve the way they conduct and use employee satisfaction surveys.

To obtain a survey instrument, an excellent place to begin is with one of the many established scales. The validity and reliability of many satisfaction scales have been tested, so it is possible to compare the survey instruments. The main reason for the organization to create its own scale would be that it wants to measure satisfaction with aspects of work that are specific to the organization (such as satisfaction with a particular health plan).

A widely used measure of job satisfaction is the Job Descriptive Index (JDI). The JDI emphasizes specific aspects of satisfaction—pay, the work itself, supervision, coworkers, and promotions. Figure 10.8 shows several items from the JDI scale. Other scales measure general satisfaction, using broad questions such as "All in all, how satisfied are you with your job?"[53] Some scales avoid language altogether, relying on pictures. The faces scale in Figure 10.9 is an example of this type of measure. Other scales exist for measuring more specific aspects of satisfaction. For example, the Pay Satisfaction Questionnaire (PSQ) measures satisfaction with specific aspects of pay, such as pay levels, structure, and raises.[54]

For a more sophisticated analysis of employee satisfaction, the researchers can sort responses according to groups of employees. For example, IndyMac Bank, a California mortgage lender, found a surprise in the relationship between performance and satisfaction as measured by employee turnover.[55] As expected, higher-performing employ-

figure 10.8

Example of Job Descriptive Index (JDI)

Instructions: Think of your present work. What is it like most of time? In the blank beside each word given below, write

   Y   for "Yes" if it describes your work
   N   for "No" if it does NOT describe your work
   ?   if you cannot decide

Work Itself	Pay	Promotion Opportunities
_____ Routine	_____ Less than I deserve	_____ Dead-end job
_____ Satisfying	_____ Highly paid	_____ Unfair policies
_____ Good	_____ Insecure	_____ Based on ablility

Supervision	Coworkers
_____ Impolite	_____ Intelligent
_____ Praises good work	_____ Responsible
_____ Doesn't supervise enough	_____ Boring

SOURCE: W. K. Balzar, D. C. Smith, D. E. Kravitz, S. E. Lovell, K. B. Paul, B. A. Reilly, and C. E. Reilly, *User's Manual for the Job Descriptive Index (JDI)* (Bowling Green, OH: Bowling Green State University, 1990).

Job Satisfaction from the Faces Scale
Consider all aspects of your job. Circle the face that best describes your feelings about your job in general.

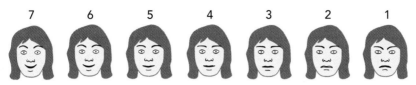

SOURCE: From R. B. Dunham and J. B. Herman, *Journal of Applied Psychology* 60 (1975), pp. 629–31. Reprinted with permission.

Figure 10.9

Example of a Simplified, Nonverbal Measure of Job Satisfaction

ees tended to be satisfied and stay with the company, but a subgroup of those employees was actually *more* likely to quit. The company rated employees' performance on a 100-point scale, and all employees at 85 or above were considered to exceed expectations. However, the company's performance awards—grants of stock—went only to employees who rated at 90 or above. Employees who scored at 85 to 89 on the rating scale were noticeably less satisfied than employees who scored high enough to receive a stock grant, suggesting that the company's reward system might not meet some of the criteria of fairness described earlier in this chapter.

The survey at IndyMac has launched a reevaluation of the bank's HR practices such as stock grants. Similarly, organizations benefit when they act on the results of their surveys. A good example of linking survey results to organizational change can be found at Cendant Mobility, a Connecticut-based global relocation service. After Cendant underwent a rocky series of mergers with two other companies, the morale of the workforce was low, and turnover was high. An employee attitude survey revealed that most of the workers were struggling with work–life balance. Most considered lack of flexibility in work schedules to be one of the top problems they faced at Cendant. The company offered a schedule with flexible starting and ending times and a small range of core time—10:00 A.M. to 2:00 P.M.—as well as an option to work a four-day compressed workweek. Turnover dropped from over 30 percent to less than 10 percent within two years. The program, which cost very little to implement, saved Cendant well over $8 million.[56]

In spite of surveys and other efforts to retain employees, some employees inevitably will leave the organization. This presents another opportunity to gather information for retaining employees: the **exit interview**—a meeting of the departing employee with the employee's supervisor and/or a human resource specialist to discuss the employee's reasons for leaving. A well-conducted exit interview can uncover reasons why employees leave and perhaps set the stage for some of them to return.[57] HR professionals can help make exit interviews more successful by arranging for the employee to talk to someone from the HR department (rather than the departing employee's supervisor) in a neutral location.[58] Questions should start out open-ended and general, to give the employee a chance to name the source of the dissatisfaction.

A recruiter armed with information about what caused a specific person to leave may be able to negotiate a return when the situation changes. And when several exiting employees give similar reasons for leaving, management should consider whether this indicates a need for change. In the war for talent, the best way to manage retention is to engage in a battle for every valued employee, even when it looks as if the battle has been lost.

exit interview
A meeting of a departing employee with the employee's supervisor and/or a human resource specialist to discuss the employee's reasons for leaving.

thinking ETHICALLY

Do Employees Have a Right to a Day Off?

"My bus broke down and was held up by robbers."
"I eloped."
"My cat unplugged the alarm clock."

These statements are actual excuses people have used when calling in to take a sick day. As the chapter described, absenteeism is costly to employers and can be demoralizing for the employees who do show up and have to carry the extra work of the absent employee. Many employees are honest and use time off only for a true illness. But a survey by the Ethics Resource Center found that more than one-third of employees admitted to calling in sick when they were actually well.

Reasons for inventing excuses differ, and so do employers' reactions. Some organizations recognize that employees face genuine role conflicts. Employees might make up work-related excuses such as an "appointment" that is really a need to be available for a child or an elderly parent. Employers can address this issue with broader paid-time-off policies in which employees have a bank of time to use for any personal need, not just illness. Other organizations are addressing the problem of absences with policies that strictly reward perfect attendance and punish unscheduled absences. At Lawson Products, a warehouse and customer service center in Addison, Illinois, employees receive points for being late or absent. After 6 points, they are reprimanded; those with 10 points are suspended without pay; and 12 points can result in firing. Employers view such "no-fault" policies as fair because the employee knows the expectations and consequences, and all employees are treated the same way.

SOURCE: Kathy Gurchiek, "'I Can't Make It to Work, Today Boss . . . Gotta Round Up My Ostriches,'" *HRMagazine,* March 2005, downloaded from Infotrac at http://web7.infotrac.gale-group.com; Sue Shellenbarger, "How and Why We Lie at the Office," *The Wall Street Journal,* March 24, 2005, http://online.wsj.com; and Barbara Rose, "Absences Make the Firms Grow Tougher," *Chicago Tribune,* April 18, 2005, sec. 1, pp. 1, 16.

Questions

1. Do employees have an ethical obligation to be honest about the reasons for their absences? Why or why not?
2. Do employers have an ethical obligation to accommodate employees who want or need time off? Explain.
3. Which seems more ethical to you—a flexible approach to time off that makes adjustments for personal needs or a no-fault policy in which all employees receive the same consequences for absences? Why? Would the most ethical approach depend on the nature of the work?

SUMMARY

1. Distinguish between involuntary and voluntary turnover, and describe their effects on an organization. Involuntary turnover occurs when the organization requires employees to leave, often when they would prefer to stay. Voluntary turnover occurs when employees initiate the turnover, often when the organization

would prefer to keep them. Both are costly because of the need to recruit, hire, and train replacements. Involuntary turnover can also result in lawsuits and even violence.

2. Discuss how employees determine whether the organization treats them fairly.

Employees draw conclusions based on the outcomes of decisions regarding them, the procedures applied, and the way managers treat employees when carrying out those procedures. Outcome fairness is a judgment that the consequences are just. The consequences should be consistent, expected, and in proportion to the significance of the behavior. Procedural justice is a judgment that fair methods were used to determine the consequences. The procedures should be consistent, unbiased, based on accurate information, and correctable. They should take into account the viewpoints of everyone involved, and they should be consistent with prevailing ethical standards. Interactional justice is a judgment that the organization carried out its actions in a way that took the employee's feelings into account—for example, by listening to the employee and treating the employee with dignity.

3. Identify legal requirements for employee discipline.

Employee discipline should not result in wrongful discharge, such as a termination that violates an implied contract or public policy. Discipline should be administered evenhandedly, without discrimination. Discipline should respect individual employees' privacy. Searches and surveillance should be for a legitimate business purpose, and employees should know about and consent to them. Reasons behind disciplinary actions should be shared only with those who need to know them. When termination is part of a plant closing, employees should receive the legally required notice, if applicable.

4. Summarize ways in which organizations can fairly discipline employees.

Discipline should follow the principles of the hot-stove rule, meaning discipline should give warning and have consequences that are consistent, objective, and immediate. A system that can meet these requirements is progressive discipline, in which rules are established and communicated, and increasingly severe consequences follow each violation of the rules. Usually, consequences range from a spoken warning through written warnings, suspension, and termination. These actions should be documented in writing. Organizations also may resolve problems through alternative dispute resolution, including an open-door policy, peer review, mediation, and arbitration. When performance problems seem to result from substance abuse or mental illness, the manager may refer the employee to an employee assistance program. When a manager terminates an employee or encourages an employee to leave, outplacement counseling may smooth the process.

5. Explain how job dissatisfaction affects employee behavior.

Circumstances involving the nature of a job, supervisors and coworkers, pay levels, or the employee's own disposition may produce job dissatisfaction. When employees become dissatisfied, they may engage in job withdrawal. This may include behavior change, as employees try to bring about changes in policy and personnel through inside action or through whistle-blowing or lawsuits. Physical job withdrawal may range from tardiness and absenteeism to job transfer or leaving the organization altogether. Especially when employees cannot find another job, they may psychologically withdraw by displaying low levels of job involvement and organizational commitment.

6. Describe how organizations contribute to employees' job satisfaction and retain key employees.

Organizations can try to identify and select employees who have personal dispositions associated with job satisfaction. They can make jobs more complex and meaningful—for example, through job enrichment and job rotation. They can use methods such as the role analysis technique to make roles clear and appropriate. They can reinforce shared values and encourage social support among employees. They can try to establish satisfactory pay levels and communicate with employees about pay structure and pay raises. Monitoring job satisfaction helps organizations identify which of these actions are likely to be most beneficial.

REVIEW AND DISCUSSION QUESTIONS

1. Give an example of voluntary turnover and an example of involuntary turnover. Why should organizations try to reduce both kinds of turnover?

2. A member of a restaurant's serving staff is chronically late to work. From the organization's point of view, what fairness issues are involved in deciding how to handle this situation? In what ways might the employee's and other servers' ideas of fairness be different?

3. For the situation in Question 2, how would a formal discipline policy help the organization address issues of fairness?

4. The progressive discipline process described in this chapter is meant to be fair and understandable, but it tends to be slow. Try to think of two or three offenses that should result in immediate discharge, rather than follow all the steps of progressive discipline. Explain why you selected these offenses. If the dismissed employee sued, do you think the organization would be able to defend its action in court?

5. A risk of disciplining employees is that some employees retaliate. To avoid that risk, what organizational policies might encourage low-performing employees to leave while encouraging high-performing employees to stay? (Consider the sources of employee satisfaction and dissatisfaction discussed in this chapter.)

6. List forms of behavior that can signal job withdrawal. Choose one of the behaviors you listed, and describe how you would respond if an otherwise valuable employee whom you supervised engaged in this kind of behavior.

7. What are the four factors that influence an employee's job dissatisfaction (or satisfaction)? Which of these do you think an employer can most easily change? Which would be the most expensive to change?

8. The section on principles of justice used noncompete agreements as an example. How would you expect the use of noncompete agreements to affect voluntary turnover? How might the use of these agreements af-fect job withdrawal and job satisfaction? Besides requiring noncompete agreements, how could an organization reduce the likelihood of employees leaving to work for competitors? Would these other methods have a better effect on employee satisfaction?

9. Consider your current job or a job you recently held. Overall, were you satisfied or dissatisfied with that job? How did your level of satisfaction or dissatisfaction affect your behavior on the job? Is your own experience consistent with this chapter's models of job withdrawal and job satisfaction?

10. Suppose you are an HR professional who convinced your company's management to conduct a survey of employee satisfaction. Your budget was limited, and you could not afford a test that went into great detail. Rather, you investigated overall job satisfaction and learned that it is low, especially among employees in three departments. You know that management is concerned about spending a lot for HR programs because sales are in a slump, but you want to address the issue of low job satisfaction. Suggest some ways you might begin to make a difference, even with a small budget. How will you convince management to try your ideas?

11. Why are exit interviews important? Should an organization care about the opinions of people who are leaving? How are those opinions relevant to employee separation and retention?

WHAT'S YOUR HR IQ?

The text Web site offers two more ways to check what you've learned so far. Use the Self-Assessment exercise to take a sample employee survey. Go online with the Web Exercise to see how well your knowledge of employee satisfaction with supervisors works in cyberspace.

BusinessWeek CASE

BusinessWeek The Costco Way

Although Costco Wholesale Corporation handily beat investors' profit expectations and forecasted higher profits for the rest of the year, the stock market drove down the price of Costco stock by 4 percent. One problem for Wall Street is that Costco pays its workers much better than archrival Wal-Mart Stores does. Analysts worry that Costco's operating expenses could get out of hand. "At Costco, it's better to be an employee or a customer than a shareholder," says Deutsche Bank analyst Bill Dreher.

The market's view of Costco speaks volumes about the so-called Wal-Martization of the U.S. economy. Although Wal-Mart has taken a public-relations pounding for paying poverty-level wages and shouldering health insurance for fewer than half of its 1.2 million U.S. workers, it re-mains the darling of Wall Street, which believes that shareholders are best served if employers do all they can to hold down costs, including the cost of labor.

Surprisingly, however, Costco's high-wage approach actually beats Wal-Mart at its own game on many measures. *BusinessWeek* ran through the numbers from each company to compare Costco and Sam's Club, the Wal-Mart warehouse unit that competes directly with Costco. We found that by compensating employees generously to motivate and retain good workers, one-fifth of whom are unionized, Costco gets lower turnover and higher productivity. Combined with a smart business strategy that sells a mix of higher-margin products to more affluent customers, Costco actually keeps its labor costs lower than Wal-

Mart's as a percentage of sales, and its 68,000 hourly workers in the United States sell more per square foot. Also, Costco's operating income grew at an average of 10.1 percent annually, slightly besting Sam's 9.8 percent. Most of Wall Street doesn't see the broader picture, though, and only focuses on the up-front savings Costco would gain if it paid workers less.

Given Costco's performance, the question for Wall Street shouldn't be why Costco isn't more like Wal-Mart. Rather, why can't Wal-Mart deliver high shareholder returns and high living standards for its workforce? Says Costco CEO James D. Sinegal: "Paying your employees well is not only the right thing to do but it makes for good business."

Look at how Costco pulls it off. Although Sam's $11.52 hourly average wage for full-timers tops the $9.64 earned by a typical Wal-Mart worker, it's still nearly 40 percent less than Costco's $15.97. Costco also shells out thousands more a year for workers' health and retirement and includes more of them in its health care, 401(k) retirement savings, and profit-sharing plans. "They take a very pro-employee attitude," says Rome Aloise, chief Costco negotiator for the Teamsters, which represents 14,000 Costco workers.

In return for all this generosity, Costco gets one of the most productive and loyal workforces in all of retailing. Only 6 percent of employees leave after the first year, compared with 21 percent at Sam's. That saves tons, since Wal-Mart says it costs $2,500 per worker just to test, interview, and train a new hire. Costco's motivated employees also sell more: $795 of sales per square foot, versus only $516 at Sam's and $411 at BJ's Wholesale Club, its other primary club rival. "Employees are willing to do whatever it takes to get the job done," says Julie Molina, a 17-year Costco worker in South San Francisco, California, who makes $17.82 an hour, plus bonuses.

Costco's productive workforce more than offsets the higher expense. Its labor and overhead tab, also called its selling, general, and administrative costs (SG&A), totals just 9.8 percent of revenue. While Wal-Mart declines to break out Sam's SG&A, it's likely higher than Costco's but lower than Wal-Mart's 17 percent. At Target, it's 24 percent. "Paying higher wages translates into more efficiency," says Costco's chief financial officer, Richard Galanti.

Of course, it's by no means as simple as that sounds, and management has to hustle to make the high-wage strategy work. It's constantly looking for ways to repackage goods into bulk items, which reduces labor, speeds up Costco's just-in-time inventory and distribution system, and boosts sales per square foot. Costco is also savvier than Sam's and BJ's about catering to small shop owners and more affluent customers, who are more likely to buy in bulk and purchase higher-margin goods. Neither rival has been able to match Costco's innovative packaging or merchandising mix, either. Costco was the first wholesale club to offer fresh meat, pharmacies, and photo labs.

Wal-Mart defenders often focus on the undeniable benefits its lower prices bring consumers, while ignoring the damage it does to U.S. wages. Costco shows that with enough smarts, companies can help consumers and workers alike.

SOURCE: Excerpted from S. Holmes and W. Zellner, "The Costco Way," *BusinessWeek*, April 12, 2004, pp. 76–77.

Questions

1. How can Costco be more profitable than Sam's Club even though it pays higher wages? What role does employee retention seem to play?
2. For Sam's Club to match Costco's wages yet continue to compete with Costco, in what areas would it have to improve performance? How could the ideas in this chapter help?
3. Do you think Costco's strategy of retaining loyal employees by compensating them more generously than the competition does will continue to work in the long run? Why or why not?

CASE: Are "Family-Friendly" Policies Unfriendly to Some?

Raising children has never been easy, and the task is even trickier in families where both parents work or when a single parent has children. Many employers have responded to these challenges with "family-friendly" policies to help recruit and retain valued workers. Over time, these programs have become more sophisticated. Today, the support can take many different forms, including referral services, company-sponsored community child care centers, company-owned on-site child care centers, on-site backup emergency care centers (for when the caregiver is unavailable), after-school care, and employer matching of tax-deferred spending accounts earmarked for child care.

The programs have been effective, according to some measures. For example, more than 40 percent of the workers at companies that provided on-site care cited this as one of the main reasons they chose their current employer. Over 20 percent said they rejected outside offers from competing employers because they wanted to keep their children at their current company-sponsored day care center. Child care centers also reduce absenteeism among employees. In addition, child care programs can help keep people in the workforce. Particularly among the working poor, the biggest contributor to chronic tardiness and absenteeism is failure to find affordable and reliable child care. This, in turn, often leads to employee dismissals and spotty work histories, which makes it harder for these people to find and keep jobs.

These programs are not universally praised, however. Increasingly, critics consider family-friendly work practices such as child care benefits, benefits to employees' spouses, and even company-sponsored "family picnics" as a form of unfair compensation that enriches workers who are spouses and parents but gives nothing to single, childless employees. In effect, two employees doing exactly the same work receive a different total package of pay and benefits. One is receiving benefits for a spouse and children, which make the total package much more valuable than that received by the single, childless employee. In the words of Tom Coleman, director of the advocacy group Unmarried America, "Employees without children have lives outside of work and consider their needs and responsibilities just as important as those of workers with kids."

In fact, changes in society are resulting in a large increase in the number of individuals who are classified as "singletons," that is, people living alone. This shift can be attributed to the fact that people are marrying much later in life or not at all, are postponing having children or not having them at all, and are more likely to divorce. Also, people are retiring later, in which case they are more likely to live alone, without children in the household. Taking these trends together, an estimated 30 percent of U.S. households are expected to be single-person households by the year 2010.

Responding to this growing diversity in the workforce poses a challenge for employers. On the one hand, trying to cover every possible contingency in a highly centralized, formal HR policy is impossible. The ways in which one group can be slighted relative to another are endless. On the other hand, creating decentralized systems that leave too much discretion in the hands of individual supervisors also can lead to problems. If supervisors arrange personal deals supporting particular workers with families and different arrangements for workers without families, employees are likely to perceive favoritism toward those individuals. Clearly, keeping everyone happy is difficult. Those who can successfully meet this challenge can gain a competitive edge in recruiting and retaining employees.

SOURCE: P. J. Kiger, "A Case for Child-Care," *Workforce*, April 2004, pp. 34–40; M. Conlin and A. Bernstein, "Working and Poor," *BusinessWeek*, October 20, 2003, pp. 58–68; M. Conlin, "Unmarried America," *BusinessWeek*, October 20, 2003, pp. 106–16; M. Hammers, "Family-Friendly Benefits Prompt Non-parent Backlash," *Workforce*, August 2003, pp. 77–79; and A. Fisher, "The Rebalancing Act," *Fortune*, October 6, 2003, pp. 110–13.

Questions

1. Based on the chapter's description of outcome justice, procedural justice, and interactional justice, do you think family-friendly policies are just or unjust? Explain.
2. Suggest some ways of making family-friendly policies fairer to employees who have no spouse or children.
3. What sources of job satisfaction and dissatisfaction are family-friendly policies aimed at addressing? How can job design and benefits policies address these sources of satisfaction and dissatisfaction among employees without spouses or children?

NOTES

1. D. Fenn, "Rescuing Tradition," *Inc.*, August 2001, pp. 48–49.
2. M. L. Schmit and S. P. Allscheid, "Employee Attitudes and Customer Satisfaction: Making Theoretical and Empirical Connections," *Personnel Psychology* 48 (1995), pp. 521–36; F. Reichheld, *The Loyalty Effect* (Cambridge, MA: Harvard Business School Press, 1996).
3. D. J. Koys, "The Effects of Employee Satisfaction, Organizational Citizenship Behavior, and Turnover on Organizational Effectiveness: A Unit-Level Longitudinal Study," *Personnel Psychology* 54 (2001), pp. 101–14; R. Batt, "Managing Customer Services: Human Resource Practices, Quit Rates, and Sales Growth," *Academy of Management Journal* 45 (2002), pp. 587–97; and I. S. Fulmer, B. Gerhart, and K. S. Scott, "Are the 100 Best Better? An Empirical Investigation of the Relationship between Being a 'Great Place to Work' and Firm Performance," *Personnel Psychology* 56 (2003), pp. 965–93.
4. M. Heller, "A Return to At-Will Employment," *Workforce*, May 2001, pp. 42–46.
5. M. M. Le Blanc and K. Kelloway, "Predictors and Outcomes of Workplace Violence and Aggression," *Journal of Applied Psychology*, 87, 2002, pp. 444-53.
6. B. J. Tepper, "Relationship among Supervisors' and Subordinates' Procedural Justice Perceptions and Organizational Citizenship Behaviors," *Academy of Management Journal* 46 (2003), pp. 97–105; and T. Simons and Q. Roberson, "Why Managers Should Care about Fairness: The Effects of Aggregate Justice Perception on Organizational Outcomes," *Journal of Applied Psychology* 88 (2003), pp. 432–43.
7. D. Spencer, "Soothing the Sting," *Human Resource Executive*, June 1, 2001, pp. 30–34; M. Conlin, "Revenge of the Downsized Nerds," *BusinessWeek*, July

30, 2001, p. 40; M. Boyle, "The Not-So-Fine Art of the Layoff," *Fortune*, March 19, 2001, pp. 209–10.

8. J. J. Myers, D. V. Radack, and P. M. Yenerall, "Making the Most of Employment Contracts," *HR Magazine* 43, no. 9 (August 1998), pp. 106–9; *Toussaint v. Blue Cross and Blue Shield of Michigan*, 408 Mich. 579, 292 N.W.2d 880 (1980).

9. *Harmon v. Thornburgh*, CA, DC No. 88-5265 (July 30, 1989); *Treasury Employees Union v. Von Raab*, U.S. Sup. Ct. No. 86-18796 (March 21, 1989); *City of Annapolis v. United Food & Commercial Workers Local 400*, Md. Ct. App. No. 38 (November 6, 1989); *Skinner v. Railway Labor Executives Association*, U.S. Sup. Ct. No. 87-1555 (March 21, 1989); *Bluestein v. Skinner*, 908 F.2d 451, 9th Cir. (1990).

10. D. J. Hoekstra, "Workplace Searches: A Legal Overview," *Labor Law Journal* 47, no. 2 (February 1996), pp. 127–38.

11. G. Henshaw and K. Youmans, "Employee Privacy in the Workplace and an Employer's Right to Conduct Workplace Searches and Surveillance," *SHRM Legal Report*, Spring 1990, pp. 1–5; B. K. Repa, *Your Rights in the Workplace* (Berkeley, CA: Nolo Press, 1997).

12. L. Conley, "The Privacy Arms Race," *Fast Company*, July 2004, http://web1.infotrac.galegroup.com; D. Cadrain, "GPS on Rise; Workers' Complaints May Follow," *HRMagazine*, April 2005, http://web1.infotrac.galegroup.com; and G. Webster, "Respecting Employee Privacy," *Association Management*, January 1994, pp. 142–43, 146.

13. J. Schramm, "Privacy at Work," *HRMagazine*, April 2005, downloaded from Infotrac at http://web1.infotrac.galegroup.com; M. Denis and J. Andes, "Defamation—Do You Tell Employees Why a Co-worker Was Discharged?" *Employee Relations Law Journal* 16, no. 4 (Spring 1991), pp. 469–79; R. S. Soderstrom and J. R. Murray, "Defamation in Employment: Suits by At-Will Employees," *FICC Quarterly*, Summer 1992, pp. 395–426; and R. J. Posch Jr., "Your Personal Exposure for Interoffice Communications," *Direct Marketing* 61 (August 1998).

14. N. Orkin and M. Heise, "Weingarten through the Looking Glass," *Labor Law Journal* 48, no. 3 (March 1997), pp. 157–63.

15. K. Karl and C. Sutton, "A Review of Expert Advice on Employment Termination Practices: The Experts Don't Always Agree," in *Dysfunctional Behavior in Organizations*, ed. R. Griffin, A. O'Leary-Kelly, and J. Collins (Stanford, CT: JAI Press, 1998).

16. "Dow Employees Fired over E-mail Misuse Win Their Jobs Back," *Miami.com*, April 3, 2002.

17. "Arbitration's Popularity Still Growing," *HRNext*, March 18, 2002, www.hrnext.com; J. Howard-Martin, "Arbitration Can Speed Resolution of Grievances," *USA Today*, March 26, 2002, http://careers.usatoday.com.

18. S. Caudron, "Blowing the Whistle on Employee Disputes," *Workforce*, May 1997, pp. 50–57.

19. S. Johnson, "Results, Relapse Rates Add to Cost of Non-Hospital Treatment," *Employee Benefit Plan Review* 46 (1992), pp. 15–16.

20. C. Mulcany, "Experts Eye Perils of Mental Health Cuts," *National Underwriter* 96 (1992), pp. 17–18; A. Meisler, "Mind Field," *Workforce*, September 2003, pp. 57–60; and S. Sonnenberg and C. McEnerney, "Medical Leave: A Prescription," *Workforce*, April 2004, pp. 16–17.

21. J. Jones, "How to Bounce Back if You're Bounced Out," *BusinessWeek*, January 27, 1998, pp. 22–23.

22. D. W. Baruch, "Why They Terminate," *Journal of Consulting Psychology* 8 (1944), pp. 35–46; J. G. Rosse, "Relations among Lateness, Absence and Turnover: Is There a Progression of Withdrawal?" *Human Relations* 41 (1988), pp. 517–31; C. Hulin, "Adaptation, Persistence and Commitment in Organizations," in *Handbook of Industrial & Organizational Psychology*, 2nd ed., ed. M. D. Dunnette and L. M. Hough (Palo Alto, CA: Consulting Psychologists Press, 1991), pp. 443–50; C. Hulin, M. Roznowski, and D. Hachiya, "Alternative Opportunities and Withdrawal Decisions," *Psychological Bulletin* 97 (1985), pp. 233–50.

23. D. Watson, L. A. Clark, and A. Tellegen, "Development and Validation of Brief Measures of Positive and Negative Affect: The PANAS Scales," *Journal of Personality and Social Psychology* 54 (1988), pp. 1063–70.

24. T. A. Judge, E. A. Locke, C. C. Durham, and A. N. Kluger, "Dispositional Effects on Job and Life Satisfaction: The Role of Core Evaluations," *Journal of Applied Psychology* 83 (1998), pp. 17–34.

25. B. M. Staw, N. E. Bell, and J. A. Clausen, "The Dispositional Approach to Job Attitudes: A Lifetime Longitudinal Test," *Administrative Science Quarterly* 31 (1986), pp. 56–78; B. M. Staw and J. Ross, "Stability in the Midst of Change: A Dispositional Approach to Job Attitudes," *Journal of Applied Psychology* 70 (1985), pp. 469–80; R. P. Steel and J. R. Rentsch, "The Dispositional Model of Job Attitudes Revisited: Findings of a 10-Year Study," *Journal of Applied Psychology* 82 (1997), pp. 873–79.

26. T. A. Judge and J. E. Bono, "Relationship of Core Self-Evaluation Traits—Self-Esteem, Generalized Self-Efficacy, Locus of Control, and Emotional Stability—with Job Satisfaction and Job Performance: A Meta-Analysis," *Journal of Applied Psychology* 86 (2001), pp. 80–92.

27. T. A. Judge, J. E. Bono, and E. A. Locke, "Personality and Job Satisfaction: The Mediating Role of Job

Characteristics," *Journal of Applied Psychology* 85 (2000), pp. 237–49.

28. S. C. Douglas and M. J. Martinko, "Exploring the Role of Individual Differences in the Prediction of Workplace Aggression," *Journal of Applied Psychology* 86 (2001), pp. 547–59.

29. B. A. Gerhart, "How Important Are Dispositional Factors as Determinants of Job Satisfaction? Implications for Job Design and Other Personnel Programs," *Journal of Applied Psychology* 72 (1987), pp. 493–502.

30. E. F. Stone and H. G. Gueutal, "An Empirical Derivation of the Dimensions along Which Characteristics of Jobs Are Perceived," *Academy of Management Journal* 28 (1985), pp. 376–96.

31. L. W. Porter and R. M. Steers, "Organizational Work and Personal Factors in Employee Absenteeism and Turnover," *Psychological Bulletin* 80 (1973), pp. 151–76; S. Melamed, I. Ben-Avi, J. Luz, and M. S. Green, "Objective and Subjective Work Monotony: Effects on Job Satisfaction, Psychological Distress, and Absenteeism in Blue Collar Workers," *Journal of Applied Psychology* 80 (1995), pp. 29–42.

32. D. R. Ilgen and J. R. Hollenbeck, "The Structure of Work: Job Design and Roles," in *Handbook of Industrial & Organizational Psychology*, 2nd ed.

33. J. A. Breaugh and J. P. Colihan, "Measuring Facets of Job Ambiguity: Construct Validity Evidence," *Journal of Applied Psychology* 79 (1994), pp. 191–201.

34. M. A. Shaffer and D. A. Harrison, "Expatriates' Psychological Withdrawal from Interpersonal Assignments: Work, Non-work, and Family Influences," *Personnel Psychology* 51 (1998), pp. 87–118.

35. J. M. Brett and L. K. Stroh, "Working 61 Plus Hours a Week: Why Do Managers Do It?" *Journal of Applied Psychology* 88 (2003), pp. 67–78; and V. S. Major, K. J. Klein, and M. G. Ehrhart, "Work Time, Work Interference with Family, and Psychological Distress," *Journal of Applied Psychology* 87 (2002), pp. 427–36.

36. S. M. Lilienthal, "Screen and Glean," *Workforce*, October 2000, downloaded from FindArticles.com.

37. Ibid., citing M. Buckingham and C. Coffman, *First Break All the Rules* (New York: Simon & Schuster, 1999).

38. J. Cook, "Positively Negative," *Human Resource Executive*, June 15, 2001, pp. 101–4.

39. S. F. Gale, "Sickened by Costs of Absenteeism, Companies Look for Solutions," *Workforce*, September 2003, pp. 72–75.

40. R. T. Mowday, R. M. Steers, and L. W. Porter, "The Measurement of Organizational Commitment," *Journal of Vocational Behavior* 14 (1979), pp. 224–47.

41. E. A. Locke, "The Nature and Causes of Job Dissatisfaction," in *The Handbook of Industrial & Organizational Psychology*, ed. M. D. Dunnette (Chicago: Rand McNally, 1976), pp. 901–69.

42. E. Tanouye, "Depression Takes Annual Toll of $70 Billion on Employers," *The Wall Street Journal*, June 13, 2001, p. 1; E. Tanouye, "Mental Illness in the Workplace Afflicts Bosses, Can Affect Business," *The Wall Street Journal*, June 13, 2001, pp. 1–2; J. Vennochi, "When Depression Comes to Work," *Working Woman*, August 1995, pp. 43–51.

43. G. R. Oldham, A. Cummings, L. J. Mischel, J. M. Schmidtke, and J. Zhou, "Listen While You Work? Quasi-experimental Relations between Personal-Stereo Headset Use and Employee Work Responses," *Journal of Applied Psychology* 80 (1995), pp. 547–64.

44. B. Kaye, "Wake Up and Smell the Coffee: People Flock to Family Friendly," *BusinessWeek Online*, January 28, 2001, pp. 1–2.

45. G. Flynn, "The Legalities of Flextime," *Workforce*, October 2001, pp. 62–66; G. Weber, "Flexible Jobs Mean Fewer Absences," *Workforce*, November 2003, pp. 26–28; and M. Hammers, "Babies Deliver a Loyal Workforce," *Workforce*, April 2003, p. 52.

46. J. E. Perry-Smith, "Work Family Human Resource Bundles and Perceived Organizational Performance," *Academy of Management Journal* 43 (2000), pp. 801–15; and M. M. Arthur, "Share Price Reactions to Work-Family Initiatives: An Institutional Perspective," *Academy of Management Journal* 46 (2003), pp. 497–505.

47. B. Sorrell, "Many U.S. Employees Feel Overworked, Stressed, Study Says," *CNN.com*, May 16, 2001, pp. 1–2.

48. M. Conlin, "Revenge of the Managers," *BusinessWeek*, March 12, 2001, pp. 60–61.

49. B. M. Meglino, E. C. Ravlin, and C. L. Adkins, "A Work Values Approach to Corporate Culture: A Field Test of the Value Congruence Process and Its Relationship to Individual Outcomes," *Journal of Applied Psychology* 74 (1989), pp. 424–33.

50. G. C. Ganster, M. R. Fusilier, and B. T. Mayes, "Role of Social Support in the Experience of Stress at Work," *Journal of Applied Psychology* 71 (1986), pp. 102–11.

51. R. Eisenberger, F. Stinghamber, C. Vandenberghe, I. L. Sucharski, and L. Rhoades, "Perceived Supervisor Support: Contributions to Perceived Organizational Support and Employee Retention," *Journal of Applied Psychology* 87 (2002), pp. 565–73.

52. R. T. Keller, "A Test of the Path-Goal Theory of Leadership with Need for Clarity as a Moderator in Research and Development Organizations," *Journal of Applied Psychology* 74 (1989), pp. 208–12.

53. R. P. Quinn and G. L. Staines, *The 1977 Quality of Employment Survey* (Ann Arbor, MI: Survey Research

Center, Institute for Social Research, University of Michigan, 1979).

54. T. Judge and T. Welbourne, "A Confirmatory Investigation of the Dimensionality of the Pay Satisfaction Questionnaire," *Journal of Applied Psychology* 79 (1994), pp. 461–66.

55. P. Babcock, "Find What Workers Want," *HRMagazine*, April 2005, www.shrm.org/hrmagazine.

56. E. Zimmerman, "The Joy of Flex," *Workforce* , March 2004, pp. 38–40.

57. J. Applegaste, "Plan an Exit Interview," *CNN-Money.com*, November 13, 2000, pp. 1–2.

58. H. E. Allerton, "Can Teach Old Dogs New Tricks," *Training & Development*, November 2000, downloaded from FindArticles.com.

If you are using the Manager's Hot Seat DVD with this book, consider finishing case 5: Whistleblowing: Code Red or Red Ink? for this chapter.

4

COMPENSATING HUMAN RESOURCES

ESTABLISHING A PAY STRUCTURE

❧ INTRODUCTION

When you call a company's customer service line, the person who answers the phone might be working in India. An important reason, as we discussed in Chapter 2, is that employers can find qualified Indian workers who have much lower rates of pay than comparable individuals would accept in the United States. Organizations have latitude in deciding what they will pay workers, but they have to consider the impact on their profits and their ability to recruit and keep workers. They also have to consider customers' reactions. Sometimes customers have been dissatisfied when talking to an employee in another part of the world. So, U.S. employers are looking within the United States for customer service help again and finding that they can afford to operate in small towns in the South and Northwest—including Nacogdoches, Texas, and Coeur d'Alene, Idaho—where a large pool of workers are eager to take call center jobs paying $7 or $8 an hour. The cost of living in these areas is relatively low, and unemployment is relatively high. So, companies can quickly fill jobs, and the workers are pleased to have employment. A recent study found that call centers in rural areas outperformed those in cities, because the rural workers had fewer job opportunities, so the companies could attract better workers.[1]

From the employer's point of view, pay is a powerful tool for meeting the organization's goals. Pay has a large impact on employee attitudes and behaviors. It influences which kinds of employees are attracted to (and remain with) the organization. By rewarding certain behaviors, it can align employees' interests with the organization's goals. Employees care about policies affecting earnings because the policies affect the employees' income and standard of living. Besides the level of pay, employees care about its fairness compared with what others earn. Also, employees consider pay a sign of status and success. They attach great importance to pay decisions when they evaluate their relationship with their employer. For these reasons, organizations must carefully manage and communicate decisions about pay.

At the same time, pay is a major cost. Its share of total costs varies widely, but across all industries, pay averages almost one-fourth of a company's revenues.[2] Some companies spend 40 percent or more of their revenues on paying employees. Managers have to keep this cost reasonable.

This chapter describes how managers weigh the importance and costs of pay to arrive at a structure for compensation and levels of pay for different jobs. We first define the basic decisions in terms of pay structure and pay level. Next, we look at several considerations that influence these decisions: legal requirements related to pay, economic forces, the nature of the organization's jobs, and employees' judgments about the fairness of pay levels. We describe methods for evaluating jobs and market data to arrive at a pay structure. We then summarize alternatives to the usual focus on jobs. The chapter closes with a look at two issues of current importance—pay for employees on leave to serve in the military and pay for executives.

◈ DECISIONS ABOUT PAY

Because pay is important both in its effect on employees and on account of its cost, organizations need to plan what they will pay employees in each job. An unplanned approach, in which each employee's pay is independently negotiated, will likely result in unfairness, dissatisfaction, and rates that are either overly expensive or so low that positions are hard to fill. Organizations therefore make decisions about two aspects of pay structure: job structure and pay level. **Job structure** consists of the relative pay for different jobs within the organization. It establishes relative pay among different functions and different levels of responsibility. For example, job structure defines the difference in pay between an entry-level accountant and an entry-level assembler, as well as the difference between an entry-level accountant, the accounting department manager, and the organization's comptroller. **Pay level** is the average amount (including wages, salaries, and bonuses) the organization pays for a particular job. Together, job structure and pay levels establish a **pay structure** that helps the organization achieve goals related to employee motivation, cost control, and the ability to attract and retain talented human resources. The "Best Practices" box describes the pay structure of Babcock and Wilcox in terms of its business objectives.

The organization's job structure and pay levels are policies of the organization, rather than the amount a particular employee earns. For example, an organization's pay structure could include the range of pay that a person may earn in the job of entry-level accountant. An individual accountant could be earning an amount anywhere within that range. Typically, the amount a person earns depends on the individual's qualifications, accomplishments, and experience. The individual's pay may also depend partly on how well the organization performs. This chapter focuses on the organization's decisions about pay structure, and the next chapter will explore decisions that affect the amount of pay an individual earns.

Especially in an organization with hundreds or thousands of employees, it would be impractical for managers and the human resource department to make an entirely

LO1
Identify the kinds of decisions involved in establishing a pay structure.

job structure
The relative pay for different jobs within the organization.

pay level
The average amount (including wages, salaries, and bonuses) the organization pays for a particular job.

pay structure
The pay policy resulting from job structure and pay-level decisions.

BEST PRACTICES

BABCOCK & WILCOX GETS PHILOSOPHICAL ABOUT PAY

Babcock & Wilcox (B&W), headquartered in Barberton, Ohio, provides equipment and services primarily for companies in the energy business. The company started as a partnership of two longtime friends, and today it employs more than 10,000 people, including more than 6,000 in North America. As it has grown, it has developed a formal plan for compensation decisions. Those decisions are now based on a compensation "philosophy," which states the values and principles of the company's pay structure.

The B&W compensation philosophy calls for pay decisions to be equitable and balanced. The objective of meeting economic demands is balanced against a primary emphasis on tying pay increases and bonuses to individual and group performance. In the words of the company's own statement of this philosophy, posted on B&W's in-

tranet, "The most important aspect of our [compensation] philosophy is to differentiate salary increases and incentive bonuses based on performance without regard to race, color, religion, gender, sexual orientation, national origin, citizenship, age, disability or status as a disabled veteran, other veteran, recently separated veteran, or Vietnam-Era veteran." With these words, the B&W compensation philosophy addresses business needs (rewarding performance) and legal requirements (avoidance of discrimination), as well as stating its intent to be fair.

B&W's emphasis on paying for performance is only a few years old. So, the company had to communicate this emphasis to obtain the commitment of managers and demonstrate the fairness of the policy. Managers and employees weren't used to talking openly about compensation and its relation to performance.

Vickie Davis, B&W's manager of compensation and benefits, worked with the company's communications staff to write the compensation philosophy. Davis explains that the "driving force" behind posting the philosophy on the intranet is "the feeling that the employees needed to see it in writing, needed to understand it, so that they would understand it wasn't arbitrary." HR staff also coached supervisors on how to talk about pay with their employees. Says Davis, "We've gone from a culture that didn't talk about compensation to one that does." As a result, she adds, employees now see the system as fair because it is based on the common purpose of achieving business success.

SOURCE: Charlotte Garvey, "Philosophizing Compensation," *HRMagazine*, January 2005, downloaded from Infotrac at http://web6.infotrac.galegroup.com; and Babcock & Wilcox Web site, www.babcock.com, accessed May 24, 2005.

unique decision about each employee's pay. The decision would have to weigh so many factors that this approach would be expensive, difficult, and often unsatisfactory. Establishing a pay structure simplifies the process of making decisions about individual employees' pay by grouping together employees with similar jobs. As shown in Figure 11.1, human resource professionals develop this pay structure based on legal requirements, market forces, and the organization's goals, such as attracting a high-quality workforce and meeting principles of fairness.

LO2
Summarize legal requirements for pay policies.

⬥ LEGAL REQUIREMENTS FOR PAY

Government regulation affects pay structure in the areas of equal employment opportunity, minimum wages, pay for overtime, and prevailing wages for federal contractors. All of an organization's decisions about pay should comply with the applicable laws.

Figure 11.1

Issues in Developing a Pay Structure

Equal Employment Opportunity

Under the laws governing Equal Employment Opportunity, described in Chapter 3, employers may not base differences in pay on an employee's age, sex, race, or other protected status. Any differences in pay must instead be tied to such business-related considerations as job responsibilities or performance. The goal is for employers to provide *equal pay for equal work*. For example, the government of Wicomico County, Maryland, was able to defend itself against a recent discrimination claim made by its director and deputy director of emergency services that they were paid less because they were female.[3] The women argued that they should be paid as much as the county's male directors and deputy directors because all employees at those levels of the organization are responsible for preparing budgets, supervising employees, and conducting meetings. However, the county successfully replied that directors and deputy directors of other departments have different jobs because their departments perform much different functions, requiring their managers to have different qualifications. As in this situation, job descriptions, job structures, and pay structures can help organizations demonstrate that they are upholding these laws.

These laws do not guarantee equal pay for men and women, whites and minorities, or any other groups, because so many legitimate factors, from education to choice of occupation, affect a person's earnings. In fact, numbers show that women and racial minorities in the United States tend to earn less than white men. Among full-time workers in 2004, women on average earned 80 cents for every dollar earned by men, while black workers on average earned 80 cents for every dollar earned by white workers.[4] Even when these figures are adjusted to take into account education, experience, and occupation, the earnings gap does not completely close.[5]

One explanation for historical lower pay for women has been that employers have undervalued work performed by women—in particular, placing a lower value on occupations traditionally dominated by women. Some policy makers have proposed a remedy for this called equal pay for *comparable worth*. This policy uses job evaluation (described later in the chapter) to establish the worth of an organization's jobs in terms of

Two employees who do the same job cannot be paid different wages because of gender, race, or age. It would be illegal to pay these two employees differently because one is male and the other is female. Only if there are differences in their experience, skills, seniority, or job performance are there legal reasons why their pay might be different.

such criteria as their difficulty and their importance to the organization. The employer then compares the evaluation points awarded to each job with the pay for each job. If jobs have the same number of evaluation points, they should be paid equally. If they are not, pay of the lower-paid job is raised to meet the goal of comparable worth.

Comparable-worth policies are controversial. From an economic standpoint, the obvious drawback of such a policy is that raising pay for some jobs places the employer at an economic disadvantage relative to employers that pay the market rate. In addition, a free-market economy assumes people will take differences in pay into account when they choose a career. The courts allow organizations to defend themselves against claims of discrimination by showing that they pay the going market rate.[6] Businesses are reluctant to place themselves at an economic disadvantage, but many state governments adjust pay to achieve equal pay for comparable worth. Also, at both private and government organizations, policies designed to shatter the "glass ceiling" (discussed in Chapter 9) can help to address the problem of unequal pay.

Minimum Wage

minimum wage
The lowest amount that employers may pay under federal or state law, stated as an amount of pay per hour.

In the United States, employers must pay at least the **minimum wage** established by law. (A *wage* is the rate of pay per hour.) At the federal level, the 1938 **Fair Labor Standards Act (FLSA)** establishes a minimum wage that now stands at $5.15 per hour. In a 1990 amendment to the FLSA, Congress established a lower "training wage," which employers may pay to workers under the age of 20 for a period of up to 90 days. This subminimum wage is approximately 85 percent of the minimum wage. Some states have laws specifying minimum wages; in these states, employers must pay whichever rate is higher.

Fair Labor Standards Act (FLSA)
Federal law that establishes a minimum wage and requirements for overtime pay and child labor.

From the standpoint of social policy, an issue related to the minimum wage is that it tends to be lower than the earnings required for a full-time worker to rise above the poverty level. A number of cities have therefore passed laws requiring a so-called *living wage*, essentially a minimum wage based on the cost of living in a particular region. These local laws usually cover businesses with government contracts, but some cities have recently been considering laws to extend the living-wage requirements to the private sector.[7] Because labor costs influence the cost of providing a product or service, these laws may contribute to higher local taxes and raise the cost of doing business in an area with living-wage laws. Also, higher labor costs may result in employers choosing to employ fewer people.

Overtime Pay

Another requirement of the FLSA is that employers must pay higher wages for overtime, defined as hours worked beyond 40 hours per week. The overtime rate under the FLSA is one and a half times the employee's usual hourly rate, including any bonuses and piece-rate payments (amounts paid per item produced). The overtime rate applies to the hours worked beyond 40 in one week. Time worked includes not only hours spent on production or sales but also time on such activities as attending required classes, cleaning up the work site, or traveling between work sites. Figure 11.2 shows how this applies to an employee who works 50 hours to earn a base rate of $10 per hour plus a weekly bonus of $30. The overtime pay is based on the base pay ($400) plus the bonus ($30), for a rate of $10.75 per hour. For each of the 10 hours of overtime, the employee would earn $16.13, so the overtime pay is $161.30 ($16.13 times 10). When employees are paid per unit produced or when they receive a monthly or quarterly bonus, those payments must be converted into wages per hour, so that the employer can include these amounts when figuring the correct overtime rate.

The FLSA requires overtime pay for hours worked beyond 40, whether or not the employer specifically asked or expected the employee to work those extra hours.[8] In other words, if the employer knows the employee is working overtime but does not pay time and a half, the employer may be violating the FLSA.

Not everyone is eligible for overtime pay. Under the FLSA, executive, professional, administrative, and highly compensated white-collar employees are considered **exempt employees,** meaning employers need not pay them one and a half times their regular pay for working more than 40 hours per week. Exempt status depends on the employee's job responsibilities, salary level (at least $455 per week), and "salary basis," meaning that the employee is paid a given amount regardless of the number of hours worked or quality of the work.[9] Paying an employee on a salary basis means the organization expects that this person can manage his or her own time to get the work done, so the employer may deduct from the employee's pay only in certain limited circumstances, such as disciplinary action or for unpaid leave for personal reasons. Additional exceptions apply to certain occupations, including outside salespersons, teachers, and computer professionals (if they earn at least $27.63 per hour). Thus, the standards are fairly complicated. For more details about the standards for exempt employees, contact the Wage and Hour Division of the Labor Department's Employment Standards Administration or refer to its Web site at **www.dol.gov/esa.** Any employee who is not in one of the exempt categories is called a **nonexempt employee.** Most workers paid on an hourly basis are nonexempt and therefore subject to the laws governing overtime pay. However, paying a salary does not necessarily mean a job is exempt.

exempt employees
Managers, outside salespeople, and any other employees not covered by the FLSA requirement for overtime pay.

nonexempt employees
Employees covered by the FLSA requirements for overtime pay.

Figure 11.2
Computing Overtime Pay

Employee's Base Pay: $10/hr. + $30/wk. (bonus)
Employee's Hours: 50 (40 regular, 10 overtime)

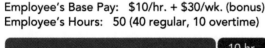

Pay for First 40 Hours	Overtime Rate
$10/hr. × 40 hr.= $400	$10.75 × 1.5 = $16.13
Bonus @ $30 = 30	
Total = $430	

Hourly Rate	Overtime Pay
$430 ÷ 40 = $10.75/hr.	$16.13/hr. × 10 hr. = $161.30

Total Pay for Week
$430.00 + $161.30 = $591.30

Child Labor

In the early years of the Industrial Revolution, employers could pay low wages by hiring children. The FLSA now sharply restricts the use of child labor, with the aim of protecting children's health, safety, and educational opportunities.[10] The restrictions apply to children younger than 18. Under the FLSA, children aged 16 and 17 may not be employed in hazardous occupations defined by the Department of Labor, such as mining, meatpacking, and certain kinds of manufacturing using heavy machinery. Children aged 14 and 15 may work only outside school hours, in jobs defined as nonhazardous, and for limited time periods. A child under age 14 may not be employed in any work associated with interstate commerce, except work performed in a non-hazardous job for a business entirely owned by the child's parent or guardian. A few additional exemptions from this ban include acting, baby-sitting, and delivering newspapers to consumers.

Besides the FLSA, state laws also restrict the use of child labor. Many states have laws requiring working papers or work permits for minors, and many states restrict the number of hours or times of day that minors aged 16 and older may work. Before hiring any workers under the age of 18, employers must ensure they are complying with the child labor laws of their state, as well as the FLSA requirements for their industry.

Prevailing Wages

Two additional federal laws, the Davis-Bacon Act of 1931 and the Walsh-Healy Public Contracts Act of 1936, govern pay policies of federal contractors. Under these laws, federal contractors must pay their employees at rates at least equal to the prevailing wages in the area. The calculation of prevailing rates must be based on 30 percent of the local labor force. Typically, the rates are based on relevant union contracts. Pay earned by union members tends to be higher than the pay of nonunion workers in similar jobs, so the effect of these laws is to raise the lower limit of pay an employer can offer.

These laws do not cover all companies. Davis-Bacon covers construction contractors that receive more than $2,000 in federal money. Walsh-Healy covers all government contractors receiving $10,000 or more in federal funds.

LO3
Discuss how economic forces influence decisions about pay.

❧ ECONOMIC INFLUENCES ON PAY

An organization cannot make spending decisions independent of the economy. Organizations must keep costs low enough that they can sell their products profitably, yet they must be able to attract workers in a competitive labor market. Decisions about how to respond to the economic forces of product markets and labor markets limit an organization's choices about pay structure.

Product Markets

The organization's *product market* includes organizations that offer competing goods and services. In other words, the organizations in a product market are competing to serve the same customers. To succeed in their product markets, organizations must be able to sell their goods and services at a quantity and price that will bring them a sufficient profit. They may try to win customers by being superior in a number of areas, including quality, customer service, and price. An important influence on price is the cost to produce the goods and services for sale. As we mentioned earlier, the cost of labor is a significant part of an organization's costs.

If an organization's labor costs are higher than those of its competitors, it will be under pressure to charge more than competitors charge for similar products. If one company spends $50 in labor costs to make a product and its competitor spends only $35, the second company will be more profitable unless the first company can justify a higher price to customers. Of course, higher-earning employees might be delivering greater value, such as making a finer product. In the *BusinessWeek* case for Chapter 10, we saw that Costco employees earn a higher average wage than Sam's Club employees. But Costco employees also sell more in each square foot of their stores than Sam's Club employees do, so Costco's average profit per employee is actually greater than that for Sam's Club.[11] Still, investors have pressured Costco to become even more profitable by reducing wages.

In this way, product markets place an upper limit on the pay an organization will offer. This upper limit is most important when labor costs are a large part of an organization's total costs and when the organization's customers place great importance on price. Organizations that want to lure top-quality employees by offering generous salaries therefore have to find ways to automate routine activities (so that labor is a smaller part of total costs) or to persuade customers that high quality is worth a premium price. Organizations under pressure to cut labor costs may respond by reducing staff levels, freezing pay levels, postponing hiring decisions, or requiring employees to bear more of the cost of benefits such as insurance premiums.

Labor Markets

Besides competing to sell their products, organizations must compete to obtain human resources in *labor markets*. In general, workers prefer higher-paying jobs and avoid employers that offer less money for the same type of job. In this way, competition for labor establishes the minimum an organization must pay to hire an employee for a particular job. If an organization pays less than the minimum, employees will look for jobs with other organizations.

An organization's competitors in labor markets typically include companies with similar products and companies in other industries that hire similar employees. For example, a truck transportation firm would want to know the pay earned by truck drivers at competing firms as well as truck drivers for manufacturers that do their own shipping, drivers for moving and storage companies, and drivers for stores that provide delivery services. In setting pay levels for its bookkeepers and secretaries, the company would probably define its labor market differently, because bookkeepers and secretaries work for most kinds of businesses. The company would likely look for data on the earnings of bookkeepers

There is currently a strong demand for nurses in the labor market. What this means for hospitals is that they have to pay competitive wages and other perks to attract and retain staff. How does this differ from the current airline industry's labor market?

and secretaries in the region. For all these jobs, the company wants to know what others are paying so that it will pay enough to attract and keep qualified employees.

Another influence on labor markets is the *cost of living*—the cost of a household's typical expenses, such as house payments, groceries, medical care, and gasoline. In some parts of the country, the cost of living is higher than in others, so the local labor markets there will likely demand higher pay. Also, over time, the cost of living tends to rise. When the cost of living is rising rapidly, labor markets demand pay increases. The federal government tracks trends in the nation's cost of living with a measure called the Consumer Price Index (CPI). Following and studying changes in the CPI can help employers prepare for changes in the demands of the labor market.

Pay Level: Deciding What to Pay

Although labor and product markets limit organizations' choices about pay levels, there is a range within which organizations can make decisions.[12] The size of this range depends on the details of the organization's competitive environment. If many workers are competing for a few jobs, employers will have more choice. Similarly, employers can be more flexible about pay policies if they use technology and work design to get better results from employees than their competitors do.

When organizations have a broad range in which to make decisions about pay, they can choose to pay at, above, or below the rate set by market forces. Economic theory holds that the most profitable level, all things being equal, would be at the market rate. Often, however, all things are not equal from one employer to another. For instance, an organization may gain an advantage by paying above the market rate if it uses the higher pay as one means to attract top talent and then uses these excellent employees' knowledge to be more innovative, produce higher quality, or work more efficiently.

This approach is based on the view of employees as resources. Higher pay may be an investment in superior human resources. Having higher labor costs than your competitors is not necessarily bad if you also have the best and most effective workforce, which produces more products of better quality. Pay policies are one of the most important human resource tools for encouraging desired employee behaviors and discouraging undesired behaviors. Therefore, organizations must evaluate pay as more than a cost, but also as an investment that can generate returns in attracting, retaining, and motivating a high-quality workforce. For this reason, paying above the going rate may be advantageous for an organization that empowers employees or that cannot closely watch employees (as with repair technicians who travel to customers). Those employers might use high pay to attract and retain top candidates and to motivate them to do their best because they want to keep their high-paying jobs.[13]

Of course, employers do not always have this much flexibility. Some companies are under intense pressure to charge low prices for their products, and some companies are trying to draw workers from a pool that is too small to satisfy all employers' needs. Some companies—including the small U.S. businesses that supply big manufacturers—are in the unfortunate position of trying to do both.[14] Small U.S. manufacturers often face product market competition from companies in countries where labor costs are lower. At the same time, they are struggling to find workers in a tight labor market. For example, North East Precision, a machine shop in Vermont, has had to turn down orders because it cannot find enough employees to work at a rate that lets the company charge a competitive price.[15] For unskilled labor, North East tries to match the pay of local supermarket and fast-food employees, but work at North East is more physically difficult, so many workers would rather stick with McDonald's.

HR HOW TO

GATHERING WAGE DATA AT THE BLS WEB SITE

A convenient source of data on hourly wages is the wage query system of the Bureau of Labor Statistics (BLS). This federal agency makes data available at its Web site on an interactive basis. The data come from the BLS's National Compensation Survey. The user specifies the category of data desired, and the BLS provides tables of data almost instantly. Here's how to use the BLS system.

Visit the BLS Web site (www. bls.gov) and click on the link to Wages, Earnings, and Benefits. Find and click on the link to the National Compensation Survey (NCS). On the NCS Web page, click on "Get Detailed NCS Statistics" and then on "Create Customized Tables (one screen)" for wages. In the pop-up window that opens, you can enter a geographic area and a general or specific occupation, including different work levels for certain occupations. The search engine will provide the hourly wage for the occupation and area you specified.

You can also start by using the map to select an area. The National Compensation Survey gathers data from selected areas of the United States, designed to be representative of the entire country. Wage data cover about 90 areas, including most metropolitan areas. You can select one of these areas, or one of nine broad geographic regions, or the entire United States. When you select an area, the system allows you to select from the occupations for which the BLS has published data in that area.

The survey data cover hundreds of occupations, grouped into more general categories. For example, at the most specific level, you could look at civil engineers. More broadly, you could look at all engineers, or at the larger grouping of engineers, architects, and surveyors. Still more broadly, you could request data for all professional specialty occupations, which is part of the yet-broader group called professional specialty and technical occupations. This category is part of white-collar occupations, which is part of the "all workers" group. You should select the most specific grouping that covers the occupation you want to investigate. If you select occupation first, you can then select geographic areas for which the database includes data on that occupation.

After selecting an occupation, you may select a work level. This describes the level of such work features as knowledge required and the scope, complexity, and demands of the job. For instance, you could look only at data for entry-level or senior accountants, rather than all accountants. Some occupations, including artists, athletes, and announcers, are not classified by work level.

Click on the link to submit the request to the BLS. The system immediately processes the request and presents the table (or tables) on your computer screen.

The Bureau of Labor Statistics is planning to make the system still more useful by offering additional categories of data. For example, the BLS is working on tools for comparing government and private-sector wages, as well as wages for full-time and part-time employees. As these options become available, users should tailor their requests as much as possible to the characteristics of their jobs and organizations.

SOURCE: Bureau of Labor Statistics Web site, www.bls.gov, May 24, 2005; and M. Gittleman and W. J. Wiatrowski, "The BLS Wage Query System: A New Tool to Access Wage Data," *Monthly Labor Review*, October 2001, pp. 22–27.

Organizations being squeezed between labor and product markets need to couple pay policies with creative HR, production, and marketing management to develop new recruiting sources, desirable benefits besides pay, technology and training to make workers' contributions more valuable, and more profitable product lines.

Gathering Information about Market Pay

To compete for talent, organizations use **benchmarking,** a procedure in which an organization compares its own practices against those of successful competitors. In terms of compensation, benchmarking involves the use of pay surveys. These provide information about the going rates of pay at competitors in the organization's product and labor markets. An organization can conduct its own surveys, but the federal government and other organizations make a great deal of data available already.

Pay surveys are available for many kinds of industries (product markets) and jobs (labor markets). The primary collector of this kind of data in the United States is the Bureau of Labor Statistics, which conducts an ongoing National Compensation Survey measuring wages, salaries, and benefits paid to the nation's employees. The "HR How To" box on page 369 provides guidelines for using the BLS Web site as a source of wage data. The Society for Human Resource Management, the American Management Association, and many industry, trade, and professional groups also collect wage and salary data. Employers should check with the relevant groups to see what surveys are available. Consulting firms also will provide data, including the results of international surveys, and can tailor data to the organization's particular needs.

Human resource professionals need to determine whether to gather data focusing on particular industries or on job categories. Industry-specific data are especially relevant for jobs with skills that are specific to the type of product. For jobs with skills that can be transferred to companies in other industries, surveys of job classifications will be more relevant.

❧ EMPLOYEE JUDGMENTS ABOUT PAY FAIRNESS

In developing a pay structure, it is important to keep in mind employees' opinions about fairness. After all, one of the purposes of pay is to motivate employees, and they will not be motivated by pay if they think it is unfair.

Judging Fairness

Employees evaluate their pay relative to the pay of other employees. Social scientists have studied this kind of comparison and developed *equity theory* to describe how people make judgments about fairness.[16] According to equity theory, people measure outcomes such as pay in terms of their inputs. For example, an employee might think of her pay in terms of her master's degree, her 12 years of experience, and her 60-hour workweeks. To decide whether a level of pay is equitable, the person compares her ratio of outcomes and inputs with other people's outcome/input ratios, as shown in Figure 11.3. The person in the previous example might notice that an employee with less education or experience is earning more than she is (unfair) or that an employee who works 80 hours a week is earning more (fair). In general, employees compare their pay and contributions against several yardsticks:

- What they think employees in other organizations earn for doing the same job.
- What they think other employees holding different jobs within the organization earn for doing work at the same or different levels.
- What they think other employees in the organization earn for doing the same job as theirs.

Employees' conclusions about equity depend on what they choose as a standard of comparison. The results can be surprising. For example, some organizations have set

Equity: Pay Seems Fair   **Inequity: Pay Seems Unfair**

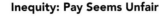

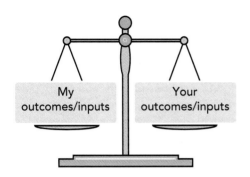

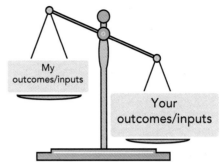

Figure 11.3

Opinions about Fairness: Pay Equity

up two-tier wage systems as a way to cut labor costs without cutting employees' existing salaries. Typically, employers announce these programs as a way to avoid moving jobs out of the country or closing down altogether. In a two-tier wage system, existing employees continue on at their current (upper-tier) pay rate while new employees sign on for less pay (the lower tier). One might expect reaction among employees in the lower tier that the pay structure is unfair. But a study of these employees found that they were *more* satisfied than the top-tier employees.[17] The lower-tier employees were not comparing their pay with that of the upper-tier employees but with the other alternatives they saw for themselves: lower-paying jobs or unemployment.

The ways employees respond to their impressions about equity can have a great impact on the organization. Typically, if employees see their pay as equitable, their attitudes and behavior continue unchanged. If employees see themselves as receiving an advantage, they usually rethink the situation to see it as merely equitable. But if employees conclude that they are underrewarded, they are likely to make up the difference in one of three ways. They might put forth less effort (reducing their inputs), find a way to increase their outcomes (for example, stealing), or withdraw by leaving the organization or refusing to cooperate. Employees' beliefs about fairness also influence their willingness to accept transfers or promotions. For example, if a job change involves more work, employees will expect higher pay.

Communicating Fairness

Equity theory tells organizations that employees care about their pay relative to what others are earning and that these feelings are based on what the employees *perceive* (what they notice and form judgments about). An organization can do much to contribute to what employees know and, as a result, what they perceive. If the organization researches salary levels and concludes that it is paying its employees generously, it should communicate this. If the employees do not know what the organization learned from its research, they may reach an entirely different conclusion about their pay.

Knowing this, most organizations communicate their pay structures openly, right? Actually, until recently, few of them did. In a poll by HRNext, one-third of the 345 companies that responded said they forbid workplace discussions about pay.[18] Still, that number is smaller than five years earlier, when more than half banned such discussions, perhaps out of fear that employees would perceive inequities in their pay. Besides wanting to be more open with employees when the labor market is tight, these companies may have been responding to a ruling by the National Labor

Relations Board that employees must be free to talk about pay in the workplace. These organizations also may realize that many employees prefer to work for a company with a policy of openness.

Employers must also recognize that employees know much more about what other employers pay now than they did before the Internet became popular. In the past, when gathering wage and salary data was expensive and difficult, employers had more leeway in negotiating with individual employees. Today's employees can go to Web sites like jobstar.org or salary.com to find hundreds of links to wage and salary data. For a fee, executive search firms provide data, such as the information at www.futurestep.com, operated by Korn/Ferry. Resources like these give employees information about what other workers are earning, along with the expectation that information will be shared. This means employers will face increased pressure to clearly explain their pay policies.

Managers play the most significant role in communication because they interact with their employees each day. The HR department should prepare them to explain why the organization's pay structure is designed as it is and to judge whether employee concerns about the structure indicate a need for change. A common issue is whether to reclassify a job because its content has changed. If an employee takes on more responsibility, the employee will often ask the manager for help in seeking more pay for the job.

Organizations can also contribute to a sense of fairness by including employees in decision making about pay structures. Employee participation can take many forms. Employees may serve on task forces charged with recommending and designing a pay structure. The organization may ask them to help communicate the structure and explain its rationale. As with open communications about pay, however, employee participation in decisions about pay is fairly rare.

LO5
Explain how organizations design pay structures related to jobs.

job evaluation
An administrative procedure for measuring the relative internal worth of the organization's jobs.

❧ JOB STRUCTURE: RELATIVE VALUE OF JOBS

Along with market forces and principles of fairness, organizations consider the relative contribution each job should make to the organization's overall performance. In general, an organization's top executives have a great impact on the organization's performance, so they tend to be paid much more than entry-level workers. Executives at the same level of the organization—for example, the vice president of marketing and the vice president of information systems—tend to be paid similar amounts. Creation of a pay structure requires that the organization develop an internal structure showing the relative contribution of its various jobs.

One typical way of doing this is with a **job evaluation,** an administrative procedure for measuring the relative worth of the organization's jobs. Usually, the organization does this by assembling and training a job evaluation committee, consisting of people familiar with the jobs to be evaluated. The committee often includes a human resource specialist and, if its budget permits, may hire an outside consultant.

To conduct a job evaluation, the committee identifies each job's *compensable factors,* meaning the characteristics of a job that the organization values and chooses to pay for. As shown in Table 11.1, an organization might value the experience and education of people performing computer-related jobs, as well as the complexity of those jobs. Other compensable factors might include working conditions and responsibility. Based on the job attributes defined by job analysis (discussed in Chapter 4), the jobs are rated for each factor. The rater assigns each factor a certain number of points, giving more points to factors when they are considered more important and when the job requires a high level of that factor. Often the number of points comes from one of the *point manuals* published by trade groups and management consultants. If neces-

	COMPENSABLE FACTORS			
JOB TITLE	EXPERIENCE	EDUCATION	COMPLEXITY	TOTAL
Computer operator	40	30	40	110
Computer programmer	40	50	65	155
Systems analyst	65	60	85	210

TABLE 11.1

Job Evaluation of Three Jobs with Three Factors

sary, the organization can adapt the scores in the point manual to the organization's situation or even develop its own point manual. As in the example in Table 11.1, the scores for each factor are totaled to arrive at an overall evaluation for each job.

The organization may evaluate its managerial and professional jobs separately, using a method designed for this purpose. One of the most popular methods is the **Hay Guide-Chart Profile method,** often referred to as the Hay plan. Named for the Hay Group, the consulting firm that developed it, the Hay plan creates a profile for each position based on three variables:[19]

1. *Know-how*—the required skills, area of knowledge, and abilities.
2. *Problem solving*—the required degree of analysis, creativity, and reasoning.
3. *Accountability*—the level of responsibility and the job's impact on the organization.

A trained analyst interviews supervisors and reviews job descriptions to evaluate the organization's jobs, scoring them on one of Hay's Guide Charts developed for this purpose. The result is a score for each managerial or professional job, stated as a percentage factor for each of the three variables. These percentages can be used to rank the jobs and arrange them into a job structure.

Job evaluations provide the basis for decisions about relative internal worth. According to the sample assessments in Table 11.1, the job of systems analyst is worth

Hay Guide-Chart Profile method
Method of job evaluation that creates a profile for each position based on its required know-how, degree of problem solving, and accountability.

Popular actors, such as Denzel Washington, are evaluated by their impact on box office receipts and other revenues and then compensated based on these evaluations.

almost twice as much to this organization as the job of computer operator. Therefore, the organization would be willing to pay almost twice as much for the work of a systems analyst as it would for the work of a computer operator.

The organization may limit its pay survey to jobs evaluated as *key jobs*. These are jobs that have relatively stable content and are common among many organizations, so it is possible to obtain survey data about what people earn in these jobs. Organizations can make the process of creating a pay structure more practical by defining key jobs. Research for creating the pay structure is limited to the key jobs that play a significant role in the organization. Pay for the key jobs can be based on survey data, and pay for the organization's other jobs can be based on the organization's job structure. A job with a higher evaluation score than a particular key job would receive higher pay than that key job.

❧ PAY STRUCTURE: PUTTING IT ALL TOGETHER

hourly wage
Rate of pay for each hour worked.

piecework rate
Rate of pay for each unit produced.

salary
Rate of pay for each week, month, or year worked.

As we described in the first section of this chapter, the pay structure reflects decisions about how much to pay (pay level) and the relative value of each job (job structure). The organization's pay structure should reflect what the organization knows about market forces, as well as its own unique goals and the relative contribution of each job to achieving the goals. By balancing this external and internal information, the organization's goal is to set levels of pay that employees will consider equitable and motivating. Organizations typically apply the information by establishing some combination of pay rates, pay grades, and pay ranges. Within this structure, they may state the pay in terms of a rate per hour, commonly called an **hourly wage;** a rate of pay for each unit produced, known as a **piecework rate;** or a rate of pay per month or year, called a **salary.**

Pay Rates

If the organization's main concern is to match what people are earning in comparable jobs, the organization can base pay directly on market research into as many of its key jobs as possible. To do this, the organization looks for survey data for each job title. If it finds data from more than one survey, it must weight the results based on their quality and relevance. The final number represents what the competition pays. In light of that knowledge, the organization decides what it will pay for the job.

The next step is to determine salaries for the nonkey jobs, for which the organization has no survey data. Instead, the person developing the pay structure creates a graph like the one in Figure 11.4. The vertical axis shows a range of possible pay rates, and the horizontal axis measures the points from the job evaluation. The analyst plots points according to the job evaluation and pay rate for each key job. Finally, the analyst fits a line, called a **pay policy line,** to the points plotted. (This can be done statistically on a computer, using a procedure called regression analysis.) Mathematically, this line shows the relationship between job evaluation and rate of pay. Using this line, the analyst can estimate the market pay level for a given job evaluation. Looking at the graph gives approximate numbers, or the regression analysis will provide an equation for calculating the rate of pay.

pay policy line
A graphed line showing the mathematical relationship between job evaluation points and pay rate.

The pay policy line reflects the pay structure in the market, which does not always match rates in the organization (see key job F in Figure 11.4). Survey data may show that people in certain jobs are actually earning significantly more or less than the amount shown on the pay policy line. For example, some kinds of expertise are in

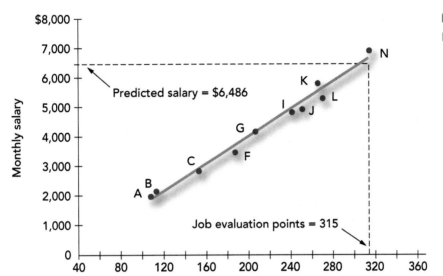

short supply. People with that expertise can command higher salaries, because they can easily leave one employer to get higher pay somewhere else. Suppose, in contrast, that local businesses have laid off many warehouse employees. Because so many of these workers are looking for jobs, organizations may be able to pay them less than the rate that job evaluation points would suggest.

When job structure and market data conflict in these ways, organizations have to decide on a way to resolve the two. One approach is to stick to the job evaluations and pay according to the employees' worth to the organization. Organizations that do so will be paying more or less than they have to, so they will likely have more difficulty competing for customers or employees. A way to moderate this approach is to consider the importance of each position to the organization's goals.[20] If a position is critical for meeting the organization's goals, paying more than competitors pay may be worthwhile.

At the other extreme, the organization could base pay entirely on market forces. However, this approach also has some practical drawbacks. One is that employees may conclude that pay rates are unfair. Two vice presidents or two supervisors will expect to receive similar pay because their responsibilities are similar. If the differences between their pay are large, because of different market rates, the lower-paid employee will likely be dissatisfied. Also, if the organization's development plans include rotating managers through different assignments, the managers will be reluctant to participate if managers in some departments receive lower pay. Organizations therefore must weigh all the objectives of their pay structure to arrive at suitable rates.

Pay Grades

A large organization could have hundreds or even thousands of different jobs. Setting a pay rate for each job would be extremely complex. Therefore, many organizations group jobs into **pay grades**—sets of jobs having similar worth or content, grouped together to establish rates of pay. For example, the organization could establish five pay grades, with the same pay available to employees holding any job within the same grade.

A drawback of pay grades is that grouping jobs will result in rates of pay for individual jobs that do not precisely match the levels specified by the market and the

pay grades
Sets of jobs having similar worth or content, grouped together to establish rates of pay.

organization's job structure. Suppose, for example, that the organization groups together its senior accountants (with a job evaluation of 255 points) and its senior systems analysts (with a job evaluation of 270 points). Surveys might show that the market rate of pay for systems analysts is higher than that for accountants. In addition, the job evaluations give more points to systems analysts. Even so, for simplicity's sake, the organization pays the same rate for the two jobs because they are in the same pay grade. The organization would have to pay more than the market requires for accountants or pay less than the market rate for systems analysts (so it would probably have difficulty recruiting and retaining them).

Pay Ranges

pay ranges
A set of possible pay rates defined by a minimum, maximum, and midpoint of pay for employees holding a particular job or a job within a particular pay grade.

Usually, organizations want some flexibility in setting pay for individual jobs. They want to be able to pay the most valuable employees the highest amounts and to give rewards for performance, as described in the next chapter. Flexibility also helps the organization balance conflicting information from market surveys and job evaluations. Therefore, pay structure usually includes a **pay range** for each job or pay grade. In other words, the organization establishes a minimum, maximum, and midpoint of pay for employees holding a particular job or a job within a particular pay grade. Employees holding the same job may receive somewhat different pay, depending on where their pay falls within the range.

A typical approach is to use the market rate or the pay policy line as the midpoint of a range for the job or pay grade. The minimum and maximum values for the range may also be based on market surveys of those amounts. Pay ranges are most common for white-collar jobs and for jobs that are not covered by union contracts. Figure 11.5 shows an example of pay ranges based on the pay policy line in Figure 11.4. Notice that the jobs are grouped into five pay grades, each with its own pay range. In this example, the range is widest for employees who are at higher levels in terms of their job evaluation points. That is because the performance of these higher-level employees will likely have more effect on the organization's performance, so the organization needs more latitude to reward them. For instance, as discussed earlier, the organization may want to select a higher point in the range to attract an employee who is more critical to achieving the organization's goals.

Usually pay ranges overlap somewhat, so that the highest pay in one grade is somewhat higher than the lowest pay in the next grade. Overlapping ranges gives the organization more flexibility in transferring employees among jobs, because transfers need not always involve a change in pay. On the other hand, the less overlap, the more important it is to earn promotions in order to keep getting raises. Assuming the organization wants to motivate employees through promotions (and assuming enough opportunities for promotion are available), the organization will want to limit the overlap from one level to the next.

red-circle rate
Pay at a rate that falls above the pay range for the job.

When the organization develops a pay structure, it may find that a few employees are being paid at rates that are above or below the range for their jobs. For example, an employee with exceptionally high seniority might earn above his range. Rates above the range are often called **red-circle rates.** In some cases, employees earning red-circle rates would receive no pay increases until they receive a promotion or until cost-of-living adjustments raise the pay range to include their pay rate. At the other extreme are **green-circle rates,** that is, rates below the pay range for a job. These employees usually would receive raises when the pay structure is put into practice; otherwise, their current pay rate signals that they are being paid less than their worth to the organization.

green-circle rate
Pay at a rate that falls below the pay range for the job.

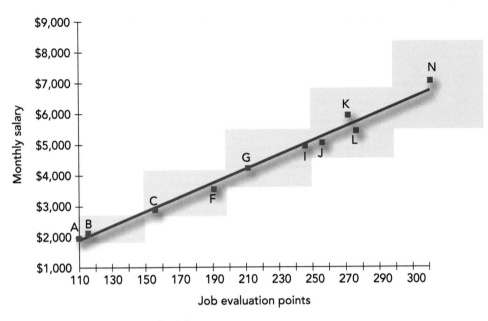

figure 11.5
Sample Pay Grade Structure

Pay Differentials

In some situations organizations adjust pay to reflect differences in working conditions or labor markets. For example, an organization may pay extra to employees who work the night shift, because night hours are less desirable for most workers. Similarly, organizations may pay extra to employees in locations where living expenses are higher. These adjustments are called **pay differentials.**

A survey of businesses in the United States found that over half have a formal or informal policy of providing pay differentials based on geographic location.[21] These differentials are intended as a way to treat employees fairly, without regard to where they work. The most common approach is to move an employee higher in the pay structure to compensate for higher living costs. For instance, the American Chamber of Commerce Research Association estimates that the cost of living in New York City is more than twice that of the average metropolitan area. An organization with employees in New York City and in an average U.S. city might pay its New York office manager substantially more than its office manager in the average city. This pay policy can become expensive for organizations that must operate in high-cost locations.

pay differential
Adjustment to a pay rate to reflect differences in working conditions or labor markets.

Night hours are less desirable for most workers. Therefore, some companies pay a differential for night work to compensate them.

Also, organizations need to handle the delicate issue of how to pay employees transferred to lower-cost areas.

LO6
Describe alternatives to job-based pay.

Alternatives to Job-Based Pay

The traditional and most widely used approach to developing a pay structure focuses on setting pay for jobs or groups of jobs.[22] This emphasis on jobs has some limitations. The precise definition of a job's responsibilities can contribute to an attitude that some activities "are not in my job description," at the expense of flexibility, innovation, quality, and customer service. Also, the job structure's focus on higher pay for higher status can work against an effort at empowerment. Organizations may avoid change because it requires repeating the time-consuming process of creating job descriptions and related paperwork. Another change-related problem is that when the organization needs a new set of knowledge, skills, and abilities, the existing pay structure may be rewarding the wrong behaviors. Finally, a pay structure that rewards employees for winning promotions may discourage them from gaining valuable experience through lateral career moves.

Organizations have responded to these problems with a number of alternatives to job-based pay structures. Some organizations have found greater flexibility through **delayering,** or reducing the number of levels in the organization's job structure. By combining more assignments into a single layer, organizations give managers more flexibility in making assignments and awarding pay increases. These broader groupings often are called *broad bands*. IBM recently changed from a pay structure with 5,000 job titles and 24 salary grades to one with 1,200 jobs and 10 bands. When IBM began using broad bands, it replaced its point-factor job evaluation system with an approach based on matching jobs to descriptions. Figure 11.6 provides an example of how this works. Broad bands reduce the opportunities for promoting employees, so organizations that eliminate layers in their job descriptions must find other ways to reward employees.

Another way organizations have responded to the limitations of job-based pay has been to move away from the link to jobs and toward pay structures that reward employees based on their knowledge and skills.[23] **Skill-based pay systems** are pay structures that set pay according to the employees' level of skill or knowledge and what they are capable of doing. Paying for skills makes sense at organizations where changing technology requires employees to continually widen and deepen their knowledge. For example, modern machinery often requires that operators know how to program and monitor computers to perform a variety of tasks. Skill-based pay also supports efforts to empower employees and enrich jobs because it encourages employees to add to their knowledge so they can make decisions in many areas. In this way, skill-based pay helps organizations become more flexible and innovative. More generally, skill-based pay can encourage a climate of learning and adaptability and give employees a broader view of how the organization functions. These changes should help employees use their knowledge and ideas more productively. A field study of a manufacturing plant found that changing to a skill-based pay structure led to better quality and lower labor costs.[24]

Of course, skill-based pay has its own disadvantages.[25] It rewards employees for acquiring skills but does not provide a way to ensure that employees can use their new skills. The result may be that the organization is paying employees more for learning skills that the employer is not benefiting from. The challenge for HRM is to design work so that the work design and pay structure support one another. Also, if employees learn skills very quickly, they may reach the maximum pay level so quickly that it

delayering
Reducing the number of levels in the organization's job structure.

skill-based pay systems
Pay structures that set pay according to the employees' levels of skill or knowledge and what they are capable of doing.

Figure 11.6

IBM's New Job Evaluation Approach

Below is an abbreviated schematic illustration of the new—and simple—IBM job evaluation approach:

POSITION REFERENCE GUIDE

Band	Skills required	Leadership/Contribution	Scope/Impact
1			
2			
3			
4			
5			
6			
7			
8			
9			
10			

Factors: Leadership/Contribution

Band 06: Understand the mission of the professional group and vision in own area of competence.

Band 07: Understand the departmental mission and vision.

Band 08: Understand departmental/functional mission and vision.

Band 09: Has vision of functional or unit mission.

Band 10: Has vision of overall strategies.

Both the bands and the approach are global. In the U.S., bands 1–5 are nonexempt; bands 6–10 are exempt. Each cell in the table contains descriptive language about key job characteristics. Position descriptions are compared to the chart and assigned to bands on a "best fit" basis. There are no points or scoring mechanisms. Managers assign employees to bands by selecting a position description that most closely resembles the work being done by an employee using an online position description library.

That's it!

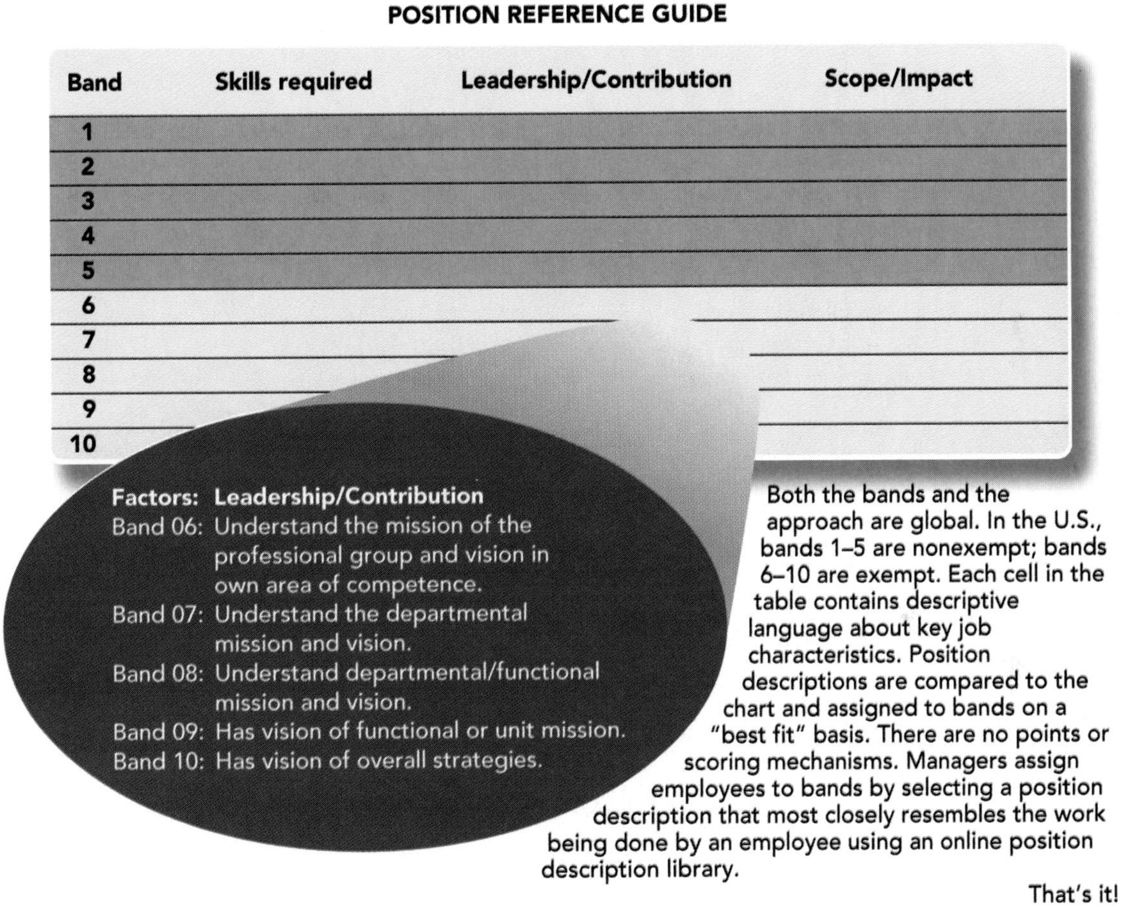

SOURCE: A. S. Richter, "Paying the People in Black at Big Blue," *Compensation and Benefits Review*, May–June 1998, pp. 51–59. Reprinted with permission of Sage Publications, Inc.

will become difficult to reward them appropriately. Skill-based pay does not necessarily provide an alternative to the bureaucracy and paperwork of traditional pay structures, because it requires records related to skills, training, and knowledge acquired. Finally, gathering market data about skill-based pay is difficult, because most wage and salary surveys are job-based.

PAY STRUCTURE AND ACTUAL PAY

Usually, the human resource department is responsible for establishing the organization's pay structure. But building a structure is not the end of the organization's decisions about pay structure. The structure represents the organization's policy, but what the organization actually does may be different. As part of its management responsibility, the HR department therefore should compare actual pay to the pay structure, making sure that policies and practices match.

LO7

Summarize how to ensure that pay is actually in line with the job structure.

Figure 11.7

Finding a Compa-Ratio

Pay Grade: 1
Midpoint of Range: $2,175 per month

Salaries of Employees in Pay Grade
Employee 1 $2,306
Employee 2 $2,066
Employee 3 $2,523
Employee 4 $2,414

Average Salary of Employees
$2,306 + $2,066 + $2,523 + $2,414 = $9,309
$9,309 ÷ 4 = $2,327.25

Compa-Ratio

$$\frac{\text{Average}}{\text{Midpoint}} = \frac{\$2,327.25}{\$2,175.00} = 1.07$$

A common way to do this is to measure a *compa-ratio*, the ratio of average pay to the midpoint of the pay range. Figure 11.7 shows an example. Assuming the organization has pay grades, the organization would find a compa-ratio for each pay grade: the average paid to all employees in the pay grade divided by the midpoint for the pay grade. If the average equals the midpoint, the compa-ratio is 1. More often, the compa-ratio is somewhat above 1 (meaning the average pay is above the midpoint for the pay grade) or below 1 (meaning the average pay is below the midpoint).

Assuming that the pay structure is well planned to support the organization's goals, the compa-ratios should be close to 1. A compa-ratio greater than 1 suggests that the organization is paying more than planned for human resources and may have difficulty keeping costs under control. A compa-ratio less than 1 suggests that the organization is underpaying for human resources relative to its target and may have difficulty attracting and keeping qualified employees. When compa-ratios are more or less than 1, the numbers signal a need for the HR department to work with managers to identify whether to adjust the pay structure or the organization's pay practices. The compa-ratios may indicate that the pay structure no longer reflects market rates of pay. Or maybe performance appraisals need to be more accurate, as discussed in Chapter 8.

LO8
Discuss issues related to paying employees serving in the military and paying executives.

❧ CURRENT ISSUES INVOLVING PAY STRUCTURE

An organization's policies regarding pay structure greatly influence employees' and even the general public's opinions about the organization. Issues affecting pay structure therefore can hurt or help the organization's reputation and ability to recruit, motivate, and keep employees. Recent issues related to pay structure include decisions about paying employees on active military duty and decisions about how much to pay the organization's top executives.

Pay during Military Duty

As we noted in Chapter 3, the Uniformed Services Employment and Reemployment Rights Act (USERRA) requires employers to make jobs available to their workers when they return after fulfilling military duties for up to five years. During the time these employees are performing their military service, the employer faces decisions related to paying these people. The armed services pay service members during their time of duty, but military pay often falls short of what they would earn in their civilian jobs. Some employers have chosen to support their employees by paying the difference between their military and civilian earnings for extended periods. Recent surveys have found that during the military actions in Afghanistan and Iraq, over half of U.S. employers have provided compensation to Reservists on active duty.[26] Some make up the full difference in pay, while others might provide health insurance. One company that makes up the full difference is Home Depot, which had about 1,800 employees called up in 2003 alone.[27]

Policies to make up the difference between military pay and civilian pay are costly. The employer is paying employees while they are not working for the organization, and it may have to hire temporary employees as well. This challenge has posed a significant hardship on some employers since 2002, as hundreds of thousands of Reservists and National Guard members have been mobilized. Even so, as the nation copes with this challenge, hundreds of employers have decided that maintaining positive relations with employees—and the goodwill of the American public—makes the expense worthwhile.

Pay for Executives

The media have drawn public attention to the issue of executive pay. The issue attracts notice because of the very high pay that the top executives of major U.S. companies have received in recent years. A significant form of executive compensation comes in the form of company stock (a type of compensation discussed in the next chapter). Stock prices soared during the 1990s and then fell at the beginning of this decade. Likewise, as shown in Figure 11.8, total CEO compensation soared and then declined. Pay in the form of salaries and bonuses remained quite stable, with most of the change in total compensation coming from other compensation—primarily from increases in the value of the company's stock given to the CEO. Also keep in mind

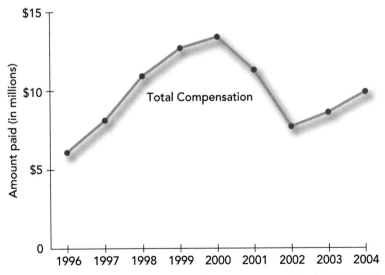

Figure 11.8

CEO Compensation at 365 of the Largest U.S. Companies

SOURCE: *BusinessWeek* survey of executive compensation, as reported April 21, 1997; April 20, 1998; April 19, 1999; April 17, 2000; April 5, 2002; April 19, 2004; and April 18, 2005.

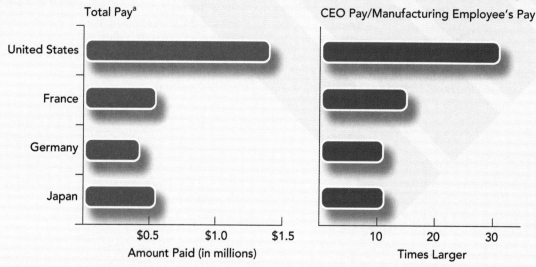

? DID YOU KNOW?

U.S. COMPANIES ARE GENEROUS TO CEOS

According to a survey by HR consulting firm Towers Perrin, U.S. chief executive officers earned far more than their colleagues in three other industrialized countries (France, Germany, and Japan). U.S. companies were also generous to CEOs relative to their average manufacturing worker. In the United States, the average CEO earned more than 30 times the pay of an average manufacturing worker; in the other three countries, the typical CEO earned about 10 times more than a manufacturing worker.

[a]Includes salary, bonus, company contributions, perquisites, and long-term incentives. Data based on company with $500 million in sales.
SOURCE: Towers Perrin, "2000 Worldwide Total Remuneration," New York: Towers Perrin, 2000.

that the numbers do not represent many managers; *BusinessWeek* surveyed "365 of the country's largest companies" to arrive at the data in Figure 11.8. A more representative survey of 2003 compensation found that average CEO compensation ranged from $988,000 for CEOs in the transportation industry to just under $3 million for CEOs in the construction industry.[28]

Although these high amounts apply to only a small proportion of the total workforce, the issue of executive pay is relevant to pay structure in terms of equity theory. As we discussed earlier in the chapter, employees draw conclusions about the fairness of pay by making comparisons among employees' inputs and outcomes. By many comparisons, U.S. CEOs' pay is high. The "Did You Know . . . ?" box compares CEO pay in several countries and shows that the pay of a U.S. CEO is noticeably greater. According to equity theory, employees would see this as fair if the U.S. CEOs also do more for their organizations than CEOs in other countries do. The situation becomes more complex for international organizations, where executives compare their pay to other executives in the same country, as well as to other executives in the same organization. Larry Fish, the chief executive of Citizens Financial Group in Providence, Rhode Island, made $3.2 million in 2001 and $13.8 million the year before (much higher in 2000 because of a one-time bonus).[29] His company is a subsidiary of Royal

Bank of Scotland Group, whose Scots chief executive earned far less—$2.2 million in 2001 and $3.2 million in 2000. A spokesman for the company says this pay structure "brings us absolutely no management issues," but HR consultants predict that U.S.-style pay will become the global norm as companies compete internationally for top talent.

Another way to think about the equity of CEO pay is to compare it with the pay of other employees in the organization. As shown in the "Did You Know . . . ?" box, chief executives of large U.S. businesses earn over 30 times as much as manufacturing employees in their companies. This multiple is over twice that enjoyed by CEOs in the other countries shown. Again, equity theory would consider not only the size of executive pay relative to pay for other employees but also the amount the CEOs contribute. An organization's executives potentially have a much greater effect on the organization's performance than other employees have. But if they do not seem to contribute 30 times more, employees will see the compensation as unfair. Researchers at Stanford University tried evaluating CEOs' contributions by comparing individual companies' performance within industries.[30] By their measures, there was a strong link between high CEO pay and high CEO performance at small firms. At big companies, the relationship between pay and performance was more complex. Applying this analysis, it would be easier for small companies to justify the fairness of their executive compensation.

Top executives help to set the tone or culture of the organization, and employees at all levels are affected by behavior at the top. As a result, the equity of executive pay can affect more employees than, say, equity among warehouse workers or sales clerks. One study that investigated this issue compared the pay of rank-and-file employees and executives in various business units.[31] In business units where the difference in pay was greater, customer satisfaction was lower. The researchers speculated that employees thought pay was inequitable and adjusted their behavior to provide lower inputs by putting forth less effort to satisfy customers. To avoid this type of situation, organizations need to plan not only *how much* to pay managers and executives, but also *how* to pay them. In the next chapter, we will explore many of the options available.

thinking ETHICALLY

Shedding Light on Executive Compensation

At the end of the 1990s, WorldCom seemed to be an incredible success story. Under the leadership of Bernard Ebbers, a small Mississippi company called Long Distance Discount Service made a series of acquisitions that helped it grow into the telecommunications giant called WorldCom. But in 2002, observers saw that WorldCom's success was literally too good to be true. The company was cutting its growth forecasts, and the Securities and Exchange Commission began investigating whether the company had been committing fraud in its accounting by overstating earnings and understating expenses. Ebbers resigned, and WorldCom admitted fraud and declared bankruptcy.

The accounting fraud was the largest in U.S. legal history, and a jury in 2005 held Ebbers responsible for conspiring to commit that fraud. The prosecution argued that Ebbers had a motivation related to his pay: Most of his assets were in the form of WorldCom stock that he received as compensation in his role as CEO. If the stock reflected its true value, Ebbers would be financially ruined.

The WorldCom case was the largest of several scandals that moved Congress to enact the Sarbanes-Oxley Act of 2002. Under Sarbanes-Oxley, corporations must establish a code of ethics for senior financial officers. Chief executives and chief financial officers must certify the accuracy of corporate financial reports, which must meet stricter standards for disclosing financial data. Corporations may not make personal loans to their officers and directors, and these people may not buy, sell, or transfer stock during pension plan "blackout" periods (during which pension plan participants and beneficiaries are not allowed to trade the corporation's stock). Corporations also must undergo audits of their internal controls to show that they are prepared to detect accounting fraud. Auditors are expected to investigate whether people are in place to take responsibility for financial reporting. Jobs related to financial reporting need precautions to ensure honesty. For example, every five years, companies must get new lead accountants for their audits.

The Sarbanes-Oxley Act is a complicated law aimed at protecting investors from being misled about corporations' financial health—a goal that ethical, competent management also could have achieved.

SOURCE: Almar Latour, Shawn Young, and Li Yuan, "Ebbers Is Convicted in Massive Fraud," *The Wall Street Journal*, March 16, 2005, http://online.wsj.com; Erik Sherman, "Use Technology to Stay in SOX Compliance," *HRMagazine*, May 2005, downloaded from Infotrac at http://web6.infotrac.galegroup.com; Rebecca Jarvis, "Sarbanes-Oxley Reminder," *Crain's Chicago Business*, March 21, 2005, downloaded from Business & Company Resource Center at http://galenet.galegroup.com; and J. Segal, "The 'Joy' of Uncooking," *HRMagazine* 47, no. 11 (2002).

Questions

1. The WorldCom scandal took place at a time when executive compensation was soaring, along with corporate stock prices. Do pay structures that reward executives with stock encourage unethical behavior? Explain.
2. Who was hurt by the WorldCom scandal? How does the Sarbanes-Oxley Act protect these groups in the future?
3. Companies say complying with the Sarbanes-Oxley requirements is expensive and time-consuming. Yet without the scandals at WorldCom, Enron, and other companies, there would have been no reason for Congress to enact such a law. What does this situation say about the significance of ethical behavior by businesspeople?

SUMMARY

1. Identify the kinds of decisions involved in establishing a pay structure.

Organizations make decisions to define a job structure, or relative pay for different jobs within the organization. They establish relative pay for different functions and different levels of responsibility for each function. Organizations also must establish pay levels, or the average paid for the different jobs. These decisions are based on the organization's goals, market data, legal requirements, and principles of fairness. Together, job structure and pay level establish a pay structure policy.

2. Summarize legal requirements for pay policies.

To meet the standard of equal employment opportunity, employers must provide equal pay for equal work, regardless of an employee's age, race, sex, or other protected status. Differences in pay must relate to factors such as a person's qualifications or market levels of pay. Under the Fair Labor Standards Act (FLSA), the employer must pay at least the minimum wage established by law. Some state and local governments have established higher minimum wages. The FLSA also requires overtime pay—at one and a half times the employee's regular pay rate, including bonuses—for hours worked beyond 40 in each week. Managers, professionals, and outside salespersons are exempt from the overtime pay requirement. Employers must meet FLSA requirements concerning child labor. Federal contractors also must meet requirements to pay at least the prevailing wage in the area where their employees work.

3. Discuss how economic forces influence decisions about pay.

To remain competitive, employers must meet the demands of product and labor markets. Product markets seek to buy at the lowest price, so organizations must limit their costs as much as possible. In this way, product markets place an upper limit on the pay an employer can afford to offer. Labor markets consist of workers, who want to earn as much as possible. To attract and keep workers, employers must pay at least the going rate in their labor markets. Organizations make decisions about whether to pay at, above, or below the pay rate set by these market forces. Paying above the market rate may make the organization less competitive in product markets but give it an advantage in labor markets. The organization benefits only if it can attract the best candidates and provide the systems that motivate and enable them to do their best work. Organizations that pay below the market rate need creative practices for recruiting and training workers so that they can find and keep enough qualified people.

4. Describe how employees evaluate the fairness of a pay structure.

According to equity theory, employees think of their pay relative to their inputs, such as training, experience, and effort. To decide whether their pay is equitable, they compare their outcome (pay)/input ratio with other people's outcome/input ratios. Employees make these comparisons with people doing the same job in other organizations and with people doing the same or different jobs in the same organization. If employees conclude that their outcome/input ratio is less than the comparison person's, they conclude that their pay is unfair and may engage in behaviors to create a situation they think is fair.

5. Explain how organizations design pay structures related to jobs.

Organizations typically begin with a job evaluation to measure the relative worth of their jobs. A job evaluation committee identifies each job's compensable factors and rates each factor. The committee may use a point manual to assign an appropriate number of points to each job. The committee can research market pay levels for key jobs, then identify appropriate rates of pay for other jobs, based on their number of points relative to the key jobs. The organization can do this with

a pay policy line, which plots a salary for each job. The organization can combine jobs into several groups, called pay grades. For each pay grade or job, the organization typically establishes a pay range, using the market rate or pay policy line as the midpoint. Differences in working conditions or labor markets sometimes call for the use of pay differentials to adjust pay levels.

6. Describe alternatives to job-based pay.

To obtain more flexibility, organizations may reduce the levels in the organization's job structure. This process of delayering creates broad bands of jobs with a pay range for each. Other organizations reward employees according to their knowledge and skills. They establish skill-based pay systems, or structures that set pay according to the employees' level of knowledge and what they are capable of doing. This encourages employees to be more flexible and adapt to changing technology. However, if the organization does not also provide systems in which employees can apply new skills, it may be paying them for skills they do not actually use.

7. Summarize how to ensure that pay is actually in line with the pay structure.

The human resource department should routinely compare actual pay with the pay structure to see that policies and practices match. A common way to do this is to measure a compa-ratio for each job or pay grade. The compa-ratio is the ratio of average pay to the midpoint of the pay range. Assuming the pay structure supports the organization's goals, the compa-ratios should be close to 1. When compa-ratios are more or less than 1, the HR department should work with managers to identify whether to adjust the pay structure or the organization's pay practices.

8. Discuss issues related to paying employees serving in the military and paying executives.

The Uniformed Services Employment and Reemployment Rights Act requires employers to make jobs available to any of their employees who leave to fulfill military duties for up to five years. While these employees are performing their military service, many are earning far less. To demonstrate their commitment to these employees and to earn the public's goodwill, many companies pay the difference between their military and civilian earnings, even though this policy is costly. Executive pay has drawn public scrutiny because top executive pay is much higher than average workers' pay. The great difference is an issue in terms of equity theory. Chief executive officers have an extremely large impact on the organization's performance, but critics complain that when performance falters, executive pay does not decline as fast as the organization's profits or stock price. Top executives help to set the organization's tone or culture, and employees at all levels are affected by the behavior of the people at the top. Therefore, employees' opinions about the equity of executive pay can have a large effect on the organization's performance.

REVIEW AND DISCUSSION QUESTIONS

1. In setting up a pay structure, what legal requirements must an organization meet? Which of these do you think would be most challenging for a small start-up business? Why?
2. In gathering data for its pay policies, what product markets would a city's hospital want to use as a basis for comparison? What labor markets would be relevant? How might the labor markets for surgeons be different from the labor markets for nursing aides?
3. Why might an organization choose to pay employees more than the market rate? Why might it choose to pay less? What are the consequences of paying more or less than the market rate?
4. Suppose you work in the HR department of a manufacturing company that is planning to enrich jobs by having production workers work in teams and rotate through various jobs. The pay structure will have to be adjusted to fit this new work design. How would you expect the employees to evaluate the fairness of their pay in their redesigned jobs? In terms of equity theory, what comparisons would they be likely to make?
5. Summarize the way organizations use information about jobs as a basis for a pay structure.
6. Imagine that you manage human resources for a small business. You have recently prepared a report on the market rate of pay for salespeople, and the company's owner says the market rate is too high. The company cannot afford this level of pay, and furthermore, paying that much would cause salespeople to earn more than most of the company's managers. Suggest three possible measures the company might take to help resolve this conflict.
7. What are the advantages of establishing pay ranges, rather than specific pay levels, for each job? What are the drawbacks of this approach?
8. Suppose the company in Question 1 wants to establish a skills-based pay structure. What would be some advantages of this approach? List the issues the company should be prepared to address in setting up this system. Consider the kinds of information you will need and the ways employees may react to the new pay structure.
9. Why do some employers subsidize the pay of military reserve members called up to active duty? If the military instead paid these people the wage they command in the civilian market (that is, the salary they earn at their regular jobs), who would bear the cost? When neither the reserve members' employers nor the military pays reserve members their civilian wage, reserve members and their families bear the cost. In your opinion, who *should* bear this cost—employers, taxpayers, or service members (or someone else)?
10. Do you think U.S. companies pay their chief executives too much? Why or why not?

WHAT'S YOUR HR IQ?

The text Web site offers two more ways to check what you've learned so far. Use the Self-Assessment exercise to test your expectations of salary brackets. Go online with the Web Exercise to experiment with salary calculators and to view cost of living comparisons for U.S. cities.

BusinessWeek CASE

BusinessWeek What Could Take a Bite out of Whole Foods

I don't know about you, but I can't recall when I last saw two employees hugging in a supermarket. I don't mean a phony air-kiss-with-grazing-shoulders thing, but something more, um, full-bodied. The other morning, I witnessed two such hugs. Then, right as I was leaving, I saw a pair of shoppers actually making out.

This was no Winn-Dixie, but the Whole Foods Market in Winter Park, Florida, one of 167 locations run by the Austin, Texas–based grocer with a mission. All the lovin' left me feeling good. So did the seventies sounds (Carole King, Brothers Johnson) instead of Muzak; the meats, seafood, and produce (gorgeous berries, nine kinds of peppers); the helpful, smiling clerks; the choice of frozen pizzas (a 9.1-ounce American Flatbread All Natural Pizza Baked in a Primitive Wood-Fired Earthen Oven Organic Tomato and Three-Cheese pizza for $6.79, or a Whole Foods' private-label 16.5-ounce spinach and feta pie at $3.69). Best of all was lunch: a big bowl of green split pea with soy bacon bits, one of six choices of soup at the deli, plus a mini baguette, for $4.41.

Yes, there's a lot to like at Whole Foods. So it leaves me feeling more of a killjoy than usual to suggest you think twice before buying the stock. This is not just because it's at record levels. The stock zoomed past 104, or 47 times past earnings, after the company posted 11.4 percent growth in its latest quarterly comparable-store sales. (Whole Foods is amending its results as it changes accounting for leases.) What really gives me pause is a fresh drag on earnings as Whole Foods strives to justify investors' lofty hopes.

Like other companies, Whole Foods this summer will be required by new accounting rules to deduct from earnings the costs of paying employees with stock or stock options. Unlike most other companies—especially unlike most other nontechnology companies—Whole Foods has been a heavy user of stock-based pay. Giving its 32,000 employees, or in Whole Foods–speak, its "team members," a direct stake in the chain's profitability is a key to its guiding philosophy of serving customers, employees, and investors, in that order. This is clicking: Contented customers and employees have made ecstatic shareholders.

Now, however, the new accounting rules have prompted Whole Foods to begin rationing its awards of stock and options so earnings eventually are dented no more than 10 percent. Whole Foods isn't saying how much this will cut team members' compensation. But we can guesstimate. In the past four quarters, Whole Foods posted earnings of $147.5 million. Had the costs of its stock-based pay been deducted from profits, earnings

would have come to $120.4 million, more than 18 percent less. Had Whole Foods wanted to limit the earnings hit to 10 percent, it would have had to cut the value of its option awards by perhaps 40 or 50 percent.

Whole Foods declined to discuss this with me, and it has yet to explain its plan to employees. It told Wall Street analysts that by accelerating the vesting of outstanding options—forcing a $10 million extraordinary charge against earnings this year—and by paying team members a bit more in cash, it may soften the blow. After calling the accounting rule "stupid," CEO John Mackey on February 9, 2005, assured analysts that Whole Foods will be growing so fast that the drag on earnings will barely be felt.

That could happen. Or, if management doesn't balance the hopes of its employees and Wall Street quite right, the team members whom Mackey credits with creating Whole Foods' success won't feel so rich. Then some on the team might start whistling another of my seventies favorites, the Roberta Flack and Donny Hathaway duet, "Where Is the Love?"

SOURCE: Robert Barker, "What Could Take a Bite out of Whole Foods," *BusinessWeek*, March 14, 2005, downloaded from Infotrac at http://web6.infotrac.galegroup.com.

Questions
1. According to the case, why does Whole Foods pay its employees with company stock as well as money? What business goals does this pay structure support?
2. Why is the company planning to reduce the amount of stock paid to employees? What do you expect to be the consequences of this change?
3. How can HRM help Whole Foods carry out this change in pay structure in a way that avoids negative consequences?

CASE: American Airlines Pay Deal Doesn't Fly with Employees

AMR Corporation's American Airlines unit infuriated employees by negotiating pay cuts at the same time it was offering generous pay to its top executives. The company, like many airlines, had been struggling financially since the travel industry's downturn in 2001. American asked its employees to accept pay cuts ranging between 15.6 and 23 percent, beginning in May 2003. The unions were also asked to accept more limited benefits plans and more flexible work rules. The changes were necessary, said American, to prevent the company from filing for bankruptcy.

Because the company has a union workforce, the unions put these requests to a vote. The Transport Workers Union barely accepted the changes, with 53 percent voting to make the concessions.

Just hours after the voting ended, AMR filed its annual report with the Securities and Exchange Commission. But it had held back on the filing during the union's vote. The report disclosed payments to executives, and the top six executives were offered "retention bonuses" for staying with American through January 2005. Those bonuses were double the amount of each executive's salary. In addition, the company set up a trust to hold supplemental pension benefits of 45 senior executives.

The reaction? Employees were furious. Representatives of the flight attendants union and Transport Workers Union both commented that if workers had known about the payments, they would have been much less likely to support concessions. An American crew chief, Joseph

Szubryt, told a *Wall Street Journal* reporter, "On the day we voted for all this stuff, giving up $10,000 a year when we only make $45,000 or $50,000, they disclose this? How the heck could these guys do that?"

In fact, managers had agreed to givebacks as well. But the disclosure of the benefits in the annual report overshadowed their goodwill gesture. Still, American insisted that there was a valid reason for the benefits. The company needed consistent leadership during difficult times, and it didn't want to risk having key executives leave, taking pension benefits with them.

In the years following that tense period leading up to the 2003 labor contracts, the airline has been able to show some signs of progress in its business performance and ability to reward employees. In April 2005, the company announced it would be granting all nonunion employees a 1.5 percent raise to signal that its financial condition had improved. Union employees also were scheduled to receive a raise under the terms of the company's labor agreement. In addition, in February 2005 the company improved its on-time performance from ninth among the 14 large airlines to second place. The company rewarded each of its employees with a $50 bonus. The bonus was a promise made at the time of the 2003 negotiations. In 2004, employees earned a total of $200 each for on-time performance.

Since 2003, the unions and management have been working together on teams to cut costs and improve profits. Union leaders hope that if they help the company do better, they can win back some of the concessions they made during earlier, bitter days.

SOURCE: Scott McCartney, "AMR Unions Express Fury over Management Benefits," *The Wall Street Journal*, April 17, 2003, http://online.wsj.com; "American Airlines to Give All Employees 1.5% Raise," *Airline Industry Information*, April 25, 2005, http://web6.infotrac.galegroup.com; Eric Torbenson, "American Airlines' Truce with Its Labor Unions Pays Off in Cost-Cutting," *Dallas Morning News*, April 28, 2005, http://web6.infotrac. galegroup.com; and Trebor Banstetter, "AA Workers to Get Bonus for On-Time Performance," *Fort Worth Star-Telegram*, April 7, 2005, http://web6. infotrac.galegroup.com.

Questions

1. This case describes several decisions about pay levels at American Airlines. How do they reflect economic influences on pay?
2. How have the company's decisions about pay affected employees' opinions of the company's fairness?
3. Does American seem to have a good match between its pay structure and its business goals? Explain.

NOTES

1. R. Chittum, "Call Centers Phone Home," *The Wall Street Journal*, June 9, 2004, pp. B1, B8.
2. Saratoga Institute, *2000 Human Capital Benchmarking Report* (Santa Clara, CA: Saratoga Institute, 2000).
3. Declan C. Leonard, "'Virtually Identical' Job Duties Needed for Equal Pay Claim," *HRMagazine*, February 2005, downloaded from Infotrac at http://web6. infotrac.galegroup.com.
4. Bureau of Labor Statistics, "Women in the Labor Force: A Databook," Report 985, http://www.bls.gov/cps/ wlf-databook2005.htm, last modified May 9, 2005.
5. B. Morris, K. Bonamici, S. M. Kaufman, and P. Neering, "How Corporate America Is Betraying Women," *Fortune*, January 10, 2005, downloaded from Infotrac at http://web6.infotrac.galegroup.com; B. Gerhart, "Gender Differences in Current and Starting Salaries: The Role of Performance, College Major, and Job Title," *Industrial and Labor Relations Review* 43 (1990), pp. 418–33; G. G. Cain, "The Economic Analysis of Labor Market Discrimination: A Survey," in *Handbook of Labor Economics*, ed. O. Ashenfelter and R. Layard (New York: North-Holland, 1986), pp. 694–785.
6. S. L. Rynes and G. T. Milkovich, "Wage Surveys: Dispelling Some Myths about the 'Market Wage,'" *Personnel Psychology* 39 (1986), pp. 71–90; G. T. Milkovich and J. Newman, *Compensation* (Homewood, IL: BPI/ Irwin, 1993).
7. C. Tejada, "Supporters of a Living Wage Push to Expand Current Laws," *The Wall Street Journal Online*, May 22, 2002, http://online.wsj.com.
8. U.S. Department of Labor, Employment Standards Division, "Overtime Requirements of the FLSA," Fact Sheet 23, www.dol.gov/esa, accessed May 19, 2005.
9. M. M. Clark, "Step by Step," *HRMagazine*, February 2005, downloaded from Infotrac at http://web6. infotrac.galegroup.com.
10. U.S. Department of Labor, Employment Standards Administration, "Child Labor Provisions of the Fair Labor Standards Act (FLSA) for Nonagricultural Occupations," Fact Sheet #43, Labor Department Web site, www.dol.gov, downloaded August 15, 2002.
11. S. Holmes and W. Zellner, "The Costco Way," *BusinessWeek*, April 12, 2004, pp. 76–77; and M. V. Rafter, "Welcome to the Club," *Workforce Management*, April 2005, pp. 40–46.
12. B. Gerhart and G. T. Milkovich, "Organizational Differences in Managerial Compensation and Financial Performance," *Academy of Management Journal* 33 (1990), pp. 663–91; E. L. Groshen, "Why Do Wages Vary among Employers?" *Economic Review* 24 (1988), pp. 19–38.

13. G. A. Akerlof, "Gift Exchange and Efficiency-Wage Theory: Four Views," *American Economic Review* 74 (1984), pp. 79–83; J. L. Yellen, "Efficiency Wage Models of Unemployment," *American Economic Review* 74 (1984), pp. 200–5.

14. R. Breeden, "Labor Costs Squeeze Small Manufacturers," *The Wall Street Journal Online*, June 25, 2002, http://online.wsj.com.

15. R. Rosenwein, "Help (Still) Wanted," *Inc.*, April 2001, pp. 51–55.

16. J. S. Adams, "Inequity in Social Exchange," in *Advances in Experimental Social Psychology*, ed. L. Berkowitz (New York: Academic Press, 1965); P. S. Goodman, "An Examination of Referents Used in the Evaluation of Pay," *Organizational Behavior and Human Performance* 12 (1974), pp. 170–95; J. B. Miner," *Theories of Organizational Behavior* (Hinsdale, IL: Dryden Press, 1980).

17. P. Capelli and P. D. Sherer, "Assessing Worker Attitudes under a Two-Tier Wage Plan," *Industrial and Labor Relations Review* 43 (1990), pp. 225–44.

18. K. J. Dunham, "Employers Ease Bans on Workers Asking, 'What Do They Pay You?'" *The Wall Street Journal*, May 1, 2001, pp. B10+.

19. R. I. Henderson, *Compensation Management in a Knowledge-Based World* (Englewood Cliffs, NJ: Prentice Hall, 1998).

20. J. P. Pfeffer and A. Davis-Blake, "Understanding Organizational Wage Structures: A Resource Dependence Approach," *Academy of Management Journal* 30 (1987), pp. 437–55.

21. Runzheimer International, *1997–1998 Survey of Geographic Pay Differential Policies and Practices* (Rochester, WI: Runzheimer, 1998).

22. This section draws freely on B. Gerhart and R. D. Bretz, "Employee Compensation," in *Organization and Management of Advanced Manufacturing*, ed. W. Karwowski and G. Salvendy (New York: Wiley, 1994), pp. 81–101.

23. E. E. Lawler III, *Strategic Pay* (San Francisco: Jossey-Bass, 1990); G. Ledford, "3 Cases on Skill-Based Pay: An Overview," *Compensation and Benefits Review*, March–April 1991, pp. 11–23; G. E. Ledford, "Paying for the Skills, Knowledge, Competencies of Knowledge Workers," *Compensation and Benefits Review*, July–August 1995, p. 55.

24. B. C. Murray and B. Gerhart, "An Empirical Analysis of a Skill-Based Pay Program and Plant Performance Outcomes," *Academy of Management Journal* 41, no. 1 (1998), pp. 68–78.

25. Ibid.; N. Gupta, D. Jenkins, and W. Curington, "Paying for Knowledge: Myths and Realities," *National Productivity Review*, Spring 1986, pp. 107–23.

26. B. Leonard, "Majority of Reservists' Families Report More Income during Service," *HRMagazine*, May 2003; and B. Leonard, "Data Indicate Strong Employer Support for Activated Reservists," *HRMagazine*, October 2003, both downloaded from Infotrac at http://web4.infotrac.galegroup.com.

27. R. Allen, "Open Arms for Returning Reservists," *Workforce Management*, February 2004, downloaded from Infotrac at http://web4.infotrac.galegroup.com.

28. The Conference Board, "CEO and Outside Director Pay Rises in All Industries, in Annual Compensation Studies," news release, October 19, 2004, www.conference-board.org.

29. K. J. Dunham, "Home Disadvantage," *The Wall Street Journal Online*, May 6, 2002, http://online.wsj.com.

30. Stanford University Graduate School of Business, "CEO Skill and Excessive Pay: A Breakdown in Corporate Governance?" Research section of Stanford GSB News page, February 2005, www.gsb.stanford.edu (citing research by Robert Daines, Vinay B. Nair, and Lewis Kornhauser).

31. D. M. Cowherd and D. I. Levine, "Product Quality and Pay Equity between Lower-Level Employees and Top Management: An Investigation of Distributive Justice Theory," *Administrative Science Quarterly* 37 (1992), pp. 302–20.

If you are using the Manager's Hot Seat DVD with this book, consider finishing case 3: Negotiation: Thawing the Salary Freeze for this chapter.

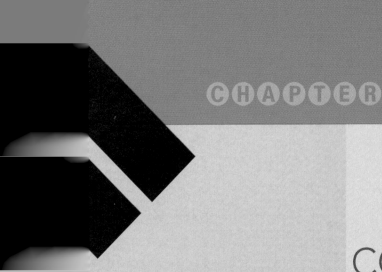

CHAPTER 12

RECOGNIZING EMPLOYEE CONTRIBUTIONS WITH PAY

What Do I Need to Know?

1. Discuss the connection between incentive pay and employee performance.

2. Describe how organizations recognize individual performance.

3. Identify ways to recognize group performance.

4. Explain how organizations link pay to their overall performance.

5. Describe how organizations combine incentive plans in a "balanced scorecard."

6. Summarize processes that can contribute to the success of incentive programs.

7. Discuss issues related to performance-based pay for executives.

❧ INTRODUCTION

The 7,500 employees of Jamba Juice Company know how to earn more money. They know that their pay raises depend on how well they performed their jobs the previous year. Supervisors rank employees according to whether their performance was outstanding, above requirements, meeting requirements, or below requirements. Those in the top category receive the largest raises. Those rated as performing below requirements receive no raise at all, and they don't have a chance to earn a bonus. According to Russ Testa, Jamba Juice's vice president of human resources, this pay system is a practical matter of allocating the company's money to the company's best employees: "If you're devoting dollars to underperformers, that simply means you're taking away from your high performers."[1] Employees consider the process fair because they understand how their performance will be measured and how it will affect their pay.

The pay earned by each Jamba Juice employee depends on the starting pay for a particular job (the topic of the preceding chapter) and pay raises tied to the employee's performance. In this chapter we focus on using pay to recognize and reward employees' contributions to the organization's success. Employees' pay does not depend solely on the jobs they hold. Instead, organizations vary the amount paid according to differences in performance of the individual, group, or whole organization, as well as differences in employee qualities such as seniority and skills.[2]

In contrast to decisions about pay structure, organizations have wide discretion in setting performance-related pay, called **incentive pay.** Organizations can tie incentive pay to individual performance, profits, or many other measures of success. They select incentives based on their costs, expected influence on performance, and fit with the organization's broader HR and company policies and goals. These decisions are significant. A study of 150 organizations found that the way organizations paid employees was strongly associated with their level of profitability.[3]

This chapter explores the choices available to organizations with regard to incentive pay. First, the chapter describes the link between pay and employee performance. Next, we discuss ways organizations provide a variety of pay incentives to individuals. The following two sections describe pay related to group and organizational performance. We then explore the organization's processes that can support the use of incentive pay. Finally, we discuss incentive pay for the organization's executives.

incentive pay
Forms of pay linked to an employee's performance as an individual, group member, or organization member.

✎ INCENTIVE PAY

Along with wages and salaries, many organizations offer *incentive pay*—that is, pay specifically designed to energize, direct, or control employees' behavior. Incentive pay is influential because the amount paid is linked to certain predefined behaviors or outcomes. For example, as we will see in this chapter, an organization can pay a salesperson a *commission* for closing a sale, or the members of a production department can earn a *bonus* for meeting a monthly production goal. Usually, these payments are in addition to wages and salaries. Knowing they can earn extra money for closing sales or meeting departmental goals, the employees often try harder or get more creative than they might without the incentive pay. In addition, the policy of offering higher pay for higher performance may make an organization attractive to high performers when it is trying to recruit and retain these valuable employees.[4]

For incentive pay to motivate employees to contribute to the organization's success, the pay plans must be well designed. In designing incentive pay plans, organizations should consider whether the pay encourages the kinds of behavior that are most needed, whether employees believe they have the ability and resources to meet the performance standards, and whether they value the rewards and think the pay plan is fair. These principles are summarized in Figure 12.1.

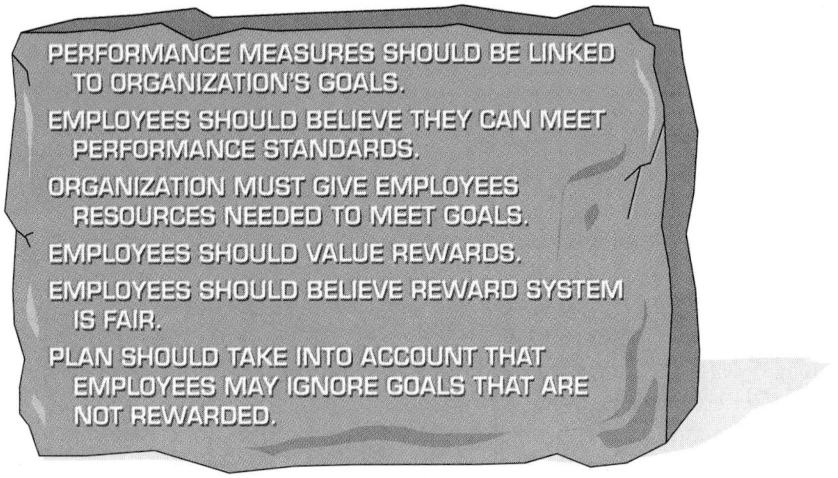

LO1
Discuss the connection between incentive pay and employee performance.

Figure 12.1
Principles of Effective Incentive Pay Plans

PERFORMANCE MEASURES SHOULD BE LINKED TO ORGANIZATION'S GOALS.

EMPLOYEES SHOULD BELIEVE THEY CAN MEET PERFORMANCE STANDARDS.

ORGANIZATION MUST GIVE EMPLOYEES RESOURCES NEEDED TO MEET GOALS.

EMPLOYEES SHOULD VALUE REWARDS.

EMPLOYEES SHOULD BELIEVE REWARD SYSTEM IS FAIR.

PLAN SHOULD TAKE INTO ACCOUNT THAT EMPLOYEES MAY IGNORE GOALS THAT ARE NOT REWARDED.

Since incentive pay is linked to particular outcomes or behaviors, the organization is encouraging employees to demonstrate those chosen outcomes and behaviors. As obvious as that may sound, the implications are more complicated. If incentive pay is extremely rewarding, employees may focus on only the performance measures rewarded under the plan and ignore measures that are not rewarded. Suppose an organization pays managers a bonus when employees are satisfied; this policy may interfere with other management goals. A manager who doesn't quite know how to inspire employees to do their best might be tempted to fall back on overly positive performance appraisals, letting work slide to keep everyone happy. Similarly, many call centers pay employees based on how many calls they handle, as an incentive to work quickly and efficiently. However, speedy call handling does not necessarily foster good customer relationships. Gallup Organization depends on good relationships to keep the people in its research samples from hanging up on its telephone pollsters, so its incentive pay is based on customer evaluations, rather than number of calls.[5] As we will see in this chapter, organizations may combine a number of incentives so employees do not focus on one measure to the exclusion of others. Also, as described in the "e-HRM" box, technology is enabling companies to track a wider variety of performance measures so that incentive pay can better match the desired areas of performance.

Employees must also believe they have the ability and resources to meet the performance standards. For rewards to be motivating, employees have to believe they can earn them. Failure to meet this requirement sank the incentive program Scott Testa once devised for Mindbridge Software, where he is chief operating officer. The prize for meeting sales goals was attractive: up to $3,000 for airfare and lodging for a long weekend at *any* destination. The problem was that salespeople had to more than double their performance. They had been selling on average $200,000 a month, and to win the trip, they had to bring in $500,000 a month for an entire year. When Testa discovered that the program was actually demoralizing salespeople, he had to abandon it.[6] In general, if organizations want to reward employees for meeting goals, they must give the employees access to the resources needed for meeting those goals. If rewards are tied to customer satisfaction, for example, employees must be empowered to satisfy customers.

Other attitudes that influence the success of incentive pay include whether employees value the rewards and think the pay plan is fair. Offering money as an incentive avoids the pitfall of inappropriate rewards. An insurance company in California once rewarded salespeople with tickets to a Christmas program at a nearby cathedral. One-third of the salespeople were Jewish, and they were more than unenthusiastic—they were offended.[7] Although most, if not all, employees value pay, it is important to remember that earning money is not the only reason people try to do a good job. As we have discussed in other chapters (see Chapters 4, 8, and 13), people also want interesting work, appreciation for their efforts, flexibility, and a sense of belonging to the work group—not to mention the inner satisfaction of work well done. Therefore, a complete plan for motivating and compensating employees has many components, from pay to work design to developing managers so they can exercise positive leadership.

With regard to the fairness of incentive pay, the preceding chapter described equity theory, which explains how employees form judgments about the fairness of a pay structure. The same process applies to judgments about incentive pay. In general, employees compare their efforts and rewards with other employees', considering a plan to be fair when the rewards are distributed according to what the employees contribute.

The remainder of this chapter identifies elements of incentive pay systems. We consider each option's strengths and limitations with regard to these principles. The

HIGH-TECH MEASURES FOR PERFORMANCE AND PAY

When companies are enjoying strong sales and the money is flowing in, it's easy to pass around pay raises to make everyone feel part of the success. But when sales slow, companies have to look more carefully at the ways they reward employees. They can't afford to overload their compensation budgets with more and more dollars.

During the leaner years of the past decade, some companies have approached the budget problem by looking for more precise ways to measure employees' performance. The detailed information helps them allocate raises, bonuses, and other rewards to the best performers. Companies that link pay to precise measures include Hewlett-Packard, General Electric, Du Pont, and Sun Microsystems.

British Airways uses computer software to measure the performance of its customer service representatives. The software measures the precise time these employees spend answering customer calls, to see that they are not being paid for time spent on breaks or personal phone calls. The program also calculates how many customer complaints each employee resolves and the amount the person generates in ticket sales. Until British Airways installed the software, it didn't have a way of measuring its office employees' performance as it did for the performance of its flight crews. Now it can award its customer service reps merit pay according to their contribution to the company.

At Hewlett-Packard, software helps sales and marketing managers boost their earnings along with their goals. They can use an "incentive calculator" that shows the link the company has established between higher goals and higher incentive pay.

Bayer used technology to improve the way it calculates commissions paid to its salespeople. The traditional approach is to reward salespeople based on the dollar value of the amount they sell. However, sales can increase for reasons that have nothing to do with salespeople's contributions. For example, in 2001, an incident in which letters were poisoned with anthrax caused a rush to buy the antibiotic Cipro, a Bayer product. Bayer wanted to reward the salespeople who performed best, not just those who happened to be filling Cipro orders. So, it set up its software to count hours spent on calls to physicians and hospitals, not just dollar sales.

Employees are not always happy with having the details of their activities monitored, however. Some worry that companies will use the information in ways that violate individuals' privacy. Yet, the interest in high-tech monitoring is likely to grow as companies find that they can identify and reward the employees they most want to keep.

SOURCE: Michelle Conlin, "The Software Says You're Just Average," *BusinessWeek*, February 25, 2002, p. 126.

many kinds of incentive pay fall into three broad categories: incentives linked to individual, group, or organizational performance. Choices from these categories should consider not only their strengths and weaknesses, but also their fit with the organization's goals. The choice of incentive pay may affect not only the level of motivation but also the kinds of employees who are attracted to and stay with the organization. For example, there is some evidence that organizations with team-based rewards will tend to attract employees who are more team-oriented, while rewards tied to individual performance make an organization more attractive to those who think and act independently, as individuals.[8]

❧ PAY FOR INDIVIDUAL PERFORMANCE

Organizations may reward individual performance with incentives such as piecework rates, standard hour plans, merit pay, individual bonuses, and sales commissions. These alternatives are summarized in Figure 12.2.

Piecework Rates

piecework rate
A wage based on
the amount workers
produce.

As an incentive to work efficiently, some organizations pay production workers a **piecework rate,** a wage based on the amount they produce. The amount paid per unit is set at a level that rewards employees for above-average production volume. For example, suppose that on average, assemblers can finish 10 components in an hour. If the organization wants to pay its average assemblers $8 per hour, it can pay a piecework rate of $8/hour divided by 10 components/hour, or $.80 per component. An assembler who produces the average of 10 components per hour earns an amount equal to $8 per hour. An assembler who produces 12 components in an hour would earn $.80 × 12, or $9.60 each hour. This is an example of a **straight piecework plan,** because the employer pays the same rate per piece, no matter how much the worker produces.

straight piecework plan
Incentive pay in
which the employer
pays the same rate
per piece, no matter
how much the
worker produces.

A variation on straight piecework is **differential piece rates** (also called *rising and falling differentials*), in which the piece rate depends on the amount produced. If the worker produces more than the standard output, the piece rate is higher. If the worker produces at or below the standard, the amount paid per piece is lower. In the preceding example, the differential piece rate could be $1 per component for components exceeding 12 per hour and $.80 per component for up to 12 components per hour.

differential piece rates
Incentive pay in
which the piece rate
is higher when a
greater amount is
produced.

In one study, the use of piece rates increased production output by 30 percent—more than any other motivational device evaluated.[9] An obvious advantage of piece rates is the direct link between how much work the employee does and the amount the employee earns. This type of pay is easy to understand and seems fair to many people, if they think the production standard is reasonable. In spite of their advantages, piece rates are relatively rare for several reasons.[10] Most jobs, including those of managers, have no physical output, so it is hard to develop an appropriate performance measure. This type of incentive is most suited for very routine, standardized jobs with

Figure 12.2

Types of Pay for Individual Performance

| Piecework Rates (Straight or Differential) | Standard Hours Plan | Merit Pay | Performance Bonus | Sales Commissions |

Figure 12.3

How Incentives Sometimes "Work"

SOURCE: DILBERT reprinted by permission of United Features Syndicate, Inc.

output that is easy to measure. For complex jobs or jobs with hard-to-measure outputs, piecework plans do not apply very well. Also, unless a plan is well designed to include performance standards, it may not reward employees for focusing on quality or customer satisfaction if it interferes with the day's output. In Figure 12.3, the employees quickly realize they can earn huge bonuses by writing software "bugs" and then fixing them, while writing bug-free software affords no chance to earn bonuses. More seriously, a bonus based on number of faucets produced gives production workers no incentive to stop a manufacturing line to correct a quality-control problem. Production-oriented goals may do nothing to encourage employees to learn new skills or cooperate with others. Therefore, individual incentives such as these may be a poor incentive in an organization that wants to encourage teamwork. They may not be helpful in an organization with complex jobs, employee empowerment, and team-based problem solving.

Standard Hour Plans

Another quantity-oriented incentive for production workers is the **standard hour plan,** an incentive plan that pays workers extra for work done in less than a preset "standard time." The organization determines a standard time to complete a task, such as tuning up a car engine. If the mechanic completes the work in less than the standard time, the mechanic receives an amount of pay equal to the wage for the full standard time. Suppose the standard time for tuning up an engine is 2 hours. If the mechanic finishes a tune-up in 1½ hours, the mechanic earns 2 hours' worth of pay in 1½ hours. Working that fast over the course of a week could add significantly to the mechanic's pay.

In terms of their pros and cons, standard hour plans are much like piecework plans. They encourage employees to work as fast as they can, but not necessarily to care about quality or customer service. Also, they only succeed if employees want the extra money more than they want to work at a pace that feels comfortable.

Merit Pay

Almost all organizations have established some program of **merit pay**—a system of linking pay increases to ratings on performance appraisals. (Chapter 8 described the content and use of performance appraisals.) Merit pay is most common for white-collar employees. To make the merit increases consistent, so they will be seen as fair, many

standard hour plan
An incentive plan that pays workers extra for work done in less than a preset "standard time."

merit pay
A system of linking pay increases to ratings on performance appraisals.

merit pay programs use a *merit increase grid*, such as the sample for Merck, the giant drug company, in Table 12.1. As the table shows, the decisions about merit pay are based on two factors: the individual's performance rating and the individual's compa-ratio (pay relative to average pay, as defined in Chapter 11). This system gives the biggest pay increases to the best performers and to those whose pay is relatively low for their job. At the highest extreme, an exceptional employee earning 80 percent of the average pay for his job could receive a 15 percent merit raise. An employee rated as having "room for improvement" would receive a raise only if that employee was earning relatively low pay for the job (compa-ratio of .95 or less).

By today's standards, all of these raises are large, because they were created at a time when inflation was strong and economic forces demanded big pay increases to keep up with the cost of living. The range of percentages for a policy used today would be lower. Organizations establish and revise merit increase grids in light of changing economic conditions. When organizations revise pay ranges, employees have new compa-ratios. A higher pay range would result in lower compa-ratios, causing employees to become eligible for bigger merit increases. An advantage of merit pay is therefore that it makes the reward more valuable by relating it to economic conditions. A drawback is that conditions can shrink the available range of increases. During recent years, budgets for merit pay increases were about 3 to 5 percent of pay, so average performers could receive a 4 percent raise, and top performers perhaps as much as 6 percent. The 2-percentage-point difference, after taxes and other deductions, would amount to only a few dollars a week on a salary of $40,000 per year. Over an entire career, the bigger increases for top performers can grow into a major change, but viewed on a year-by-year basis, they are not much of an incentive to excel.[11]

Another advantage of merit pay is that it provides a method for rewarding performance in all of the dimensions measured in the organization's performance management system. If that system is appropriately designed to measure all the important job behaviors, then the merit pay is linked to the behaviors the organization desires. This link seems logical, although so far there is little research showing the effectiveness of merit pay.[12]

TABLE 12.1

Sample Merit Increase Grid

	SUGGESTED MERIT INCREASE PERCENTAGE			
PERFORMANCE RATING	COMPA-RATIO 80.00–95.00	COMPA-RATIO 95.01–110.00	COMPA-RATIO 110.01–120.00	COMPA-RATIO 120.01–125.00
EX (Exceptional within Merck)	13–15%	12–14%	9–11%	To maximum of range
WD (Merck Standard with Distinction)	9–11	8–10	7–9	—
HS (High Merck Standard)	7–9	6–8	—	—
RI (Merck Standard Room for Improvement)	5–7	—	—	—
NA (Not Adequate for Merck)	—	—	—	—

SOURCE: K. J. Murphy, "Merck & Co., Inc. (B)," Boston: Harvard Business School, Case 491-006. Copyright © 1990 by the President & Fellows of Harvard College. Reprinted with permission.

A drawback of merit pay, from the employer's standpoint, is that it can quickly become expensive. Managers at a majority of organizations rate most employees' performance in the top two categories (out of four or five).[13] Therefore, the majority of employees are eligible for the biggest merit increases, and their pay rises rapidly. This cost is one reason that some organizations have established guidelines about the percentage of employees that may receive the top rating, as discussed in Chapter 8.

Another drawback of merit pay is that it makes assumptions that may be misleading. Rewarding employees for superior performance ratings assumes that those ratings depend on employees' ability and motivation. But performance may actually depend on forces outside the employee's control, such as managers' rating biases, the level of cooperation from coworkers, or the degree to which the organization gives employees the authority, training, and resources they need. Under these conditions, employees will likely conclude that the merit pay system is unfair.

Quality guru W. Edwards Deming also criticizes merit pay for discouraging teamwork. In Deming's words, "Everyone propels himself forward, or tries to, for his own good, on his own life preserver. The organization is the loser."[14] For example, if employees in the purchasing department are evaluated based on the number or cost of contracts they negotiate, they may have little interest in the quality of the materials they buy, even when the manufacturing department is having quality problems. In reaction to such problems, Deming advocated the use of group incentives. Another alternative is for merit pay to include ratings of teamwork and cooperation. Some employers ask coworkers to provide such ratings.

The "HR How To" box suggests ways to set up a merit pay system so that it maximizes the advantages of this type of pay while minimizing the drawbacks.

Performance Bonuses

Like merit pay, performance bonuses reward individual performance, but bonuses are not rolled into base pay. The employee must re-earn them during each performance period. In some cases, the bonus is a one-time reward. Bonuses may also be linked to objective performance measures, rather than subjective ratings.

Bonuses for individual performance can be extremely effective and give the organization great flexibility in deciding what kinds of behavior to reward. For example, as we saw in Chapter 2, Continental Airlines pays employees a quarterly bonus for ranking in the top three airlines for on-time arrivals, a measure of service quality. In many cases, employees receive bonuses for meeting such routine targets as sales or production numbers. Such bonuses encourage hard work. But an organization that focuses on growth and innovation may get better results from rewarding employees for learning new skills than from linking bonuses to mastery of existing jobs.

Adding to this flexibility, organizations also may motivate employees with one-time bonuses. For example, when one organization acquires another, it usually wants to retain certain valuable employees in the organization it is buying. Therefore, it is common for organizations involved in an acquisition to pay *retention bonuses*—one-time incentives paid in exchange for remaining with the company—to top managers, engineers, top-performing salespeople, and information technology specialists. When AMR Corporation, the parent company of American Airlines, acquired Trans World Airlines, it paid key TWA managers bonuses if they stayed on after the acquisition.[15] Each manager who stayed received a bonus equaling 15 to 30 percent of his or her salary.

HR HOW TO

IMPLEMENTING A MERIT PAY PROGRAM

Increasingly, companies are linking bonuses and pay increases to employees' performance. That means employees will see the money only if they can show they have met or exceeded goals. One reason is that in times of low growth and low inflation, the budgets available to reward employees are smaller. For the pay to have an impact, companies need to ensure that the money is directed toward the best performers.

An important requirement for merit pay is that the employees understand what they have to do to receive it. Employers should provide frequent written information about the company's merit pay. Employees and their supervisors should be sure they understand how to define excellent performance. They also need to know when failure to meet standards will result in their receiving no pay increase. When the measures are clear, managers are better able to withstand the temptation to reward everyone in order to

avoid the discomfort of telling certain employees that they will not be receiving merit pay. At the same time, the employees can see that the system is fair.

Throughout the year, employees should be able to see whether they are making progress toward meeting those requirements. For individual performance, managers need to provide frequent personal feedback. In organizations that reward group performance, managers can post charts showing both goals and progress toward those goals. This feedback gives employees a chance to improve before merit pay decisions are made.

When pay increases or bonuses are awarded, employees should not be surprised. A surprise means the communication throughout the year was not adequate. At the time employees receive information about merit pay awards, they should be fully aware of what their goals were, whether they were meeting goals, and what

the link between goal achievement and merit pay is.

Even when an organization clearly communicates its expectations and when managers give frequent feedback, it still feels uncomfortable to tell a poorly performing employee that he or she will not receive any pay raise that year. So, a merit pay system will be more successful if the company also provides managers with training and coaching in how to deliver bad news. For example, role-playing exercises can help managers develop skills in navigating difficult conversations. The company may also give managers flexibility—for example, allowing them to delay a pay increase for several months, to give the employee a chance to improve.

SOURCE: Jeff D. Opdyke, "Getting a Bonus Instead of a Raise," *The Wall Street Journal*, December 29, 2004, pp. D1–D2; and Susan J. Wells, "No Results, No Raise," *HRMagazine*, May 2005, downloaded from Infotrac at http://web6.infotrac.galegroup.com.

Sales Commissions

commissions
Incentive pay calculated as a percentage of sales.

A variation on piece rates and bonuses is the payment of **commissions,** or pay calculated as a percentage of sales. For instance, a furniture salesperson might earn commissions equaling 6 percent times the price of the furniture the person sells during the period. Selling a $2,000 couch would add $120 to the salesperson's commissions for the period. At most organizations today, commissions range from 5 percent to 20 percent of sales.[16] In a growth-oriented organization, sales commissions need not be limited to salespeople. Many of the technical experts at Scientific & Engineering Solutions are eligible for commissions and bonuses tied to the profitability of the sales they help to close. One member of the Maryland company's technical staff, Steve

Many car salespeople earn a straight commission, meaning that 100% of their pay comes from commission instead of a salary. What type of individual might enjoy a job like this?

Newcomb, helped to develop a small contract into a $700,000 sale. He earned the commission on the sale, along with an additional prize—tickets to the Super Bowl.[17]

Some salespeople earn a commission in addition to a base salary; others earn only commissions—a pay arrangement called a *straight commission plan*. Straight commissions are common among insurance and real estate agents and car salespeople. Other salespeople earn no commissions at all, but a straight salary. Paying most or all of a salesperson's compensation in the form of salary frees the salesperson to focus on developing customer goodwill. Paying most or all of a salesperson's compensation in the form of commissions encourages the salesperson to focus on closing sales. In this way, differences in salespeople's compensation directly influence how they spend their time, how they treat customers, and how much the organization sells.

The nature of salespeople's compensation also affects the kinds of people who will want to take and keep sales jobs with the organization. Hard-driving, ambitious, risk-taking salespeople might enjoy the potential rewards of a straight commission plan. An organization that wants salespeople to concentrate on listening to customers and building relationships might want to attract a different kind of salesperson by offering more of the pay in the form of a salary. Basing part or all of a salesperson's pay on commissions assumes that the organization wants to attract people with some willingness to take risks—probably a reasonable assumption about people whose job includes talking to strangers and encouraging them to spend money.

LO3
Identify ways to recognize group performance.

PAY FOR GROUP PERFORMANCE

Employers may address the drawbacks of individual incentives by including group incentives in the organization's compensation plan. To win group incentives, employees must cooperate and share knowledge so that the entire group can meet its performance targets. As shown in Figure 12.4, common group incentives include gainsharing, bonuses, and team awards.

Gainsharing

gainsharing
Group incentive program that measures improvements in productivity and effectiveness and distributes a portion of each gain to employees.

Organizations that want employees to focus on efficiency may adopt a **gainsharing** program, which measures increases in productivity and effectiveness and distributes a portion of each gain to employees. For example, if a factory enjoys a productivity gain worth $30,000, half the gain might be the company's share. The other $15,000 would be distributed among the employees in the factory. Knowing that they can enjoy a financial benefit from helping the company be more productive, employees supposedly will look for ways to work more efficiently and improve the way the factory operates.

Gainsharing addresses the challenge of identifying appropriate performance measures for complex jobs. For example, how would a hospital measure the production of its nurses—in terms of satisfying patients, keeping costs down, or completing a number of tasks? Each of these measures oversimplifies the complex responsibilities involved in nursing care. Even for simpler jobs, setting acceptable standards and measuring performance can be complicated. Gainsharing frees employees to determine how to improve their own and their group's performance. It also broadens employees' focus beyond their individual interests. But in contrast to profit sharing, discussed

Figure 12.4

Types of Pay for Group Performance

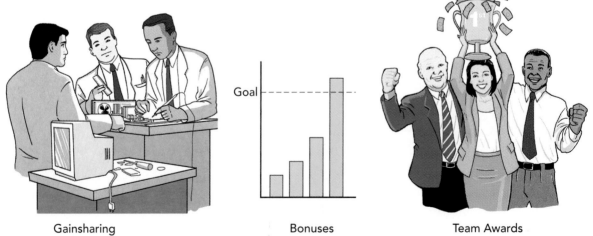

Gainsharing
• Scanlon plans
• Rucker plans
• Improshare programs

Goal

Bonuses

Team Awards

later, it keeps the performance measures within a range of activity that most employees believe they can influence. Organizations can enhance the likelihood of a gain by providing a means for employees to share knowledge and make suggestions, as we will discuss in the last section of this chapter.

Gainsharing is most likely to succeed when organizations provide the right conditions. Among the conditions identified, the following are among the most common:[18]

- Management commitment.
- Need for change or strong commitment to continuous improvement.
- Management acceptance and encouragement of employee input.
- High levels of cooperation and interaction.
- Employment security.
- Information sharing on productivity and costs.
- Goal setting.
- Commitment of all involved parties to the process of change and improvement.
- Performance standard and calculation that employees understand and consider fair and that is closely related to managerial objectives.
- Employees who value working in groups.

Gainsharing plans have many variations. Among the most widely used gainsharing plans are Scanlon plans, Rucker plans, and Improshare programs.

Scanlon Plans

A popular form of gainsharing is the **Scanlon plan,** developed in the 1930s by Joseph N. Scanlon, president of a union local at Empire Steel and Tin Plant in Mansfield, Ohio. The Scanlon plan gives employees a bonus if the ratio of labor costs to the sales value of production is below a set standard. To keep this ratio low enough to earn the bonus, workers have to keep labor costs to a minimum and produce as much as possible with that amount of labor. Figure 12.5 provides an example. In this example, the standard is a ratio of 20/100, or 20 percent, and the workers produced parts worth $1.2 million. To meet the standard, the labor costs should be less than 20 percent of $1.2 million, or $240,000. Since the actual labor costs were $210,000, the workers will get a gainsharing bonus based on the $30,000 difference between the $240,000 target and the actual cost.

Typically, an organization does not pay workers all of the gain immediately. First, the organization keeps a share of the gain to improve its own bottom line. A portion

Scanlon plan
A gainsharing program in which employees receive a bonus if the ratio of labor costs to the sales value of production is below a set standard.

$$\text{Target Ratio: } \frac{\text{Labor Costs}}{\text{Sales Value of Production}} = \frac{20}{100}$$

Sales Value of Production: $1,200,000

Goal: $\dfrac{20}{100} \times \$1,200,000 = \$240,000$

Actual: $210,000

Gain: $240,000 − $210,000 = $30,000

Figure 12.5

Finding the Gain in a Scanlon Plan

SOURCE: Example adapted from B. Graham-Moore and Timothy L. Ross, *Gainsharing: Plans for Improving Performance* (Washington, DC: Bureau of National Affairs, 1990), p. 57.

of the remainder goes into a reserve account. This account offsets losses in any months when the gain is negative (that is, when costs rise or production falls). At the end of the year, the organization closes out the account and distributes any remaining surplus. If there were a loss at the end of the year, the organization would absorb it.

Rucker Plans

Rucker plan
A gainsharing program in which the ratio measuring the gain compares labor costs to the value added in production (output minus the cost of materials, supplies, and services).

A **Rucker plan** is similar to a Scanlon plan but takes a broader view of production expenses. The ratio used as a basis for measuring the gain takes into account the use of materials, supplies, and services. These production costs are subtracted from production output to find the *value added* in production. The Rucker plan formula measures the ratio of labor costs to value added; the organization then shares gains in this ratio with employees. Since workers can improve the ratio by reducing any production costs (not just the cost of labor), as well as by increasing output, this plan offers an incentive to reduce production-related costs such as wasteful use of supplies. As with the Scanlon plan, the organization keeps a share of the gain, places a portion in a reserve account, and distributes the rest to the employees in the group.

Improshare

Improshare
A gainsharing program in which the gain is the decrease in the labor hours needed to produce one unit of product, with the gains split equally between the organization and its employees.

Industrial engineer Mitchell Fein devised a form of gainsharing he called **Improshare**, a shortened form of "improved productivity through sharing." An Improshare program is similar to a standard hour plan. The organization measures the labor hours needed to produce one unit of product. Gains in this measure—that is, the hours saved in production—are the basis for computing a bonus to be split equally between the organization and its employees.

To implement an Improshare program, the organization would use engineering procedures to determine how long it takes to produce a unit of product. Applying this rate to the amount produced, the organization establishes a baseline number of hours. If the group produces more than this baseline amount, the difference is the gain to be shared between organization and employees. Like the individual incentive of a piecework rate, Improshare focuses strictly on quantity. In contrast to piecework, Improshare counts not only production workers' time, but also the indirect hours of management and support staff. This gives employees an incentive to cooperate to get the job done.

Group Bonuses and Team Awards

In contrast to gainsharing plans, which typically reward the performance of all employees at a facility, bonuses for group performance tend to be for smaller work groups.[19] These bonuses reward the members of a group for attaining a specific goal, usually measured in terms of physical output. Team awards are similar to group bonuses, but they are more likely to use a broad range of performance measures, such as cost savings, successful completion of a project, or even meeting deadlines.

Both types of incentives have the advantage that they encourage group or team members to cooperate so that they can achieve their goal. However, depending on the reward system, competition among individuals may be replaced by competition among groups. Competition may be healthy in some situations, as when groups try to outdo one another in satisfying customers. On the downside, competition may also prevent necessary cooperation among groups. To avoid this, the organization should carefully set the performance goals for these incentives so that concern for costs or sales does not obscure other objectives, such as quality, customer service, and ethical behavior.

Group members that meet a sales goal or a product development team that meets a deadline or successfully launches a product may be rewarded with a bonus for group performance. What are some advantages and disadvantages of group bonuses?

PAY FOR ORGANIZATIONAL PERFORMANCE

Two important ways organizations measure their performance are in terms of their profits and their stock price. In a competitive marketplace, profits result when an organization is efficiently providing products that customers want at a price they are willing to pay. Stock is the owners' investment in a corporation; when the stock price is rising, the value of that investment is growing. Rather than trying to figure out what performance measures will motivate employees to do the things that generate high profits and a rising stock price, many organizations offer incentive pay tied to those organizational performance measures. The expectation is that employees will focus on what is best for the organization.

These organization-level incentives can motivate employees to align their activities with the organization's goals. For example, when Harry Kraemer joined Baxter International as chief financial officer, he observed that the executives in charge of the company's divisions operated so independently that Baxter lacked focus. To align the executives' efforts, Kraemer directed the company to change its incentive pay policy. Instead of relying on bonuses linked to divisional results, Baxter encouraged managers to purchase the company's stock and later began granting stock options to all employees.[20]

Linking incentives to the organization's profits or stock price exposes employees to a high degree of risk. Profits and stock price can soar very high very fast, but they can also fall. The result is a great deal of uncertainty about the amount of incentive pay each employee will receive in each period. Therefore, these kinds of incentive pay are likely to be most effective in organizations that emphasize growth and innovation, which tend to need employees who thrive in a risk-taking environment.[21]

LO4
Explain how organizations link pay to their overall performance.

Profit Sharing

Under **profit sharing,** payments are a percentage of the organization's profits and do not become part of the employees' base salary. For example, General Motors provides for profit sharing in its contract with its workers' union, the United Auto Workers. Depending on how large GM's profits are in relation to its total sales for the year, at least 6 percent of the company's profits are divided among the workers according to how many hours they worked during the year.[22] The formula for computing and dividing the profit-sharing bonus is included in the union contract.

Organizations use profit sharing for a number of reasons. It may encourage employees to think more like owners, taking a broad view of what they need to do in order to

profit sharing
Incentive pay in which payments are a percentage of the organization's profits and do not become part of the employees' base salary.

make the organization more effective. They are more likely to cooperate and less likely to focus on narrow self-interests. Also, profit sharing has the practical advantage of costing less when the organization is experiencing financial difficulties. If the organization has little or no profit, this incentive pay is small or nonexistent, so employers may not need to rely as much on layoffs to reduce costs.[23]

Does profit sharing help organizations perform better? The evidence is not yet clear. Although research supports a link between profit-sharing payments and profits, researchers have questioned which of these causes the other.[24] For example, Ford, Chrysler, and GM have similar profit-sharing plans in their contracts with the United Auto Workers, but the payouts are not always similar. In one year, the average worker received $4,000 from Ford, $550 from GM, and $8,000 from Chrysler. Since the plans are similar, something other than the profit sharing must have made Ford and Chrysler more profitable than GM.

Differences in payouts, as in the preceding example, raise questions not only about the effectiveness of the plans, but about equity. Assuming workers at Ford, Chrysler, and GM have similar jobs, they would expect to receive similar profit-sharing checks. In the year of this example, GM workers might have seen their incentive pay as highly inequitable unless GM could show how Chrysler workers did more to earn their big checks. Employees also may feel that small profit-sharing checks are unfair because they have little control over profits. If profit sharing is offered to all employees but most employees think only management decisions about products, price, and marketing have much impact on profits, they will conclude that there is little connection between their actions and their rewards. In that case, profit-sharing plans will have little impact on employee behavior. This problem is even greater when employees have to wait months before profits are distributed. The time lag between high-performance behavior and financial rewards is simply too long to be motivating.

An organization setting up a profit-sharing plan should consider what to do if profits fall. If the economy slows and profit-sharing payments disappear along with profits, employees may become discouraged or angry. Mission Controls Automation counters this problem with open sharing of information and a commitment to avoid layoffs whenever possible. The engineering firm, located in Costa Mesa, California, gives employees profit-sharing payments when business is profitable. When economic conditions sour, employees understand what is happening and how they can make a difference. Management calls everyone together for twice-a-year financial meetings to explain the company's performance, and employees elect representatives to the company's board of directors. The company's three founders work in cubicles alongside everyone else, so any employee can stop in with questions or ideas. During the 2001 economic slowdown, the founders took a pay cut, but the company still struggled to avoid layoffs. Employees volunteered for pay cuts instead, and they also aggressively cut costs and hunted for new business. Eventually, the company returned to its previous strong growth, thanks to the commitment of its people.[25] The open sharing of information supports the profit-sharing incentive at Mission Controls because employees understand the connection between what they are doing and how well the company performs—as well as the impact of the business cycle—so the program seems fair.

Given the limitations of profit-sharing plans, one strategy is to use them as a component of a pay system that includes other kinds of pay more directly linked to individual behavior. This increases employees' commitment to organizational goals while addressing concerns about fairness.

ANSON INDUSTRIES EMPLOYEES THINK THE WAY OWNERS DO: THAT'S WHAT THEY ARE

Many employees receive stock as part of their compensation, but Anson Industries takes the practice to the extreme. The Chicago construction company's employees own all of the company's stock. Anson has been employee owned since 1954, when its former owners retired. To keep the company running, they offered Anson's managers the opportunity to buy the stock. The managers arranged to do so, and they made a rule that only employees would be allowed to make future stock purchases. Every two years, the company makes additional stock available for purchase. (Employees also receive cash bonuses and a profit-sharing program invested in a broad base of stocks and bonds.)

Although only a few managers were in the early group that bought Anson Industries stock, today 95 percent of the company's full-time salaried employees are shareholders. Most employees hold on to the stock until they leave the company for retirement or a job elsewhere.

Owning shares in Anson Industries fosters loyalty. One administrative assistant has purchased shares over the course of three decades. She now has thousands of shares worth hundreds of thousands of dollars and says her relationship with Anson is "a lifetime career." Managers find that they make decisions with extra care, knowing that many of their employees have invested heavily in the company.

Employee ownership also keeps employees focused on the company's long-term success. Benefits manager Carol Haisoch, whose career at Anson spans more than 40 years, says owning stock in the company gives employees an added level of commitment: "You're not just doing your job and going home. . . . Everyone here has the same attitude because it's our money." Similarly, salesman Ryan Till works long hours and weekends with customers. He says employee ownership makes the difference for him: "It helps to motivate you that last little bit, just when you're starting to think, 'Why am I here?'"

Anson's chief financial officer, Dave Brueggen, notes that the stock purchase program has an additional incentive. Many companies give managers stock options, which contribute to their wealth. But Anson gives employees the ability to make purchases with their own money. The act of investing their money, rather than receiving an "extra," intensifies the commitment to making that investment pay off over the long term. So far, that incentive is working. Anson Industries' stock has grown in value even through the recent economic downturn, with only two dips in value over the past 35 years.

SOURCE: Andrew Blackman, "You're the Boss," *The Wall Street Journal*, April 11, 2005, http://online.wsj.com.

Stock Ownership

While profit-sharing plans are intended to encourage employees to "think like owners," a stock ownership plan actually makes employees part owners of the organization. Like profit sharing, employee ownership is intended as a way to encourage employees to focus on the success of the organization as a whole. The "Best Practices" box describes how employee ownership has motivated the employees of Anson Industries, a construction company. The drawbacks of stock ownership as a form of incentive pay are similar to those of profit sharing. Specifically, it may not have a strong effect on individuals' motivation. Employees may not see a strong link between their actions and the company's stock price, especially in larger organizations. The link between pay and performance is even harder to appreciate because the financial benefits mostly come when the stock is sold—typically when the employee leaves the organization.

Ownership programs usually take the form of *stock options* or *employee stock ownership plans*. These are illustrated in Figure 12.6.

Stock Options

stock options
Rights to buy a certain number of shares of stock at a specified price.

One way to distribute stock to employees is to grant them **stock options**—the right to buy a certain number of shares of stock at a specified price. (Purchasing the stock is called *exercising* the option.) Suppose that in 2000 a company's employees received options to purchase the company's stock at $10 per share. The employees will benefit if the stock price rises above $10 per share, because they can pay $10 for something (a share of stock) that is worth more than $10. If in 2005 the stock is worth $30, they can exercise their options and buy stock for $10 a share. If they want to, they can sell their stock for the market price of $30, receiving a gain of $20 for each share of stock. Of course, stock prices can also fall. If the 2005 stock price is only $8, the employees would not bother to exercise the options.

Traditionally, organizations have granted stock options to their executives. During the 1990s, many organizations pushed eligibility for options further down in the organization's structure. As Figure 12.7 shows, the share of companies granting stock options to at least half of their employees has grown from less than one-quarter to more than half. Wal-Mart and PepsiCo are among the large companies that have granted stock options to employees at all levels. Stock options were a popular way to lure employees to Internet start-ups during the last decade. Stock values were rising so fast during the 1990s that options were extremely rewarding for a time. But when stock prices tumbled in the current decade, options lost their attractiveness as a way to reward employees at all levels.

Some studies suggest that organizations perform better when a large percentage of top and middle managers are eligible for long-term incentives such as stock options. This evidence is consistent with the idea of encouraging employees to think like owners.[26] It is not clear whether these findings would hold up for lower-level employees. They may see much less opportunity to influence the company's performance in the stock market.

Recent scandals have drawn attention to another challenge of using stock options as incentive pay. As with other performance measures, employees may focus so much on stock price that they lose sight of other goals, including ethical behavior. Ideally, managers would bring about an increase in stock price by adding value in terms of ef-

Figure 12.6

Types of Pay for Organizational Performance

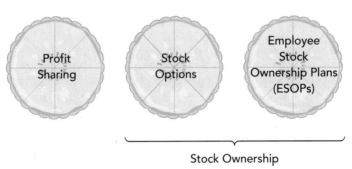

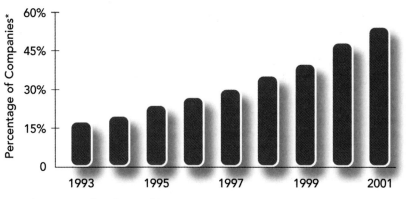

Figure 12.7

Share of Large Corporations Granting Stock Options to at Least Half Their Employees

*Based on a survey of 350 large, public companies.

SOURCE: From *The Wall Street Journal Online* by G. Hitt and J. M. Schlesinger, "Perk Police: Stock Options Come under Fire in Wake of Enron's Collapse," March 26, 2002, by Dow Jones & Co., Inc. Reproduced by permission of Dow Jones & Co., Inc. Copyright Clearance Center.

ficiency, innovation, and customer satisfaction. But there are other, unethical ways to increase stock price by tricking investors into thinking the organization is more valuable and more profitable than it actually is. Hiding losses and inflating the recorded value of revenues are just two of the ways some companies have boosted stock prices, enriching managers until these misdeeds come to light. The 2002 bankruptcy of WorldCom demonstrated on a massive scale that the short-term benefits of an inflated stock price may not be in a company's long-term best interests.

Employee Stock Ownership Plans

While stock options are most often used with top management, a broader arrangement is the **employee stock ownership plan (ESOP).** In an ESOP, the organization distributes shares of stock to its employees by placing the stock into a trust managed on the employees' behalf. Employees receive regular reports on the value of their stock, and when they leave the organization, they may sell the stock to the organization or (if it is a publicly traded company) on the open market.

ESOPs are the most common form of employee ownership, with the number of employees in such plans increasing from over 3 million in 1980 to 10 million in 2005 in the United States.[27] The "Did You Know . . . ?" box shows the growth in the number of ESOPs in the United States. In Japan, 91 percent of companies listed on Japanese stock markets have an ESOP, and these companies appear to have higher average productivity than non-ESOP companies.[28] One reason for ESOPs' popularity in the United States is that earnings of the trust holdings are exempt from income taxes.

ESOPs raise a number of issues. On the negative side, they carry a significant risk for employees. By law, an ESOP must invest at least 51 percent of its assets in the company's own stock (in contrast to other kinds of stock funds that hold a wide diversity of companies). Problems with the company's performance therefore can take away significant value from the ESOP. Many companies set up ESOPs to hold retirement funds, so these risks directly affect employees' retirement income. Adding to the risk, funds in an ESOP are not guaranteed by the Pension Benefit Guarantee Corporation (described in Chapter 13). Sometimes employees use an ESOP to buy their company when it is experiencing financial problems; this is a highly risky investment.

Still, ESOPs can be attractive to employers. Along with tax and financing advantages, ESOPs give employers a way to build pride in and commitment to the organization.

employee stock ownership plan (ESOP)
An arrangement in which the organization distributes shares of stock to all its employees by placing it in a trust.

USE OF ESOPS HAS SURGED OVER 30 YEARS

There are nearly seven times as many ESOPs today as there were in 1975. In recent years, smaller companies have set up ESOPs, so the number of plans has grown faster than the number of individuals who participate in them.

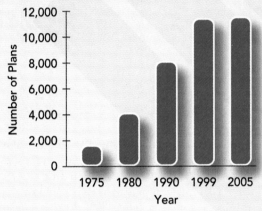

SOURCE: National Center for Employee Ownership, "A Statistical Profile of Employee Ownership," Research & Statistics page of NCEO Web site, updated March 2005, www.nceo.org.

Employees have a right to participate in votes by shareholders (if the stock is registered on a national exchange, such as the New York Stock Exchange).[29] This means employees participate somewhat in corporate-level decision making. Still, the overall level of participation in decisions appears to vary significantly among organizations with ESOPs. Some research suggests that the benefits of ESOPs are greatest when employee participation is greatest.[30]

LO5
Describe how organizations combine incentive plans in a "balanced scorecard."

balanced scorecard
A combination of performance measures directed toward the company's long- and short-term goals and used as the basis for awarding incentive pay.

◈ BALANCED SCORECARD

As the preceding descriptions indicate, any form of incentive pay has advantages and disadvantages. For example, relying exclusively on merit pay or other individual incentives may produce a workforce that cares greatly about meeting those objectives but competes to achieve them at the expense of cooperating to achieve organizational goals. Relying heavily on profit sharing or stock ownership may increase cooperation but do little to motivate day-to-day effort or to attract and retain top individual performers. Because of this, many organizations design a mix of pay programs. The aim is to balance the disadvantages of one type of incentive pay with the advantages of another type.

One way of accomplishing this goal is to design a **balanced scorecard**—a combination of performance measures directed toward the company's long- and short-term goals and used as the basis for awarding incentive pay. A corporation would have financial goals to satisfy its stockholders (owners), quality- and price-related goals to

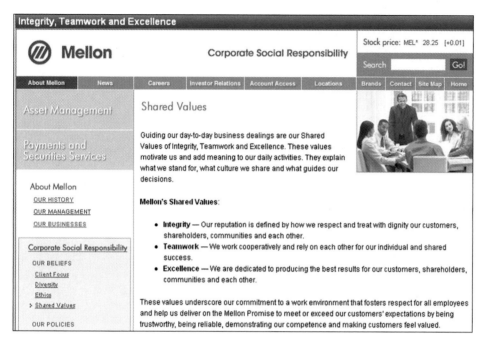

Mellon Financial Corporation has had much success using the balanced scorecard to clarify their vision and strategy and translate them into action. How can a company hope to succeed using the balanced scorecard?

satisfy its customers, efficiency goals to ensure better operations, and goals related to acquiring skills and knowledge for the future to fully tap into employees' potential. Different jobs would contribute to those goals in different ways. For example, an engineer could develop products that better meet customer needs and can be produced more efficiently. The engineer could also develop knowledge of new technologies, in order to contribute more to the organization in the future. A salesperson's goals would include measures related to sales volume, customer service, and learning about product markets and customer needs. Organizations customize their balanced scorecards according to their markets, products, and objectives. The scorecards of a company that is emphasizing low costs and prices would be different from the scorecards of a company emphasizing innovative use of new technology.

Table 12.2 shows the kinds of information that go into a balanced scorecard. This scorecard for a manager in a manufacturing company includes four performance measures. The financial performance measure is return on capital employed (that is, profits divided by capital used during the period). A higher percentage means the capital (money and equipment) generated more profits. The measure of customer satisfaction is product returns. If customers return 1 product out of 1,000, they are better satisfied than if they return 1 product out of 800. The measure of internal operations is the percentage by which the manager's group reduces *cycle time*, the amount of time required to complete the group's process, such as fulfilling an order or getting a new product into production. Finally, the manager's objective for learning and growth in the group is to reduce voluntary turnover among employees. This goal assumes that the manager can develop a more experienced, valuable group of employees by reducing turnover.

For each of these goals, the balanced scorecard assigns a target incentive payment for the manager to earn and four levels of performance. If the manager achieves the top level of performance, the manager will earn 150 percent of the target incentive.

TABLE 12.2

Sample Balanced
Scorecard for a
Production Manager

PERFORMANCE MEASURE	INCENTIVE SCHEDULE		
	TARGET INCENTIVE PER MONTH	PERFORMANCE LEVEL	% TARGET EARNED
Financial • Return on capital employed	$1000	20%+ 16–20% 12–16% Below 12%	150% 100% 50% 0%
Customer • Product returns	$ 400	1 in: 1,000 + 900–999 800–899 Below 800	1 150% 100% 50% 0%
Internal • Cycle time reduction (%)	$ 300	9%+ 6–9% 3–6% 0–3%	150% 100% 50% 0%
Learning and growth • Voluntary employee turnover	$ 300	Below 5% 5–8% 8–12%	150% 100% 50%
Total	$2000		

SOURCE: Adapted from F. C. McKenzie and M. P. Shilling, "Avoiding Performance Traps: Ensuring Effective Incentive Design and Implementation," *Compensation and Benefits Review*, July–August 1998, pp. 57–65. Reprinted with permission of Sage Publications, Inc.

The payout would fall to 100 percent of the incentive for achieving the second level of performance, 50 percent of the incentive for achieving the third level, and nothing for achieving the bottom level. In this example, the manager's target incentive is $2,000 per time period (e.g., per month), but the manager could earn $3,000 per period for exceeding all of the performance objectives—or nothing for failing to achieve all of the objectives.

Not only does the balanced scorecard combine the advantages of different incentive-pay plans, it helps employees understand the organization's goals. By communicating the balanced scorecard to employees, the organization shows employees information about what its goals are and what it expects employees to accomplish. In Table 12.2, for example, the organization not only indicates that the manager should meet the four performance objectives, but also that it is especially concerned with the financial target, because half the incentive is based on this one target.

Tellabs, which provides communication service products around the world, uses a balanced scorecard. The company tracks performance measures such as revenue growth, customer satisfaction, time to market for new products, and employee satisfaction.[31] Each department has objectives that support the goals on the scorecard. Every employee has a bonus plan; bonuses are tied to performance as measured by the objectives. The company conducts quarterly meetings at which employees learn how their performance will be evaluated according to the scorecard. The company also makes this information available on its intranet.

PROCESSES THAT MAKE INCENTIVES WORK

As we explained in Chapter 11, communication and employee participation can contribute to a belief that the organization's pay structure is fair. In the same way, the process by which the organization creates and administers incentive pay can help it use incentives to achieve the goal of motivating employees. The monetary rewards of gainsharing, for example, can substantially improve productivity,[32] but the organization can set up the process to be even more effective. In a study of an automotive parts plant, productivity rose when the gainsharing plan added employee participation in the form of monthly meetings with managers to discuss the gainsharing plan and ways to increase productivity. A related study asked employees what motivated them to participate actively in the plan (for example, by making suggestions for improvement). According to employees, other factors besides the pay itself were important—especially the ability to influence and control the way their work was done.[33]

LO6
Summarize processes that can contribute to the success of incentive programs.

Participation in Decisions

Employee participation in pay-related decisions can be part of a general move toward employee empowerment. If employees are involved in decisions about incentive pay plans and employees' eligibility for incentives, the process of creating and administering these plans can be more complex.[34] There is also a risk that employees will make decisions that are in their interests, at the expense of the organization's interests. However, employees have hands-on knowledge about the kinds of behavior that can help the organization perform well, and they can see whether individuals are displaying that behavior.[35] Therefore, in spite of the potential risks, employee participation can contribute to the success of an incentive plan. This is especially true when monetary incentives encourage the monitoring of performance and when the organization fosters a spirit of trust and cooperation.

Communication

Along with empowerment, communicating with employees is important. It demonstrates to employees that the pay plan is fair. Also, when employees understand the requirements of the incentive pay plan, the plan is more likely to influence their behavior as desired.

It is particularly important to communicate with employees when changing the plan. Employees tend to feel concerned about changes. Pay is a frequent topic of rumors and assumptions based on incomplete information, partly because of pay's importance to employees. When making any changes, the human resource department should determine the best ways to communicate the reasons for the change. Some organizations rely heavily on videotaped messages from the chief executive officer. Other means of communication include brochures that show examples of how employees will be affected. The human resource department may also conduct small-group interviews to learn about employees' concerns, then address those concerns in the communications effort.

INCENTIVE PAY FOR EXECUTIVES

Because executives have a much stronger influence over the organization's performance than other employees do, incentive pay for executives warrants special attention. Assuming that incentives influence performance, decisions about incentives for

LO7
Discuss issues related to performance-based pay for executives.

executives should have a great impact on how well the executives and the organization perform. Along with overall pay levels for executives (discussed in Chapter 11), organizations need to create incentive plans for this small but important group of employees.

To encourage executives to develop a commitment to the organization's long-term success, executive compensation often combines short-term and long-term incentives. *Short-term incentives* include bonuses based on the year's profits, return on investment, or other measures related to the organization's goals. Sometimes, to gain tax advantages, the actual payment of the bonus is deferred (for example, by making it part of a retirement plan). *Long-term incentives* include stock options and stock purchase plans. The rationale for these long-term incentives is that executives will want to do what is best for the organization because that will cause the value of their stock to grow.

Each year *BusinessWeek* publishes a list of top executives who did the most for their pay (that is, their organizations performed best) and those who did the least. The performance of the latter group has prompted much of the negative attention that executive pay has received. The problem seems to be that in some organizations, the chief executive's pay is high every year, regardless of the organization's profitability or performance in the stock market. In terms of people's judgments about equity, it seems fairer if high-paid executives must show results to justify their pay levels.

A corporation's shareholders—its owners—want the corporation to encourage managers to act in the owners' best interests. They want managers to care about the company's profits and stock price, and incentive pay can encourage this interest. One way to achieve these goals is to tie a large share of executives' pay to performance. In the *BusinessWeek* survey we discussed in Chapter 11, almost 80 percent of chief executives' pay comes in the form of stock options and other incentive pay based on long-term performance objectives. Another study has found that relying on such long-term incentives is associated with greater profitability.[36]

Performance Measures for Executives

The balanced-scorecard approach is useful in designing executive pay. Whirlpool, for example, has used a balanced scorecard that combines measures of whether the organization is delivering value to shareholders, customers, and employees. These measures are listed in Table 12.3.

TABLE 12.3

Balanced Scorecard for Whirlpool Executives

TYPE OF VALUE CREATION	MEASURES
Shareholder value	Economic value added
	Earnings per share
	Cash flow
	Total cost productivity
Customer value	Quality
	Market share
	Customer satisfaction
Employee value	High-performance culture index
	High-performance culture deployment
	Training and development diversity

SOURCE: E. L. Gubman, *The Talent Solution* (New York: McGraw-Hill, 1998).

Warren Buffet must be doing something right. In 2004, the billionaire was ranked by *BusinessWeek* magazine as being the top executive who gave shareholders the most for their pay.

Rewarding achievement of a variety of goals in a balanced scorecard reduces the temptation to win bonuses by manipulating financial data. Fannie Mae, the organization that funds home mortgages, rewarded former chief executive Franklin Raines with large incentives for meeting goals for earnings growth. Then federal regulators found problems with Fannie Mae's accounting practices, and Raines retired. In response to the scandal, the organization began tying bonuses to additional performance measures, such as making financing available for affordable housing.[37]

Regulators and shareholders have pressured companies to do a better job of linking executive pay and performance. The Securities and Exchange Commission (SEC) has required companies to more clearly report executive compensation levels and the company's performance relative to that of competitors. These reporting requirements shine a light on situations where executives of poorly performing companies receive high pay, so companies feel more pressure to link pay to performance. Some forms of incentive pay also have tax advantages. Under the Omnibus Budget Reconciliation Act of 1993, companies may not deduct executive pay that exceeds $1 million, but performance-related pay (including stock options) is exempt, so it is deductible even over $1 million.

Ethical Issues

Incentive pay for executives lays the groundwork for significant ethical issues. When an organization links pay to its stock performance, executives need the ethical backbone to be honest about their company's performance even when dishonesty or clever shading of the truth offers the tempting potential for large earnings. As recent scandals involving WorldCom, Enron, Global Crossing, and other companies have shown, the results can be disastrous when unethical behavior comes to light.

Among these issues is one we have already touched on in this chapter: the difficulty of setting performance measures that encourage precisely the behavior desired. In the case of incentives tied to stock performance, executives may be tempted to inflate the stock price in order to enjoy bonuses and valuable stock options. The intent is for the executive to boost stock value through efficient operations, technological innovation, effective leadership, and so on. Unfortunately, individuals at some companies determined that they could obtain faster results through accounting practices that stretched the norms in order to present the company's performance in the best light. When such practices are discovered to be misleading, stock prices plunge and the company's reputation is damaged, sometimes beyond repair.

A related issue when executive pay includes stock or stock options is insider trading. When executives are stockholders, they have a dual role as owners and managers. This places them at an advantage over others who want to invest in the company. An individual, a pension fund, or other investors have less information about the company than its managers do—for example, whether product development is proceeding on schedule, whether a financing deal is in the works, and so on. An executive who knows about these activities could therefore reap a windfall in the stock market by buying or selling stock based on knowledge about the company's future. The SEC places strict limits on this "insider trading," but some executives have violated these limits. In the worst cases executives have sold stock, secretly knowing their company was failing, before the stock price collapsed. The losers are the employees, retirees, and other investors who hold the now-worthless stock.

As recent news stories have reminded us, linking pay to stock price can reward unethical behavior, at least in the short term and at least in the minds of a handful of executives. Yet, given the motivational power of incentive pay, organizations cannot afford to abandon incentives for their executives. These temptations are among the reasons that executive positions demand individuals who maintain the highest ethical standards.

thinking ETHICALLY

Rewards for Cheaters?

In Chapter 11, we considered the risk that compensation practices could give executives an incentive to behave unethically. That risk is not limited to executives, of course. Whenever rewards are linked to performance, the temptation exists to make the performance look better than it really is.

Recently, that issue has played out in the domain of primary education. Under the federal No Child Left Behind law, schools are rewarded or punished based on how well children perform on standardized tests. So, administrators put teachers under pressure to meet the standards. In some states, teachers' bonuses are linked to students' test scores. Evidence suggests that some teachers have coped with that pressure by cheating—for example, changing answers or coaching students during tests. In Boston, an elementary-school principal was suspended after a group of students and their teacher said she encouraged the students to cheat. In the state of Washington, a teacher was reprimanded for showing students answers to the state's math test. During an investigation into charges against that teacher, investigators found that one child's "work" shown for a math problem was "my techre [sic] told me."

Officials have responded to these and hundreds of other complaints. Some states have passed laws against teachers interfering in the testing process. In Pittsburgh, independent monitors began observing tests in schools after several instances of cheating were exposed.

SOURCE: Brian Grow, "A Spate of Cheating—by Teachers," *BusinessWeek*, July 5, 2004, downloaded from Infotrac at http://web6.infotrac.galegroup.com.

Questions

1. In an e-mail message to *BusinessWeek*, former U.S. Education Secretary Rod Paige wrote, "It is simply a disgrace that a small minority of teachers feel the need to cheat and are blaming their own moral failings on No Child Left Behind." Comment on that statement. When teachers or schools are rewarded for high test scores and punished for low scores, whose responsibility is it if teachers manipulate test results?
2. Who is harmed by teachers manipulating test scores?
3. How can states and school districts minimize cheating by teachers? Focus on the ways performance can be rewarded, but note other aspects of human resource management that might apply to the problem.

SUMMARY

1. Discuss the connection between incentive pay and employee performance.

   Incentive pay is pay tied to individual performance, profits, or other measures of success. Organizations select forms of incentive pay to energize, direct, or control employees' behavior. It is influential because the amount paid is linked to predefined behaviors or outcomes. To be effective, incentive pay should encourage the kinds of behavior that are most needed, and employees must believe they have the ability to meet the performance standards. Employees must value the rewards, have the resources they need to meet the standards, and believe the pay plan is fair.

2. Describe how organizations recognize individual performance.

   Organizations may recognize individual performance through such incentives as piecework rates, standard hour plans, merit pay, sales commissions, and bonuses for meeting individual performance objectives. Piecework rates pay employees according to the amount they produce. Standard hour plans pay workers extra for work done in less than a preset "standard time." Merit pay links increases in wages or salaries to ratings on performance appraisals. Bonuses are similar to merit pay, because they are paid for meeting individual goals, but they are not rolled into base pay, and they usually are based on achieving a specific output, rather than subjective performance ratings. A sales commission is incentive pay calculated as a percentage of sales closed by a salesperson.

3. Identify ways to recognize group performance.

   Common group incentives include gainsharing, bonuses, and team awards. A gainsharing program measures increases in productivity and distributes a portion of each gain to employees. Types of gainsharing programs include Scanlon plans, Rucker plans, and Improshare programs. Group bonuses reward the members of a group for at-

   taining a specific goal, usually measured in terms of physical output. Team awards are more likely to use a broad range of performance measures, such as cost savings, successful completion of a project, or meeting a deadline.

4. Explain how organizations link pay to their overall performance.

   Incentives for meeting organizational objectives include profit sharing and stock ownership. Profit-sharing plans pay workers a percentage of the organization's profits; these payments do not become part of the employees' base salary. Stock ownership incentives may take the form of stock options or employee stock ownership plans. A stock option is the right to buy a certain number of shares at a specified price. The employee benefits by exercising the option at a price lower than the market price, so the employee benefits when the company's stock price rises. An employee stock ownership plan (ESOP) is an arrangement in which the organization distributes shares of its stock to employees by placing the stock in a trust managed on the employees' behalf. When employees leave the organization, they may sell their shares of the stock.

5. Describe how organizations combine incentive plans in a "balanced scorecard."

   A balanced scorecard is a combination of performance measures directed toward the company's long- and short-term goals and used as the basis for awarding incentive pay. Typically, it includes financial goals to satisfy stockholders, quality- and price-related goals for customer satisfaction, efficiency goals for improved operations, and goals related to acquiring skills and knowledge for the future. The mix of pay programs is intended to balance the disadvantages of one type of incentive with the advantages of another type. The balanced scorecard also helps employees to understand and care about the organization's goals.

6. Summarize processes that can contribute to the success of incentive programs.

   Communication and participation in decisions can contribute to employees' feeling that the organization's incentive pay plans are fair. Employee participation in pay-related decisions can be part of a general move toward employee empowerment. Employees may put their own interests first in developing the plan, but they also have firsthand insight into the kinds of behavior that can contribute to organizational goals. Communicating with employees is important because it demonstrates that the pay plan is fair and helps them understand what is expected of them. Communication is especially important when the organization is changing its pay plan.

7. Discuss issues related to performance-based pay for executives.

   Because executives have such a strong influence over the organization's performance, incentive pay for them receives special attention. Executive pay usually combines long-term and short-term incentives. By motivating executives, these incentives can significantly affect the organization's performance. The size of incentives should be motivating but also meet standards for equity. Performance measures should encourage behavior that is in the organization's best interests, including ethical behavior. Executives need ethical standards that keep them from insider trading or deceptive practices designed to manipulate the organization's stock price.

REVIEW AND DISCUSSION QUESTIONS

1. With some organizations and jobs, pay is primarily wages or salaries, and with others, incentive pay is more important. For each of the following jobs, state whether you think the pay should emphasize base pay (wages and salaries) or incentive pay (bonuses, profit sharing, and so on). Give a reason for each.
   a. An accountant at a manufacturing company.
   b. A salesperson for a software company.
   c. A chief executive officer.
   d. A physician in a health clinic.

2. Consider your current job or a job that you have recently held. Would you be most motivated in response to incentives based on your individual performance, your group's performance, or the organization's overall performance (profits or stock price)? Why?

3. What are the pros and cons of linking incentive pay to individual performance? How can organizations address the negatives?

4. Suppose you are a human resource professional at a company that is setting up work teams for production and sales. What group incentives would you recommend to support this new work arrangement?

5. Why do some organizations link incentive pay to the organization's overall performance? Is it appropriate to use stock performance as an incentive for employees at all levels? Why or why not?

6. Stock options have been called the pay program that "built Silicon Valley," because of their key role as in-

centive pay for employees in high-tech companies. They were popular during the 1990s, when the stock market was rising rapidly. Since then, stock prices have fallen.
   a. How would you expect this change to affect employees' attitudes toward stock options as incentive pay?
   b. How would you expect this change to affect the effectiveness of stock options as an incentive?

7. Based on the balanced scorecard in Table 12.2, what would be the total incentive paid to a manager if the group's return on capital employed was 12 percent, customers returned 1 product out of every 1,200 products delivered, cycle time was reduced by 5 percent, and employee turnover was 4 percent? (For each measure, find the performance level, then multiply the corresponding percentage by the target incentive to find the incentive earned.)

8. Why might a balanced scorecard like the one in Question 7 be more effective than simply using merit pay for a manager?

9. How can the way an organization creates and carries out its incentive plan improve the effectiveness of that plan?

10. In a typical large corporation, the majority of the chief executive's pay is tied to the company's stock price. What are some benefits of this pay strategy? Some risks? How can organizations address the risks?

WHAT'S YOUR HR IQ?

The text Web site offers two more ways to check what you've learned so far. Use the Self-Assessment exercise to test your money-talk skills. Go online with the Web Exercise to see information on compensation and benefits management.

BusinessWeek CASE

BusinessWeek Reinventing Motorola

It takes Motorola employees about 30 seconds after they meet Edward J. Zander to realize how different their new boss is from their last one. Where Zander's predecessor, Christopher B. Galvin, was reserved, polite, and genteel, Zander is a brash Brooklynite, incessantly pumping hands and flashing his trademark mile-wide smile.

But in March 2004, three months after taking over the chief executive post, Zander showed he also was going to be much more demanding. He gathered his top 20 execs in the company's downtown Chicago offices, some 30 miles from the Schaumburg, Illinois, headquarters, for a two-day brainstorming session on how to improve Motorola's lackluster execution. His message: Employees will be held accountable for customer satisfaction, product quality, and even collaboration among business units. "If you don't cooperate and work together, I will kill you," he said. Today, Zander laughs: "That's surviving-and-growing-up-in-Brooklyn talk. It was my way of saying, 'We're going to fix this thing.'"

Zander is about as affable as CEOs come, but he's deadly serious about restoring Motorola to the top of the communications world. The tech veteran, who spent 15 years at computer giant Sun Microsystems and eventually became its president, is trying to reinvent Motorola as a nimble, unified technology company. His most dramatic effort to date is a plan to dismantle Motorola's debilitating bureaucracy and end a culture of rivalries so intense that Motorola's own employees have referred to its business units as "warring tribes." And he's not leaving it to chance: He has made cooperation a key factor in determining raises and bonuses. "It's a damn different place," says Patrick J. Canavan, a 24-year veteran and Motorola's director for global governance. "Everyone is looking out for everyone else."

The changes are just beginning. Zander has been exploring a major reorganization. By October 2004, Zander hopes to abandon Motorola's stovepipe divisions, which are focused on products like mobile phones and broadband gear, and reorganize operations around customer markets—one for the digital home, for example, and another for corporate buyers.

The reorganization will help Zander deliver on several new initiatives. Perhaps the most important is what the chief executive calls "seamless mobility." The idea is that Motorola should make it easy for consumers to transport any digital information—music, video, e-mail, phone calls—from the house to the car to the workplace. Mastering that technology would do more than boost cellphone sales. It also could make Motorola a key player in the digital home, helping it sell flat-panel TVs and broadband modems, home wireless networks, and gateways to manage digital content. Also, Motorola is planning a major push to sell more services to corporations.

Zander is planning to trim costs by shedding employees, bringing in more handpicked executives to help execute his plans, and reducing the number of separate businesses. Analysts say he is working on a plan that could combine the wireless network unit with the company's broadband division.

Just as important as the structural changes will be the strategy that goes with them. The concept of seamless mobility was born on a flight to France in February 2004, when Zander and his chief technology officer, Padmasree Warrior, were headed to a wireless-industry conference. The strategy has been refined over [recent] months and by senior leaders from Motorola's business units gathered . . . at Motorola University, adjacent to headquarters, to discuss strategies for internal development and potential acquisitions.

The Motorola vision starts with users sitting at home watching, say, the New York Yankees battling the Chicago White Sox. To leave home, they pause the video, transfer it to their phone, walk into the garage, and transfer the video to the car as they drive away. The car would switch to audio so as not to distract the driver and then switch back to video if the driver stops at a traffic light. Motorola has the technology portfolio to pursue the entire scenario. Besides phone and cable set-top boxes, it has a $2.3 billion automotive-electronics business that develops technologies for cars to communicate with outside networks.

The key will be beating rivals to market with innovative solutions. That's why Zander's top priority has been improving execution. The main driver is a new incentive plan. In the past, workers were compensated based on the revenue, profit, and cash generated in their particular sector. If one sector did well, its employees pulled in huge bonuses. A unit that did not perform got little or nothing.

Zander has been relentless in trying to get the most out of his staff. A new bonus plan bases 25 percent on three key areas: customer satisfaction, product reliability, and the cost of poor quality. When the heads of each business unit first laid out their targets, Zander's no-nonsense roots showed: "You're sandbagging," he barked. Before long, the targets were more difficult. "We're driving for improvement year over year," says Michael J. Fenger, a vet Zander picked to improve corporate quality.

Source: Excerpted from Roger O. Crockett, "Reinventing Motorola," *BusinessWeek*, August 9, 2004, downloaded from Infotrac at http://web6.infotrac.galegroup.com.

Questions

1. Briefly summarize Motorola's goals, as described in this case. How is the company's incentive pay intended to support those goals?
2. Consider the situation of a Motorola manager whose group has been receiving large bonuses because the group works in an industry sector that has been growing rapidly. Now a large part of the group's bonuses will be based on new measures, like customer satisfaction and product reliability. How would you expect this manager to react to the changes? As a member of the HR team responsible for compensation, how could you prepare for and handle the expected response?
3. How would you expect the situation to differ with a manager whose group operates in a slow-growth industry sector? How would you prepare for and handle this response?

CASE: Microsoft Abandons Stock Options

As Microsoft Corporation became hugely successful, many of its employees became rich. One important source of their wealth was incentive pay in the form of stock options. The company would issue the options to employees, and as the value of Microsoft stock rose, the employees exercised the options to receive an immediate return and then realize enormous returns over time.

Options were extremely motivating through the 1990s because they give a right to buy stock at a fixed price. The stock price of Microsoft and other technology companies rose so fast that exercising options was extremely profitable. But when stock prices dropped in 2000 and afterward, options became worthless. It doesn't pay to exercise an option if the stock price is less than the exercise price; you would lose money on the deal.

From a high of $59.56 near the end of 1999, share prices for Microsoft tumbled during the following year to a price near $20 per share. Since then, prices have roughly ranged between $25 and $30 a share. In response to this situation, Microsoft in 2003 announced that it would no longer reward employees with stock options. Instead, it began using restricted stock, meaning shares of stock that employees could sell only at a specified point in the future and only if they still worked for Microsoft. The use of stock instead of stock options avoids the risk of options being worthless if stock prices don't rise fast enough to make the exercise price profitable. The move away from stock options signals that the company does not expect a return to the fast-growth 1990s. In the words of Microsoft's chief financial officer, John Connors, "If you think what happened in the nineties is going to happen again—it's not."

Recognizing that the personal computer industry in general and Microsoft in particular have left the early fast-growth days behind, the company's management believes that stock options no longer have a place in the company's performance-based pay. By replacing the stock options with stock grants, the company hopes that employees will continue to be rewarded by the now-mature company's long-term growth and profits.

Because Microsoft, with over 50,000 employees and revenues of almost $37 billion, is such a dominant player in the technology sector, the decision to abandon stock options signals a major change in how technology companies compensate their employees. Exceptions might be start-up companies that expect to grow fast and enjoy rapid growth in their earnings and stock prices. Despite those exceptions, in the two years since Microsoft announced its decision, the use of stock options has been declining in every industry sector. The trend has been accelerated by a recent federal government requirement that companies treat stock options as an expense, an accounting change that reduces a company's reported profits when it issues stock options. For example, Microsoft said that if it had counted stock options as an expense during the nine months ending March 31, 2003, its profits would have been one-fourth less than it had reported. Thus, the new regulations governing stock options can have a major impact on companies' financial reports.

Were stock options just a good idea whose time has passed? One person who evidently disagrees is Microsoft's own chairman, Bill Gates. Gates recently told a *BusinessWeek* reporter, "I actually regret that we ever used [stock options]. There's some benefit, but the approach we're taking now is just a better approach."

SOURCE: Robert A. Guth and Joann S. Lublin, "Microsoft Ushers Out Golden Era of Options," *The Wall Street Journal*, July 9, 2003; "MSFT Stock Chart," *MSN Money*, http://moneycentral.msn.com, accessed May 31, 2005; Microsoft Corporation, "Microsoft Reports Strong Fourth Quarter Earnings," news release, July 22, 2004, www.microsoft.com; Ira Sager, "Gates: Good Riddance to Options," *BusinessWeek*, May 16, 2005, p. 10; and Louis Lavelle, "Are Options Headed for Extinction?" *BusinessWeek*, May 2, 2005, downloaded from Infotrac at http://web3.infotrac.galegroup.com.

Questions

1. In general, stock options are most valuable if the stock price rises above the exercise price during the life of the option, and stock grants are most valuable if the stock's value rises during the entire time the person owns the stock. From the point of view of an employee receiving stock options or stock grants, is this difference significant? Would this difference affect the kind of motivation provided to Microsoft's employees?
2. Why do you think Bill Gates expressed "regret" for using stock options to reward employees? What draw-

backs of stock options might he have been thinking about?

3. In terms of skills, abilities, and other qualities, what kinds of employees would be most valuable to

Microsoft? Besides stock, what other forms of pay would you recommend Microsoft use to attract and keep the kinds of people you identified?

NOTES

1. S. J. Wells, "No Results, No Raise," *HRMagazine*, May 2005, downloaded from Infotrac at http://web6.infotrac.galegroup.com.

2. This chapter draws freely on several literature reviews: B. Gerhart and G. T. Milkovich, "Employee Compensation: Research and Practice," in *Handbook of Industrial and Organizational Psychology*, vol. 3, 2nd ed., ed. M. D. Dunnette and L. M. Hough (Palo Alto, CA: Consulting Psychologists Press, 1992); and B. Gerhart and S. L. Rynes, *Compensation: Theory, Evidence, and Strategic Implications* (Thousand Oaks, CA: Sage, 2003).

3. B. Gerhart and G. T. Milkovich, "Organizational Differences in Managerial Compensation and Financial Performance," *Academy of Management Journal* 33 (1990), pp. 663–91.

4. G. T. Milkovich and A. K. Wigdor, *Pay for Performance* (Washington, DC: National Academy Press, 1991); Gerhart and Milkovich, "Employee Compensation"; C. Trevor, B. Gerhart, and J. W. Boudreau, "Voluntary Turnover and Job Performance: Curvilinearity and the Moderating Influences of Salary Growth and Promotions," *Journal of Applied Psychology* 82 (1997), pp. 44–61.

5. "Who's Answering the Phone? Your Company's Fortunes Hang on It," *Gallup Management Journal*, Fall 2001.

6. E. Tahmincioglu, "Gifts That Gall, Part 1 of 2," *Workforce Management*, April 2004, downloaded from Infotrac at http://web7.infotrac.galegroup.com.

7. Ibid.

8. R. D. Bretz, R. A. Ash, and G. F. Dreher, "Do People Make the Place? An Examination of the Attraction-Selection-Attrition Hypothesis," *Personnel Psychology* 42 (1989), pp. 561–81; T. A. Judge and R. D. Bretz, "Effect of Values on Job Choice Decisions," *Journal of Applied Psychology* 77 (1992), pp. 261–71; D. M. Cable and T. A. Judge, "Pay Performance and Job Search Decisions: A Person-Organization Fit Perspective," *Personnel Psychology* 47 (1994), pp. 317–48.

9. E. A. Locke, D. B. Feren, V. M. McCaleb, K. N. Shaw, and A. T. Denny, "The Relative Effectiveness of Four Methods of Motivating Employee Performance," in *Changes in Working Life*, ed. K. D. Duncan, M. M. Gruenberg, and D. Wallis (New York: Wiley, 1980), pp. 363–88.

10. Gerhart and Milkovich, "Employee Compensation."

11. E. E. Lawler III, "Pay for Performance: A Strategic Analysis," in *Compensation and Benefits*, ed. L. R. Gomez-Mejia (Washington, DC: Bureau of National Affairs, 1989); A. M. Konrad and J. Pfeffer, "Do You Get What You Deserve? Factors Affecting the Relationship between Productivity and Pay," *Administrative Science Quarterly* 35 (1990), pp. 258–85; J. L. Medoff and K. G. Abraham, "Are Those Paid More Really More Productive? The Case of Experience," *Journal of Human Resources* 16 (1981), pp. 186–216; K. S. Teel, "Are Merit Raises Really Based on Merit?" *Personnel Journal* 65, no. 3 (1986), pp. 88–95.

12. R. D. Bretz, G. T. Milkovich, and W. Read, "The Current State of Performance Appraisal Research and Practice," *Journal of Management* 18 (1992), pp. 321-52; R. L. Heneman, "Merit Pay Research," *Research in Personnel and Human Resource Management* 8 (1990), pp. 203–63; Milkovich and Wigdor, *Pay for Performance*.

13. Bretz et al., "Current State of Performance Appraisal Research."

14. W. E. Deming, *Out of the Crisis* (Cambridge, MA: Center for Advanced Engineering Study, Massachusetts Institute of Technology, 1986), p. 110.

15. D. J. Hanford, "Stay, Please," *The Wall Street Journal Online*, April 12, 2001, http://interactive.wsj.com.

16. J. Bennett, "A Career on Commission Can Be a Hard Sell," *Chicago Tribune*, March 24, 2002, sec. 5, p. 5.

17. S. Greco, "Sales: What Works Now," *Inc.*, February 2002, pp. 52–59.

18. T. L. Ross and R. A. Ross, "Gainsharing: Sharing Improved Performance," in *The Compensation Handbook*, 3rd ed., ed. M. L. Rock and L. A. Berger (New York: McGraw-Hill, 1991).

19. T. M. Welbourne and L. R. Gomez-Mejia, "Team Incentives in the Workplace," in *The Compensation Handbook*, 3rd ed.

20. D. Harbrecht, "Baxter's Harry Kraemer: 'I Don't Golf,'" *BusinessWeek Online*, March 28, 2002, www.businessweek.com (interview with Harry Kraemer Jr.).

21. L. R. Gomez-Mejia and D. B. Balkin, *Compensation, Organizational Strategy, and Firm Performance* (Cincinnati: South-Western, 1992).

22. J. A. Fossum, *Labor Relations* (New York: McGraw-Hill, 2002).

23. This idea has been referred to as the "share economy." See M. L. Weitzman, "The Simple Macroeconomics of Profit Sharing," *American Economic Review* 75 (1985), pp. 937–53. For supportive research, see the following studies: J. Chelius and R. S. Smith, "Profit Sharing and Employment Stability," *Industrial and Labor Relations Review* 43 (1990), pp. 256S–73S; B. Gerhart and L. O. Trevor, "Employment Stability under Different Managerial Compensation Systems," working paper (Cornell University Center for Advanced Human Resource Studies, 1995); D. L. Kruse, "Profit Sharing and Employment Variability: Microeconomic Evidence on the Weitzman Theory," *Industrial and Labor Relations Review* 44 (1991), pp. 437–53.

24. Gerhart and Milkovich, "Employee Compensation"; M. L. Weitzman and D. L. Kruse, "Profit Sharing and Productivity," in *Paying for Productivity*, ed. A. S. Blinder (Washington, DC: Brookings Institution, 1990); D. L. Kruse, *Profit Sharing: Does It Make a Difference?* (Kalamazoo, MI: Upjohn Institute, 1993).

25. Jan Norman, "Engineering Firm Makes Layoffs the Last Option," *Orange County Register*, March 23, 2005, downloaded from Infotrac at http://web7.infotrac.galegroup.com.

26. Gerhart and Milkovich, "Organizational Differences in Managerial Compensation."

27. National Center for Employee Ownership, "A Statistical Profile of Employee Ownership," Research & Statistics page of NCEO Web site, updated March 2005, www.nceo.org.

28. D. Jones and T. Kato, "The Productivity Effects of Employee Stock Ownership Plans and Bonuses: Evidence from Japanese Panel Data," *American Economic Review* 185, no. 3 (June 1995), pp. 391–414.

29. M. A. Conte and J. Svejnar, "The Performance Effects of Employee Ownership Plans," in *Paying for Productivity*, pp. 245–94.

30. Ibid.; T. H. Hammer, "New Developments in Profit Sharing, Gainsharing, and Employee Ownership," in *Productivity in Organizations*, ed. J. P. Campbell, R. J. Campbell, et al. (San Francisco: Jossey-Bass, 1988); K. J. Klein, "Employee Stock Ownership and Employee Attitudes: A Test of Three Models," *Journal of Applied Psychology* 72 (1987), pp. 319–32.

31. E. Raimy, "A Plan for All Seasons," *Human Resource Executive*, April 2001, pp. 34–38.

32. R. T. Kaufman, "The Effects of Improshare on Productivity," *Industrial and Labor Relations Review* 45 (1992), pp. 311–22; M. H. Schuster, "The Scanlon Plan: A Longitudinal Analysis," *Journal of Applied Behavioral Science* 20 (1984), pp. 23–28; J. A. Wagner III, P. Rubin, and T. J. Callahan, "Incentive Payment and Nonmanagerial Productivity: An Interrupted Time Series Analysis of Magnitude and Trend," *Organizational Behavior and Human Decision Processes* 42 (1988), pp. 47–74.

33. C. R. Gowen III and S. A. Jennings, "The Effects of Changes in Participation and Group Size on Gainsharing Success: A Case Study," *Journal of Organizational Behavior Management* 11 (1991), pp. 147–69.

34. D. I. Levine and L. D. Tyson, "Participation, Productivity, and the Firm's Environment," in *Paying for Productivity*.

35. T. Welbourne, D. Balkin, and L. Gomez-Mejia, "Gainsharing and Mutual Monitoring: A Combined Agency–Organizational Justice Interpretation," *Academy of Management Journal* 38 (1995), pp. 881–99.

36. Gerhart and Milkovich, "Organizational Differences in Managerial Compensation."

37. M. K. Ozanian and E. MacDonald, "Paychecks on Steroids," *Forbes*, May 9, 2005, downloaded from Infotrac at http://web7.infotrac.galegroup.com.

CHAPTER 13

PROVIDING EMPLOYEE BENEFITS

What Do I Need to Know?

After reading this chapter, you should be able to:

1. Discuss the importance of benefits as a part of employee compensation.

2. Summarize the types of employee benefits required by law.

3. Describe the most common forms of paid leave.

4. Identify the kinds of insurance benefits offered by employers.

5. Define the types of retirement plans offered by employers.

6. Describe how organizations use other benefits to match employees' wants and needs.

7. Explain how to choose the contents of an employee benefits package.

8. Summarize the regulations affecting how employers design and administer benefits programs.

9. Discuss the importance of effectively communicating the nature and value of benefits to employees.

◈ INTRODUCTION

Hewitt Associates signals to its employees that it cares about them, body, mind, and spirit. Employees participate in plans that help them pay for medical, dental, and vision care expenses, stop-smoking programs, and care expenses for sick children. Employees who travel on business can receive reimbursement for overnight dependent care and overnight care for their pets. Employees enjoy paid time off for vacations and holidays, plus additional "Splash" time off in their fifth year of service and every five years after that. Through the LifeWorks referral service, Hewitt employees can find help with family, education, legal, and financial issues. A tuition reimbursement program pays 85 percent of employees' tuition for approved courses. The company also encourages employees to participate in charitable activities. Employees who wish to volunteer time in their communities can receive up to two days of paid time off. These and other benefits attract qualified employees and keep them loyal to Hewitt.[1]

Like Hewitt's employees, employees at almost every organization receive more than dollars and cents in exchange for their efforts. They also receive a package of **employee benefits**—compensation in forms other than cash. Besides the use of corporate fitness centers, examples include paid vacation time, employer-paid health insurance, and pension plans, among a wide range of possibilities.

This chapter describes the contents of an employee benefits package and the way organizations administer

employee benefits
Compensation in forms other than cash.

employee benefits. We begin by discussing the important role of benefits as a part of employee compensation. The following sections define major types of employee benefits: benefits required by law, paid leave, insurance policies, retirement plans, and other benefits. We then discuss how to choose which of these alternatives to include in an employee benefits package so that it contributes to meeting the organization's goals. The next section summarizes the regulations affecting how employers design and administer benefits programs. Finally, we explain why and how organizations should effectively communicate with employees about their benefits.

LO1
Discuss the importance of benefits as a part of employee compensation.

THE ROLE OF EMPLOYEE BENEFITS

As a part of the total compensation paid to employees, benefits serve functions similar to pay. Benefits contribute to attracting, retaining, and motivating employees. The variety of possible benefits also helps employers tailor their compensation to the kinds of employees they need. Different employees look for different types of benefits. Employers need to examine their benefits package regularly to see whether they meet the needs of today. At the same time, benefits packages are more complex than pay structures, so benefits are harder for employees to understand and appreciate. Even if employers spend large sums on benefits, if employees do not understand how to use them or why they are valuable, the cost of the benefits will be largely wasted.[2] Employers need to communicate effectively so that the benefits succeed in motivating employees.

Employees have come to expect that benefits will help them maintain economic security. Social Security contributions, pensions, and retirement savings plans help employees prepare for their retirement. Insurance plans help to protect employees from unexpected costs such as hospital bills. This important role of benefits is one reason that benefits are subject to government regulation. Some benefits, such as Social Security, are required by law. Other regulations establish requirements that benefits must meet to obtain the most favorable tax treatment. Later in the chapter, we will describe some of the most significant regulations affecting benefits.

Even though many kinds of benefits are not required by law, they have become so common that today's employees expect them. Many employers find that attracting qualified workers requires them to provide medical and retirement benefits of some sort. A large employer without such benefits would be highly unusual and would have difficulty competing in the labor market. Still, the nature of the benefits package changes over time, as we will discuss at various points throughout the chapter.

Like other forms of compensation, benefits impose significant costs. On average, out of every dollar spent on compensation, 30 cents or more go to benefits. As Figure 13.1 shows, this share has grown over the past decades. Data from the Bureau of Labor Statistics show a somewhat smaller share (slightly under 30 percent of total compensation) but also indicate the substantial and increasing cost of employee benefits. These numbers indicate that an organization managing its labor costs must pay careful attention to the cost of its employee benefits.

Why do organizations pay a growing share of compensation in the form of benefits? It would be simpler to pay all compensation in cash and let employees buy their own insurance and contribute to their own savings plans. That arrangement would also give employees greater control over what their compensation buys. However, several forces have made benefits a significant part of compensation packages. One is that laws require employers to provide certain benefits, such as contributions to Social Security and unemployment insurance. Also, tax laws can make benefits favorable. For example, employees do not pay income taxes on most benefits they receive, but

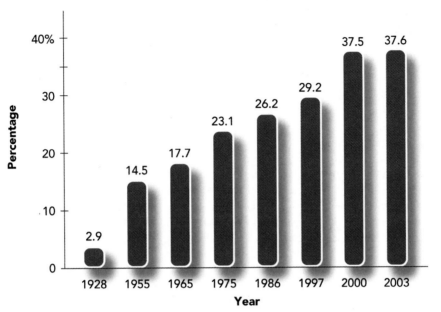

Figure 13.1

Benefits as a
Percentage of Total
Compensation

SOURCE: U.S. Chamber of Commerce, *Employee Benefits 1990, Employee Benefits 1997, Employee Benefits 2000,* and news releases dated January 31, 2003, and January 26, 2005, *www.uschamber.com.*

they pay income taxes on cash compensation. Therefore, an employee who receives a $1,000 raise "takes home" less than the full $1,000, but an employee who receives an additional $1,000 worth of benefits receives the full benefits. Another cost advantage of paying benefits is that employers, especially large ones, often can get a better deal on insurance or other programs than employees can obtain on their own. Finally, some employers assemble creative benefits packages that set them apart in the competition for talent. Examples include Hewitt Associates, described in the Introduction, and the companies that address workers' needs and their own need for efficiency by using prepaid benefits cards, described in the "e-HRM" box.

BENEFITS REQUIRED BY LAW

The federal and state governments require various forms of social insurance to protect workers from the financial hardships of being out of work. In general, Social Security provides support for retired workers, unemployment insurance assists laid-off workers, and workers' compensation insurance provides benefits and services to workers injured on the job. Employers must also provide unpaid leave for certain family and medical needs. Because these benefits are required by law, employers cannot gain an advantage in the labor market by offering them, nor can they design the nature of these benefits. Rather, the emphasis must be on complying with the details of the law. Table 13.1 summarizes legally required benefits.

LO2
Summarize the types of employee benefits required by law.

Social Security

In 1935 the federal Social Security Act established old-age insurance and unemployment insurance. Congress later amended the act to add survivor's insurance (1939), disability insurance (1956), hospital insurance (Medicare Part A, 1965), and supplementary

Social Security
The federal Old Age, Survivors, Disability, and Health Insurance (OASDHI) program, which combines old age (retirement) insurance, survivor's insurance, disability insurance, hospital insurance (Medicare Part A), and supplementary medical insurance (Medicare Part B) for the elderly.

medical insurance (Medicare Part B, 1965) for the elderly. Together, the law and its amendments created what is now the Old Age, Survivors, Disability, and Health Insurance (OASDHI) program, informally known as **Social Security.** This program covers over 90 percent of U.S. employees. The main exceptions are railroad and federal, state, and local government employees, who often have their own plans.

Workers who meet eligibility requirements receive the retirement benefits according to their age and earnings history. If they elect to begin receiving benefits at full retirement age, they can receive full benefits, or if they elect to begin receiving benefits at age 62, they receive benefits at a permanently reduced level. The full retirement age rises with birth year: a person born in 1940 reaches full retirement age at 65 years and 6 months, and a person born in 1960 or later reaches full retirement age at 67. The benefit amount rises with the person's past earnings, but the level goes up very little after a certain level. In 2005, the maximum monthly benefit was $1,939. The government increases the payments each year according to the growth in the consumer price index. Also, spouses of covered earners receive benefits, even if they have no covered earnings. They receive either the benefit associated with their own earnings or one-half of the amount received by the covered earner, whichever is greater.

Benefits may be reduced if the worker is still earning wages above a maximum, called the *exempt amount*. In 2005, the exempt amount was $12,000 for beneficiaries under the full retirement age. A beneficiary in that age range who earns more than

BENEFIT	EMPLOYER REQUIREMENT
Social Security	Flat payroll tax on employees and employers
Unemployment insurance	Payroll tax on employers that depends on state requirements and experience rating
Workers' compensation insurance	Provide coverage according to state requirements. Premiums depend on experience rating
Family and medical leave	Up to 12 weeks of unpaid leave for childbirth, adoption, or serious illness

TABLE 13.1

Benefits Required by Law

the exempt amount sees a reduction in his or her benefit. The amount of the reduction is $1 for every $2 the person earns above the exempt amount. For example a 63-year-old who earned $14,000 in 2005 would have earned $2,000 above the exempt amount, so the person's Social Security benefits would have been reduced by $1,000. During the year a worker reaches full retirement age, the maximum untaxed earnings are $31,800 (in 2005), and benefits are reduced $1 for every $3 in earnings. Beginning in the month they reach full retirement age, workers face no reduction in benefits for earning above the exempt amount. For workers below that age, the penalty increases the incentive to retire or at least reduce the number of hours worked. Adding to this incentive, Social Security benefits are free from federal income taxes and free from state taxes in about half the states.

Employers and employees share the cost of Social Security through a payroll tax. The percentage is set by law and has changed from time to time. In 2005, employers and employees each paid a tax of 7.65 percent on the first $90,000 of the employee's earnings, with 6.2 percent of earnings going to OASDI and 1.45 percent going to Medicare (Part A). For earnings above $90,000, only the 1.45 percent for Medicare is assessed.

Unemployment Insurance

Along with OASDHI, the Social Security Act of 1935 established a program of **unemployment insurance.** This program has four objectives related to minimizing the hardships of unemployment. It provides payments to offset lost income during involuntary

unemployment insurance
A federally mandated program to minimize the hardships of unemployment through payments to unemployed workers, help in finding new jobs, and incentives to stabilize employment.

One of President Bush's major goals for his second term is Social Security reform. Under this proposed reform, younger workers would shift part of their payroll taxes into private stock and bond accounts. How do you feel about this proposed reform? Why?

unemployment, and it helps unemployed workers find new jobs. The payment of unemployment insurance taxes gives employers an incentive to stabilize employment. And providing workers with income during short-term layoffs preserves investments in worker skills because workers can afford to wait to return to their employer, rather than start over with another organization. Technically, the federal government left it to each state's discretion to establish an unemployment insurance program. At the same time, the Social Security Act created a tax incentive structure that quickly led every state to establish the program.

Most of the funding for unemployment insurance comes from federal and state taxes on employers. The federal tax rate is currently 0.8 percent of the first $7,000 of each employee's wages. The state tax rate varies. For a new employer, rates range from 1.0 percent to 4.1 percent, and the taxable wage base ranges from $7,000 to $31,000, so the amount paid depends a great deal on where the company is located. Also, some states charge new employers whatever rate is the average for their industry, so the amount of tax paid in those states also depends on the type of business.

experience rating
The number of employees a company has laid off in the past and the cost of providing them with unemployment benefits.

No state imposes the same tax rate on every employer in the state. The size of the unemployment insurance tax imposed on each employer depends on the employer's **experience rating**—the number of employees the company laid off in the past and the cost of providing them with unemployment benefits. Employers with a history of laying off a large share of their workforces pay higher taxes than those with few layoffs. In some states, an employer with very few layoffs may pay no state tax. In contrast, an employer with a poor experience rating could pay a tax as high as 5.4 to 10.9 percent, depending on the state.[3] The use of experience ratings gives employers some control over the cost of unemployment insurance. Careful human resource planning can minimize layoffs and keep their experience rating favorable.

To receive benefits, workers must meet four conditions:

1. They meet requirements demonstrating they had been employed (often 52 weeks or four quarters of work at a minimum level of pay).
2. They are available for work.
3. They are actively seeking work. This requirement includes registering at the local unemployment office.
4. They were not discharged for cause (such as willful misconduct), did not quit voluntarily, and are not out of work because of a labor dispute (such as a union member on strike).

Workers who meet these conditions receive benefits at the level set by the state—typically about half the person's previous earnings—for a period of 26 weeks. States with a sustained unemployment rate above a particular threshold or significantly above recent levels also offer extended benefits for up to 13 weeks. Sometimes Congress funds emergency extended benefits, as it did with passage of the Job Creation and Worker Assistance Act of 2002. All states have minimum and maximum weekly benefit levels.

workers' compensation
State programs that provide benefits to workers who suffer work-related injuries or illnesses, or to their survivors.

Workers' Compensation

Decades ago, workers who suffered work-related injury or illness had to bear the cost unless they won a lawsuit against their employer. Those who sued often lost the case because of the defenses available to employers. Today, the states have passed **workers' compensation** laws, which help workers with the expenses resulting from job-related accidents and illnesses.[4] These laws operate under a principle of *no-fault lia-*

bility, meaning that an employee does not need to show that the employer was grossly negligent in order to receive compensation, and the employer is protected from lawsuits. The employer loses this protection if it intentionally contributes to a dangerous workplace. Employees are not eligible if their injuries are self-inflicted or if they result from intoxication or "willful disregard of safety rules."[5]

About 9 out of 10 U.S. workers are covered by state workers' compensation laws, with the level of coverage varying from state to state. The benefits fall into four major categories:

1. Disability income
2. Medical care
3. Death benefits
4. Rehabilitative services

The amount of income varies from state to state but is typically two-thirds of the worker's earnings before the disability. The benefits are tax free.

The states differ in terms of how they fund workers' compensation insurance. Some states have a single state fund. Most states allow employers to purchase coverage from private insurance companies. Most also permit self-funding by employers. The cost of the workers' compensation insurance depends on the kinds of occupations involved, the state where the company is located, and the employer's experience rating. Premiums for low-risk occupations may be less than 1 percent of payroll. For some of the most hazardous occupations, the cost may be as high as 100 percent of payroll. Costs also vary from state to state, so that one state's program requires higher premiums than another state's program. As with unemployment insurance, unfavorable experience ratings lead to higher premiums. Organizations can minimize the cost of this benefit by keeping workplaces safe and making employees and their managers conscious of safety issues, as discussed in Chapter 3.

Unpaid Family and Medical Leave

In the United States, unpaid leave is required by law for certain family needs. Specifically, the **Family and Medical Leave Act (FMLA)** of 1993 requires organizations with 50 or more employees within a 75-mile radius to provide as much as 12 weeks of unpaid leave after childbirth or adoption; to care for a seriously ill child, spouse, or parent; or for an employee's own serious illness. Employers must also guarantee these employees the same or a comparable job when they return to work. The law does not cover employees who have less than one year of service, work fewer than 25 hours per week, or are among the organization's 10 percent highest paid. The 12 weeks of unpaid leave amount to a smaller benefit than is typical of Japan and most countries in Western Europe. Japan and West European nations typically require paid family leave.

Experience with the Family and Medical Leave Act suggests that a majority of those opting for this benefit fail to take the full 12 weeks. In about one out of four situations, employees take their leave intermittently, over periods of days or even hours, creating a significant record-keeping task.[6] Other employees, especially female executives, are simply keeping parental leaves under FMLA to a minimum, less than the available 12 weeks. Many are eager to return to their careers, and others fear that staying away for three months would damage their career opportunities.[7] Of course, another reason for not taking the full 12 weeks is that not everyone can afford three months without pay, especially when responsible for the expenses that accompany childbirth, adoption, or serious illness.

Family and Medical Leave Act (FMLA)
Federal law requiring organizations with 50 or more employees to provide up to 12 weeks of unpaid leave after childbirth or adoption; to care for a seriously ill family member; or for an employee's own serious illness.

When employees experience pregnancy and childbirth, employers must also comply with the Pregnancy Discrimination Act, described in Chapter 3. If an employee is temporarily unable to perform her job due to pregnancy, the employer must treat her in the same way as any other temporarily disabled employee. For example, the employer may provide modified tasks, alternative assignments, disability leave, or leave without pay.

OPTIONAL BENEFITS PROGRAMS

Other types of benefits are optional. These include various kinds of insurance, retirement plans, and paid leave. Figure 13.2 shows the percentage of full-time workers receiving the most common employee benefits. (Part-time workers often receive fewer benefits.) The most widely offered benefits are paid leave for vacations and holidays, life and medical insurance, and retirement plans. In general, benefits packages at smaller companies tend to be more limited than at larger companies.

Benefits such as health insurance often extend to employees' dependents. Traditionally, these benefits have covered employees, their spouses, and dependent children. Today, many employers also cover *domestic partners*, defined either by local law or by the companies themselves. Typically, a domestic partner is an adult nonrelative who lives with the employee in a relationship defined as permanent and financially interdependent. Some local governments provide for registration of domestic partners. Organizations offering coverage to domestic partners generally require that the partners sign a document stating they meet the requirements for a domestic partnership. Benefits provided to domestic partners do not have the same tax advantages as benefits provided to spouses. The partner's benefits are taxed as wages of the employee receiving the benefits.

LO3
Describe the most common forms of paid leave.

Paid Leave

The major categories of paid leave are vacations, holidays, and sick leave. Employers also should establish policies for other situations that may require time off. Organizations often provide for paid leave for jury duty, funerals of family members, and military duty. Some organizations provide for other paid leave, such as time off to vote or to donate blood. Establishing policies communicates the organization's values, clarifies what employees can expect, and prevents situations in which unequal treatment leads to claims of unfairness.

At first blush, paid vacation, holidays, sick leave, and other paid leave may not seem to make economic sense. The employer pays the employee for time spent not working, so the employer receives nothing in return for the pay. Some employers may see little direct advantage. This may be the reason that Western European countries require a minimum number of paid vacation days, with new employees receiving 30 days off in many countries. The United States, in contrast, has no such legal requirement. It is up to U.S. employers to decide whether paid leave has a payoff in recruiting and retaining employees. At large U.S. companies, paid vacation is typically 10 days a year for the first few years. To receive as much vacation as European employees, U.S. workers must typically stay with an employer for 20 to 25 years.[8]

Paid holidays are time off on specified days in addition to vacation time. In Western Europe and the United States, employees typically have about 10 paid holidays each year, regardless of length of service. The most common paid holidays in the United States are New Year's Day, Memorial Day, Independence Day, Labor Day, Thanksgiving Day, and Christmas Day.

Figure 13.2

Percentage of Full-Time Workers with Access to Selected Benefit Programs

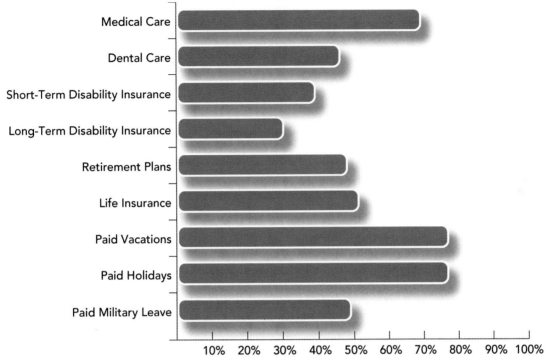

SOURCE: Bureau of Labor Statistics, "National Compensation Survey: Employee Benefits in Private Industry in the United States," Summary, March 2004, www.bls.gov.

Sick leave programs pay employees for days not worked because of illness. The amount of sick leave is often based on length of service, so that it accumulates over time—for example, one day added to sick leave for each month of service. Employers must decide how many sick days to grant and whether to let them continue accumulating year after year. If sick days accumulate without limit, employees can "save" them in case of disability. If an employee becomes disabled, the employee can use up the accumulated sick days, receiving full pay rather than smaller payments from disability insurance, discussed later. Some employers let sick days accumulate for only a year, and unused sick days "disappear" at year-end. This may provide an unintended incentive to use up sick days. Some healthy employees may call in sick near the end of the year so that they can obtain the benefit of the paid leave before it disappears. Employers may counter this tendency by paying employees for some or all of their unused sick days at year-end or when the employees retire or resign.

An organization's policies for time off may include other forms of paid and unpaid leave. For a workforce that values flexibility, the organization may offer paid *personal days*, days off that employees may schedule according to their personal needs, with the supervisor's approval. Typically, organizations offer a few personal days in addition to sick leave. *Floating holidays* are paid holidays that vary from year to year. The organization may schedule floating holidays so that they extend a Tuesday or Thursday holiday into a long weekend. Organizations may also give employees discretion over the scheduling of floating holidays.

Paid time off is a way for employees to enjoy time with their families and to refresh their bodies and spirits. Is paid time off an important criteria for you when accepting a position?

The most flexible approach to time off is to grant each employee a bank of *paid time off*, in which the employer pools personal days, sick days, and vacation days for employees to use as the need or desire arises. This flexibility is especially attractive to younger workers, who tend to rate work/life balance as one of the most important sources of job satisfaction. The flexibility also fits with the U.S. trend toward more frequent but shorter vacations. In this business environment, the use of paid-time-off plans has risen sharply from one out of five companies in 2000 to almost two-thirds in 2004.[9]

Employers should also establish policies for leaves without pay–for example, leaves of absence to pursue nonwork goals or to meet family needs. Unpaid leave is an employee benefit because the employee usually retains seniority and benefits during the leave.

Group Insurance

As we noted earlier, rates for group insurance are typically lower than for individual policies. Also, insurance benefits are not subject to income tax, as wages and salaries are. When employees receive insurance as a benefit, rather than higher pay so they can buy their own insurance, employees can get more for their money. Because of this, most employees value group insurance. The most common types of insurance offered as employee benefits are medical, life, and disability insurance.

Medical Insurance

For the average person, the most important benefit by far is medical insurance.[10] As Figure 13.2 shows, about seven out of every ten full-time employees receive medical benefits. The policies typically cover three basic types of medical expenses: hospital expenses, surgical expenses, and visits to physicians. Some employers offer additional coverage, such as dental care, vision care, birthing centers, and prescription drug programs. Under the Mental Health Parity Act of 1996, health insurance plans offered to employees must have the same maximum dollar benefits for covered mental illness as for other medical and surgical benefits. Some states have stricter requirements than the federal law. However, insurance plans can and do impose other restrictions on mental health care, such as limits on the number of days of hospitalization, and some employers avoid the restrictions by offering insurance without any mental health coverage.[11]

Employers that offer medical insurance must meet the requirements of the **Consolidated Omnibus Budget Reconciliation Act (COBRA)** of 1985. This federal law requires employers to permit employees to extend their health insurance coverage at group rates for up to 36 months following a "qualifying event." Qualifying events include termination (except for gross misconduct), a reduction in hours that leads to loss of health insurance, and the employee's death (in which case the surviv-

LO4
Identify the kinds of insurance benefits offered by employers.

Consolidated Omnibus Budget Reconciliation Act (COBRA)
Federal law that requires employers to permit employees or their dependents to extend their health insurance coverage at group rates for up to 36 months following a qualifying event, such as a layoff, reduction in hours, or the employee's death.

ing spouse or dependent child would extend the coverage). To extend the coverage, the employee or the surviving spouse or dependent must pay for the insurance, but the payments are at the group rate. These employees and their families must have access to the same services as those who did not lose their health insurance.

As we will discuss later in the chapter, health insurance is a significant and fast-growing share of benefits costs at U.S. organizations. Figure 13.3 shows that the United States spends much more of its total wealth on health care than other countries do. Most Western European countries have nationalized health systems, but the majority of Americans with coverage for health care expenses get it through their own or a family member's employer. As a result, a growing number of employees whose employers cannot afford this benefit are left without insurance to cover health care expenses. The "Best Practices" box describes how some employers have joined together to address this problem.

Managed Care. As the cost of health care coverage has risen, employers have looked for ways to control the cost while keeping this valuable benefit. To address employer concerns about cost, most insurers have offered forms of *managed care*, in which the insurer plays a role in decisions about health care, aimed at avoiding unnecessary procedures. Managed care may include claims review, in which the insurer studies claims to determine whether procedures are effective for the type of illness or injury. Patients may be required to obtain approval before hospital admissions, and the insurer may require alternatives to hospital stays—for example, outpatient surgery or home health care. Managed care often involves two variations on the design of health insurance: health maintenance organizations and preferred provider organizations.

A **health maintenance organization (HMO)** is a health care plan that requires patients to receive their medical care from the HMO's health care professionals, who

health maintenance organization (HMO)
A health care plan that requires patients to receive their medical care from the HMO's health care professionals, who are often paid a flat salary, and provides all services on a prepaid basis.

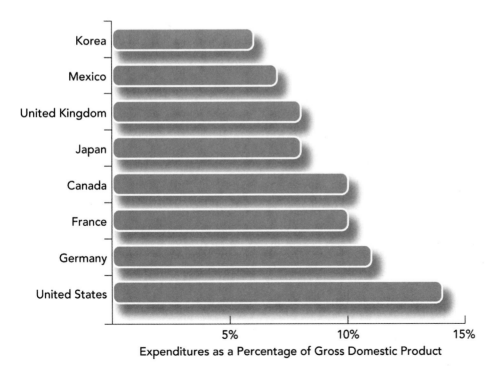

Figure 13.3

Health Care Costs in Various Countries

Expenditures as a Percentage of Gross Domestic Product

SOURCE: Organization for Economic Cooperation and Development, *OECD in Figures* (Paris: OECD, 2003).

BEST PRACTICES

HR POLICY ASSOCIATION GETS MORE EMPLOYEES INSURED

Millions of workers, especially part-time employees and contract workers, lack health insurance. Employers typically provide insurance only to full-time employees and their families. Other workers are on their own to pay for an individual insurance plan, which is beyond the reach of many household budgets.

Health care for the uninsured may be a public policy issue, but recently a group of several dozen private businesses, including General Electric, IBM, Sears, and McDonald's, has tackled this challenge. The group, working through the HR Policy Association, developed a proposal called National Health Access. Under this plan, the companies will pool their uninsured workers and invite insurance companies to offer a group policy to these workers. The association members believe that a large group of several million part-time employees, contract workers, and retirees too young for Medicare would be an attractive population for health insurers. These workers would have to pay for their policies, but at the lower premium rates charged for group insurance plans.

The idea is to provide a variety of options so that uninsured workers can find affordable choices. Options are as inexpensive as a $5 a month discount card and $300 a month for major-medical and hospital insurance with a high deductible. The employers say they cannot afford to insure the workers, but they hope to reduce the number of uninsured by placing more options within their reach.

The HR Policy Association began seeking state regulatory approval for National Health Access in 2005, hoping to open enrollment to workers later the same year.

SOURCE: Julie Appleby, "Employers Consider Insurance Pools," *USA Today*, May 9, 2004; and Mark McGraw, "National Health Access Program Introduced," *Human Resource Executive*, May 2, 2005, p. 19.

---

preferred provider organization (PPO) A health care plan that contracts with health care professionals to provide services at a reduced fee and gives patients financial incentives to use network providers.

flexible spending account Employee-controlled pretax earnings set aside to pay for certain eligible expenses such as health care expenses during the same year.

are often paid a flat salary, and provides all services on a prepaid basis. In other words, the premiums paid for the HMO cover all the patient's visits and procedures, without an additional payment from the patient. By paying physicians a salary, rather than a fee for each service, the HMO hopes to remove any incentive to provide more services than the patients really need. HMO coverage tends to cost less than traditional health insurance. The downside is that employees sometimes complain cost-control incentives work so well that they are denied access to services they actually need.

A **preferred provider organization (PPO)** is a health care plan that contracts with health care professionals to provide services at a reduced fee. Often, the PPO does not require employees to use providers in the network, but it pays a larger share of the cost of services from PPO providers. For example, the employee might pay 10 percent of the cost of a test by an in-network provider and 20 percent if the employee goes out of the PPO network. PPOs have quickly grown to become the most widely used health plan among U.S. employers. In 2000, over half of U.S. health plans were PPOs, up from 11 percent in 1990. HMOs make up most of the remaining health plans, as traditional fee-for-service plans fell from three-quarters of all plans in 1990 to less than 10 percent in 2000.[12]

Flexible Spending Accounts. Another alternative to traditional employer-provided insurance is a **flexible spending account,** in which employees may set aside a portion of pretax earnings to pay for eligible expenses. In particular, a *medical savings account* lets employees use their pretax savings to pay for qualified health care expenses (for example, payment of premiums). To avoid taxation, the money in the account must meet IRS requirements. Contributions to this account may not exceed $5,000 per year and must be designated in advance. The money in the account may be spent on health care expenses of the employee and employee's dependents during the plan year. At the end of the year, any remaining funds in the account revert to the employer.

The major advantage of flexible spending accounts is that the money in the account is not taxed, so employees will have more take-home pay. For example, if they were in a 30 percent tax bracket and saved $5,000, they could keep the $1,500 (.30 × $5,000) they otherwise would have paid in income taxes. Because of the tax savings, employees will benefit if they use a flexible spending account and actually need all the money in the account for health care expenses. But if they do not use all the money in the flexible spending account, they lose the amount they do not spend. Therefore, employees are most likely to benefit from a flexible spending account if they have predictable health care expenses, such as insurance premiums.

A form of flexible spending accounts is one part of a recent approach to providing health coverage in the form of *consumer-driven health plans* (CDHPs). These plans are intended to provide health coverage in a way that gets employees involved as consumers making decisions to lower costs. A CDHP typically brings together three elements: insurance with a high deductible, a medical savings account in which the employer contributes to employee-controlled accounts for paying expenses below the deductible, and health education aimed at helping employees improve their health and thus lower their need for health care. Whole Foods Market is one of the few companies that have offered this type of plan so far. But many others are investigating the idea, and some, including Quest Diagnostics and Lockheed Martin, have offered this type of plan as one option for employees.[13]

Wellness Programs. Another way to lower the cost of health insurance is to reduce employees' need for health care services. Employers may try to do this by offering an **employee wellness program (EWP),** a set of communications, activities, and facilities designed to change health-related behaviors in ways that reduce health risks. Typically, an EWP aims at specific health risks, such as high blood pressure, high

employee wellness program (EWP)
A set of communications, activities, and facilities designed to change health-related behaviors in ways that reduce health risks.

Kellogg's employees can use the company's "Feeling Gr-r-reat" Fitness Center to make sure the Frosted Flakes they eat don't expand their waistlines. Can you think of firms that offer other unique fringe benefits?

cholesterol levels, smoking, and obesity, by encouraging preventive measures such as exercise and good nutrition.

EWPs are either passive or active. Passive programs provide information and services, but no formal support or motivation to use the program. Examples include health education (such as lunchtime courses) and fitness facilities. These programs are passive because they rely on employees to identify the services they need and act on their own to obtain the services, such as participating in classes. Active wellness programs assume that behavior change requires support and reinforcement along with awareness and opportunity. These programs provide for outreach and follow-up. For example, the program may include counselors who tailor programs to individual employees' needs, take baseline measurements (for example, blood pressure and weight), and take follow-up measures for comparison to the baseline. Active programs often set goals and provide symbolic rewards as individuals make progress toward meeting their goals. In general, passive health education programs cost less than fitness facilities and active wellness programs.[14] All these variations have had success in reducing risk factors associated with cardiovascular disease (obesity, high blood pressure, smoking, lack of exercise), but the follow-up method is most successful.

Life Insurance

short-term disability insurance
Insurance that pays a percentage of a disabled employee's salary as benefits to the employee for six months or less.

Employers may provide life insurance to employees or offer the opportunity to buy coverage at low group rates. With a *term life insurance* policy, if the employee dies during the term of the policy, the employee's beneficiaries receive a payment called the death benefit. In policies purchased as an employee benefit, the usual death benefit is twice the employee's yearly pay. The policies may provide additional benefits for accidental death and dismemberment (loss of a body part such as a hand or foot). Along with a basic policy, the employer may give employees the option of purchasing additional coverage, usually at a nominal cost.

Disability Insurance

long-term disability insurance
Insurance that pays a percentage of a disabled employee's salary after an initial period and potentially for the rest of the employee's life.

Employees risk losing their incomes if a disability makes them unable to work. Disability insurance provides protection against this loss of income. Typically, **short-term disability insurance** provides benefits for six months or less. **Long-term disability insurance** provides benefits after that initial period, potentially for the rest of the disabled employee's life. Disability payments are a percentage of the employee's salary—typically 50 to 70 percent. Payments under short-term plans may be higher. Often the policy sets a maximum amount that may be paid each month. Because its limits make it more affordable, short-term disability coverage is offered by more employers. Fewer than half of employers offer long-term plans.

In planning an employee benefits package, the organization should keep in mind that Social Security includes some long-term disability benefits. To manage benefits costs, the employer should ensure that the disability insurance is coordinated with Social Security and any other programs that help workers who become disabled.

contributory plan
Retirement plan funded by contributions from the employer and employee.

Long-Term Care Insurance

noncontributory plan
Retirement plan funded entirely by contributions from the employer.

The cost of long-term care, such as care in a nursing home, can be devastating. Today, with more people living to an advanced age, many people are concerned about affording long-term care. Some employers address this concern by offering long-term care insurance. These policies provide benefits toward the cost of long-term care and related medical expenses.

Retirement Plans

Despite the image of retired people living on their Social Security checks, Figure 13.4 shows that those checks amount to less than half of a retired person's income. Among persons over age 65, pensions provided a significant share of income in 2000. Employers have no obligation to offer retirement plans beyond the protection of Social Security, but most offer some form of pension or retirement savings plan. About half of employees working for private businesses (that is, nongovernment jobs) have employer-sponsored retirement plans. These plans are most common for higher-earning employees. Among employees earning the top one-fifth of incomes, almost three-quarters have a pension plan, and about one out of six employees in the bottom fifth have pensions.[15] Retirement plans may be **contributory plans,** meaning they are funded by contributions from the employer and employee, or **noncontributory plans,** meaning all the contributions come from the employer.

Defined Benefit Plans

Employers have a choice of using retirement plans that define the amount to be paid out after retirement or plans that define the amount the employer will invest each year. A **defined benefit plan** guarantees a specified level of retirement income. Usually the amount of this defined benefit is calculated for each employee based on the employee's years of service, age, and earnings level (for example, the average of the employee's five highest-earnings years). These calculations typically result in pension payments that range from 20 percent of final salary for an employee who is relatively young and has few years of service to 35 percent of the final salary of an older employee who has spent many years with the organization. Using years of service as part of the basis for calculating benefits gives employees an incentive to stay with the organization as long as they can, so it can help to reduce voluntary turnover.

Defined benefit plans must meet the funding requirements of the **Employee Retirement Income Security Act (ERISA)** of 1974. This law increased the responsibility of pension plan trustees to protect retirees, established certain rights related to vesting (earning a right to receive the pension) and *portability* (being able to move retirement

LO5
Define the types of retirement plans offered by employers.

defined benefit plan
Pension plan that guarantees a specified level of retirement income.

Employee Retirement Income Security Act (ERISA)
Federal law that increased the responsibility of pension plan trustees to protect retirees, established certain rights related to vesting and portability, and created the Pension Benefit Guarantee Corporation.

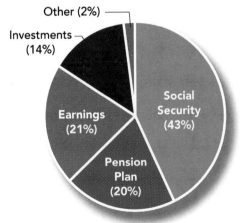

Figure 13.4

Sources of Income for Persons 65 and Older

Other (2%)
Investments (14%)
Earnings (21%)
Social Security (43%)
Pension Plan (20%)

SOURCE: Employee Benefit Research Institute, "FAQs about Benefits: Retirement Issues," www.ebri.org, citing *EBRI Notes*, November 2003.

Pension Benefit Guarantee Corporation (PBGC)
Federal agency that insures retirement benefits and guarantees retirees a basic benefit if the employer experiences financial difficulties.

savings when changing employers), and created the **Pension Benefit Guarantee Corporation (PBGC).** The PBGC is the federal agency that insures retirement benefits and guarantees retirees a basic benefit if the employer experiences financial difficulties. To fund the PBGC, employers must make annual contributions of $19 per fund participant. Plans that are *underfunded*—meaning the employer does not contribute enough to the plan each year to meet future obligations—must pay an additional premium as high as $72 per participant.[16] The PBGC's protection applies to the pensions of 44 million workers.

With a defined benefit plan, the employer sets up a pension fund to invest the contributions. As required by ERISA, the employer must contribute enough for the plan to cover all the benefits to be paid out to retirees. Defined benefit plans protect employees from the risk that the pension fund will not earn as much as expected. If the pension fund earns less than expected, the employer makes up the difference from other sources. If the employer experiences financial difficulties so that it must end or reduce employee pension benefits, the PBGC provides a basic benefit, which does not necessarily cover the full amount promised by the employer's pension plan. The PBGC establishes a maximum; in 2004, it was the lesser of $1/12$ of an employee's annual gross income or $3,699 per month.

Defined Contribution Plans

defined contribution plan
Retirement plan in which the employer sets up an individual account for each employee and specifies the size of the investment into that account.

An alternative to defined benefits is a **defined contribution plan,** which sets up an individual account for each employee and specifies the size of the investment into that account, rather than the amount to be paid out upon retirement. The amount the retiree receives will depend on the account's performance. Many kinds of defined contribution plans are available, including the following:

- *Money purchase plan*—The employer specifies a level of annual contributions (for example, 10 percent of salary). The contributions are invested, and when the employee retires, he or she is entitled to receive the amount of the contributions plus the investment earnings. ("Money purchase" refers to the fact that when employees retire, they often buy an annuity with the money, rather than taking it as a lump sum.)
- *Profit-sharing and employee stock ownership plans*—As we saw in Chapter 12, incentive pay may take the form of profit sharing and employee stock ownership plans (ESOPs). These payments may be set up so that the money goes into retirement plans. By defining its contributions in terms of stock or a share of profits, the organization has more flexibility to contribute less dollar value in lean years and more in good years.
- *Section 401(k) plans*—Employees contribute a percentage of their earnings, and employers may make matching contributions. The amount employees contribute is not taxed as part of their income until they receive it from the plan. The federal government limits the amount that may be contributed each year. In 2005 the limit was $14,000; it increases to $15,000 in 2006 and then by up to $500 a year through 2010, depending on the inflation rate. The contribution limits are higher for persons 50 and older.[17]

These plans free employers from the risks that investments will not perform as well as expected. They put the responsibility for wise investing squarely on the shoulders of each employee. A defined contribution plan is also easier to administer. The employer need not calculate payments based on age and service, and payments to the PBGC are not required. Considering the advantages to employers, it is not surprising that a growing share of retirement plans are defined contribution plans, especially at relatively small organizations. For instance, 401(k) plans covered 64 million people in 2003, four times the number enrolled in these plans in 1978.[18] While the number of defined-contribution plans soared over the past decade, the number of defined-benefit plans has declined. In the United States in 2002, there were more than 800,000 defined-contribution plans but just 32,000 defined-benefit plans (less than one-third of their 1990 level).[19] Still, many organizations offer both kinds of retirement plans.

When retirement plans make individual employees responsible for investment decisions, the employees need information about retirement planning. Retirement savings plans often give employees much control over decisions about when and how much to invest. Many employees do not appreciate the importance of beginning to save early in their careers. As Figure 13.5 shows, an employee who invests $3,000 a year ($250 a month) between the ages of 21 and 29 will have far more at age 65 than an employee who invests the same amount between ages 31 and 39. Another important lesson is to diversify investments. Based on investment performance between 1946 and 1990, stocks earned an average of 11.4 percent per year, bonds earned 5.1 percent, and bank savings accounts earned 5.3 percent. But in any given year, one of these types of investments might outperform the other. And within the categories of stocks and bonds, it is important to invest in a wide variety of companies. If one company performs poorly, the investments in other companies might perform better. However, studies of investment decisions by employees have found that many employees hold a sizable share of their retirement savings in stock of the company they work for, and few have followed basic guidelines for diversifying investments among stocks, bonds, and savings accounts according to their age and investment needs.[20] In a study by Watson Wyatt, employees who managed their own 401(k) plans earned half a percentage point less per year than professionally managed pension funds held by the same companies. (Over 30 years, half a percentage point on a $100,000 investment would mean an $88,000 difference in the total return.) To help employees handle such risks, some organizations provide financial planning as a separate benefit or offer an option to have a professional invest the funds in a 401(k) plan. For example, more than

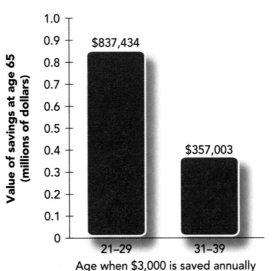

Figure 13.5

Value of Retirement Savings Invested at Different Ages

Note: Investment portfolio consists of 60 percent stocks, 30 percent bonds, and 10 percent cash (e.g., money-market funds, bank savings accounts), assuming average rates of return based on historical rates from 1946 to 1990.

two-thirds of the employees at Magnetek have opted to have investment decisions made by ProManage, a Chicago investment firm, according to their age, expected Social Security benefits, and other information.

In spite of these challenges, defined contribution plans also offer an advantage to employees in today's highly mobile workforce. They do not penalize employees for changing jobs. With these plans, retirement earnings are less related to the number of years an employee stays with a company.

Cash Balance Plans

cash balance plan
Retirement plan in which the employer sets up an individual account for each employee and contributes a percentage of the employee's salary; the account earns interest at a predefined rate.

An increasingly popular way to combine the advantages of defined benefit plans and defined contribution plans is to use a **cash balance plan.** This type of retirement plan consists of individual accounts, as in a 401(k) plan. But in contrast to a 401(k), all the contributions come from the employer. Usually, the employer contributes a percentage of the employee's salary, say, 4 or 5 percent. The money in the cash balance plan earns interest according to a predetermined rate, such as the rate paid on U.S. Treasury bills. Employers guarantee this rate as in a defined benefit plan. This arrangement helps employers plan their contributions and helps employees predict their retirement benefits. If employees change jobs, they generally can roll over the balance into an individual retirement account.

A switch from traditional defined benefit plans to cash balance plans, like any major change, requires employers to consider the effects on employees as well as on the organization's bottom line. Defined benefit plans are most generous to older employees with many years of service, and cash balance plans are most generous to young employees who will have many years ahead in which to earn interest. For an organization with many experienced employees, switching from a defined benefit plan can produce great savings in pension benefits. In that case, the older workers are the greatest losers, unless the organization adjusts the program to retain their benefits. After IBM switched to a cash benefit plan, a group of employees filed an age discrimination lawsuit, which IBM lost, potentially costing its pension fund billions of dollars.[21] The U.S. Treasury Department has recently proposed rules on cash balance plans, but it is unclear when or if Congress will act on these proposals. In this uncertain legal environment, few companies have converted their defined benefit plans to cash balance plans.

Government Requirements for Vesting and Communication

vesting rights
Guarantee that when employees become participants in a pension plan and work a specified number of years, they will receive a pension at retirement age, regardless of whether they remained with the employer.

Along with requirements for funding defined benefit plans, ERISA specifies a number of requirements related to eligibility for benefits and communication with employees. ERISA guarantees employees that when they become participants in a pension plan and work a specified number of years, they earn a right to a pension upon retirement. These rights are called **vesting rights.** Employees whose contributions are *vested* have met the requirements (enrolling and length of service) to receive a pension at retirement age, regardless of whether they remained with the employer until that time. Employees' own contributions to their pension plans are always completely vested. In most cases, the vesting of employer-funded pension benefits must take place under one of two schedules selected by the employer:

1. The employer may vest employees after five years and may provide zero vesting until that time.
2. The employer may vest employees over a three- to seven-year period, with at least 20 percent vesting in the third year and at least an additional 20 percent in each year after the third year.

These two schedules represent minimum requirements. Employers may vest employees more quickly if they wish. Two less-common situations have different vesting requirements. One is a "top-heavy" pension plan, meaning pension benefits for *key employees* (such as highly paid top managers) exceed a government-specified share of total pension benefits. A top-heavy plan requires faster vesting for nonkey employees. Another exception from the usual schedule involves multiemployer pension plans. These plans need not provide vesting until after 10 years of employment.

The intent of vesting requirements is to protect employees by preventing employers from terminating them before they meet retirement age in order to avoid paying pension benefits. In addition, it is illegal for employers to transfer or lay off employees as a way to avoid pension obligations, even if these changes are motivated partly by business need.[22] One way employers may legally try to minimize pension costs is in choosing a vesting schedule. For example, if many employees leave after three or four years of employment, the five-year vesting schedule would minimize pension costs.

ERISA's reporting and disclosure requirements involve the Internal Revenue Service, the Department of Labor, and employees.[23] Within 90 days after employees enter a plan, they must receive a **summary plan description (SPD),** a report that describes the plan's funding, eligibility requirements, risks, and other details. If the employee requests one, the employer must also make available an individual benefit statement, which describes the employee's vested and unvested benefits. Many employers provide such information regularly, without waiting for employee requests. This type of communication helps employees understand and value their retirement benefits.

summary plan description
Report that describes a pension plan's funding, eligibility requirements, risks, and other details.

"Family-Friendly" Benefits

As employers have recognized the significance of employees' need to manage conflicts between their work and family roles, many have added "family-friendly" benefits to their employee benefits. These benefits include family leave policies and child care. The programs discussed here apply directly to the subset of employees with family responsibilities. However, family-friendly benefits often have spillover effects in the form of loyalty because employees see the benefits as evidence that the organization cares about its people.[24]

LO6
Describe how organizations use other benefits to match employees' wants and needs.

Family Leave

Family-friendly benefits often include some form of family or parental leave granting employees time off to care for children and other dependents. As discussed earlier in the chapter, federal law requires 12 weeks of unpaid leave. Companies may choose to offer more generous leave policies. Paid family leave remains rare in the United States, however, despite some state laws. By contrast, more than 120 countries provide paid family leave by law. The norm in Western Europe is three to four months' maternity leave at 80 to 100 percent of pay, plus additional (often unpaid) parental leave for both parents.[25]

Child Care

Many companies provide some form of child care benefits. These benefits may take several forms, requiring different levels of organizational involvement.[26] As shown in Figure 13.6, the lowest level of involvement, offered by 36 percent of companies, is for the organization to supply and help employees collect information about the cost and quality

Figure 13.6

Percentage of Employers Offering Various Levels of Child Care Benefits

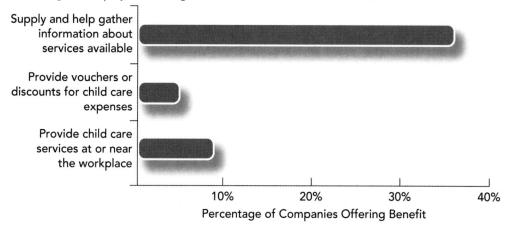

Note: Data based on a nationally representative survey of employers with 100 or more employees.

SOURCE: Families and Work Institute, "The Families and Work Institute's 1998 Business Work-Life Study," www.familiesandwork.org.

of available child care. At the next level, organizations provide vouchers or discounts for employees to use at existing child care facilities. At the highest level of involvement, the employer provides child care at or near the work site. Cisco Systems, a software company in San Jose, California, operates a day care center at company headquarters.[27] In spite of the costs of this benefit and the recent economic slowdown, Cisco continued operating the day care center because it believes the center helps employees work more productively, and productivity is especially important during difficult economic times.

An organization should not take lightly the decision to staff its own child care facility. Such an operation is costly and involves important liability concerns. At the same time, the results of this type of benefit, in terms of reducing absenteeism and enhancing productivity, have been mixed. Some organizations have simply offered day care to follow a trend in employee benefits, rather than to address the needs of specific employees.[28] One large U.S. corporation found that less than 2 percent of its workforce used a flexible spending account the company offered as its main child care benefit. Organizations can avoid such wasted benefits by conducting a thorough needs analysis before selecting programs to offer.[29] Providian Financial Corporation, a credit card company with headquarters in San Francisco, determined that for many of its employees, the big hurdle with child care and elder care was affordability. So, Providian set up flexible spending accounts for dependent care. Employees may contribute up to the legal maximum $5,000 in pretax earnings, and Providian provides matching contributions up to $2,000. The plan is targeted to meet the needs of employees earning between $25,000 and $35,000 a year, many of whom staff the company's large call centers. The share of these employees who enroll in the flexible spending accounts has grown significantly each year since Providian began offering the program.[30]

College Savings

As workers' children grow up, their needs shift from maternity leave and child care to college tuition. Some organizations have supported this concern by sponsoring tax-favored *529 savings plans*. These plans, named after the section of the Internal

Revenue Code that regulates them, let parents and other family members defer taxes on the earnings of their deposits into the 529 account. Some states also provide a (limited) tax deduction for these contributions. As an employee benefit, organizations can arrange with a broker to offer direct deposit of a portion of employees' paychecks into their accounts. Besides offering the convenience of direct deposit, employers can negotiate lower management fees. For example, Merrill Lynch charges half its usual management fee on 529 accounts set up through employers.[31]

Elder Care

As the population of the nation's elderly grows, so do the demands on adult children to care for elderly parents, aunts, and uncles. When these people become ill or disabled, they rely on family or professional caregivers. Responsibilities such as providing assistance, paying for professional caregivers, and locating services can be expensive, time-consuming, and exhausting, often distracting employees from their work roles. In response, many employers have added elder care benefits. These benefits typically emphasize information and support, rather than direct financial assistance. For example, organizations may provide access to counseling, flexible schedules, and printed resources. Even companies that cannot afford to offer counseling or referral services can use intranets to provide links to helpful Web sites such as the National Alliance for Caregiving (www.caregiving.org), the National Council on Aging (www.benefitscheckup.org), and the federal government's benefits information site (govbenefits.gov).[32]

Other Benefits

The scope of possible employee benefits is limited only by the imagination of the organization's decision makers. Organizations have developed a wide variety of benefits to meet the needs of employees and to attract and keep the kinds of workers who will be of value to the organization. Traditional extras include subsidized cafeterias, on-site

In order to provide a relaxed environment for their employees, one of the perks Neversoft Entertainment offers is allowing employees to bring their pets to work. What other incentives do companies offer their employees?

health care for minor injuries or illnesses, and moving expenses for newly hired or relocating employees. Stores and manufacturers may offer employee discounts on their products.

To encourage learning and attract the kinds of employees who wish to develop their knowledge and skills, many organizations offer *tuition reimbursement* programs. A typical program covers tuition and related expenses for courses that are relevant to the employee's current job or future career at the organization. Employees are reimbursed for these expenses after they demonstrate they have completed an approved course.

Especially for demanding, high-stress jobs, organizations may look for benefits that help employees put in the necessary long hours and alleviate stress. Recreational activities such as on-site basketball courts or company-sponsored softball teams provide for social interaction as well as physical activity. Employers may reward hardworking groups or individuals with a trip for a weekend, a meal, or any activity employees are likely to enjoy. At one accounting firm, a manager made a practice of occasionally taking her team of women to a manicure salon for a break to relax and converse.[33]

◈ SELECTING EMPLOYEE BENEFITS

LO7
Explain how to choose the contents of an employee benefits package.

Although the government requires certain benefits, employers have wide latitude in creating the total benefits package they offer employees.[34] Decisions about which benefits to include should take into account the organization's goals, its budget, and the expectations of the organization's current employees and those it wishes to recruit in the future. Employees have come to expect certain things from employers. An organization that does not offer the expected benefits will have more difficulty attracting and keeping talented workers. Also, if employees believe their employer feels no commitment to their welfare, they are less likely to feel committed to their employer.

The Organization's Objectives

A logical place to begin selecting employee benefits is to establish objectives for the benefits package. This helps an organization select the most effective benefits and monitor whether the benefits are doing what they should. Table 13.2 is an example of one organization's benefits objectives. Unfortunately, research suggests that most organizations do not have written benefits objectives.

Analytical Graphics Inc. (AGI), based in Exton, Pennsylvania, develops software that analyzes data from military equipment to help the equipment operate better. For a company that produces products that are so technical, complex, and critical, a chief objective is keeping the loyalty of talented professionals. The challenge is not so much to motivate them to get their work done as it is to create a work environment in which they feel respected and free to contribute. The company's benefits policy supports these objectives by going beyond such standards as health insurance, vacations, and a 401(k) plan with employer matching contributions to such privileges as flextime, free catered meals, an exercise room, and a policy of allowing children to visit anytime and use the well-stocked playroom. Other services that make life easier for employees include oil changes in the parking lot, weekly pickup and delivery of dry cleaning, and shipping of personal packages, at cost, through the company's shipping department. AGI's chief executive, Paul L. Graziani, says, "If you can remove a couple of the stresses, especially for people with families here, they can come in and be really productive. . . . They get more productive, and the company gets more productive, and then you have the resources to do more things for them."[35]

TABLE 13.2

An Organization's
Benefits Objectives

- To establish and maintain an employee benefit program that is based primarily on the employees' needs for leisure time and on protection against the risks of old age, loss of health, and loss of life.
- To establish and maintain an employee benefit program that complements the efforts of employees on their own behalf.
- To evaluate the employee benefit plan annually for its effect on employee morale and productivity, giving consideration to turnover, unfilled positions, attendance, employees' complaints, and employees' opinions.
- To compare the employee benefit plan annually with that of other leading companies in the same field and to maintain a benefit plan with an overall level of benefits based on cost per employee that falls within the second quintile of these companies.
- To maintain a level of benefits for nonunion employees that represents the same level of expenditures per employee as for union employees.
- To determine annually the costs of new, changed, and existing programs as percentages of salaries and wages and to maintain these percentages as much as possible.
- To self-fund benefits to the extent that a long-run cost savings can be expected for the firm and catastrophic losses can be avoided.
- To coordinate all benefits with social insurance programs to which the company makes payments.
- To provide benefits on a noncontributory basis except for dependent coverage, for which employees should pay a portion of the cost.
- To maintain continual communications with all employees concerning benefit programs.

SOURCE: Adapted from B. T. Beam Jr. and J. J. McFadden, *Employee Benefits*, 3rd ed. © 1992 by Dearborn Financial Publishing, Inc. Published by Dearborn Financial Publishing, Inc., Chicago. All rights reserved.

Employees' Expectations and Values

Employees expect to receive benefits that are legally required and widely available, and they value benefits they are likely to use. To meet employee expectations about benefits, it can be helpful to see what other organizations offer. Employers can purchase survey information about benefits packages from private consultants. In addition, the Bureau of Labor Statistics gathers benefits data. The BLS Web site (www.bls.gov) is therefore a good place to check for free information about employee benefits in the United States. With regard to value, medical insurance is a high-value benefit because employees usually realize that a surgery or major illness can be financially devastating. Vision and dental care tend to be much less expensive, but many employees appreciate this type of coverage because so many people receive dental or vision care in the course of a year. As a result, many employers are finding that employees are even happy to pay the modest premiums for dental and vision coverage themselves because of the value they place on this benefit.[36]

Employers should also consider that the value employees place on various benefits is likely to differ from one employee to another. At a broad level, basic demographic factors such as age and sex can influence the kinds of benefits employees want. An older workforce is more likely to be concerned about (and use) medical coverage, life insurance, and pensions. A workforce with a high percentage of women of childbearing age may care more about disability or family leave. Young, unmarried men and women often place more value on pay than on benefits. However, these are only general observations;

organizations should check which considerations apply to their own employees and identify more specific needs and differences. One approach is to use surveys to ask employees about the kinds of benefits they value. The survey should be carefully worded not to raise employees' expectations by seeming to promise all the benefits asked about at no cost to the employee.

The choice of benefits may influence current employees' satisfaction and may also affect the organization's recruiting, in terms of both the ease of recruiting and the kinds of employees attracted to the organization. For example, a benefits package that has strong medical benefits and pensions may be particularly attractive to older people or to those with many dependents. Such benefits may attract people with extensive experience and those who wish to make a long-term commitment to the organization. This strategy may be especially beneficial when turnover costs are very high. On the other hand, offering generous health care benefits may attract and retain people with high health care costs. Thus, organizations need to consider the signals sent by their benefits package as they set goals for benefits and select benefits to offer.

cafeteria-style plan
A benefits plan that offers employees a set of alternatives from which they can choose the types and amounts of benefits they want.

Organizations can address differences in employees' needs and empower their employees by offering flexible benefits plans in place of a single benefits package for all employees. These plans, often called **cafeteria-style plans,** offer employees a set of alternatives from which they can choose the types and amounts of benefits they want. The plans vary. Some impose minimum levels for certain benefits, such as health care coverage; some allow employees to receive money in exchange for choosing a "light" package; and some let employees pay extra for the privilege of receiving more benefits. For example, some plans let employees give up vacation days for more pay or to purchase extra vacation days in exchange for a reduction in pay.

Cafeteria-style plans have a number of advantages.[37] The selection process can make employees more aware of the value of the benefits, particularly when the plan assigns each employee a sum of money to allocate to benefits. Also, the individual choice in a cafeteria plan enables each employee to match his or her needs to the company's benefits, increasing the plan's actual value to the employee. And because employees would not select benefits they don't want, the company avoids the cost of providing employees with benefits they don't value. Another way to control costs is to give employees incentives to choose lower-cost options. For example, the employee's deductible on a higher-cost health plan could be larger than on a relatively low-cost HMO.

A drawback of cafeteria-style plans is that they have a higher administrative cost, especially in the design and start-up stages. Organizations can avoid some of the higher cost, however, by using software packages and standardized plans that have been developed for employers wishing to offer cafeteria-style benefits. Another possible drawback is that employee selection of benefits will increase rather than decrease costs because employees will select the kinds of benefits they expect to need the most. For example, an employee expecting to need a lot of dental work is more likely to sign up for a dental plan. The heavy use of the dental coverage would then drive up the employer's premiums for that coverage. Costs can also be difficult to estimate when employees select their benefits.

Benefits' Costs

Employers also need to consider benefits costs. One place to start is with general information about the average costs of various benefits types. Widely used sources of cost data include the Bureau of Labor Statistics (BLS), Employee Benefit Research Institute, and U.S. Chamber of Commerce. Annual surveys by the Chamber of Commerce state

LEGALLY REQUIRED BENEFITS ARE THE COSTLIEST

At the end of 2004, the average amount spent on employee compensation (pay and benefits costs) for civilian workers was $25.57 per hour, with benefits accounting for almost 30 percent of that amount. Of the spending on benefits, the biggest share went to legally required benefits, including Social Security and Medicare. However, the cost of insurance is close behind and growing fast, driven by the rising cost of health care.

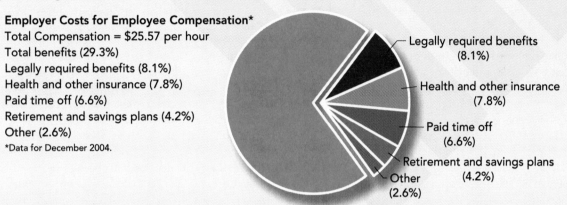

Employer Costs for Employee Compensation*
Total Compensation = $25.57 per hour
Total benefits (29.3%)
Legally required benefits (8.1%)
Health and other insurance (7.8%)
Paid time off (6.6%)
Retirement and savings plans (4.2%)
Other (2.6%)
*Data for December 2004.

Legally required benefits (8.1%)
Health and other insurance (7.8%)
Paid time off (6.6%)
Retirement and savings plans (4.2%)
Other (2.6%)

SOURCE: Bureau of Labor Statistics, "Employer Costs for Employee Compensation—December 2004," news release, March 16, 2005, downloaded at www.bls.gov; and Employee Benefit Research Institute, "Compensation Costs in Private Industry: March 1987 to December 2002," *EBRI Fact Sheet*, July 2003, www.ebri.org.

the cost of benefits as a percentage of total payroll costs and in dollar terms. The "Did You Know . . . ?" box shows information from the BLS about benefits costs.

Employers can use data about costs to help them select the kinds of benefits to offer. But in balancing these decisions against organizational goals and employee benefits, the organization may decide to offer certain high-cost benefits while also looking for ways to control the cost of those benefits. The highest-cost items tend to offer the most room for savings, but only if the items permit choice or negotiation. Also, as we noted earlier, organizations can control certain costs such as workers' compensation by improving their experience ratings. Cost control is especially important—and difficult—when economic growth slows or declines. The "HR How To" box provides some guidelines for coping with this challenge.

In recent years, benefits related to health care have attracted particular attention because these costs have risen very rapidly and because employers have a number of options. Concern over costs has prompted many employers to shift from traditional health insurance to HMOs and PPOs. Some employers shift more of the cost to employees. They may lower the employer's payments by increasing the amounts employees pay for deductibles and coinsurance (the employee's share of the payment for services). Or they may require employees to pay some or all of the difference in cost between traditional insurance and an HMO or PPO plan. Excluding or limiting coverage for certain types of claims also can slow the increase in health insurance costs. Employee wellness programs,

HR HOW TO

CONTROLLING THE COST OF BENEFITS

Even though organizations are still competing for high-quality, talented workers, competitive pressures are also forcing them to cut back on certain perks without losing their employees' trust or loyalty. Much of the cost-cutting efforts involve health insurance. Some employers are doubling the deductibles and raising copayments on their insurance policies. Many have asked employees to start paying a share of the monthly premiums or to pay a larger share than they have been.

Dave Stum, president of Aon Consulting's Loyalty Institute, suggests, "Organizations need to take a good, hard look at the basics before launching new and trendy benefits or other human resources packages. Start by ensuring that you offer a safe, secure work environment and equitable compensation and benefits packages." According to Stum, these basics form the foundation of the employer's compensation system. Any additional benefits should be laid on a firm foundation.

Jean Wilson, membership director of the Employee Services Management Association in Oak Brook, Illinois, advises comparing benefits costs to the potential cost of higher employee turnover. According to Wilson, the cost of a benefit is often much less than that of replacing an employee coaxed away by a more generous employer.

Even so, organizations must sometimes cut back on some of their employee services. When this happens, says Cathy Ohmes, owner of Creative Perks LLC, organizations should clearly communicate the decision to employees before the change occurs. The communication prepares employees to understand and absorb the information before the services are eliminated.

To make the communication more effective, organizations should get input from employees. Employers need to know

especially when they are targeted to employees with risk factors and include follow-up and encouragement, can reduce risk factors for disease.[38] A study published by the President's Council on Physical Fitness and Sports found that fitness programs provided by employers saved between $1.15 and $5.52 for every dollar spent.[39] As a result, employee wellness programs should contribute to lower health insurance costs.

Since the 1990s, efforts to control the growth in health care costs have borne fruit only temporarily. From 1980 through 1993, the growth rate in health care costs was in the double digits, but employer expenses for health care fell by 17 percent from 1994 through 1999. The trend reversed again in this decade, with costs increasing 22 percent from 1999 to 2003.[40] The Health Care Financing Administration projects that health care spending in the United States will continue to grow. Already 85 percent of working Americans with health care coverage participate in some form of managed care, so employers cannot repeat the savings of switching to managed care. Also, the profit margins of many managed-care providers are already slim, so they are limited in how to find new savings.

LO8
Summarize the regulations affecting how employers design and administer benefits programs.

❧ LEGAL REQUIREMENTS FOR EMPLOYEE BENEFITS

As we discussed earlier in this chapter, some benefits are required by law. This requirement adds to the cost of compensating employees. Organizations looking for ways to control staffing costs may look for ways to structure the workforce so as to what their employees understand about benefits costs and what benefits they value. The timing of the message is also important. For example, employees will be actively listening for information about health benefits during the period when they enroll, especially if the employer offers several choices. This is a good time to show practical benefits of medical savings accounts, healthy living habits, and other issues related to the cost of health care.

Cost-cutting efforts can also appeal to employees' sense of fairness. Ford Motor Company conducted audits of its health plans and found that tens of thousands of individuals listed as dependents were not actually eligible. Cutting them from the program saved Ford money, but it also made this benefit fairer.

Instead of cutting services altogether, organizations can look for new, cheaper ways to offer comparable services. At Intel, HR managers were frustrated that the company was offering lunchtime seminars on health topics but no one was attending them. Concerned that many workers were already skipping meals, exercise, and sleep, Intel didn't want to give up its health program. So the company linked its intranet to the Mayo Clinic HealthQuest service, which creates personalized Web pages detailing how individuals can improve their health habits. Information covers exercise programs, healthful recipes, and more. The site is cheaper to manage than the lunchtime lectures, and employees are more apt to use it.

SOURCE: "Benefits for Your Workers," *Business Owner's Toolkit,* October 30, 2001, www.toolkit.cch.com; L. Lawrence, "Companies Still Offering Perks, but HR's Taking Another Look," *HR News,* June 2001, p. 4; B. Brady, "The Cost of Health," *Business 2.0,* January 2000, www.business2.com.; L. Wiener, "The Big Benefit Squeeze," *U.S. News & World Report,* March 21, 2005, p. 47; and R. Stolz, "Healthy Encouragement," *Human Resource Executive,* May 2, 2005, pp. 1, 22–28.

minimize the expense of benefits. They may require overtime rather than adding new employees, hire part-time rather than full-time workers (because part-time employees generally receive much smaller benefits packages), and use independent contractors rather than hire employees. Some of these choices are limited by legal requirements, however. For example, the Fair Labor Standards Act requires overtime pay for nonexempt workers, as discussed in Chapter 11. Also, the Internal Revenue Service strictly limits the definition of "independent contractors," so that employees cannot avoid legal obligations by classifying workers as self-employed when the organization receives the benefits of a permanent employee. Other legal requirements involve tax treatment of benefits, antidiscrimination laws, and accounting for benefits.

Tax Treatment of Benefits

The IRS provides more favorable tax treatment of benefits classified as *qualified plans*. The details vary from one type of benefit to another. In the case of retirement plans, the advantages include the ability for employees to immediately take a tax deduction for the funds they contribute to the plans, no immediate tax on employees for the amount the employer contributes, and tax-free earnings on the money in the retirement fund.[41]

To obtain status as a qualified plan, a benefit plan must meet certain requirements.[42] In the case of pensions, these involve vesting and nondiscrimination rules. The nondiscrimination rules provide tax benefits to plans that do not discriminate in favor of the organization's "highly compensated employees." To receive the benefits, the organization cannot set up a retirement plan that provides benefits exclusively to the organization's owners and top managers. The requirements encourage employers to provide important benefits such as pensions to a broad spectrum of employees. Before offering pension plans and other benefits, organizations should have them reviewed by an expert who can advise on whether the benefits are qualified plans.

Antidiscrimination Laws

As we discussed in Chapter 3, a number of laws are intended to provide equal employment opportunity without regard to race, sex, age, disability, and several other protected categories. Some of these laws apply to the organization's benefits policies.

Legal treatment of men and women includes equal access to benefits, so the organization may not use the employee's gender as the basis for providing more limited benefits. That is the rationale for the Pregnancy Discrimination Act, which requires that employers treat pregnancy as it treats any disability. If an employee needs time off for conditions related to pregnancy or childbirth, the employee would receive whatever disability benefits the organization offers to employees who take disability leave for other reasons. Another area of concern in the treatment of male and female employees is pension benefits. On average, women live longer than men, so on average, pension benefits for female employees are more expensive (because the organization pays the pension longer), other things being equal. Some organizations have used this difference as a basis for requiring that female employees contribute more than male employees to defined benefit plans. The Supreme Court in 1978 determined that such a requirement is illegal.[43] According to the Supreme Court, the law is intended to protect individuals, and when women are considered on an individual basis (not as averages), not every woman outlives every man.

Age discrimination is also relevant to benefits policies. Two major issues have received attention under the Age Discrimination in Employment Act (ADEA) and amendments. First, employers must take care not to discriminate against workers over age 40 in providing pay or benefits. For example, employers may not set an age at which retirement benefits stop growing as a way to pressure older workers to retire.[44] Also, early-retirement incentive programs need to meet certain standards. The programs may not coerce employees to retire, they must provide accurate information about the options available, and they must give employees enough time to make a decision. In effect, employees must really have a choice about whether they retire.

When employers offer early retirement, they often ask employees to sign waivers saying they will not pursue claims under the ADEA. The Older Workers Benefit Protection Act of 1990 set guidelines for using these waivers.[45] The waivers must be voluntary and understandable to the employee and employer, and they must spell out the employee's rights under the ADEA. Also, in exchange for signing the waiver, the employee must receive "compensation," that is, greater benefits than he or she would otherwise receive upon retirement. The employer must inform employees that they may consult a lawyer before signing, and employees must have time to make a decision about signing—21 days before signing plus 7 days afterward in which they can revoke the agreement.

The Americans with Disabilities Act imposes requirements related to health insurance. Under the ADA, employees with disabilities must have "equal access to whatever health insurance coverage the employer provides other employees." Even so, the terms and conditions of health insurance may be based on risk factors—as long as the employer does not use this basis as a way to escape offering health insurance to someone with a disability. From the standpoint of avoiding legal challenges, an employer who has risk-based insurance and then hires an employee with a disability is in a stronger position than an employer who switches to a risk-based policy after hiring a disabled employee.[46]

Antidiscrimination laws may also apply to situations in which employers offer benefits to their retirees. In a recent case, a federal judge ruled that an employer offering health benefits to retirees could not cut back those benefits when retirees became eligible for Medicare. In other words, if some retirees are eligible for employer-provided insurance, the employer may not require that others receive Medicare coverage instead, based on their age. Some employers have addressed this requirement by eliminating health coverage for retirees.[47]

Accounting Requirements

Companies' financial statements must meet the many requirements of the Financial Accounting Standards Board (FASB). These accounting requirements are intended to ensure that financial statements are a true picture of the company's financial status and that outsiders, including potential lenders and investors, can understand and compare financial statements. Under FASB standards, employers must set aside the funds they expect to need for benefits to be paid after retirement, rather than funding those benefits on a pay-as-you-go basis. On financial statements, those funds must appear as future cost obligations.[48] For companies with substantial retirement benefits, reporting those benefits as future cost obligations greatly lowers income each year. Along with rising benefits costs, this reporting requirement has encouraged many companies to scale back benefits to retirees.

❧ COMMUNICATING BENEFITS TO EMPLOYEES

LO9
Discuss the importance of effectively communicating the nature and value of benefits to employees.

Organizations must communicate benefits information to employees so that they will appreciate the value of their benefits. This is essential so that benefits can achieve their objective of attracting, motivating, and retaining employees. Employees are interested in their benefits, and they need a great deal of detailed information to take advantage of benefits such as health insurance and 401(k) plans. It follows that electronic technology such as the Internet and supporting databases can play a significant role in modern benefit systems. Many companies are putting benefits information on their intranets.

In actuality, employees and job applicants often have a poor idea of what benefits they have and what the market value of their benefits is. Research asking employees about their benefits has shown that employees significantly underestimate the cost and value of their benefits.[49] Probably a major reason for their lack of knowledge is a lack of communications from employers. Employees don't know what employers are spending for benefits, so many of them doubt employers' complaints about soaring costs and their impact on the company's future.[50] In one study, employees said their company neglected to tell them how to be better consumers of health care, and they would be willing to make changes in their lifestyle if they had a financial incentive to do so. Such research suggests to employers that better communication, coupled with well-designed benefits plans, will pay off in practical terms.

Employers have many options for communicating information about benefits. To increase the likelihood that employees will receive and understand the messages, employers can combine several media, such as brochures, question-and-answer meetings, intranet pages, memos, and e-mail. Figure 13.7 identifies a variety of options for

Figure 13.7

Techniques for
Communicating
Employee Benefits

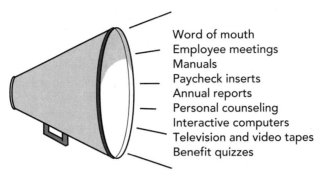

Word of mouth
Employee meetings
Manuals
Paycheck inserts
Annual reports
Personal counseling
Interactive computers
Television and video tapes
Benefit quizzes

Booklets
Computerized statements
Letters to employees
Posters
Check stubs
Benefits fairs
Annual benefits review
Slide presentations
Telephone hot lines

SOURCE: From "An Evaluation of Benefit Communication Strategy," by Michael C. Giallorakis and G. Stephen Taylor reprinted with permission from *Employee Benefits Journal*, 4th Quarter 1991 published by the International Foundation of Employee Benefit Plans (www.ifebp.org), Brookfield, WI. All rights reserved. No further transmission or electronic distribution of this material is permitted.

communicating messages to employees about their benefits. An investment of creativity in communications to employees can reap great returns in the form of committed, satisfied employees.

thinking ETHICALLY

Who Will Pay for Pensions?

Pensions have been a blessing and a curse to employers. Companies invest the money they set aside for pension funds. When the investments perform well, they may bring in so much more money that the plan is overfunded—that is, it grows larger than is required by law and is needed to meet its obligations. The overfunding can become a source of income for the company, or the company may be able to borrow from the fund or use it to pay retirees' medical expenses. But when investments don't live up to expectations, the plan may become underfunded, as happened at a majority of large companies at the end of 1999.

Recently, several companies have announced that they no longer can meet their pension fund obligations. Companies including U.S. Airways, Kaiser Aluminum Corporation, United Airlines, and Bethlehem Steel Corporation have defaulted on their pensions and turned them over to the Pension Benefit Guarantee Corporation. Retirees lose out because PBGC payments are less than what their employer had promised. At United, for example, union leaders said retirees would lose 20 to 50 percent of their expected pension payments. United's position was that it could not emerge from bankruptcy without eliminating its pension obligations. And with several major defaults to cover, the PBGC itself has reported a $30 billion deficit. One possible consequence is that employers might be required to meet stricter funding standards or pay higher premiums for PBGC protection.

Source: Ellen E. Schultz, "Ten Ways Employers Benefit from Benefits Plans," *The Wall Street Journal*, January 24, 2005, http://online.wsj.com; Keith L. Alexander, "United Can End Pensions, Judge Says," *Washington Post*, May 11, 2005, www.washingtonpost.com; and Alexandra Marks, "Why Pensions Are Becoming Even Scarcer," *Christian Science Monitor*, May 16, 2005, www.csmonitor.com.

Questions

1. When a corporation offers its employees a pension plan, who benefits from that arrangement? If the plan becomes underfunded, who is harmed?

2. What issues of fairness are involved in United Airlines' decision to default on its pension plan? Does fairness conflict with United's business interests?

3. For a bankrupt corporation such as United, what do you recommend that the company do to handle its pension funding problem ethically?

SUMMARY

1. Discuss the importance of benefits as a part of employee compensation.

   Like pay, benefits help employers attract, retain, and motivate employees. The variety of possible benefits also helps employers tailor their compensation packages to attract the right kinds of employees. Employees expect at least a minimum level of benefits, and providing more than the minimum helps an organization compete in the labor market. Benefits are also a significant expense, but employers provide benefits because employees value them and many benefits are required by law.

2. Summarize the types of employee benefits required by law.

   Employers must contribute to the Old Age, Survivors, Disability, and Health Insurance program known as Social Security through a payroll tax shared by employers and employees. Employers must also pay federal and state taxes for unemployment insurance, based on each employer's experience rating, or percentage of employees a company has laid off in the past. State laws require that employers purchase workers' compensation insurance. Under the Family and Medical Leave Act, employees who need to care for a baby following birth or adoption or for an ill family member must be granted unpaid leave of up to 12 weeks.

3. Describe the most common forms of paid leave.

   The major categories of paid leave are vacations, holidays, and sick leave. Paid time off may seem uneconomical, which may be the reason U.S. employers tend to offer much less vacation time than is common in Western Europe. At large U.S. companies, paid vacation is typically 10 days. The typical number of paid holidays is 10 in both Western Europe and the United States. Sick leave programs often provide full salary replacement for a limited period of time, with the amount of sick leave usually based on length of service. Policies are needed to determine how the organization will handle unused sick days at the end of each year. Some organizations let employees roll over some or all of the unused sick days into the next year, and others let un-used days expire at the end of the year. Other forms of paid leave include personal days and floating holidays.

4. Identify the kinds of insurance benefits offered by employers.

   Medical insurance is one of the most valued employee benefits. Such policies typically cover hospital expenses, surgical expenses, and visits to physicians. Some employers offer additional coverage, such as dental care, vision care, birthing centers, and prescription drug programs. Under the Consolidated Omnibus Budget Reconciliation Act of 1985, employees must be permitted to extend their health insurance coverage at group rates for up to 36 months after they leave the organization. To manage the costs of health insurance, many organizations offer coverage through a health maintenance organization or preferred provider organization, or they may offer flexible spending accounts. Some encourage healthy behaviors through an employee wellness program. Life insurance usually takes the form of group term life insurance, with the usual benefit being two times the employee's yearly pay. Employers may also offer short-term and/or long-term disability insurance, with disability payments being a percentage of the employee's salary. Some employers provide long-term care insurance to pay the costs associated with long-term care such as nursing home care.

5. Define the types of retirement plans offered by employers.

   Retirement plans may be contributory, meaning funded by contributions from employer and employee, or noncontributory, meaning funded only by the employer. These plans may be defined benefit plans, which guarantee a specified level of retirement income, usually based on the employee's years of service, age, and earnings level. Benefits under these plans are protected by the Pension Benefit Guarantee Corporation. An alternative is to set up a defined contribution plan, such as a 401(k) plan. The employer sets up an individual account for each employee and guarantees the size of the investment into that account, rather than the amount to be paid out on retirement. Because employees have control over investment decisions, the organization may also offer financial planning services as an employee benefit. A cash balance plan combines some advantages of defined benefit plans and defined contribution plans. The employer sets up individual accounts and contributes a percentage of each employee's salary. The account earns interest at a predetermined rate, so the contributions and benefits are easier to predict.

6. Describe how organizations use other benefits to match employees' wants and needs.
   Employers have responded to work-family role conflicts by offering family-friendly benefits, including paid family leave, child care services or referrals, college savings plans, and elder care information and support. Other employee benefits have traditionally included subsidized cafeterias, on-site health clinics, and reimbursement of moving expenses. Stores and manufacturers may offer discounts on their products. Tuition reimbursement encourages employees to continue learning. Recreational services and employee outings provide social interaction as well as stress relief.

7. Explain how to choose the contents of an employee benefits package.
   A logical place to begin is to establish organizational objectives and select benefits that support those objectives. Organizations should also consider employees' expectations and values. At a minimum, organizations offer the benefits employees have come to view as basic; some organizations go so far as to match extra benefits to individual employees' needs and interests. Cafeteria-style plans are an intermediate step that gives employees control over the benefits they receive. Employers must also weigh the costs of benefits, which are significant.

8. Summarize the regulations affecting how employers design and administer benefits programs.
   Employers must provide the benefits that are required by law, and they may not improperly classify employees as "independent contractors" to avoid paying benefits. Tax treatment of qualified plans is favorable, so organizations need to learn the requirements for setting up benefits as qualified plans—for example, ensuring that pension plans do not discriminate in favor of the organization's highly compensated employees. Employers may not use employees' gender as the basis for discriminating against anyone, as in pension benefits on the basis that women as a group may live longer. Nor may employers discriminate against workers over age 40 in providing pay or benefits, such as pressuring older workers to retire by limiting retirement benefits. When employers offer early retirement, they must meet the requirements of the Older Workers Benefit Protection Act of 1990. Under the Americans with Disabilities Act, employers must give disabled employees equal access to health insurance. To meet the requirements of the Financial Accounting Standards Board, employers must set aside the funds they expect to need for retirement benefits ahead of time, rather than funding the benefits on a pay-as-you-go basis.

9. Discuss the importance of effectively communicating the nature and value of benefits to employees.
   Communicating information about benefits is important so that employees will appreciate the value of their benefits. Communicating their value is the main way benefits attract, motivate, and retain employees. Employers have many options for communicating information about benefits, such as brochures, meetings, intranets, memos, and e-mail. Using a combination of such methods increases employees' understanding.

REVIEW AND DISCUSSION QUESTIONS

1. Why do employers provide employee benefits, rather than providing all compensation in the form of pay and letting employees buy the services they want?
2. Of the benefits discussed in this chapter, list the ones you consider essential—that is, the benefits you would require in any job offer. Why are these benefits important to you?
3. Define the types of benefits required by law. How can organizations minimize the cost of these benefits while complying with the relevant laws?
4. What are some advantages of offering a generous package of insurance benefits? What are some drawbacks of generous insurance benefits?
5. Imagine that you are the human resource manager of a small architectural firm. You learn that the monthly premiums for the company's existing health insurance policy will rise by 15 percent next year. What can you suggest to help your company manage this rising cost?
6. In principle, health insurance would be most attractive to employees with large medical expenses, and retirement benefits would be most attractive to older employees. What else might a company include in its benefits package to appeal to young, healthy employees? How might the company structure its benefits so these employees can take advantage of the benefits they care about most?

7. What issues should an organization consider in selecting a package of employee benefits? How should an employer manage the trade-offs among these considerations?

8. How do tax laws and accounting regulations affect benefits packages?

9. What legal requirements might apply to a family leave policy? Suggest how this type of policy should be set up to meet those requirements.

10. Why is it important to communicate information about employee benefits? Suppose you work in the HR department of a company that has decided to add new benefits—dental and vision insurance plus an additional two days of paid time off for "personal days." How would you recommend communicating this change? What information should your messages include?

WHAT'S YOUR HR IQ?

The text Web site offers two more ways to check what you've learned so far. Use the Self-Assessment Exercise to determine if you're likely to find a job that provides the benefits you want. Go online with the Web Exercise to evaluate a company that helps businesses to set up intranets.

BusinessWeek CASE

BusinessWeek Akron Children's Hospital Treats Doctors to Malpractice Insurance

For the past few years, the insurance industry has been running Dr. Stephen W. Crane's practice into the ground. A perinatologist, Crane treats expectant moms who have complications that endanger their pregnancies. Malpractice insurance premiums for such high-risk specialists run as high as $150,000 a year in Ohio—triple what Crane paid when he moved to Akron seven years ago from Syracuse, New York. And with many insurers dropping their malpractice coverage, Crane feared he would be ditched altogether. So when Akron Children's Hospital offered him a full-time job last December, he jumped, thanks to a tantalizing perk: The hospital would foot the entire bill for his malpractice coverage through its own in-house insurance company. "At some point, you can't afford to be in private practice anymore," Crane says.

Doctors and hospitals have been in a squeeze for some time, of course, as malpractice premiums have soared. Now they're also getting inventive. To keep more physicians from bailing out, hospitals are increasingly offering doctors malpractice insurance through not-for-profit entities known as "captives." The captive at Akron Children's can cover Crane and his colleagues for 50 percent less than doctors pay on the open market, estimates CEO William H. Considine. That's because, unlike traditional insurers, hospitals don't have to calculate premiums based on industrywide losses. Instead hospitals, which often supplement coverage through reinsurers, can design coverage around the hospital's track record, a much smaller risk pool.

Today, only 7 percent of doctors actually work for hospitals; the majority just obtain privileges to practice at them. That could change rapidly as hospitals learn they can make an end run around insurers. Among the 2,369 hospitals in 19 "crisis states," where the malpractice insurance situation is most serious, 11 percent had in-house insurance in 2004—up from 9 percent in 2002. That number is expected to multiply. "Interest is skyrocketing," says S. Allan Adelman, a partner with law firm Adelman, Scheff & Smith LLC in Annapolis, Maryland, which advises hospitals on setting up captives.

Hiring doctors also gets hospitals around anti-kickback laws which bar hospitals from providing financial incentives to independent doctors who refer patients to those hospitals. Insurance could be construed as a kickback. But "if you employ them, you can insure them," Adelman says.

The malpractice insurance conundrum has also emboldened hospitals to give the doctor business another try. In the 1990s, hospitals bought up physician practices in droves, hoping to gain specialties that would make them more competitive. It was a disaster. Doctors resented hospital execs watching over them like Big Brother. For their part, the execs griped that doctors grew complacent. Now hospital CEOs are learning from these failures. For example, many hospitals are drawing up job contracts that allow doctors to nab bonuses based on productivity.

Washington understands the bind doctors and hospitals are finding themselves in. President George W. Bush is pushing legislation that would cap so-called noneconomic damages—for emotional distress, for instance—in malpractice cases at $250,000. But experts doubt that reduced jury awards will motivate profit-driven insurers to lower their prices much. That's why hospitals are taking matters into their own hands. Akron Children's Considine says he plans to add three more perinatologists over the next 18 months. They'll join more than 50 pediatricians and other specialists he has hired. "We need physicians to be there for the kids," Considine says, "and we're going to be aggressive about employing them." With no end to the medical malpractice insurance crisis in sight, he won't be alone.

SOURCE: Arlene Weintraub, "A Remedy for Malpractice Malaise," *BusinessWeek*, February 7, 2005, downloaded from Infotrac at http://web7. infotrac.galegroup.com.

Questions

1. Why do physicians value the benefit of hospital-paid malpractice insurance?
2. What do physicians give up by becoming hospital employees rather than operating their own practice?
3. Imagine that you work in the HR department of Akron Children's Hospital, and the hospital's executives want to improve their recruitment and retention of doctors as employees. Suggest at least three additional benefits or policies that would make hospital employment an attractive option to physicians. List your suggestions along with your reasons why each idea will succeed.

CASE: Will Retiree Benefits Drive General Motors Out of Business?

At the 2005 meeting of shareholders, Rick Wagoner, the chief executive officer of General Motors Corporation, announced that GM was planning to eliminate 25,000 U.S. jobs over a three-year period. Much of the blame focused on marketing problems. Demand for the company's big SUVs, which had been the source of most profits, has declined. However, the company has other problems as well, including higher-than-average costs to make its vehicles. In particular, the labor costs to make each vehicle include $1,525 in health care benefits. The company forecasts that total costs for health insurance covering GM's active employees, retirees, and their dependents will reach $5.6 billion in 2005. Of that amount, only about 31 percent goes for current employees and their families; the rest is retiree coverage.

One way to reduce expenses is to set up facilities to run more efficiently, requiring fewer labor hours. GM is also working with the employees' unions on various ways to reduce spending related to health care. One proposal is that hourly employees will pay a greater share of their health care expenses. The company has also set up various wellness programs.

GM's role in promoting employee health is a delicate one because unions resist actions they see as negative. For example, smoking has traditionally been tolerated, so no-smoking policies are difficult to introduce. A majority of GM factories allow workers to smoke while working on assembly lines. Many facilities also have installed cigarette machines. However, attitudes may be changing. In Janesville, Wisconsin, workers voted in favor of a new smoking policy that restricts smoking to designated areas. One of the Janesville employees is Rick Austin, who told a reporter, "I don't smoke and I don't want to stand on the line next to somebody that smokes all day long." Carolyn Markey, the media relations specialist at the Janesville plant, says the new smoking policy represented "a huge cultural change." Can that cultural change work companywide? GM spokesman Stefan Weinmann cautions that

"it's a local issue" and "not something that we can influence centrally." Former union official Michael Kelley explains that workers "don't want to be told that they can't do what they've been doing all along."

Along with curbing smoking, GM hopes it can reduce the impact of obesity and stress on health care expenses. Company statistics indicate that over one-fourth of the people covered by its health insurance are obese according to federal weight guidelines and that these individuals cost the company $1,000 to $3,000 more in terms of using health services. Some of GM's major health-related expenses are drugs used to treat high cholesterol, high blood pressure, and diabetes, conditions that have been linked to excess weight and stress. Of the $5.2 billion GM spent on health care in 2004, $1.5 billion paid for prescription drugs.

To address these problems, GM and the United Auto Workers in 1996 launched a program called LifeSteps, which includes health classes and other wellness services. The program, offered to employees and retirees, was expanded in 2003. In addition, some GM locations offer workout facilities. Planners of the LifeSteps program try to come up with courses and activities geared to employees' interests. For example, many GM workers enjoy hunting, so LifeSteps offers classes that focus on the fitness needs of hunters. Charlie Estey, a consultant involved in LifeSteps comments, "These are 300 guys that would never come to an aerobics class or yoga, yet we were able to do some things with deer hunting and conditioning." Those "things" included conditioning advice, safety guidelines, and healthful recipes for preparing venison. Denny Geurink, a former writer for *Field & Stream* magazine, spoke to the employees about how to get in shape for hunting season.

With health care spending rising year after year, GM will have to continue to be this creative.

SOURCE: Lee Hawkins Jr., "As GM Battles Surging Costs, Workers' Health Becomes Issue," *The Wall Street Journal*, April 7, 2005, http://online.wsj.com; and "GM Plans to Cut 25,000 Jobs as Part of Turnaround Plan," *The Wall Street Journal*, June 7, 2005, http://online.wsj.com.

Questions

1. What do you think is GM's greatest challenge in reducing its spending for health care benefits? Explain.
2. If you worked in GM's HR department, what information would you want employees to know about the

company's spending for health care? How could you convey that information to employees?
3. Besides the ideas described in this case, describe another way GM might be able to reduce spending on health benefits.

NOTES

1. "Benefits—United States," Hewitt Associates Web site, http://was.hewitt.com, downloaded August 27, 2002.
2. B. Gerhart and G. T. Milkovich, "Employee Compensation: Research and Practice," in *Handbook of Industrial and Organizational Psychology*, vol. 3, 2nd ed., ed. M. D. Dunnette and L. M. Hough (Palo Alto, CA: Consulting Psychologists Press, 1992); and J. Swist, "Benefits Communications: Measuring Impact and Values," *Employee Benefit Plan Review*, September 2002, pp. 24–26.
3. U.S. Department of Labor, Employment and Training Administration, "Unemployment Insurance (UI) Taxable Wage Bases and Tax Rates," http://workforcesecurity.doleta.gov, accessed June 2, 2005.
4. J. V. Nackley, *Primer on Workers' Compensation* (Washington, DC: Bureau of National Affairs, 1989); T. Thomason, T. P. Schmidle, and J. F. Burton, *Workers' Compensation* (Kalamazoo, MI: Upjohn Institute, 2001).
5. B. T. Beam Jr. and J. J. McFadden, *Employee Benefits*, 6th ed. (Chicago: Dearborn Financial Publishing, 2000).
6. S. S. Muñoz, "A Good Idea, but . . . ," *The Wall Street Journal*, January 24, 2005, p. R6.
7. P. Hardin, "Women Execs Should Feel at Ease about Taking Full Maternity Leave," *Personnel Journal*, September 1995, p. 19; U.S. Department of Labor Web site, www.dol.gov, 2000.
8. "Summer Vacation Highlights Global Differences in Paid Time Off," Hewitt Associates, June 6, 2001.
9. G. Weber, "Lost Time: Vacation Days Go Unused Despite More Liberal Time-Off Policies," *Workforce Management*, December 2004, pp. 66–67.
10. Employee Benefit Research Institute, "Value of Employee Benefits Constant in a Changing World," March 28, 2002, www.ebri.org.
11. J. D. Morton and P. Aleman, "Trends in Employer-Provided Mental Health and Substance Abuse Benefits," *Monthly Labor Review*, April 2005, pp. 25–35.
12. Employee Benefit Research Institute, "FAQs about Benefits: Health Spending and Insurance Issues," www.ebri.org, citing *EBRI Issue Brief*, May 2003.
13. R. Lieber, "New Way to Curb Medical Costs: Make Employees Feel the Sting," *The Wall Street Journal*,

June 23, 2004, pp. A1, A6; and R. Stolz, "Healthy Encouragement," *Human Resource Executive*, May 2, 2005, pp. 1, 22–31.
14. J. C. Erfurt, A. Foote, and M. A. Heirich, "The Cost-Effectiveness of Worksite Wellness Programs for Hypertension Control, Weight Loss, Smoking Cessation and Exercise," *Personnel Psychology* 45 (1992), pp. 5–27.
15. D. Wessel, "Enron and a Bigger Ill: Americans Don't Save," *The Wall Street Journal Online*, March 7, 2002, http://online.wsj.com.
16. M. Slate, "The Retirement Protection Act," *Labor Law Journal*, April 1995, pp. 245–50.
17. Internal Revenue Service Web site, www.irs.gov.
18. R. A. Ippolito, "Toward Explaining the Growth of Defined Contribution Plans," *Industrial Relations* 34 (1995), pp. 1–20; and Employee Benefit Research Institute, "Historical Statistics," EBRI May 2004 Policy Forum, www.ebri.org.
19. Employee Benefit Research Institute, "FAQs about Benefits: Retirement Issues," www.ebri.org, accessed June 1, 2005.
20. T. Lauricella, "A Lesson for Social Security: Many Mismanage Their 401(k)s," *The Wall Street Journal*, December 1, 2004, http://online.wsj.com.
21. E. E. Schultz, "IBM Settles Small Part of Pension Suit," *The Wall Street Journal*, September 17, 2004, p. A2.
22. "Supreme Court Lets Stand Third Circuit Ruling That Pension Avoidance Scheme Is ERISA Violation," *Daily Labor Report*, no. 234 (December 8, 1987), p. A-14, summarizing *Continental Can Company v. Gavalik*.
23. Beam and McFadden, *Employee Benefits*.
24. S. L. Grover and K. J. Crooker, "Who Appreciates Family Responsive Human Resource Policies: The Impact of Family-Friendly Policies on the Organizational Attachment of Parents and Non-parents," *Personnel Psychology* 48 (1995), pp. 271–88; M. A. Arthur, "Share Price Reactions to Work-Family Initiatives: An Institutional Perspective," *Academy of Management Journal* 46 (2003), p. 497; and J. E. Perry-Smith and T. Blum, "Work-Family Human Resource Bundles and Perceived Organizational Performance," *Academy of Management Journal* 43 (2000), pp. 1107–17.

25. Clearinghouse on International Developments in Child, Youth and Family Policies, "Comparative Policies and Programs," Section 1.1, Maternity, Paternity, Parental and Family Leave Policies, www.childpolicyintl.org, last updated November 2004.

26. Families and Work Institute (FWI), "The Families and Work Institute's 1998 Business Work-Life Study," FWI Web site, www.familiesandwork.org.

27. "Benefits and the Bottom Line," (Raleigh, N.C.) *News and Observer*, October 14, 2001.

28. E. E. Kossek, "Diversity in Child Care Assistance Needs: Employee Problems, Preferences, and Work-Related Outcomes," *Personnel Psychology* 43 (1990), pp. 769–91.

29. E. E. Kossek, *The Acceptance of Human Resource Innovation: Lessons from Management* (Westport, CT: Quorum, 1989).

30. B. Shutan, "Lending a Hand," *Human Resource Executive*, May 2, 2005, pp. 46–49.

31. T. Cullen, "Workplace 529 Plans May Have Lower Fees, but Also Drawbacks," *The Wall Street Journal Online*, May 9, 2002, http://online.wsj.com.

32. S. Shellenbarger, "Web Sites Can Help to Ease Burden of Caring for Elders," *The Wall Street Journal Online*, February 27, 2002, http://online.wsj.com.

33. S. Shellenbarger, "From Catnaps to Lunchtime Jobs: Tales about 'Undertime' at Work," *The Wall Street Journal Online*, May 16, 2002, http://online.wsj.com.

34. R. Broderick and B. Gerhart, "Nonwage Compensation," in *The Human Resource Management Handbook*, ed. D. Lewin, D. J. B. Mitchell, and M. A. Zadi (San Francisco: JAI Press, 1996).

35. J. M. Von Bergen, "Pampering Employees Benefits Company," *Philadelphia Inquirer*, August 1, 2004, pp. F1–F2.

36. V. Colliver, "Balancing the Benefit Bite," *San Francisco Chronicle*, January 19, 2005, www.sfgate.com.

37. Beam and McFadden, *Employee Benefits*.

38. D. A. Harrison and L. Z. Liska, "Promoting Regular Exercise in Organizational Fitness Programs: Health-Related Differences in Motivational Building Blocks," *Personnel Psychology* 47 (1994), pp. 47–71; Erfurt et al., "The Cost-Effectiveness of Worksite Wellness Programs."

39. D. Beck, "Your Company Needs Its Own Best Practices," *The Wall Street Journal* (Career Journal, July 30–August 5, 2001), www.careerjournal.com; and M. Chase, "Healthy Assets," *The Wall Street Journal*, May 1, 2000, http://interactive.wsj.com.

40. U.S. Bureau of Labor Statistics, www.bls.gov.

41. Beam and McFadden, *Employee Benefits*, p. 359.

42. For a description of these rules, see M. M. Sarli, "Nondiscrimination Rules for Qualified Plans: The General Test," *Compensation and Benefits Review* 23, no. 5 (September–October 1991), pp. 56–67.

43. *Los Angeles Department of Water & Power v. Manhart*, 435 U.S. S. Ct. 702 (1978), 16 E.P.D. 8250.

44. S. K. Hoffman, "Discrimination Litigation Relating to Employee Benefits," *Labor Law Journal*, June 1992, pp. 362–81.

45. P. J. Kennedy, "Take the Money and Sue," *HRMagazine* 43, no. 5 (April 1998), pp. 105–8.

46. Hoffman, "Discrimination Litigation," p. 375.

47. A. B. Crenshaw, "Retiree Benefits Can't Be Cut at 65, Judge Says," *Washington Post*, March 31, 2005, www.washingtonpost.com.

48. A. Tergesen, "The Hidden Bite of Retiree Health," *BusinessWeek*, January 19, 2004; D. Welch, "Has GM Outrun Its Pension Problems?" *BusinessWeek*, January 19, 2004.

49. M. Wilson, G. B. Northcraft, and M. A. Neale, "The Perceived Value of Fringe Benefits," *Personnel Psychology* 38 (1985), pp. 309–20; H. W. Hennessey, P. L. Perrewe, and W. A. Hochwarter, "Impact of Benefit Awareness on Employee and Organizational Outcomes: A Longitudinal Field Experiment," *Benefits Quarterly* 8, no. 2 (1992), pp. 90–96.

50. M. C. Giallourakis and G. S. Taylor, "An Evaluation of Benefit Communication Strategy," *Employee Benefits Journal* 15, no. 4 (1991), pp. 14–18; and J. Mehring, "Health Care: Trust Issues," *BusinessWeek*, August 2, 2004, p. 28.

If you are using the Manager's Hot Seat DVD with this book, consider finishing case 13: Listening Skills: Yeah, Whatever for this chapter.

5

MEETING OTHER HR GOALS

14

COLLECTIVE BARGAINING AND LABOR RELATIONS

≈ INTRODUCTION

As organizations try to do more with less and as employees struggle with the challenge of balancing work and personal lives, many disputes between employees and employers involve demands on workers' time. In particular, unions representing workers have increasingly emphasized limits on overtime when they are bargaining with employers. Occasionally, that issue even fuels a strike. In 2005, workers in Local 369 of the Utility Workers of America went on strike against NStar, which provides electrical service to customers in eastern and central Massachusetts. They complained that NStar had eliminated about 120 maintenance positions, so employees had to work longer hours, compromising safety. Lineman Tim Morrissey complained, "I work constantly, and I'm on call 24 hours per day, seven days a week," adding that his pay of $97,000 a year was so high "only because we're forced to be here." The company replied that long hours are sometimes necessary in the power industry because emergencies can cause power outages. After three weeks, the strike was settled with compromises on both sides, including the hiring of 150 new workers, many of them for maintenance positions. Pushing the two sides toward an agreement was mediator John Martin, who started the conversation by getting negotiators to begin by discussing issues the workers and company agreed on and then moving to the more controversial matters. Their efforts produced a four-year contract, which the union workers voted for by a wide margin.[1]

In contrast to the discussion of work design in Chapter 4, the changes in work rules by NStar were prompted in part by workers' demands as a group—that is, by their union. The presence of unions at NStar changes this aspect of human resource management by directing more attention to the interests of employees as a group. The majority of employees wanted maintenance tasks to be accomplished by more employees working fewer hours, reducing the amount of mandatory overtime for each employee. In general, employees and employers share the same interests. They both benefit when the organization is strong and growing, providing employees with jobs and employers with profits. But although the interests of employers and employees overlap, they obviously are not identical. In the case of pay, workers benefit from higher pay, but high pay cuts into the organization's profits, unless pay increases are associated with higher productivity or better customer service. Workers may negotiate differences with their employers individually, or they may form unions to negotiate on their behalf. This chapter explores human resource activities in organizations where employees belong to unions or where employees are seeking to organize unions.

We begin by formally defining unions and labor relations, and then describe the scope and impact of union activity. We next summarize government laws and regulations affecting unions and labor relations. The following three sections detail types of activities involving unions: union organizing, contract negotiation, and contract administration. Finally, we identify ways in which unions and management are working together in arrangements that are more cooperative than the traditional labor-management relationship.

ROLE OF UNIONS AND LABOR RELATIONS

In the United States today, most workers act as individuals to select jobs that are acceptable to them and to negotiate pay, benefits, flexible hours, and other work conditions. Especially when there is stiff competition for labor and employees have hard-to-replace skills, this arrangement produces satisfactory results for most employees. At times, however, workers have believed their needs and interests do not receive enough consideration from management. One response by workers is to act collectively by forming and joining labor **unions,** organizations formed for the purpose of representing their members' interests and resolving conflicts with employers.

Unions have a role because some degree of conflict is inevitable between workers and management.[2] As we commented earlier, for example, managers can increase profits by lowering workers' pay, but workers benefit in the short term if lower profits result because their pay is higher. Still, this type of conflict is more complex than a simple trade-off, such as wages versus profits. Rising profits can help employees by driving up profit sharing or other benefits, and falling profits can result in layoffs and a lack of investment. Although employers can use programs like profit sharing to help align employee interests with their own, some remaining divergence of interests is inevitable. Labor unions represent worker interests and the collective bargaining process provides a way to manage the conflict. In other words, through systems for hearing complaints and negotiating labor contracts, unions and managers resolve conflicts between employers and employees.

As unionization of workers became more common, universities developed training in how to manage union-management interactions.[3] This specialty, called **labor relations,** emphasizes skills that managers and union leaders can use to foster effective labor-management cooperation, minimize costly forms of conflict (such as strikes), and seek win-win solutions to disagreements. Labor relations involves three levels of decisions:[4]

LO1
Define unions and labor relations and their role in organizations.

unions
Organizations formed for the purpose of representing their members' interests in dealing with employers.

labor relations
Field that emphasizes skills managers and union leaders can use to minimize costly forms of conflict (such as strikes) and seek win-win solutions to disagreements.

1. *Labor relations strategy*—For management, the decision involves whether the organization will work with unions or develop (or maintain) nonunion operations. This decision is influenced by outside forces such as public opinion and competition. For unions, the decision involves whether to fight changes in how unions relate to the organization or accept new kinds of labor-management relationships.

2. *Negotiating contracts*—As we will describe later in the chapter, contract negotiations in a union setting involve decisions about pay structure, job security, work rules, workplace safety, and many other issues. These decisions affect workers' and the employer's situation for the term of the contract.

3. *Administering contracts*—These decisions involve day-to-day activities in which union members and the organization's managers may have disagreements. Issues include complaints of work rules being violated or workers being treated unfairly in particular situations. A formal grievance procedure is typically used to resolve these issues.

Later sections in this chapter describe how managers and unions carry out the activities connected with these levels of decisions, as well as the goals and legal constraints affecting these activities.

National and International Unions

craft union
Labor union whose members all have a particular skill or occupation.

industrial union
Labor union whose members are linked by their work in a particular industry.

Most union members belong to a national or international union. Figure 14.1 shows the membership of the 10 largest national unions in the United States. Half of these have memberships of over a million workers.

These unions may be either craft or industrial unions. The members of a **craft union** all have a particular skill or occupation. Examples include the International Brotherhood of Electrical Workers for electricians and the United Brotherhood of Carpenters and Joiners of America for carpenters. Craft unions are often responsible for training their members through apprenticeships and for supplying craft workers to employers. For example, an employer would send requests for carpenters to the union hiring hall, which would decide which carpenters to send out. In this way, craft workers may work for many employers over time but have a constant link to the union. A craft union's bargaining power depends greatly on its control over the supply of its workers.

Andrew Stern, left, is president of the Service Employees International Union, one of the fastest growing unions that recently withdrew from the AFL-CIO. Stern intends to create a new and more dynamic labor movement by spending half the SEIU's budget on helping more workers unite in the union and gain a voice on the job.

Figure 14.1

10 Largest Unions in the United States

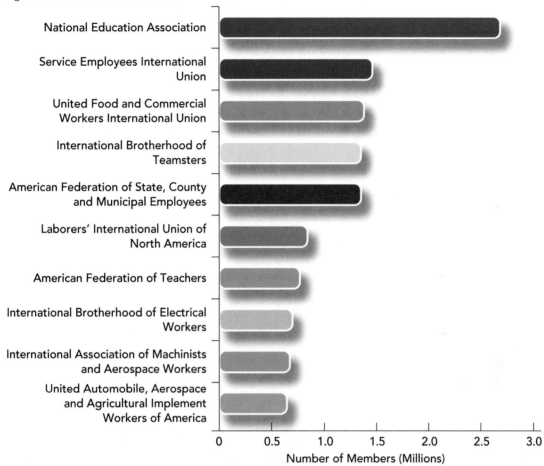

SOURCE: Labor Research Association, "Unions in U.S. with More than 100,000 Members (2002)," *LRA Online*, www.laborresearch.org, citing *Directory of U.S. Labor Organizations*, Bureau of National Affairs, 2004.

In contrast, **industrial unions** consist of members who are linked by their work in a particular industry. Examples include the United Steelworkers of America and the Communication Workers of America. Typically, an industrial union represents many different occupations. Membership in the union is the result of working for a particular employer in the industry. Changing employers is less common than it is among craft workers, and employees who change employers remain members of the same union only if they happen to move to other employers covered by that union. Another difference is that whereas a craft union may restrict the number of skilled craftsmen—say, carpenters—to maintain higher wages, industrial unions try to organize as many employees in as wide a range of skills as possible.

Most national unions are affiliated with the **American Federation of Labor and Congress of Industrial Organizations (AFL-CIO).** The AFL-CIO is not a labor union but an association that seeks to advance the shared interests of its member unions at the national level, much as the Chamber of Commerce and the National Association of Manufacturers do for their member employers. Approximately 55 national and

American Federation of Labor and Congress of Industrial Organizations (AFL-CIO)
An association that seeks to advance the shared interests of its member unions at the national level.

international unions are affiliated with the AFL-CIO. An important responsibility of the AFL-CIO is to represent labor's interests in public policy issues such as labor law, economic policy, and occupational safety and health. The organization also provides information and analysis that member unions can use in their activities. The AFL-CIO is currently an organization in crisis. Three of the largest affiliated unions, the Service Employees International Union, Teamsters, and the United Food and Commercial Workers voted to leave the AFL-CIO removing over 25% of its membership.[5] Leaders of these unions believe a new strategy is needed to increase union membership and impact (such as focusing organizing efforts on service employees).

Local Unions

Most national unions consist of multiple local units. Even when a national union plays the most critical role in negotiating the terms of a collective bargaining contract, negotiation occurs at the local level for work rules and other issues that are locally determined. In addition, administration of the contract largely takes place at the local union level. As a result, most day-to-day interaction between labor and management involves the local union.

Membership in the local union depends on the type of union. For an industrial union, the local may correspond to a single large facility or to a number of small facilities. In a craft union, the local may cover a city or a region.

Typically, the local union elects officers, such as president, vice president, and treasurer. The officers may be responsible for contract negotiation, or the local may form a bargaining committee for that purpose. When the union is engaged in bargaining, the national union provides help, including background data about other settlements, technical advice, and the leadership of a representative from the national office.

Individual members participate in local unions in various ways. At meetings of the local union, they elect officials and vote on resolutions to strike. Most of workers' contact is with the **union steward,** an employee elected by union members to represent them in ensuring that the terms of the contract are enforced. The union steward helps to investigate complaints and represents employees to supervisors and other managers when employees file grievances alleging contract violations.[6] When the union deals with several employers, as in the case of a craft union, a *business representative* performs some of the same functions as a union steward. Because of union stewards' and business representatives' close involvement with employees, it is to management's advantage to cultivate positive working relationships with them.

union steward
An employee elected by union members to represent them in ensuring that the terms of the labor contract are enforced.

Trends in Union Membership

Union membership in the United States peaked in the 1950s, reaching over one-third of employees. Since then, the share of employees who belong to unions has fallen. It now stands at 12.5 percent overall and 9 percent of private-sector employment.[7] As Figure 14.2 indicates, union membership fell steadily during the 1980s and 1990s. Union membership among government workers has held steady, with the decline occurring in the private sector.

The decline in union membership has been attributed to several factors.[8] The factor that seems to be cited most often is change in the structure of the economy. Much recent job growth has occurred among women and youth in the service sector of the economy, while union strength has traditionally been among urban blue-collar workers, especially middle-aged workers. Women are less likely than men to belong to

Figure 14.2

Union Membership Density among U.S. Wage and Salary Workers, 1973–2004

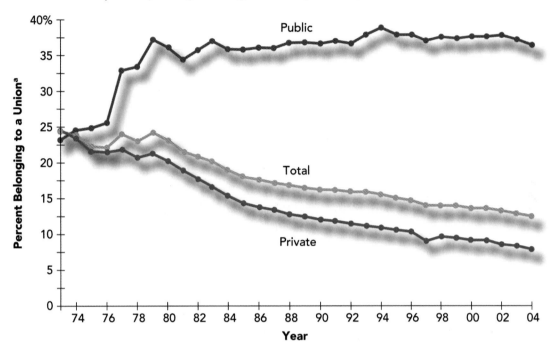

[a]Percentage of total, private-sector, and public-sector wage and salary workers who are union members. Beginning in 1977, workers belonging to "an employee association similar to a union" are included as members.

SOURCE: Data for 1973–2001 from B. T. Hirsch and D. A. MacPherson, *Union Membership and Earnings Data Book 2001* (Washington, DC: Bureau of National Affairs, 2002), using data from U.S. Current Population Surveys. Data for 2002 and 2003 from U.S. Census Bureau, *Statistical Abstract of the United States, 2004–2005*, p. 419. Data for 2004 from Bureau of Labor Statistics, "Union Members in 2004," news release, January 27, 2005, www.bls.gov.

unions, and services industries such as finance, insurance, and real estate have lower union representation than manufacturing. Also, much business growth has been in the South, where workers are less likely to join unions.[9]

Another force working against union membership is management efforts against union organizing. In a survey, almost half of large employers said their most important labor goal was to be union-free. Efforts to control costs have contributed to employer resistance to unions.[10] On average, unionized workers receive higher pay than their nonunionized counterparts, and the pressure is greater because of international competition. In the past, union membership across an industry such as automobiles or steel resulted in similar wages and work requirements for all competitors. Today, U.S. producers must compete with companies that have entirely different pay scales and work rules, often placing the U.S. companies at a disadvantage. Another way in which management may contribute to the decline in union membership is by adopting human resource practices that increase employees' commitment to their job and employer. Competition for scarce human resources can lead employers to offer much of what employees traditionally sought through union membership. Government regulations, too, can make unions seem less important. Stricter regulation in such areas as workplace safety and equal employment opportunity leaves fewer areas in which unions can show an advantage over what employers must already offer.

Figure 14.3

Union Membership
Rates and Coverage
in Selected
Countries

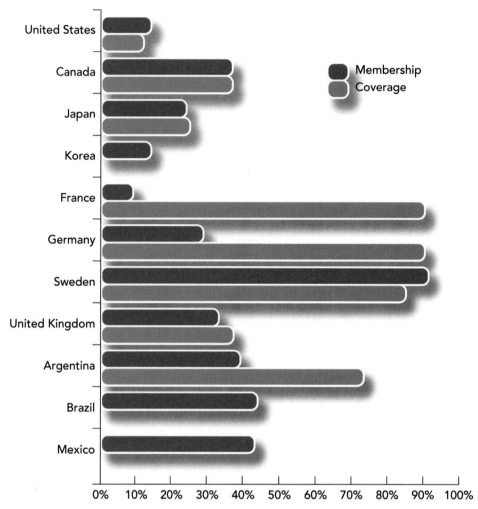

SOURCE: International Labour Office, *World Labour Report, 1997–98* (Geneva, Switzerland).

As Figure 14.3 indicates, the percentage of U.S. workers who belong to unions is lower than in many countries. More dramatic is the difference in "coverage"—the percentage of employees whose terms and conditions of employment are governed by a union contract, whether or not the employees are technically union members. In Western Europe, it is common to have coverage rates of 80 to 90 percent, so the influence of labor unions far outstrips what membership levels would imply.[11] Also, employees in Western Europe tend to have a larger formal role in decision making than in the United States. This role, including worker representatives on boards of directors, is often mandated by the government. But as markets become more and more global, pressure to cut labor costs and increase productivity is likely to be stronger in every country. Unless unions can help companies improve productivity or organize new production facilities opened in lower-wage countries, union influence may decline in countries where it is now strong.

Although union members are a smaller share of the U.S. workforce, they are a significant part of many industries' labor markets. Along with strength in numbers, large unions have strength in dollars. Union retirement funds, taken together, are huge.

Unions try to use their investment decisions in ways that influence businesses. Before the stock market's rebound in 2003, unions directly controlled roughly $250 billion in pension funds and shared control with employers over another $1 trillion, with government-employee pension funds controlling another $2 trillion. The AFL-CIO and the United Steelworkers have set up a separate fund, the Heartland Labor Capital Network, which directs its investments to worker-friendly companies.[12]

Unions in Government

Unlike union membership for workers in businesses, union membership among government workers has remained strong. Union membership in the public sector grew during the 1960s and 1970s and has remained steady ever since. Over one-third of government employees are union members, and a larger share are covered by collective bargaining agreements. One reason for this strength is that government regulations and laws support the right of government workers to organize. In 1962 Executive Order 10988 established collective bargaining rights for federal employees. By the end of the 1960s, most states had passed similar laws.

An interesting aspect of union growth among government workers is that much of it has occurred in the service industry and among white-collar employees—groups that have been viewed as difficult to organize. The American Federation of State, County and Municipal Employees (AFSCME) has over 1.3 million members. These include 230,000 members in health care and 243,000 in education. A majority of AFSCME employees have at least some college education, and over one-third hold at least a bachelor's degree.[13]

Labor relations with government workers is different in some respects, such as regarding the right to strike. Strikes are illegal for federal workers and for state workers in most states. At the local level, all states prohibit strikes by police (Hawaii being a partial exception) and firefighters (Idaho being the exception). Teachers and state employees are somewhat more likely to have the right to strike, depending on the state. Legal or not, strikes by government workers do occur. Of the 39 strikes involving 1,000 or more workers in 2000, eight involved workers in state and local government.

Impact of Unions on Company Performance

Organizations are concerned about whether union organizing and bargaining will hurt their performance, in particular, unions' impact on productivity, profits, and stock performance. Researchers have studied the general relationship between unionization and these performance measures. Through skillful labor relations, organizations can positively influence outcomes.

There has been much debate regarding the effects of unions on productivity.[14] One view is that unions decrease productivity because of work rules and limits on workloads set by union contracts and production lost to such union actions as strikes and work slowdowns. At the same time, unions can have positive effects on productivity.[15] They can reduce turnover by giving employees a route for resolving problems.[16] Unions emphasize pay systems based on seniority, which remove incentives for employees to compete rather than cooperate. The introduction of a union also may force an employer to improve its management practices and pay greater attention to employee ideas.

Although there is evidence that unions have both positive and negative effects on productivity, most studies have found that union workers are more productive than nonunion workers. Still, questions remain. Are highly productive workers more likely

Harley-Davidson and the International Association of Machinists and Aerospace Workers have cooperated to produce good results. In general, though, companies wishing to become more competitive need to continually monitor their labor relations strategies.

to form unions, or does a union make workers more productive? The answer is unclear. In theory, if unions caused greater productivity, we would expect union membership to be rising, not falling as it has been.[17]

Even if unions do raise productivity, a company's profits and stock performance may still suffer if unions raise wage and benefits costs by more than the productivity gain. On average, union members receive higher wages and more generous benefits than nonunion workers, and evidence shows that unions have a large negative effect on profits. Also, union coverage tends to decline faster in companies with a lower return to shareholders.[18] In summary, companies wishing to become more competitive must continually monitor their labor relations strategy.

The studies tend to look at the average effects of unions, not at individual companies or innovative labor relations. Some organizations excel at labor relations, and some have worked with unions to meet business needs. For example, even though U.S. manufacturers have outsourced or automated many jobs, a study by the National Association of Manufacturers found that 8 out of 10 had at least a moderate shortage of production workers, machinists, and craft workers. Many of these companies traditionally depended on unions to recruit and train new workers through apprenticeship programs. Some still do. At U.S. Steel, the United Steelworkers of America trains apprentices in trades including metalworking; 150 apprentices were in the program in 2005.[19]

❦ GOALS OF EACH GROUP

LO2
Identify the labor relations goals of management, labor unions, and society.

Resolving conflicts in a positive way is usually easiest when the parties involved understand each other's goals. Although individual cases vary, we can draw some general conclusions about the goals of labor unions and management. Society, too, has goals for labor and business, given form in the laws regulating labor relations.

Goals of Management

Management goals are to increase the organization's profits. Managers tend to prefer options that lower costs and raise output. When deciding whether to discourage employees from forming a union, a concern is that a union will create higher costs in wages and benefits, as well as raise the risk of work stoppages. Managers may also fear that a union will make managers and workers into adversaries or limit management's discretion in making business and employment decisions.

When an employer has recognized a union, management's goals continue to emphasize restraining costs and improving output. Managers continue to prefer to keep the organization's operations flexible, so they can adjust activities to meet competitive challenges and customer demands. Therefore, in their labor relations managers prefer to limit increases in wages and benefits and to retain as much control as they can over work rules and schedules.

Goals of Labor Unions

In general, labor unions have the goals of obtaining pay and working conditions that satisfy their members and of giving members a voice in decisions that affect them. Traditionally, they obtain these goals by gaining power in numbers. The more workers who belong to a union, the greater the union's power. More members translates into greater ability to halt or disrupt production. Larger unions also have greater financial resources for continuing a strike; the union can help to make up for the wages the workers lose during a strike. The threat of a long strike—stated or implied—can make an employer more willing to meet the union's demands.

As we noted earlier, union membership is indeed linked to better compensation. In 2000, private-sector unionized workers received, on average, wages 19 percent higher than nonunion workers in similar jobs.[20] Union membership has an even greater effect on benefits packages. Total compensation (pay plus benefits) was 36 percent higher for union members in 2000. Taking into account other influences, such as the greater ease with which unions are able to organize relatively highly paid, productive workers, researchers estimate that the total "union effect" on wages is about 10 percent.[21] In other words, for every $1 paid to a nonunion worker, a union worker in the same job would earn about $1.10.

Unions typically want to influence the *way* pay and promotions are determined. Unlike management, which tries to consider employees as individuals so that pay and promotion decisions relate to performance differences, unions try to build group solidarity and avoid possible arbitrary treatment of employees. To do so, unions focus on equal pay for equal work. They try to have any pay differences based on seniority, on the grounds that this measure is more objective than performance evaluations. As a result, where workers are represented by a union, it is common for all employees in a particular job classification to be paid at the same rate.

The survival and security of a union depend on its ability to ensure a regular flow of new members and member dues to support the services it provides. Therefore, unions typically place high priority on negotiating two types of contract provisions with an employer that are critical to a union's security and viability: checkoff provisions and provisions relating to union membership or contribution.

Under a **checkoff provision,** the employer, on behalf of the union, automatically deducts union dues from employees' paychecks. Security provisions related to union membership are *closed shop, union shop, agency shop,* and *maintenance of membership.*

The strongest union security arrangement is a **closed shop,** under which a person must be a union member before being hired. Under the National Labor Relations Act, discussed later in this chapter, closed shops are illegal. A legal membership arrangement that supports the goals of labor unions is the **union shop,** an arrangement that requires an employee to join the union within a certain time (30 days) after beginning employment. A similar alternative is the **agency shop,** which requires the payment of union dues but not union membership. **Maintenance of membership** rules do not require union membership but do require that employees who join the union remain members for a certain period of time, such as the length of the contract. As we will discuss later in the chapter, some states forbid union shops, agency shops, and maintenance of membership.

checkoff provision
Contract provision under which the employer, on behalf of the union, automatically deducts union dues from employees' paychecks.

closed shop
Union security arrangement under which a person must be a union member before being hired; illegal for those covered by the National Labor Relations Act.

union shop
Union security arrangement that requires employees to join the union within a certain amount of time (30 days) after beginning employment.

agency shop
Union security arrangement that requires the payment of union dues but not union membership.

maintenance of membership
Union security rules not requiring union membership but requiring that employees who join the union remain members for a certain period of time.

All these provisions are ways to address unions' concern about "free riders"—employees who benefit from union activities without belonging to a union. By law, all members of a bargaining unit, whether union members or not, must be represented by the union. If the union must offer services to all bargaining unit members but some of them are not dues-paying union members, the union may not have enough financial resources to operate successfully.

Goals of Society

The activities of unions and management take place within the context of society, with society's values driving the laws and regulations that affect labor relations. As long ago as the late 1800s and early 1900s, industrial relations scholars saw unions as a way to make up for individual employees' limited bargaining power.[22] At that time, clashes between workers and management could be violent, and many people hoped that unions would replace the violence with negotiation. Since then, observers have expressed concern that unions in certain industries have become too strong, achieving their goals at the expense of employers' ability to compete or meet other objectives. But even Senator Orrin Hatch, described by *BusinessWeek* as "labor's archrival on Capitol Hill," has spoken of a need for unions:

> There are always going to be people who take advantage of workers. Unions even that out, to their credit. We need them to level the field between labor and management. If you didn't have unions, it would be very difficult for even enlightened employers not to take advantage of workers on wages and working conditions, because of [competition from less-enlightened] rivals. I'm among the first to say I believe in unions.[23]

Senator Hatch's statement implies that society's goal for unions is to ensure that workers have a voice in how they are treated by their employers. As we will see in the next section, this view has produced a set of laws and regulations intended to give workers the right to join unions if they so wish.

LO3
Summarize laws and regulations that affect labor relations.

❧ LAWS AND REGULATIONS AFFECTING LABOR RELATIONS

The laws and regulations pertaining to labor relations affect unions' size and bargaining power, so they significantly affect the degree to which unions, management, and society achieve their varied goals. These laws and regulations set limits on union structure and administration and the ways in which unions and management interact.

National Labor Relations Act (NLRA)

National Labor Relations Act (NLRA)
Federal law that supports collective bargaining and sets out the rights of employees to form unions.

Perhaps the most dramatic example of labor laws' influence is the 1935 passage of the Wagner Act (also known as the **National Labor Relations Act,** or **NLRA),** which actively supported collective bargaining. After Congress passed the NLRA, union membership in the United States nearly tripled, from 3 million in 1933 to 8.8 million (19.2 percent of employment) in 1939.[24]

Before the 1930s, the U.S. legal system was generally hostile to unions. The courts tended to view unions as coercive organizations that hindered free trade. Unions' focus on collective voice and collective action (such as strikes and boycotts) did not fit well with the U.S. emphasis on capitalism, individualism, freedom of contract, and property rights.[25] Then the Great Depression of the 1930s shifted public attitudes toward business and the free-enterprise system. Unemployment rates as high as 25 percent and a steep fall in production between 1929 and 1933 focused attention on employee rights and the shortcomings of the economic system of the time. The nation was in crisis, and President Franklin Roosevelt responded dramatically with the New Deal. On the labor front, the 1935 NLRA ushered in an era of public policy for labor unions, enshrining collective bargaining as the preferred way to settle labor-management disputes.

Section 7 of the NLRA sets out the rights of employees, including the "right to self-organization, to form, join, or assist labor organizations, to bargain collectively through representatives of their own choosing, and to engage in other concerted activities for the purpose of collective bargaining."[26] Employees also have the right to refrain from these activities, unless union membership is a condition of employment. The following activities are among those protected under the NLRA:

- Union organizing.
- Joining a union, whether recognized by the employer or not.
- Going out on strike to secure better working conditions.
- Refraining from activity on behalf of the union.

Most employees in the private sector are covered by the NLRA. As shown in Table 14.1, however, certain workers are excluded, including supervisors, independent contractors, agricultural workers, and government employees. State or local laws may provide additional coverage. For example, California's 1975 Agricultural Labor Relations Act covers agricultural workers in that state.

In Section 8(a), the NLRA prohibits certain activities by employers as unfair labor practices. In general, employers may not interfere with, restrain, or coerce employees in exercising their rights to join or assist a labor organization or to refrain from such activities. Employers may not dominate or interfere with the formation or activities of a labor union. They may not discriminate in any aspect of employment that attempts to encourage or discourage union activity, nor may they discriminate against employees for providing testimony related to enforcement of the NLRA. Finally, employers may not refuse to bargain collectively with a labor organization that has standing under the act. For more guidance in complying with the NLRA, see the examples in the "HR How To" box.

When employers or unions violate the NLRA, remedies typically include ordering that unfair labor practices stop. Employers may be required to rehire workers, with or without back pay. The NLRA is not a criminal law, and violators may not be assigned punitive damages (fines to punish, rather than merely make up for the harm done).

TABLE 14.1

Workers Excluded from the NLRA's Coverage

Workers employed under the following conditions are not covered by the NLRA:
- Employed as a supervisor.
- Employed by a parent or spouse.
- Employed as an independent contractor.
- Employed in the domestic service of any person or family in a home.
- Employed as agricultural laborers.
- Employed by an employer subject to the Railway Labor Act.
- Employed by a federal, state, or local government.
- Employed by any other person who is not an employer as defined in the NLRA.

SOURCE: National Labor Relations Board Web site, www.nlrb.gov.

HR HOW TO

AVOIDING UNFAIR LABOR PRACTICES

The National Labor Relations Act prohibits employers and unions from engaging in unfair labor practices. For employers, this means they must not interfere with employees' decisions about whether to join a union and engage in union-related activities. Employers may not discriminate against employees for being involved in union activities or testifying in court about actions under the NLRA. Here are some specific examples of unfair labor practices that *employers must avoid:*

- Threatening employees with loss of their jobs or benefits if they join or vote for a union.
- Threatening to close down a plant if it is organized by a union.
- Questioning employees about their union membership or activities in a way that restrains or coerces them.

- Spying or pretending to spy on union meetings.
- Granting wage increases timed to discourage employees from forming or joining a union.
- Taking an active part in organizing a union or committee to represent employees.
- Providing preferential treatment or aid to one of several unions trying to organize employees.
- Discharging employees for urging other employees to join a union.
- Refusing to hire applicants because they are union members.
- Refusing to reinstate workers when job openings occur, on the grounds that the workers participated in a lawful strike.
- Ending operations at one facility and opening the same operations at another facility with new employees because employees at the first joined a union.

- Demoting or firing employees for filing an unfair labor practice complaint or testifying at an NLRB meeting.
- Refusing to meet with employees' representatives because the employees are on strike.
- Refusing to supply the employees' representative with cost and other data concerning a group insurance plan covering employees.
- Announcing a wage increase without consulting the employees' representative.
- Failing to bargain about the effects of a decision to close one of the employer's facilities.

SOURCE: National Labor Relations Board, *Basic Guide to the Law and Procedures under the National Labor Relations Act* (Washington, DC: U.S. Government Printing Office, 1997); National Labor Relations Board Web site, www.nlrb.gov.

Laws Amending the NLRA

Originally, the NLRA did not list any unfair labor practices by unions. In later amendments to the NLRA—the Taft-Hartley Act of 1947 and the Landrum-Griffin Act of 1959—Congress established some restrictions on union practices deemed unfair to employers and union members.

Under the Taft-Hartley Act, unions may not restrain employers through actions such as the following:[27]

- Mass picketing in such numbers that nonstriking employees physically cannot enter the workplace.
- Engaging in violent acts in connection with a strike.

Figure 14.4
States with Right-to-Work Laws

SOURCE: National Right to Work Legal Defense Foundation, cited in K. Chen, "Wooing Companies: Do 'Right-to-Work' Laws Make a Difference?" *The Wall Street Journal Online*, July 10, 2002, http://online.wsj.com.

- Threatening employees with physical injury or job loss if they do not support union activities.
- During contract negotiations, insisting on illegal provisions, provisions that the employer may hire only workers who are union members or "satisfactory" to the union, or working conditions to be determined by a group to which the employer does not belong.
- Terminating an existing contract and striking for a new one without notifying the employer, the Federal Mediation and Conciliation Service, and the state mediation service (where one exists).

The Taft-Hartley Act also allows the states to pass so-called **right-to-work laws,** which make union shops, maintenance of membership, and agency shops illegal. The idea behind such laws is that requiring union membership or the payment of union dues restricts the employees' right to freedom of association. In other words, employees should be free to choose whether they join a union or other group. Of course, unions have a different point of view. The union perspective is that unions provide services to all members of a bargaining unit (such as all of a company's workers), and all members who receive the benefits of a union should pay union dues. Figure 14.4 indicates which states currently have right-to-work laws.

The Landrum-Griffin Act regulates unions' actions with regard to their members, including financial disclosure and the conduct of elections. This law establishes and protects rights of union members. These include the right to nominate candidates for union office, participate in union meetings and secret-ballot elections, and examine unions' financial records.

right-to-work laws
State laws that make union shops, maintenance of membership, and agency shops illegal.

National Labor Relations Board (NLRB)

Enforcement of the NLRA rests with the **National Labor Relations Board (NLRB).** This federal government agency consists of a five-member board, the general counsel, and 52 regional and other field offices. Because the NLRB is a federal agency, its enforcement actions are limited to companies that have an impact on interstate commerce,

National Labor Relations Board (NLRB)
Federal government agency that enforces the NLRA by conducting and certifying representation elections and investigating unfair labor practices.

but as a practical matter, this extends to all but purely local businesses. For federal government workers under the Civil Service Reform Act of 1978, Title VII, the Federal Labor Relations Authority has a role similar to that of the NLRB. Many states have similar agencies to administer their laws governing state and local government workers.

The NLRB has two major functions: to conduct and certify representation elections and to prevent unfair labor practices. It does not initiate either of these actions but responds to requests for action.

Representation Elections

The NLRB is responsible for ensuring that the organizing process follows certain steps, described in the next section. Depending on the response to organizing efforts, the NLRB conducts elections. When a majority of workers vote in favor of a union, the NLRB certifies it as the exclusive representative of a group of employees. The NLRB also conducts elections to decertify unions, following the same process as for representation elections.

The NLRB is also responsible for determining the appropriate bargaining unit and the employees who are eligible to participate in organizing activities. As we stated earlier, bargaining units may not include certain types of employees, such as agricultural laborers, independent contractors, supervisors, and managers. Beyond this, the NLRB attempts to group together employees who have a community of interest in their wages, hours, and working conditions. A unit may cover employees in one facility or multiple facilities within a single employer, or the unit may cover multiple employers. In general, employees on the payroll just before the ordering of an election are eligible to vote, although this rule is modified in some cases, for example, when employment in the industry is irregular. Most employees who are on strike and who have been replaced by other employees are eligible to vote in an election (such as a decertification election) that occurs within 12 months of the onset of the strike.

Prevention of Unfair Labor Practices

The handling of complaints regarding unfair labor practices begins when someone files a charge. The deadline for filing a charge is six months after the alleged unfair practice. All parties must be served with a copy of the charge. (Registered mail is recommended.) The charge is investigated by a regional office. If, after investigating, the NLRB finds the charge has merit and issues a complaint, two actions are possible. The NLRB may defer to a grievance procedure agreed on by the employer and the union; grievances are discussed later in this chapter. Or a hearing may be held before an administrative law judge. The judge makes a recommendation, which either party may appeal.

The NLRB has the authority to issue cease-and-desist orders to halt unfair labor practices. It also can order the employer to reinstate workers, with or without back pay. The NLRB can set aside the results of an election if it believes either the union or the employer has created "an atmosphere of confusion or fear of reprisals."[28] If an employer or union refuses to comply with an NLRB order, the board has the authority to petition the U.S. Court of Appeals. The court may enforce the order, recommend it to the NLRB for modification, change the order itself, or set it aside altogether.

LO4
Describe the union organizing process.

✎ UNION ORGANIZING

Unions begin their involvement with an organization's employees by conducting an organizing campaign. To meet its objectives, a union needs to convince a majority of workers that they should receive better pay or other employment conditions and that the union will help them do so. The employer's objectives will depend on its strategy—whether it seeks to work with a union or convince employees that they are better off without union representation.

The Process of Organizing

The organizing process begins with authorization cards, such as the example shown in Figure 14.5. Union representatives make contact with employees, present their message about the union, and invite them to sign an authorization card. For the organization process to continue, at least 30 percent of the employees must sign an authorization card.

If over half the employees sign an authorization card, the union may request that the employer voluntarily recognize the union. If the employer agrees, the NLRB certifies the union as the exclusive representative of employees. If the employer refuses, or if only 30 to 50 percent of employees signed cards, the NLRB conducts a secret-ballot election. The arrangements are made in one of two ways:

1. For a *consent election,* the employer and the union seeking representation arrive at an agreement stating the time and place of the election, the choices included on the ballot, and a way to determine who is eligible to vote.
2. For a *stipulation election,* the parties cannot agree on all of these terms, so the NLRB dictates the time and place, ballot choices, and method of determining eligibility.

On the ballot, workers vote for or against union representation, and they may also have a choice from among more than one union. If the union (or one of the unions on the ballot) wins a majority of votes, the NLRB certifies the union. If the ballot includes more than one union and neither gains a simple majority, the NLRB holds a runoff election.

Figure 14.5
Authorization Card

SOURCE: From J. A. Fossum, *Labor Relations: Development, Structure and Process, 2002.*
Copyright © 2002 The McGraw-Hill Companies, Inc. Reprinted with permission.

As noted earlier, if the NLRB finds the election was not conducted fairly, it may set aside the results and call for a new election. Conduct that may lead to an election result's being set aside include the following examples:[29]

- Threats of loss of jobs or benefits by an employer or union to influence votes or organizing activities.
- A grant of benefits or a promise of benefits as a means of influencing votes or organizing activities.
- Campaign speeches by management or union representatives to assembled groups of employees on company time less than 24 hours before an election.
- The actual use or threat of physical force or violence to influence votes or organizing activities.

After certification, there are limits on future elections. Once the NLRB has certified a union as the exclusive representative of a group of employees, it will not permit additional elections for one year. Also, after the union and employer have finished negotiating a contract, an election cannot be held for the time of the contract period or for three years, whichever comes first. The parties to the contract may agree not to hold an election for longer than three years, but an outside party (another union) cannot be barred for more than three years.

Management Strategies

Sometimes an employer will recognize a union after a majority of employees have signed authorization cards. More often, there is a hotly contested election campaign. During the campaign, unions try to persuade employees that their wages, benefits, treatment by employers, and chances to influence workplace decisions are too poor or small and that the union will be able to obtain improvements in these areas. Management typically responds with its own messages providing an opposite point of view. Management messages say the organization has provided a valuable package of wages and benefits and has treated employees well. Management also argues that the union will not be able to keep its promises but will instead create costs for employees, such as union dues and lost income during strikes.

Employers use a variety of methods to oppose unions in organizing campaigns.[30] Their efforts range from hiring consultants to distributing leaflets and letters to presenting the company's viewpoint at meetings of employees. Some management efforts go beyond what the law permits, especially in the eyes of union organizers. This impression is supported by an increase in charges of employer unfair labor practices and awards of back pay since the late 1960s.[31] Why would employers break the law? One explanation is that the consequences, such as reinstating workers with back pay, are small compared to the benefits.[32] If coercing workers away from joining a union saves the company the higher wages, benefits, and other costs of a unionized workforce, management may feel an incentive to accept costs like back pay. In this competitive environment, a union election victory is far from assured. The "Did You Know . . . ?" box shows the industries in which unions most often win elections and those in which they most often lose.

Supervisors have the most direct contact with employees. Thus, as Table 14.2 indicates, it is critical that they establish good relationships with employees even before there is any attempt at union organizing. Supervisors also must know what *not* to do if a union drive takes place. They should be trained in the legal principles discussed earlier in this chapter.

? DID YOU KNOW?

UNION ELECTIONS ARE WON MOST IN SERVICES INDUSTRIES

For workers who want union representation, it helps to be in a service industry such as building maintenance, education, or health care, and it hurts to be in manufacturing. The graph shows the industries in which unions were most and least successful in NLRB certification elections. Other industries
in which more than half the elections were union victories include schools, nursing homes, universities, and restaurants.

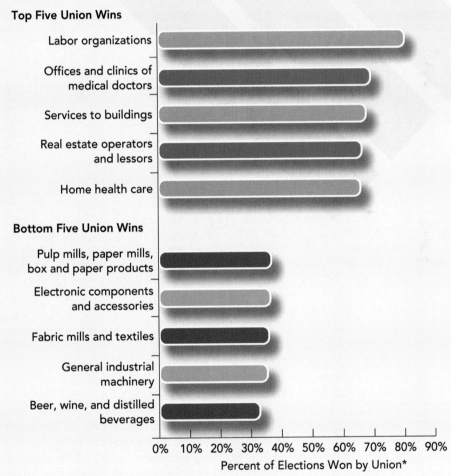

Top Five Union Wins

- Labor organizations
- Offices and clinics of medical doctors
- Services to buildings
- Real estate operators and lessors
- Home health care

Bottom Five Union Wins

- Pulp mills, paper mills, box and paper products
- Electronic components and accessories
- Fabric mills and textiles
- General industrial machinery
- Beer, wine, and distilled beverages

0% 10% 20% 30% 40% 50% 60% 70% 80% 90%

Percent of Elections Won by Union*

*NLRB certification elections held January 1990–September 2002

SOURCE: Labor Research Association, "25 Highest Win-Rates by Industry" and "25 Lowest Win-Rates by Industry," *LRA
Online*, www.laborresearch.org, accessed June 9, 2005.

TABLE 14.2
What Supervisors
Should and Should
Not Do to
Discourage Unions

WHAT TO DO:

Report any direct or indirect signs of union activity to a core management group.

Deal with employees by carefully stating the company's response to pro-union arguments. These responses should be coordinated by the company to maintain consistency and to avoid threats or promises. Take away union issues by following effective management practices all the time:

    Deliver recognition and appreciation.

    Solve employee problems.

    Protect employees from harassment or humiliation.

    Provide business-related information.

    Be consistent in treatment of different employees.

    Accommodate special circumstances where appropriate.

    Ensure due process in performance management.

    Treat all employees with dignity and respect.

WHAT TO AVOID:

Threatening employees with harsher terms and conditions of employment or employment loss if they engage in union activity.

Interrogating employees about pro-union or anti-union sentiments that they or others may have or reviewing union authorization cards or pro-union petitions.

Promising employees that they will receive favorable terms or conditions of employment if they forgo union activity.

Spying on employees known to be, or suspected of being, engaged in pro-union activities.

SOURCE: From J. A. Segal, "Unshackle Your Supervisors to Stay Union Free," *HR Magazine*, June 1998. Copyright © 1998 by Society for Human Resource Management. Reproduced with permission of Society for Human Resource Management via Copyright Clearance Center.

Union Strategies

The traditional union organizing strategy has been for organizers to call or visit employees at home, when possible, to talk about issues like pay and job security. For a young, educated workforce, unions have been learning new tactics. In Madison, Wisconsin, the United Food and Commercial Workers union organized the employees of the local Whole Foods Market when regional union leaders learned that many employees felt their concerns were being ignored by management. The union arranged for interested workers to develop their own Web site, research the relevant labor laws, and invite their coworkers out for coffee or beer after work. Whole Foods unintentionally reinforced the union message that the company was pushy and insensitive by requiring that employees attend meetings to discuss the union. The union's strategy emphasized speed, personal attention, and employee empowerment, and it succeeded when employees voted 65 to 54 in favor of the union.[33] Subsequently, employees at the Madison store petitioned to remove the union as their representative and Whole Foods withdrew its recognition of the union. This example shows that a successful organizing drive by a union is not necessarily the end of the story. Maintaining employee support and negotiating a contract are major challenges that follow.

Beyond encouraging workers to sign authorization cards and vote for the union, organizers use some creative alternatives to traditional organizing activities. They sometimes offer workers **associate union membership,** which is not linked to an em-

associate union membership
Alternative form of union membership in which members receive discounts on insurance and credit cards rather than representation in collective bargaining.

ployee's workplace and does not provide representation in collective bargaining. Rather, an associate member receives other services, such as discounts on health and life insurance or credit cards.[34] In return for these benefits, the union receives membership dues and a broader base of support for its activities. Associate membership may be attractive to employees who wish to join a union but cannot because their workplace is not organized by a union.

Another alternative to traditional organizing is to conduct **corporate campaigns**— bringing public, financial, or political pressure on employers during union organization and contract negotiation.[35] For example, the Building and Construction Trades Department of the AFL-CIO successfully lobbied Congress to eliminate $100 million in tax breaks for a Toyota truck plant in Kentucky until Toyota agreed to use union construction workers and pay union wages.[36] The Amalgamated Clothing and Textile Workers Union (ACTWU) corporate campaign against textile maker J. P. Stevens during the late 1970s was one of the first successful corporate campaigns and served as a model for those that followed. The ACTWU organized a boycott of J. P. Stevens products and threatened to withdraw its pension funds from financial institutions where J. P. Stevens officers acted as directors. The company eventually agreed to a contract with ACTWU.[37]

In some recent success stories unions have eschewed elections in favor of strikes and negative publicity to pressure corporations to accept a union.[38] The Hotel Employees and Restaurant Employees (HERE) organized 9,000 workers in 2001, with 80 percent of these memberships resulting from pressure on employers rather than a vote. The Union of Needletrade, Industrial and Textile Employees (UNITE), which organized 15,000 workers in 2001, has also succeeded with this approach. After losing an election by just two votes among employees of Up-to-Date Laundry, which cleans linens for Baltimore hotels and hospitals, UNITE decided to try other tactics, including a corporate campaign. It called a strike to demand that Up-to-Date recognize the union. It

corporate campaigns
Bringing public, financial, or political pressure on employers during union organization and contract negotiation.

The Communications Workers of America (CWA) is currently campaigning to organize former AT&T Wireless employees following a merger with unionized Cingular so that they can have voice in their workplace. This campaign also sparked a new twist to organizing a campaign by having part of it online.

also persuaded several major customers of the laundry to threaten to stop using the laundry's services, shared claims of racial and sexual harassment with state agencies and the NAACP, and convinced the Baltimore city council to require testimony from Up-to-Date. Eventually, the company gave in, recognized the union, and negotiated a contract that raised the workers' $6-an-hour wages and gave them better benefits.

Another winning union organizing strategy is to negotiate employer neutrality and card-check provisions into a contract (see the CWA-Cingular example on the previous page). Under a *neutrality provision*, the employer pledges not to oppose organizing attempts elsewhere in the company. A *card-check provision* is an agreement that if a certain percentage—by law, at least a majority—of employees sign an authorization card, the employer will recognize their union representation. An impartial outside agency, such as the American Arbitration Association, counts the cards. Evidence suggests that this strategy can be very effective for unions.[39]

Decertifying a Union

The Taft-Hartley act expanded union members' right to be represented by leaders of their own choosing to include the right to vote out an existing union. This action is called *decertifying* the union. Decertification follows the same process as a representation election. An election to decertify a union may not take place when a contract is in effect.

Research indicates that when decertification elections are held, unions typically do not fare well.[40] During the mid-1990s, unions lost about 7 out of 10 decertification elections. In another blow to unions, the number of decertification elections has increased from about 5 percent of all elections in the 1950s and 1960s to about 14 percent in the mid-1990s.

COLLECTIVE BARGAINING

When the NLRB has certified a union, that union represents employees during contract negotiations. In **collective bargaining,** a union negotiates on behalf of its members with management representatives to arrive at a contract defining conditions of

LO5
Explain how management and unions negotiate contracts.

collective bargaining
Negotiation between union representatives and management representatives to arrive at a contract defining conditions of employment for the term of the contract and to administer that contract.

TABLE 14.3
Typical Provisions in Collective Bargaining Contracts

Establishment and administration of the agreement	Bargaining unit and plant supplements Contract duration and reopening and renegotiation provisions Union security and the checkoff Special bargaining committees Grievance procedures Arbitration and mediation Strikes and lockouts Contract enforcement
Functions, rights, and responsibilities	Management rights clauses Plant removal Subcontracting Union activities on company time and premises Union–management cooperation Regulation of technological change Advance notice and consultation

TABLE 14.3

Concluded

Wage determination and administration	General provisions
	Rate structure and wage differentials
	Allowances
	Incentive systems and production bonus plans
	Production standards and time studies
	Job classification and job evaluation
	Individual wage adjustments
	General wage adjustments during the contract period
Job or income security	Hiring and transfer arrangements
	Employment and income guarantees
	Reporting and call-in pay
	Supplemental unemployment benefit plans
	Regulation of overtime, shift work, etc.
	Reduction of hours to forestall layoffs
	Layoff procedures; seniority; recall
	Worksharing in lieu of layoff
	Attrition arrangements
	Promotion practices
	Training and retraining
	Relocation allowances
	Severance pay and layoff benefit plans
	Special funds and study committees
Plant operations	Work and shop rules
	Rest periods and other in-plant time allowances
	Safety and health
	Plant committees
	Hours of work and premium pay practices
	Shift operations
	Hazardous work
	Discipline and discharge
Paid and unpaid leave	Vacations and holidays
	Sick leave
	Funeral and personal leave
	Military leave and jury duty
Employee benefit plans	Health and insurance plans
	Pension plans
	Profit-sharing, stock purchase, and thrift plans
	Bonus plans
Special groups	Apprentices and learners
	Workers with disabilities and older workers
	Women
	Veterans
	Union representatives
	Nondiscrimination clauses

SOURCE: T. A. Kochan, *Collective Bargaining and Industrial Relations* (Homewood, IL: Richard D. Irwin, 1980), p. 29. Original data from J. W. Bloch, "Union Contracts—A New Series of Studies," *Monthly Labor Review* 87 (October 1964), pp. 1184–85.

employment for the term of the contract and to resolve differences in the way they interpret the contract. Typical contracts include provisions for pay, benefits, work rules, and resolution of workers' grievances. Table 14.3 shows typical provisions negotiated in collective bargaining contracts.

Collective bargaining differs from one situation to another in terms of *bargaining structure*—that is, the range of employees and employers covered by the contract. A contract may involve a narrow group of employees in a craft union or a broad group in an industrial union. Contracts may cover one or several facilities of the same employer, or the bargaining structure may involve several employers. Many more interests must be considered in collective bargaining for an industrial union with a bargaining structure that includes several employers than in collective bargaining for a craft union in a single facility.

The majority of contract negotiations take place between unions and employers that have been through the process before. In the typical situation, management has come to accept the union as an organization it must work with. The situation can be very different when a union has just been certified and is negotiating its first contract. In over one-fourth of negotiations for a first contract, the parties are unable to reach an agreement.[41]

Bargaining over New Contracts

Clearly, the outcome of contract negotiations can have important consequences for labor costs, productivity, and the organization's ability to compete. Therefore, unions and management need to prepare carefully for collective bargaining. Preparation includes establishing objectives for the contract, reviewing the old contract, gathering data (such as compensation paid by competitors and the company's ability to survive a strike), predicting the likely demands to be made, and establishing the cost of meeting the demands.[42] This preparation can help negotiators develop a plan for how to negotiate. Different situations and goals call for different approaches to bargaining, such as the following alternatives proposed by Richard Walton and Robert McKersie:[43]

- *Distributive bargaining* divides an economic "pie" between two sides—for example, a wage increase means giving the union a larger share of the pie.
- *Integrative bargaining* looks for win-win solutions, or outcomes in which both sides benefit. If the organization's labor costs hurt its performance, integrative bargaining might seek to avoid layoffs in exchange for work rules that improve productivity.
- *Attitudinal structuring* focuses on establishing a relationship of trust. The parties are concerned about ensuring that the other side will keep its part of any bargain.
- *Intraorganizational bargaining* addresses conflicts within union or management groups or objectives, such as between new employees and workers with high seniority or between cost control and reduction of turnover.

The collective bargaining process may involve any combination of these alternatives.

Negotiations go through various stages.[44] In the earliest stages, many more people are often present than in later stages. On the union side, this may give all the various internal interest groups a chance to participate and voice their goals. Their input helps communicate to management what will satisfy union members and may help the union achieve greater solidarity. At this stage, union negotiators often present a long list of proposals, partly to satisfy members and partly to introduce enough issues that they will have flexibility later in the process. Management may or may not present proposals of its own. Sometimes management prefers to react to the union's proposals.

In May 2004, Communications Workers of America staged a four-day strike against SBC telecommunications company due to the criticisms surrounding SBC's position on wages, healthcare costs and job security.

During the middle stages of the process, each side must make a series of decisions, even though the outcome is uncertain. How important is each issue to the other side? How likely is it that disagreement on particular issues will result in a strike? When and to what extent should one side signal its willingness to compromise?

In the final stage of negotiations, pressure for an agreement increases. Public negotiations may be only part of the process. Negotiators from each side may hold one-on-one meetings or small-group meetings where they escape some public relations pressures. A neutral third party may act as a go-between or facilitator. In some cases, bargaining breaks down as the two sides find they cannot reach a mutually acceptable agreement. The outcome depends partly on the relative bargaining power of each party. That power, in turn, depends on each party's ability to withstand a strike, which costs the workers their pay during the strike and costs the employer lost production and possibly lost customers.

When Bargaining Breaks Down

The intended outcome of collective bargaining is a contract with terms acceptable to both parties. If one or both sides determine that negotiation alone will not produce such an agreement, bargaining breaks down. To bring this impasse to an end, the union may strike, or the parties may bring in outside help to resolve their differences.

Strikes

strike

A collective decision by union members not to work until certain demands or conditions are met.

A **strike** is a collective decision of the union members not to work until certain demands or conditions are met. The union members vote, and if the majority favors a strike, they all go on strike at that time or when union leaders believe the time is right. Strikes are typically accompanied by *picketing*—the union stations members near the worksite with signs indicating the union is on strike. During the strike, the union members do not receive pay from their employer, but the union may be able to make up for some of the lost pay. The employer loses production unless it can hire replacement workers, and even then, productivity may be reduced. Often, other unions support striking workers by refusing to cross their picket line—for example, refusing to make deliveries to a company during a strike.

The vast majority of labor-management negotiations do not result in a strike, and the number of strikes has plunged since the 1950s, as shown in Figure 14.6. The percentage of total working time lost to strikes in 2004 was a mere 0.01 percent—that is, one-hundredth of 1 percent of working time. A primary reason strikes are rare is that a strike is seldom in the best interests of either party. Not only do workers lose wages and employers lose production, but the negative experience of a strike can make future interactions more difficult. When strikes do occur, the conduct of each party during the strike can do lasting harm to labor-management relations. Violence by either side or threats of job loss or actual job loss because jobs went to replacement workers can make future relations difficult. Finally, many government employees do not have a right to strike, and their percentage among unionized employees overall has risen in recent decades, as we discussed earlier.

Figure 14.6

Strikes Involving 1,000 or More Workers

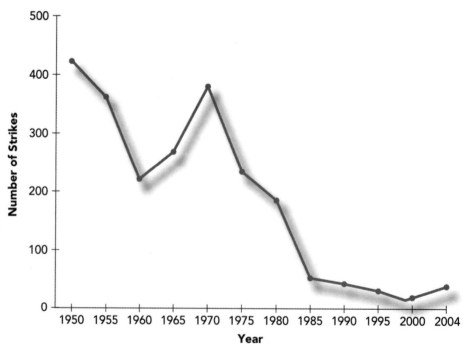

Note: Because strikes are most likely in large bargaining units, these numbers represent most lost working time in the United States.

SOURCE: Bureau of Labor Statistics Web site, www.bls.gov/cba; U.S. Census Bureau, *Statistical Abstract of the United States, 2004–2005*.

Alternatives to Strikes

Because strikes are so costly and risky, unions and employers generally prefer other methods for resolving conflicts. Three of the most common alternatives are mediation, fact finding, and arbitration. All of these rely on a neutral third party, who usually is provided by the Federal Mediation and Conciliation Service (FMCS).

The least formal and most widely used of these procedures is **mediation.** In this procedure, a mediator hears the views of both sides and facilitates the negotiation process. The mediator has no formal authority to dictate a resolution, so a strike remains a possibility. In a survey studying negotiations between unions and large businesses, mediation was used in almost 4 out of 10 negotiation efforts.[45]

A **fact finder,** most often used for negotiations with governmental bodies, typically reports on the reasons for the dispute, the views and arguments of both sides, and (sometimes) a recommended settlement, which the parties may decline. The public nature of these recommendations may pressure the parties to reach a settlement. Even if they do not accept the fact finder's recommended settlement, the hope of this process is that the fact finder will identify or frame issues in a way that makes agreement easier. Sometimes merely devoting time to this process gives the parties a chance to reach an agreement. Again, however, there is no guarantee that a strike will be avoided.

The most formal type of outside intervention is **arbitration,** under which an arbitrator or arbitration board determines a settlement that is *binding,* meaning the parties have to accept it. In conventional arbitration, the arbitrator fashions the solution. In "final-offer arbitration," the arbitrator must choose either management's or the union's final offer for each issue or for the contract as a whole. There is wide acceptance of "rights arbitration," which focuses on enforcing or interpreting contract terms, but arbitration in the writing of contracts or setting of contract terms has traditionally been reserved for special circumstances such as negotiations between unions and government agencies, where strikes may be illegal or especially costly. Occasionally, arbitration has also been used with businesses in situations where strikes have been extremely damaging. Arbitration is uncommon in the private sector and one reason is the general opinion that union and management representatives are in the best position to resolve conflicts themselves, because they are closer to the situation than an arbitrator can be.

❧ CONTRACT ADMINISTRATION

Although the process of negotiating a labor agreement (including the occasional strike) receives the most publicity, other union-management activities occur far more often. Bargaining over a new contract typically occurs only about every three years, but administering labor contracts goes on day after day, year after year. The two activities are linked, of course. Vague or inconsistent language in the contract can make administering the contract more difficult. The difficulties can create conflict that spills over into the next round of negotiations.[46] Events during negotiations—strikes, the use of replacement workers, or violence by either side—also can lead to difficulties in working successfully under a conflict.

Contract administration includes carrying out the terms of the agreement and resolving conflicts over interpretation or violation of the agreement. Under a labor contract, the process for resolving these conflicts is called a **grievance procedure.** This procedure has a key influence on success in contract administration. A grievance procedure may be started by an employee or discharged employee who believes the employer violated the contract or by a union representative on behalf of a group of workers or union representatives.

mediation
Conflict resolution procedure in which a mediator hears the views of both sides and facilitates the negotiation process but has no formal authority to dictate a resolution.

fact finder
Third party to collective bargaining who reports the reasons for a dispute, the views and arguments of both sides, and possibly a recommended settlement, which the parties may decline.

arbitration
Conflict resolution procedure in which an arbitrator or arbitration board determines a binding settlement.

LO6
Summarize the practice of contract administration.

grievance procedure
The process for resolving union-management conflicts over interpretation or violation of a collective bargaining agreement.

For grievances launched by an employee, a typical grievance procedure follows the steps shown in Figure 14.7. The grievance may be settled during any of the four steps. In the first step, the employee talks to his or her supervisor about the problem. If this conversation is unsatisfactory, the employee may involve the union steward in further discussion. The union steward and employee decide whether the problem has been resolved and, if not, whether it is a contract violation. If the problem was not resolved and does seem to be a contract violation, the union moves to step 2, putting the grievance in writing and submitting it to a line manager. The union steward meets with a management representative to try to resolve the problem. Management consults with the industrial relations staff and puts its response in writing too at this second stage. If step 2 fails to resolve the problem, the union appeals the grievance to top line management and representatives of the industrial relations staff. The union may involve more local or international officers in discussions at this stage (see step 3 in Figure 14.7). The decision resulting from the appeal is put into writing. If the grievance is still not resolved, the union may decide (step 4) to appeal the grievance to an arbitrator. If the grievance involves a discharged employee, the process may begin at step 2 or 3, however, and the time limits between steps may be shorter. Grievances filed by the union on behalf of a group may begin at step 1 or step 2.

figure 14.7

Steps in an Employee-Initiated Grievance Procedure

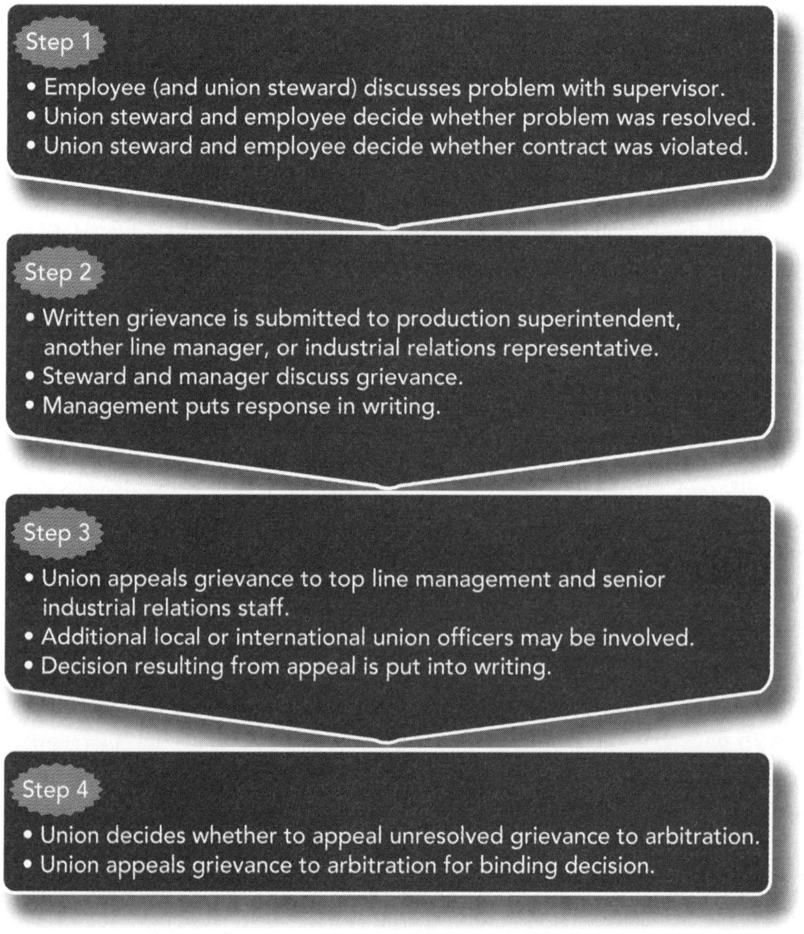

Step 1
• Employee (and union steward) discusses problem with supervisor.
• Union steward and employee decide whether problem was resolved.
• Union steward and employee decide whether contract was violated.

Step 2
• Written grievance is submitted to production superintendent, another line manager, or industrial relations representative.
• Steward and manager discuss grievance.
• Management puts response in writing.

Step 3
• Union appeals grievance to top line management and senior industrial relations staff.
• Additional local or international union officers may be involved.
• Decision resulting from appeal is put into writing.

Step 4
• Union decides whether to appeal unresolved grievance to arbitration.
• Union appeals grievance to arbitration for binding decision.

SOURCE: Adapted from T. A. Kochan, *Collective Bargaining and Industrial Relations* (Homewood, IL: Richard D. Irwin, 1980), p. 395; J. A. Fossum, *Labor Relations* (Boston: McGraw-Hill/Irwin, 2002), pp. 448-52.

The majority of grievances are settled during the earlier steps of the process. This reduces delays and avoids the costs of arbitration. If a grievance does reach arbitration, the arbitrator makes the final ruling in the matter. Based on a series of Supreme Court decisions, courts generally avoid reviewing arbitrators' decisions and focus only on whether the grievance involved an issue that is subject to arbitration under the contract.[47]

From the point of view of employees, the grievance procedure is an important means of getting fair treatment in the workplace. Its success depends on whether it provides for all the kinds of problems that are likely to arise (such as how to handle a business slowdown), whether employees feel they can file a grievance without being punished for it, and whether employees believe their union representatives will follow through. Under the National Labor Relations Act, the union has a *duty of fair representation*, which means the union must give equal representation to all members of the bargaining unit, whether or not they actually belong to the union. Too many grievances may indicate a problem—for example, the union members or line supervisors do not understand how to uphold the contract or have no desire to do so. At the same time, a very small number of grievances may also signal a problem. A very low grievance rate may suggest a fear of filing a grievance, a belief that the system does not work, or a belief that employees are poorly represented by their union.

What types of issues most commonly reach arbitration? According to data from the Federal Mediation and Conciliation Service, the majority of arbitration cases involved discharge or other disciplinary actions.[48] Other issues that often reach arbitration are subcontracting; the use of seniority in decisions about promotions, layoffs, transfers, work assignments, and scheduling; and the distribution of overtime or requirement of overtime. In reaching decisions about these and other issues, arbitrators consider a number of criteria, such as employees' understanding of the rules, the employer's consistency and fairness, and the employees' chance to present a defense and appeal a decision.[49]

❧ LABOR-MANAGEMENT COOPERATION

The traditional understanding of union-management relations is that the two parties are adversaries, meaning each side is competing to win at the expense of the other. There have always been exceptions to this approach. And since at least the 1980s, there seems to be wider acceptance of the view that greater cooperation can increase employee commitment and motivation while making the workplace more flexible.[50] Also, evidence suggests that employees who worked under traditional labor relations systems and then under the new, more cooperative systems prefer the cooperative approach.[51]

Cooperation between labor and management may feature employee involvement in decision making, self-managing employee teams, labor-management problem-solving teams, broadly defined jobs, and sharing of financial gains and business information with employees.[52] The search for a win-win solution requires that unions and their members understand the limits on what an employer can afford in a competitive marketplace. The nearby "Best Practices" box describes how Goodyear Tire and Rubber Company has met this challenge.

Without the union's support, efforts at employee empowerment are less likely to survive and less likely to be effective if they do survive.[53] Unions have often resisted employee empowerment programs, precisely because the programs try to change workplace relations and the role that unions play. Union leaders have often feared that such programs will weaken unions' role as independent representatives of employee interests. Indeed, the National Labor Relations Act makes it an unfair labor

LO7
Describe more cooperative approaches to labor-management relations.

BEST PRACTICES

UNION COOPERATION HELPS GOODYEAR ROLL TO SUCCESS

In April 2003, when Goodyear Tire & Rubber Company entered into contract negotiations with the United Steelworkers (USW), both sides knew that the company was in trouble. During the previous year, instead of earning profits, Goodyear had lost more than a billion dollars. Failed efforts to expand into new markets generated $5 billion in debt as the company lost market share. Turnover among company executives was high. With so much trouble at the top, could the union and company resolve contract issues without destroying what was left of the company?

Goodyear's management, seeing tire sales shift to competitors with cheaper tires made in countries where wages are low, wanted to move its operations overseas as well. If the union went along with the plan in order to save the company, 14 U.S. plants could be closed, with the jobs transferred to Asia. If the union fought the

plan, a strike could bankrupt Goodyear, possibly leaving workers even worse off. But the USW's president, Leo Gerard, had a better idea. The union hired an investment banking firm to develop a long-term strategic plan for Goodyear that would make the company more competitive and preserve as many union jobs as possible.

That plan provided guidance for union and management to develop a new labor contract balancing worker protection with corporate health. The union would permit changes, including elimination of 3,000 (out of 19,000) jobs and reduction of labor costs by more than $1 billion over a three-year period. Goodyear promised to invest in and continue operating 12 of its 14 U.S. factories and limit imports from its facilities in Brazil and Asia. Goodyear's management also agreed to financial guidelines developed by the union's advisers. If the company does not meet debt goals by

2007, it has agreed to pay $1,000 to each union worker and $500 to each retiree.

According to union president Gerard, the objective of this kind of involvement in strategy is to help companies improve the profitability of their domestic operations so that they don't need to move jobs overseas. It's a difficult challenge, given the huge difference between union wages in the United States and the pay earned in Asia and South America. The early evidence for Goodyear is promising, however. The company returned to profitability and reduced its debt in 2004, helped by a stronger focus on customer needs.

SOURCE: David Welch, "What Goodyear Got from Its Union," *BusinessWeek*, October 20, 2003, www.businessweek.com; and "Working to Bounce Back," *Crain's Cleveland Business*, May 16, 2005, downloaded from Business & Company Resource Center, http://galenet.galegroup.com.

practice for an employer to "dominate or interfere with the formation or administration of any labor organization or contribute financial or other support to it."

This legal requirement gave rise to concern that self-managing work teams set up by an employer could violate the NLRA. Several widely publicized rulings by the National Labor Relations Board in the mid-1990s found that worker-management committees were illegal when they were dominated by management and dealt with issues such as wages, grievances, and working conditions.[54] Table 14.4 provides some guidance on when the use of teams might be illegal.

Although employers must be careful to meet legal requirements, the NLRB has clearly supported employee involvement in decision making. For example, in a 2001 ruling, the NLRB found that employee participation committees at Crown Cork &

Primary factors to look for that could mean a team violates national labor law:	
Representation	Does the team address issues affecting nonteam employees? (Does it represent other workers?)
Subject matter	Do these issues involve matters such as wages, grievances, hours of work, and working conditions?
Management involvement	Does the team deal with any supervisors, managers, or executives on any issue?
Employer domination	Did the company create the team or decide what it would do and how it would function?

TABLE 14.4

When Teams May Be Illegal

SOURCE: T. Kochan and P. Osterman, *The Mutual Gains Enterprise* (Boston: Harvard Business School Press, 1994), p. 202; originally from A. Bernstein, "Making Teamwork Work—And Appeasing Uncle Sam," *BusinessWeek*, January 25, 1993, p. 101.

Seal's aluminum-can factory did not violate federal labor law.[55] Those committees make and carry out decisions regarding a wide range of issues, including production, quality, training, safety, and certain types of discipline. The NLRB determined that the committees were not employer dominated. Instead of "dealing with" management, where employees make proposals for management to accept or reject, the committees exercise authority within boundaries set by management, similar to the authority of a first-line supervisor. In spite of the legal concerns, cooperative approaches to labor relations seem to contribute to an organization's success.[56]

Beyond avoiding any taint of misuse of employee empowerment, employers build cooperative relationships by the way they treat employees—with respect and fairness, in the knowledge that attracting talent and minimizing turnover are in the employer's best interests. A business owner who appreciates this approach is Kenn Ricci, founder of Flight Options, which offers clients the use of a private plane.[57] Clients buy a share in the ownership of a plane, and Flight Options provides a pilot to fly the plane. A pilot himself, Ricci built his company on values many pilots share, including flexibility and trust. When Flight Options prepared to acquire Raytheon Travel Air, Ricci inherited a union organizing effort at that company. In a climate of rumors and mistrust, a Travel Air pilot sent Ricci an e-mail message asking if he planned to lay off the Travel Air pilots if they voted in favor of the union. Ricci replied with a simple *no*—and the pilots voted down the union. When it came time to merge the two company's seniority lists (the basis for assigning pilots to aircraft and routes), Ricci called together a group of pilots representing both companies to identify alternatives. He posted the ideas on the Flight Options Web site, gathered reactions, and narrowed the choices to two, which pilots voted on. Ricci's active involvement with employees and the company's culture of trust have kept pilot turnover at a fraction of the industry average and made labor relations positive in an industry racked with disputes.

thinking ETHICALLY

Is the Seniority System Fair?

Traditionally, union contracts have called for pay systems that reward employees with higher pay as they achieve greater seniority, that is, more years on the job. In a company with a unionized workforce, employees with comparable amounts of experience would have comparable earnings. Employees with greater seniority would earn more than newer employees.

Some people have questioned whether tying pay to seniority is effective or even fair. In a survey of federal workers, many of whom are unionized, fewer than half said their agency succeeds in recognizing high achievers, and slightly more than one-fourth said their manager effectively addresses poor performance. According to Doris Hausser, a senior adviser at the Office of Personnel Management, which conducted the survey, the survey shows a need to link pay more closely to individual performance. However, unions representing federal employees say efforts to give managers more discretion in discipline and tie pay more directly to federal employees' performance will interfere with employees' rights and allow managers to distribute rewards unfairly to the employees they like best.

SOURCE: Christopher Lee, "In Survey, Most Workers Are Critical of Management," *Washington Post*, May 20, 2005, www.washingtonpost.com.

Questions

1. Why do you think unions have traditionally favored a system of linking pay to seniority? Who benefits? Why do you think management has favored a system of linking pay to performance? Who benefits?
2. What employee rights does seniority-based pay fulfill? What standards for ethical behavior does it meet? (See Chapter 1 to review a description of employee rights and ethical standards.)
3. What employee rights does performance-based pay fulfill? What standards for ethical behavior does it meet?

SUMMARY

1. Define unions and labor relations and their role in organizations.
   A union is an organization formed for the purpose of representing its members in resolving conflicts with employers. Labor relations is the management specialty emphasizing skills that managers and union leaders can use to minimize costly forms of conflict and to seek win-win solutions to disagreements. Unions—often locals belonging to national and international organizations—engage in organizing, collective bargaining, and contract administration with businesses and government organizations. In the United States, union membership has been declining among businesses but has held steady with government employees. Unionization is associated with more generous compensation and higher productivity but lower profits. Unions may reduce a business's flexibility and economic performance.

2. Identify the labor relations goals of management, labor unions, and society.
   Management goals are to increase the organization's profits. Managers generally expect that unions will make

these goals harder to achieve. Labor unions have the goal of obtaining pay and working conditions that satisfy their members. They obtain these results by gaining power in numbers. Society's values have included the hope that the existence of unions will replace conflict or violence between workers and employers with fruitful negotiation.

3. Summarize laws and regulations that affect labor relations.
   The National Labor Relations Act supports the use of collective bargaining and sets out the rights of employees, including the right to organize, join a union, and go on strike. The NLRA prohibits unfair labor practices by employers, including interference with efforts to form a labor union and discrimination against employees who engage in union activities. The Taft-Hartley Act and Landrum-Griffin Act establish restrictions on union practices that restrain workers, such as their preventing employees from working during a strike or determining who an employer may hire. The Taft-Hartley Act also permits state right-to-work laws.

4. Describe the union organizing process.

   Organizing begins when union representatives contact employees and invite them to sign an authorization card. If over half the employees sign a card, the union may request that the employer voluntarily recognize the union. If the employer refuses or if 30 to 50 percent of employees signed authorization cards, the NLRB conducts a secret-ballot election. If the union wins, the NLRB certifies the union. If the union loses but the NLRB finds that the election was not conducted fairly, it may set aside the results and call a new election.

5. Explain how management and unions negotiate contracts.

   Negotiations take place between representatives of the union and the management bargaining unit. The majority of negotiations involve parties that have been through the process before. The process begins with preparation, including research into the other side's strengths and demands. In the early stages of negotiation, many more people are present than at later stages. The union presents its demands, and management sometimes presents demands as well. Then the sides evaluate the demands and the likelihood of a strike. In the final stages, pressure for an agreement increases, and a neutral third party may be called on to help reach a resolution. If bargaining breaks down, the impasse may be broken with a strike, mediation, fact finder, or arbitration.

6. Summarize the practice of contract administration.

   Contract administration is a daily activity under the labor agreement. It includes carrying out the terms of the agreement and resolving conflicts over interpretation or violation of the contract. Conflicts are resolved through a grievance procedure. Typically, the grievance procedure begins with an employee talking to his or her supervisor about the problem and possibly involving the union steward in the discussion. If this does not resolve the conflict, the union files a written grievance with a line manager, and union and management representatives meet to discuss the problem. If this effort fails, the union appeals the grievance to top line management and the industrial relations staff. If the appeal fails, the union may appeal the grievance to an arbitrator.

7. Describe more cooperative approaches to labor-management relations.

   In contrast to the traditional view that labor and management are adversaries, some organizations and unions work more cooperatively. Cooperation may feature employee involvement in decision making, self-managing employee teams, labor-management problem-solving teams, broadly defined jobs, and sharing of financial gains and business information with employees. If such cooperation is tainted by attempts of the employer to dominate or interfere with labor organizations, however, such as by dealing with wages, grievances, or working conditions, it may be illegal under the NLRA. In spite of such legal concerns, cooperative labor relations seem to contribute to an organization's success.

REVIEW AND DISCUSSION QUESTIONS

1. Why do employees join labor unions? Did you ever belong to a labor union? If you did, do you think union membership benefited you? If you did not, do you think a union would have benefited you? Why or why not?

2. Why do managers at most companies prefer that unions not represent their employees? Can unions provide benefits to an employer? Explain.

3. How has union membership in the United States changed over the past few decades? How does union membership in the United States compare with union membership in other countries? How might these patterns in union membership affect the HR decisions of an international company?

4. What legal responsibilities do employers have regarding unions? What are the legal requirements affecting unions?

5. Suppose you are the HR manager for a chain of clothing stores. You learn that union representatives have been encouraging the stores' employees to sign authorization cards. What events can follow in this process of organizing? Suggest some ways that you might respond in your role as HR manager.

6. If the parties negotiating a labor contract are unable to reach an agreement, what actions can resolve the situation?

7. Why are strikes uncommon? Under what conditions might management choose to accept a strike?

8. What are the usual steps in a grievance procedure? What are the advantages of resolving a grievance in the first step? What skills would a supervisor need so grievances can be resolved in the first step?

9. The "Best Practices" box near the end of the chapter gives an example of union-management cooperation at Goodyear Tire & Rubber. What does the company gain from this effort? What do workers gain?

10. What are the legal restrictions on labor-management cooperation?

WHAT'S YOUR HR IQ?

The text Web site offers two more ways to check what you've learned so far. Use the Self-Assessment exercise to test your judgments about labor relations. Go online with the Web Exercise to understand more about labor unions.

BusinessWeek CASE

BusinessWeek How Briggs Is Revving the Engines

Briggs & Stratton Corporation was at a crossroads. Since 1955, the company had been cranking out small gasoline-powered engines by the millions at a titanic 2-million-square-foot factory in Wauwatosa, Wisconsin, outside Milwaukee. The setup paid off for the longest time, enabling Briggs to claim two-thirds of the U.S. lawn-mower market and helping it post a profit every year except 1988, when drought scorched sales.

In 1993, though, Briggs executives concluded that the plant had become a millstone. Organized labor had pushed up costs just as retailers, trawling the global market for cheaper goods, were demanding lower prices. The facility itself had grown so unwieldy that no one could even tell which products were making money. "We had become a battleship," says John S. Shiely, chairman and chief executive officer.

Check out Briggs today. The company by 2003 was on track to build 10.4 million engines—more than any other manufacturer in the world. Despite a lackluster economy, Briggs has made money every year since 1988. In fact, net income was forecast to surge 32 percent to $75 million in the fiscal year ending June 30, 2003, on record revenue of $1.6 billion, with exports accounting for 25 percent of sales. Briggs is also getting into new products, including outboard boat motors and portable power generators, at prices that undercut those of Japanese competitors by nearly half.

The secret? Instead of scurrying to China and other low-wage countries as many other U.S. manufacturers have done, the Wauwatosa, Wisconsin–based company relocated its assembly work to a clutch of factories in America's rural South. The facilities are all nonunion, which means much lower labor expenses. The new plants are also smaller and focus on only one or two product lines, making them more manageable. And they're highly automated, allowing Briggs to cut jobs and bring the union at its headquarters plant to heel. "Briggs wouldn't be in business today with the old system," says L. Michael Braig, an equity analyst with A. G. Edwards & Sons in Saint Louis.

Management decided to go all out with its Southern strategy in 1993, after the company's union—now Local 7-232 of the Paper, Allied-Industrial, Chemical & Energy Workers International Union (PACE)—refused to go along with pay and benefit concessions. Briggs now operates a total of six "focus factories." They may not match China's rock-bottom wages, but the plants keep Briggs in the game.

Take its Murray, Kentucky, factory, which each year produces about 3.4 million basic 3- and 4.5-horsepower engines for walk-behind mowers. The plant employs about 950 people, including 80 to 90 students from Murray State University, who are let go every summer when demand ebbs. Pay starts at $9.64 an hour, plus productivity bonuses that add $1.72 an hour to the base wage. Because of that incentive, "our workers go to extremes to take even a half a cent of cost out of each engine," notes Paul M. Neylon, senior vice president for engine products. Engines that took one hour to build at the old plant now require just 30 minutes.

The company's new ways have also hurt many people. To compete with the nonunion shops, PACE now allows Briggs to pay new hires at Wauwatosa $11 an hour—instead of the going union rate of $16 an hour or more—and to exclude them from retiree health care benefits. Still, Briggs continues to shrink the facility's payroll. By 2004, headcount was predicted to fall to roughly 1,000, down from 6,000 hourly workers in 1984. "It just seems like corporate greed," charges Local 7-232 president Gregory Gorecki. He warns the company's nonunion workers that Briggs will abandon them, too, if their pay and benefits rise too high.

CEO Shiely acknowledges that Briggs may, in fact, transfer assembly work to Asia one day. Already, the company outsources components from low-wage foreign manufacturers and has a joint venture in China that builds engines, primarily for Asian markets. But for now, he says, Briggs intends to rely on its new plants. Granted, the company's payroll is smaller, but its factory jobs are still largely in America. That's something fewer and fewer U.S. manufacturers can claim.

SOURCE: Michael Arndt, "How Briggs Is Revving the Engines," *BusinessWeek*, May 5, 2003.

Questions

1. Why did Briggs & Stratton move manufacturing operations from one factory in Wisconsin to six factories,

with five in the South? What are the benefits of this arrangement?

2. When the company moved operations to its new factories, what role would HRM have played in the changes? For example, what were the needs for HR planning, recruitment, compensation, and other HR functions in order for this change to succeed?

3. Imagine that you work in Briggs's HRM department. After the change to focus factories, what changes would you expect to see in your department? How, if at all, would the functions and goals of HRM be different? What about practical matters, such as the number and geographic location of HRM staff? Would you expect the company's greater use of outsourcing to affect HRM staff?

CASE: The Governor Squares Off against the Teachers

In the United States today, the vast majority of union members work for the government, and many of them are teachers. As a result, negotiating with unions often becomes the job of politicians and government officials. Under the public's gaze, these efforts often play out in ways that are as colorful as they are well publicized. Recently, some of the most powerful conflicts have taken place in California. There, Governor Arnold Schwarzenegger has been trying to change the way that state's teachers are selected and paid. And the teachers are resisting every step of the way.

Governor Schwarzenegger asked the California legislature to enact three changes. First, he wants teachers' pay to be directly related to their performance in terms of student test scores and other measures. So, when their students score well on standardized tests, teachers would get higher pay. Second, he wants teachers to work for five rather than two years before they become eligible for tenure (tenured teachers cannot be fired except under strict circumstances). Finally, the governor asked for cuts in spending for schools. He added that if the legislature did not pass those measures, he would support an effort to have them placed on a fall 2005 ballot as a referendum.

Schwarzenegger's argument is that these measures are necessary because reforming schools is possible only if administrators have a way to reward successful teachers and punish bad ones. Under the current system, pay hikes are tied to seniority, so even poor performers get raises year after year. That makes educating children more expensive without necessarily improving outcomes.

The two unions representing California teachers—the American Federation of Teachers (AFT) and the National Education Association (NEA)—both oppose the idea of linking teachers' pay to test scores. They argue that this would intensify an already too great focus on teaching students to pass tests, rather than exploring a broader or deeper curriculum. Still, the AFT has been open to the general idea of merit pay as part of a larger effort to improve teacher quality with training as well as incentive pay.

Both sides are doing much of their communication in public. Schwarzenegger actively campaigns for his propos-

als, stating, "The more we tolerate ineffective teachers, the more our teachers will be ineffective." The teachers' unions have raised millions of dollars to bring their own campaigns to California and several other states considering pay for performance. Their efforts focus on the proposal for linking pay to test scores; the tenure issue is seen as less significant. Both sides have been broadcasting advertisements. Teachers and other union members have demonstrated noisily at the governor's appearances. Schwarzenegger replies that the demonstrators do not represent average Californians.

In the early months of these campaigns, public support for performance-based pay was mixed. A strong majority support the general idea of merit pay, but far fewer want pay linked specifically to students' test scores. Also, a majority support a longer wait for tenure status.

SOURCE: Ronald Grover and Aaron Bernstein, "Arnold Gets Strict with the Teachers," *BusinessWeek*, May 2, 2005, downloaded from Business & Company Resource Center, http://galenet.galegroup.com; "Unions Protest at Schwarzenegger Event," *Yahoo News*, April 6, 2005, http://story.news.yahoo.com; and John Gittelsohn, "Schwarzenegger Submits Signatures for Initiative on Teachers' Tenure," *Orange County Register*, May 5, 2005, downloaded from Business & Company Resource Center, http://galenet.galegroup.com.

Questions

1. Why is building public support such an important part of labor negotiations for public-sector jobs?

2. Why do you think the teachers' unions object to linking teachers' pay to their students' performance on standardized tests? Why do you think the governor favors this kind of merit pay?

3. Imagine that you are an adviser for either Governor Schwarzenegger or one of the teachers' unions—choose one side or the other. Write a memo to the governor or the union based on which side you choose. Summarize areas of this controversy where you see potential for an agreement. Then, for matters on which you think your side should not compromise, give reasons why the public should accept your point of view. As much as possible, apply what you have learned about HRM to strengthen your case.

NOTES

1. D. E. Lewis, "Mandatory Overtime Rises as a Major Issue for Labor," *Boston Globe*, May 17, 2005, www.boston.com; G. Sukiennik, "NStar, Labor Union Reach Tentative Contract Agreement," *Seacoast Online*, June 9, 2005, www.seacoastonline.com; and NStar, "NStar Set to Welcome Employees Back to Work," news release, May 31, 2005, www.nstaronline.com.

2. J. T. Dunlop, *Industrial Relations Systems* (New York: Holt, 1958); C. Kerr, "Industrial Conflict and Its Mediation," *American Journal of Sociology* 60 (1954), pp. 230–45.

3. See A. M. Glassman and T. G. Cummings, *Industrial Relations: A Multidimensional View* (Glenview, IL: Scott, Foresman, 1985); W. H. Holley Jr. and K. M. Jennings, *The Labor Relations Process* (Chicago: Dryden Press, 1984).

4. T. A. Kochan, *Collective Bargaining and Industrial Relations* (Homewood, IL: Richard D. Irwin, 1980), p. 25; H. C. Katz and T. A. Kochan, *An Introduction to Collective Bargaining and Industrial Relations*, 3rd ed. (New York: McGraw-Hill, 2004).

5. G. Fields, K. Maher, and A. Zimmerman, "Two Unions Quit AFL-CIO, Casting Cloud on Labor," *Wall Street Journal*, July 26, 2005, A1 and A22.

6. Whether the time the union steward spends on union business is paid for by the employer, the union, or a combination is a matter of negotiation between the employer and the union.

7. B. T. Hirsch and D. A. MacPherson, *Union Membership and Earnings Data Book 2001* (Washington, DC: Bureau of National Affairs, 2002).

8. Katz and Kochan, *An Introduction to Collective Bargaining*, building on J. Fiorito and C. L. Maranto, "The Contemporary Decline of Union Strength," *Contemporary Policy Issues* 3 (1987), pp. 12–27; G. N. Chaison and J. Rose, "The Macrodeterminants of Union Growth and Decline," in *The State of the Unions*, ed. G. Strauss et al. (Madison, WI: Industrial Relations Research Association, 1991).

9. Bureau of Labor Statistics Web site, www.bls.gov; AFL-CIO Web site, www.aflcio.org.

10. T. A. Kochan, R. B. McKersie, and J. Chalykoff, "The Effects of Corporate Strategy and Workplace Innovations in Union Representation," *Industrial and Labor Relations Review* 39 (1986), pp. 487–501; Chaison and Rose, "The Macrodeterminants of Union Growth and Decline"; J. Barbash, *Practice of Unionism* (New York: Harper, 1956), p. 210; W. N. Cooke and D. G. Meyer, "Structural and Market Predictors of Corporate Labor Relations Strategies," *Industrial and Labor Relations Review* 43 (1990), pp. 280–93; T. A. Kochan and P. Capelli, "The Transformation of the Industrial Relations and Personnel Function," in *Internal Labor Markets*, ed. P. Osterman (Cambridge, MA: MIT Press, 1984).

11. C. Brewster, "Levels of Analysis in Strategic HRM: Questions Raised by Comparative Research," Conference on Research and Theory in HRM, Cornell University, October 1997.

12. A. Fung, T. Hebb, and J. Rogers, eds., *Working Capital: The Power of Labor's Pensions* (Ithaca, NY: Cornell University Press, 2001); A. Bernstein, "Working Capital: Labor's New Weapon?" *BusinessWeek*, September 27, 1997; and A. Michaud, "Investments with the Union Label," *BusinessWeek*, August 22, 2001.

13. American Federation of State, County and Municipal Employees Web site, www.afscme.org.

14. J. T. Addison and B. T. Hirsch, "Union Effects on Productivity, Profits, and Growth: Has the Long Run Arrived?" *Journal of Labor Economics* 7 (1989), pp. 72–105; R. B. Freeman and J. L. Medoff, "The Two Faces of Unionism," *Public Interest* 57 (Fall 1979), pp. 69–93.

15. L. Mishel and P. Voos, *Unions and Economic Competitiveness* (Armonk, NY: M. E. Sharpe, 1991); Freeman and Medoff, "Two Faces"; S. Slichter, J. Healy, and E. R. Livernash, *The Impact of Collective Bargaining on Management* (Washington, DC: Brookings Institution, 1960).

16. A. O. Hirschman, *Exit, Voice, and Loyalty* (Cambridge, MA: Harvard University Press, 1970); R. Batt, A. J. S. Colvin, and J. Keefe, "Employee Voice, Human Resource Practices, and Quit Rates: Evidence from the Telecommunications Industry," *Industrial and Labor Relations Review* 55 (1970), pp. 573–94.

17. R. B. Freeman and J. L. Medoff, *What Do Unions Do?* (New York: Basic Books, 1984); Addison and Hirsch, "Union Effects on Productivity"; M. Ash and J. A. Seago, "The Effect of Registered Nurses' Unions on Heart-Attack Mortality," *Industrial and Labor Relations Review* 57 (2004), p. 422; and C. Doucouliagos and P. Laroche, "What Do Unions Do to Productivity? A Meta-Analysis," *Industrial Relations* 42 (2003), pp. 650–91.

18. B. E. Becker and C. A. Olson, "Unions and Firm Profits," *Industrial Relations* 31, no. 3 (1992), pp. 395–415; B. T. Hirsch and B. A. Morgan, "Shareholder Risks and Returns in Union and Nonunion Firms," *Industrial and Labor Relations Review* 47, no. 2 (1994), pp. 302–18.

19. K. Maher, "Skills Shortage Gives Training Programs New Life," *The Wall Street Journal*, May 3, 2005, http://online.wsj.com.

20. Bureau of Labor Statistics Web site, http://stats.bls.gov.

21. S. B. Jarrell and T. D. Stanley, "A Meta-Analysis of the Union-Nonunion Wage Gap," *Industrial and Labor Relations Review* 44 (1990), pp. 54–67; and L. Mishel and M. Walters, "How Unions Help All Workers," Economic Policy Institute Briefing Paper, August 2003, www.epinet.org.

22. S. Webb and B. Webb, *Industrial Democracy* (London: Longmans, Green, 1897); J. R. Commons, *Institutional Economics* (New York: Macmillan, 1934).

23. "Why America Needs Unions, but Not the Kind It Has Now," *BusinessWeek,* May 23, 1994, p. 70.

24. E. E. Herman, J. L. Schwartz, and A. Kuhn, *Collective Bargaining and Labor Relations* (Englewood Cliffs, NJ: Prentice Hall, 1992).

25. Kochan, *Collective Bargaining and Industrial Relations,* p. 61.

26. National Labor Relations Board, *Basic Guide to the National Labor Relations Act* (Washington, DC: U.S. Government Printing Office, 1997).

27. Ibid.

28. Ibid.

29. Ibid.

30. R. B. Freeman and M. M. Kleiner, "Employer Behavior in the Face of Union Organizing Drives," *Industrial and Labor Relations Review* 43, no. 4 (April 1990), pp. 351–65.

31. Freeman and Medoff, *What Do Unions Do?*; National Labor Relations Board annual reports for 1980s and 1990s.

32. J. A. Fossum, *Labor Relations,* 8th ed. (New York: McGraw-Hill, 2002), p. 149.

33. C. Tejada, "Young, Educated Employees Are Seen as Boon for Union," *The Wall Street Journal Online,* August 21, 2002, http://online.wsj.com.

34. Herman et al., *Collective Bargaining;* P. Jarley and J. Fiorito, "Associate Membership: Unionism or Consumerism?" *Industrial and Labor Relations Review* 43 (1990), pp. 209–24.

35. Katz and Kochan, *An Introduction to Collective Bargaining;* R. L. Rose, "Unions Hit Corporate Campaign Trail," *The Wall Street Journal,* March 8, 1993, p. B1.

36. P. Jarley and C. L. Maranto, "Union Corporate Campaigns: An Assessment," *Industrial and Labor Relations Review* 44 (1990), pp. 505–24.

37. Katz and Kochan, *An Introduction to Collective Bargaining.*

38. D. Wessel, "Aggressive Tactics by Unions Target Lower-Paid Workers," *The Wall Street Journal Online,* January 31, 2002, http://online.wsj.com.

39. A. E. Eaton and J. Kriesky, "Union Organizing under Neutrality and Card Check Agreements," *Industrial and Labor Relations Review* 55 (2001), pp. 42–59.

40. National Labor Relations Board annual reports.

41. Chaison and Rose, "The Macrodeterminants of Union Growth and Decline."

42. Fossum, *Labor Relations,* p. 262.

43. R. E. Walton and R. B. McKersie, *A Behavioral Theory of Negotiations* (New York: McGraw-Hill, 1965).

44. C. M. Steven, *Strategy and Collective Bargaining Negotiations* (New York: McGraw-Hill, 1963): Katz and Kochan, *An Introduction to Collective Bargaining.*

45. Kochan, *Collective Bargaining and Industrial Relations,* p. 272.

46. Katz and Kochan, *An Introduction to Collective Bargaining.*

47. *United Steelworkers v. American Manufacturing Company,* 363 U.S. 564 (1960); *United Steelworkers v. Warrior Gulf and Navigation Company,* 363 U.S. 574 (1960); *United Steelworkers v. Enterprise Wheel and Car Corporation,* 363 U.S. 593 (1960).

48. U.S. Federal Mediation and Conciliation Service, *Fiftieth Annual Report, Fiscal Year 1997* (Washington, DC: U.S. Government Printing Office, 1997).

49. J. R. Redecker, *Employee Discipline: Policies and Practices* (Washington, DC: Bureau of National Affairs, 1989).

50. T. A. Kochan, H. C. Katz, and R. B. McKersie, *The Transformation of American Industrial Relations* (New York: Basic Books, 1986), chap. 6; E. Appelbaum, T. Bailey, and P. Berg, *Manufacturing Advantage: Why High-Performance Work Systems Pay Off* (Ithaca, NY: Cornell University Press, 2000).

51. L. W. Hunter, J. P. MacDuffie, and L. Doucet, "What Makes Teams Take? Employee Reactions to Work Reforms," *Industrial and Labor Relations Review* 55 (2002), pp. 448–472.

52. J. B. Arthur, "The Link between Business Strategy and Industrial Relations Systems in American Steel Minimills," *Industrial and Labor Relations Review* 45 (1992), pp. 488–506; M. Schuster, "Union Management Cooperation," in *Employee and Labor Relations,* ed. J. A. Fossum (Washington, D.C.: Bureau of National Affairs, 1990); E. Cohen-Rosenthal and C. Burton, *Mutual Gains: A Guide to Union-Management Cooperation,* 2nd ed. (Ithaca, NY: ILR Press, 1993); T. A. Kochan and P. Osterman, *The Mutual Gains Enterprise* (Boston: Harvard Business School Press, 1994); E. Applebaum and R. Batt, *The New American Workplace* (Ithaca, NY: ILR Press, 1994).

53. A. E. Eaton, "Factors Contributing to the Survival of Employee Participation Programs in Unionized Settings," *Industrial and Labor Relations Review* 47, no. 3 (1994), pp. 371–89.

54. A. Bernstein, "Putting a Damper on That Old Team Spirit," *BusinessWeek,* May 4, 1992, p. 60; Bureau of National Affairs, "Polaroid Dissolves Employee Committee in Response to Labor Department Ruling," *Daily Labor Report,* June 23, 1992, p. A-3; K. G. Salwen, "DuPont Is Told It Must Disband Nonunion Panels," *The Wall Street Journal,* June 7, 1993, p. A2.

55. "NLRB 4–0 Approves Crown Cork & Seal's Use of Seven Employee Participation Committees," *HR News*, September 3, 2001.

56. Kochan and Osterman, *The Mutual Gains Enterprise*; J. P. MacDuffie, "Human Resource Bundles and Manufacturing Performance: Organizational Logic and Flexible Production Systems in the World Auto Industry," *Industrial and Labor Relations Review* 48, no. 2 (1995), pp. 197–221; W. N. Cooke, "Employee Participation Programs, Group-Based Incentives, and Company Performance: A Union-Nonunion Comparison," *Industrial and Labor Relations Review* 47, no. 4 (1994), pp. 594–609; C. Doucouliagos, "Worker Participation and Productivity in Labor-Managed and Participatory Capitalist Firms: A Meta-Analysis," *Industrial and Labor Relations Review* 49, no. 1 (1995), pp. 58–77.

57. P. Thomas, "Aviation Firm Learns to Deal with Strained Labor Relations," *The Wall Street Journal Online*, July 30, 2002, http://online.wsj.com.

If you are using the Manager's Hot Seat DVD with this book, consider finishing case 7: Partnership: The Unbalancing Act for this chapter.

CHAPTER 15

MANAGING HUMAN RESOURCES GLOBALLY

After reading this chapter, you should be able to:

What Do I Need to Know?

1. Summarize how the growth in international business activity affects human resource management.

2. Identify the factors that most strongly influence HRM in international markets.

3. Discuss how differences among countries affect HR planning at organizations with international operations.

4. Describe how companies select and train human resources in a global labor market.

5. Discuss challenges related to compensating employees from other countries.

6. Explain how employers prepare managers for international assignments and for their return home.

❖ INTRODUCTION

Students receiving their master's degrees from the top U.S. business schools are lining up for jobs in China, India, and Singapore as never before. The economies are booming in those parts of the world, and the graduates want to be part of the excitement while gaining valuable expertise in what are likely to be some of the world's most important markets. The employers—including investment banks, consulting firms, and multinational corporations selling consumer products, high-tech goods, and health care—are looking for people who know about business principles and also about the language and culture of the country where they will be working. Those requirements can place U.S.-born candidates at a disadvantage, but some qualify. Joseph Kauffman, for example, learned to speak Mandarin in college and worked at Coca-Cola in China between earning his undergraduate degree and enrolling in business school. His language skills and work experience helped him land a summer job with Morgan Stanley in Hong Kong.[1] At the same time that Morgan Stanley and other U.S. companies are hiring employees for assignments in other countries, foreign companies are setting up operations in the United States. Today, human resource management truly takes place on an international scale.

This chapter discusses the HR issues that organizations must address in a world of global competition. We begin by describing how the global nature of business is affecting human resource management in modern organizations. Next, we identify how global differences among countries affect the organization's decisions about human resources. In the following sections we explore HR planning, selection, training, and compensation practices in international settings. Finally, we examine guidelines for managing employees sent on international assignments.

LO1
Summarize how the growth in international business activity affects human resource management.

❦ HRM IN A GLOBAL ENVIRONMENT

The environment in which organizations operate is rapidly becoming a global one. More and more companies are entering international markets by exporting their products, building facilities in other countries, and entering into alliances with foreign companies. At the same time, companies based in other countries are investing and setting up operations in the United States. Indeed, most organizations now function in the global economy.

What is behind the trend toward expansion into global markets? Foreign countries can provide a business with new markets in which there are millions or billions of new customers; developing countries often provide such markets, but developed countries do so as well. In addition, companies set up operations overseas because they can operate with lower labor costs—for example, in Mexico near the U.S. border, thousands of manufacturing plants called *maquiladoras*, most of them owned by U.S. companies, employ Mexican laborers at an average wage of less than $3 per hour.[2] Finally, thanks to advances in telecommunications and information technology, companies can more easily spread work around the globe, wherever they find the right mix of labor costs and abilities. College graduates in India, for example, offer high intelligence and technical know-how at pay scales that are one-sixth or less the

As companies in the United States and Britain cut software jobs and outsource to other countries in order to drive down costs, countries such as India continue to see employment rates rise.

rate paid to a typical U.S. worker. A company that hires technical workers in both countries can move projects along around the clock. When one country's employees are leaving for the day, they can electronically share their work with employees in the other country, who are fresh and ready to get started.[3]

Global activities are simplified and encouraged by trade agreements among nations; for example, most countries in Western Europe belong to the European Union and have begun to share a common currency, the euro. Canada, Mexico, and the United States have encouraged trade among themselves with the North American Free Trade Agreement (NAFTA). The World Trade Organization (WTO) resolves trade disputes among more than 100 participating nations.

As these trends and arrangements encourage international trade, they increase and change the demands on human resource management. Organizations with customers or suppliers in other countries need employees who understand those customers or suppliers. Organizations that operate facilities in foreign countries need to understand the laws and customs that apply to employees in those countries. They may have to prepare managers and other personnel to take international assignments. They have to adapt their human resource plans and policies to different settings. Even if some practices are the same worldwide, the company now has to communicate them to its international workforce. A variety of international activities require managers to understand HRM principles and practices prevalent in global markets.

Employees in an International Workforce

When organizations operate globally, their employees are very likely to be citizens of more than one country. Employees may come from the employer's parent country, a host country, or a third country. The **parent country** is the country in which the organization's headquarters is located. For example, the United States is the parent country of General Motors, because GM's headquarters is in Michigan. A GM employee who was born in the United States and works at GM's headquarters or one of its U.S. factories is therefore a *parent-country national.*

A **host country** is a country (other than the parent country) in which an organization operates a facility. Great Britain is a host country of General Motors because GM has operations there. Any British workers hired to work at GM's British facility would be *host-country nationals,* that is, employees who are citizens of the host country.

A **third country** refers to a country that is neither the parent country nor the host country. (The organization may or may not have a facility in the third country.) In the example of GM's operations in Great Britain, the company could hire an Australian manager to work there. The Australian manager would be a *third-country national* because the manager is neither from the parent country (the United States) nor from the host country (Great Britain).

When organizations operate overseas, they must decide whether to hire parent-country nationals, host-country nationals, or third-country nationals for the overseas operations. Usually, they hire a combination of these. In general, employees assigned to work in another country are called **expatriates.** In the GM example, the U.S. and Australian managers working in Great Britain would be expatriates during those assignments.

The extent to which organizations use parent-country, host-country, or third-country nationals varies. In Japan, Canon is keeping the majority of its production facilities in the parent country as a way to foster close ties between product development and production teams. The goal is for designers and production engineers to collaborate on improving quality and efficiency. In China, a challenge for companies

parent country
The country in which an organization's headquarters is located.

host country
A country (other than the parent country) in which an organization operates a facility.

third country
A country that is neither the parent country nor the host country of an employer.

expatriates
Employees assigned to work in another country.

MONSTER ADVANCING INTO CHINA

By now, most U.S. companies realize the advantages of recruiting online, where they can quickly sort through résumés from applicants who have expressed interest in their industry and location. What about companies that have operations overseas? The search for applicants in another country is even more complicated, so the need for Web-based recruiting tools is that much greater.

In China, where economic growth is strong and the potential for the future even stronger, Internet recruiting services are already playing an important role. Recently, Monster Worldwide, one of the domi-

nant players in U.S. recruiting sites, acquired 40 percent ownership of ChinaHR.com, a Chinese job search site. The acquisition gives Monster an opening into the massive—population 1.3 billion—market and helps ChinaHR.com improve its methods.

The challenges for expansion into China are greater than in another top spot, India, where the business language is English. Most of the job postings and résumés on ChinaHR.com are in Chinese characters, so the information cannot easily be shared with non-Chinese Web sites. As a result, recruiters need to be able

to read and write in Chinese characters. They also should consider including company logos in their listings, as a way to communicate their identity across language systems. Finally, recruiters need to understand that Chinese employees with strong technical skills may lack knowledge or skill in preparing English-language résumés. Matching key terms may be more important than looking for the fine details of a well-crafted résumé.

SOURCE: John Zappe, "Monster Makes a Play for the Chinese Market," *Workforce Management,* March 2005, downloaded from Infotrac at http://web5.infotrac.galegroup.com.

is the limited supply of people with management expertise, so Chinese companies often recruit managers working in the United States. These managers may be U.S. citizens, Chinese citizens gaining experience in the United States, or third-country nationals, including Malaysians (many of whom are ethnic Chinese and able to communicate in their employer's language).[4] In all of these situations, human resource management across national borders is complex, but modern technology is helping. The "e-HRM" box describes online recruiting services in China.

Employers in the Global Marketplace

Just as there are different ways for employees to participate in international business—as parent-country, host-country, or third-county nationals—so there are different ways for employers to do business globally, ranging from simply shipping products to customers in other countries to transforming the organization into a truly global one, with operations, employees, and customers in many countries. Figure 15.1 shows the major levels of global participation.

Most organizations begin by serving customers and clients within a domestic marketplace. Typically, a company's founder has an idea for serving a local, regional, or national market. The business must recruit, hire, train, and compensate employees to produce the product, and these people usually come from the business owner's local labor market. Selection and training focus on employees' technical abilities and, to some extent, on interpersonal skills. Pay levels reflect local labor conditions. If the product

Figure 15.1

Levels of Global Participation

succeeds, the company might expand operations to other domestic locations, and HRM decisions become more complex as the organization draws from a larger labor market and needs systems for training and motivating employees in several locations. As the employer's workforce grows, it is also likely to become more diverse. Even in small domestic organizations, a significant share of workers may be immigrants. In this way, even domestic companies are affected by issues related to the global economy.

As organizations grow, they often begin to meet demand from customers in other countries. The usual way that a company begins to enter foreign markets is by *exporting*, or shipping domestically produced items to other countries to be sold there. Eventually, it may become economically desirable to set up operations in one or more foreign countries. An organization that does so becomes an **international organization.** The decision to participate in international activities raises a host of HR issues, including the basic question of whether a particular location provides an environment where the organization can successfully acquire and manage human resources.

While international companies build one or a few facilities in another country, **multinational companies** go overseas on a broader scale. They build facilities in a number of different countries as a way to keep production and distribution costs to a minimum. In general, when organizations become multinationals, they move production facilities from relatively high-cost locations to lower-cost locations. The lower-cost locations may have lower average wage rates, or they may reduce distribution costs by being nearer to customers. The HRM challenges faced by a multinational company are similar to but larger than those of an international organization, because more countries are involved. More than ever, the organization needs to hire managers who can function in a variety of settings, give them necessary training, and provide flexible compensation systems that take into account the different pay rates, tax systems, and costs of living from one country to another.

At the highest level of involvement in the global marketplace are **global organizations.** These flexible organizations compete by offering top products tailored to segments of the market while keeping costs as low as possible. A global organization locates each facility based on the ability to effectively, efficiently, and flexibly produce a product or service, using cultural differences as an advantage. Rather than treating differences in other countries as a challenge to overcome, a global organization treats

international organization
An organization that sets up one or a few facilities in one or a few foreign countries.

multinational company
An organization that builds facilities in a number of different countries in an effort to minimize production and distribution costs.

global organization
An organization that chooses to locate a facility based on the ability to effectively, efficiently, and flexibly produce a product or service, using cultural differences as an advantage.

different cultures as equals. It may have multiple headquarters spread across the globe, so decisions are more decentralized. This type of organization needs HRM practices that encourage flexibility and are based on an in-depth knowledge of differences among countries. Global organizations must be able to recruit, develop, retain, and use managers who can get results across national boundaries.

A global organization needs a **transnational HRM system**[5] that features decision making from a global perspective, managers from many countries, and ideas contributed by people from a variety of cultures. Decisions that are the outcome of a transnational HRM system balance uniformity (for fairness) with flexibility (to account for cultural and legal differences). This balance and the variety of perspectives should work together to improve the quality of decision making. The participants from various countries and cultures contribute ideas from a position of equality, rather than the parent country's culture dominating.

transnational HRM system
Type of HRM system that makes decisions from a global perspective, includes managers from many countries, and is based on ideas contributed by people representing a variety of cultures.

LO2
Identify the factors that most strongly influence HRM in international markets.

❧ FACTORS AFFECTING HRM IN INTERNATIONAL MARKETS

Whatever their level of global participation, organizations that operate in more than one country must recognize that the countries are not identical and differ in terms of many factors. To simplify this discussion, we focus on four major factors: culture, education, economic systems, and political-legal systems. These influences on human resource management are shown in Figure 15.2.

Culture

By far the most important influence on international HRM is the culture of the country in which a facility is located. *Culture* is a community's set of shared assumptions about how the world works and what ideals are worth striving for.[6] Cultural influences may be expressed through customs, languages, religions, and so on.

Figure 15.2
Factors Affecting Human Resource Management in International Markets

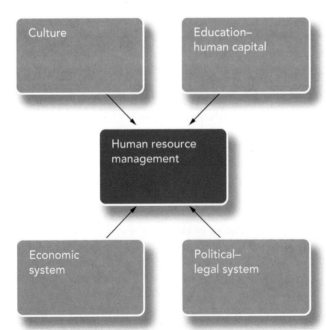

Culture is important to HRM for two reasons. First, it often determines the other three international influences. Culture can greatly affect a country's laws, because laws often are based on the culture's definitions of right and wrong. Culture also influences what people value, so it affects people's economic systems and efforts to invest in education.

Even more important for understanding human resource management, culture often determines the effectiveness of various HRM practices. Practices that are effective in the United States, for example, may fail or even backfire in a country with different beliefs and values.[7] Consider the five dimensions of culture that Geert Hofstede identified in his classic study of culture:[8]

1. *Individualism/collectivism* describes the strength of the relation between an individual and other individuals in the society. In a culture that is high in individualism, such as the United States, Great Britain, and the Netherlands, people tend to think and act as individuals rather than as members of a group. People in these countries are expected to stand on their own two feet, rather than be protected by the group. In a culture that is high in collectivism, such as Colombia, Pakistan, and Taiwan, people think of themselves mainly as group members. They are expected to devote themselves to the interests of the community, and the community is expected to protect them when they are in trouble.

2. *Power distance* concerns the way the culture deals with unequal distribution of power and defines the amount of inequality that is normal. In countries with large power distances, including India and the Philippines, the culture defines it as normal to maintain large differences in power. In countries with small power distances, such as Denmark and Israel, people try to eliminate inequalities. One way to see differences in power distance is in the way people talk to one another. In the high-power-distance countries of Mexico and Japan, people address one another with titles (Señor Smith, Smith-san). At the other extreme, in the United States, in most situations people use one another's first names—behavior that would be disrespectful in other cultures.

3. *Uncertainty avoidance* describes how cultures handle the fact that the future is unpredictable. High uncertainty avoidance refers to a strong cultural preference for structured situations. In countries such as Greece and Portugal, people tend to rely heavily on religion, law, and technology to give them a degree of security and clear rules about how to behave. In countries with low uncertainty avoidance, including Singapore and Jamaica, people seem to take each day as it comes.

4. *Masculinity/femininity* is the emphasis a culture places on practices or qualities that have traditionally been considered masculine or feminine. A "masculine" culture is a culture that values achievement, money making, assertiveness, and competition. A "feminine" culture is one that places a high value on relationships, service, care for the weak, and preserving the environment. In this model, Germany and Japan are examples of masculine cultures, and Sweden and Norway are examples of feminine cultures.

5. *Long-term/short-term orientation* suggests whether the focus of cultural values is on the future (long term) or the past and present (short term). Cultures with a long-term orientation value saving and persistence, which tend to pay off in the future. Many Asian countries, including Japan and China, have a long-term orientation. Short-term orientations, as in the cultures of the United States, Russia, and West Africa, promote respect for past tradition, and for fulfilling social obligations in the present. Figure 15.3 summarizes these five cultural dimensions.

Figure 15.3

Five Dimensions of
Culture

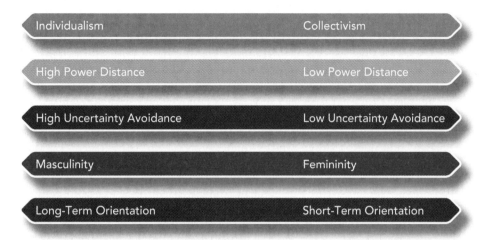

SOURCE: G. Hofstede, "Dimensions of National Cultures in Fifty Countries and Three Regions," in *Expectations in Cross-Cultural Psychology*, eds. J. Deregowski, S. Dziurawiec, and R. C. Annis (Lisse, Netherlands: Swets and Zeitlinger, 1983); G. Hofstede, "Cultural Constraints in Management Theories," *Academy of Management Executive* 7 (1993), pp. 81–90.

Such cultural characteristics as these influence the ways members of an organization behave toward one another, as well as their attitudes toward various HRM practices. For instance, cultures differ strongly in their opinions about how managers should lead, how decisions should be handled, and what motivates employees. In Germany, managers achieve their status by demonstrating technical skills, and employees look to managers to assign tasks and resolve technical problems. In the Netherlands, managers focus on seeking agreement, exchanging views, and balancing the interests of the people affected by a decision.[9] Clearly, differences like these would affect how an organization selects and trains its managers and measures their performance. The "Best Practices" box describes how such differences can affect the success of a global ethics policy.

Cultures strongly influence the appropriateness of HRM practices. For example, the extent to which a culture is individualist or collectivist will affect the success of a compensation program. Compensation tied to individual performance may be seen as fairer and more motivating by members of an individualist culture; a culture favoring individualism will be more accepting of great differences in pay between the organization's highest- and lowest-paid employees. Collectivist cultures tend to have much flatter pay structures.

Job design aimed at employee empowerment can be problematic in cultures with high "power distance." In a Mexican slipper-manufacturing plant, an effort to expand the decision-making authority of production workers stumbled when the workers balked at doing what they saw as the supervisor's proper responsibility.[10] Realizing they had moved too quickly, the plant's managers narrowed the scope of the workers' decision-making authority so they could adapt to the role. On the other hand, a factor in favor of empowerment at that plant was the Mexican culture's high collectivism. The workers liked discussing team-related information and using the information to benefit the entire team. As in this example, a culture does not necessarily rule out a particular HRM practice, such as employee empowerment, but it should be a consideration in deciding how to carry out the practice.

Finally, cultural differences can affect how people communicate and how they coordinate their activities. In collectivist cultures, people tend to value group decision

BEST PRACTICES

ETHICS WITHOUT BOUNDARIES AT DELOITTE TOUCHE TOHMATSU

The name Deloitte Touche Tohmatsu (DTT) invokes the international origins of a firm founded by accountants who started practices in England, the United States, and Japan. The practices grew and later merged to form a global consulting giant offering services in accounting, auditing, and financial advice. For a firm to succeed in delivering such services, its clients must feel confident they can trust the firm. So, DTT must establish, sustain, and communicate high ethical standards to clients worldwide.

DTT has identified nine ethical principles required of all its member firms: honesty and integrity, professional behavior (compliance with laws), competence, objectivity, confidentiality, fair business practices, responsibility to society, respect and fair treatment of colleagues, and accountability (leading by example). To ensure that all employees understand these principles, the company provides Web-based training through a program it calls the Integrity Compass. The Integrity Compass teaches by presenting ethical dilemmas employees might encounter. The company has appointed a chief ethics partner for at least one member firm in each country where it operates. Employees also may call a toll-free telephone hot line if they suspect they have evidence of unethical conduct.

Internal reporting systems, especially anonymous hot lines, can be the most difficult part of an ethics program for an international company. In some cultures, history and values make this type of reporting unacceptable. For example, in France and Italy, employees associate anonymous tips with their memories of people collaborating with Axis occupiers during World War II. Many Russians make negative associations with Stalinist tactics. In parts of the Middle East, employees might accept the idea of making reports to a local office but not to an international headquarters. Besides these value differences come the challenges of providing accurate and understandable ethics materials in several languages. Examples also need to be realistic for the cultures who use them.

William G. Parrett, DTT's chief executive, recognizes these challenges, noting that "in some cultures a 1-800 hotline would not be culturally acceptable." So, the firm has customized elements of the ethics program for the culture of each country. The nine ethical principles, however, are shared globally. The accountant's duty to be trustworthy is a requirement that knows no national boundaries.

SOURCE: Kris Maher, "Global Companies Face Reality of Instituting Ethics Programs," *The Wall Street Journal*, November 9, 2004, p. B8; and Deloitte Touche Tohmatsu, "About Us," www.deloitte.com, accessed June 20, 2005.

making, as in the previous example. When a person raised in an individualistic culture must work closely with people from a collectivist culture, communication problems and conflicts often occur. People from the collectivist culture tend to collaborate heavily and may evaluate the individualistic person as unwilling to cooperate and share information with them. Cultural differences in communication affected the way a North American agricultural company embarked on employee empowerment at its facilities in the United States and Brazil.[11] Empowerment requires information sharing, but in Brazil, high power distance leads employees to expect managers to make decisions, so they do not desire information that is appropriately held by managers. Empowering the Brazilian employees required involving managers directly in giving and sharing information to show that this practice was in keeping with the traditional chain of command. Also, because uncertainty avoidance is another aspect of Brazilian culture, managers explained that greater information sharing would reduce uncertainty about their work. At the same time, greater collectivism in Brazil made employees comfortable with the day-to-day communication of teamwork. The individualistic U.S. employees needed to be sold more on this aspect of empowerment.

Because of these challenges, organizations must prepare managers to recognize and handle cultural differences. They may recruit managers with knowledge of other cultures or provide training, as described later in the chapter. For expatriate assignments, organizations may need to conduct an extensive selection process to identify individuals who can adapt to new environments. At the same time, it is important to be wary of stereotypes and avoid exaggerating the importance of cultural differences. Recent research that examined Hofstede's model of cultural differences found that differences among organizations within a particular culture were sometimes larger than differences from country to country.[12] This finding suggests that it is important for an organization to match its HR practices to its values; individuals who share those values are likely to be interested in working for the organization.

Education and Skill Levels

Countries also differ in the degree to which their labor markets include people with education and skills of value to employers. As discussed in Chapter 1, the United States suffers from a shortage of skilled workers in many occupations, and the problem is expected to increase. For example, the need for knowledge workers (engineers, teachers, scientists, health care workers) is expected to grow almost twice as fast as the overall rate of job growth in the United States.[13] On the other hand, the labor markets in many countries are very attractive because they offer high skills and low wages.

Educational opportunities also vary from one country to another. In general, spending on education is greater per pupil in high-income countries than in poorer countries.[14] Poverty, illnesses such as AIDS, and political turmoil may keep children away from school in some areas. In sub-Saharan Africa, only 59 percent of eligible children finish primary school. However, some countries, including Guinea, Ethiopia, and Chad, have made significant gains in educating children. In contrast, children in East Asia and the Pacific are much more likely to complete primary school, although poor children are less likely to enroll and to stay in school.[15]

Companies with foreign operations locate in countries where they can find suitable employees. The education and skill levels of a country's labor force affect how and the extent to which companies want to operate there. In countries with a poorly educated population, companies will limit their activities to low-skill, low-wage jobs. In contrast, India's large pool of well-trained technical workers is one reason that the country has become a popular location for outsourcing computer programming jobs.

Economic System

A country's economic system whether capitalist or socialist, as well as the government's involvement in the economy through taxes or compensation, price controls, and other activities, influences human resource management practices in a number of ways.

As with all aspects of a region's or country's life, the economic system and culture are likely to be closely tied, providing many of the incentives or disincentives for developing the value of the labor force. Socialist economic systems provide ample opportunities for educational development because the education system is free to stu-

Students at the University of Warsaw in Poland are provided with a government-supported education. In general, former Soviet bloc countries tend to be generous in funding education, so they tend to have highly educated and skilled labor forces. Capitalist countries such as the United States generally leave higher education up to individual students to pay for, but the labor market rewards students who earn a college degree.

dents. At the same time, socialism may not provide economic rewards (higher pay) for increasing one's education. In capitalist systems, students bear more of the cost of their education, but employers reward those who invest in education.

The health of an economic system affects human resource management. In developed countries with great wealth, labor costs are relatively high. Such differences show up in compensation systems and in recruiting and selection decisions.

In general, socialist systems take a higher percentage of each worker's income as the worker's income increases. Capitalist systems tend to let workers keep more of their earnings. In this way, socialism redistributes wealth from high earners to the poor, while capitalism apparently rewards individual accomplishments. In any case, since the amount of take-home pay a worker receives after taxes may thus differ from country to country, in an organization that pays two managers in two countries $100,000 each, the manager in one country might take home more than the manager in the other country. Such differences make pay structures more complicated when they cross national boundaries, and they can affect recruiting of candidates from more than one country.

Political-Legal System

A country's political-legal system—its government, laws, and regulations—strongly impinges on human resource management. The country's laws often dictate the requirements for certain HRM practices, such as training, compensation, hiring, firing, and layoffs. As we noted in the discussion of culture, the political-legal system arises to a large degree from the culture in which it exists, so laws and regulations reflect cultural values.

For example, the United States has led the world in eliminating discrimination in the workplace. Because this value is important in U.S. culture, the nation has legal safeguards such as the equal employment opportunity laws discussed in Chapter 3, which affect hiring and other HRM decisions. As a society, the United States also has strong beliefs regarding the fairness of pay systems. Thus, the Fair Labor Standards Act (discussed in Chapter 11), among other laws and regulations, sets a minimum wage for a variety of jobs. Other laws and regulations dictate much of the process of negotiation between unions and management. All these are examples of laws and regulations that affect the practice of HRM in the United States.

Similarly, laws and regulations in other countries reflect the norms of their cultures. In Western Europe, where many countries have had strong socialist parties, some laws have been aimed at protecting the rights and benefits of workers. Until recently, France and Germany had 35-hour workweeks, although workers have recently begun to accept contracts with more flexibility. However, the European Parliament in 2005 voted in favor of a 48-hour ceiling on the number of hours worked per week in European Union countries. Under that requirement, regular hours plus overtime could not exceed 48 hours in a single week.[16]

An organization that expands internationally must gain expertise in the host country's legal requirements and ways of dealing with its legal system, often leading organizations to hire one or more host-country nationals to help in the process. Some countries have laws requiring that a certain percentage of the employees of any foreign-owned subsidiary be host-country nationals, and in the context of our discussion here, this legal challenge to an organization's HRM may hold an advantage if handled creatively.

LO3
Discuss how differences among countries affect HR planning at organizations with international operations.

❧ HUMAN RESOURCE PLANNING IN A GLOBAL ECONOMY

As economic and technological change creates a global environment for organizations, human resource planning is involved in decisions about participating as an exporter or as an international, multinational, or global company. Even purely domestic companies may draw talent from the international labor market. As organizations consider decisions about their level of international activity, HR professionals should provide information about the relevant human resource issues, such as local market pay rates and labor laws. When organizations decide to operate internationally or globally, human resource planning involves decisions about where and how many employees are needed for each international facility.

Decisions about where to locate include HR considerations such as the cost and availability of qualified workers. In addition, HR specialists must work with other members of the organization to weigh these considerations against financial and operational requirements. For example, while many companies are arranging to have goods produced in China, where labor costs are low, China's largest maker of appliances, Haier Group, has recently opened facilities in the United States. Haier and other Chinese manufacturers have grown by making appliances inexpensively for foreign companies and then by selling their own products in the Chinese market. Beginning in the mid-1990s, Haier began designing and selling compact refrigerators for U.S. consumers. When these products succeeded, the company decided to expand into full-size models. However, the larger refrigerators are too expensive to ship across the Pacific. Because of the products' size, building them in the United States is more economical, even though labor costs are greater. Haier America originally sent Chinese employees to its Camden, South Carolina, plant to train workers, but most of the employees are now Americans.[17]

Other location decisions involve outsourcing, described in Chapter 2. Many companies have boosted efficiency by arranging to have specific functions performed by outside contractors. As described in the "Did You Know . . . ?" box, many—but not

MOST U.S. OUTSOURCED JOBS GO TO INDIA— AND THE UNITED STATES

The largest percentage of companies outsourcing jobs today are using workers in India, with the United States a close second. Other popular countries for outsourced jobs are the United Kingdom, Canada, and the Philippines. All of these countries have a sizable English-speaking workforce. However, 40 percent of companies say they expect to outsource jobs to China in the future; 32 percent expect some outsourcing to use workers in Eastern Europe.

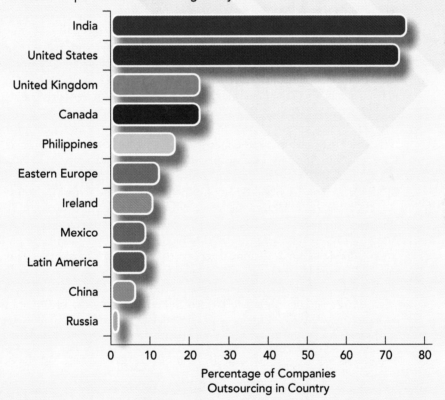

Where Companies Are Outsourcing Today

SOURCE: Aaron Rutkoff, "Firms Expect to Increase IT Outsourcing, Survey Shows," *The Wall Street Journal*, June 7, 2005, http://online.wsj.com.

all—of these arrangements involve workers outside the United States in lower-wage countries.

In Chapter 5, we saw that human resource planning includes decisions to hire and lay off workers to prepare for the organization's expected needs. Compared with other countries, the United States allows employers wide latitude in reducing their workforce, giving U.S. employers the option of hiring for peak needs, then laying off employees if needs decline. Other governments place more emphasis on protecting workers' jobs. European countries, and France in particular, tend to be very strict in this regard.

LO4
Describe how companies select and train human resources in a global labor market.

◈ SELECTING EMPLOYEES IN A GLOBAL LABOR MARKET

Many companies such as Microsoft have headquarters in the United States plus facilities in locations around the world. To be effective, employees in the Microsoft Mexico operations in Mexico City must understand that region's business and social culture. Organizations often meet this need by hiring host-country nationals to fill most of their foreign positions. A key reason is that a host-country national can more easily understand the values and customs of the local workforce than someone from another part of the world can. Also, training for and transporting families to foreign assignments is more expensive than hiring people in the foreign country. Employees may be reluctant to take a foreign assignment because of the difficulty of moving overseas. Sometimes the move requires the employee's spouse to quit a job, and some countries will not allow the employee's spouse to seek work, even if jobs might be available.

Even so, organizations fill many key foreign positions with parent-country or third-country nationals. Sometimes a person's technical and human relations skills outweigh the advantages of hiring locally. In other situations, such as the shortage of U.S. knowledge workers, the local labor market simply does not offer enough qualified people. At organizations located where needed skills are in short supply, hiring immigrant employees may be part of an effective recruitment and selection strategy.[18] Of the two largest categories of foreign workers employed in the United States, one group consists of professionals with the particular qualifications needed to fill a job.[19] The other group comprises employees of multinational companies who are transferred to the United States from their employer's facilities in another country. The terrorist attacks of September 11, 2001, have not changed the basics of selecting these employees, but they have raised some security issues. One is that the government may move more deliberately (and thus more slowly) in approving visas for immigrants. Employers may be required to provide more paperwork, such as annual reports to show they can pay the immigrant's salary and, for some kinds of positions, job descriptions clarifying that the worker will not be in a situation where he or she could harm the United States. Another issue is that foreign travelers to and from the United States, including the organization's immigrant workers, may have to contend with more delays and red tape. The primary impact on employers is that they must be more patient in completing the hiring process.[20]

Qualities associated with success in foreign assignments are the ability to communicate in the foreign country, flexibility, enjoying a challenging situation, and support from family members. What would persuade you to take a foreign assignment?

Whether the organization is hiring immigrants or selecting parent-country or third-country nationals for foreign assignments, some basic principles of selection apply. Selection of employees for foreign assignments should reflect criteria that have been associated with success in working overseas:

- Competency in the employee's area of expertise.
- Ability to communicate verbally and nonverbally in the foreign country.
- Flexibility, tolerance of ambiguity, and sensitivity to cultural differences.
- Motivation to succeed and enjoyment of challenges.
- Willingness to learn about the foreign country's culture, language, and customs.
- Support from family members.[21]

In research conducted a number of years ago, the factor most strongly influencing whether an employee completed a foreign assignment was the comfort of the employee's spouse and family.[22] Personality may also be important. Research has found successful completion of overseas assignments to be most likely among employees who are extroverted (outgoing), agreeable (cooperative and tolerant), and conscientious (dependable and achievement oriented).[23]

Qualities of flexibility, motivation, agreeableness, and conscientiousness are so important because of the challenges involved in entering another culture. The emotions that accompany an overseas assignment tend to follow a cycle like that in Figure 15.4.[24] For a month or so after arriving, the foreign worker enjoys a "honeymoon" of fascination and euphoria as the employee enjoys the novelty of the new culture and compares its interesting similarities to or differences from the employee's own culture. Before long, the employee's mood declines as he or she notices more unpleasant differences and experiences feelings of isolation, criticism, stereotyping, and even hostility. As the mood reaches bottom, the employee is experiencing **culture shock,** the disillusionment and discomfort that occur during the process of adjusting to a new culture and its norms, values, and perspectives. Eventually, if employees persist and continue learning about their host country's culture, they develop a greater understanding and a support network. As the employee's language skills and comfort increase, the employee's mood should improve as well. Eventually, the employee reaches a stage of adjustment in which he or she accepts and enjoys the host country's culture.

Even if the organization determines that the best candidate for a position is someone from another country, employers often have difficulty persuading candidates to accept foreign assignments. Not only do the employee and employee's family have to contend with culture shock, but the employee's spouse commonly loses a job when an employee makes a foreign move. Some organizations solve this problem with a compromise: the use of **virtual expatriates,** or employees who manage an operation abroad without locating permanently in that country.[25] They take frequent trips to the foreign country, and when they are home, they use modern technology such as videoconferencing and e-mail to stay in touch. An assignment as a virtual expatriate may be less inconvenient to family members and less costly to the employer. The arrangement

culture shock
Disillusionment and discomfort that occur during the process of adjusting to a new culture.

virtual expatriates
Employees who manage an operation abroad without permanently locating in the country.

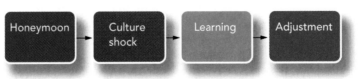

figure 15.4

Emotional Cycle Associated with a Foreign Assignment

SOURCE: Adapted from C. Lachnit, "Low-Cost Tips for Successful Inpatriation," *Workforce,* August 2001, p. 44.

does have disadvantages. Most notably, by limiting personal contact to sporadic trips, the virtual expatriate will likely have a harder time building relationships.

◈ TRAINING AND DEVELOPING A GLOBAL WORKFORCE

In an organization whose employees come from more than one country, some special challenges arise with regard to training and development: (1) Training and development programs should be effective for all participating employees, regardless of their country of origin. (2) When organizations hire employees to work in a foreign country or transfer them to another country, the employer needs to provide the employees with training in how to handle the challenges associated with working in the foreign country.

Training Programs for an International Workforce

Developers of effective training programs for an international workforce must ask certain questions.[26] The first is to establish the objectives for the training and its content. Decisions about the training should support those objectives. The developers should next ask what training techniques, strategies, and media to use. Some will be more effective than others, depending on the learners' language and culture, as well as the content of the training. For example, in preparation U.S. employees might expect to discuss and ask questions about the training content, whereas employees from other cultures might consider this level of participation to be disrespectful, so for them some additional support might be called for. Language differences will require translations and perhaps a translator at training activities. Next, the developers should identify any other interventions and conditions that must be in place for the training to meet its objectives. For example, training is more likely to meet its objectives if it is linked to performance management and has the full support of management. Finally, the developers of a training program should identify who in the organization should be involved in reviewing and approving the training program.

The plan for the training program must consider international differences among trainees. For example, economic and educational differences might influence employees' access to and ability to use Web-based training. Cultural differences may influence whether they will consider it appropriate to ask questions and whether they expect the trainer to spend time becoming acquainted with employees or to get down to business immediately. Table 15.1 provides examples of how cultural characteristics can affect training design. These differences may call for extra planning and creativity on the part of the training program's developer. Mattel, the toy maker known for Barbie dolls and Hot Wheels cars, meets the challenge of training employees in 36 countries by combining the adaptability of e-learning with the consistency of leadership training at its headquarters. The goal is to make sure managers in every location have skills in leading and motivating employees, including ways to discuss their performance, so that everyone is focused on the company's strategy.[27]

Another example of successful international training was a unit on avoiding sexual harassment presented to employees of four multinational companies working on the Sea Launch vessel, a rocket launch platform located in the Pacific Ocean.[28] The Sea Launch employees came from the United States, Norway, Russia, Ukraine, and the Philippines. The training was essential because one of the employers in this joint venture, the Boeing Company, is a U.S. business and therefore must comply with U.S. laws forbidding sex discrimination. However, the other three companies partic-

TABLE 15.1

Effects of Culture on
Training Design

CULTURAL DIMENSION	IMPACT ON TRAINING
Individualism	Culture high in individualism expects participation in exercises and questioning to be determined by status in the company or culture.
Uncertainty avoidance	Culture high in uncertainty avoidance expects formal instructional environments. Less tolerance for impromptu style.
Masculinity	Culture low in masculinity values relationships with fellow trainees. Female trainers less likely to be resisted in low-masculinity cultures.
Power distance	Culture high in power distance expects trainer to be expert. Trainers expected to be authoritarian and controlling of session.
Time orientation	Culture with a long-term orientation will have trainees who are likely to accept development plans and assignments.

SOURCE: Based on B. Filipczak, "Think Locally, Act Globally," *Training*, January 1997, pp. 41–48.

ipating in the joint venture are based in other countries, so the law did not apply to them, and they had differing standards on what is appropriate in male-female interactions. The objective of the training was therefore to explain how employees should behave to succeed in an American work environment, emphasizing shared values of personal responsibility and respect for individuals, rather than "right" or "wrong" behavior. The trainers selected the most common and accepted training methods for their audience: a lecture followed by a question-and-answer session. To establish the training's importance and credibility, the training sessions included an introduction by top executives and presentations by experts in the subject matter. Also, upper management was involved in the design of the program, which helped to demonstrate management's commitment to the training content. Classes brought together participants from all the cultures, and a translator enabled the material to be presented in the two dominant languages, English and Russian. Employee satisfaction surveys later showed a positive contribution to the attitudes of Boeing's Sea Launch employees.

Cross-Cultural Preparation

When an organization selects an employee for a position in a foreign country, it must prepare the employee for the foreign assignment. This kind of training is called **cross-cultural preparation,** preparing employees to work across national and cultural boundaries, and it often includes family members who will accompany the employee on the assignment. The training is necessary for all three phases of an international assignment:

1. Preparation for *departure*—language instruction and an orientation to the foreign country's culture.
2. The *assignment* itself—some combination of a formal program and mentoring relationship to provide ongoing further information about the foreign country's culture.
3. Preparation for the *return* home—providing information about the employee's community and home-country workplace (from company newsletters, local newspapers, and so on).

cross-cultural preparation
Training to prepare employees and their family members for an assignment in a foreign country.

Methods for providing this training may range from lectures for employees and their families to visits to culturally diverse communities.[29] Employees and their families may also spend time visiting a local family from the country where they will be working. In the later section on managing expatriates, we provide more detail about cross-cultural preparation.

U.S.-based companies sometimes need to be reminded that foreign employees who come to the United States ("inpatriates") need cross-cultural preparation as much as U.S. employees sent on foreign assignments.[30] In spite of the many benefits of living in the United States, relocation can be challenging for inpatriates. In fact, in the Global Relocation Trends 2000 Survey Report, the United States was listed as among the most challenging foreign assignments.[31] For example, inpatriates exposed to the United States through Hollywood and TV shows often worry about safety in their new homes. In many parts of the world, a middle manager or professional's lifestyle may include servants, and the cost of rental housing is far less. As with expatriates, organizations can prepare inpatriate employees by providing information about getting the resources they need to live safely and comfortably in their new surroundings. HR personnel may be able to identify local immigrant communities where their inpatriate employees can go to shop for familiar foods and hear their native language.

Global Employee Development

At global organizations, international assignments are a part of many career paths. The organization benefits most if it applies the principles of employee development in deciding which employees should be offered jobs in other countries. Career development helps expatriate and inpatriate employees make the transitions to and from their assignments and helps the organization apply the knowledge the employees obtain from these assignments.

❧ PERFORMANCE MANAGEMENT ACROSS NATIONAL BOUNDARIES

The general principles of performance management may apply in most countries, but the specific methods that work in one country may fail in another. Therefore, organizations have to consider legal requirements, local business practices, and national cultures when they establish performance management methods in other countries. Differences may include which behaviors are rated, how and the extent to which performance is measured, who performs the rating, and how feedback is provided.[32]

For example, National Rental Car uses a behaviorally based rating scale for customer service representatives. To measure the extent to which customer service representatives' behaviors contribute to the company's goal of improving customer service, the scale measures behaviors such as smiling, making eye contact, greeting customers, and solving customer problems. Depending on the country, different behaviors may be appropriate. In Japan, culturally defined standards for polite behavior include the angle of bowing as well as proper back alignment and eye contact. In Ghana and many other African nations, appropriate measures would include behaviors that reflect loyalty and repaying of obligations as well as behaviors related to following regulations and procedures.

The extent to which managers measure performance may also vary from one country to another. In rapidly changing regions, such as Southeast Asia, the organization may have to update its performance plans more often than once a year.

Feedback is another area in which differences can occur. Employees around the world appreciate positive feedback, but U.S. employees are much more used to direct feedback than are employees in other countries. In Mexico managers are expected to provide positive feedback before focusing the discussion on behaviors the employee needs to improve.[33] At the Thai office of Singapore Airlines, managers resisted giving negative feedback to employees because they feared this would cause them to have bad karma, contributing to their reincarnation at a lower level in their next life.[34] The airlines therefore allowed the managers to adapt their feedback process to fit local cultures.

❧ COMPENSATING AN INTERNATIONAL WORKFORCE

LO5
Discuss challenges related to compensating employees from other countries.

The chapters in Part 4 explained that compensation includes decisions about pay structure, incentive pay, and employee benefits. All these decisions become more complex when an organization has an international workforce. In a recent survey of employers with international operations, 85 percent said they have a global compensation strategy to guide compensation decisions for employees at all levels and in all countries where they operate.[35] Still, HR specialists may need to make extra efforts to administer these systems effectively. In half of the companies surveyed, the person in charge of HRM in one country reports to the head of that company's operations, rather than to the leader of HRM at headquarters.

Pay Structure

As Figure 15.5 shows, market pay structures can differ substantially across countries in terms of both pay level and the relative worth of jobs. For example, compared with the labor market in Frankfurt, Germany, the markets in Budapest, Hungary, and in Bombay, India, provide much lower pay levels overall. The latter two labor markets also exhibit less of a pay difference for jobs requiring greater skill and education.

Differences such as these create a dilemma for global companies: Should pay levels and differences reflect what workers are used to in their own countries? Or should they reflect the earnings of colleagues in the country of the facility, or earnings at the company headquarters? For example, should a German engineer posted to Bombay be paid according to the standard in Frankfurt or the standard in Bombay? If the standard is Frankfurt, the engineers in Bombay will likely see the German engineer's pay as unfair. If the standard is Bombay, the company will likely find it impossible to persuade a German engineer to take an assignment in Bombay. Dilemmas such as these make a global compensation strategy important as a way to show employees that the pay structure is designed to be fair and related to the value that employees bring to the organization.

These decisions affect a company's costs and ability to compete. The average hourly labor costs in industrialized countries such as the United States, Germany, and Japan are far higher than these costs in newly industrialized countries such as Mexico, Hong Kong, and Korea.[36] As a result, we often hear that U.S. labor costs are too high to allow U.S. companies to compete effectively unless the companies shift operations to low-cost foreign subsidiaries. That conclusion oversimplifies the situation for many companies. Merely comparing wages ignores differences in education, skills, and productivity.[37] If an organization gets more or higher-quality output from a higher-wage workforce, the higher wages may be worth the cost. Besides this, if the organization

Figure 15.5

Earnings in Selected Occupations in Seven Cities

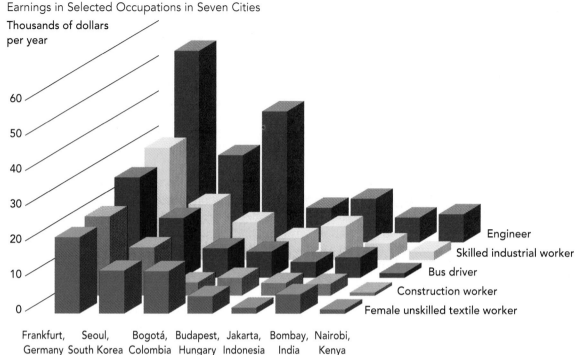

Note: Earnings are adjusted to reflect purchasing power.

SOURCE: From *World Development Report 1995*. Workers in an Integrating World by World Bank. Copyright 1995 by World Bank. Reprinted with permission of World Bank via Copyright Clearance Center.

has many positions requiring highly skilled workers, it may need to operate in (or hire immigrants from) a country with a strong educational system, regardless of labor costs. Finally, labor costs may be outweighed by other factors, such as transportation costs or access to resources or customers. When a production process is highly automated, differences in labor costs may not be significant.

At the same time, the challenge of competing with organizations in low-wage countries can be very difficult. China, for example, has invested in vocational schools, which provide training for skilled factory jobs. Chinese universities graduate a much larger share of engineers than U.S. universities. These schools are flooding the Chinese labor market with talent, so that even as high-tech manufacturing spreads to many Chinese cities, the need for workers is easy to fill. For Chinese workers, even experienced engineers, the result is that pay is growing but remains low compared to rates in other countries. An example is Li Guangxiang, a senior engineer and assistant manager at a Flextronics International computer parts factory, who earns just $10,000 a year.[38]

Incentive Pay

Besides setting a pay structure, the organization must make decisions with regard to incentive pay, such as bonuses and stock options. Although stock options became a common form of incentive pay in the United States during the 1990s, European businesses did not begin to embrace this type of compensation until the end of that decade. European companies with North American operations have felt the greatest pressure to join the stock option "club."[39] For instance, executives at Alcatel, a French manufacturer of telecommunications equipment, recently realized they needed to broaden the scope of their compensation when they began to acquire North American firms such as Canada's Newbridge Networks. Afraid that failure to offer stock options would result in a loss of qualified employees, Alcatel announced a plan that would award options to over one-third of its engineers and middle managers outside the United States (and three-quarters of them inside the United States).

The United States and Europe differ in the way they award stock options. European companies usually link the options to specific performance goals, such as the increase in a company's share price compared with that of its competitors. German law actually requires this, and British firms such as Barclays are beginning to enforce stricter guidelines. Belgium and Switzerland still discourage the use of stock options by imposing high taxes on this form of compensation. Italy and Norway have passed laws and tax changes that make stock options more attractive to employers and employees. As competition in European labor markets increases, experts predict that companies not offering options will have a harder time recruiting the best employees.

Employee Benefits

As in the United States, compensation packages in other countries include benefits. Decisions about benefits must take into account the laws of each country involved, as well as employees' expectations and values in those countries. Some countries require paid maternity leave, and some countries have nationalized health care systems, which would affect the value of private health insurance in a compensation package. Pension plans are more widespread in parts of Western Europe than in the United States and Japan. Over 90 percent of workers in Switzerland have pension plans, as do all workers in France. Among workers with pension plans, U.S. workers are significantly less likely to have defined benefit plans than workers in Japan or Germany.

Paid vacation, discussed in Chapter 13, tends to be more generous in Western Europe than in the United States. Figure 15.6 compares the number of hours the average manufacturing employee works in various countries. Of these countries, only in

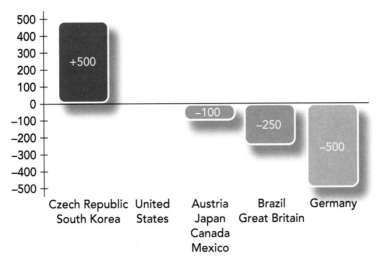

Figure 15.6

Normal Annual Hours Worked in Manufacturing Relative to United States

SOURCE: *Key Indicators of the Labor Market 2001–2002* (Geneva, Switzerland: International Labour Office, 2001).

the Czech Republic and South Korea do manufacturing workers put in more hours than U.S. workers—500 more hours per year. In the other countries, the norm is to work 100 to 500 hours less than a U.S. worker over the course of a year.

✧ INTERNATIONAL LABOR RELATIONS

Companies that operate across national boundaries often need to work with unions in more than one country. Organizations establish policies and goals for labor relations, overseeing labor agreements, and monitoring labor performance (for example, output and productivity).[40] The day-to-day decisions about labor relations are usually handled by each foreign subsidiary. The reason is that labor relations on an international scale involve differences in laws, attitudes, and economic systems, as well as differences in negotiation styles.

At least in comparison with European organizations, U.S. organizations exert more centralized control over labor relations in the various countries where they operate.[41] U.S. management therefore must recognize differences in how various countries understand and regulate labor relations. For example, in the United States, collective bargaining usually involves negotiations between a union local and an organization's management, but in Sweden and Germany, collective bargaining generally involves negotiations between an employers' organization and a union representing an entire industry's employees.[42] Legal differences range from who may form a union to how much latitude an organization is allowed in laying off workers. In China, for example, efforts at economic reform have resulted in many thousands of layoffs. In the spring of 2002, as many as 20,000 workers at a time have rallied to protest layoffs by PetroChina, angry that early-retirement packages did not include expected medical insurance and social security payments. The workers resort to public protest because the country's legal and economic system allows only government-controlled unions and does not provide them with recourse when the government does not support their position.[43] In Germany, because labor representatives participate on companies' boards of directors, the way management handles labor relations can affect a broad range of decisions.[44] Management therefore has an incentive to build cooperative relationships.

International labor relations must also take into account that negotiations between labor and management take place in a different social context, not just different economic and legal contexts. Cultural differences that affect other interactions come into play in labor negotiations as well. Negotiators will approach the process differently depending on whether the culture views the process as primarily cooperative or competitive and whether it is local practice to negotiate a deal by starting with

Due to the Multi Fibre Agreement which governs trade in the textile and clothing industry, the once prosperous clothing industry in Cambodia is falling to competitors in countries such as China. Many fear employees being laid off will be pushed to prostitution or become victims of human trafficking.

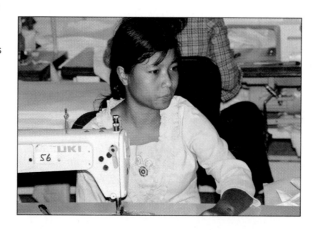

the specifics or agreeing on overall principles.[45] Working with host-country nationals can help organizations navigate such differences in negotiation style.

❧ MANAGING EXPATRIATES

At some point, most international and global organizations assign managers to foreign posts. These assignments give rise to significant human resource challenges, from selecting managers for these assignments to preparing them, compensating them, and helping them adjust to a return home. In a global marketplace, expatriate assignments are important, but evidence suggests that U.S. companies have not yet learned to select and use expatriates. Out of every hundred U.S. expatriates, between 16 and 40 return before their assignment is complete, a rate about two to three times that of foreign nationals.[46] The same kinds of HRM principles that apply to domestic positions can help organizations avoid mistakes in managing expatriates: planning and goal setting, selection aimed at achieving the HR goals, and performance management that includes evaluation of whether the overseas assignment delivered value relative to the costs involved.[47] The "HR How To" box lists guidelines for successful management of expatriates.

Selecting Expatriate Managers

The challenge of managing expatriate managers begins with determining which individuals in the organization are most capable of handling an assignment in another country. Expatriate managers need technical competence in the area of operations, in part to help them earn the respect of subordinates. Of course, many other skills are also necessary for success in any management job, especially one that involves working overseas. Depending on the nature of the assignment and the culture where it is located, the organization should consider each candidate's skills, learning style, and approach to problem solving. Each of these should be related to achievement of the organization's goals, such as solving a particular problem, transferring knowledge to host-country employees, or developing future leaders for the organization.[48]

A successful expatriate manager must be sensitive to the host country's cultural norms, flexible enough to adapt to those norms, and strong enough to survive the culture shock of living in another culture. In addition, if the manager has a family, the family members must be able to adapt to a new culture. Adaptation requires three kinds of skills:[49]

1. Ability to maintain a positive self-image and feeling of well-being.
2. Ability to foster relationships with the host-country nationals.
3. Ability to perceive and evaluate the host country's environment accurately.

In a study that drew on the experience of people holding international assignments, expatriates told researchers that the most important qualities for an expatriate manager are, in order of importance, family situation, flexibility and adaptability, job knowledge and motivation, relational skills, and openness to other cultures.[50] To assess candidates' ability to adapt to a new environment, interviews should address topics such as the ones listed in Table 15.2. The interviewer should be certain to give candidates a clear and complete preview of the assignment and the host-country culture. This helps the candidate evaluate the assignment and consider it in terms of his or her family situation, so the employer does not violate the employee's privacy.[51]

Of course, selection decisions are not just about finding employees who can do the job; the organization needs to select people who *want* an expatriate assignment. It is

HR HOW TO

ENSURING SUCCESS OF EXPATRIATES

The following HRM practices support the effectiveness of expatriates:

Staffing and Selection

- Communicate the value of international assignments for the company's global mission.
- Ensure that those with the highest potential move internationally.
- Provide short-term assignments to increase the pool of employees with international experience.
- Recruit employees who have lived or who were educated abroad.

Training and Career Development

- Make international assignment planning a part of the career development process.
- Encourage early international experience.

- Create learning opportunities during the assignment.
- Use international assignments as a leadership development tool.

Performance Appraisal and Compensation

- Differentiate performance management based on expatriate roles.
- Align incentives with objectives for expatriation.
- Tailor benefits to the expatriate's needs.
- Focus on equality of opportunities, not cash.
- Emphasize rewarding careers rather than short-term outcomes.

Expatriation and Repatriation Activities

- Involve the family in the orientation program at the beginning and the end of the assignment.

- Establish mentor relationships between expatriates and executives from the home country.
- Provide support for dual careers.
- Secure opportunities for the returning manager to use knowledge and skills learned while on the international assignment.

SOURCE: P. Evans, V. Pucik, and J. Barsoux, *The Global Challenge: Framework for International Human Resource Management*, 2002. Copyright © 2002 The McGraw-Hill Companies, Inc. Reprinted with permission.

nothing new that many people are reluctant to move to a foreign country. Since the terrorist attacks of September 2001 and the subsequent war on terrorism, however, the reluctance of some employees has grown, because they fear being targets of another attack or civil unrest related to anger about U.S. policies. Organizations can and should address these concerns.[52] They should prepare evacuation plans in case of emergency and should tell the employees about those plans. They should provide strong channels of communication for expatriate workers, as well as access to employee assistance plans (EAPs). Above all, they should ensure that employees are well trained for their assignments, prepared for the culture, and knowledgeable about the transportation and geography in their host country, so that they do not unintentionally draw negative attention to themselves or expose themselves unduly. Finally, employers should take a global perspective that recognizes the present heightened anxiety felt by all—"inpatriates" (foreign workers in the United States) as well as expatriates abroad.

TABLE 15.2

Topics for Assessing Candidates for Overseas Assignments

Motivation
- Investigate reasons and degree of interest in wanting to be considered.
- Determine desire to work abroad, verified by previous concerns such as personal travel, language training, reading, and association with foreign employees or students.
- Determine whether the candidate has a realistic understanding of what working and living abroad requires.
- Determine the basic attitudes of the spouse toward an overseas assignment.

Health
- Determine whether any medical problems of the candidate or his or her family might be critical to the success of the assignment.
- Determine whether he or she is in good physical and mental health, without any foreseeable change.

Language ability
- Determine potential for learning a new language.
- Determine any previous language(s) studied or oral ability (judge against language needed on the overseas assignment).
- Determine the ability of the spouse to meet the language requirements.

Family considerations
- How many moves has the family made in the past among different cities or parts of the United States?
- What problems were encountered?
- How recent was the last move?
- What is the spouse's goal in this move?
- What are the number of children and the ages of each?
- Has divorce or its potential, or death of a family member, weakened family solidarity?
- Will all the children move? Why or why not?
- What are the location, health, and living arrangements of grandparents and the number of trips normally made to their home each year?
- Are there any special adjustment problems that you would expect?
- How is each member of the family reacting to this possible move?
- Do special educational problems exist within the family?

Resourcefulness and initiative
- Is the candidate independent; can he make and stand by his decisions and judgments?
- Does she have the intellectual capacity to deal with several dimensions simultaneously?
- Is he able to reach objectives and produce results with whatever personnel and facilities are available, regardless of the limitations and barriers that might arise?
- Can the candidate operate without a clear definition of responsibility and authority on a foreign assignment?
- Will the candidate be able to explain the aims and company philosophy to the local managers and workers?
- Does she possess sufficient self-discipline and self-confidence to overcome difficulties or handle complex problems?
- Can the candidate work without supervision?
- Can the candidate operate effectively in a foreign environment without normal communications and supporting services?

Adaptability
- Is the candidate sensitive to others, open to the opinions of others, cooperative, and able to compromise?
- What are his reactions to new situations, and efforts to understand and appreciate differences?

(Continued)

TABLE 15.2 Concluded

Adaptability *(continued)*
- Is she culturally sensitive, aware, and able to relate across the culture?
- Does the candidate understand his own culturally derived values?
- How does the candidate react to criticism?
- What is her understanding of the U.S. government system?
- Will he be able to make and develop contacts with peers in the foreign country?
- Does she have patience when dealing with problems?
- Is he resilient; can he bounce back after setbacks?

Career planning
- Does the candidate consider the assignment anything other than a temporary overseas trip?
- Is the move consistent with her progression and that planned by the company?
- Is his career planning realistic?
- What is the candidate's basic attitude toward the company?
- Is there any history or indication of interpersonal problems with this employee?

Financial
- Are there any current financial and/or legal considerations that might affect the assignment, such as house purchase, children and college expenses, car purchases?
- Are financial considerations negative factors? Will undue pressures be brought to bear on the employee or her family as a result of the assignment?

SOURCE: Excerpted with permission, pages 55–57 from *"Multinational People Management: A Guide for Organizations and Employees,"* by David M. Noer. Copyright © 1975 by The Bureau of National Affairs, Inc. Washington, DC 20037. Published by The Bureau of National Affairs, Inc., Washington, DC 20037. For copies of BNA Books publications call toll free 1-800-960-1220.

LO6

Explain how employers prepare managers for international assignments and for their return home.

Preparing Expatriates

Once the organization has selected a manager for an overseas assignment, it is necessary to prepare that person through training and development. Because expatriate success depends so much on the entire family's adjustment, the employee's spouse should be included in the preparation activities. Employees selected for expatriate assignments already have job-related skills, so preparation for expatriate assignments often focuses on cross-cultural training—that is, training in what to expect from the host country's culture. The general purpose of cross-cultural training is to create an appreciation of the host country's culture so expatriates can behave appropriately.[53] Paradoxically, this requires developing a greater awareness of one's own culture, so that the expatriate manager can recognize differences and similarities between the cultures and, perhaps, home-culture biases. Consider, for example, the statements in Figure 15.7, which are comments made by visitors to the United States. Do you think these observations accurately describe U.S. culture?

On a more specific level, cross-cultural training for foreign assignments includes the details of how to behave in business settings in another country—the ways people behave in meetings, how employees expect managers to treat them, and so on. As an example, Germans value promptness for meetings to a much greater extent than do Latin Americans—and so on. How should one behave when first meeting one's business counterparts in another culture? The "outgoing" personality style so valued in the United States may seem quite rude in other parts of the world.[54]

Employees preparing for a foreign assignment also need information about such practical matters as housing, schools, recreation, shopping, and health care facilities in the country where they will be living. This is a crucial part of the preparation.

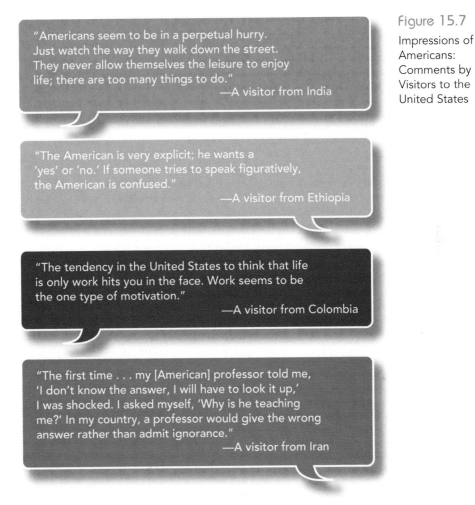

"Americans seem to be in a perpetual hurry. Just watch the way they walk down the street. They never allow themselves the leisure to enjoy life; there are too many things to do."
—A visitor from India

"The American is very explicit; he wants a 'yes' or 'no.' If someone tries to speak figuratively, the American is confused."
—A visitor from Ethiopia

"The tendency in the United States to think that life is only work hits you in the face. Work seems to be the one type of motivation."
—A visitor from Colombia

"The first time . . . my [American] professor told me, 'I don't know the answer, I will have to look it up,' I was shocked. I asked myself, 'Why is he teaching me?' In my country, a professor would give the wrong answer rather than admit ignorance."
—A visitor from Iran

SOURCE: J. Feig and G. Blair, *There Is a Difference*, 2nd ed. (Washington, DC: Meridian House International, 1980), cited in N. Adler, *International Dimensions of Organizational Behavior*, 2nd ed. (Boston: PWS-Kent, 1991).

Communication in another country often requires a determined attempt to learn a new language. Some employers try to select managers who speak the language of the host country, and a few provide language training. Most companies assume that employees in the host country will be able to speak the host country's language. Even if this is true, host country nationals are not likely to be fluent in the home country's language, so language barriers remain.

Along with cross-cultural training, preparation of the expatriate should include career development activities. Before leaving for a foreign assignment, expatriates should discuss with their managers how the foreign assignment fits into their career plans and what types of positions they can expect upon their return. This prepares the expatriate to develop valuable skills during the overseas assignment and eases the return home when the assignment is complete.

When the employee leaves for the assignment, the preparation process should continue.[55] Employees need a chance to discuss their experiences with other expatriates, so they can learn from their failures and successes. The organization may provide a host-country mentor or "assimilator" to help expatriates understand their experiences. Successful expatriates tend to develop a bicultural or multicultural point of view, so as they spend more time in the host country, the value of their connections to other expatriates may actually increase.

Managing Expatriates' Performance

Performance management of expatriates requires clear goals for the overseas assignment and frequent evaluation of whether the expatriate employee is on track to meet those goals. Steven Miranda, vice president of human resources at Lucent Technologies, recommends using phone calls, e-mail, and face-to-face meetings to assess the expatriate's performance frequently during the first five or six months of the assignment. The information can help management decide whether to give the expatriate employee additional authority. When the goal of the overseas assignment is to prepare host-country nationals to manage the operation, the evaluations should consider those employees' performance as well.[56]

Compensating Expatriates

One of the greatest challenges of managing expatriates is determining the compensation package. Most organizations use a *balance sheet approach* to determine the total amount of the package. This approach adjusts the manager's compensation so that it gives the manager the same standard of living as in the home country plus extra pay for the inconvenience of locating overseas. As shown in Figure 15.8, the balance sheet approach begins by determining the purchasing power of compensation for the same type of job in the manager's own country—that is, how much a person can buy, after taxes, in terms of housing, goods and services, and a reserve for savings. Next, this amount is compared with the cost (in dollars, for a U.S. company) of these same expenses in the foreign country. In Figure 15.8, the greater size of the second column means the costs for a similar standard of living in the foreign country are much higher in every category except the reserve amount. For the expatriate in this situation, the employer would pay the additional costs, as shown by the third column. Finally, the expatriate receives additional purchasing power from premiums and incentives. Because of these added incentives, the expatriate's purchasing power is more than what the manager could buy at home with the salary for an equivalent job. (Compare the fourth column with the first.) In practice, the total cost of an international assignment is three to five times the employee's salary in the host country.[57] To restrain spending, some organizations are sending expatriates on shorter assignments. For instance, on an assignment of less than a year, an expatriate generally would not move his or her family, substantially reducing the cost of relocation and eliminating the need to cover children's education expenses.

After setting the total pay, the organization divides this amount into the four components of a total pay package. First, there is a base salary. Determining the base salary is complex because different countries use different currencies (dollars, yen, euros, and so on). The exchange rate—the rate at which one currency may be exchanged for another—constantly shifts in response to a host of economic forces, so the real value of a salary in terms of dollars is constantly changing. Also, as discussed earlier, the base salary may be comparable to the pay of other managers at headquarters or comparable to other managers at the foreign subsidiary. Because many organizations pay a salary premium as an incentive to accept an overseas assignment, expatriates'

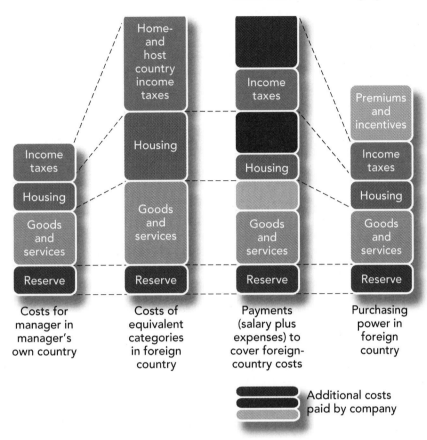

SOURCE: C. Reynolds, "Compensation of Overseas Personnel," in *Handbook of Human Resource Administration*, 2nd ed., J. J. Famularo, ed. (New York: McGraw-Hill, 1986), p. 51. Reprinted with permission. Copyright © 1986 by The McGraw-Hill Companies, Inc.

salaries are often higher than pay for staying at headquarters. This incentive role of pay has been especially important in recruiting expatriate managers for the Mexican *maquiladoras*. As demand for manufacturing in these facilities has increased, so has the need for qualified managers. To meet the demand, salaries for managers of *maquiladoras* have risen much faster than the average salary growth in the United States.[58]

A second component of total pay is a *tax equalization allowance*. Companies have different systems for taxing income, and in many countries, tax rates are much higher than in the United States. Usually, the employer of an expatriate withholds the amount of tax to be paid in the parent country, then pays all of the taxes due in the country where the expatriate is working.

A third component, benefits, presents additional challenges. Most of these have to do with whether an employee can use the same benefits in the foreign country. For example, if an expatriate has been contributing to a pension plan in the United States, does this person have a new pension in the foreign country? Or can the expatriate continue to contribute to the U.S. pension plan? Similarly, health benefits may involve receiving care at certain health facilities. While the person is abroad, does the same health plan cover services received in the foreign country? In one case, flying a manager back to the United States for certain procedures actually would have cost less than having the procedures done in the country where the person was working. But the company's health plans did not permit this alternative.

An employer may offer expatriates additional benefits to address the problem of uprooting the spouse when assigning an employee overseas. Pfizer, a pharmaceutical company, provides a $10,000 allowance that the spouse can use in many different ways.[59] A person in the foreign country helps the spouse with professional development and locating educational or other resources. In countries where the spouse is allowed to work, Pfizer tries to find him or her a job within the company. Pfizer also provides cross-cultural counseling and language assistance and tries to connect the family with the area's expatriate community.

The final component of pay packages is some set of allowances to make a foreign assignment more attractive. Cost-of-living allowances make up the differences in expenses for day-to-day needs. Housing allowances ensure that the expatriate can maintain the same standard of living as in the United States. Education allowances reimburse expatriates who pay tuition for their children to attend private English-speaking schools. Relocation allowances cover the expenses of making the move to the foreign country, including transportation, shipping or storage of possessions, and expenses for temporary housing until the employee can rent or purchase a home. Figure 15.9 is an example of a summary sheet for an expatriate manager's compensation package, showing a variety of allowances.

Helping Expatriates Return Home

repatriation
The process of preparing expatriates to return home from a foreign assignment.

As the expatriate's assignment nears its end, the human resource department faces a final challenge: helping the expatriate make the transition back to his or her home country. The process of preparing expatriates to return home from a foreign assignment is called **repatriation.** Reentry is not as simple as it might sound. Culture shock takes place in reverse. The experience has changed the expatriate, and the company's and expatriate's home culture have changed as well. Also, because of differences in economies and compensation levels, a returning expatriate may experience a decline in living standards. The standard of living for an expatriate in many countries includes maid service, a limousine, private schools, and clubs.

Companies are increasingly making efforts to help expatriates through this transition. Two activities help the process along: communication and validation.[60] Communication refers to the expatriate receiving information and recognizing changes while abroad. The more the organization keeps in contact with the expatriate, the more effective and satisfied the person will be upon return. The expatriate plays a role in this process as well. Expatriates should work at maintaining important contacts in the company and industry. Communication related to career development before and during the overseas assignment also should help the employee return to a position that is challenging and interesting. Validation means giving the expatriate recognition for the overseas service when this person returns home. Expatriates who receive praise and recognition from colleagues and top managers for their overseas service and future contribution have fewer troubles with reentry than those whose contributions are disregarded. Validation should also include planning for how the returning employee will contribute to the organization. What skills will this person bring back? What position will he or she fill? The new skills may be much more than knowledge of a particular culture. For example, the person may have learned how to lead or negotiate with a diverse group of people.[61]

Figure 15.9
International
Assignment
Allowance Form

John H. Doe		1 October 2005	
Name		**Effective date**	
Singapore		Manager, SLS./Serv. AP/ME	
Location of assignment		**Title**	

Houston, Texas	1234	202	202
Home base	**Emp. no.**	**LCA code**	**Tax code**

Reason for Change: ___ International Assignment ___

	Old	New
Monthly base salary		$5,000.00
Living cost allowance		$1,291.00
Foreign service premium		$ 750.00
Area allowance		- 0 -
Gross monthly salary		$7,041.00
Housing deduction		$ 500.00
Hypothetical tax		$ 570.00
Other		
Net monthly salary		$5,971.00

Prepared by _____   **Date** _____

Vice President, Human Resources _____   **Date** _____

thinking ETHICALLY

Carrying Ethics Standards Abroad

The "Best Practices" box in this chapter described how Deloitte Touche Tohmatsu is applying ethical standards to its employees, who work in almost 150 different countries. The firm has one advantage, at least: Its professional employees share the values of their profession, even if they come from a variety of cultural backgrounds. For other companies, the political, cultural, and economic realities of a host country may be extremely different from those of the parent country, causing ethical dilemmas.

Consider companies that market clothing in the United States that is manufactured in low-wage countries where living standards are far from those in the United States. Critics have objected to the practice of selling goods made in "sweatshops," factories where working conditions are unhealthy and unsafe. Typically, the U.S. marketer doesn't hire its own manufacturing employees but instead contracts with manufacturing firms in low-wage countries, so the U.S. company has limited direct control over working conditions. Nike has addressed the criticism by joining the Fair Labour Association, an international group that monitors factory conditions, and it issues reports of working conditions. For example, in 2005, the company published a report indicating, for example, that abuses of employees occurred in one-fourth of its factories in South Asia and that over one-fourth of those factories restricted access to toilets and drinking water during the workday. The Gap has issued similar reports about working conditions in the factories of its suppliers. The retailer conducts initial evaluations of potential suppliers and has reported that about 90 percent fail that evaluation. The Gap also trains suppliers in its requirements for working conditions, and it helps them set up compliance programs.

Paul Fireman, the chairman and chief executive officer of Reebok International, says disclosing information is not always sufficient in extreme situations. He notes that human rights in Burma are in a deplorable state under its current rulers. Noting that the Burmese government's record includes the use of slave labor, removal of over a million people from their homelands, and rape as a weapon of war, Fireman urges companies to uphold ethical standards by publicly refusing to operate in Burma, as a way to force political change in that country. Companies that have joined Reebok in making that decision include adidas-Salomon, IKEA, and British Petroleum.

SOURCE: David Teather, "Nike Lists Abuses at Asian Factories," *The Guardian*, April 14, 2005, www.guardian.co.uk; Amy Merrick, "Gap Offers Unusual Look at Factory Conditions," *The Wall Street Journal*, May 12, 2004, pp. A1, A12; and Paul Fireman, "What We Can Do about Burma," *The Wall Street Journal*, June 7, 2005, http://online.wsj.com.

Questions

1. Does a company bear responsibility for the ethical practices of its suppliers? Why or why not?
2. Suppose you work in the HR department of Nike or The Gap. How does the decision to publicize information about working conditions in overseas factories affect HRM at your company? How can your department support the principles behind this decision?
3. How is HRM affected when a company such as Reebok takes an ethics-based position not to operate in certain countries? Will it be easier or harder to find and keep talented people? Why?

SUMMARY

1. Summarize how the growth in international business activity affects human resource management.

   More and more companies are entering international markets by exporting and operating foreign facilities. Organizations therefore need employees who understand customers and suppliers in other countries. They need to understand local laws and customs and be able to adapt their plans to local situations. To do this organizations may hire a combination of parent-country, host-country, and third-country nationals. They may operate on the scale of an exporter or an international, global, or multinational organization. A global organization needs a transnational HRM system, which makes decisions from a global perspective, includes managers from many countries, and is based on ideas contributed by people representing a variety of cultures.

2. Identify the factors that most strongly influence HRM in international markets.

   By far the most important influence is the culture of each market—its set of shared assumptions about how the world works and what ideals are worth striving for. A culture has the dimensions of individualism/collectivism, high or low power distance, high or low uncertainty avoidance, masculinity/femininity, and long-term or short-term orientation. Countries also differ in the degree to which their labor markets include people with education and skills of value to employers. Another influence on international HRM is the foreign country's political-legal system—its government, laws, and regulations. Finally, a country's economic system, capitalist or socialist, as well as the government's involvement in the country's economy, such as through taxes and price controls, is a strong factor determining HRM practices.

3. Discuss how differences among countries affect HR planning at organizations with international operations.

   As organizations consider decisions about their level of international activity, HR professionals should provide information about the relevant human resource issues. When organizations decide to operate internationally or globally, HR planning involves decisions about where and how many employees are needed for each international facility. Some countries limit employers' ability to lay off workers, so organizations would be less likely to staff for peak periods. Other countries allow employers more flexibility in meeting human resource needs. HRM professionals need to be conversant with such differences.

4. Describe how companies select and train human resources in a global labor market.

   Many organizations with foreign operations fill most positions with host-country nationals. These employees can more easily understand the values and customs of the local workforce, and hiring locally tends to be less expensive than moving employees to new locations. Organizations also fill foreign positions with parent-country and third-country nationals who have human relations skills associated with success in foreign assignments. They also may use "virtual expatriates," who do not go abroad for an extended period. When sending employees on foreign assignments, organizations prepare the employees (and often their families) through cross-cultural training. Before the assignment, the training provides instruction in the foreign country's language and culture. During the assignment, there is communication with the home country and mentoring. For the return home the employer provides further training.

5. Discuss challenges related to compensating employees from other countries.

   Pay structures can differ substantially among countries in terms of pay level and the relative worth of jobs. Organizations must decide whether to set pay levels and differences in terms of what workers are used to in their own countries or in terms of what employees' colleagues earn at headquarters. Typically, companies have resolved this dilemma by linking pay and benefits more closely to those of the employee's country, but this practice may be weakening so that it depends more on the nature and length of the foreign assignment. These decisions affect the organization's costs and ability to compete, so organizations consider local labor costs in their location decisions. Along with the basic pay structure, organizations must make decisions regarding incentive pay, such as bonuses and stock options. Laws may dictate differences in benefit packages, and the value of benefits will differ if a country requires them or makes them a government service.

6. Explain how employers prepare managers for international assignments and for their return home.

   When an organization has selected a manager for an overseas assignment, it must prepare the person for the experience. In cross-cultural training the soon to-be expatriate learns about the foreign culture he or she is heading to, and studies her or his own home-country culture as well for insight. The trainee is given a detailed briefing on how to behave in business settings in the new country. Along with cross-cultural training, preparation of the expatriate should include career development activities to help the individual acquire valuable career skills during the foreign assignment and at the end of the assignment to handle repatriation successfully. Communication of changes at home and validation of a job well done abroad help the expatriate through the repatriation process.

REVIEW AND DISCUSSION QUESTIONS

1. Identify the parent country, host country(ies), and third country(ies) in the following example: A global soft-drink company called Cold Cola has headquarters in Atlanta, Georgia. It operates production facilities in Athens, Greece, and in Jakarta, Indonesia. The company has assigned a manager from Boston to head the Athens facility and a manager from Hong Kong to manage the Jarkarta facility.

2. What are some HRM challenges that arise when a U.S. company expands from domestic markets by exporting? When it changes from simply exporting to operating as an international company? When an international company becomes a global company?

3. In recent years, many U.S. companies have invested in Russia and sent U.S. managers there in an attempt to transplant U.S.-style management. According to Hofstede (see Figure 15.3), U.S. culture has low power distance, uncertainty avoidance, and long-term orientation and high individuality and masculinity. Russia's culture has high power distance and uncertainty avoidance, low masculinity and long-term orientation, and moderate individuality. In light of what you know about cultural differences, how well do you think U.S. managers can succeed in each of the following U.S.-style HRM practices? (Explain your reasons.)
   a. Selection decisions based on extensive assessment of individual abilities.
   b. Appraisals based on individual performance.
   c. Systems for gathering suggestions from workers.
   d. Self-managing work teams.

4. Besides cultural differences, what other factors affect human resource management in an organization with international operations?

5. Suppose you work in the HR department of a company that is expanding into a country where the law and culture make it difficult to lay off employees. How should your knowledge of that difficulty affect human resource planning for the overseas operations?

6. Why do multinational organizations hire host-country nationals to fill most of their foreign positions, rather than sending expatriates for most jobs?

7. Suppose an organization decides to improve collaboration and knowledge sharing by developing an intranet to link its global workforce. It needs to train employees in several different countries to use this system. List the possible cultural issues you can think of that the training program should take into account.

8. For an organization with operations in three different countries, what are some advantages and disadvantages of setting compensation according to the labor markets in the countries where the employees live and work? What are some advantages and disadvantages of setting compensation according to the labor market in the company's headquarters? Would the best arrangement be different for the company's top executives and its production workers? Explain.

9. What abilities make a candidate more likely to succeed in an assignment as an expatriate? Which of these abilities do you have? How might a person acquire these abilities?

10. In the past, a large share of expatriate managers from the United States have returned home before successfully completing their foreign assignments. Suggest some possible reasons for the high failure rate. What can HR departments do to increase the success of expatriates?

WHAT'S YOUR HR IQ?

The text Web site offers two more ways to check what you've learned so far. Use the Self-Assessment exercise to test your knowledge of global HRM. Go online with the Web Exercise to compare labor statistics for different countries.

BusinessWeek CASE

BusinessWeek China Unchains Ad Agencies

The ad campaign left shoemaker Nike Inc. flatfooted. The company's "Chamber of Fear" spot featured LeBron James of the NBA's Cleveland Cavaliers battling—and defeating—a computer-generated Kung Fu master. It might not have raised eyebrows elsewhere, but Chinese consumers found the concept insulting, and Beijing banned the ad in 2004.

The bad news for Nike, though, was great news for advertisers. The fact that the ad ignited a national debate highlighted the growing power of advertising in China. The industry has grown from virtually nothing in 1979, when the communist government lifted a ban on ads, to as much as $16 billion in 2004—an increase of at least 20 percent over the year before, according to MindShare, a media buying company. China was forecasted to be the third-largest ad market in the world by 2006, with the numbers continuing to climb as the nation gears up for the 2008 Beijing Olympics.

The potential has international ad agencies scrambling for position. Since the market opened more than a quarter-century ago, virtually every major industry player has set up shop in China. Until now they have been confined to operating joint ventures with local partners. That restriction, though, is to be lifted at the end of 2005 under commitments China made when it joined the World Trade Organization. While some agencies have good relationships with their local partners and value the cultural background they provide, others feel constrained by the regulations. The rule change "will be liberating for a lot of [agencies] that have been boxed in with a bad or mediocre partner," says David Droga, global creative director for Publicis Group, the giant ad agency conglomerate.

International ad agencies control the biggest accounts, but there's plenty of local competition. The country has some 80,000 ad shops doing everything from designing fliers and renting space on local taxis to placing ads on the Internet—and charging cutthroat prices for their services. The best of those agencies—and myriad companies in other industries hungry for experienced marketing hands—are also attracting many of the young Chinese execs that the global giants have schooled. "The biggest problem we have is finding more people to hire and keeping the ones we train," says Shelly Lazarus, chairman of New York–based Ogilvy & Mather Worldwide, which has 1,000 employees in four cities in China.

One challenge for global agencies is tailoring ads to the regional sensibilities of China's 1.3 billion citizens. As the divide between the rich coastal cities and the poorer interior grows, companies must make sure their messages fit the audience. "In Shanghai, where women are more cosmopolitan and sophisticated, we cater to a daily regimen of skin care with Oil of Olay," says Alfonso de Dios, media director for Greater China at consumer-goods giant Procter & Gamble Company. "But in Urumqi we sell women Safeguard soap and Crest first. It's a question of needs."

Those concerns have spurred big foreign agencies to seek out local expertise. J. Walter Thompson Company has taken a 30 percent stake in Guangzhou's Newsun Insight, while Ogilvy & Mather bought Fujian Effort Advertising.

While multinationals have driven the market until now—P&G's Oil of Olay skin cream was the most advertised brand in China last year—local clients are coming on strong. Last year four local brands were among the top 10 advertisers in China. J. Walter Thompson gets about 35 percent of its billings from Chinese companies, as it has signed up the likes of computer maker Lenovo, cellular carrier China Mobile, and TV manufacturer Konka.

China's advertising industry may remain decades behind the West in sophistication and creativity. But most Chinese put the highest value on low price and reliability, so ads need a straightforward message that tells the consumer exactly what to expect. That helps explain the tremendous success of products such as Gai Zhong Gai, a brand of calcium tablets. Although many in the industry pooh-poohed Gai Zhong Gai's simplistic approach and constant repetition of the same message, "They did everything that an advertising textbook in the U.S. would tell you not to do, but it worked," says Quinn Taw, managing partner of MindShare. "They created a whole awareness about calcium and bones."

And what works elsewhere in the world doesn't always translate well in China. Nike's "Just Do It" campaign doesn't work because it emphasizes individualistic youthful irreverence—a no-no in Confucian China. Instead, Nike runs ads such as a 10-second spot that features a school kid impressing classmates by spinning the globe on his finger. While the ad expresses playfulness and a certain bravado, "there's no rebellion," says Tom Doctoroff, CEO of Greater China for J. Walter Thompson, which made the spot.

SOURCE: Frederik Balfour and David Kiley, "China Unchains Ad Agenices," *BusinessWeek*, April 25, 2005, www.businessweek.com.

Questions

1. If you worked for an international advertising agency and were involved in HR planning for positions that involve serving the Chinese market, would you recommend that the firm look for parent-country nationals, host-country nationals, or third-country nationals? Explain.
2. What qualifications are necessary in an employee who creates advertising for a Chinese audience?
3. Imagine that you are sending a manager from your advertising agency's headquarters to set up an office in China. Suggest several ways to prepare the manager for this assignment.

CASE: Employees Under Fire: Working in Iraq

Workplace safety takes on a special significance for employees working in Iraq since 2003. Along with the usual hazards of construction or transportation jobs, employees encounter such dangers as kidnapping or assassination by the insurgents operating in that country. For example, Thomas Hamill, a truck driver for Kellogg, Brown and Root, was captured in May 2004 when insurgents attacked his convoy, which was delivering food and fuel to U.S. soldiers. A widely played videotape showed Hamill being forced into a car, in which he was driven to an unknown location. Eventually Hamill escaped from his captors and made it to a U.S. military checkpoint, where he was treated for injuries before being flown home. Hamill was lucky compared with some others, including Nicholas Berg, a contractor who was beheaded by his captors, and Leslie Davis, a Halliburton Company employee who was killed when a suicide bomber struck the mess hall of the U.S. military base in Mosul.

In mid-2004, James M. Taylor of Aon Consulting (which has provided contract services for rebuilding Serbia, Kosovo, and Afghanistan) said, "We haven't seen anything to match the size and scope of the operations in Iraq since probably the first Gulf War and possibly even Vietnam." Tens of thousands of Americans work for contractors in the effort to provide reconstruction services in Iraq. According to workers' compensation records, more than 200 civilians working on U.S. government contracts or subcontracts died in Iraq between the spring of 2003 and early 2004.

Why are so many people working under such dangerous conditions? One reason is restructuring of the work done by the U.S. armed forces. In effect, outsourcing has changed military as well as civilian work. Between 1991 and 2004, the U.S. armed forces were reduced by 29 percent, with contractors now handling many of the tasks once performed by the military, from serving food to hauling away trash. Civilian workers also are carrying out many security tasks.

One of the challenges of outsourcing is that the civilian workers do not go through the same recruiting and rigorous training process as soldiers. That difference raises questions about how the contractors are selected and trained. For the types of work involved, the contractors' pay tends to be very high, to compensate for the risks the workers accept. Pay for mechanics and warehouse workers for Aerotek runs as high as $100,000 per year. Federal law also requires that civilian workers receive certain benefits such as health and life insurance. Consequently, these jobs are attractive to people who are desperate enough for the money that they will accept the danger. Thomas Hamill, for example, was a dairy farmer who had to sell the family farm when the price of milk fell. His wife underwent surgery. Being unemployed and burdened with debt may have been a strong motivator for Hamill to take the job, but his circumstances did not necessarily make him well qualified for driving convoys through areas that would come under attack.

Of people in Hamill's situation, security specialist Philip Deming says, "They're not in constant surveillance mode [as a soldier would be] and take risks they cannot fully appreciate because they're desperate." Deming believes that better-suited candidates would be people attracted to work in Iraq because they are motivated by a sense of adventure or patriotism or are highly committed to their employer. Ideally, workers would have experience working in hostile environments, along with the qualities of confidence, flexibility, innovativeness, and cultural sensitivity to the region where they work. At Creative Associates International, HR manager Wendy Bradford says, "All of our employees who currently are in Iraq volunteered to go." Bradford calls them "truly . . . a dedicated group of people."

Some people have given up on this challenge. In December 2004, Contrack International pulled out of Iraq, where it had been leading a group of companies trying to rebuild Iraq's transportation system. Contrack said the reason was that security costs had become excessive. The contractors had originally planned to spend up to 15 percent of the contract value on security, but by 2005, they were spending closer to 50 percent for security. Before its pullout, Contrack had been unable to carry out some parts of its planned work because conditions were so dangerous.

Other companies have fared better. Fluor Corporation, an engineering and construction firm, had 300 employees in Iraq as of February 2005. During the year leading up to that date, the number of job applicants in its database doubled. Although the company agreed that the security situation in Iraq was difficult, it had increased protection and improved living conditions. To avoid roadside bombs, Fluor transports employees to work in Black Hawk helicopters.

SOURCE: S. E. Ante, "The Other Military," *BusinessWeek*, May 31, 2004, pp. 76–78; J. Kahn and N. D. Schwartz, "Private Sector Soldiers," *Fortune*, May 3, 2004, pp. 33–36; S. A. Feeney, "Dangerous Business," *Workforce*, June 2004, pp. 32–40; Bill Leonard, "Workplace as War Zone," *HRMagazine*, June 2004, http://web5.infotrac.galegroup.com; and Matthew Heller, "Deaths, Danger Mount," *Workforce Management*, February 2005, http://web5.infotrac.galegroup.com.

Questions

1. Of the HR functions described in this book, which do you think would be most challenging in an organization that is providing reconstruction services in Iraq? Explain.
2. To fill positions in a company that is rebuilding schools in Iraq, what employee knowledge, skills, abilities, and other characteristics would be most important? How would you recruit candidates with these qualities?
3. To attract and keep the kind of employee you identified in Question 2, what types of pay and benefits do you think would be most important? Besides providing an attractive compensation plan, how else can HRM help to keep qualified people working in Iraq?

NOTES

1. E. White, "For M.B.A. Students, a Good Career Move Means a Job in Asia," *The Wall Street Journal*, May 10, 2005, http://online.wsj.com.

2. B. P. Sunoo, "Over the Border," *Workforce*, July 2000, pp. 40–44; C. Sparks, T. Bikoi, and L. Moglia, "A Perspective on U.S. and Foreign Compensation Costs

in Manufacturing," *Monthly Labor Review*, June 2002, pp. 36–50.

3. D. Kirkpatrick, "The Net Makes It All Easier—Including Exporting U.S. Jobs," *Fortune*, May 2003, www.fortune.com.

4. S. Moffett, "Separation Anxiety," *The Wall Street Journal*, September 27, 2004, p. R11; and A. Browne, "Chinese Recruit Top Executives Trained Abroad," *The Wall Street Journal*, November 30, 2004, pp. B1, B8.

5. N. Adler and S. Bartholomew, "Managing Globally Competent People," *The Executive* 6 (1992), pp. 52–65.

6. V. Sathe, *Culture and Related Corporate Realities* (Homewood, IL: Richard D. Irwin, 1985); M. Rokeach, *Beliefs, Attitudes, and Values* (San Francisco: Jossey-Bass, 1968).

7. N. Adler, *International Dimensions of Organizational Behavior*, 2nd ed. (Boston: PWS-Kent, 1991).

8. G. Hofstede, "Dimensions of National Cultures in Fifty Countries and Three Regions," in *Expectations in Cross-Cultural Psychology*, eds. J. Deregowski, S. Dziurawiec, and R. C. Annis (Lisse, Netherlands: Swets and Zeitlinger, 1983); G. Hofstede, "Cultural Constraints in Management Theories," *Academy of Management Executive* 7 (1993), pp. 81–90.

9. Hofstede, "Cultural Constraints in Management Theories."

10. W. A. Randolph and M. Sashkin, "Can Organizational Empowerment Work in Multinational Settings?" *Academy of Management Executive* 16, no. 1 (2002), pp. 102–15.

11. Ibid.

12. B. Gerhart and M. Fang, "National Culture and Human Resource Management: Assumptions and Evidence," *International Journal of Human Resource Management* (forthcoming).

13. L. A. West Jr. and W. A. Bogumil Jr., "Foreign Knowledge Workers as a Strategic Staffing Option," *Academy of Management Executive* 14, no. 4 (2000), pp. 71–83.

14. National Center for Education Statistics (NCES), "International Comparisons of Education," *Digest of Education Statistics*, 2000, chapter 6, NCES Web site, http://nces.ed.gov, downloaded September 23, 2002.

15. World Bank, "Facts and Figures from World Development Indicators," www.worldbank.org, accessed June 16, 2005.

16. "France Abolishing Its 35-Hour Workweek," *Yahoo News*, March 22, 2005, http://news.yahoo.com; M. Karnitschnig, "Clock Ticks on Germany's 35-Hour Week," *The Wall Street Journal*, April 29, 2004, p. A14; and J. Sliva, "Parliament OKs 48-Hour Maximum Work Week," *Yahoo News*, May 11, 2005, http://news.yahoo.com.

17. K. K. Spors, "Against the Grain," *The Wall Street Journal*, September 27, 2004, p. R6.

18. West and Bogumil, "Foreign Knowledge Workers as a Strategic Staffing Option."

19. G. Flynn, "Hiring Foreign Workers in a Post-9/11 World," *Workforce*, July 2002, pp. 78–79.

20. Ibid; and S. Ladika, "Unwelcome Changes," *HRMagazine*, February 2005, downloaded from Infotrac at http://web5.infotrac.galegroup.com.

21. W. A. Arthur Jr. and W. Bennett Jr., "The International Assignee: The Relative Importance of Factors Perceived to Contribute to Success," *Personnel Psychology* 48 (1995), pp. 99–114; G. M. Spreitzer, M. W. McCall Jr., and J. D. Mahoney, "Early Identification of International Executive Potential," *Journal of Applied Psychology* 82 (1997), pp. 6–29.

22. J. S. Black and J. K. Stephens, "The Influence of the Spouse on American Expatriate Adjustment and Intent to Stay in Pacific Rim Overseas Assignments," *Journal of Management* 15 (1989), pp. 529–44.

23. P. Caligiuri, "The Big Five Personality Characteristics as Predictors of Expatriates' Desire to Terminate the Assignment and Supervisor-Rated Performance," *Personnel Psychology* 53 (2000), pp. 67–88.

24. C. Lachnit, "Low-Cost Tips for Successful Inpatriation," *Workforce*, August 2001, pp. 42–44, 46–47.

25. J. Flynn, "E-mail, Cell Phones, and Frequent-Flier Miles Let 'Virtual' Expats Work Abroad but Live at Home," *The Wall Street Journal*, October 25, 1999, p. A26.

26. D. M. Gayeski, C. Sanchirico, and J. Anderson, "Designing Training for Global Environments: Knowing What Questions to Ask," *Performance Improvement Quarterly* 15, no. 2 (2002), pp. 15–31.

27. L. G. Klaff, "Many People, One Mattel," *Workforce Management*, March 2004, www.workforce.com.

28. B. Filipczak, "Think Locally, Train Globally," *Training*, January 1997, pp. 41–48.

29. J. S. Black and M. Mendenhall, "A Practical but Theory-Based Framework for Selecting Cross-Cultural Training Methods," in *Readings and Cases in International Human Resource Management*, eds. M. Mendenhall and G. Oddou (Boston: PWS-Kent, 1991), pp. 177–204.

30. Lachnit, "Low-Cost Tips for Successful Inpatriation."

31. Ibid., citing research jointly sponsored by GMAC Global Relocation Services/Windham International, the National Foreign Trade Council, and SHRM Global Forum.

32. D. D. Davis, "International Performance Measurement and Management," in *Performance Appraisal: State of the Art in Practice*, ed. J. W. Smither (San Francisco: Jossey-Bass, 1998), pp. 95–131.

33. M. Gowan, S. Ibarreche, and C. Lackey, "Doing the Right Things in Mexico," *Academy of Management Executive* 10 (1996), pp. 74–81.

34. L. S. Chee, "Singapore Airlines: Strategic Human Resource Initiatives," in *International Human Resource*

Management: Think Globally, Act Locally, ed. D. Torrington (Upper Saddle River, NJ: Prentice Hall, 1994), pp. 143–59.

35. "Global Compensation Strategies and HR," *HRMagazine,* May 2005, downloaded from Infotrac at http://web5.infotrac.galegroup.com.

36. Sparks, Bikoi, and Moglia, "A Perspective on U.S. and Foreign Compensation Costs in Manufacturing."

37. See, for example, A. E. Cobet and G. A. Wilson, "Comparing 50 Years of Labor Productivity in U.S. and Foreign Manufacturing," *Monthly Labor Review,* June 2002, pp. 51–63; and M. Hayes, "Precious Connection," *Information Week Online,* October 20, 2003, www.informationweek.com.

38. P. Wonacott, "China's Secret Weapon: Smart, Cheap Labor for High-Tech Goods," *The Wall Street Journal,* March 14, 2002, pp. A1, A6.

39. "Taxation of European Stock Options," *The European Commission,* June 26, 2001, http://europa.eu.int; D. Woodruff, "Europe: A Latecomer, Embraces Options Even as Market Swoons," *The Wall Street Journal,* May 15, 2001, www.wsj.com; "Eager Europeans Press Their Noses to the Glass," *BusinessWeek Online,* April 19, 1999, www.businessweek.com.

40. P. J. Dowling, D. E. Welch, and R. S. Schuler, *International Human Resource Management,* 3rd ed. (Cincinnati: South-Western, 1999), pp. 235–36.

41. Ibid.; J. La Palombara and S. Blank, *Multinational Corporations and National Elites: A Study of Tensions* (New York: Conference Board, 1976); A. B. Sim, "Decentralized Management of Subsidiaries and Their Performance: A Comparative Study of American, British and Japanese Subsidiaries in Malaysia," *Management International Review* 17, no. 2 (1977), pp. 45–51; Y. K. Shetty, "Managing the Multinational Corporation: European and American Styles," *Management International Review* 19, no. 3 (1979), pp. 39–48; J. Hamill, "Labor Relations Decision-Making within Multinational Corporations," *Industrial Relations Journal* 15, no. 2 (1984), pp. 30–34.

42. Dowling, Welch, and Schuler, *International Human Resource Management,* p. 231.

43. P. Wonacott, "PetroChina Unit, after Job Cuts, Is Besieged by Protesters," *The Wall Street Journal,* March 14, 2002, pp. A9, A12.

44. J. K. Sebenius, "The Hidden Challenge of Cross-Border Negotiations," *Harvard Business Review,* March 2002, pp. 76–85.

45. Ibid.

46. R. Tung, "Selection and Training Procedures of U.S., European, and Japanese Multinational Corporations," *California Management Review* 25, no. 1 (1982), pp. 57–71.

47. E. Krell, "Evaluating Returns on Expatriates," *HRMagazine,* March 2005, downloaded from Infotrac at http://web5.infotrac.galegroup.com.

48. Ibid.; and M. Harvey and M. M. Novicevic, "Selecting Expatriates for Increasingly Complex Global Assignments," *Career Development International* 6, no. 2 (2001), pp. 69–86.

49. M. Mendenhall and G. Oddou, "The Dimensions of Expatriate Acculturation," *Academy of Management Review* 10 (1985), pp. 39–47.

50. Arthur and Bennett, "The International Assignee."

51. J. I. Sanchez, P. E. Spector, and C. L. Cooper, "Adapting to a Boundaryless World: A Developmental Expatriate Model," *Academy of Management Executive* 14, no. 2 (2000), pp. 96–106.

52. A. Freedman, "Alien Nation," *Human Resource Executive,* February 2002, pp. 51–54; B. McConnell, "Terrorism Changes Managers' Thinking about Overseas Assignments," *HR News,* January 2002, p. 14.

53. P. Dowling and R. Schuler, *International Dimensions of Human Resource Management* (Boston: PWS-Kent, 1990).

54. Sanchez, Spector, and Cooper, "Adapting to a Boundaryless World."

55. Ibid.; Lachnit, "Low-Cost Tips for Successful Inpatriation."

56. F. Jossi, "Successful Handoff," *HRMagazine,* October 2002, pp. 49–52.

57. Krell, "Evaluating Returns on Expatriates"; and L. G. Klass, "Fed Up with High Costs, Companies Thin the Ranks of 'Career Expats,'" *Workforce Management,* October 2004, downloaded from Infotrac at http://web5.infotrac.galegroup.com.

58. Sunoo, "Over the Border," p. 42.

59. J. Flynn, "Multinationals Help Career Couples Deal with Strains Affecting Expatriates," *The Wall Street Journal,* August 8, 2000, p. A19; C. Solomon, "The World Stops Shrinking," *Workforce,* January 2000, pp. 48–51; C. Solomon, "Unhappy Trails," *Workforce,* August 2000, pp. 36–41.

60. Adler, *International Dimensions of Organizational Behavior.*

61. L. G. Klaff, "The Right Way to Bring Expats Home," *Workforce,* July 2002, pp. 40–44.

If you are using the Manager's Hot Seat DVD with this book, consider finishing case 8: Cultural Differences: Let's Break a Deal for this chapter.

CHAPTER 16

CREATING AND MAINTAINING HIGH-PERFORMANCE ORGANIZATIONS

What Do I Need to Know?

After reading this chapter, you should be able to:

1. Define high-performance work systems and identify the elements of such a system.

2. Summarize the outcomes of a high-performance work system.

3. Describe the conditions that create a high-performance work system.

4. Explain how human resource management can contribute to high performance.

5. Discuss the role of HRM technology in high-performance work systems.

6. Summarize ways to measure the effectiveness of human resource management.

◈ INTRODUCTION

Blackmer/Dover Resources, which makes heavy-duty pumps, experienced some resistance while trying to get performance improvements flowing.[1] To boost efficiency and cut inventory costs, the company redesigned its production process. Replacing jobs in which assemblers built most of each pump at a single workstation, Blackmer set up an assembly line. The redesign was done by consultants without input from the production workers. The results included slower production, higher costs, and lower job satisfaction. Workers who intimately knew their machines and products felt that their expertise no longer mattered.

With sales declining, the company hired a new president, Carmine Bosco. Bosco brought a desire to learn from workers. Under Bosco, workers provided ideas for correcting problems in the production system. Production workers still learn different jobs so that they can move to different parts of the factory as needed. Not everyone likes the change. Bill Fowler, whose job involves the precision cutting of metal shafts for the pumps, says, "I don't want to move around, because I love my routine—it helps me get through the day." To avoid unfamiliar assignments, Fowler—a 24-year veteran with a track record of working faster than his coworkers—keeps his extensive knowledge to himself. He figures his strategy also prevents management from using his knowledge against him by raising production standards. In spite of Fowler's reaction, Blackmer's management believes that most employees will be won over to the spirit of knowledge sharing. The company intends to convince them by building trust and setting up the right incentives so that employees know they will be rewarded, not punished, for sharing their know-how.

Blackmer's efforts at achieving high performance show that technology alone cannot do the trick. Someone in the organization has to recognize how changes will affect the organization's people. The organization must design work and performance management systems so that they bring out the best in the employees. These challenges are some of the most crucial responsibilities of human resource management.

This chapter summarizes the role of human resource management in creating an organization that achieves a high level of performance, measured in such terms as long-term profits, quality, and customer satisfaction. We begin with a definition of *high-performance work systems* and a description of these systems' elements and outcomes. Next, we identify the conditions that contribute to high performance. We explain how the various HRM functions can contribute to high performance. Finally, we introduce ways to measure the effectiveness of human resource management.

HIGH-PERFORMANCE WORK SYSTEMS

LO1
Define high-performance work systems and identify the elements of such a system.

high-performance work system
The right combination of people, technology, and organizational structure that makes full use of the organization's resources and opportunities in achieving its goals.

The challenge facing managers today is how to make their organizations into **high-performance work systems,** with the right combination of people, technology, and organizational structure to make full use of resources and opportunities in achieving their organizations' goals. To function as a high-performance work system, each of these elements must fit well with the others in a smoothly functioning whole. Many manufacturers use the latest in processes including flexible manufacturing technology, total quality management, and just-in-time inventory control (meaning parts and supplies are automatically restocked as needed), but of course, these processes do not work on their own; they must be run by qualified people. Organizations need to determine what kinds of people fit their needs, and then locate, train, and motivate those special people.[2] According to research, organizations that introduce integrated high-performance work practices usually experience increases in productivity and long-term financial performance.[3]

Creating a high-performance work system contrasts with traditional management practices. In the past, decisions about technology, organizational structure, and human resources were treated as if they were unrelated. An organization might acquire a new information system, restructure jobs, or add an office in another country without considering the impact on its people.[4] More recently, managers have realized that success depends on how well all the elements work together. For instance, after visiting hundreds of manufacturing facilities to prepare his company's annual Harbour Report on the state of the automotive industry, Ron Harbour has found that manufacturing is first of all a "people system" that depends on clear processes and worker involvement, not just sophisticated machinery. Harbour has also concluded that the most productive operations apply ideas from line workers and use strategies that work well with their own people, rather than simply copying other companies.

Elements of a High-Performance Work System

As shown in Figure 16.1, in a high-performance work system, the elements that must work together include organizational structure, task design, people (the selection, training, and development of employees), reward systems, and information systems, and human resource management plays an important role in establishing all these.

Figure 16.1

Elements of a High-Performance Work System

Organizational structure is the way the organization groups its people into useful divisions, departments, and reporting relationships. The organization's top management makes most decisions about structure, for instance, how many employees report to each supervisor and whether employees are grouped according to the functions they carry out or the customers they serve. Such decisions affect how well employees coordinate their activities and respond to change. In a high-performance work system, organizational structure promotes cooperation, learning, and continuous improvement.

Task design determines how the details of the organization's necessary activities will be grouped, whether into jobs or team responsibilities. In a high-performance work system, task design makes jobs efficient while encouraging high quality. In Chapter 4, we discussed how to carry out this HRM function through job analysis and job design.

The right *people* are a key element of high-performance work systems. HRM has a significant role in providing people who are well suited and well prepared for their jobs. Human resource personnel help the organization recruit and select people with the needed qualifications. Training, development, and career management ensure that these people are able to perform their current and future jobs with the organization.

Reward systems contribute to high performance by encouraging people to strive for objectives that support the organization's overall goals. Reward systems include the

In a high-performance work system, all the elements—people, technology, and organizational structure—work together for success.

performance measures by which employees are judged, the methods of measuring performance, and the incentive pay and other rewards linked to success. Human resource management plays an important role in developing and administering reward systems, as we saw in Chapters 8 through 12.

The final element of high-performance work systems is the organization's *information systems*. Managers make decisions about the types of information to gather and the sources of information. They also must decide who in the organization should have access to the information and how they will make the information available. Modern information systems, including the Internet, have enabled organizations to share information widely. HR departments take advantage of this technology to give employees access to information about benefits, training opportunities, job openings, and more, as we will describe later in this chapter.

LO2
Summarize the outcomes of a high-performance work system.

Outcomes of a High-Performance Work System

Consider the practices of steel minimills in the United States. Some of these mills have strategies based on keeping their costs below competitors' costs; low costs let them operate at a profit while winning customers with low prices. Other steel minimills focus on "differentiation," meaning they set themselves apart in some way other than low price—for example, by offering higher quality or unusual product lines. Research has found that the minimills with cost-related goals tend to have highly centralized structures, so managers can focus on controlling through a tight line of command. These organizations have low employee participation in decisions, relatively low wages and benefits, and pay highly contingent on performance.[5] At minimills that focus on differentiation, structures are more complex and decentralized, so authority is more spread out. These minimills encourage employee participation and have higher wages and more generous benefits. They are high-performance work systems. In general, these differentiator mills enjoy higher productivity, lower scrap rates, and lower employee turnover than the mills that focus on low costs.

Outcomes of a high-performance work system thus include higher productivity and efficiency. These outcomes contribute to higher profits. A high-performance work system may have other outcomes, including high product quality, great customer satisfaction, and low employee turnover. Some of these outcomes meet intermediate goals that lead to higher profits (see Figure 16.2). For example, high quality contributes to customer satisfaction, and customer satisfaction contributes to growth of the business. Likewise, improving productivity lets the organization do more with less, which satisfies price-conscious customers and may help the organization win over customers from its competitors. Other ways to lower cost and improve quality are to reduce absenteeism and turnover, providing the organization with a steady supply of experienced workers. In the previous example of minimills, some employers keep turnover and scrap rates low. Meeting those goals helps the minimills improve productivity, which helps them earn more profits.

In a high-performance work system, the outcomes of each employee and work group contribute to the system's overall high performance. The organization's individuals and groups work efficiently, provide high-quality goods and services, and so on, and in this way, they contribute to meeting the organization's goals. When the organization adds or changes goals, people are flexible and make changes as needed to meet the new goals. For example, an especially important outcome of human resource departments during the high-growth 1990s was obtaining enough talented employees. When the economy began to slow in 2000 and 2001, many organizations relied on HR departments to help them focus more on the efficiency of their workforces. Yet another issue surfaced fol-

Figure 16.2

Outcomes of a High-Performance Work System

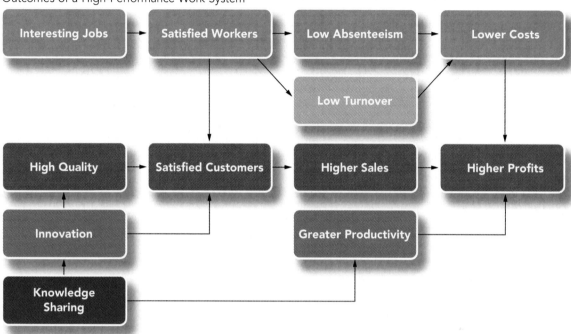

lowing the September 2001 terrorist attacks on the Pentagon and World Trade Center: knowing that all the organization's employees are safe and accounted for.[6] As employers of people working at those locations struggled to locate their employees on September 11, 2001, they appreciated more than ever the importance of having accurate data about all personnel, including up-to-date emergency contact information. This tragic lesson illustrates the importance of good HR information systems as an outcome that helps an organization perform even under the worst circumstances.

≫ CONDITIONS THAT CONTRIBUTE TO HIGH PERFORMANCE

LO3
Describe the conditions that create a high-performance work system.

Certain conditions underlie the formation of a high-performance work system. Table 16.1 shows examples of such conditions—common practices in high-performing organizations. These practices, such as those involving rewards, employee empowerment, and jobs with variety, contribute to high performance by giving employees skills, incentives, knowledge, anatomy—and satisfaction, another condition associated with high performance. Finally, ethical behavior is a necessary condition of high performance because it contributes to good long-term relationships with employees, customers, and the public.

Teamwork and Empowerment

As we discussed in Chapter 2, today's organizations empower employees. They expect employees to make more decisions about how they perform their jobs. One of the most popular ways to empower employees is to design work so that it is performed by

TABLE 16.1

Conditions for High Performance

- Teams perform work.
- Employees participate in selection.
- Employees receive formal performance feedback and are actively involved in the performance improvement process.
- Ongoing training is emphasized and rewarded.
- Employees' rewards and compensation relate to the company's financial performance.
- Equipment and work processes are structured and technology is used to encourage maximum flexibility and interaction among employees.
- Employees participate in planning changes in equipment, layout, and work methods.
- Work design allows employees to use a variety of skills.
- Employees understand how their jobs contribute to the finished product or \ service.
- Ethical behavior is encouraged.

SOURCE: Based on J. A. Neal and C. L. Tromley, "From Incremental Change to Retrofit: Creating High-Performance Work Systems," *Academy of Management Executive* 9 (1995), pp. 42–54; M. A. Huselid, "The Impact of Human Resource Management Practices on Turnover, Productivity, and Corporate Financial Performance," *Academy of Management Journal* 38 (1995), pp. 635–72.

teams. On a work team, employees bring together various skills and experiences to produce goods or provide services. The organization may charge the team with making decisions traditionally made by managers, such as hiring team members and planning work schedules. Teamwork and empowerment contribute to high performance when they improve job satisfaction and give the organization fuller use of employees' ideas and expertise.

For empowerment to succeed, managers must serve in linking and coordinating roles[7] and provide the team with the resources it needs to carry out its work. The manager should help the team and its members interact with employees from other departments or teams and should make sure communication flows in both directions—the manager keeps the team updated on important issues and ensures that the team shares information and resources with others who need them. At Genencor International, which makes health care products and commercial enzymes, management has empowered employees to make decisions about working conditions and benefits. When the company built its Palo Alto, California, headquarters, it encouraged input from its employees and then applied their suggestions. Labs are arranged around the building's exterior, so that scientists can work in natural light. A "main street" provides a traffic area where employees can interact naturally throughout the day. Genencor regularly conducts employee surveys to help identify which benefits are most valued. Adapting benefits to employees' needs has not been expensive and contributes to keeping loyal and productive employees.[8]

learning organization
An organization that supports lifelong learning by enabling all employees to acquire and share knowledge.

Knowledge Sharing

For more than a decade, managers have been interested in creating a **learning organization,** that is, an organization in which the culture values and supports lifelong learning by enabling all employees to continually acquire and share knowledge. The people in a learning organization have resources for training, and they are encouraged to share their knowledge with colleagues. Managers take an active role in identifying training needs and encouraging the sharing of ideas.[9] An organization's information systems, discussed later in this chapter, have an important role in making this learning activity possible. Information systems capture knowledge and make it available even after individual employees who provided the knowledge have left the organization. Ultimately, people are the essential ingredients in a learning organization. They must be committed to learning and willing to share what they have learned. A learning organization has the key features identified in Figure 16.3: continuous learning, generation and sharing of knowledge, thinking that is critical and systematic, a culture that values learning, encouragement of flexibility and experimentation, and appreciation of the value of each employee.

Continuous learning is each employee's and each group's ongoing efforts to gather information and apply the information to their decisions. In many organizations, the process of continuous learning is aimed at improving quality. To engage in continuous learning, employees must understand the entire work system they participate in, the relationships among jobs, their work units, and the organization as a whole. Employees who continuously learn about their work system are adding to their ability to improve performance.

Knowledge is most valuable to the organization when it is *shared*. Therefore, to create a learning organization, one challenge is to shift the focus of training away from merely teaching skills and toward a broader focus on generating and sharing knowledge.[10] In this view, training is an investment in the organization's human resources; it increases employees' value to the organization. Also, training content should be related to the organization's goals. Human resource departments can support the creation of a learning organization by planning training programs that meet these criteria, and they can help to create systems for creating, capturing, and sharing knowledge.

Critical, systematic thinking occurs when organizations encourage employees to see relationships among ideas and to test assumptions and observe the results of their actions. Reward systems can be set up to encourage employees and teams to think in new ways.

A *learning culture* is an organizational culture in which learning is rewarded, promoted, and supported by managers and organizational objectives. This culture may be

continuous learning
Each employee's and each group's ongoing efforts to gather information and apply the information to their decisions in a learning organization.

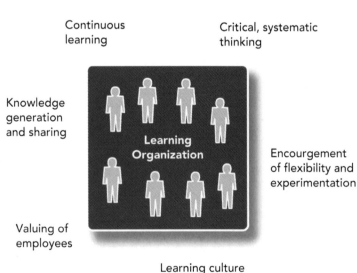

Continuous learning

Critical, systematic thinking

Knowledge generation and sharing

Learning Organization

Encourgement of flexibility and experimentation

Valuing of employees

Learning culture

Figure 16.3

Key Features of a Learning Organization

SOURCE: Adapted from M. A. Gephart, V. J. Marsick, M. E. Van Buren, and M. S. Spiro, "Learning Organizations Come Alive," *Training and Development* 50 (1996), pp. 34–45.

reflected in performance management systems and pay structures that reward employees for gathering and sharing more knowledge. A learning culture creates the conditions in which managers encourage *flexibility* and *experimentation*. The organization should encourage employees to take risks and innovate, which means it cannot be quick to punish ideas that do not work out as intended.

Finally, in a learning organization, *employees are valued*. The organization recognizes that employees are the source of its knowledge. It therefore focuses on ensuring the development and well-being of each employee.

An example of a learning organization is Viant, a consulting firm that specializes in building e-businesses.[11] When employees join the company, they start in the home office in Boston, where they learn team skills, the company's consulting strategy, and the organization's culture. There they meet members of upper management. On the job, Viant employees work in settings that encourage interaction; no walls separate desks, and snack areas are located conveniently nearby. Performance reviews emphasize growth in employees' skills, and the company rewards knowledge sharing with incentives in the form of stock options. Before each project, consultants complete a brief document describing the knowledge they need, the knowledge they can use from other projects, what they need to create, and what they hope to learn that they can share with their colleagues. These documents are posted on Viant's internal Web site. Every six weeks, Viant's knowledge management group posts an online summary of what has been learned.

Job Satisfaction

A condition underpinning any high-performance organization is that employees experience job satisfaction—they experience their jobs as fulfilling or allowing them to fulfill important values. Research supports the idea that employees' job satisfaction and job performance are related.[12] Higher performance at the individual level should contribute to higher performance for the organization as a whole. One study looked at job satisfaction in teachers and the overall performance of their schools.[13] It found a significant link between teachers' satisfaction and their schools' performance according to a variety of measures, including students' behavior and academic achievement. More recently, a study by Watson Wyatt Worldwide found that companies with high employee commitment (which includes employees' satisfaction with their jobs and the company) enjoyed higher total returns to shareholders, a basic measure of a company's financial performance.[14]

Chapter 10 described a number of ways organizations can promote job satisfaction. They include making jobs more interesting, setting clear and challenging goals, and providing valued rewards that are linked to performance in a performance management sys-

Research has found that teachers' job satisfaction is associated with high performance of the schools where they teach. What are other ways in which organizations can promote and foster job satisfaction?

DID YOU KNOW?

EMPLOYEE SATISFACTION IS WEAK BY SOME MEASURES

Monster Worldwide, which in the United States operates the Monster.com recruiting and job-hunting Web site, recently reported survey results showing that 86 percent of employees are dissatisfied with their jobs and 82 percent are dissatisfied with their work/life balance. These numbers suggest plenty of room for organizations that want to carve out a niche for themselves as desirable employers. Still, it's important to remember that these numbers come from online polls of visitors to Monster.com; presumably, employees who are satisfied with their positions are less likely to visit the Web site.

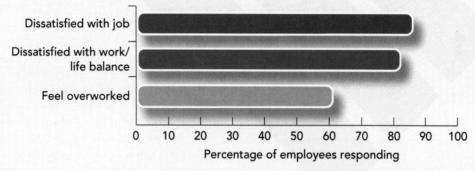

SOURCE: Monster Worldwide, "61 Percent of Americans Consider Themselves Overworked and 86 Percent Are Not Satisfied with Their Job, According to Monster's 2004 Work/Life Balance Survey," news release, August 3, 2004, http://pr.monsterworldwide.com.

tem that employees consider fair. Effective promotion of employee satisfaction can distinguish an organization from its competitors. As the "Did You Know . . . ?" box reports, there are many organizations at which employees feel dissatisfied and overstressed.

Some organizations are moving beyond concern with mere job satisfaction and are trying to foster employees' *passion* for their work. Passionate people are fully engaged with something so that it becomes part of their sense of who they are. Feeling this way about one's work has been called *occupational intimacy*.[15] People experience occupational intimacy when they love their work, when they and their coworkers care about one another, and when they find their work meaningful. Human resource managers have a significant role in creating these conditions. For example, they can select people who care about their work and customers, provide methods for sharing knowledge, design work to make jobs interesting, and establish policies and programs that show concern for employees' needs. Such efforts may become increasingly important as the business world increasingly uses employee empowerment, teamwork, and knowledge sharing to build flexible organizations.[16]

These trends rely on positive employee relationships. Perhaps that is why, when the Gallup Organization studied more than 105,000 employees, it found that one of the 13 circumstances associated with high productivity was "having a best friend at work."[17] A case in point is David Liggett, who developed important friendships at work. Those friends encouraged him, provided helpful feedback, and pitched in whenever one of the friends needed help to meet a deadline. Fifteen years after meeting, the friends continue to get together.

Ethics

In the long run, a high-performance organization meets high ethical standards. Ethics, defined in Chapter 1, establishes fundamental principles for behavior, such as honesty and fairness. Organizations and their employees must meet these standards if they are to maintain positive long-term relationships with their customers and their community.

Ethical behavior is most likely to result from values held by the organization's leaders combined with systems that promote ethical behavior. Charles O. Holliday Jr., the chairman and chief executive officer of Du Pont Company, is an example of an executive who cares about ethics. For Holliday, ethics is a matter of behaving in ways that promote trust: "Just saying you're ethical isn't very useful. You have to earn trust by what you do every day."[18] Holliday experienced this kind of leadership himself when he first joined Du Pont. The CEO at that time, Dick Heckert, told him, "This company lives by the letter of its contracts and the intent of those contracts," speaking with such conviction that he imprinted the lesson on Holliday's mind.

A number of organizational systems can promote ethical behavior.[19] These include a written code of ethics that the organization distributes to employees and expects them to use in decision making. Publishing a list of ethical standards is not enough, however. The organization should reinforce ethical behavior. For example, performance measures should include ethical standards, and misdeeds should receive swift discipline, as described in Chapter 10. The organization should provide channels employees can use to ask questions about ethical behavior or to seek help if they are expected to do something they believe is wrong. Organizations also can provide training in ethical decision making.

As these examples suggest, ethical behavior is a human resource management concern. The systems that promote ethical behavior include such HRM functions as training, performance management, and discipline policies. A reputation for high ethical standards can also help a company attract workers—and customers—who share those high standards. UPS is committed to living up to the words of its founder, Jim Casey: "We have become known to all who deal with us as a people of integrity, and that priceless asset is more valuable than anything we possess." UPS has a written code of conduct, published in a detailed booklet that offers regularly updated examples. All employees must read and give their written acceptance of that code when they join the company. Employees who have questions about particular situations or who see ethical problems within the company may call a hotline, staffed by a vendor. The vendor compiles information from the calls and forwards it to the UPS compliance department, which distributes the issues to the appropriate departments. The majority of situations are handled by the human resource department; other departments, including legal and security, handle the other concerns. Unit managers receive summary reports, and their responses to concerns play a role in their performance evaluations. Even if their unit has relatively few complaints, managers are expected to take action.[20]

❧ HRM'S CONTRIBUTION TO HIGH PERFORMANCE

Management of human resources plays a critical role in determining companies' success in meeting the challenges of a rapidly changing, highly competitive environment.[21] Compensation, staffing, training and development, performance management, and other HRM practices are investments that directly affect employees'

- HRM practices match organization's goals.
- Individuals and groups share knowledge.
- Work is performed by teams.
- Organization encourages continuous learning.
- Work design permits flexibility in where and when tasks are performed.
- Selection system is job related and legal.

- Performance management system measures customer satisfaction and quality.
- Organization monitors employees' satisfaction.
- Discipline system is progressive.
- Pay systems reward skills and accomplishments.
- Skills and values of a diverse workforce are valued and used.
- Technology reduces time and costs of tasks while preserving quality.

TABLE 16.2

HRM Practices That Can Help Organizations Achieve High Performance

motivation and ability to provide products and services that are valued by customers. A study by Watson Wyatt Worldwide found that significant improvements in major HR practices, including reward systems, recruitment, and employee retention, led to significant increases in the value of a company's stock.[22] Table 16.2 lists examples of HRM practices that contribute to high performance.

Research suggests that it is more effective to improve HRM practices as a whole than to focus on one or two isolated practices, such as the organization's pay structure or selection system.[23] Also, to have the intended influence on performance, the HRM practices must fit well with one another and the organization as a whole.[24] An example of an organization that has achieved this fit is SYSCO Corporation, described in the "Best Practices" box.

Job Design

For the organization to benefit from teamwork and employee empowerment, jobs must be designed appropriately. Often, a high-performance work system places employees in work teams where employees collaborate to make decisions and solve problems. Individual employees also may be empowered to serve on teams that design jobs and work processes. For example, the members of the staff of a ThedaCare health clinic in Wisconsin evaluated the process of office visits, looking for a way to shrink the average length of a visit from an hour to 30 minutes. They drew a chart showing the typical steps involved in serving a patient with pneumonia and discovered that of the 68 steps identified, only 17 were considered valuable. They determined that instead of requiring patients to walk down the hall to a laboratory to have blood drawn, they could have a technician visit the examination room to draw blood. Changes such as these cut patients' waiting time from 30 minutes to just 9. The nature of certain jobs also changed. Six assistants had been assigned to work with individual doctors; in the redesigned process, these assistants were pooled to work wherever they were needed most.[25]

Recruitment and Selection

At a high-performance organization, recruitment and selection aim at obtaining the kinds of employees who can thrive in this type of setting. These employees are enthusiastic about and able to contribute to teamwork, empowerment, and knowledge sharing. Qualities such as creativity and ability to cooperate as part of a team may play a large role in selection decisions. High-performance organizations need selection methods that

SYSCO SERVES UP HRM THAT'S WELL WORTH THE PRICE

Hamburgers don't just deliver themselves, and SYSCO Corporation has prospered by capitalizing on this fact. Founded in 1970, SYSCO has become North America's leading food-service provider, with approximately 400,000 customers from mom-and-pop diners to large chains like Hilton Hotels and Wendy's International.

Several factors explain SYSCO's success. One is its principle of "Earned Autonomy," in which each of the company's 150 businesses operates independently as long as it is successful. SYSCO also tries to keep its people close to their customers by limiting the size of each business unit. When a unit approaches 700 employees, SYSCO splits it into separate businesses. The result is a corporation with a decentralized structure in which many managers have a significant degree of control, so they can encourage innovation and customer service. The company also empowers its sales force by making employees more than salespeople. These "marketing associates" not only take orders but also help customers with food handling, inventory management, and recipe ideas.

In such a decentralized company with so many individuals

empowered to act creatively, running an HRM organization presents a host of challenges. Ken Carrig, SYSCO's vice president of human resources, wants his staff to provide services that contribute to high performance. But his group cannot simply design one set of services to force on the other business units.

So, Carrig developed what he calls "market-based" human resource management. This approach treats SYSCO as a market and its business unit leaders as customers, who are free to select the HRM services they actually pay for, based on their decisions about which services are valuable. For example, if a business unit wants to conduct a survey of employees, that unit has a choice between using the company's own HRM staff or the research capabilities of an outside firm. Corporate HRM, as a result, has an incentive to ensure that its services are effective and reasonably priced.

Under Carrig's leadership, HRM at SYSCO has focused on identifying and providing the services the company's business units want. It also focuses on collecting data that help the HRM team learn how it can help business units succeed. Carrig and his associates study the company's most successful

business units to learn what they are doing that other units might copy. They also collect data on HR programs so that they can demonstrate to business unit leaders the value provided by their services. For example, HR programs have boasted a 30 percent reduction in claims for workers' compensation—saving $10 million a year—and 20 percent improvement in retention of night-shift warehouse employees—saving about $15 million a year.

Executives can look up such performance data on the company's intranet to learn about the programs that are producing results in SYSCO's business units. The readily available database informs decision making all the way to the top of SYSCO. The company's chief executive, Richard J. Schnieders, tracks data from the company's workplace climate survey, which has shown a strong link with units' profits.

SOURCE: R. Stoltz, "Ah, to Be Strategic," *Human Resource Executive*, November 2003, pp. 1, 20–30; P. Kiger, "HR Proves Its Value," *Workforce*, March 2002, pp. 28–33; and Richard F. Stolz, "CEOs Who 'Get It,'" *Human Resource Executive*, March 16, 2005, pp. 1, 18–19, 22–24.

identify more than technical skills like ability to perform accounting and engineering tasks. Employers may use group interviews, open-ended questions, and psychological tests to find employees who innovate, share ideas, and take initiative.

Training and Development

When organizations base hiring decisions on qualities like decision-making and teamwork skills, training may be required to teach employees the specific skills they need to perform the duties of their job. Extensive training and development also are part of a learning organization, described earlier in this chapter. And when organizations delegate many decisions to work teams, the members of those teams likely will benefit from participating in team development activities that prepare them for their roles as team members.

Employee development is an important factor in IBM's top ranking in a study of the "Top 20 Companies for Leaders," jointly conducted by Hewitt Associates and *Chief Executive* magazine. According to Randall MacDonald, IBM's senior vice president of human resources, IBM had determined that leadership was one of four areas it had to focus on to achieve high performance. So the company charged all its existing leaders with developing future leaders. Once a year, IBM calls together its top managers to select candidates for leadership development, and they work with the candidates to create a development plan that meets their personal goals. By making leadership development a part of the company's routine processes, IBM removes the fear that coaching one's replacement threatens one's own career. MacDonald points out that planning for leadership is at least as important as other types of planning: "The [chief financial officer], when he gives one of our line guys $3 billion to go build a new plant, he doesn't say, 'Go build the plant and do what you want with it.' No, that CFO and that line person are going to manage that asset. . . . Whatever happened to the concept of people being our most important asset? Well if they are, we ought to manage them."[26]

Performance Management

In a high-performance organization, employees know the organization's goals and what they must do to help achieve those goals. HR departments can contribute to this ideal through the design of the organization's performance management system. As

To develop future leaders, new IBM managers participate in IBM's Basic Blue program for an intensive nine-month training program. IBM is considered one of the best companies in the development of future leaders.

we discussed in Chapter 8, performance management should be related to the organization's goals. For example, teamwork is central to the success of GE Fanuc Automation, a joint venture between General Electric and FANUC Ltd. of Japan. The company organized its work force into more than 40 self-directed work teams to encourage employees to contribute their ideas. Therefore, managers must support their teams, and support of teamwork is one performance measure in the managers' performance evaluations.[27] At Extreme Logic, high performance comes from clear communication about what kinds of behavior are needed. On its intranet, the Atlanta-based software company publishes attributes and behaviors associated with success in each job, as well as the performance standard for each attribute and behavior. Employees can go online at any time to gauge whether they are meeting those standards.[28]

To set up a performance management system that supports the organization's goals, managers need to understand the process of employee performance. As shown in Figure 16.4, individual employees bring a set of skills and abilities to the job, and by applying a set of behaviors, they use those skills to achieve certain results. But success is more than the product of individual efforts. The organization's goals should influence each step of the process. The organization's culture and other factors influence the employees' abilities, behaviors, and results. Sometimes uncontrollable forces such as the current economic conditions enter the picture, it mustn't be forgotten—for example, a salesperson can probably sell more during an economic expansion than during an economic slowdown.

This model suggests some guidelines for performance management. First, each aspect of performance management should be related to the organization's goals. Business goals should influence the kinds of employees selected and their training, the requirements of each job, and the measures used for evaluating results. Generally, this means the organization identifies what each department must do to achieve the desired results, then defines how individual employees should contribute to their department's goals. More specifically, the following guidelines describe how to make the performance management system support organizational goals:[29]

- *Define and measure performance in precise terms.* Focus on outcomes that can be defined in terms of how frequently certain behaviors occur. Include criteria that describe ways employees can add value to a product or service (such as through quan-

Figure 16.4

Employee Performance as a Process

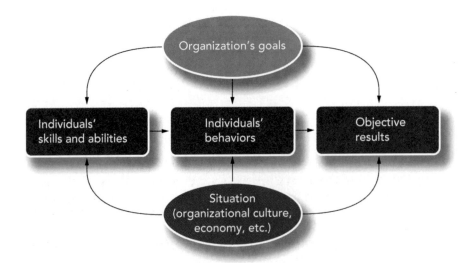

tity, quality, or timeliness). Include behaviors that go beyond the minimum required to perform a job (such as helping coworkers).

- *Link performance measures to meeting customer needs.* "Customers" may be the organization's external customers, or they may be internal customers (employees receiving services from a coworker). Service goals for internal customers should be related to satisfying external customers.
- *Measure and correct for the effect of situational constraints.* Monitor economic conditions, the organization's culture, and other influences on performance. Measures of employees' performance should take these influences into account.

This approach gives employees the information they need to behave in ways that contribute to high performance. In addition, organizations should help employees identify and obtain the abilities they need to meet their performance goals.

Compensation

Organizations can reinforce the impact of this kind of performance management by linking compensation in part to performance measures. Chapter 12 described a number of methods for doing this, including merit pay, gainsharing, and profit sharing. A small manufacturer called Headsets.com improved productivity by linking bonuses to sales volume; employees share a fixed percentage of the company's total sales.[30] Employees at Headsets.com can see that if the company grows by hiring more workers, rather than by using the same number of workers to produce and sell more, the bonus will be divided among more people. They can earn a bigger bonus if they get the same results by working more efficiently. Since starting this bonus plan, Headsets.com has been able to grow more profitably. Compensation systems also can help to create the conditions that contribute to high performance, including teamwork, empowerment, and job satisfaction. For example, as discussed in Chapter 12, compensation can be linked to achievement of team objectives.

Organizations can increase empowerment and job satisfaction by including employees in decisions about compensation and by communicating the basis for decisions about pay. When the organization designs a pay structure, it can set up a task force that includes employees with direct experience in various types of jobs. Some organizations share financial information with their employees and invite them to recommend pay increases for themselves, based on their contributions. Employees also may participate in setting individual or group goals for which they can receive bonuses. Research has found that employee participation in decisions about pay policies is linked to greater satisfaction with the pay and the job.[31] And as we discussed in Chapter 11, when organizations explain their pay structures to employees, the communication can enhance employees' satisfaction and belief that the system is fair.

HRM Technology

Human resource departments can improve their own and their organization's performance by appropriately using new technology. New technology usually involves *automation*—that is, using equipment and information processing to perform activities that had been performed by people. Over the last few decades, automation has improved HRM efficiency by reducing the number of people needed to perform routine tasks. Using automation can free HRM experts to concentrate on ways to determine how human resource management can help the organization meet its goals, so technology also can make this function more valuable.[32] For example, information

LO5
Discuss the role of HRM technology in high-performance work systems.

HR HOW TO

USING INFORMATION SYSTEMS IN A LEARNING ORGANIZATION

A learning organization uses information technology to encourage employees to share information with each other, and HR professionals can help establish these applications. Here are some ideas:

- Set up an intranet that allows employees to store and share knowledge through Web pages and e-mail.
- Publish directories listing what employees do, what kinds of knowledge they have, and how to contact them.
- Develop "informational maps," or charts that identify where specific knowledge is stored in the organization.
- Create the position of chief information officer, which includes the responsibility for cataloging information and enabling the sharing of information within the organization.
- When employees attend training programs, require that they give their coworkers presentations or post summaries on the intranet of what they have learned from the programs.
- Allow employees to take time off from work to acquire knowledge or study problems. Establish policies for sabbaticals, attendance at training programs, and other time away from the workplace for learning, and communicate these on the intranet.
- Create an online library of learning resources, such as journals, technical manuals, training opportunities, and seminars. These can be available through the organization's intranet.

---

technology provides ways to build and improve systems for knowledge generation and sharing, as part of a learning organization. The "HR How To" box describes some ways of using information technology to create and share knowledge.

HRM Applications

transaction processing
Computations and calculations involved in reviewing and documenting HRM decisions and practices.

decision support systems
Computer software systems designed to help managers solve problems by showing how results vary when the manager alters assumptions or data.

As computers become ever more powerful, new technologies continue to be introduced. In fact, so many HRM applications are developed for use on personal computers that publications serving the profession (such as *HR Magazine* and *Personnel Journal*) devote annual issues to reviewing this software. Some of the technologies that have been widely adopted are transaction processing, decision support systems, and expert systems.[33]

Transaction processing refers to computations and calculations involved in reviewing and documenting HRM decisions and practices. It includes documenting decisions and actions associated with employee relocation, training expenses, and enrollments in courses and benefit plans. Transaction processing also includes the activities required to meet government reporting requirements, such as filling out EEO-1 reports, on which employers report information about employees' race and gender by job category. Computers enable companies to perform these tasks more efficiently. Employers can fill out computerized forms and store HRM information in databases (data stored electronically in user-specified categories), so that it is easier to find, sort, and report.

Decision support systems are computer software systems designed to help managers solve problems. They usually include a "what if?" feature that managers can use to enter different assumptions or data and see how the likely outcomes will change.

This type of system can help managers make decisions for human resource planning. The manager can, for example, try out different assumptions about turnover rates to see how those assumptions affect the number of new employees needed. Or the manager can test a range of assumptions about the availability of a certain skill in the labor market, looking at the impact of the assumptions on the success of different recruiting plans. Possible applications for a decision support system include forecasting (discussed in Chapter 5) and succession planning (discussed in Chapter 9).

Expert systems are computer systems that incorporate the decision rules used by people who are considered to have expertise in a certain area. The systems help users make decisions by recommending actions based on the decision rules and the information provided by the users. An expert system is designed to recommend the same actions that a human expert would in a similar situation. For example, an expert system could guide an interviewer during the selection process. Some organizations use expert systems to help employees decide how to allocate their money for benefits (as in a cafeteria plan) and help managers schedule the labor needed to complete projects. Expert systems can deliver both high quality and lower costs. By using the decision processes of experts, an expert system helps many people to arrive at decisions that reflect the expert's knowledge. An expert system helps avoid the errors that can result from fatigue and decision-making biases, such as biases in appraising employee performance, described in Chapter 8. An expert system can increase efficiency by enabling fewer or less-skilled employees to do work that otherwise would require many highly skilled employees.

In modern HR departments, transaction processing, decision support systems, and expert systems often are part of a human resource information system. Also, these technologies may be linked to employees through a network such as an intranet. Information systems and networks have been evolving rapidly; the following descriptions provide a basic introduction.

expert systems
Computer systems that support decision making by incorporating the decision rules used by people who are considered to have expertise in a certain area.

Human Resource Information Systems

A standard feature of a modern HRIS is the use of *relational databases*, which store data in separate files that can be linked by common elements. These common elements are fields identifying the type of data. Commonly used fields for an HR database include name, Social Security number, job status (full- or part-time), hiring date, position, title, rate of pay, citizenship status, job history, job location, mailing address, birth date, and emergency contacts. A relational database lets a user sort the data by any of the fields. For example, depending on how the database is set up, the user might be able to look up tables listing employees by location, rates of pay for various jobs, or employees who have completed certain training courses. This system is far more sophisticated than the old-fashioned method of filing employee data by name, with one file per employee.

The ability to locate and combine many categories of data has a multitude of uses in human resource management. Databases have been developed to track employee benefit costs, training courses, and compensation. The system can meet the needs of line managers as well as the HR department. On an oil rig, for example, management might look up data listing employee names along with safety equipment issued and appropriate skill certification. HR managers at headquarters might look up data on the same employees to gather information about wage rates or training programs needed. Another popular use of an HRIS is applicant tracking, or maintaining and retrieving records of job applicants. This is much faster and easier than trying to sort through stacks of résumés. With relational databases, HR staff can retrieve information about specific applicants or obtain lists of applicants with specific skills, career goals, work history, and employment background. Such information is useful for HR planning, recruitment, succession planning, and career development. Taking the process a step further, the system could store information related to hiring and terminations. By analyzing such data, the HR department could measure the long-term success of its recruiting and selection processes.

Human Resource Management Online: E-HRM

During the last decade or so, organizations have seen the advantages of sharing information in computer networks. At the same time, the widespread adoption of the Internet has linked people around the globe. As we discussed in Chapter 2, more and more organizations are engaging in e-HRM, providing HR-related information over the Internet. Because much human resource information is confidential, organizations may do this with an intranet, which uses Internet technology but allows access only to authorized users (such as the organization's employees). For HR professionals, Internet access also offers a way to research new developments, post job openings, trade ideas with colleagues in other organizations, and obtain government documents. In this way, e-HRM combines company-specific information on a secure intranet with links to the resources on the broader Internet.

A benefit of e-HRM is that employees can help themselves to the information they need when they need it, instead of contacting an HR staff person. For example, employees can go online to enroll in or select benefits, submit insurance claims, or fill out employee satisfaction surveys. This can be more convenient for the employees, as well as more economical for the HR department. At Cisco Systems, many HR activities are automated online.[34] When employees join the company, they log on, visit the "New Hire" page, and sign up for benefits. They also see that the Web site is the place to file expense reports, look up project information, and more. The site lets employees know when it is time for their performance review and lets them start the process with their supervisor. The employee reviews an evaluation form, studies the expected behaviors, fills in needed information, and sends the form to the supervisor. If the form requires information from someone else in the company, the supervisor clicks on a link to request that information. The supervisor receives any requested information, completes the appraisal form, and meets with the employee to discuss the review. So much of the

Online recruiting offers many benefits to the company and the potential employee. Companies are able to easily post job openings, retrieve résumés and most importantly, it allows them to voice the message of their company. Potential employees also benefit by having the ability to research the company, search for job openings and submit their résumé. The Internet is fast becoming an excellent source for recruiting.

E-HRM

WAL-MART GETS CONNECTED WITH HR TECHNOLOGY

With a one-and-a-half million employees in an industry characterized by high turnover and entry-level wages, Wal-Mart has faced extraordinary HR challenges. In recent months, the company has responded by upgrading its HR services, including the adoption of some high-tech solutions.

Online, Wal-Mart has set up a career portal for its employees. They use the portal to submit applications for management jobs. Using the career portal enables employees to apply for jobs in other stores and other geographic areas. They can receive automatic notification when specified positions open up.

In addition, Wal-Mart has an automated system for requesting time off. The online system is more efficient and accurate than the previous approach, which used requests on paper. Automating this process also makes it efficient for Wal-Mart to fine-tune schedules to meet its demand for human resources with temporary and part-time, as well as full-time, employees.

These high-tech solutions are backed up by more traditional forms of HR support for Wal-Mart's store managers and headquarters staff. The company has been hiring HR staff members to improve recruiting, interviewing, and selection. Their success is to be measured

in terms of reduced turnover among store employees. In addition, the company has set up a team of HR professionals with legal expertise to answer HR-related questions from headquarters around the clock. The goal is to have someone always available to advise store managers when a question related to employment law arises.

SOURCE: Jessica Marquez, "Wal-Mart Throws Lifeline to Managers," *Workforce Management*, April 15, 2005, www.workforce.com; and Jeff Madrick, "Wal-Mart May Be the New Model of Productivity, but It Isn't Always Wowing Workers," *New York Times*, September 2, 2004, downloaded from Business & Company Resource Center, http://galenet.galegroup.com.

process is automated that supervisors have more time to focus on the actual meeting with the employee. The "e-HRM" box describes how Wal-Mart is using Internet technology and automation to improve its human resource management.

Most administrative and information-gathering activities in human resource management can be part of e-HRM. For example, online recruiting has become a significant part of the total recruiting effort, as candidates submit résumés online. Employers go online to retrieve suitable résumés from job search sites or retrieve information from forms they post at their own Web sites. For selection decisions, the organization may have candidates use one of the online testing services available; these services conduct the tests, process the results, and submit reports to employers. Online appraisal systems can help managers make pay decisions consistent with company policies and employee performance. Many types of training can be conducted online, as we discussed in Chapter 7. Online surveys of employee satisfaction can be quick and easy to fill out. Besides providing a way to administer the survey, an intranet is an effective vehicle for communicating the results of the survey and management's planned response.

Not only does e-HRM provide efficient ways to carry out human resource functions, it also poses new challenges to employees and new issues for HR managers to address. The Internet's ability to link people anytime, anywhere has accelerated such trends as globalization, the importance of knowledge sharing within organizations, and the need for flexibility.[35] These trends, in turn, change the work environment for employees. For example, employees in the Internet age are expected to be highly committed but flexible, able to move from job to job. Employees also may be connected to the organization 24/7. In the car, on vacation, in airports, and even in the bathroom, employees with handheld computers can be interrupted by work demands. Organizations depend on their human resource departments to help prepare employees for this changing work world through such activities as training, career development, performance management, and benefits packages that meet the need for flexibility and help employees manage stress.

LO6
Summarize ways to measure the effectiveness of human resource management.

❖ EFFECTIVENESS OF HUMAN RESOURCE MANAGEMENT

In recent years, human resource management at some organizations has responded to the quest for total quality management by taking a customer-oriented approach. For an organization's human resource division, "customers" are the organization as a whole and its other divisions. They are customers of HRM because they depend on HRM to provide a variety of services that result in a supply of talented, motivated employees. Taking this customer-oriented approach, human resource management defines its customer groups, customer needs, and the activities required to meet those needs, as shown in Figure 16.5. These definitions give an organization a basis for defining goals and measures of success.

One company that uses this approach is Whirlpool Corporation. The company's HR managers identify their customer, define the need they can satisfy or the value they can provide, and identify the methods they must use to satisfy the customer. When Whirlpool planned to start a centralized service center, its plan called for hiring of 100 to 150 employees as call takers to process service requests from customers owning Whirlpool appliances and to schedule service calls. Whirlpool gave an HR manager the responsibility for developing a selection system for call takers. The man-

Figure 16.5

Customer-Oriented Perspective of Human Resource Management

Who Are Our Customers?
Line managers
Strategic planners
Employees

What Do Our Customers Need?
Committed employees
Competent employees

How Do We Meet Customer Needs?
Qualified staffing
Performance management
Rewards
Training and development

Human Resource Management

ager determined the customer in this instance was the operations manager in charge of phone service and the need was the delivery of qualified call takers. To meet this need, the HR manager decided to use a combination of structured interviews and paper-and-pencil tests. The company can evaluate the success of this program in terms of whether it efficiently produces enough qualified call takers.

Depending on the situation, a number of techniques are available for measuring HRM's effectiveness in meeting its customers' needs. These techniques include reviewing a set of key indicators, measuring the outcomes of specific HRM activity, and measuring the economic value of HRM programs.

Human Resource Management Audits

An **HRM audit** is a formal review of the outcomes of HRM functions. To conduct the audit, the HR department identifies key functions and the key measures of business performance and customer satisfaction that would indicate each function is succeeding. Table 16.3 lists examples of these measures for a variety of HRM functions: staffing, compensation, benefits, training, appraisal and development, and overall effectiveness. The audit may also look at any other measure associated with successful management of human resources—for instance, compliance with equal employment opportunity laws, succession planning, maintaining a safe workplace, and positive labor relations. An HRM audit using customer satisfaction measures supports the customer-oriented approach to human resource management.

After identifying performance measures for the HRM audit, the staff carries out the audit by gathering information. The information for the key business indicators is usually available in the organization's documents. Sometimes the HR department has to create new documents for gathering specific types of data. The usual way to measure customer satisfaction is to conduct surveys. Employee attitude surveys, discussed in Chapter 10, provide information about the satisfaction of these internal customers. Many organizations conduct surveys of top line executives to get a better view of how HRM practices affect the organization's business success.

HRM audit
A formal review of the outcomes of HRM functions, based on identifying key HRM functions and measures of business performance.

Analyzing the Effect of HRM Programs

Another way to measure HRM effectiveness is to analyze specific programs or activities. The analysis can measure a program's success in terms of whether it achieved its objectives and whether it delivered value in an economic sense. For example, if the organization sets up a training program, it should set up goals for that program, such as the training's effects on learning, behavior, and performance improvement (results). The analysis would then measure whether the training program achieved the preset goals.

The analysis can take an economic approach that measures the dollar value of the program's costs and benefits. Successful programs should deliver value that is greater than the programs' costs. Costs include employees' compensation as well as the costs to administer HRM programs such as training, employee development, or satisfaction surveys. Benefits could include a reduction in the costs associated with employee absenteeism and turnover, as well as improved productivity associated with better selection and training programs.

In general, HR departments should be able to improve their performance through some combination of greater efficiency and greater effectiveness. Greater efficiency means the HR department uses fewer and less-costly resources to perform its functions. Greater effectiveness means that what the HR department does—for example, selecting

TABLE 16.3

Key Measures of Success for an HRM Audit

BUSINESS INDICATORS	CUSTOMER SATISFACTION MEASURES
Staffing Average days taken to fill open requisitions Ratio of acceptances to offers made Ratio of minority/women applicants to representation in local labor market Per capita requirement costs Average years of experience/education of hires per job family	Anticipation of personnel needs Timeliness of referring qualified workers to line supervisors Treatment of applicants Skill in handling terminations Adaptability to changing labor market conditions
Compensation Per capita (average) merit increases Ratio of recommendations for reclassification to number of employees Percentage of overtime hours to straight time Ratio of average salary offers to average salary in community	Fairness of existing job evaluation system in assigning grades and salaries Competitiveness in local labor market Relationship between pay and performance Employee satisfaction with pay
Benefits Average unemployment compensation payment (UCP) Average workers' compensation payment (WCP) Benefit cost per payroll dollar Percentage of sick leave to total pay	Promptness in handling claims Fairness and consistency in the application of benefit policies Communication of benefits to employees Assistance provided to line managers in reducing potential for unnecessary claims
Training Percentage of employees participating in training programs per job family Percentage of employees receiving tuition refunds Training dollars per employee	Extent to which training programs meet the needs of employees and the company Communication to employees about available training opportunities Quality of introduction/orientation programs
Employee appraisal and development Distribution of performance appraisal ratings Appropriate psychometric properties of appraisal forms	Assistance in identifying management potential Organizational development activities provided by HRM department
Overall effectiveness Ratio of personnel staff to employee population Turnover rate Absenteeism rate Ratio of per capita revenues to per capita cost Net income per employee	Accuracy and clarity of information provided to managers and employees Competence and expertise of staff Working relationship between organizations and HRM department

SOURCE: Excerpted with permission, Chapter 1.5, "Evaluating Human Resource Effectiveness," (pp. 187–227) by Anne S. Tsui and Luis R. Gomez-Mejia from "Human Resource Management: Evolving Roles & Responsibilities," edited by Lee Dyer. Copyright © 1988 by The Bureau of National Affairs, Inc., Washington, DC. For copies of BNA Books publications call toll free 1-800-960-1200.

employees or setting up a performance management system—has a more beneficial effect on employees' and the organization's performance. For example, Home Depot tracks a variety of measures to see whether it is effective at meeting goals for attracting, motivating, and keeping skilled employees. The company uses a database that includes data on job applications, career paths, performance ratings, employee satisfaction, and attrition (employees leaving the company). Managers can analyze the data by region, district, and store, as well as compare numbers over time.[36]

HRM's potential to affect employees' well-being and the organization's performance makes human resource management an exciting field. As we have shown throughout the book, every HRM function calls for decisions that have the potential to help individuals and organizations achieve their goals. For HR managers to fulfill that potential, they must ensure that their decisions are well grounded. As an example, we discussed telework in Chapter 4, as an option for work design that many organizations have embraced to promote greater productivity and job satisfaction. At the same time, a review of the research literature shows that these assumptions about telework's benefits are largely untested.[37] Telework is but one example of an issue that can dramatically affect employees' lives and organizations' success yet remains open for future investigation. The field of human resource management provides tremendous opportunity to future researchers and managers who want to make a difference in many people's lives.

thinking ETHICALLY

Do Employers Have a Right to Know How Their Employees Feel?

As technology has advanced, so have HRM applications, and so have the questions about ethical issues such as employee privacy. Consider the case of SAS Human Capital Management, a software package that combines databases, a Web-based decision support system, and other features to create a system for maintaining and analyzing data about the organization's human resources. The system includes an advanced search feature known as data mining that lets users search for collections of characteristics and patterns.

One possible application of SAS Human Capital Management is that an organization can search for qualities associated with employees likely to leave the organization, such as education levels, salary, or length of service. The system can rank employees according to their likelihood of quitting and can even compute the probabilities that each will leave the company. The aim is to help employers carry out human resource planning. However, some employees might worry that they would be treated unfairly by managers who—perhaps incorrectly—expect them to quit in the near future.

SOURCE: Kathleen Sibley, "SAS Says Software Can Spot Employee Angst," *Technology in Government*, January/February 2004, www.findarticles.com; and SAS, "SAS Human Capital Management," www.sas.com, accessed June 27, 2005.

Questions

1. How might a computer system such as SAS Human Capital Management help an organization be more competitive? Can employees benefit from such a system as well?

2. Explain whether you think it is ethical for an organization to use this system in HR planning. Under what conditions is it fair to use the information to make decisions about individual employees?
3. Imagine that you work in the HR department of an organization that is preparing to install SAS Human Capital Management. How can you assure employees that the system will be used in an ethical manner?

SUMMARY

1. Define high-performance work systems and identify the elements of such a system.

A high-performance work system is the right combination of people, technology, and organizational structure that makes full use of the organization's resources and opportunities in achieving its goals. The elements of a high-performance work system are organizational structure, task design, people, reward systems, and information systems. These elements must work together in a smoothly functioning whole.

2. Summarize the outcomes of a high-performance work system.

A high-performance work system achieves the organization's goals, typically including growth, productivity, and high profits. On the way to achieving these overall goals, the high-performance work system meets such intermediate goals as high quality, innovation, customer satisfaction, job satisfaction, and reduced absenteeism and turnover.

3. Describe the conditions that create a high-performance work system.

Many conditions contribute to high-performance work systems by giving employees skills, incentives, knowledge, autonomy, and employee satisfaction. Teamwork and empowerment can make work more satisfying and provide a means for employees to improve quality and productivity. Organizations can improve performance by creating a learning organization, in which people constantly learn and share knowledge so that they continually expand their capacity to achieve the results they desire. In a high-performance organization, employees experience job satisfaction or even "occupational intimacy." For long-run high performance, organizations and employees must be ethical as well.

4. Explain how human resource management can contribute to high performance.

Jobs should be designed to foster teamwork and employee empowerment. Recruitment and selection should focus on obtaining employees who have the qualities necessary for teamwork, empowerment, and

knowledge sharing. When the organization selects for teamwork and decision-making skills, it may have to provide training in specific job tasks. Training also is important because of its role in creating a learning organization. The performance management system should be related to the organization's goals, with a focus on meeting internal and external customers' needs. Compensation should include links to performance, and employees should be included in decisions about compensation. Research suggests that it is more effective to improve HRM practices as a whole than to focus on one or two isolated practices.

5. Discuss the role of HRM technology in high-performance work systems.

Technology can improve the efficiency of the human resource management functions and support knowledge sharing. HRM applications involve transaction processing, decision support systems, and expert systems, often as part of a human resource information system using relational databases, which can improve the efficiency of routine tasks and the quality of decisions. With Internet technology, organizations can use e-HRM to let all the organization's employees help themselves to the HR information they need whenever they need it.

6. Summarize ways to measure the effectiveness of human resource management.

Taking a customer-oriented approach, HRM can improve quality by defining the internal customers who use its services and determining whether it is meeting those customers' needs. One way to do this is with an HRM audit, a formal review of the outcomes of HRM functions. The audit may look at any measure associated with successful management of human resources. Audit information may come from the organization's documents and surveys of customer satisfaction. Another way to measure HRM effectiveness is to analyze specific programs or activities. The analysis can measure success in terms of whether a program met its objectives and whether it delivered value in an economic sense, such as by leading to productivity improvements.

REVIEW AND DISCUSSION QUESTIONS

1. What is a high-performance work system? What are its elements? Which of these elements involve human resource management?
2. As it has become clear that HRM can help create and maintain high-performance work systems, it appears that organizations will need two kinds of human resource professionals: One kind focuses on identifying how HRM can contribute to high performance. The other kind develops expertise in particular HRM functions, such as how to administer a benefits program that complies with legal requirements. Which aspect of HRM is more interesting to you? Why?
3. How can teamwork, empowerment, knowledge sharing, and job satisfaction contribute to high performance?
4. If an organization can win customers, employees, or investors through deception, why would ethical behavior contribute to high performance?

5. How can an organization promote ethical behavior among its employees?
6. Summarize how each of the following HR functions can contribute to high performance.
   a. Job design
   b. Recruitment and selection
   c. Training and development
   d. Performance management
   e. Compensation
7. How can HRM technology make a human resource department more productive? How can technology improve the quality of HRM decisions?
8. Why should human resource departments measure their effectiveness? What are some ways they can go about measuring effectiveness?

WHAT'S YOUR HR IQ?

The text Web site offers two more ways to check what you've learned so far. Use the Self-Assessment to help you consider whether managing human resources to build or maintain a high-performance organization sounds like a career you wish to pursue. Then go online with the Web Exercise to learn more about organizations that have high-performance work systems.

BusinessWeek CASE

BusinessWeek Greater Chicago Food Depository: A High-Performance Nonprofit

When Brigadier General Michael P. Mulqueen left the Marine Corps to take command of the Greater Chicago Food Depository, one of the nation's biggest hunger-relief outfits, he ran into a lot of skeptics. Wouldn't someone accustomed to barking out orders clash with the nonprofit world's cooperative culture? And what value could a Vietnam veteran bristling with medals bring to the fight against hunger? "There were a couple of people on the board [of directors] who were actually offended by the idea," recalls William A. Rudnick, a former general counsel at the Chicago depository. "A lot of people in the social-service world don't view the military as a breeding ground for people who want to do good in society."

Now, nearly 14 years after the genial Mulqueen signed on, his operation has emerged as a model of efficiency for the country's food-assistance industry, which helps more than 23 million Americans every year. And Mulqueen, to the surprise of some, never barks out orders and insists on being called Mike. But to no one's surprise, the ex-Marine

runs the depository more like a business than a nonprofit. He recruited heavily from the private sector: His chief financial officer is a certified public accountant from Arthur Andersen, the felled accounting giant; the operations director has a Ph.D in aeronautical engineering and ran logistics for the *Chicago Sun-Times*; and the director of food resources was an engineer at a local utility. Mulqueen also established competitive bids on every purchase over $500 and set performance standards and rewards for his staff, to whom he pays for-profit market salaries ranging up to $150,000 a year (he himself earns about $200,000).

The result is a spit-and-polish operation that attracts food bank officials from around the country eager to learn how the depository does it. Among its successes: a training program in which welfare moms learn restaurant cooking while feeding hungry children through a chain of Kids Cafes; Pantry University, which teaches hundreds of volunteers to run food pantries efficiently; and the depository's new $29 million warehouse in southwest Chicago, built with the guidance of corporate logistics experts to serve some 600 local pantries and soup kitchens. "He's a leader and always willing to share ideas that make us all better," says Lynn Brantley, chief executive of the Capital Area Food Bank of Washington.

Mulqueen, who once commanded some 7,000 Marines and sailors in a provisioning group on Okinawa, is as demanding as any no-nonsense CEO. To keep his people in touch with the depository's mission, he insists they spend at least one day a year working at a food pantry or soup kitchen. He did his latest stint in December, helping volunteers repackage and distribute food in a mixed-income suburb near the Indiana border. "When you're in your nice office here, it's easy to forget why you're doing what you're doing," says Mulqueen.

His secret is combining cordiality and efficiency. Even in the military, he says, leaders don't get troops to rally around them by dictating. Leaving room for autonomy works better than simply issuing orders. And recognition matters, whether it's another stripe on a uniform or a simple "attaboy."

Mulqueen also won over the critics by setting up innovative programs. Mindful of the charge that food banks amount to Band-Aids on America's poverty problems, he and his team work to get some of the hungry off the food lines. Chicago's Community Kitchens is a rigorous 12-week program that trains scores of unemployed or underemployed people, often welfare moms who have never held jobs before, to work in restaurants and institutional kitchens. Almost all the 295 graduates since 1998 found jobs soon after leaving. Some 63 percent stayed in their posts for at least a year, a big number in the usually high-turnover food industry.

While they learn, Community Kitchens trainees support another big depository program. They prepare hundreds of meals each day for Kids Cafes, an after-school hot-meal, mentoring, and fitness program for poor children in 26 sites around Chicago. The cafes, an idea pioneered at another food bank, are designed to give children refuge from gangs and troubled homes. Such programs are aimed at "the cause of the problem, not just the symptom," says Lori Fey, a grant officer at the Michael & Susan Dell Foundation, which contributed to the depository.

With his businesslike approach and an array of military decorations, Mulqueen has won support from Corporate America, too. When he and his staff designed the new warehouse, they got pointers from top executives at CDW Corporation, an electronics distribution outfit that knows how to move goods. The depository's board includes top execs from McDonald's, Sodexho, Credit Suisse First Boston, and Citigroup, along with local grocery store officials and religious leaders. Mulqueen "is open, and he's honest, which is what any businessperson wants," says Peter L. Schaefer, a McDonald's vice president on the depository board.

SOURCE: Joseph Weber, "Waging War on Hunger," *BusinessWeek*, May 16, 2005, downloaded from Infotrac at http://web4.infotrac.galegroup.com.

Questions

1. In this description of the Greater Chicago Food Depository, what elements of a high-performance work system are present?
2. Which of the conditions that contribute to high performance exist at this organization?
3. Imagine that you work in the food depository's HR department. Identify a way your department can contribute to higher performance, and write a paragraph explaining your idea, including how and why it will add value to the organization.

CASE: Determining the Value of Training Programs

Can anyone question the value of training employees? Employees want training; in surveys, they have placed it among the top three benefits they desire. Training makes them more effective to their employers and opens up career opportunities. That feeling is especially strong among young employees and those in professional and technical positions. Organizations want to provide training because they see it as a way to satisfy employees and build a more skilled workforce at the same time.

However, evidence about the value of training is not universally favorable. A study of 750 large, publicly traded companies conducted by Watson Wyatt Worldwide, an HR consulting firm, looked for a link between shareholder value and various HRM practices. They found that total shareholder value was higher in companies that offered employee stock ownership, above-market pay, and effective performance management. But organizations that provided training related to employee development actually saw a lower shareholder value. How can that be?

Several explanations can be offered. One is that companies may not pay enough attention to the quality of the training they offer. They may send employees to whatever classes are close at hand or pull together an in-house program quickly without carefully selecting staff or outside trainers. They may not clearly identify the training goals or even understand what needs the training can meet. Entire departments may be assigned to training programs without carefully matching programs to needed skills.

A related concern is that many organizations are lax about measuring the impact of training programs. "Measurement" may consist of a brief survey asking participants whether they enjoyed the program, were satisfied with it, and believe they learned something. Objective measures of training's impact on performance are more difficult, so these measures are more often neglected.

Another explanation for the negative association seen between training and shareholder value is that training at some companies is part of a broader approach to HR planning that is inefficient. Specifically, some organizations have a policy of hiring employees with "potential" and then developing them for high performance, rather than hiring people who already have the necessary skills and experience to perform at the outset. The Watson Wyatt researchers have concluded that selecting this HR strategy is a major part of the problem with training. They say selection practices should focus more accurately on identifying people who can perform the job right away, without developmental training. Doing this avoids two potential costs of hiring and then developing employees: (1) the likelihood that employees will expect a pay increase after they have learned new skills and (2) the greater turnover among employees who have received developmental training without an opportunity for advancement. Besides these costs, the hire-then-develop approach starts with a major difficulty: employees' potential to perform tends to be harder to measure than observable skills and past accomplishments.

To illustrate the problems with this strategy, the researchers describe the experience of a financial services company. During an economic boom, the company was having difficulty filling all its sales positions through traditional channels, which drew recruits with financial backgrounds. The company decided to expand its recruiting to include successful salespeople in industries outside financial services. The new hires would receive training in financial services so that they could use their broad selling skills to sell financial products. Soon, training costs skyrocketed, salespeople performed worse than expected, and many gave up and left the company.

This experience suggests that careful planning and measurement must be part of any training program. Also, training programs must be linked to other HR decisions such as selection, determination of career paths, and performance management. Training programs must also focus on achieving a business's key outcomes—including skills that trainees can use right away, not after they leave a company for another job. For management training, this practical emphasis could involve helping a manager solve an immediate business problem, rather than conveying

general knowledge to solve some future problem. Success at solving problems at hand can provide more opportunity for development than a simulated classroom exercise, even one that is skillfully taught.

However, adhering rigidly to hiring people with a precise skill set in place of developing employees can also backfire. An organization's long-term planning for human resource needs could—and perhaps should—include acquiring people now so that they can gain experience and knowledge to lead the company in the future. The more competitive the labor market, the less likely an employer will be to find all the people it needs who already have all the skills for the organization's present and future needs.

SOURCE: Bruce Pfau, "Playing the Training Game and Losing," *HRMagazine*, August 2002, www.findarticles.com; John Murphy, "Link Training to Results," *HRMagazine*, August 2002, www.findarticles.com; Cydney Kilduff, "Look to the Future," *HRMagazine*, August 2002, www.findarticles.com; and Watson Wyatt Worldwide, "Research: Human Capital Index," www.watsonwyatt.com, accessed June 28, 2005.

Questions

1. The study described in this case found relationships between companies' value to shareholders and certain HRM practices. Do you think the HRM practices caused the companies' value to be higher, or does it seem more likely that the high-value companies just had skillful leaders who excel at managing financial, human, and other resources? Explain.

2. Suppose you work in the HR department of a large store chain that has conducted an employee satisfaction survey. The chain's sales have slumped recently, and the top managers are looking for ways to motivate employees and make them more effective. The survey asked employees what additional benefits they would value, and the most votes were for additional training and development opportunities. You have been asked to prepare suggestions for management. Write a proposal related to employees' desire for training and justify its need to management. What information do you need to include about the program? What elements of high-performance work systems would you focus on (see Figure 16.1)? Remember that top managers will be interested in the organization's performance, and employees will be watching to see whether you follow through on the survey results.

3. What outcomes of this training initiative will be important to measure? How can you measure those results?

NOTES

1. T. Aeppel, "On Factory Floors, Top Workers Hide Secrets to Success," *The Wall Street Journal*, July 1, 2002, pp. A1, A10.

2. S. Snell and J. Dean, "Integrated Manufacturing and Human Resource Management: A Human Capital Perspective," *Academy of Management Journal* 35 (1992), pp. 467–504.

3. M. A. Huselid, "The Impact of Human Resource Management Practices on Turnover, Productivity, and Corporate Financial Performance," *Academy of*

Management Journal 38 (1995), pp. 635–72; U.S. Department of Labor, *High-Performance Work Practices and Firm Performance* (Washington, DC: U.S. Government Printing Office, 1993).

4. R. N. Ashkenas, "Beyond the Fads: How Leaders Drive Change with Results," *Human Resource Planning* 17 (1994), pp. 25–44; and C. Slater, "The Truth Shall Set You Free," *Fast Company*, May 2004, pp. 78–79, 82–83.

5. J. Arthur, "The Link between Business Strategy and Industrial Relations Systems in American Steel Minimills," *Industrial and Labor Relations Review* 45 (1992), pp. 488–506.

6. "9/11: A Look Back," *Human Resource Executive*, 2002, pp. 1, 26+.

7. D. McCann and C. Margerison, "Managing High-Performance Teams," *Training and Development Journal*, November 1989, pp. 52–60.

8. F. Haley, "Mutual Benefit," *Fast Company*, October 2004, pp. 98–99.

9. D. Senge, "The Learning Organization Made Plain and Simple," *Training and Development Journal*, October 1991, pp. 37–44.

10. T. T. Baldwin, C. Danielson, and W. Wiggenhorn, "The Evolution of Learning Strategies in Organizations: From Employee Development to Business Redefinition," *Academy of Management Executive* 11 (1997), pp. 47–58; J. J. Martocchio and T. T. Baldwin, "The Evolution of Strategic Organizational Training," in *Research in Personnel and Human Resource Management* 15, ed. G. R. Ferris (Greenwich, CT: JAI Press, 1997), pp. 1–46.

11. T. Stewart, "The House That Knowledge Built," *Fortune*, October 2, 2000, pp. 278–80; Viant Web site, www.viant.com.

12. T. A. Judge, C. J. Thoresen, J. E. Bono, and G. K. Patton, "The Job Satisfaction-Job Performance Relationship: A Qualitative and Quantitative Review," *Psychological Bulletin* 127 (2001), pp. 376–407; R. A. Katzell, D. E. Thompson, and R. A. Guzzo, "How Job Satisfaction and Job Performance Are and Are Not Linked," *Job Satisfaction*, ed. C. J. Cranny, P. C. Smith, and E. F. Stone (New York: Lexington Books, 1992), pp. 195–217.

13. C. Ostroff, "The Relationship between Satisfaction, Attitudes, and Performance," *Journal of Applied Psychology* 77, no. 6 (1992), pp. 963–74.

14. Watson Wyatt Worldwide, *WorkUSA 2002: Weathering the Storm* (Watson Wyatt, October 2002, www.humancapitalonline.com).

15. P. E. Boverie and M. Kroth, *Transforming Work: The Five Keys to Achieving Trust, Commitment, and Passion in the Workplace* (Cambridge, MA: Perseus, 2001), pp. 71–72, 79.

16. R. P. Gephart Jr., "Introduction to the Brave New Workplace: Organizational Behavior in the Electronic Age," *Journal of Organizational Behavior* 23 (2002), pp. 327–44.

17. S. Shellenbarger, "Along with Benefits and Paychecks, Employees Value Workplace Friends," *The Wall Street Journal Online*, February 20, 2002, http://online.wsj.com.

18. C. Hymowitz, "CEOs Must Work Hard to Maintain Faith in the Corner Office," *The Wall Street Journal*, July 9, 2002, p. B1.

19. K. Maher, "Wanted: Ethical Employer," *The Wall Street Journal*, July 9, 2002, pp. B1, B8.

20. R. F. Stolz, "What HR Will Stand For," *Human Resource Executive*, January 2003, pp. 1, 20–28.

21. W. F. Cascio, *Costing Human Resources: The Financial Impact of Behavior in Organizations*, 3rd ed. (Boston: PWS-Kent, 1991); Watson Wyatt Worldwide, *Watson Wyatt's Human Capital Index: Human Capital as a Lead Indicator of Shareholder Value*, 2001/2002 Survey Report (Watson Wyatt, October 2002, www.humancapitalonline.com).

22. Watson Wyatt, *Watson Wyatt's Human Capital Index*.

23. B. Becker and M. A. Huselid, "High-Performance Work Systems and Firm Performance: A Synthesis of Research and Managerial Implications," in *Research in Personnel and Human Resource Management* 16, ed. G. R. Ferris (Stamford, CT: JAI Press, 1998), pp. 53–101.

24. B. Becker and B. Gerhart, "The Impact of Human Resource Management on Organizational Performance: Progress and Prospects," *Academy of Management Journal* 39 (1996), pp. 779–801.

25. B. Wysocki Jr., "To Fix Health Care, Hospitals Take Tips from Factory Floor," *The Wall Street Journal*, April 9, 2004, pp. A1, A6.

26. "Leadership: Ripe for Change," *Human Resource Executive*, 2002, pp. 60, 62+ (interview with Randall MacDonald).

27. G. Flynn, "HR Leaders Stay Close to the Line," *Workforce*, February 1997, p. 53; General Electric Company, "World Class Excellence," GE Fanuc Corporate Profile, GE Web site, www.ge.com/gemis/gefanuc.

28. C. M. Solomon, "HR's Push for Productivity," *Workforce*, August 2002, pp. 28–33.

29. H. J. Bernardin, C. M. Hagan, J. S. Kane, and P. Villanova, "Effective Performance Management: A Focus on Precision, Customers, and Situational Constraints," in *Performance Appraisal: State of the Art in Practice*, ed. J. W. Smither (San Francisco: Jossey-Bass, 1998), p. 56.

30. J. Bailey, "Entrepreneurs Share Their Tips to Boost a Firm's Productivity," *The Wall Street Journal*, July 9, 2002, p. B4.

31. L. R. Gomez-Mejia and D. B. Balkin, *Compensation, Organizational Strategy, and Firm Performance* (Cincinnati: South-Western, 1992); G. D. Jenkins and E. E. Lawler III, "Impact of Employee Participation in Pay Plan Development," *Organizational Behavior and Human Performance* 28 (1981), pp. 111–28.

32. S. Shrivastava and J. Shaw, "Liberating HR through Technology," *Human Resource Management* 42, no. 3 (2003), pp. 201–17.

33. R. Broderick and J. W. Boudreau, "Human Resource Management, Information Technology, and the Competitive Edge," *Academy of Management Executive* 6 (1992), pp. 7–17.

34. Solomon, "HR's Push for Productivity," p. 31.

35. Gephart, "Introduction to the Brave New Workplace."

36. R. F. Stolz, "CEOs Who 'Get It,'" *Human Resource Executive*, March 16, 2005, pp. 1, 18–25.

37. D. E. Bailey and N. B. Kurland, "A Review of Telework Research: Findings, New Directions, and Lessons for the Study of Modern Work," *Journal of Organizational Behavior* 23 (2002), pp. 383–400.

If you are using the Manager's Hot Seat DVD with this book, consider finishing case 6: Change: More Pain than Gain? for this chapter.

GLOSSARY

achievement tests Tests that measure a person's existing knowledge and skills.

action learning Training in which teams get an actual problem, work on solving it and commit to an action plan, and are accountable for carrying it out.

adventure learning A teamwork and leadership training program based on the use of challenging, structured outdoor activities.

affirmative action An organization's active effort to find opportunities to hire or promote people in a particular group.

agency shop Union security arrangement that requires the payment of union dues but not union membership.

alternative dispute resolution (ADR) Methods of solving a problem by bringing in an impartial outsider but not using the court system.

alternative work arrangements Methods of staffing other than the traditional hiring of full-time employees (for example, use of independent contractors, on-call workers, temporary workers, and contract company workers).

American Federation of Labor and Congress of Industrial Organizations (AFL-CIO) An association that seeks to advance the shared interests of its member unions at the national level.

apprenticeship A work-study training method that teaches job skills through a combination of on-the-job training and classroom training.

aptitude tests Tests that assess how well a person can learn or acquire skills and abilities.

arbitration Conflict resolution procedure in which an arbitrator or arbitration board determines a binding settlement.

assessment center A wide variety of specific selection programs that use multiple selection methods to rate applicants or job incumbents on their management potential.

assessment Collecting information and providing feedback to employees about their behavior, communication style, or skills.

associate union membership Alternative form of union membership in which members receive discounts on insurance and credit cards rather than representation in collective bargaining.

balanced scorecard A combination of performance measures directed toward the company's long- and short-term goals and used as the basis for awarding incentive pay.

behavior description interview (BDI) A structured interview in which the interviewer asks the candidate to describe how he or she handled a type of situation in the past.

behavioral observation scale (BOS) A variation of a BARS which uses all behaviors necessary for effective performance to rate performance at a task.

behaviorally anchored rating scale (BARS) Method of performance measurement that rates behavior in terms of a scale showing specific statements of behavior that describe different levels of performance.

benchmarking A procedure in which an organization compares its own practices against those of successful competitors.

Benchmarks A measurement tool that gathers ratings of a manager's use of skills associated with success in managing.

bona fide occupational qualification (BFOQ) A necessary (not merely preferred) qualification for performing a job.

cafeteria-style plan A benefits plan that offers employees a set of alternatives from which they can choose the types and amounts of benefits they want.

cash balance plan Retirement plan in which the employer sets up an individual account for each employee and contributes a percentage of the employee's salary; the account earns interest at a predefined rate.

central tendency Incorrectly rating all employees at or near the middle of a rating scale.

checkoff provision Contract provision under which the employer, on behalf of the union, automatically deducts union dues from employees' paychecks.

closed shop Union security arrangement under which a person must be a union member before being hired; illegal for those covered by the National Labor Relations Act.

coach A peer or manager who works with an employee to motivate the employee, help him or her develop skills, and provide reinforcement and feedback.

cognitive ability tests Tests designed to measure such mental abilities as verbal skills, quantitative skills, and reasoning ability.

collective bargaining Negotiation between union representatives and management representatives to arrive at a contract defining conditions of employment for the term of the contract and to administer that contract.

commissions Incentive pay calculated as a percentage of sales.

compensatory model Process of arriving at a selection decision in which a very high score on one type of assessment can make up for a low score on another.

concurrent validation Research that consists of administering a test to people who currently hold a job, then comparing their scores to existing measures of job performance.

Consolidated Omnibus Budget Reconciliation Act (COBRA) Federal law that requires employers to permit employees or their dependents to extend their health insurance coverage at group rates for up to 36 months following a qualifying event, such as a layoff, reduction in hours, or the employee's death.

construct validity Consistency between a high score on a test and high level of a construct such as intelligence or leadership ability, as well as between mastery of this construct and successful performance of the job.

content validity Consistency between the test items or problems and the kinds of situations or problems that occur on the job.

continuous learning Each employee's and each group's ongoing efforts to gather information and apply the information to their decisions in a learning organization.

contributory plan Retirement plan funded by contributions from the employer and employee.

coordination training Team training that teaches the team how to share information and make decisions to obtain the best team performance.

core competency A set of knowledges and skills that make the organization superior to competitors and create value for customers.

corporate campaigns Bringing public, financial, or political pressure on employers during union organization and contract negotiation.

craft union Labor union whose members all have a particular skill or occupation.

criterion-related validity A measure of validity based on showing a substantial correlation between test scores and job performance scores

critical-incident method Method of performance measurement based on managers' records of specific examples of the employee acting in ways that are either effective or ineffective.

cross-cultural preparation Training to prepare employees and their family members for an assignment in a foreign country.

cross-training Team training in which team members understand and practice each other's skills so that they are prepared to step in and take another member's place.

culture shock Disillusionment and discomfort that occur during the process of adjusting to a new culture.

decision support systems Computer software systems designed to help managers solve problems by showing how results vary when the manager alters assumptions or data.

defined benefit plan Pension plan that guarantees a specified level of retirement income.

defined contribution plan Retirement plan in which the employer sets up an individual account for each employee and specifies the size of the investment into that account.

delayering Reducing the number of levels in the organization's job structure.

development The acquisition of knowledge, skills, and behaviors that improve an employee's ability to meet changes in job requirements and in customer demands.

Dictionary of Occupational Titles Created by the Department of Labor in the 1930s, the DOT listed over 12,000 jobs and requirements.

differential piece rates Incentive pay in which the piece rate is higher when a greater amount is produced.

direct applicants People who apply for a vacancy without prompting from the organization.

disability Under the Americans with Disabilities Act, a physical or mental impairment that substantially limits one or more major life activities, a record of having such an impairment, or being regarded as having such an impairment.

disparate impact A condition in which employment practices are seemingly neutral yet disproportionately exclude a protected group from employment opportunities.

disparate treatment Differing treatment of individuals, where the differences are based on the individuals' race, color, religion, sex, national origin, age, or disability status.

diversity training Training designed to change employee attitudes about diversity and/or develop skills needed to work with a diverse workforce.

downsizing The planned elimination of large numbers of personnel with the goal of enhancing the organization's competitiveness.

downward move Assignment of an employee to a position with less responsibility and authority.

due-process policies Policies that formally lay out the steps an employee may take to appeal the employer's decision to terminate that employee.

EEO-1 report The EEOC's Employer Information Report, which details the number of women and minorities employed in nine different job categories.

e-learning Receiving training via the Internet or the organization's intranet.

electronic business (e-business) Any process that a business conducts electronically, especially business involving use of the Internet.

electronic human resource management (e-HRM) The processing and transmission of digitized HR information, especially using computer networking and the Internet.

employee assistance program (EAP) A referral service that employees can use to seek professional treatment for emotional problems or substance abuse.

employee benefits Compensation in forms other than cash.

employee development The combination of formal education, job experiences, relationships, and assessment of personality and abilities to help employees prepare for the future of their careers.

employee empowerment Giving employees responsibility and authority to make decisions regarding all aspects of product development or customer service.

Employee Retirement Income Security Act (ERISA) Federal law that increased the responsibility of pension plan trustees to protect retirees, established certain rights related to vesting and portability, and created the Pension Benefit Guarantee Corporation.

employee stock ownership plan (ESOP) An arrangement in which the organization distributes shares of stock to all its employees by placing it in a trust.

employee wellness program (EWP) A set of communications, activities, and facilities designed to change health-related behaviors in ways that reduce health risks.

employment at will Employment principle that if there is no specific employment contract saying otherwise, the employer or employee may end an employment relationship at any time, regardless of cause.

equal employment opportunity (EEO) The condition in which all individuals have an equal chance for employment, regardless of their race, color, religion, sex, age, disability, or national origin.

Equal Employment Opportunity Commission (EEOC) Agency of the Department of Justice charged with enforcing Title VII of the Civil Rights Act of 1964 and other antidiscrimination laws.

ergonomics The study of the interface between individuals' physiology and the characteristics of the physical work environment.

ethics The fundamental principles of right and wrong.

exempt employees Managers, outside salespeople, and any other employees not covered by the FLSA requirement for overtime pay.

exit interview A meeting of a departing employee with the employee's supervisor and/or a human resource specialist to discuss the employee's reasons for leaving.

expatriates Employees assigned to work in another country.

experience rating The number of employees a company has laid off in the past and the cost of providing them with unemployment benefits.

experiential programs Training programs in which participants learn concepts and apply them by simulating behaviors involved and analyzing the activity, connecting it with real-life situations.

expert systems Computer systems that support decision making by incorporating the decision rules used by people who are considered to have expertise in a certain area.

external labor market Individuals who are actively seeking employment.

externship Employee development through a full-time temporary position at another organization.

fact finder Third party to collective bargaining who reports the reasons for a dispute, the views and arguments of both sides, and possibly a recommended settlement, which the parties may decline.

Fair Labor Standards Act (FLSA) Federal law that establishes a minimum wage and requirements for overtime pay and child labor.

Family and Medical Leave Act (FMLA) Federal law requiring organizations with 50 or more employees to provide up to 12 weeks of unpaid leave after childbirth or adoption; to care for a seriously ill family member; or for an employee's own serious illness.

Fleishman Job Analysis System   Job analysis technique that asks subject-matter experts to evaluate a job in terms of the abilities required to perform the job.

flexible spending account   Employee-controlled pretax earnings set aside to pay for certain eligible expenses such as health care expenses during the same year.

flextime   A scheduling policy in which full-time employees may choose starting and ending times within guidelines specified by the organization.

forced-distribution method   Method of performance measurement that assigns a certain percentage of employees to each category in a set of categories.

forecasting   The attempts to determine the supply of and demand for various types of human resources to predict areas within the organization where there will be labor shortages or surpluses.

four-fifths rule   Rule of thumb that finds evidence of discrimination if an organization's hiring rate for a minority group is less than four-fifths the hiring rate for the majority group.

gainsharing   Group incentive program that measures improvements in productivity and effectiveness objectives and distributes a portion of each gain to employees.

generalizable   Valid in other contexts beyond the context in which the selection method was developed.

glass ceiling   Circumstances resembling an invisible barrier that keep most women and minorities from attaining the top jobs in organizations.

global organization   An organization that chooses to locate a facility based on the ability to effectively, efficiently, and flexibly produce a product or service, using cultural differences as an advantage.

graphic rating scale   Method of performance measurement that lists traits and provides a rating scale for each trait; the employer uses the scale to indicate the extent to which an employee displays each trait.

green-circle rate   Pay at a rate that falls below the pay range for the job.

grievance procedure   The process for resolving union-management conflicts over interpretation or violation of a collective bargaining agreement.

group-building methods   Training methods in which trainees share ideas and experiences, build group identity, understand interpersonal relationships, and learn the strengths and weaknesses of themselves and their coworkers.

halo error   Rating error that occurs when the rater reacts to one positive performance aspect by rating the employee positively in all areas of performance.

hands-on methods   Training methods which actively involve the trainee in trying out skills being taught.

Hay Guide-Chart Profile method   Method of job evaluation that creates a profile for each position based on its required know-how, degree of problem solving, and accountability.

health maintenance organization (HMO)   A health care plan that requires patients to receive their medical care from the HMO's health care professionals, who are often paid a flat salary, and provides all services on a prepaid basis.

high-performance work system   An organization in which technology, organizational structure, people, and processes all work together to give an organization an advantage in the competitive environment.

horns error   Rating error that occurs when the rater responds to one negative aspect by rating an employee low in other aspects.

host country   A country (other than the parent country) in which an organization operates a facility.

hot-stove rule   Principle of discipline that says discipline should be like a hot stove, giving clear warning and following up with consistent, objective, immediate consequences.

hourly wage   Rate of pay for each hour worked.

HRM audit   A formal review of the outcomes of HRM functions, based on identifying key HRM functions and measures of business performance.

human capital   An organization's employees, described in terms of their training, experience, judgment, intelligence, relationships, and insight.

human resource information system (HRIS)   A computer system used to acquire, store, manipulate, analyze, retrieve, and distribute information related to an organization's human resources.

human resource management (HRM)   The policies, practices, and systems that influence employees' behavior, attitudes, and performance.

human resource planning   Identifying the numbers and types of employees the organization will require in order to meet its objectives.

Improshare   A gainsharing program in which the gain is the decrease in the labor hours needed to produce one unit of product, with the gains split equally between the organization and its employees.

incentive pay Forms of pay linked to an employee's performance as an individual, group member, or organization member.

industrial engineering The study of jobs to find the simplest way to structure work in order to maximize efficiency.

industrial union Labor union whose members are linked by their work in a particular industry.

instructional design A process of systematically developing training to meet specified needs.

interactional justice A judgment that the organization carried out its actions in a way that took the employee's feelings into account.

internal labor force An organization's workers (its employees and the people who have contracts to work at the organization).

international organization An organization that sets up one or a few facilities in one or a few foreign countries.

internship On-the-job learning sponsored by an educational institution as a component of an academic program.

involuntary turnover Turnover initiated by an employer (often with employees who would prefer to stay).

job A set of related duties.

job analysis The process of getting detailed information about jobs.

job description A list of the tasks, duties, and responsibilities (TDRs) that a particular job entails.

job design The process of defining how work will be performed and what tasks will be required in a given job.

job enlargement Broadening the types of tasks performed in a job.

job enrichment Empowering workers by adding more decision-making authority to jobs.

job evaluation An administrative procedure for measuring the relative internal worth of the organization's jobs.

job experiences The combination of relationships, problems, demands, tasks, and other features of an employee's jobs.

job extension Enlarging jobs by combining several relatively simple jobs to form a job with a wider range of tasks.

job hazard analysis technique Safety promotion technique that involves breaking down a job into basic elements, then rating each element for its potential for harm or injury.

job involvement The degree to which people identify themselves with their jobs.

job posting The process of communicating information about a job vacancy on company bulletin boards, in employee publications, on corporate intranets, and anywhere else the organization communicates with employees.

job rotation Enlarging jobs by moving employees among several different jobs.

job satisfaction A pleasant feeling resulting from the perception that one's job fulfills or allows for the fulfillment of one's important job values.

job sharing A work option in which two part-time employees carry out the tasks associated with a single job.

job specification A list of the knowledge, skills, abilities, and other characteristics (KSAOs) that an individual must have to perform a particular job.

job structure The relative pay for different jobs within the organization.

job withdrawal A set of behaviors with which employees try to avoid the work situation physically, mentally, or emotionally.

knowledge workers Employees whose main contribution to the organization is specialized knowledge, such as knowledge of customers, a process, or a profession.

labor relations Field that emphasizes skills managers and union leaders can use to minimize costly forms of conflict (such as strikes) and seek win-win solutions to disagreements.

leaderless group discussion An assessment center exercise in which a team of five to seven employees is assigned a problem and must work together to solve it within a certain time period.

leading indicators Objective measures that accurately predict future labor demand.

learning organization An organization that supports lifelong learning by enabling all employees to acquire and share knowledge.

leniency error Rating error of assigning inaccurately high ratings to all employees.

long-term disability insurance Insurance that pays a percentage of a disabled employee's salary after an initial period and potentially for the rest of the employee's life.

maintenance of membership Union security rules not requiring union membership but requiring that employees who join the union remain members for a certain period of time.

management by objectives (MBO) A system in which people at each level of the organization set goals in a process that flows from top to bottom, so employees at all levels are contributing to the organization's overall goals;

these goals become the standards for evaluating each employee's performance.

material safety data sheets (MSDSs) Forms on which chemical manufacturers and importers identify the hazards of their chemicals.

mediation Conflict resolution procedure in which a mediator hears the views of both sides and facilitates the negotiation process but has no formal authority to dictate a resolution.

mentor An experienced, productive senior employee who helps develop a less experienced employee (a protégé).

merit pay A system of linking pay increases to ratings on performance appraisals.

minimum wage The lowest amount that employers may pay under federal or state law, stated as an amount of pay per hour.

mixed-standard scales Method of performance measurement that uses several statements describing each trait to produce a final score for that trait.

multinational company An organization that builds facilities in a number of different countries in an effort to minimize production and distribution costs.

multiple-hurdle model Process of arriving at a selection decision by eliminating some candidates at each stage of the selection process.

Myers-Briggs Type Indicator (MBTI) Psychological test that identifies individuals' preferences for source of energy, means of information gathering, way of decision making, and lifestyle, providing information for team building and leadership development.

National Labor Relations Act (NLRA) Federal law that supports collective bargaining and sets out the rights of employees to form unions.

National Labor Relations Board (NLRB) Federal government agency that enforces the NLRA by conducting and certifying representation elections and investigating unfair labor practices.

needs assessment The process of evaluating the organization, individual employees, and employees' tasks to determine what kinds of training, if any, are necessary.

nepotism The practice of hiring relatives.

noncontributory plan Retirement plan funded entirely by contributions from the employer.

nondirective interview A selection interview in which the interviewer has great discretion in choosing questions to ask each candidate.

nonexempt employees Employees covered by the FLSA requirements for overtime pay.

Occupational Safety and Health Act (OSH Act) U.S. law authorizing the federal government to establish and enforce occupational safety and health standards for all places of employment engaging in interstate commerce.

Occupational Safety and Health Administration (OSHA) Labor Department agency responsible for inspecting employers, applying safety and health standards, and levying fines for violation.

Office of Federal Contract Compliance Procedures (OFCCP) The agency responsible for enforcing the executive orders that cover companies doing business with the federal government.

offshoring Moving operations from the country where a company is headquartered to a country where pay rates are lower but the necessary skills are available.

on-the-job training (OJT) Training methods in which a person with job experience and skill guides trainees in practicing job skills at the workplace.

open-door policy An organization's policy of making managers available to hear complaints.

organization analysis A process for determining the appropriateness of training by evaluating the characteristics of the organization.

organizational behavior modification (OBM) A plan for managing the behavior of employees through a formal system of feedback and reinforcement.

organizational commitment The degree to which an employee identifies with the organization and is willing to put forth effort on its behalf.

orientation Training designed to prepare employees to perform their jobs effectively, learn about their organization, and establish work relationships.

outcome fairness A judgment that the consequences given to employees are just.

outplacement counseling A service in which professionals try to help dismissed employees manage the transition from one job to another.

outsourcing Contracting with another organization (vendor, third party provider or consultant) to provide services.

paired-comparison method Method of performance measurement that compares each employee with each other employee to establish rankings.

panel interview Selection interview in which several members of the organization meet to interview each candidate.

parent country The country in which an organization's headquarters is located.

pay differential Adjustment to a pay rate to reflect differences in working conditions or labor markets.

pay grades Sets of jobs having similar worth or content, grouped together to establish rates of pay.

pay level The average amount (including wages, salaries, and bonuses) the organization pays for a particular job.

pay policy line A graphed line showing the mathematical relationship between job evaluation points and pay rate.

pay ranges A set of possible pay rates defined by a minimum, maximum, and midpoint of pay for employees holding a particular job or a job within a particular pay grade.

pay structure The pay policy resulting from job structure and pay level decisions.

peer review Process for resolving disputes by taking them to a panel composed of representatives from the organization at the same levels as the people in the dispute.

Pension Benefit Guarantee Corporation (PBGC) Federal agency that insures retirement benefits and guarantees retirees a basic benefit if the employer experiences financial difficulties.

performance appraisal The measurement of specified areas of an employee's performance.

performance management The process through which managers ensure that employees' activities and outputs contribute to the organization's goals.

person analysis A process for determining individuals' needs and readiness for training.

personnel selection The process through which organizations make decisions about who will or will not be allowed to join the organization.

piecework rate: Rate of pay for each unit produced.

Position Analysis Questionnaire (PAQ) A standardized job analysis questionnaire containing 194 questions about work behaviors, work conditions, and job characteristics that apply to a wide variety of jobs.

position The set of duties (job) performed by a particular person.

predictive validation Research that uses the test scores of all applicants and looks for a relationship between the scores and future performance of the applicants who were hired.

preferred provider organization (PPO) A health care plan that contracts with health care professionals to provide services at a reduced fee and gives patients financial incentives to use network providers.

presentation methods Training methods in which trainees receive information provided by instructors or via computers or other media.

procedural justice A judgment that fair methods were used to determine the consequences an employee receives.

profit sharing Incentive pay in which payments are a percentage of the organization's profits and do not become part of the employees' base salary.

progressive discipline A formal discipline process in which the consequences become more serious if the employee repeats the offense.

promotion Assignment of an employee to a position with greater challenges, more responsibility, and more authority than in the previous job, usually accompanied by a pay increase.

protean career A career that frequently changes based on changes in the person's interests, abilities, and values and in the work environment.

psychological contract A description of what an employee expects to contribute in an employment relationship and what the employer will provide the employee in exchange for those contributions.

readability The difficulty level of written materials.

readiness for training A combination of employee characteristics and positive work environment that permit training.

realistic job preview Background information about a job's positive and negative qualities.

reality check Information employers give employees about their skills and knowledge and where these assets fit into the organization's plans.

reasonable accommodation An employer's obligation to do something to enable an otherwise qualified person to perform a job.

recruiting Any activity carried on by the organization with the primary purpose of identifying and attracting potential employees.

recruitment The process through which the organization seeks applicants for potential employment.

red-circle rate Pay at a rate that falls above the pay range for the job.

reengineering   A complete review of the organization's critical work processes to make them more efficient and able to deliver higher quality.

referrals   People who apply for a vacancy because someone in the organization prompted them to do so.

reliability   The extent to which a measurement is from random error.

repatriation   The process of preparing expatriates to return home from a foreign assignment.

right-to-know laws   State laws that require employers to provide employees with information about the health risks associated with exposure to substances considered hazardous.

right-to-work laws   State laws that make union shops, maintenance of membership, and agency shops illegal.

role ambiguity   Uncertainty about what the organization expects from the employee in terms of what to do or how to do it.

role analysis technique   A process of formally identifying expectations associated with a role.

role conflict   An employee's recognition that demands of the job are incompatible or contradictory.

role overload   A state in which too many expectations or demands are placed on a person.

role   The set of behaviors that people expect of a person in a particular job.

Rucker plan   A gainsharing program in which the ratio measuring the gain compares labor costs to the value added in production (output minus the cost of materials, supplies, and services).

sabbatical   A leave of absence from an organization to renew or develop skills.

salary   Rate of pay for each week, month, or year worked.

Scanlon plan   A gainsharing program in which employees receive a bonus if the ratio of labor costs to the sales value of production is below a set standard.

selection   The process by which the organization attempts to identify applicants with the necessary knowledge, skills, abilities, and other characteristics that will help the organization achieve its goals.

self-assessment   The use of information by employees to determine their career interests, values, aptitudes, and behavioral tendencies.

self-service   System in which employees have online access to information about HR issues and go online to enroll themselves in programs and provide feedback through surveys.

sexual harassment   Unwelcome sexual advances as defined by the EEOC.

short-term disability insurance   Insurance that pays a percentage of a disabled employee's salary as benefits to the employee for six months or less.

similar-to-me error   Rating error of giving a higher evaluation to people who seem similar to oneself.

simple ranking   Method of performance measurement that requires managers to rank employees in their group from the highest performer to the poorest performer.

simulation   A training method that represents a real-life situation, with trainees making decisions resulting in outcomes that mirror what would happen on the job.

situational interviews   A structured interview in which the interviewer describes a situation likely to arise on the job, then asks the candidate what he or she would do in that situation.

skill-based pay systems   Pay structures that set pay according to the employees' levels of skill or knowledge and what they are capable of doing.

Social Security   The federal Old Age, Survivors, Disability, and Health Insurance (OASDHI) program, which combines old age (retirement) insurance, survivor's insurance, disability insurance, hospital insurance (Medicare Part A), and supplementary medical insurance (Medicare Part B) for the elderly.

standard hour plan   An incentive plan that pays workers extra for work done in less than a preset "standard time."

stock options   Rights to buy a certain number of shares of stock at a specified price.

straight piecework plan   Incentive pay in which the employer pays the same rate per piece, no matter how much the worker produces.

strictness error   Rating error of giving low ratings to all employees, holding them to unreasonably high standards.

strike   A collective decision by union members not to work until certain demands or conditions are met.

structured interview   A selection interview that consists of a predetermined set of questions for the interviewer to ask.

succession planning   The process of identifying and tracking high-potential employees who will be able to fill top management positions when they become vacant.

summary plan description Report that describes a pension plan's funding, eligibility requirements, risks, and other details.

task analysis inventory Job analysis method that involves listing the tasks performed in a particular job and rating each task according to a defined set of criteria.

task analysis The process of identifying and analyzing tasks to be trained for.

team leader training Training in the skills necessary for effectively leading the organization's teams.

teamwork The assignment of work to groups of employees with various skills who interact to assemble a product or provide a service.

technic of operations review (TOR) Method of promoting safety by determining which specific element of a job led to a past accident.

third country A country that is neither the parent country nor the host country of an employer.

360-degree performance appraisal Performance measurement that combines information from the employee's managers, peers, subordinates, self, and customers.

total quality management (TQM) A companywide effort to continuously improve the ways people, machines, and systems accomplish work.

training An organization's planned efforts to help employees acquire job-related knowledge, skills, abilities, and behaviors, with the goal of applying these on the job.

transaction processing Computations and calculations involved in reviewing and documenting HRM decisions and practices.

transfer of training On-the-job use of knowledge, skills, and behaviors learned in training.

transfer Assignment of an employee to a position in a different area of the company, usually in a lateral move.

transitional matrix A chart that lists job categories held in one period and shows the proportion of employees in each of those job categories in a future period.

transnational HRM system Type of HRM system that makes decisions from a global perspective, includes managers from many countries, and is based on ideas contributed by people representing a variety of cultures.

trend analysis Constructing and applying statistical models that predict labor demand for the next year, given relatively objective statistics from the previous year.

unemployment insurance A federally mandated program to minimize the hardships of unemployment through payments to unemployed workers, help in finding new jobs, and incentives to stabilize employment.

Uniform Guidelines on Employee Selection Procedures Guidelines issued by the EEOC and other agencies to identify how an organization should develop and administer its system for selecting employees so as not to violate antidiscrimination laws.

union shop Union security arrangement that requires employees to join the union within a certain amount of time (30 days) after beginning employment.

union steward An employee elected by union members to represent them in ensuring that the terms of the labor contract are enforced.

unions Organizations formed for the purpose of representing their members' interests in dealing with employers.

utility The extent to which something provides economic value greater than its cost.

validity The extent to which performance on a measure (such as a test score) is related to what the measure is designed to assess (such as job performance).

vesting rights Guarantee that when employees become participants in a pension plan and work a specified number of years, they will receive a pension at retirement age, regardless of whether they remained with the employer.

virtual expatriates Employees who manage an operation abroad without permanently locating in the country.

virtual reality A computer-based technology that provides an interactive, three-dimensional learning experience.

voluntary turnover Turnover initiated by employees (often when the organization would prefer to keep them).

work flow design The process of analyzing the tasks necessary for the production of a product or service.

workers' compensation State programs that provide benefits to workers who suffer work-related injuries or illnesses, or to their survivors.

workforce utilization review A comparison of the proportion of employees in protected groups with the proportion that each group represents in the relevant labor market.

yield ratio A ratio that expresses the percentage of applicants who successfully move from one stage of the recruitment and selection process to the next.

PHOTO CREDITS

NAME/COMPANY INDEX

SUBJECT INDEX